EARLY SETTLERS AND INDIAN FIGHTERS

OF

SOUTHWEST TEXAS

BY

A. J. SOWELL
Author of "Texas Rangers", "Big Foot Wallace", etc.

*FACTS GATHERED FROM SURVIVORS OF
FRONTIER DAYS*

A Facsimile Reproduction of the Original

*Published by
State House Press
Austin, Texas
1986*

Sowell, A. J. (Andrew Jackson), 1848-1921.
  Early settlers and Indian fighters of southwest Texas.
  Reprint. Originally published: Austin, Tex.:
B. C. Jones & Co., Printers, 1900.
  Includes index.
  1. Pioneers—Texas—Biography. 2. Texas—Biography.
3. Frontier and pioneer life—Texas. 4. Indians of
North America—Texas—Wars. 5. Indians of North
America—Wars—1815-1875. I. Title.
F385.S7   1986   976.4 [B]   86-61776
ISBN 0-938349-05-8
ISBN 0-938349-06-6 (lim. ed.)

State House Press
P.O. Box 15247
Austin, Texas 78761

EARLY SETTLERS AND INDIAN FIGHTERS

OF

SOUTHWEST TEXAS

BY

A. J. SOWELL

AUTHOR OF "TEXAS RANGERS" "BIG-FOOT WALLACE," ETC.

FACTS GATHERED FROM SURVIVORS OF
FRONTIER DAYS

AUSTIN, TEXAS:
BEN C. JONES & CO., PRINTERS
1900

PREFACE.

In the following pages the author has attempted to recite what is yet the unwritten history of life on the border, especially in Southwest Texas. Many brave and heroic men have lived and died, and did their country glorious service upon the frontier of Texas, whose names as yet have found no place in history. They were the men who cut the brush and blazed the way for immigration, and drove the wild beast and wilder men from the path of civilization. They bore the heat and burden of the day, and their deeds should live like monuments in the hearts of their countrymen. Where commerce now holds its busy and prosperous marts was then the camping ground and rendezvous of these rangers and pioneers. The incidents of history herein contained have been gathered from sources most reliable, and he who peruses this volume may feel assured that he is not reading fiction, but facts which form a part of the frontier history of Texas. If this work serves one of the purposes for which it was written, i. e., that the names of these good and brave men and women be not forgotten and the writer occupy one fresh, green spot in the folds of their memory, he will not think his labor has been in vain. And now, to the pioneers of Texas and to their descendants is this work dedicated by

THE AUTHOR.

CONTENTS.

BENJ. F. HIGHSMITH.

TEXAS INDIAN FIGHTERS.

BENJAMIN F. HIGHSMITH.

Came to Texas in 1823.

"Uncle Ben" Highsmith, as he is familiarly called by all who know him, is one of the most interesting characters at this time (1899) in Southwest Texas. He lives in Bandera County, on Blanket Creek, between Sabinal and Frio Canyons. In 1897, when the writer went to interview the old veteran for the purpose of getting a sketch of his life for publication in the Galveston News, he found him sitting in front of his door, with his hat pulled down, shading his eyes, for he is nearly blind, and he has to almost feel his way when stirring about. His general health, however, is good, and he has one of the most remarkable memories of incidents, names, and dates. To my greeting, he called out, "How are you, Jack? I know your voice, but I can not see you. Get down."

Uncle Ben was born in Lincoln County, Mississippi, on the 11th day of September, 1817. His father, A. M. Highsmith, was in the British war of 1812, and served as scout and ranger. Mr. Highsmith came to Texas with his father in 1823, and crossed the Sabine River on a raft the day before Christmas of the above date. There were four other families along, thirty-three persons in all, and all relatives except one.

The Highsmiths moved on up the country after landing on Texas soil, and first settled on the Colorado River two miles above the present town of La Grange, on the west side of the river. This place was afterwards called Manton's Big Spring. At that time it was called Castleman's Spring. It was named for John Castleman.

The Indians soon gave trouble, and these outside pioneers had to come back to the settlement below, where lived the families of Zaddock Woods and Stephen Cottle. This settlement was

1

finally abandoned on account of Indians, and all went to Rabb's
Mill. The settlement here and those who came for mutual protection now numbered six families. Bread was a very scarce article, as farming at this time was on a very small scale.

The Comanche Indians, who had up to this time been on
friendly terms with the whites, now informed them that they
must leave or they would come next moon and kill all of them.
The settlers were not strong enough to disregard such a warning as this, and consequently broke up and scattered. Most of
them went down to Old Caney and Columbus. The Cottles
stopped at Jesse Burnham's and the Highsmiths at Elliot C.
Buckner's. This was in 1829.

Mr. Highsmith first visited San Antonio in 1830. On this
occasion he went on a trading trip in company with James Bowie,
W. B. Travis, Ben McCulloch, Winslow Turner, Sam Highsmith,
and George Kimble. They arrived there on the first day of
April. It was far out on the frontier, and consisted of scattered grass-covered houses, mostly.

After returning from this trip, Mr. Highsmith moved with
the other members of the family to Cedar Lake and stopped on
the Harrison place, and was the only family there at that time.

In 1832 a disturbance commenced with the Mexicans, which
culminated in the

BATTLE OF VELASCO.

The causes which brought about the collision were these: In
1831 Bustamante had overthrown Zacatecas, who was President of Mexico, and who had formulated the famous Constitution of 1824, which guaranteed to Americans the right to govern themselves. Bustamante told his followers that it gave the
Americans the right to govern Mexico also, and at once sent
troops to garrison San Antonio, La Bahia, Velasco, Anahuac,
and Nacogdoches. General Cos was sent to San Antonio, Fili-
sola to La Bahia (Goliad), Ugartechea to Velasco, and Bradburn to Anahuac. Santa Anna now arose against Bustamante
and the Americans espoused his cause, thinking he was their
friend and would uphold the Constitution of 1824.

To show their fidelity to the cause of Santa Anna, the American settlers began to raise men to attack the garrisons which had

been placed in the Texas towns by Bustamante. Capt. Elliot C. Buckner raised one of the companies and proceeded with other captains against Velasco. Uncle Ben joined this company, having to run away from home to do so on account of his youth, being then only 15 years of age. The following are the names of those whom Mr. Highsmith can still remember who belonged to this company: Peter Powell, Joe and Horace Yeamans, Billy Kingston, Moses Morrison, Isaac Van Dorn, Hamilton Cook, Caleb R. Bostick, Tom Tone, Dan Ralls, Andrew Castleman, Leander Woods, and a Mexican named Hosea, who lived with. Captain Buckner.

When the Americans under Buckner, about 100 in number, arrived at Velasco they went into the town at a full charge, and being supported by other troops the battle commenced with great fury. The Mexicans numbered about 500, and met the Americans with a heavy fire of musketry and artillery. In less than an hour the battle of Velasco was over and the Mexicans defeated. While many Mexicans were killed, the Americans did not come unscathed out of the fight. Out of Buckner's company, he himself was killed, the Mexican, Hosea, Leander Woods, and Andrew Castleman. One man of this company ran when the firing commenced, but soon checked up and seemed about to come back, but about this time the Mexican artillery fire commenced, and away he went again and returned not. When the boys joked him about it afterwards he said: "Boys, I will tell you the truth. I have got as brave a heart in me as any man that lives, but the most cowardly pair of legs that was ever fastened on to a man. Now, while my legs were carrying me off I was protesting and trying to persuade them to bring me back into the fight, and did actually get them to stop and turn me around, but at that critical moment the cannon fired, and away they went again, and I failed to get them to hold up any more within range of the battle."

About the middle of November, 1833, Ben Highsmith and his father were camped at Croft's prairie, eight miles below Bastrop, cutting logs to build a house, when the "stars fell," as that extraordinary meteoric display which occurred at that time was called.

BATTLE OF GONZALES.

In 1835 Santa Anna, who had overthrown Bustamante, was now President of Mexico, and wanted to govern Texas also. He went about to bring this to pass by ordering General Cos, his brother-in-law, who was still in command at San Antonio, to send a company of soldiers to Gonzales and bring off a little cannon which the Americans had in their possession, and which had been furnished them by the Mexican government for defense against the Indians. The settlers at Gonzales refused to' give up the cannon, and the soldiers went back to San Antonio and reported the same to their commander. Another company was sent with an order from Santa Anna to take it by force. In the meantime a runner had been sent from Gonzales to the settlements on the Colorado, informing them of the action of the Mexican government, and calling on the settlers for assistance to repel with force this plain violation of the Constitution of 1824. The fact of the business was that Santa Anna had become alarmed at the number of Americans that were settling in Texas and wished to disarm and drive them out, although this immigration had been invited and extra inducements offered to get it, and these settlers were actual citizens of Mexico.

The appeal from Gonzales was responded to with alacrity by the Colorado men, and companies were formed and moved with great dispatch. Mr. Highsmith left his home on the Colorado, and on arriving at Gonzales joined the company of Capt. John Alley, the whole being under the command of Col. John H. Moore. The cannon in question was a small affair, had never been used by the settlers against an enemy, and they had no balls to fit it, and did not know how it would shoot if occasion offered. However, they concluded to try it before the Mexicans came. John Sowell, a gunsmith of Gonzales, hammered out a ball on his anvil to fit the cannon, and it was loaded at his shop. Col. James Neill, an experienced artillerist, was present, and he aimed the gun at a small sycamore tree which grew on the bank of the Guadalupe River, about 300 yards distant from the shop. The tree was hit and considerably splintered, and part of the top fell off. When the Mexicans came they crossed the river above town and the settlers went up there before day to fight them, carrying the cannon with them, which had been loaded with slugs at Sowells' shop. It was not yet daylight when they arrived in the vicinity of the Mexicans, and very foggy,—the strangest fog, Mr. Highsmith says, he ever saw. It was clear of the ground a short distance of half a foot or more, and by lying down one could see the legs of the Mexicans, who were on the ground, and also that of the horses of those who were mounted, 150 yards away . Mr. Highsmith found this out by dropping something and stooping down to pick it up. He called the attention of Colonel Neill to this fact, and the colonel said that it beat anything in the fog line that he had ever witnessed. Colonel Neill had charge of the cannon, and was about to direct its fire on the Mexicans, when the battle very unexpectedly and accidentally commenced. This was brought about by two scouts, one from each of the opposing forces, coming in contact and firing at each other at close range in the fog. The fight was of short duration. The cannon was fired five times, mixed with rifle shots, and the Mexicans retreated across the river. The fog lifted, and shots were exchanged after they crossed. Dr. John T. Tinsley got a fair bead on one who had stopped to take a look back, and, from the way he cursed in choice Spanish as he continued his retreat, must have hit him. The gunsmith John Sowell brought his shop apron full of slugs to the battleground to load the cannon with. The Mexicans continued their retreat to San Antonio, and most of the Colorado men went back home.

BATTLE OF MISSION CONCEPCION.

Captain Alley's company and a good many of the Gonzales men after the fight at Gonzales joined Gen. Stephen F. Austin, who, seeing war was inevitable now with Mexico, was raising a force to capture San Antonio. Mr. Highsmith remained with his company, and says one night the command camped on the Cibolo Creek while en route to assault the city, and that two of the men ate so many green pecans that it killed them. This was in the fall of 1835.

General Austin went into camp on the San Antonio River below the city, and then sent Colonels Fannin and Bowie up to near the old Mission Concepcion with ninety-two men, as an advance guard. They went into camp in a pecan grove in a bend of the

river and put out guards. Next morning, about the break of day,
as some of the men had arisen and were kindling fires, 400 Mexican morales troops attacked them. It was foggy, and the Mexicans had advanced a nine-pound cannon and placed it in close
range of the position of the Texans and commenced firing before the guards discovered them. At the first fire of the gun,
one of the Texans sang out, "That cannon is ours!" Fannin
and Bowie were cool, brave men, and soon had their small force
well in hand and to some extent protected by the bank of the
river, where they were told to form and shoot when they liked,
and not to wait for orders. The cannon shots had no effect, as
the Texans were sheltered also by pecan and hackberry trees.
The rifles soon cleared the gunners from the piece, and as the
fog lifted they could see the Mexican infantry coming with
trailed arms to protect it. This line was soon checked by a
deadly rifle fire, and then a portion of the Texans made a charge
from their position and captured the cannon. The Mexican infantry fired and then retreated, but formed again and still continued to fire at longer range. The cannon was only fired three
times before it was captured and brought into the Texan camp.

When the firing commenced Dave Kent, Jesse Robinson, and
John Henry Brown had just arrived at the Mission San Jose
with some beef cattle, and at once hurried to the battle.

There has been some controversy as to who was in command
of the Texans in this fight, Bowie or Fannin. Mr. Highsmith
says that on the morning of the fight Bowie gave the order to
"Get your guns, boys; here they come," when the Mexicans first
fired on them. Only one man on the side of the Americans was
killed. His name was Richard Andrews. He and Ben Highsmith stood beside the same hackberry tree during the hottest of
the fire, and Andrews exposed himself in getting a shot. His
companion said, "Look out, Dick; they will hit you." He fired,
however, and stepped back to reload, and then leaned from the
tree again to look and to shoot. Highsmith said again, "Look
out; you will get shot." About this time a ball struck the side
of the tree, and, glancing, went through Andrews, going in at the
right and coming out at the left side, lacerating the bowels in
its progress. The wounded man lived until night and died in
great agony. So great was his pain that he would place a finger
in each bullet hole and try to tear them larger in the vain effort

to get relief. He was buried on the battleground, under a large pecan tree. During the battle the Mexican cavalry was stationed back east in the prairie on the La Bahia road, about half a mile from the battleground, with their ropes ready to lasso the Texans when they were driven out of the timber across the open flats. The Mexicans had not learned yet what it was to round up a bunch of Texans. In the end the infantry and cavalry retreated back to San Antonio, with the loss of one cannon and about sixty men.

THE GRASS FIGHT.

After the Concepcion fight General Austin came up with the main body of his troops and all moved to the head of the San Antonio River above the city and began to invest the place. General Burleson had arrived with the Colorado men, and Ben Milam was also there. The Mexicans were in a precarious situation. They could not leave the city, and no supplies could reach them. Their cavalry horses were nearly starving. One night a party was sent out west of town to cut grass and bring it in for the horses. They succeeded in loading about fifty burros with the prairie grass, but daylight came upon them before they could get back to town, and they were discovered by Colonel Bowie, who with part of his men were on the lookout for a reinforcement which was expected from Mexico to relieve the beleaguered city. Bowie at once attacked them, although a large force of soldiers was with the grass cutters. The Mexicans commenced a rapid retreat to town, followed by the yelling Texans, and a lively fight and chase took place. The grass-laden jacks kept the road, braying at every jump, and the Mexicans fired back as they ran. One Texan was hit a glancing shot in the forehead and he fell from his horse. When the suburbs of the town was reached the Texans turned back, as the firing was attracting a reinforcement with artillery. The fight commenced on the Alazan Creek, and the road to Castroville now crosses the battleground. A party came back to see about the man that fell from his horse, and he was found sitting on the bank of a small ravine and holding his forehead with both hands. One of the party, John McGuffin, said, "Hello, here; what are you doing? Catching your brains in your hands?" The wounded man was tenderly cared for and recovered. Uncle Ben was in the fight, but does not remember the man's name. In writing this sketch I only give accounts of battles that Mr. Highsmith participated in, and only allude to others in a general way.

General Somerville was present during the siege, and one day a sentinel named Winslow Turner made him mark time for trying to pass him without the countersign. It is more than likely the officer was trying the soldier to see what kind of a guard he was.

STORMING OF SAN ANTONIO.

On the 5th day of December, 1835, while the siege was dragging slow and the men impatient and inactive, Col. Ben Milam called for volunteers to storm San Antonio. General Austin, who was not a military man, but a statesman, and who was at the head of the great immigration scheme of bringing colonists from the States to Texas, had quit the service, and Gen. Edward Burleson was in command of the Texans now before San Antonio. When Milam made the call for men to enter the city, 300 responded and were led in by Milam and Col. Frank W. Johnson. General Burleson held the reserves up at the old mill. Bowie also, with part of his men, was there ready to give assistance at a moment's notice. Mr. Highsmith went in with Milam, but was not by him when he was killed, being on the west side of Soledad Street, and the gallant old colonel was killed on the east side at the Veramendi House. After Milam was killed Colonel Johnson took command and continued the assault to a successful finish. Col. J. C. Neill made a demonstration against the Alamo with artillery to draw the attention of the Mexicans to the east side of the river, while Milam and his men were entering on the other.

Mr. Highsmith noticed two men get peculiar shots near him while a storming party were making their way toward the plaza. Sam Evitts was shot in the mouth and the ball came out under his right ear, and James Belden had his right eye shot out. Both men recovered. John Harvey was killed, and Captain Ware and "Deaf" Smith were wounded at the Veramendi House when Milam was killed.

General Cos surrendered his men, and they were all paroled and sent back to Mexico.

FRONT OF THE VERAMENDI HOUSE ON SOLEDAD STREET, SAN ANTONIO,
TEXAS, WHERE COL. BEN MILAM WAS KILLED.
The marks of bullets are seen on the doors, which are of cedar, heavy and thick, and
have swung there since 1720.

THE GRAVE OF BEN MILAM, SAN ANTONIO, TEXAS.

After the surrender many of the Texans went back home, thinking the war was over. Colonel Fannin had been sent to La Bahia, or Goliad, before the taking of San Antonio, and was in command there. Col. James Neill was placed in command of the Alamo until relieved by Col. William B. Travis. Mr. Highsmith stayed in the Alamo with Colonel Travis until the approach of Santa Anna from Mexico with a large army, and he was then sent by his commander with a dispatch to Colonel Fannin ordering that officer to blow up the fort at Goliad and come to him with his men. Mr. Highsmith was gone five days, and on his return Santa Anna's advance of 600 cavalry was on the east side of the river, riding around the Alamo and on the lookout for messengers whom they knew the Texan commander was sending from the doomed fort.

Mr. Highsmith sat on his horse on Powderhouse Hill and took in the situation. The Mexican flag was waving from the Church of Bexar across the river, and the flag of Travis from the Alamo. The country was open and nearly all prairie in the valley around San Antonio, and objects could be seen some distance from the elevated points. There was a great stir and perceptible activity in the town, and the forms of some of the doomed men at the Alamo could be plainly seen as from the walls of the fort they watched the Mexican cavalry.

The daring messenger saw there was no chance for him to communicate with his gallant commander, and slowly rode north towards the San Antonio and Gonzales road. The Mexican cavalrymen saw him, and a dense body of them rode parallel with and closely watched him. Finally they spurred their horses into a gallop and came rapidly towards him. Highsmith took one last look towards the Alamo and the trapped heroes within, and then, turning his horse east, dashed off towards Gonzales. He is the last man alive to-day who talked with Bowie and Travis at the Alamo. The Mexicans pursued Uncle Ben six miles—two miles beyond the Salado Creek—and then gave up the chase. He went on to the Cibolo Creek, eighteen miles from San Antonio, and then halted on a ridge to rest his horse. While here his quick ear caught the sound of cannon as the dull boom was wafted across the prairie. The siege and bombardment of the Alamo had commenced. Mr. Highsmith thinks that David Crockett went into the Alamo with George Kimble, A. J. Kent, Abe Darst,

Tom Jackson, Tom Mitchell, Wash Cottle, and two 16-year-old boys named Albert Fuqua and John Gaston. Crockett had a few men who came with him to Texas, and some think he did not come by Gonzales, but straight across from Bastrop to San Antonio. The men mentioned above all came from Gonzales and were led by Captain Kimble. The names are not all given here. There were thirty two of them in all. They came down the river in the night and fought their way into the Alamo by a sudden dash.

When Mr. Highsmith arrived at Gonzales he found Gen. Sam Houston there with about 300 men on his way to succor Travis, and Highsmith's report was the last reliable news before the fall. Scouts were sent back to within a few miles of San Antonio to listen for the signal gun which Travis said he would fire at sunup each morning as long as held the fort. On Monday morning, March 7, 1836, the scouts listened in vain for the welcome signal. The sun arose and began to mount into the heavens, and still no token came; all was silent in the west. The scouts mounted their horses and set off again for Gonzales to inform General Houston that the Alamo had fired her last gun. On the 6th the Alamo had been stormed and all the defenders perished.

When Mr. Highsmith reported to General Houston the situation at the Alamo, he sent Uncle Ben and a boy named David B. Kent again to Colonel Fannin, ordering him to demolish the fort of Goliad and retire to the east bank of the Guadalupe River and form a junction with him. When they arrived at Goliad and handed the message to Fannin he read it, but said nothing. When asked what reply they must carry back he said, "Tell him that I will not desert the fort." Colonel Fannin had made an attempt to join Travis at the Alamo, but his frail transportation carts had broken down and he had to return to Goliad, having no means to convey his supplies or artillery. The readers of Texas history are familiar with the terrible scenes that were enacted around the fort of Goliad after the departure of these last messengers to Fannin. A large Mexican army came and the commands of Ward, King, and others were massacred. Fannin attempted also to leave, but was cut off and surrounded in the Coleta prairie, and after a hard battle against largely superior numbers, surrendered the remnant of his command, who were then massacred, only a few escaping the general slaughter.

The young lad Kent, who was sent with Highsmith to Fannin,

THE OLD CHURCH OF BEXAR.
From which waved the blood-red flag of Santa Anna during the
siege and storming of the Alamo.

was the son of David Kent, who was killed in the Alamo. The writer has seen this messenger Kent, and had many talks with him. He died a few years ago in Frio Canyon, Uvalde County.

Highsmith and Kent returned to Gonzales and found General Houston and his men still there, and made their report. Houston was greatly distressed. There was great commotion in town. Mrs. Dickinson had arrived and confirmed the report that the Alamo had fallen and its defenders been all slain. There was wailing and weeping among wives and mothers. The Gonzales men and boys to the number of thirty-two had perished with Travis. Mrs. Dickinson was the wife of Lieut. Almon Dickinson, who was killed in the Alamo. She had been spared and had made her way to Gonzales.

BATTLE OF SAN JACINTO.

The Mexican army divided at San Antonio after the Alamo was taken, Santa Anna coming to Gonzales, Cos by Bastrop, and Urrea to Goliad. It was the latter that fought Fannin. Mr. Highsmith went on with the army from Gonzales, and blames General Houston for several things. In the first place, he said, they should have fought the Mexicans at the Colorado, as more men were together there than at any subsequent time, and that the burning of Gonzales, Columbus, San Felipe, Harrisburg, and New Washington by order of Houston was useless, as the Mexicans could have done no more. He said if the battle could have been fought at Columbus it would have saved much property. Be this as it may, however, all is well that ends well. The Texans under Houston, few as they were, gained a great and glorious victory when they did fight on the historic plain of San Jacinto.

Uncle Ben went into the battle in the company of Capt. William Ware. He says the dead Mexicans lay thickest around the breastwork and were considerably scattered on the prairie. The breastwork, he said, was composed of brush, dirt, packs, etc. A great many prisoners were taken, and he says they held them in camp that night by stretching ropes around the trees, building large fires so as to keep a good light, and by keeping guards posted on the outside circle of ropes. During the night the grass caught fire and burned among some boxes of captured paper cartridges, and many of them exploded. When the cartridges commenced to go off the Mexican prisoners, 700 in number, became greatly alarmed, not knowing the cause of the fusilade, and thinking the Texans had commenced to shoot the prisoners.

After the battle and pursuit was over the wounded Mexicans who were able to travel were marched to the camp of the Texans, some having to travel two miles. They never groaned or complained, and a casual observer would not have known they were wounded except by their bloody clothes. There were about 300 of them in all, and thirty of them died in the Texan camp that night.

Mr. Highsmith says, from the amount of guns picked up on the field, there could not have been less than 2200 Mexicans in line of battle. Their line was twice the length of that of the Texans and more densely packed.

There was a man named Bob Love in the battle, and during the first charge the men were ordered to fall forward at the flash of the cannon to avoid the shots; but Love had not heard this order, and when the men went down at the flash he turned back and ran to camp and told the guard detail there that all of Houston's men had been killed at the first fire except himself. He then went on towards the Sabine and told all the people that he saw the same tale. The date of the battle was April 21, 1836.

FIGHT BETWEEN INDIANS AND SURVEYORS.

In 1838 Mr. Highsmith went out with a surveying party under the leadership of Captain Lynch. Their course was westward, and they finally established their camp between Salt and Cherokee creeks, where the land lay which they wanted to run off. This place is now covered by Lampasas County. There were twenty-five white men in the party, including the hunters. Work progressed all right. Game was plentiful and no signs of Indians. Nothing occurred worthy of note until the morning, when preparations were being made to break up camp and return to the settlements, the work having been completed. At this time the men were surprised and thrown into momentary confusion by the furious onslaught of about forty Indians who had approached their camp through some thickets. The most of the white men were frontiersmen and good Indian fighters, and order was soon restored and the Indians driven back to cover by a well-directed rifle fire. The men had time to reload before another charge came, and the Indians were again driven off after circling around the position of the whites, yelling and discharging a good many arrows, but without much effect. This kind of fighting was kept up for nearly an hour, when the Comanches, seeing it was going to cost them too much to continue it longer, drew off. There was but one white man killed, and that was the brave Captain Lynch. He was shot through the body with a bullet, and died instantly, without speaking. His body was buried on the battleground by his comrades, and they then returned to the settlement without further incident.

FEDERATION WAR.

This is the name Mr. Highsmith gives to the disturbances which occurred along the Rio Grande in 1839. He says the Mexicans were raiding on the Americans who had commenced to settle on the lower Nueces between that stream and the Rio Grande. These Mexicans were in some force, and were led by one of their countrymen named Parbon. John N. Seguin, a Mexican of Spanish descent, but loyal to Texas at that time, raised a company of ninety-five men to go and fight Parbon and his party. Sixty of this company were Americans and the balance Mexicans. Mr. Highsmith, ever ready to go on an expedition, joined the force under Seguin. The latter had a fine ranch below San Antonio on the river of the same name. On a creek called Santiago, between San Patricio and Laredo, they met Parbon and his men, and a fight occurred in the brush and prickly pears. A parley was finally agreed on, and while this was in progress one of Parbon's men told Juan Cantu, who belonged to Seguin's company, that the latter intended to sell his company out. When the men heard this they broke up and came back to San Antonio. Captain Seguin had some trouble with the Americans near his ranch, and thinking he had been wronged by them, turned traitor to Texas, removed to Mexico, and returned with the invading armies of Vasquez and Wall in 1842.

When Vasquez made his raid Mr. Highsmith joined the company of Capt. H. M. Childress. The Mexicans held San Antonio a few days and then went back to Mexico without a fight, not waiting until the Texans could assemble. The latter kept their forces in the city a while before disbanding. While here, Highsmith learned through Juan Cantu, who was loyal to the Texans, that Seguin was at the Calaveras ranch, thirty miles down the river, and applied to Captain Childress for twenty-five men to go and capture him. This was granted, and Captain Highsmith set out for the Calaveras ranch, guided by Juan Cantu.

The party arrived at the ranch in the night and surrounded it. The owner, Calaveras, was called out and asked if Seguin was there. He said "No." "You lie," said Cantu, and proposed then and there to hang him. A rope was produced, put around his neck, and he was drawn up, but was told he would be let down when he told where Seguin was. Calaveras, however, persisted in his first statement that Seguin was not there, and that he did not know where he was. He was drawn up three times, but finally released and left nearly dead. No doubt Seguin had been there, but was gone. Highsmith and his men went back to San Antonio and disbanded.

It is a pity that Captain Seguin should have had any trouble with the Texans. He commanded a small company of Mexicans at San Jacinto, fighting against Santa Anna, and it was he and his men who collected the bones of the men who were killed and partly burned at the Alamo. They buried these remains about seventy-five yards from the northeast corner of the Alamo.

CHEROKEE WAR.

In 1839 an attempt to remove the Cherokee Indians from East Texas to the Indian Territory, which had been set aside as the home of the Indian tribes, caused a short conflict, in which the Indians were defeated and the intentions of the government carried out. Two chiefs, Bowles and Big Mush, commanded the Indians, and the whites were led by Gen. Thomas J. Rusk. The battle was fought near Nacogdoches in a thick woods of pine, white oak, gum, etc. Both Indian chiefs were killed, and among the whites killed was Capt. John C. Crane, one of the captains under Milam at the storming of San Antonio in 1835, and who was well known to Mr. Highsmith, who was near him when he fell and helped to bury him. Uncle Ben in this fight belonged to Capt. Ed. Burleson's company.

THE FIGHT AT MILL CREEK.

In 1839 Gen. Vincent Cordova, a disaffected Mexican living at Nacogdoches, raised a motley crowd of Mexicans, Indians, and negroes and started to Mexico. Gen. Ed. Burleson got wind of him on the Colorado, and went with a company of rangers to intercept him. Ben Highsmith and Winslow Turner were members of the company. The trail of Cordova was struck between Webber's Prairie and Austin, and the band overtaken on Mill Creek, in Guadalupe County, about five miles east of the little village of Seguin, then just starting. It was a running fight and did not last long, as it was nearly sundown when it commenced. It could not be ascertained how many of the enemy were killed, as they fell as they ran and were badly scattered. The father of the writer lived at Seguin at the time, and was on the battle-ground next morning. He said there were two negroes, one Mexican, and one Indian dead on the ground where the fight first commenced. Cordova intended to capture and pillage Seguin. The dead Indian had his head cut off. Mr. Highsmith says that Dr. Venters, who was with the rangers, had a personal combat with an Indian and killed him. I have heard my father say that a doctor who was in this fight cut off the head of a dead Indian and carried it away with him for medical examination. Likely this was the one.

INDIAN FIGHT ON BRUSHY CREEK.

In 1839 the Comanche Indians in large force made a raid on the settlement below Austin, and after killing some of the Coleman family and robbing the house of Dr. Robinson in his absence, traveled a northerly course towards Brushy Creek, carrying one of the doctor's negroes with them. Mr. Highsmith was at Bastrop, and when he heard the news of the raid set out for Austin in company with his old comrade of many battles, Winslow Turner. When they arrived at Austin Capt. James Rogers was raising men to pursue the Indians, and the two Bastrop men joined him. Gen. Ed. Burleson, the Indian fighter and leader on the Colorado, was away at the time. Captain Rogers with thirty men left Austin in pursuit and came up with the Indians twenty miles northeast from Austin, on Brushy Creek, not far

from the present town of Taylor. The Indians saw the white
men coming across the prairie and made ready to fight them.
The Indians charged when Rogers and his men came near, and
after firing the captain saw that his force was not sufficient to
cope with them, especially in open ground, and ordered a retreat
to a mott of timber on a hill. Here his intention was to dismount
his men and make a fight. As soon as the men started the Indians followed with fearful yells, and by the time the timber was
reached considerable confusion prevailed among the white men.
Only three men dismounted in obedience to orders, and the balance passed on. Captain Rogers, seeing he could not carry out
his plans, also passed on. The three men who had dismounted
at the trees were Ben Highsmith, Winslow Turner, and Jacob
Burleson. The Indians were crowding the settlers closely and
firing at them, and the dismounted men, seeing the stand was
not going to be made, hastily remounted and followed. Their
order as they left the trees was Turner in front, Burleson next,
and Highsmith last. About this time the Indians, who were
close upon them, fired a volley with rifles. Highsmith felt the
wind of a ball close to his ear, and at the same time saw the dust
rise from the crown of Burleson's hat, who was directly in front
of him. The next instant the gallant young man reeled and fell
from his saddle, shot in the back of the head. The men were not
to blame for making this retreat, as they were greatly outnumbered, and many more would have been slain had they stayed.
Some were young men who had never seen Indians before.

The Indians did not pursue far, and the men all got together
and went back towards Austin. Captain Rogers was greatly de-
jected. Before getting back, however, they met Gen. Ed. Burleson coming rapidly with twenty men. He was informed of the
disastrous fight, and that his brother Jacob was killed. General
Burleson now took command of all the men and went back to
give the Indians another fight. He, like Jack Hays, had never
been defeated by Indians. They first went to the spot where
Jake Burleson fell, and there found his body, stripped and badly
mutilated. He was shot through the head, as Highsmith had
told them, and his right hand and right foot cut off, scalped, and
his heart cut out. The Indians went back to Brushy Creek and
there strongly posted themselves. The creek here made an acute

bend, and the Indians were in the lower part of it and concealed from view except when some of them showed themselves in order to watch the movements of the white men.

General Burleson moved his men around the position of the Comanches and occupied the upper bend of the creek, and the fight soon commenced across the space between them, which was in short rifle range. The battle lasted a long time and was hotly contested—rifle against rifle. The Indians seemed to be nearly all armed with guns and were good shots, and still outnumbered the white men. The latter, some of whom were old Indian fighters, were cautious, exposing themselves as little as possible. The Indians did the same. They evidently recognized Burleson as their old enemy, and they dared not leave cover and charge his position. One Indian crawled out of the bed of the creek unperceived and took a position behind a large bunch of prickly pears, where he lay flat on the ground and watched his opportunity to shoot as some settler would expose some part of his body. He did execution, and it was some time before he was located, but the smoke of his gun finally betrayed him. Winslow Turner saw where the smoke came from, and quickly ascending a small tree at great risk of his life, got sight of the Indian, fired quickly, and came down again. The Comanche jumped at the crack of the gun and tumbled over the creek bank. This Indian had on Dr. Robinson's coat and vest, as was noticed when he jumped away from his position. The coat and vest were found when the fight was over, covered with blood and a bullet hole in them. The Indians, after losing many of their warriors, gave up the fight and retreated down the creek and then into the hills. They carried off their dead, but the bloody ground they occupied told the tale of their loss.

After the battle was over the loss of Burleson in killed was Jack Walters, Ed. Blakey, and James Gilleland. The latter was a Methodist preacher. Of the four men killed three were shot in the head. Gilleland was shot between the point of the shoulder and neck, the ball ranging down and going through the lungs. Mr. Highsmith helped to carry Blakey to the house of Noah Smithwick, at Webber's Prairie, twenty miles distant from the battleground. Smithwick was brother-in-law of the wounded man. They carried the dying youth on a blanket stretched between two poles, between a pair of horses. He was shot late in

2

the evening, and died at sundown on the next evening. The other dead were carried off to their respective homes by friends. Heartrending scenes were enacted when the bloody remains were slowly brought to their homes by sorrowing comrades. Walters was a young man and his mother was a widow.

BATTLE OF PLUM CREEK.

In 1840 a large body of Comanche Indians, about 500 in number, made a most daring raid through Texas and burned and sacked the town of Linnville on the coast. When the news of this raid was generally circulated men began to gather from all points where there was a settlement to intercept and fight them on their way back to the mountains from whence they came. Mr. Highsmith heard the news at his home in Bastrop, and at once saddled his horse, got his gun, and started. Among the leaders who were gathering men to fight the Indians were Felix Huston, Ed. Burleson, Jack Hays, Matthew Caldwell ("Old Paint"), and the McCullochs, Henry and Ben.

Mr. Highsmith joined the company of General Burleson. The Indians came up Peach Creek and then across Tinny's Prairie towards Plum Creek. Scouts kept Burleson informed as to the route of the Indians, and he cut across with his men to intercept and fight them at Plum Creek, but when he arrived there the Comanches had crossed the creek and were out in the prairie. They had many pack animals, besides squaws and warriors, and presented an imposing spectacle as they moved along singing and exploiting on their horses, and altogether covering a mile in extent. Burleson moved out towards them and charged, commencing the fight with eighty-two men. The warriors divided and moved towards Burleson, firing and yelling, which was spiritedly replied to by the men from the Colorado. About this time a reinforcement arrived of 125 men under Gen. Felix Huston, who were following on the trail from below. The fight now became general and quite extended, as the Indians began to quail before the fire and to move off, following in the wake of the squaws and pack animals. Other reinforcements in small squads continued to arrive, attracted by the firing to the course the battle was following. The pursuit lasted many miles, and wound up where the present town of Kyle is situated, between San Marcos and

Austin. It commenced three miles east of the present town of Lockhart, in Caldwell County.

Many personal encounters took place during the long-extended and scattered battle. One Indian in the chase has his horse killed, and after leaving him and running a short distance on foot, returned to the dead horse to secure his bridle, but was killed and fell across the horse's neck with the bridle in his hand. Another Indian presented a very humorous and grotesque appearance. When the stores at Linnville were looted this fellow proceeded to rig himself from head to foot in regular full dress fashion, except the pants, having on a beegum hat, fine calf boots on over his naked legs, and a broadcloth long forked-tail coat, which was resplendent with a double row of brass buttons in front. This dusky dude, however, had no valet de chambre to put on his coat for him, and consequently got it on wrong, having the front behind and closely buttoned up to the back of his neck. He also had an umbrella hoisted, and was riding with head erect and a little thrown back, singing loudly, when the battle commenced. The sight of him and the humorous figure he cut caused loud laughter among the Texans who were near him. He lost his hat and umbrella during the fight, but himself escaped, although fired at repeatedly. He was a dexterous rider and dodger. Mr. Highsmith saw a white woman lying under a tree with an arrow in her breast. Some men had dismounted beside her, and a doctor from Gonzales was extracting the arrow. One of the men was well known to Mr. Highsmith. He was Z. N. Morrell, the noted pioneer Baptist preacher. The wounded woman was a captive, and the Indians shot her when they commenced to run from the whites.

The horse which was killed when the Indian also lost his life trying to save his bridle belonged to Colonel Bell, who was killed off of him at Kitchen's ranch as the Indians were coming back from Linnville. Several men shot at this Indian when he was killed, among whom were Mr. Highsmith and Andrew Sowell. The latter's ball hit the shield.

During the charge across the hogwallow prairie many horses fell and threw their riders. Bones of Indians were found years after along the route of pursuit.

BATTLE OF BANDERA PASS.

Soon after the Plum Creek battle President Houston commissioned the famous Jack Hays to raise a company of Texas rangers for the protection of the frontier against Indians and lawless characters. The latter were thick around San Antonio, and did pretty much as they pleased. Jack Hays at the time was a young surveyor, and not much known. He distinguished himself at the battle of Plum Creek. General Houston, who had been elected President of the young Republic of Texas, recognized his ability, and seeing the necessity of having such a man with a company of like spirits around him, at once put him in the field, and well did he sustain the trust and confidence which the hero of San Jacinto placed in him. Under Hays the Texas rangers gained a name and reputation which was world-wide.

Mr. Highsmith joined the company of Hays, and they were stationed at San Antonio. They soon established law and order in the Alamo City, and the name of Hays and his rangers soon become a terror to evildoers. The red man of the plains felt the weight of his mailed hand and learned to dread an encounter with him. In four pitched battles they were utterly routed, namely, Nueces Canyon, Pinta Trail Crossing, Enchanted Rock and Bandera Pass. No account of these battles will be given in this sketch except those Mr. Highsmith was engaged in. The main scouting ground of the rangers was in the mountains west and northwest of San Antonio, up the Guadalupe, Medina, Sabinal, Frio, and Nueces rivers.

In the spring of 1841 Captain Hays started on a scout with forty men. His camp at this time was seven miles west of San Antonio, on Leon Creek. They went a northwest direction up Medina River and camped for the night at a point about where the center of Bandera town now is. Guards were well posted, and the night passed without any disturbance. Some people would be surprised to know that the Texas rangers under Hays were many of them men of education and refinement. Around the campfire at night it was not uncommon to hear men quoting from the most popular poets and authors, and talking learnedly on ancient and modern history. It is true they looked rough in the garb they wore. The wide hat was to protect them from the sun in long scouts across the prairies. The leggings of buckskin or cowskin protected the legs from the thorny brush and cactus. The large clinking spurs put new life into a tardy pony if occasion demanded. The intention of Hays was to turn north from this place and go out through the famous Bandera Pass and into the Guadalupe valley, and then scout up the river to the divide. The pass was about ten miles from the night camp of the rangers.

After the rangers left camp and were riding over the open country towards the pass, which could be seen plainly, quite a different looking crowd were assembling there. A large band of Comanche Indians were also on the warpath, and had started across the country by way of the pass to the Medina valley. They arrived there first, and, seeing the rangers coming, laid in ambush and awaited there to fight them.

The pass was named for General Bandera of the Spanish army, who was stationed at San Antonio when the missions were first built there. All of this country and Mexico then belonged to Spain. The pass was the home of the Apache Indians, and they raided upon San Antonio. General Bandera was ordered to follow them to their stronghold and chastise them. He found them at home in the pass and strongly fortified among the rocks. A long and desperate battle took place and many were killed on both sides, but at last the Spanish arms prevailed and the Indians gave way and retreated through the hills further towards the west. They never came back, but settled in New Mexico. Now, after the lapse of a century or more, another bloody battle was about to be fought here.

Hays and his men arrived at the pass about 11 o'clock in the morning and began to ride through it, as yet having seen no sign of Indians. The pass was 500 yards in length by 125 in width, and from 50 to 75 feet high on both sides, very steep, and covered with rocks and bushes. The Indian chief dismounted his men and placed them among the rocks and bushes on both sides of the pass, leaving their horses in the rear, and also concealed in a deep gulch which cut into the pass from the west and well up towards the north end.

The first intimation the rangers had of the presence of Indians was being fired on by bullets and arrows on all sides, and the terrible warwhoop of the Comanche resounded through the gorge. For a few moments there was some confusion among the rangers

on account of the plunging of frightened and wounded horses,
who would turn and try to run back through the pass in spite
almost of all their riders could do. This was a trying and most
critical time and the Indians knew it. They charged down into
the pass and almost mixed up with the rangers and plunging
horses. The white men could not well use their guns and hold
their horses, too. To add to the disadvantage and confusion,
some of the rangers were killed and wounded and were falling
from their horses. As soon as a horse would find himself free of
his rider he would gallop madly back through the pass.

All this took place in less time than it takes to write, and it
was the first time Jack Hays was ever caught in a trap; but he
was equal to the occasion. His clear voice now rang out sharp
and quick, "Steady there, boys; dismount and tie those horses;
we can whip them; no doubt about that." Order was soon restored, and in a moment the rangers were on the ground, and
the Indians were falling and giving back before a deadly rifle and
pistol fire. They came again, however, and several hand to hand
conflicts took place. Mr. Highsmith, who was in the fight, dismounted near a ranger named Sam Luckey, who was soon shot
through by a bullet. It entered under the left shoulder blade
and came out below the right nipple. Highsmith caught him
when he commenced falling and let him down to the ground easy.
At this time the rangers had fastened their horses near the south
entrance of the pass and were fighting in front of them. The
wounded Luckey called for water, and Highsmith gave him some
out of a canteen. At this time the fight was raging and the pass
was full of Indians, rangers, and horses. The Comanche chief
during this close fight attacked Sergt. Kit Ackland and wounded
him. Ackland also shot the chief with a pistol, and then they
clinched and both went down. Both were large, powerful men,
and the combat was terrific. Both had out their long knives and
rolled over and over on the ground, each trying to avoid the
thrust of the other and himself give the deadly wound. The
ranger was finally the victor. He got up covered with blood and
dirt, with the bloody knife in hand. The chief lay dead, literally
cut to pieces.

Mr. Highsmith loaded and fired his rifle many times, and was
finally wounded in the leg with an arrow. The wound did not
disable him, but after getting the arrow out he continued to load

and fire until the fight was over, which lasted an hour. The Indians finally gave way, retreated to the upper end of the pass, and left the rangers masters of the situation. It was a dear bought victory. Five rangers lay dead and as many more wounded. Many horses were also wounded and killed. Of the wounded were Highsmith, Ackland, Tom Galbreath, James Dunn ("Red"), Sam Luckey, and one other whose name is not now remembered. While the fight was going on some of the Indians were carrying their dead back to where their horses were, at the north end of the pass. Hays carried his dead and wounded men back to the south entrance of the pass, where there was a large water hole, and there spent the night burying the dead rangers and taking care of the wounded. The writer was not able to get the names of those killed except one, whose name was Jackson. It has been fifty-six years since the battle was fought, and Mr. Highsmith can not now remember the others. At the time of the fight he had not been in the company long, and the names of those killed were not as familiar to him as the survivors became in after years.

From the pass Hays carried his wounded men to San Antonio, where they could get good medical attention.

Jack Hays never had a better crowd of fighting men than was with him in the Bandera Pass fight. Some of them are as follows: Sam Walker, Ad. Gillispie, P. H. Bell, Ben McCulloch, Kit Ackland, Sam Luckey, James Dunn, Tom Galbreath, George Neill, Mike Chevallier. Some of these became noted men in after years, but were then all young Texas rangers. Sam Walker was a lieutenant-colonel in the Mexican war of 1846, and was killed at the battle of Humantla. Gillispie commanded a company also, and was killed at the storming of Monterey. Ben McCulloch commanded a company, and was also a Confederate general in the civil war, and was killed at the battle of Elkhorn. George Neill was the son of Col. James Neill, who commanded the artillery at the storming of San Antonio. Chevalier was a captain in the Mexican war, as was also Ackland. Sam Luckey was a famous humorist, singer, and story-teller around the camp-fires. P. H. Bell was afterwards Governor of Texas. Ben Highsmith participated in eighteen battles, and was the last man to carry a dispatch from Travis at the Alamo. All of them made records as good fighters.

The Comanches buried their chief at the upper end of the pass, and the spot can still be pointed out by some rocks that are over the grave.

BATTLE OF SALADO.

In 1842 Mr. Highsmith was still a member of Jack Hays' ranging company, and stationed at San Antonio. In September of the above year Gen. Adrian Wall came from Mexico with about 1200 men and captured San Antonio. The rangers were out on a scout at the time, and failed to discover the approach of the Mexicans. Some of them came in, not being aware of the changed conditions, put up their horses, and were captured after some slight resistance. The balance of the rangers had gone down the Medina River with Captain Hays, and when they came back discovered there were Mexican soldiers in town, and made their escape, although hotly pursued by a large body of cavalry. Mr. Highsmith was with this party with Hays. The rangers went into camp on the Salado, and Captain Hays sent runners to Seguin and Gonzales and other points informing the people of the situation and calling for help. Lieut. H. E. McCulloch was very active in spreading the news and raising men. Spies from the ranger camp kept watch on the Mexicans around San Antonio. The people east, as was their wont in time of danger, responded with alacrity, and soon Gen. Matthew Caldwell took the field with a force and established his camp on the Salado, seven miles northeast from San Antonio. Captain Hays was then sent with part of his rangers to draw the Mexicans out to Caldwell's position. They advanced to within half a mile of the Alamo, and cut up many antics on their horses in a bantering way to get the Mexican cavalry to pursue them. In this they succeeded, for soon 400 cavalry came out and charged them. A lively chase now commenced back to the position of Caldwell. Mr. Highsmith was not in this chase, but remembers the following names of those who were: H. E. McCulloch, Kit Ackland, Stuart Foley, Creed Taylor, Andrew Sowell, Big Foot Wallace, Ad Gillispie, Sam Walker, Sam Luckey, and a man named Jett, who was killed in the battle which followed on the creek. The Mexican army soon came out and a severe battle was fought, in which Wall was defeated. Caldwell's force has been variously estimated. The writer once heard Gen. Henry McCulloch say that there were 201.

Before the fight commenced, and while the Mexicans were preparing to charge, the Baptist preacher, Z. N. Morrell, asked permission of Caldwell to make the men a short talk. The request was granted, and the general added, "I wish you would; it will do the boys good."

The preacher was listened to with profound respect, and he wound up the address with these words: "And now, boys, my impression before God is that we will win the fight." The men cheered their appreciation. The Mexicans made some desperate charges, but shot wild. Sometimes they would come within fifteen yards of the Texans, yelling like Indians. General Cordova, who had the fight with Burleson's rangers on Mill Creek in 1839, was killed in this fight by Wilson Randle of Seguin. John N. Seguin was also here in command of a company fighting the Texans. Capt. Nicholas Dawson, from Fayette County, tried to get to Caldwell's position with fifty-two men, but was cut to pieces and himself and thirty-two of his men were killed and the balance captured, except two—Gon. Woods and Aulcy Miller. Woods fought his way through the Mexicans and got to Caldwell; Miller went the other way to Seguin. Wall, being defeated by Caldwell, went back to San Antonio, but did not tarry there long, and set out for Mexico. He was followed by the Texans and overtaken, and a skirmish took place called

THE FIGHT ON THE HONDO.

The Mexican army in their retreat from San Antonio traveled towards the foot of the mountains and crossed the Medina River two miles above the present town of Castroville, and then traveled up between two ravines to a high ridge near the Hondo River. The advance of the Texans was led by Jack Hays and his rangers, who crowded close on the rear of the retreating Mexicans. The Texans were badly scattered, coming on in companies under their respective leaders. This want of order and a thorough understanding in regard to commanders and plan of battle caused the pursuit to be a failure. Captain Hays and his men came upon the Mexicans at the ridge where they had halted to give battle, and he halted his men to await the arrival of the remainder of the American forces, but they came in disordered squads, and the Mexican commander, seeing that he was not going to be immediately attacked, moved on across the Hondo and made another stand there. One battery was placed in position on the east side of the creek with twenty men with it, supported by infantry, and the main army formed in the flats on the west side with a cannon in position to bear upon any approach to the one on the east.

Captain Hays had sent a runner back to inform General Caldwell of the fact when the Mexicans made the first halt on the ridge. When the general came up he told Hays to follow on with his men, and when he came upon them again to charge and bring on the battle, and he would support him with the rest of the men. In the meantime Hays had sent Ben Highsmith, Sam Luckey, Tom Galbreath, and some others to follow close after Wall's army so that he could get accurate information as to the disposition of their forces in case a stand was made to fight. When the scouts arrived at a point a short distance above where the little village of New Fountain is now, in Medina County, they halted, for they were close upon the rear of the Mexicans. There was a great commotion among the latter, and they made a great deal of noise,—a perfect babel of voices, carts rattling across the rocky bed of the Hondo, officers giving commands, teamsters and artillerymen shouting and cursing, mules braying, and the occasional yelling of a lot of Cherokee Indians who were with the Mexicans. While the rangers were sitting here on their horses listening to all this they were startled by a rifle shot, and Sam Luckey reeled in his saddle and would have fallen to the ground had not Ben Highsmith caught him. The shot came from a dry branch of the Verde Creek, and the spot was located by the smoke of the rifle of the hidden marksman. Some of the rangers charged in that direction, but only the glimpse of a fleeing Cherokee Indian who did the work could be seen. These Indians were good shots and armed with rifles. They did more damage to the Texans at Salado and at Dawson's massacre than the Mexicans.

Luckey was hit under the right shoulder blade, and the ball came out just below the left nipple, barely missing the heart. This shot was just the reverse to the one he received the year before at the Bandera Pass, and by a strange coincidence Ben

Highsmith was near him on both occasions and caught him before falling, laid him down, and each time gave him water. Captain Hays and quite a lot of his men now came up, and he told the men that he was going to attack the rear guard of the enemy, and that the troops in the rear would support them. One man was left with the wounded Luckey, and the balance advanced to the attack. Hays soon found out the position of the enemy and told his men to charge and capture the battery on the east side of the creek, and then turn it upon the Mexicans beyond.

Quite a large force of Texans were now close by, and Hays though it was all right to make the charge. The men, about fifty in number, who now collected around their gallant captain to make this desperate charge were men who had been beside him in many bloody conflicts, and he knew they could be depended upon. One inducement that nerved the men to make this daring attack was the fact that in the Mexican lines on the other side of the creek, held as prisoners, were twelve of Dawson's men who had been captured at the massacre, many of the citizens of San Antonio, including members of the district court which was in session when the town was taken, and a few of Hays' rangers— their own comrades. When all was ready Hays led the way and the charge commenced. The rangers fired as they went and were soon among the cannons, which raked them with grape shot as they came up. The work was short and quick at the guns. The men who worked them either ran or were killed. Some sought refuge under the pieces to avoid the fearful rush of the mounted rangers, and Mr. Highsmith says he saw Kit Ackland lean from his saddle with pistol in hand and shoot some of them between the spokes of the cannon wheels. Although the rangers had driven in this force and captured the guns, they could not hold them. They were exposed to a severe fire of musketry and also a cannon from the other side of the creek. In vain the rangers looked for help from the rear and listened for the answering shout to their wild yells as they were spurring their horses among the cannon and artillerymen. This help did not come, and after holding their position a short time they were forced to retreat. Mr. Highsmith rode his horse under a mesquite tree and stopped after the Mexicans had been killed and driven from the cannon. While here a solid shot from the cannon beyond the Hondo struck the top of the tree and cut it off. The fragments fell upon him and his horse, which badly frightened the latter, and he wheeled and ran off with the limbs hanging all over him.

The rangers wounded in the charge were Arch. Gibson, "Dutch" Perry, John Castleman, Anderson Herrell, and William G. Cook. Herrell's horse was badly wounded, and Nick Wren's horse was killed under him in forty yards of the cannon. A grape shot hit him in the breast and went lengthwise through him. Captain Hays' horse was also wounded. Big Foot Wallace was in the charge on a mule.

While all this was going on there were more than 200 men a few hundred yards in the rear, idle spectators. It seems at the very last moment there was a misunderstanding as to who would lead the charge as commander of the whole force. The Baptist preacher, Z. N. Morrell, had a son who was a prisoner, having been captured with Dawson's men. He learned also in San Antonio that he was wounded. This man of God was in the desperate charge, hoping to rescue his son, and when the rangers returned to the main body bitterly reproached the latter for not coming to their assistance. What was the feelings of the Texas prisoners when they saw the assault fail? No doubt some of the captured rangers recognized their comrades and captain when the cannon was taken by such a bold dash, and felt sure of their liberation.

No further attempt was made on the Mexican position, and some time during the night the Mexican commander continued his retreat. A council of the Texan officers was held and the pursuit abandoned. The volunteer companies scattered back to their various homes, and the rangers went back to their quarters at San Antonio. The failure to defeat General Wall on the Hondo caused the prisoners in his hands to spend three years in the dungeons of Mexico before they were released.

Mr. Highsmith was in the Somervell expedition in 1843, but came back with Captain Hays when the expedition was abandoned, and missed the chance of drawing a bean for his life, as others did who selected commanders and went on to the invasion of Mexico after the expedition was declared off. A full account of this expedition will be given in the sketch of Big Foot Wallace, who was with it.

BATTLE OF PALO ALTO.

When the war broke out between Mexico and the United States, in 1846, Jack Hays raised a regiment of Texas rangers and joined General Taylor's army. Some of the old rangers who had been with Hays so long on the frontier raised companies for his regiment and many others went as privates. Among those who raised companies were Ad Gillispie, Kit Ackland, Ben McCulloch, Mike Chevalier, and some others. Sam Walker was lieutenant-colonel. Mr. Highsmith joined the company of Gillispie.

The cause of this war was the boundary line of Texas. When Texas applied for admission into the Union of States she claimed the Rio Grande River as her boundary line in the southwest. Mexico asserted that the Nueces River was the line, and would fight for that boundary. War was declared, and both countries began to raise armies and to march towards the disputed territory. The consequence was that the two armies came into collision on May 8th at a place called Palo Alto, on the east side of the Rio Grande. While the battle was not of long duration, there were so many cannons fired, coupled with that of the small arms, that a great deal of smoke was produced, and Mr. Highsmith says that in some charges that were made the Mexicans and Americans became badly mixed and separated from their commands. There was no breeze stirring, and the smoke lay close to the ground like a fog.

The Mexicans retreated from Palo Alto towards the Rio Grande, but halted next day at Resaca de la Palma and again gave General Taylor battle. During this battle Mr. Highsmith was helping to support a battery led by Captain May, and his horse was killed. In order to keep from being run over by the dragoon he stepped aside into a chaparal thicket. A Mexican officer saw him go in there and came to get him. The latter, however, did not know what it was to go into a thicket after an old Texas ranger. Highsmith killed him and got his horse, and rode the captured steed back into the battle. He kept this horse all during the war and rode him back to Texas.

The Mexican army being defeated here, retreated into Mexico and the Americans followed. Matamoros was taken without much fighting, and the next battle Mr. Highsmith was in was

AT MONTEREY.

This was a hard-fought battle, and many American soldiers were killed. Here Mr. Highsmith lost his captain, the brave and gallant Gillespie. He did not see him killed.

During the battle Capt. Ben McCulloch got into a very close place and was about to be cut off by some Mexican lancers. A ranger named Boseman Kent went to his assistance, but with an empty gun. The lancer who was crowding McCulloch the closest turned and ran when Kent aimed his gun at him, and then the ranger pursued him. All at once horse and Mexican went out of sight and Kent saw a deep gulley in front of him, but could not check up in time to avoid it. He pulled on his horse, gave him the spur, and leaped it. As he went over he saw the gay lancer and his horse at the bottom.

The next and last battle Uncle Ben participated in was

BUENA VISTA.

This battle was fought the 23d of February, 1847. General Taylor had 5000 men, opposed by Santa Anna with 20,000. The battle commenced early in the morning and lasted all day. The rangers and many other volunteers from the States made some most desperate charges. In one of these, about the middle of the forenoon, Uncle Ben was hit by a large musket ball in the leg. He had a large silk handkerchief around his neck, and with this he bound up his leg and went on after the command. It soon became so painful, however, he was obliged to stop. When the doctor dressed the wound he pulled the handkerchief through it four times in order to cleanse it of clotted blood. When the war was over Uncle Ben came back to Texas and joined a company of rangers commanded by Capt. J. S. Sutton. They scouted out towards the Rio Grande, but had no fights.

He made Bastrop his home from 1833 to 1882, when he came west and settled in Sabinal Canyon, near the place where he once killed a buffalo while on a scout with Jack Hays in 1842. He draws a pension as a Mexican war veteran and for two wounds. He has many relatives about Bastrop who are prominent men in legal and official circles. Uncle Ben has a whetrock in his possession which he has owned ever since 1830, and carried it in his shot pouch in all the battles he was engaged in. It was given to him by Jacob C. Trask, at Matagorda. It is about three inches in length by one and a half in width, and is much smaller than when he first came in possession of it. On one side is a deep groove, made there by sharpening his awl in the days when he made moccasins and buckskin clothes. The following old-timers have sharpened their knives on it around the campfires and elsewhere: Sam Houston, James Bowie, Thos. J. Rusk, W. B. Travis, Ben Milam, Jack Hays, Ben McCulloch, P. H. Bell, Stephen F. Austin, James W. Fannin, Deaf Smith, M. B. Lamar, Ed. Burleson, and Asa, John, and Andrew Sowell, three of McCulloch and Hays rangers.

Uncle Ben saw the first paper published in Texas, the Telegraph, issued at Columbia by Gail and Thomas Borden.

CAPTAIN JOHN TOM.

Came to Texas in 1835.

The writer, while on a trip in Frio Canyon in 1898, had the pleasure of spending a few hours with the old veteran Capt. John F. Tom, one of the few survivors of the famous battle of San Jacinto. Captain Tom has a beautiful home in the Frio valley a few miles above the town of Leakey, where he is spending the evening of life in quiet and peace, surrounded by a pleasant family and genial neighbors. He was born in Maury County, Middle Tennessee, in 1818. His father, William Tom, was a soldier under Gen. Andrew Jackson in the war with the Indians, and was present at the famous battle of Horseshoe Bend. His uncle John Files on his mother's side was a soldier under Jackson in the British war of 1812, and was killed at the battle of New Orleans on the 8th of January, 1815. His great-grandfather was killed by the tories in South Carolina during the revolutionary war of 1776.

Captain Tom came to Texas with his father in 1835, landing at the mouth of the Brazos in February. Quite a lot of people came to Texas in those days who were refugees from justice and bore bad characters generally. Mr. William Tom brought with him the following recommendations of good character and citizenship, which were shown the writer and allowed to be copied:

"State of Tennessee, Maury County, November 15, 1834.— Whereas William Tom, a citizen of the State of Tennessee and county of Maury, is about to remove from here to the province of Texas with his family, consisting of the following members: His wife Kissiah, his oldest son John, second Charles, third Alfred, fourth James, fifth a daughter named Sarah, these being children of his first wife, Mary Files; Hughes, Caroline, and William, children of his second and present wife, Kissiah.

"And whereas, we whose names are assigned below, being citizens of the State and county aforementioned, and being neighbors and acquaintances of said William Tom, and some of us knowing him as a citizen of said State and county for the most part of twenty years, do hereby certify said William Tom is an orderly citizen of honest character and industrious habits, and that the above respecting his family and all herein mentioned is correct.

"Samuel Whiteside,	B. Erwin,
"Eli Asken,	John Kingston,
"James Lusk,	James Lessoms,
"James Cathey,	Henry Higgins,
"John Prewitt,	Archibald Brown,
"Thomas Kindrick,	William Brown,
"W. J. Young,	William Gounett,
"Samuel Lusk,	Gideon Strickland,
"James Lusk,	Wm. C. Malone,
"Samuel Johnes,	Jonathan Talle,
"S. C. Aydetalatt,	S. Whiteside,
"Robert L. Brown,	Isaac O. Whiteside,
"Dudley A. Lobeston,	Milton Whiteside,
"Pen Gill,	John Eddring,
"Robertson Whitehead,	George W. Sessums,
"Michael Higgin,	Jourdan Thompson,
"Joseph Tom,	John Neilser,
"Francis Bell,	Daniel Neilser."

Following this is a certificate of County Clerk Thomas J. Porter and Justice of the Peace Alexander Cathey, of good character, etc. Also the following from the Governor of the State, showing that these certificates were by proper authority:

"State of Tennessee, Executive Department.—I, William Carroll, Governor in and over the said State, do hereby certify that Thomas J. Porter, whose signature is annexed to the foregoing certificate, is now and was on the day of the date thereof the clerk of the court of pleas and quarter sessions for the county of Maury, in the said State, and that his official acts as such are entitled to full faith and credit, and that said certificate is in due form of law. In testimony whereof, I have hereunto set my hand and caused the great seal of the State to be affixed, at Nashville, the 22d day of December, 1834. By the Governor,

"WILLIAM CARROLL.

"SAMUEL G. SMITH, Secretary."

This is rather a unique document, and I do not suppose there is another of the same character in the State of Texas. It is carefully preserved and highly prized by the Tom family, as it should be.

In the summer of 1835 the Tom family were living in Washington County, where they settled after leaving the mouth of the Brazos. In the fall of the same year the Mexicans came to Gonzales, on the Guadalupe River, which place had been settled by Green DeWitt's colony, and demanded a small cannon which had been furnished to the settlers by the Mexican government for their defense against Indian attacks. The Texans refused to give up the cannon, and a fight ensued in which the Mexicans were defeated, and they went back to San Antonio, from which place they came, without accomplishing their mission.

Gen. Stephen F. Austin, who was called the "Father of Texas," then raised a small army and proceeded to San Antonio, where General Cos was in command of the Mexican forces. William Tom and his son John, the subject of this sketch, joined Austin's command and went out to San Antonio to fight Cos and his army. They participated in the battles of Mission Concepcion and the "Grass fight," and then father and son joined the artillery under Colonel Neill, who was an old comrade of the elder Tom in the Creek war under General Jackson.

Some ditching was done and cannon planted within 600 yards of the Alamo and fire opened upon it, but the pieces were too light and no impression was made upon it. When the Mexicans opened fire on their position the Texans lay low and avoided their shots, and when night came they retired to the old mill at the head of the river. This demonstration against the fort of the Alamo was to draw the attention of the Mexicans from Col. Ben Milam, who was entering the city with about 300 men west of the river. After some terrible fighting the city was taken and Cos and his men surrendered. Before this was accomplished, however, the brave Milam lost his life, with many others who followed him.

After the capture of the city William Tom and his son went back home, and in March, 1836, John joined the army of Gen. Sam Houston on the Colorado.

On the release of General Cos and his men they went back to Mexico, and President Santa Anna, who was a brother-in-law to Cos, at once invaded Texas with a large army and recaptured San Antonio and stormed the Alamo, which was garrisoned by

CAMP GROUND OF THE TEXANS THE NIGHT BEFORE THE BATTLE OF
SAN JACINTO. From a Photo.

less than 200 men under Col. William B. Travis, all of whom
perished, fighting to the last.

Colonel Fannin met a like fate at Goliad, and none now were
left of the defenders of Texas except the small army that had
assembled under General Houston.

Young Tom joined the company commanded by Capt. W. W.
Hill. However, when the battle of San Jacinto came off, the
captain was sick, and the men were led into the fight by Bob
Stephenson.

When the final day for battle came the Texans were impatient.
They had retreated constantly before the dictator of Mexico, and
had now made a stand between Buffalo Bayou and the San Jacinto River. John Tom at this time was only 17 years of age,
boyish in appearance, and wore a pair of girl's stockings and
buckskin moccasins.

Santa Anna crossed the bayou and encamped with the men
under his immediate command, about 1500, and that night was
joined by the treacherous Cos with 500 more. He had violated
the parole granted him after the surrender at San Antonio, and
returned with the invading army under the Mexican president.
To oppose this force Houston had 732 men.

The Texan commander seemed to be in no hurry to bring on
the battle, although both armies were in close proximity. He
sat quietly and calmly in his tent until 4 o'clock in the evening
of the 21st of April. In the meantime, however, he had sent
Deaf Smith, his trusty scout, with one companion to cut down
the bridge across Vince's Bayou, which was the only outlet of
escape for a defeated army. When the general thought ample
time had elapsed for this to be accomplished, he ordered the
twenty-two captains who commanded the companies present to
come before him. There was a great stir now in the patriot
camp when the men saw their captains assemble and the horse
of their general saddled in front of his tent. He came out with
his sword buckled around him, and in a few words told the captains to parade their men in line. When the order was communi-
cated to the respective companies the men obeyed with alacrity,
and soon formed in one rank and quite extended out into the
prairie. General Houston rode down the line and gave his orders, telling the men that he was going to attack the enemy, and
for them to move slowly and orderly at first, and not to crowd

or pass the two small cannons which were in the center, and
which were to be loaded and fired as they advanced when they
came within range of the enemy. One of these guns was commanded by Ben McCulloch, afterwards Confederate general in
the civil war, and who was killed at the battle of Elkhorn. As
the men stood in line grasping their guns, with eager, expectant
faces, listening to their commander, they presented a strange
and motley group in individual contrast. Beside the gray-
haired veteran of other wars stood the beardless youth, with wide
open eyes, throbbing heart, and quick, short breath, anticipating
his first battle. Shoulder to shoulder with the better dressed
men from the towns in the east stood the buckskin-clad hunter
from the west; the merchant had left his counter and stood by
the farmer in line with gun in hand; the doctor had left his
office and drugs behind, and was handling a long rifle instead of
his pill boxes, with shotpouch and powderhorn over his shoulder;
the lawyer had quit his briefs and clients, and was parading in
line gun in hand and pistol in belt, with his patent leather boots
touching the moccasined foot of the plainsman. All were there
with but one object in view—love of liberty. The cowards, tories,
and scallawags had long since deserted Houston's ranks, and the
men who now stood in line with their faces to the foe were the
true patriots and heroes. When the advance was ordered the
men started with a firm step in good order. When they came
in view of the Mexicans they noticed them in great confusion,
and their cannon soon began to play on the advancing line of
Texans. The "Twin Sisters" replied, and soon things began to
get lively. The men commenced to double-quick and yell, and
soon passed the cannons. They were left behind on the prairie,
one of them loaded. The Mexicans sent a plunging fire of
musketry at the yelling Texans as they came sweeping towards
them, and men began to get hit and fall out of line. General
Houston shouted his orders for no man to stop to assist a fallen
friend or comrade, but to press on straight ahead and not to
fire until they could see the Mexicans' eyes, and to penetrate the
Mexican line and engage them hand to hand. The men went
at a full running charge, with trailed arms and yelling loudly.
Their comrades dropped out here and there stricken by the musket balls that were dropping among them like hail. John F.
Tom, the boy with the moccasins, was in all this wild charge, but

was finally hit and knocked out of line. The men were true to
the orders they had received and pressed on. Some of his neighbors only gave him a quick glance as he went down with his left
leg badly shattered by a musket ball. The hand-to-hand fight,
pursuit, and great slaughter of the Mexicans has already been
written many times and needs no repetition here. Mr. Tom lay
on the field until the battle was over, but two of his friends—
Milt Swisher and Louis Clemens—remembered where he fell,
and coming back to the spot bore him away to the camp. The
young soldier suffered great pain for many days and was carried
home as soon as possible, where kind and affectionate hands
dressed his wound and nursed him until the limb was cured.
Mr. Tom still limps from that shot.

In 1846 Captain Tom moved to Guadalupe County, before
it was organized, and in 1856 was elected sheriff of the county,
which office he held four years, that being the limit in that day
and time. In 1862 he moved to Atascosa County, which was
then just being settled and which was on the frontier. The Indians were very hostile and made many raids through this
county, and in 1863 Mr. Tom received a commission to raise a
company of rangers for frontier protection. While acting in
this capacity the Indians made a raid and killed some people,
besides carrying off a lot of stock. Captain Tom pursued them
with his rangers and came upon the hostiles at the head of San
Miguel Creek, and a fight ensued. Both parties attempted to
get to a pile of rocks for their protection during the battle, and
the Indians beat the rangers to the coveted spot. In the fight
that followed the Comanches were defeated with loss. Of the
men in the fight the old captain could only remember Calvin S.
Turner, Lot Miller, and a boy named McCombs. After the fight
the rangers followed the Indians to the Frio waterhole on the
divide, but could not again bring them to battle, and the pursuit
was abandoned.

In 1873 Captain Tom was sent to the Legislature from Atascosa County and made a true and faithful representative for his
people. He moved to Frio Canyon several years ago, and in 1893
had the misfortune to get a leg broken in attempting to dismount from his horse. This, coupled with the old Mexican
wound, compels him to use crutches. Captain Tom was made
a Mason in 1867, Pleasanton lodge No. 383.

CAPTAIN JAMES W. WINTERS.

SAN JACINTO VETERAN.

Came to Texas in 1834.

Once in a great while and badly scattered, the writer, while in pursuit of Texas history, comes upon a San Jacinto veteran. One of these, Capt. James W. Winters, lives near the Big Foot postoffice, in Frio County.

Mr. Winters was born in Giles County, Tennessee, on the 21st of January, 1817, near the town of Pelasca. His father, James Winters, was born in North Carolina, and came to Tennessee at an early day. He was married to Miss Rhoda Beal, daughter of Benjamin Beal, during the war with the Creek Indians. The marriage took place in a fort while the people were gathered there to make a defense against the Indians.

Before the war was over he joined General Jackson's army and took part in the battle of Talladega. While with the army Mr. Winters made the acquaintance of Sam Houston, and afterwards met him in Texas, and they recognized each other.

During the revolutionary war the house of the Winters family was robbed by the tories in North Carolina. The grandmother of the subject of this sketch had a sugar bowl full of silver money, and when she saw the tories coming carried the bowl to a trunk, but instead of putting it inside slipped it underneath. The trunk was one of the old colonial kind, heavy and on rollers, and standing several inches from the floor on short legs. When the tories came into the house they took everything out of the trunk and carried it away, but failed to find the money. They took the feather beds into the yard, and, emptying the feathers, carried away the cloth, like our western Indians here in Texas. The elder Winters moved from Giles County, Tennessee, and settled on the Forked Deer River, and then from there to Shelby County, near Memphis. From this place the family came to Texas in 1834. A family named Bankhead came with them. James W. Winters had six brothers,—William C., Orin L., John F. W., Benjamin Franklin, Elisha Willis, and

Billington Taylor. James W. was the fourth son, coming between John and Benjamin. All of these came to Texas at the same time except Orin, who was engaged to be married when the family left the old States, and did not arrive in Texas until 1840.

The Winters family first settled in Texas at a place called Big Thicket, twelve miles below where Huntsville now stands. At that time all was a wilderness. When counties were first organized the place where they settled came within the limits of Montgomery County, and they lived on a little creek now called Winters Bayou. When James W. was about grown he left home and worked at the blacksmith trade at the new town of Montgomery, which was about twenty miles from home. He set in to learn the trade with Thomas Adams, but the latter on one occasion went off to buy tools and failed to return. Trouble with the Mexicans commenced in 1835, and young Winters left Montgomery and set out for San Antonio in company with his father and brother John to join the army of Gen. Stephen F. Austin, who was investing the place with a small and hastily gathered army. On arriving at San Felipe they learned that the Mexicans had surrendered. Here also they met Gen. Sam Houston, and he and the elder Winters recognized each other, and they talked about the battle of Talladega. The general also told him at parting to go back home and raise all the corn he could, for "next spring," said he, "we are going to have it out with the Mexicans, sure." James W. went back to Montgomery and stayed there until the spring of 1836, but when the news came of the fall of the Alamo he again started to meet the Mexican invaders. On again arriving at San Felipe and learning the particulars of the fierce fight at the Alamo as given by Mrs. Dickinson, who was present during the assault, and that Santa Anna was overrunning the country, a small company was at once formed on the Bernard and Capt. William Ware was elected to command. The elder Winters stayed at home during this time, but two more sons, William C. and John F. W., were present. The first lieutenant of the company was Job Collard, George Lamb second, with Albert Gallatin first sergeant and William C. Winters second. The company went on to the Colorado and there waited a few days, and by this time 200 men had collected there. General Houston was coming on from the west with the main army, and struck the river at Mercer's farm below Columbus, which then consisted of but a few houses. Ware's company with the others were at Dewees' ford, above Columbus, and remained there to prevent the Mexicans from crossing if they came that way. They did come to the opposite side of the river and shots were exchanged with them. Not being able to hold the ford, the Texans retreated and went on to the Brazos and stayed there several days in a bottom at a place called "Groce's Retreat."

Here they formed a junction with the main army under General Houston when he arrived. While here news came that the Mexicans were on the river below San Felipe, but Houston waited several days for some cannon to arrive which he expected. They finally came—two brass six-pounders ("Twin Sisters")—and the army moved on to Dunman's, where Hempstead is now. Only one night was spent here. Next morning they went to the head of a prairie which runs down to Houston; stayed one night in the prairie, and the next, on the 18th, opposite Harrisburg, which had been burned.

Deaf Smith the day before while out on a scout had captured a Mexican mail rider, and General Houston found out where Santa Anna was. On the 19th he went down Buffalo Bayou three miles and crossed, and then went down to Lynch's ferry at the mouth of the bayou where it empties into the San Jacinto River. Vince's bridge was crossed on the way down. It spanned a small bayou on the west side of Buffalo. The Mexicans went from Harrisburg to New Washington, on the bay, and then came up into the prairie and went into camp on the San Jacinto. Houston's men were now ahead of the Mexicans, having moved back up the bayou to a skirt of timber and there went into camp. Scouts came in and reported the Mexicans in camp three-quarters of a mile away, south. On the 20th the Mexicans made an attack on the camp of the Texans at long range from a mott of timber bordering a marsh 200 yards away. The Texans replied, but little damage was done. Two or three Texans were wounded, one of whom was Col. J. C. Neill, severely.

Another portion of the Mexican army was in a low depression of the prairie where cannon were planted and breastworks made. General Houston went to all the messes of his men, encouraging them and telling them that if they gained this battle all of them would be captains. After the battle, and while Santa Anna was a prisoner in the camp he expressed his surprise at the quick annihilation of his army by an inferior force. "Nothing curious about that," said the Texan general, "my whole command were captains."

Next day, the 21st, General Houston late in the evening moved his men out and made an attack on the Mexican camp. The Winters brothers were in the second regiment, commanded by Colonel Sherman, and on the extreme left of the formation in the charge, and which brought them in contact with the Mexican right, which was posted in the timber and high grass. Colonel Sherman bore to the left to rout these. They were lying down and commenced firing on the Texans in that position as they came towards them at a double-quick charge. Mr. Winters says he heard the order to fire three times before he saw anything to shoot at, and all the men ran up close to the enemy before firing. They could see the smoke from the Mexican guns coming out of the grass near the ground in the edge of the timber, but none of them moved until they arose to run.

In the meantime, however, the bullets from the Mexicans were striking among the Texans and several had already gone down, among whom was Lieutenant Lamb and Sergeant Winters. James W. did not see his brother William fall, and kept on in the charge. When the Texans came within fifty or sixty yards of the Mexicans they sprang up quickly and ran away, and seemed to be very numerous. The Texans now opened up a rapid fire with terrible effect. The ground was almost covered with dead and disabled Mexicans. Those not hit went in rapid flight through the timber towards the breastworks, followed by the Texans, who by this time were yelling loudly. The fight was hard at the cannon, and the bullets flew among and over the Texans as thick as hail. Mr. Winters had a long flintlock rifle, and stopped beside a Spanish oak tree to ram a tight ball, and while so doing a large ball struck the side of the tree and threw so much bark in his face and with such force that for a few moments he thought he was wounded from the pain it created. At this time the right wing of the Texans had reached the works and a terrible hand-to-hand fight was taking place with clubbed rifles, bayonets, and sabers. Mexicans and Texans were one writhing, surging mass. This, however, did not last long, as the Mexicans soon ran, some in one direction and some in another.

Part of them went to Vince's bridge, hoping to escape across that; but "Deaf" Smith had destroyed it that morning, and they huddled there like a bunch of cattle, and many were killed. Some of them tried to keep in the timber along the marsh and escape towards the bay shore. Nearly all of them, however, were overtaken and killed or captured.' Many ran into the marsh to escape the Texans, and forty of them were taken out of there the next day. Mr. Winters loaded and fired his rifle eight times during the battle and pursuit. He was with those who cut off the Mexicans towards the bay shore, and it was nearly night when he returned to the main battleground. He became separated from his brothers during the fight, but saw John just as the pursuit ended, and asked him if he knew anything of William. He said no he had not seen him since the fight commenced. The two brothers now hastily went to camp, but hearing no tidings there, hurriedly returned to the bloody field and began a diligent search there until darkness put an end to all further work in that place. Once more they returned to camp, greatly distressed. They knew William too well to entertain the thought for an instant that he had shirked the battle, and grave fears were now entertained that he had been slain in some out-of-the-way place during the pursuit, fallen perhaps in high, marshy grass, and his body would never be recovered. On arriving at camp this time, however, they found the missing brother, who had just been brought into camp ·badly wounded. He was hit in the charge before reaching the timber and fell out of line without being seen by either of the other brothers. When the ball struck him he had his foot clear of the ground and leg bent, charging, and the missile, which was a large musket ball, struck just above the knee and ranged back, coming out at the large part of the thigh on the under side. In its course the ball grazed the thigh bone and so paralyzed the limb that Sergeant Winters was unable to arise from the ground after he fell, and had to lie there until dark before being carried away.

Captain Ware's company was small—only eighteen—but they were under a close fire and suffered more than some of the larger companies. The casualties were as follows: Second Lieut. George A. Lamb, killed; Sergt. William Winters, severely wounded; Sergt. Albert Gallatin, slightly wounded; Private E. G. Rector, slightly wounded; Private G. W. Robinson, severely

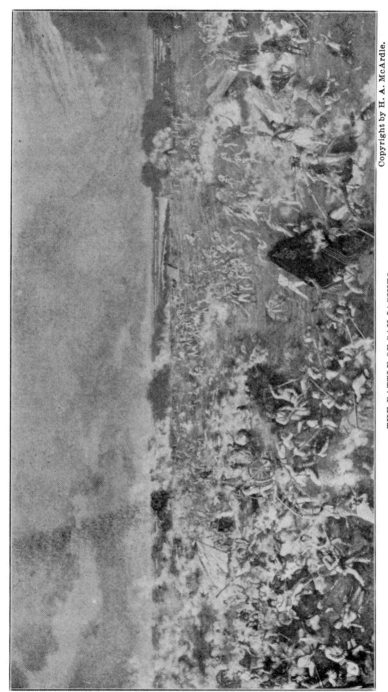

THE BATTLE OF SAN JACINTO.
From a painting.

wounded. The ball which hit Albert Gallatin first struck his powderhorn, cut through the shotpouch, and entered the side, carrying the strap of the shotpouch into the wound.

Mr. Winters says that Captain Ware was like a wild mustang, and when the charge was ordered leaped to his place in front and shouted, "Come on, boys!" Mr. Winters remained seven days on the battleground attending to his wounded brother, and at times going over the battleground. He said the Mexicans had made their breastworks out of brush and packs of camp equipage. The Mexicans lay thick in many places, and none of them were buried. The Texans had to move their camp on account of the stench emanating from the dead bodies which lay thickly south of of them. In a few days the Mexicans presented a fearful sight, swelling to enormous sizes. No buzzard or wolf came about them. From the battlefield the army went up to Harrisburg, and here Mr. Winters left them and went home. The wounded brother was carried home by John from the battleground. The elder Winters died in the Big Thicket on the first place settled by him in Texas. He had a good farm there.

In 1837 the Indians made a raid in that country and killed a Mrs. Taylor, whose husband also had been killed by Indians a month before that time. Mrs. Taylor, at the time she met her death, was at the house of a neighbor named Hadley. The attack was made in the night, and Mrs. Taylor tried to leave the house with her children, three in number—two boys and a girl. The Indians found them out in their flight, and killed the mother and little girl and shot one of the boys in the hand with an arrow. This occurred near where the town of Anderson now is. Mrs. Taylor was delivered of another child in her dying struggle after being shot. A man named Kindred went to Montgomery to give the alarm and made a most remarkable ride. It was thirty-five miles to the town, and he started from Hadley's after daylight, rode there, raised twenty-five men, and was back at Hadley's on the following night. Mr. Winters was one of the twenty-five men who went from Montgomery. After an organization took place Jerry Washam was chosen captain, and the pursuit of the Indians commenced. They had taken a westerly course out of the country. The command crossed the Navasota River and went up between that stream and the Brazos, passing within three miles of Fort Parker. Twenty-five miles beyond the fort, at a horseshoe-shaped prairie belted by timber, the Indians scattered and the trail was hard to keep. Finally buzzards were seen in a point of timber where the prairie circled around it, and the men cautiously went in. The Indians had seen the white men and hastily left, leaving bows, shields, arrows, etc. While making a close examination of the camp Mrs. Taylor's scalp was found. There was also a large amount of cooked meat in camp. The Indians were all on foot and not more than ten in number. They were trailed across the prairie on the other side of the timber, and here they again scattered and it was impossible to follow them, so the pursuers commenced their return. There was one timid man along, named Hardwick. One night he and Winters were on guard at the same time but in different places. Hardwick fired at something (or nothing) and raised an alarm. Winters saw the fire from Hardwick's gun, but not knowing what the matter was, remained at his post and awaited developments. Hardwick when he fired ran into camp with all the balance of the guards, ten in number, except Winters. The roll of the guards was called and all answered except Winters. A man by the name of Tullis said he would bet that Hardwick had killed Winters. The frightened guard had said that he did not know what he shot at. He was then asked what the thing was doing when he fired—walking upright or crawling. "Both," he says; "kinder pokin." At this they all laughed, and some of them went to hunt for Winters, whom they soon found all right.

Not long after this Indian chase Mr. Winters married Miss Pearcy Tullis, near Montgomery. Her father and brother were both in the Indian pursuit above mentioned.

In 1842, when General Wall captured San Antonio, Mr. Winters with others went to aid in defeating him. When they arrived at San Antonio their force amounted to 200 men, but the battle had been fought and the Mexicans gone back to Mexico. Mr. Winters, however, stayed out and went on with the Somervell expedition. His captain was Albert Gallatin, who was wounded at San Jacinto. Winters came back when the command had the split on the Rio Grande, and missed drawing a bean for his life,—a chance which befell those who went over into Mexico.

In 1850 he came out further west and settled on the San Marcos River, three miles above Prairie Lea, and helped his brother

William to build a mill. He stayed here two years, when he went into the mercantile business and got broke up. He moved further west then, and went into the stock business on shares with Berry Crane and others, and settled on the Nueces, near Oakville, in Liveoak County. Here he had to contend with Indians, Mexicans, and white cow-thieves. One party of six Indians made a raid and, getting into a fight with cowmen, were all killed.

When the civil war broke out Mr. Winters raised a company of ninety men and offered them to the Confederacy. They were accepted, but Mr. Winters did not go with it as captain, but was kept back as an enrolling officer, and was also commissioned as provost marshal. Guards were kept between the Nueces and Rio Grande as mounted rangers. Mr. Winters went with them part of the time. He remained on the border during the war with the rank of captain. On one occasion horse-thieves made a raid and were followed by Captain Winters with two men. They rode sixty miles in one day and caught the thieves, who were Mexicans, at sundown, charged them, killed one, and rescued eight head of horses and brought them back.

After the war he went to Tuxpan, Mexico, and lived there eight years, farming, etc. He came back to Bee County, Texas, stayed there two years, and then came to Frio County, where he still resides, eight miles southeast from Devine.

Mr. Winters had three sons in the Confederate army,—James, Josephus, and Francis Marion. James, the eldest, was captured at Arkansas Post, and was in Bragg's army after the exchange. Marion died in San Antonio before leaving Texas. Josephus was in the Fort Donelson fight, and also helped to capture the Harriet Lane at Galveston.

The old veteran, now in his eighty-second year, lives with his son William on an adjoining farm to his own. His first wife died in Mexico, and the second died in 1895.

MRS. HANNAH BERRY.

Came to Texas in 1828.

One of the most interesting characters now in Texas is Mrs. Hannah Berry, who lives in the Upper Sabinal country, in Bandera County. Mrs. Berry was born in Catahoula Parish, Louisiana, on the 2d day of November, 1812, and is the daughter of Jesse Devoe. Her father and a company of men were in hearing of the battle of New Orleans, and made all haste to get there to take part in the engagement, but were too late. They were greatly stimulated in their exertions to reach the battleground by the constant roar of cannon, which was heard for many miles.

Mrs. Berry moved to Mississippi when quite a small child, and started to Texas from "Jackson's new purchase," 150 miles above Vicksburg, in 1826. The family made several stops on the route, and arrived in Texas and settled in Liberty County in 1828. In 1831 she married John Berry, of Kentucky, who came to Texas in 1826. Mr. Berry was a gunsmith by trade, and his services in the new country were almost indispensable. He received a league of land from the Mexican government as one of Robinson's colonists.

In 1834 the family moved to Bastrop, and Mr. Berry made knives, guns, and pistols, and mended all the broken ones in the country. In 1836, when Col. David Crockett of Tennessee came to Bastrop on his way to join Col. William B. Travis at the Alamo, in San Antonio, he had with him a very fine gun, but it had been broken off at the breech, and he was very anxious to have it mended before reaching San Antonio. Some one said to Colonel Crockett when the broken gun was mentioned, "Take it to John Berry; he can fix it for you." Crockett came to Berry's shop in company with John McGee and brought the gun with him. Mr. Berry examined it, and saying he could fix it all right, at once set about the work. A large silver band was placed around the broken place, and so securely fastened that it was as strong as ever and very ornamental when polished and flowered off. Colonel Crockett was well pleased, and said it was now better than it was at first. The gun was lost in the Alamo when

Crockett was killed in the famous battle. Mention has been made several times of Crockett's beautiful silver mounted rifle which was taken by the Mexican army to Mexico when the war was over. The silver part of it was the band over the broken place put there by John Berry. Mrs. Berry says she would know the gun now if she could see it by the silver band she watched her husband put there. She remembers well how Colonel Crockett looked, and says he did not wear a cap while at Bastrop.

Mrs. Berry heard many an Indian yell during the "bloody days of Bastrop," and once saw 500 Comanche Indians at one sight. She saw Wilbarger after he was scalped by the Indians, and says he lived ten years after. When the Alamo was taken a messenger came and told the people to retreat back out of danger until the settlers who were rallying under Gen. Sam Houston could meet the victorious Mexicans in battle. The people of Bastrop left the town and traveled by various methods and to different places. Mr. Berry's family and a few others went to Fort Parker. Gen. Edward Burleson was in the Texan army, and his stepmother and her five children and one of the Burleson children went in Mr. Berry's wagon. Also of the party were the Harris and McKinney families. Dr. McKinney it was said was the cause of the Indians being so hostile in those days and killing so many Bastrop settlers. In some transaction with the Indians he made a present to them of a keg of sugar which he had poisoned, and which caused the death of a great many of them. The Indians in revenge for this killed Dr. McKinney and some companions at a place afterwards called Bone Hollow. The bones of the men had been found and buried there, hence the name. Mrs. Berry says she saw the rail pen which had been placed around them. During the stay of the fugitive families at Fort Parker Col. Benjamin Parker, who was in command of the fort and who was also a Baptist preacher, held services regularly and preached to the people. These were long, anxious days to those in the fort, especially to those who had sons and husbands in Houston's army. Mr. Berry did not go to the army, as he was getting old; but three of his sons by his first wife had gone to strike a blow for liberty.

The families stayed three weeks at the fort. Mrs. Berry knew the famous Cynthia Ann Parker well, who was then a very small girl. Mrs. Plummer was also there, who suffered so much as a captive among the Comanche Indians afterwards. There was also a strange boy at this fort named Robert Foster, whom the people who lived there called "the prophet." It was said that he told many things which had come to pass. Every morning while awaiting news from the seat of war some one would ask this boy what news he could tell them, but for a long time he would say that he had nothing to tell. One morning, however, he arose early and told the people that they could go home if they wished, as the men of General Houston had killed nearly all of the Mexican army, and that a beardless boy had captured Santa Anna. The same evening two men came in sight running their horses and firing pistols. Mr. Berry answered with several shots from the fort, and in a few minutes the men came up. They were messengers from San Jacinto, bringing news of the victory. There was great rejoicing, and those who did not live at the fort soon made preparations to go home. When the Berrys arrived at Bastrop they found their house burned and all of their stock driven off by the Mexicans. Three of the Berry boys were in the army, to wit, John Bates, Andrew Jackson, and Joseph. The two first took part in the battle, but Joseph arrived too late. Cornelius Devoe, brother of Mrs. Berry, was also in the battle. He was from Liberty County, and had not seen the Berry boys for a long time. They recognized each other during the heat of the combat, but having no time to talk or shake hands, shouted their greetings amid booming cannons and rattling musketry.

The boy Foster at Fort Parker, three days before the fearful massacre at that place, arose early one morning and told all the people to leave the fort if they did not want to get killed, as the Indians were coming and would take the place. They did not do so, and Mrs. Berry says she supposes the boy was killed with the balance, as she never heard of him afterwards.

In 1840, when the Comanches made the famous raid through Texas and burned the town of Linnville on the coast, the Berrys were living in Burleson County. When they heard the news, John Bates Berry and his brother Andrew Jackson mounted their horses and took a prominent part in the battle of Plum Creek, where the Indians were badly defeated. This battle was fought about three miles east of the present town of Lockhart, in Caldwell County.

In 1842 Bates and Joe Berry joined the Somervell expedition

and were with the party who crossed over into Mexico and fought the battle of Mier. Just before the battle Joe had the misfortune of falling into a ditch and breaking his leg while acting as a scout to ascertain something of the enemy. His brother Bates and some others carried him into an old outhouse in the town, and while there the battle commenced. The Mexicans were trying to storm Cameron's position where he had barricaded the streets and houses, and were in rifle shot of the old house in which Joe and his three companions were. It was agreed that they would not let themselves be known until the battle was over, as they would be at the mercy of the Mexicans. One of the men, however, in the excitement during a charge on the position of the Texans, aimed his rifle through an opening and fired. Joe now told them to all run and save themselves if they could and leave him alone to his fate, as the house would now be attacked and all killed. The men acted on this advice of the brave, unselfish boy, and, opening the door, made a desperate run for Cameron's position. They were met by a volley from the Mexicans, who were advancing with a small force under the command of a lieutenant to assault the house. One of the men fell dead in his tracks, but John Berry and the other man fought their way through the Mexicans and gained the position of the Texans.

In making the run and fight through the Mexicans, John Berry recognized the lieutenant in command as a man whom he knew in San Antonio. The fate of poor Joe was sealed. The Mexican officer went into the room where he lay helpless and killed him with his sword. He then came out flourishing the bloody weapon and bragging about the deed. He was afterwards killed in Texas by the Berry boys. John Berry was captured with the balance of the Texans when the surrender took place, and was in the desperate chance of drawing a bean for his life at Salado. He drew a white one, but one of his neighbors named Porter drew a black one, and bewailed his fate in such a forcible way that Berry, rendered almost desperate by the death of his brother and the terrible scenes through which he had passed, thought of swapping beans with him and being shot in his place. After the fight he had passed many long, weary hours in prison. Then came the fight at Salado, where, unarmed, they rushed upon the guards, wrenched the weapons from their hands, and fought their way

4

to liberty. Then came days of famine and thirst, lost in the mountains, trying to make their way to Texas. The recapture, brutal treatment, and being marched from town to town, exhibited like so many wild beasts, and at last to stand up and draw beans for the little miserable life that was left in them. No wonder he thought of taking his comrade's black bean and ending it all. The thought of home, however, and the old mother watching and waiting for her boys, one of whom was already gone, decided him, and he stood by and saw his neighbor shot. After twenty-two months of hard labor on the streets of the towns in Mexico, he was released and made his way back home. A man named Whitfield Clark made his escape and informed the Berry family of Joe's death before John got back.

Mrs. Berry's husband drew a pension for services in the war of 1812, and when he died it was transferred to her, which she still receives—one of the very few left who draws a pension of that character. Mr. Berry served also against the Indians under General Harrison, and fought at the battles of Tippecanoe and the Thames. He volunteered from Kentucky and served in the company commanded by Capt. William Smithers, Hopkins' regiment. Mrs. Berry was the mother of twelve children, as follows: Mary, the eldest, married John Compton; Emanuel, married Delilah Cox; John, married Hixa Jane Donnell; Jane, married Lieut. James Ramsey, now of Corn Hill, in Williamson County; Julia and Catherine, twins; the first named married Robins; the second Jackson. Joseph, a Confederate soldier, who died at the age of 18 years at Bayou Boeuff, La.; Silas, married Sarah Hutchinson; Clarissa, married Henson Mitchell; Patrick Henry and Virginia, twins; the former died young, and Virginia married George Murphy; the last George Washington, making the twelve. The Joseph mentioned above was her own son, and the one killed at Mier in Mexico was her stepson, and on account of their great love and attachment for him this one was named Joseph also. Two of her sons, Emanuel and John, went through the civil war and helped to capture the Harriet Lane at Galveston. Emanuel limps now from injuries received in crossing the long bridge going from the mainland to the city. He is a Missionary Baptist preacher and has been for more than twenty-five years. During the battle of Galveston he saw a woman going through the street with two children, one of whom was killed by a piece of bombshell. Mrs. Berry also had two nephews in the battle, Cornelius Hampshire and Barney Hampshire. Old man John Hampshire lived on elevated ground at Bolivar Point, and two shells from the Harriet Lane fell in his yard but did not explode. While Mrs. Berry was on a visit to the Hampshires some years later, these shells were shown her. Young Joseph Berry, who died in the Confederate service, belonged to Captain Hally's company, of Belton. Lieutenant Emory of the same company was also from Belton. Colonel Mullins, who commanded the regiment, was from Florence, Williamson County. Grandma Berry has belonged to the Baptist Church ever since 1841. The first Missionary Baptist Church in Williamson County was organized in her house by Revs. Garrett and Talafero. The latter preached there fourteen months. Mrs. Berry knew the old pioneer Baptist preacher, Z. N. Morrell, well.

One of the daughters-in-law of Mrs. Berry, who was a Donnell, had a brother killed during the war at Yellow Bayou. In the old family Bible the writer found the following entry:

"Wiley H. Donnell was wounded in the fight on Yellow Bayou on the 18th of May, 1864, and died of his wound on the same night at 9 o'clock, aged 24 years, 2 months and 11 days. Had been in the Confederate service two years and nine months."

Donnell was killed by a wounded Federal soldier while lying on the ground and not able to get up.

Grandma Berry has seventy-four grandchildren that she knows of, and one hundred and twenty-four great-grandchildren, and two great-great-grandchildren. Her oldest daughter is 64 years old. Emanuel, her oldest son, is 64. Her next, John, is 60, and her youngest is 40 years old. Very few people live to see their children become old and gray around them, or such a numerous offspring of grandchildren. She is a small woman, with hair white as snow and a healthy-looking round face without many wrinkles, considering her age.

"BIG FOOT" WALLACE.

"BIG FOOT" WALLACE.

Came to Texas in 1837.

William Alexander Anderson Wallace, better known as "Big Foot," was born in Lexington, Rockbridge County, Virginia, on the 3d day of April, 1817. His ancestors came from the highlands of Scotland at an early day, and took part in the war for American independence on the side of the colonists. He had two uncles killed at the battle of Guilford Courthouse. The Wallaces were all powerful men physically. The subject of this sketch when in his prime was 6 feet 2 inches in his moccasins, and weighed 240 pounds. He had one uncle who was nearly 7 feet, and one brother who was 6 feet 5 inches. "Big Foot" had long arms and large hands, and his hair was black, thick, and inclined to curl.

Nothing of interest occurred in the life of Wallace until he was about 20 years of age. At that time war had commenced in Texas between the American colonists and the Mexicans. Many brave young men went from the States to assist the Texans against the dictator, Santa Anna, and among these was Samuel Wallace, brother of Big Foot, or William, as he was then only known. Samuel was killed in the massacre of Fannin's men at Goliad, as were three other relatives. When the news reached Lexington, Va.; great was the grief in the Wallace family, and William took an oath that he was going to Texas and spend his life killing Mexicans. One reason of this bitter hatred was the fact that his brother and all the others were killed after they had surrendered and been disarmed.

As soon as he could get ready William set out for New Orleans, and from there took shipping for Galveston. A terrible storm occurred on the way and many vessels were wrecked. The one Wallace was on, the Diadem, rode out the gale well and arrived safe and sound at her destined port. Galveston, however, had nearly been destroyed, and ships were high and dry in the town. The Diadem came to anchor in Galveston Bay on the 5th day of October, 1837, and Wallace for the first time set foot on Texas soil.

The war was over in Texas. Santa Anna had been defeated and captured the year before at the famous battle of San Jacinto, and Texas was now an independent republic. Wallace drifted up to Bastrop, on the Colorado, and only found a few families there. Among them were Egglestone, Manlove, and Mays. After a short stay here he went on up to where a settlement was starting at La Grange. Col. John H. Moore owned the land where the town was afterwards built, but was the only resident there when Wallace arrived.

Shortly after coming here Big Foot had his first experience with Indians. They made a raid among the scattered settlers in the vicinity of La Grange or the Moore settlement, and were pursued by five men, among whom were Gorman Woods, William Wallace, and a man named Black. The Indians were overtaken and a running fight of several miles across a prairie took place, in which two of the Indians were killed and one wounded. Wallace killed one of them.

Wallace was fond of the woods, and hunted almost continually while at La Grange. On one occasion, while out on Buckner's Creek alone, he was suddenly surrounded by a large party of Lipan Indians and captured. They carried him to their camp and kept him for a week or more, but at the end of that time he eluded them and got back to the settlement.

In 1838 Wallace made his first trip to San Antonio, arriving there on the 14th day of April. Shortly after arriving he went and took a look at the Alamo. Signs of the fierce battle were on every side. An outer wall inclosed the fort in front and reached out into the plaza, where was an entrance through two large gates. The walls had been partly demolished by cannon shots, and the gates had been torn and twisted around and piles of rock had been thrown up here and there. The ashes were still to be seen where the slain Texans were burned, with small pieces of charred bones among them. Wallace stayed in San Antonio some time and killed many deer in the prairie around. When Austin was selected for the capital in 1839, Wallace went there and found a town of small cabins and tents. As many new buildings were going up, Wallace obtained a job to hew logs at a salary of $200 per month and board. He worked at this two months, and then went into a partnership with a man named William Leggett to raft cedar down the Colorado from high up

in the mountains. Austin was on the extreme frontier, and
nothing but one vast wilderness beyond, in which Wallace delighted. It best suited his roving disposition and hermit-like
nature. He loved the wild woods and gloried in all the primeval
scenes of nature,—her lofty rock and cedar-capped mountains,
deep canyons, dark brakes and forest, clear springs and swift-
rushing river. The deer, turkey, buffalo, wild horses, and the
painted savage all had charms for him. He would take extensive rambles up the Colorado and then make wide circles back to
the settlements, shooting game by the way, and eating and sleeping when and where he felt disposed to do so.

In Austin at this time was a good natured, jolly Irishman,
named William Fox, who went into partnership with Wallace,
and, renting a small cabin in town, kept "bach" there together.
They took contracts for work, and one of these was to haul rock
from the mountains to build houses, and they made a great deal
of money. Also in this country at that time was a noted Indian
called Big Foot, who gave the settlers much trouble. He was a
Waco, and had a band of eight with him. He would come into
the town at night, kill who he could, and carry off horses and
other property. He was a wily rascal, and the settlers tried in
vain to kill him. His tracks measured fourteen inches with his
moccasins on; hence his name. He was also powerful physically,
being 6 feet 7 inches in height, muscular, and weighing about
300 pounds. Wallace was anxious to kill him, and many miles he
trailed him. He saw him three times, but never was close enough
at those times to shoot. A man named Thomas Green shot him
once and wounded him in the knee. This man Green was afterwards Gen. Tom Green, and was killed at the battle of Blair's
Landing during the civil war. Some think that Wallace received
the name of Big Foot from killing this Indian, but when the
writer interviewed the old captain a few years ago and asked the
question, he said: "No; Ed Westfall killed him on the Llano. I
trailed him many times and saw him three times at a distance,
but never shot at him."

"Then," said I, "there is another account in circulation that
the Mexicans gave you that name while a prisoner in their hands
in Mexico after the battle of Mier, because they could not find
a pair of shoes large enough for you in the City of Mexico."

"No," said he, "that is not so. There were men in the command who had larger feet than I. The Mexicans all have small feet, and they could not find shoes to fit any of us. My feet are not large in proportion to my body. See? (and he held them out for my inspection, and it was even so—No. 9½). But 10's," he said, "fit easy. But," the old man continued, "I did get my name from the Big Foot Indian, but not because I killed him."

The story is this: One night in 1839 the Big Foot Indian came into the town of Austin, and in prowling about committed some theft on the premises of a man named Gravis, and then went to the cabin occupied by Fox and Wallace. Next morning Gravis trailed the Indian to the doorstep of Wallace, and without trying to trace it any further roused Wallace and accused him as the depredator. Wallace also were moccasins and made a large track, but he was so incensed at Gravis that he was about to whip him on the spot, and made a grab at him. Gravis got out of the way and told Wallace to prove himself clear and he would apologize, and there would be no fight. Wallace said he could do that, and at once went to the Indian's track and placed his foot in it with the moccasin on, and made Gravis come up close enough to look at it, and showed him how much longer the Indian's track was than his. This was convincing, so Gravis begged pardon and walked off. During this episode Fox came to the door and took notice of the whole transaction, and while Wallace was standing in the Indian's track, laughed and said, "Now, Wallace, when the Big Foot Indian is not around we will call you Big Foot." Others took up the name, and so it came about that when some one would make a remark about Big Foot another would ask, "Which do you mean, the Indian or Big Foot Wallace?" So the name stuck to him and has been famous along the border for more than half a century.

It is a strange coincidence that the man who gave Wallace the name of Big Foot was finally killed by the Big Foot Indian. Fox was one day hoeing a small patch of corn surrounded by a brush fence in the suburbs of the town, when Big Foot shot him from the fence. Wallace wanted now more than ever to kill the Indian, and after burying his partner took the trail, but was unsuccessful. He killed one of the band, however, at Mount Bonnell on the Colorado, above Austin. We will have to skip over many interesting incidents in the life of Wallace, and only mention the most important of battles, etc.

In 1840 William Wallace, now known as Big Foot, once more visited the historic city of San Antonio. His restless spirit, however, could not be confined to the streets of a city. He soon went further southwest and camped and hunted along the Medina River. Finally he built a cabin on the west bank of the stream, ten miles below the present town of Castroville, in Medina County.

We now come to that period in the life of Big Foot Wallace when he began to serve the young republic in the capacity of a Texas ranger under the famous Jack Hays, who stands pre-eminently at the head of that long list of ranger captains. In 1840 the situation around San Antonio, which was then on the extreme frontier, was anything but encouraging to those who wished to settle in the country and lead quiet lives and make good citizens. Besides the numerous raids of hostile bands of Indians who roamed at will from the line of New Mexico to the coast region of Texas, horsethieves, desperadoes, gamblers, and fugitives from justice who had fled from other States, swarmed around all the border towns, and more especially San Antonio. No one was safe who was in opposition to this element. It was almost impossible to keep horses. They would dig through adobe houses to get them. A strong hand was needed here to awe this class and hold them in check. There was one man in western Texas at the time who was equal to the emergency. His name was John Coffee Hays, better known to history as Jack Hays, the famous Texas ranger. He was a surveyor by profession, brave and energetic. He had already made himself known and felt at the famous batle of Plum Creek. General Houston recognized the ability of the young surveyor, and seeing the necessity of an armed active force at San Antonio to hold both Indians and lawless characters in check, commissioned Jack Hays to raise a company, to be stationed at-San Antonio as headquarters, and to follow horsethieves or Indians anywhere he wished, and to shoot horsethieves on the spot if necessary.

Big Foot Wallace heard of the organization, and at once applied for admission and was enrolled as one of the company. Captain Hays was very particular as to the kind of men he enlisted, and that is one reason why he had the best set of Indian fighters, taken as a whole, that Texas ever produced. A man had to have courage, good character, be a good rider, good shot, and have a horse worth $100. In this first company the writer has learned the names of Wallace, Woolfork, Joe Tivey, Mark Rapier, Kit Ackland, Jim Galbreth, Tom Buchanan, Coho Jones, Peter Poe, Mike Chevalier, and Ad Gillespie. Among those who came later and followed the fortunes of Hays, and helped to fight his battles and gain a reputation for him as an Indian fighter which is almost world-wide, were Sam Walker, Sam Lucky, George Neill (or Nail as he was called), James Dunn, Ben McCulloch, Henry McCulloch, Ben Highsmith, Tom Galbreth, Andrew Sowell, John Sowell, P. H. Bell, Creed Taylor, Sam Cherry, Noah Cherry, John Carlin, Rufus Perry, Joe Davis, Pipkin Taylor, Josiah Taylor, Rufus Taylor, James Nichols, Calvin Turner. Milford Day, Lee Jackson, and many other gallant men whose names can not now be obtained.

During the years 1840-41 Hays and his men captured many horsethieves in and around San Antonio and shot several of them. On one occasion they captured a notorious Mexican freebooter named Antonio Corao, and such was the nature of his crimes that it was decided to put an end to his existence. Four men were detailed to shoot him, namely, Big Foot Wallace, Chapman Woolfork, Sam Walker, and William Powell. The execution took place at the head of the San Antonio River.

During the stay of the rangers in San Antonio they did a great deal of scouting and fought several battles with the Indians. Things went on in this way until the fall of 1842, when the Mexicans under Gen. Adrian Wall made a sudden descent from Mexico and captured San Antonio. Prior to this event, however, there was a suspicion that something was wrong, from the fact that all at once no ammunition could be bought in San Antonio by the Americans. It had all been secured by Mexicans at various times. Wallace also told Captain Hays that there were at least a dozen strange Mexicans in town who did not live there. Hays now sent Wallace and another ranger named Nathan Mallon to Austin to get a supply of powder and lead. Captain Wallace told the writer that Mallon was afterwards sheriff of Bexar County. While in Austin the Indians made a raid and killed Capt. William Pyron and a man named Donovan, north of Austin about two miles. Wallace and Mallon went out and helped to bring the bodies in and bury them. They then obtained their ammunition and started back to San Antonio. Wallace had a full keg of powder rolled up in a blanket and tied to the pommel of his saddle. Mallon had a supply of caps and lead. As there were no settlements between Austin and San Antonio, they providentially went back by way of Seguin to get corn for their horses. San Antonio had been captured during their absence, and if they had gone directly back, they and their ammunition would have fallen into the hands of the Mexicans. At Seguin they found Captain Hays and his lieutenant, Henry E. McCulloch. The town (San Antonio) was suddenly captured, and part of the ranger force fell into the hands of the Mexicans. Hays and some of his men escaped. The whole country east was now rallying under Gen. Matthew Caldwell to advance upon San Antonio and give battle to this large band of 1500 freebooters and robbers. The Texans, 200 in number, advanced to the Salado Creek, seven miles northeast of the city, and Captain Hays with what rangers he had under his command was sent to draw the Mexicans out. What few rangers there were in town when the Mexicans entered made a short fight, in which the bandmaster was killed, and also the horse of General Wall.

Hays and his men went so near town and gave the Mexicans such a dare that the whole force of cavalry and infantry came out. An exciting chase now commenced across the prairie back to the position of the Texans. Four hundred cavalry chasing and firing at the small squad under the gallant Hays. When the infantry arrived with cannon the main battle came off, and the Mexicans were badly defeated.

When the Mexicans captured the quarters of the rangers in San Antonio they obtained among other things a pair of pantaloons belonging to Big Foot Wallace. During the battle now he was on the lookout to kill a big Mexican and get another pair to replace them and get even. During a close charge by the Mexicans one daring fellow charged Wallace, and presenting his carbine at him, cried out, "Take that, you d—d cowthief," and fired in his face. The large ounce ball from the escopet grazed the nose of Wallace and almost blinded him with smoke. Big Foot fired, but missed. Henry Whaling, standing near, said, "D—n such shooting as that," and aiming his rifle, quickly sent a ball through the Mexican's body, who fell against a mesquite tree and soon died.

During the next charge, one of the rangers said to Wallace:

"Big Foot, yonder is a Mexican who has on a pair of pants large enough to fit you." The Mexican in question was at this time assisting some of the wounded back to the rear. Wallace was a conspicuous figure during the fight. His dress, massive frame, and actions, while talking about the big Mexican, attracted the attention of General Caldwell, who rode up to him and said, "What command do you hold, sir?" "None," says Wallace. "I am one of Jack Hays' rangers, and want that fellow's breeches over yonder," at the same time pointing out his intended victim. Before the battle was over he killed him and secured the coveted prize, which was made of splendid material, and Wallace wore them the following year while a prisoner in Mexico after the unfortunate battle of Mier.

The saddest finale to the battle of Salado was the massacre of Dawson's men, who were cut off and nearly all killed or captured while trying to make their way to Caldwell.

The Mexicans soon left for Mexico, and were followed as far as the Hondo River, and the rear guard attacked by the rangers under Hays and some cannon captured, but failing to be supported by the main body had to retreat back. Wallace was in this fight, and the mule he rode was slightly wounded.

In 1843, in retaliation for the invasion of Texas under Wall, an expedition started to Mexico under General Somervell. Captain Hays and his rangers were along, but the expedition went to pieces on the Rio Grande and most of the men came back. Among these were Captain Hays and most of his men. Five captains, however, determined to go on in the invasion of Mexico if they could get men enough. Three hundred men came over to them. Among these were Big Foot Wallace, Sam Walker, and others of the rangers. The captains were William S. Fisher, Ewing Cameron, Eastland, Reese, and Pierson. After the separation they went down the river four miles and went into camp. Next day they elected Captain Fisher to the command and continued their march down the river. On the 21st of December, 1842, they encamped opposite the town of *Mier.* Ominous name! How the hearts of the readers of Texas history now thrill at the mention of it. Then it had no significance.

The town of Mier was six miles from the camp of the Texans. On the following morning they crossed the Rio Grande, marched to the town, and made a requisition on the alcalde for provisions and clothing. He promised that the articles should be delivered the next day at the river, but below the camp of the Texans. The Texans, however, when they went back to their camp brought the alcalde along with them as surety for the delivery of the goods. On the 23d the Texans moved their camp opposite the place where the goods were to be delivered, but the day passed off, and the next, and still the goods did not come. The Texas spies who had been kept on the west side of the river on the morning of the 24th captured a Mexican, who reported that General Ampudia had arrived in Mier with troops and prevented the fulfillment of the alcalde's promise. The Texans then determined to again cross the river and give them battle. By 4 o'clock in the evening they had all crossed and were on their march to the town. Captain Baker had command of the spies, and first met the Mexicans who sallied out from Mier. Ampudia retreated before the Texans, and at dark again entered the town.

The Texans advanced to the Alcantra Creek, east of the town, and halted for some time. This little stream ran very rapidly and it was difficult to find a crossing in the night. They finally succeeded, however, in getting over. By this time a lively fight had commenced between Baker's spies and the Mexican cavalry. Five of the Texans were cut off and captured. Among these were Dr. Sinnickson, Sam Walker, Beasley, and "Legs" Lewis. Others made narrow escapes. It was a hand to hand fight, and the Texans who were cut off were compelled to abandon their horses and take themselves across fences and ditches. Sam Walker was caught by a powerful Mexican and held down, while others tied him. One man named McMullins was caught by the legs while getting over a fence, but his boots pulled off and he made his escape. They had all emptied their guns and pistols in the fight and had no time to reload. Wallace had advanced to the edge of town, but saw the Mexican cavalry coming and went back. He passed "Legs" Lewis and said to him, "You had better run; the Mexicans will get you, sure."

After the main body of the Texans had passed the creek they advanced to the town and Wallace came in with them. They passed down a street leading to the public square, where the Mexicans had planted cannon. While doing so they were fired on and a man named Jones was killed. He was the next man in the rear of Wallace as they came in single file, and Big Foot felt the wind of the bullet that killed him. He was a well dressed man, and the Mexicans attempted to strip his body. The Texans halted and turned back, and a sharp fight ensued in which twenty Mexicans were killed. When the Texans arrived at a point near the cannon they received a discharge of grape shot which swept the street and caused them to seek shelter behind the buildings. It was now dark, Christmas evening, 1842. The only chance for the Texans to advance was by opening passage ways through the buildings and advance in this way towards the cannons. All night they worked, and when daylight came they were in fifty yards of the cannon. Their horses had been left in camp under a guard. While engaged in this work Wallace found a Mexican baby that had been abandoned during the hasty exit of the occupants of the house on the approach of the Texans. It set up a terrible squall when the white men got into the room where it was, and Big Foot took it up, and advancing to a wall inclosing a yard, climbed up and dropped it over, at the same time shouting out in Spanish for some one to come and get the muchacho. He soon heard a woman's voice on the outside and supposed it was taken care of.

At daylight portholes were opened in the various rooms the men had gotten into, and soon the deadly crack of the rifles were heard as they commenced firing on the artillerymen. The cannons were soon silenced, for it was death for a Mexican to go near them. During the day three desperate attempts were made by the enemy to storm and carry the position of the Texans, but each failed with fearful loss. Wallace said the Mexicans came so thick it was impossible to miss them, and the bravest of them were the presidio ales (town guards) who wore black hats with white bands around them. They were nearly all killed. In one of the rooms occupied by the Texans, and where Wallace was, a strong Mexican drink "aguadente" was found. The men at once commenced drinking it to excess, and even one of their officers drank so much he fell on the floor and was wounded by a bullet while in that condition. The men were so worn with the night's work that when they found this liquor they drank it out of tin cups like water. Wallace, seeing it would render them unfit for service, although he loved it as well as any of them, turned the balance of the firewater out on the floor.

Before the fight commenced, Captain Wallace says one of their scouts, Joe Berry, fell down a bluff and broke his leg. His brother Bates Berry and some others who were with him carried Joe to a vacant house in the outskirts of town. During the battle they were discovered and attacked by Mexicans. A rush was made by the Texans to reach the position of their comrades, but were all killed except Bates. He only left his wounded or crippled brother when he saw there was no chance to save him, and at the earnest solicitation of the latter, who no doubt thought the Mexicans would spare him. One of the men killed in the sally was a bugler named Austin. A Mexican lieutenant named Algerette, who was in command of the party who assaulted the position where the unfortunate Joe Berry lay, went in and killed him with his sword as he lay helpless, and then bragged about it after the surrender and exhibited the blood-stained sword. During the night battle, bugles were constantly sounding, and it was reported that the Mexicans were being largely reinforced. The Texans, however, were undismayed, and continued to load and fire their rifles with such deadly effect that great confusion prevailed among the Mexicans, who continually uttered cries of rage and pain amidst a constant blast of bugles. After it was no longer possible for the Mexicans to go near the cannons, and their charges had been repulsed, they occupied the house tops and other places convenient to shoot from, and kept their bodies hid as much as possible. Many of those killed were shot in the head. Wallace said he loaded and fired his rifle fifteen times, always waited for a good chance, and had a bead on a Mexican every time he touched the trigger. The Mexicans tried to recover their cannon by throwing ropes around them from the corners of buildings, and succeeded in getting some of them away.

During the fight after daylight on the 26th the small guard which had been left on the east side of the Alcantra Creek attacked about sixty of the Mexican cavalry and routed them, but seeing a large reinforcement coming, made a desperate attempt to join their comrades in the town. Out of the nine men who made this attempt two succeeded, four were killed, and three were captured.

During one close charge many were killed and wounded on both sides. Colonel Fisher himself was severely wounded. Captain Cameron had fortified himself and men in the rear of the building occupied by Fisher and his men, and had also been exposed to a fearful fire, during which he had three men killed and seven wounded. The bugles of the Mexicans began sounding a charge from different parts of the town, and Cameron hastily entered the room occupied by Fisher and asked for reinforcements to help defend his position. About that time a white flag was brought out by Dr. Sinnickson, one of the Texans who had been captured as before stated. He was ordered to do so by General Ampudia, and to tell the Texans he had 1700 troops in the city and 300 more on the road from Monterey, and that it would be useless for them to continue to resist, and that if they would surrender they would be treated as prisoners of war; if not, no quarter would be given. The prospect was gloomy for the Texans, and although they had fought as men worthy the name of Texan, and had caused the streets of Mier to almost run with Mexican blood, they still saw no chance to win. They were on foreign soil, hemmed in on all sides by their enemies, their number reduced, and the survivors almost worn out. Some, however, were not in favor of a surrender, and thought they could make a sally from their barricaded positions, and by keeping together fight their way out of town and back across the Rio Grande. This would have been child's play compared with what they did attempt later on. Many among Fisher's men were in favor of a surrender, and Cameron hurried back to his own and exhorted them to continue the fight. Others under the different captains favored a surrender, and commenced leaving their positions and giving up their guns in the streets. When Fisher's men commenced going out to surrender, Wallace, who had been with them most of the time, left and ran to the position of Cameron. Others now left their commands and came to Cameron, until forty or fifty stood around him and asked him to take command and continue the battle or make a rush and fight their way out. At this time great confusion prevailed; some were surrendering and others firing. Every few minutes barricades would be torn away and men would march out four or five at a time and surrender. Cameron held his position until all the balance had surrendered, and seeing that all hope was gone, said to his men, who with stern but anxious faces stood around him: "Boys, it is no use for us to continue the fight any longer; they are all gone but us." The men stood for a few minutes and looked at the hordes of Mexicans, who were now making a grand display, the cavalry charging up and down the streets, and others carrying away the guns of the Texans, who were now prisoners and herded together on the plaza. The Mexican soldiers and the citizens of the town were making a great outcry and cheering for victory. A gallant officer named Thomas J. Green, who was with Cameron, broke his sword before he would give it up. Wallace was opposed to the surrender. He remembered the fate of his brother and other relatives after the surrender at Goliad, and expected nothing else for himself and those with him on this occasion, and told them so. The gallant Cameron, however, wishing to save the lives of his men, took the lead and they followed. They were met by a strong detachment of Mexicans as they emerged from their position into the street, and the painful work commenced of handing over their guns, pistols, and knives. Wallace stayed back until the last, closely watching every incident of the surrender, thinking it might be necessary to kill another Mexican if the slaughter which he expected should commence too soon. Finally, however, he handed up his arms and was the last man to do so at Mier. Big Foot said as they were marched to the plaza his shoes became red with blood where the Mexicans bled who were killed or wounded in those desperate charges. He also saw blood in the gutters and on the house tops. He says a Mexican whom General Somervell raised and educated was killed in the fight on the Mexican side, and had the general's rifle with him.

The Mexican loss in the battle, considering the numbers engaged, was fearful. Their own report was 500 killed out of a force of 2000. The Texans had 260 men in the town, sixteen of whom were killed and thirty wounded. The Mexicans had forty artillerymen killed.

Captain Wallace told the writer he thought 800 Mexicans were killed, and while the results were not so great, it was a harder fought battle than San Jacinto. The Texans were carried up to the square from where the surrender took place, and Wallace says he saw four rows of dead Mexicans reaching across the plaza, and the priests were among them saying mass.

While this was being done the bodies of the slain Texans, stripped of their clothing, were being dragged through the streets by the cavalry, followed by crowds of yelling Mexicans of all sizes and ages.

5

During the last days of December General Ampudia set out
with his prisoners for the City of Mexico, leaving the wounded
at Mier in charge of Dr. Sinnickson. On January 9, 1843, the
captive Texans arrived at Matamoros, and on the 14th set out
from that place for Monterey, guarded by a troop of cavalry. On
the march it was one grand jubilee with the Mexicans. They
starved the prisoners and made them travel on foot all the distance until their shoes were worn out, and they were thin and
haggard. The Mexicans made grand demonstrations in passing
through the towns, their approach being heralded with bugles
and prancing, charging cavalry. The Texans were marched
through the principal streets, followed by yelling mobs of men
and boys. The women with but few exceptions pitied the half-
starved, healf-dead Americans, some of whom were beardless
boys, and when they arrived at Monterey the women came with
provisions and fed them. They stayed here from the 18th to the
20th, and were then started to Saltillo. At this place they found
six of the Texans who were captured at San Antonio in September of the year before, when Wall captured that place. Big
Foot was at this time still wearing the pants of the Mexican
whom he killed at the battle of Salado.

At Saltillo Colonel Barragan took charge of the prisoners and
proceeded with them to the Hacienda Salado, 100 miles further
on, where they arrived on the 10th of February, and were there
placed in prison. For some time the Texans had contemplated
making an attempt to escape and had formulated a plan at Monterey, but one of their own officers disclosed the plot to the Mexicans and the attempt was not made. Now it was set on foot
again without detection, and carried out. There had been an addition to the number of Texas prisoners by a portion of the Santa
Fe prisoners who had gone on the ill-starred expedition to New
Mexico and had all been captured and sent over into Old Mexico
and confined with the Mier prisoners. A few survivors of the
Dawson massacre had also been placed with them. Among the
Santa Fe prisoners were Drs. Brennan and Lyons, who were
anxious to make the attempt to escape. When all was ready,
Captain Cameron gave the signal by throwing up his hat, and
Lyons and Brennan led the charge on the guards. Cameron and
Samuel H. Walker, who was captured before the battle of Mier,

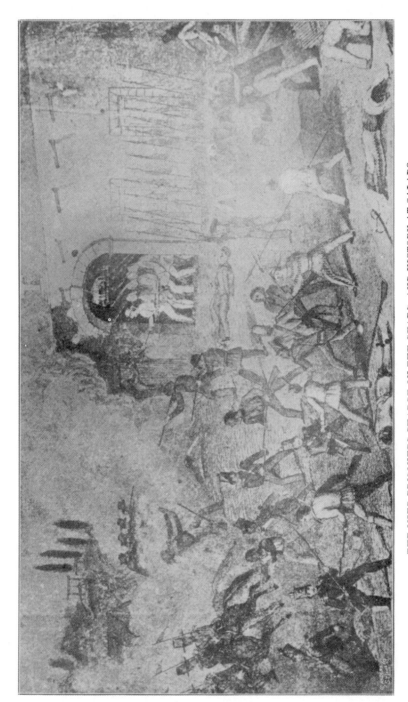

THE MIER PRISONERS CHARGE ON THE GUARD, AND VICTORY AT SALADO.

each charged a guard and succeeded in disarming him. This was at sunrise on the 11th day of February, 1843.

As soon as the first charge was made and the guards were disarmed at the door of the prison, the Texans rushed into the outer court of the building, where 150 infantry were guarding the arms and cartridge boxes. There were about 200 Texans and without hesitating an instant they rushed upon the Mexican soldiers with their naked hands, and a most desperate struggle commenced for the possession of the guns and cartridges. Where in all the world's history will we find deeds recorded of any braver men than these who, on that February morning in the prison yard of Salado, rushed empty-handed on regular soldiers, faced the leveled muskets with unflinching eye, received their fire, and then closed in on them? The Mexicans inside the prison court surrendered or fled after the first fire, but still the Texans were not masters of the situation. Another company of infantry was stationed at the gate, and a force of cavalry outside. Without hesitating, the desperate men rushed on these and a terrible fight ensued. Most of the prisoners had secured guns when this second hand to hand fight took place. Big Foot Wallace had as yet secured no gun; but he rushed upon a Mexican who had fired his gun and tried to disarm him. The fellow had a bayonet on his musket, however, and made a vicious thrust at the big Texan, who seized the bayonet, and a hard struggle commenced for the mastery. The bayonet came off in the hands of Wallace, and another unarmed prisoner came up behind and seized the gun by the breech and obtained possession of it. The Mexican then fell to his knees, held up his hands, and in Spanish called for mercy, which was granted him.

The fight at this time was fiercely raging, and Wallace went into the thick of it, brandishing his bayonet, which he used until the fight was over. In vain the Mexicans tried to keep the Texans from going through the gate, which would give them their liberty. The contest was short but bloody, and the noise and confusion was awful. The Mexicans uttered screams and yells of terror and surprise as the Texans rushed among them with clubbed guns after the first discharge, and delivered blows right and left. The cavalry became terror-stricken and fled, and the infantry at the gate began to throw down their arms and try to surrender, but for a time no stop could be put to the carnage.

At length the voice of Cameron was heard calling on his men to desist as he went among them and begged for the disarmed guards. This put a stop to it. They all loved the brave, unselfish Cameron, whose ancestors came from the highlands of Scotland. Many Mexicans lay dead on every side, while others were moaning with broken heads and gunshot wounds. Lieutenant Barragan, son of the commander of the Mexican force, displayed great bravery during the fight, and refused to surrender except to an officer. Six Texans who had secured guns with bayonets on them confronted him and demanded his surrender. Backing against a wall, he brandished his sword and refused to do so except to an officer. Six bayonets were now thrust at him, but he so successfully parried all of them that not one point touched him. His saber made such rapid movements that it was hardly visible. About this time Big Foot Wallace came up, and some one told him to get a loaded gun and shoot the fellow. Wallace said no; that a brave man like him should be spared. The brave young Mexican now called for Captain Cameron. He came at once, and the sword was then turned over to him. With a proud look the Mexican stepped back and folded his arms. His father, Colonel Barragan, had quit the field in cowardly flight some time before. Other Mexicans who had surrendered and were looking on during this episode said the lieutenant did not derive his courage from his father, but from his mother, and that he looked like her. The Texans did not come unscathed out of the fight; five lay still and motionless among their dead foes, and many more were wounded. Among the dead were the brave and fearless Brennan and Lyons, who led the charge at the prison door. The Texans now being masters of the situation, dictated terms to the Mexicans, one of which was that their wounded should be taken care of. Those who were able to travel prepared for instant flight. This was their only chance for safety, as they knew a large force would soon be on their trail.

Some of the Mexican cavalrymen who had tied their horses and were not by them when the onset was made ran away without mounting, and other horses were found in the town, so that all the men were mounted by 10 o'clock a. m., and set out towards the Rio Grande. Now, kind reader, if you have tears to shed, "prepare to shed them now." We will see these gallant men back again ere long in chains, all walking skeletons, drawing beans for their lives.

Big Foot Wallace secured a fine dun pacing mule which belonged to Captain Arroyo, who had run away on foot and left
him. By midnight the Texans were fifty miles from the scene
of their battle, and a short halt was made and the horses fed.
Twelve miles more were traveled and another halt was made, and
the men slept two hours. Early the next morning they left the
main road so as to go around the city of Saltillo. On the 13th
they struck the road leading from Saltillo to Monclova, but on
the next night abandoned it and took to the mountains on the
left. This was a fatal mistake, as events which followed will
show.

The troubles and hardships of these brave men now commenced in earnest. When too late they saw the mistake which
they had made. The country was a barren waste of mountains,
without water or anything in the shape of food. Six days were
spent in trying to get through. The men were perishing with
thirst and starvation. Horses were killed and eaten and their
blood drank by the desperate Texans. Wallace killed the mule of
Captain Arroyo, and he and others devoured quantities of it with
a most ravenous appetite and quaffed cupfuls of the red blood
with a gusto and apparent relish, as if they were drinking to
one another's health in the saloons of San Antonio.

Sitting around our firesides at home, surrounded by our families and home comforts, we can hardly realize the gravity or
horribleness of the situation, and turn from it with loathing.
The dry, lonely canyon where the horses were killed to sustain
human life; the bloody feast, akin to savage orgies, can only be
understood rightly by those who participated in it, and knew what
hunger and thirst means after days of abstinence, coupled with
anxious, toilsome flight. They could not long remain here;
swarms of cavalry with pack mules carrying provisions and water
were on their trail. Leaving the remains of the slaughtered
horses for the coyotes and buzzards to finish, the Texans once
more plunged into the dark mountains in a vain endeavor to
reach the Rio Grande, many of them now on foot, and soon all
of them, for the poor horses also failed and died of thirst. They
were hopelessly lost, and once more thirst began to torment them.
They could no longer keep together as a body.

All were now on foot, the horses which had not died being abandoned. Many became delirious, wandered away, and died in lonely, dry ravines, or on top of lofty mountains amid huge rocks. Most of the guns were cast away, and the men toiled on. Some would sink down with their heads dropped on their breasts and their feet pointing in the direction they wished to go. Big Foot Wallace had partly dried some of his mule meat in the sun and was carrying it in a haversack, and would from time to time partake of it until thirst became so intense he could no longer do so. His tongue was dry and swollen. Five more days he spent without water, but during that time his legs never failed him. The men were now badly scattered. Wallace and three companions stayed together and toiled on with their faces in the direction, as they thought, of the Rio Grande. His comrades were Captain Cameron, Tom Davis, and James Ogden.

The Mexican cavalry who were on the trail of the Texans finally began to come upon those who were behind and to capture them. The main body, which had remained together and still had some guns with them, refused to surrender when overtaken unless they could do so as prisoners of war. It was a strange sight, this small force of half-dead men, with hollow eyes and sunken cheeks, boldly facing their robust, well-fed foes, and demanding of them an honorable capitulation, saying they would fight if it was not granted. The Mexicans promised them all these things, and the surrender was made. Wallace and his three companions were headed off and captured within 150 yards of a pool of water. They surmised from the looks of the country that water was near, and were using their last remaining strength to get to it. The Mexicans doled out the water sparingly to the Texans, fearing they would kill themselves if allowed to drink all they wanted at once. While they were dispensing a small cupful to each man, Wallace noticed a cavalryman near him who had the water gourd which had been taken from him at Mier, and thinking they would all be shot anyway, sprang at him and said in Spanish, "That is my gourd; give it up." The Mexican soldier at once complied, saying, "Pobrecito" (poor fellow). Wallace turned up the gourd, and said that first swallow of water was the best he ever tasted. He continued to gurgle it down, and Tom Davis ran up to him and said, "Give me some, Big Foot." Wallace said he could not turn it loose, and Davis was unable to pull it away from him. A Mexican officer now took notice of what was going on in regard to the gourd episode, and said in Spanish, "Hell, take the water away from that fellow; he will kill himself." Three or four soldiers then tried to take the gourd away from the big Texan, but were unable to do so until he had emptied it. He was so much taller than the Mexicans he could hold it almost out of their reach and drink, and kept whirling around while doing so, and stretched his neck and held his head as high as he could. It was a gallon gourd, and was nearly full when Wallace commenced on it. After the water was drank Wallace dropped down on his knapsack and said he never felt as good in his life. In a few moments he was asleep. He had not slept any for five nights, except in short, troubled naps, with visions of running water constantly before him. When he fell down the officer said, "See, now, he is dead."

It seems that the officers in command of this squad were humane men and treated these four prisoners well, even Captain Cameron. They camped here for the night, so that the worn and weary men could rest. Through the night a little more water was given occasionally to all except Wallace. He slept all night without once rousing up, and the soldiers said he would never wake, but die that way. When morning came, however, Big Foot waked up refreshed and hungry, and opening his knapsack began to make a hearty meal of his remaining mule meat. One of the Mexicans said: "Look at that man; he is not dead; watch him eat." Another one came to him and asked what he was eating. "Mule meat," said Wallace, as he looked the Mexican in the face. "Whose mule was it?" was the next question. "My mule," says Wallace. "It was not," said the Mexican. "He belonged to Captain Arroyo." "Why did he not stay with him, then?" said Big Foot, as he continued to eat, and then resumed: "The coward ran off and left him, and I got him. So then he belonged to me, and when I got hungry I killed him and ate him. .Mule meat is good—better than horse meat."

The Mexicans made diligent search and brought in all they could find, but of the 193 who made their escape, five died of thirst and starvation, four got through to Texas, and three were never found or heard of.

The party who had Wallace and his companions next day after their capture went back to the main body, who by this time were taken. A few were taken and brought in every day for several days, and then the march commenced for Saltillo. The Texans, 160 in number, were tied together with ropes and marched in strings. On the 27th they were brought into the city, and an order was there to the commanding officer from Santa Anna to have the Texans shot. The officer refused to comply, and said he would resign his commission before he would do so. The British consul also interfered and had it stopped. One of the prisoners, James C. Wilson, was a British subject, and the consul proposed to set him at liberty, but he refused to accept it, saying he was a Texan and would die with his comrades if necessary. He lived to get back to Texas, and was honored by all who knew him. He died in Gonzales County. Wilson County was named for him. His son, Judge James C. Wilson, lives in Karnes County, and is judge of the district in which he lives.

The prisoners were now all ironed and marched back to Salado, the scene of the fight. It was now the 24th day of March. What a sad return,—haggard, poor, half dead, and in irons! Here another order was received from Santa Anna. This was to shoot every tenth man. The irons were kept on them and the guards doubled. When the prisoners arrived at the scene of their recent break for liberty, Wallace and Henry Whaling were near each other, and noticed some Mexicans digging a ditch. Whaling remarked, "That ditch is for us." The words were prophetic, as far as he was concerned. He drew a black bean, was shot, and buried in the ditch with his companions who met the same fate.

In decimating the prisoners, it was decided among the Mexican officers to let them draw lots, so that each man would have a chance for his life. The lots were to be determined by drawing black and white beans,—the white life, the black death. A pitcher (or jar, Big Foot Wallace called it, and says it was shaped like a ninepin) was procured and ten white beans to one black one was placed in it, corresponding to the number of men.

When all was ready the Texans were marched out a short distance and formed in line. An officer now approached bearing the fatal jar, in which were 159 white beans and 17 black ones. Few men even in regular war times pass through such a fearful ordeal as did the men who drew beans for their lives at Salado.

For a few moments the men stood in silence, and then the drawing commenced. No severer test could have been made of men's nerve than on this occasion. Soldiers will rush to almost certain death in the excitement of battle, but to stand and decide their fate in a second by the drawing of a bean was worse than charging to the muzzle of a blazing cannon. The Mexican officers were very anxious to kill Captain Cameron, and were in hopes that he would draw a black bean. To make this almost certain the black beans were placed on top and he was made to draw first, but the balance came in alphabetical order. As he reached for the pitcher, which was held high so that no one could see into it, one of the captives (William F. Wilson) said, "Dip deep, captain." He was a close observer, and no doubt had an idea of the job that was put up. Cameron acted on the suggestion, ran his fingers to the bottom, and pulled out a white bean. A look of satisfaction passed over the faces of the Texans, for they all loved the brave and unselfish Cameron. The Mexicans scowled. The drawing now went on rapidly. All "dipped deep," and it was some time before a black bean was drawn.

Although the men knew that some would be compelled to draw the black beans, they could not help showing their satisfaction as friend after friend brought forth the bean which gave them life. What keen pangs, however, wrenched their hearts when a fatal black bean was brought to light, held by a dear comrade who had stood by them in the midst of battle or in the desolate mountain wilds, now compelled to die—shot like a dog, far from home and the loved ones there. Most of the men showed the utmost coolness, scarcely a tremor passing over their faces as the drawing went on. One noted gambler from Austin, when his time came to draw, stepped up with a smile and said, "Boys, this is the largest stake I ever played for." When he drew forth his hand a black bean was between his thumb and forefinger. Without changing the smile on his face, he took his place in the death line and remarked, "Just my luck." The prisoners were chained together in couples, and as fast as the black beans were drawn the unfortunate holder was placed in the death line. If two chained together both drew black beans they were not separated, but moved together to the fatal line. "When one was taken and the other left" the chains were taken off and the condemned fastened to one of his companions in distress.

Young Robert Beard was sick and not able to stand in line to draw his bean, and the pitcher had to be carried to where he lay on a blanket guarded by a Mexican soldier. Before his time came to draw he told his brother, who was present, that if he himself drew a white bean and his brother a black one, he wanted to exchange and be shot instead of his brother. The brother refused, but both drew white beans and lived to return home.

It is generally believed and told that Big Foot Wallace drew two beans at Salado; that one of his comrades, a young man, expressed such great fear that he would draw a black bean, that Wallace gave him his white one and said he would take another chance. When the writer asked the old captain about this matter, he said: "No, I never drew but one, and had no idea of giving it away;" and continuing said: "I could not have done so if I wished, for I heard a Mexican officer say that there would be no swapping of beans when the Beard brothers were talking about doing so, and I suppose it was from this incident that the story started in regard to me."

One young fellow, almost a boy, drew a black bean, and giving one appealing look to his comrades, asked them to avenge his death.

"Talking" Bill Moore, when it came to his turn to draw, said, "Boys, I had rather draw for a Spanish horse and lose him." He was a lively fellow, and helped to keep up the spirits of the balance. Good fortune favored him, and he drew a white bean. While the drawing was in progress some of the petty Mexican officers did all in their power to annoy the prisoners. When one drew a black bean they expressed great sorrow, hypocritically of course, and then said, "Cheer up; better luck next time," when they knew this was the last chance the poor fellow would ever have.

Wallace was chained to a man named Sesinbaugh, and said if there ever was a Christian it was him. His time came first to draw, and as he put his hand forward to get his bean he prayed for himself and Big Foot Wallace. He drew a white bean. Wallace said that afterwards, in the dark dungeon of Perote, chained to the floor, at the midnight hour he sang and prayed and thanked God that it was as well with him as it was.

As the drawing went on the chances for Wallace grew less, his letter (W) coming at the bottom of the list. The boys had "dipped deep" until nearly all the white beans had been dipped out. When he drew there was as many black beans in the jar as white ones. When his time came his hand was so large he had difficulty in squeezing it down to the beans, and they were so scarce he scooped two up against the side of the vessel and got them between his fingers and carefully felt of them. He was under the impression that the black beans were a little larger than the white ones. The Mexicans were watching him closely, and one of them told him to hurry up, and that if he pulled out two beans and one was a black one he would have to take it. Big Foot paid no attention to this. Life was at stake now. After feeling the beans a few seconds one seemed to be a little larger than the other, and he let it go. The one he pulled out was white, but he was satisfied the other was black. When Wallace drew his hand out of the jar a Mexican officer took hold of it to examine it, and called up several others to look how large it was. The next two men to draw after Wallace both drew black beans. They were Henry Whaling and W. C. Wing.

The black beans were now all out, and the last three men on the list did not draw. An officer turned up the jar and three white beans fell to the ground.

W. C. Wing, the last man to draw a black bean, was visibly affected. He was young, and when at home was very religious, but had left the beaten track of christianity and had gone sadly astray, which fact seemed to trouble him very much. He referred to it repeatedly during the short time before his execution.

When the drawing was over and the condemned men stood in the death rank, chained two and two together, their roll stood as follows: L. L. Cash, J. D. Cocke, Robert Durham, William N. Eastland, Edward Este, Robert Harris, S. L. Jones, Patrick Mahan, James Ogden, Charles Roberts, William Rowan, J. L. Shepard (cousin of the writer), J. M. N. Thompson, James N. Torrey, James Turnbull, Henry Whaling, and W. C. Wing.

Henry Whaling asked for something to eat, saying, "I do not wish to starve and be shot, too." Strange to say, the Mexicans complied with his request and two soldiers' rations was issued to him. He ate it with relish, and then said he was ready to die. During a few minutes before the execution, while preliminaries were being arranged, the decimated men stood in silence, intently watching their captors. Not a movement escaped their notice. When the firing squad was detailed and counted off, some little sign of emotion was seen on the countenances of a few. There was a nervous twitching about the mouth. Their bosoms heaved and their breath came short and quick. Others stood as calmly as if on parade.

The irons were now taken off and they were led away to execution, bidding their more fortunate comrades farewell as they marched off. Many tears were seen running down the cheeks of the emaciated and sun-burned faces of the fortunate ones as they responded to this last good-bye.

When they arrived at the place of execution, which was just outside of the village, the Texans asked permission to be shot in front, but this was refused. Henry Whaling asked to not be blindfolded, saying he wished to look the man in the face that shot him, and show them how a Texan could die. This was also refused. The Mexicans stood close to their backs when they fired, and all fell to the ground. The bodies were then stripped and piled up like a cord of wood. The firing party then went back to the town. The Texans were all dead except J. L. Shepard. His wound was in the shoulder, although the muzzle of the Mexican's gun was in a few feet of him when discharged. He feigned death so well that he was stripped and stacked up with the balance and escaped detection of having life. When the Mexicans left he went away into the mountains, but in ten days was retaken and shot. The Mexicans discovered one was gone when they came to remove the bodies to the ditch which had been prepared for them, and scouts were sent out in all directions to hunt for him.

After the execution of the Texans, the survivors, heavily ironed, were started on foot for the City of Mexico. It is impossible to describe their sufferings. They were carried through the principal cities and towns on the route, driven like so many cattle, and half starved. They were derided, hooted at, and maltreated all the way by the populace. The shackles on Big Foot Wallace were too small, and cut deep into the flesh. His arms swelled and turned black, and when they arrived at San Luis Potosi the Governor's wife came to look at the prisoners and noticed the condition of Wallace. Her woman's sympathies were at once aroused, and she ordered the chains taken off. The officer in command refused to do so, saying only the Governor had authority to give such an order. The woman replied that she was the Governor's wife, and ordered him again to take them off.

This time he complied, and sent for a blacksmith, who removed them. The good woman then, with her own hands, bathed the swollen arms of Wallace with brandy. Seeing signs of suffering among other prisoners who had gathered around, she had the chains taken off of all of them. Before she did this, however, she asked the officer if he was afraid of his prisoners without chains on, to which he replied that he was not. Big Foot Wallace told her that she ought to be President of Mexico.

On the march to the capital, after the chains were taken off, Wallace made good use of his long arms. The writer will say here that Captain Wallace had the longest arms of any man he ever saw outside of a show. He would reach and get cakes and tamales from stands as they passed them. The owners would make a great outcry, but the soldiers would laugh. Sometimes they would meet one carrying a tray or board of good things on his head. Wallace was so much taller than the Mexican that he could get a handful of things and the owner would be none the wiser. Big Foot, with his powerful frame and long arms, was a great curiosity to them. He could pass a cake stand and then reach back and get the articles off it.

When they arrived at a little Indian village eighteen miles from the City of Mexico an order came from Santa Anna to shoot Capt. Ewing Cameron. This order was kept a secret from the balance of the prisoners for fear they would make a demonstration. That night they put Cameron in a room alone under a separate guard. The balance of the prisoners were crowded together in a small room, and they almost suffocated. They were suspicious, however, from the transaction in regard to Cameron that foul play was intended, and when they were all marched out on the following morning to a tank for the purpose of washing each Texan filled his bosom full of rocks, determined to fight for their captain and die with him if an attempt was made on his life. The guards asked them why they were getting the rocks, and were told that it was for ballast, so that they could walk better. They made no attempt to take them away—in fact they were afraid to, as they saw the Texans looked desperate. The march was again commenced early in the morning. The prisoners asked about Cameron, and wanted to know if he was going to be shot. The Mexicans said no, and for them to go on and he would soon follow. When the prisoners got one mile from this place, on rising ground, they heard a platoon of guns fire back at the village, and knew that the gallant Cameron had met his fate. It was a refinement of cruelty on the part of Santa Anna to have Cameron executed after he had drawn a white bean. He met his fate unflinchingly, and died as none but the brave can die.

Before arriving at the capital the captives were again put in irons and convict garbs placed upon them. In this condition, and with grand display, they were marched into the historic city of the Montezumas.

Before leaving San Antonio Wallace had some long shirts made which almost came down to his knees, and when his pantaloons wore out until there was but little left except the waistband, and before the convict garb was put upon him, some of the Mexicans along the route thought he was a priest, and called him "padre," and some would give him bread.

While being conveyed up the streets of the capital the populace were unusually noisy—hooting, yelling, and offering many insults. One old woman ("squaw," Wallace called her) singled him out for her especial taunts and jeers. She was very ugly, bare headed, and had a long, grizzled neck. Her hair was loose, parted on the back of her neck, and hung down in front. She would come in front of him, walk backwards, grin, and make all kinds of wry faces at him. The shackled Texan was desperate and smarting with his chain, and would have struck her if he could, but his hands were chained together behind him. Watching his chance, however, when her back was turned, he sprang forward and caught the back of her neck with his teeth, thinking to bite a piece out, but the old woman squalled like a panther and jerked loose from him. Wallace says that was the toughest meat he ever tried to bite. He could make no impression on it, and his teeth slipped off and popped like a horse pulling his foot out of a bog. The soldiers laughed very heartily at this, ridiculed the old woman, and bravoed the tall "gringo" (name for Americans).

The British consul had a good deal to say about the killing of Cameron, and had a personal interview with Santa Anna in regard to it, condemning his action.

It will be remembered by our readers that Texas was not one of the United States at this time, but was an independent Republic. The United States had nothing to do with protecting citizens of Téxas, and the young Republic was not able to invade Mexico with an army and release her citizens. The Texas prisoners arrived at the City of Mexico on the 1st day of May and remained there until the following October. During this time they were confined and closely guarded at night, and worked the streets in chains during the day. Part of their work was to carry sand in sacks to make a fine road up a hill to the bishop's palace, where President Santa Anna lived. The work was slow and tedious, walking the lock-step with chains around their ankles. Even at this, however, the Texans played off a good deal by punching holes in their sacks and letting the sand run out as they went along. Part of the time they worked at Molino del Rey, one and a half miles from the city, and here four prisoners made their escape by scaling a wall. They were Samuel H. Walker, James C. Wilson, and one Thompson and Gatis. It was late in the evening, just before sundown, and all the prisoners had been brought in for the night and placed in different rooms, but all surrounded by a wall. Before the regular guard was put on for the night, which was always doubled, the four men above mentioned scaled the wall while the sentinel's back was turned.

The man Thompson had played off on the march and while at work by wrapping bloody rags, which he managed to secure in some way, around his feet and legs, and limping terribly and making many wry faces. The Mexicans let him ride all the way coming to the city. He would grimace and fall as soon as they put him on his feet. The men all knew there was nothing the matter with him, and thought it strange the Mexicans did not investigate his lameness. Wallace said that he would rather walk or work than to make the faces and contortions of body that Thompson went through. When the sentinel went into the room where he had left the prisoners a few seconds before and found it empty the truth flashed across his mind at once, and bringing the butt of his gun down on the floor with considerable force exclaimed, "Caraja!" (Mexican oath). He, however, did not report the loss, through fear, and it was not found out until the following morning; then no one knew how it occurred. What most surprised the Mexicans was that the crippled man had got away —scaled a wall. The four Texans all made their way safely back to Texas. In October the prisoners were all sent to Perote, distant about 300 miles from the capital. Here they were confined

in a damp, loathsome dungeon. They had walked all the way
there, but without chains on. The air was so foul in the dungeon
that forty of them died. Wallace, with ten others, went wild and
had to be tied down. All died but Wallace, and he was tied down
fourteen days. The Mexican doctors who were in attendance
had their assistants to rub Big Foot to keep up circulation. In
doing so one of them rubbed a plaster off of his sore back, and
he knocked the one who did it clear across the room. This was
after reason had returned again. The sore was made on his back
in his struggles when tied down on the stone floor of the dungeon.
The writer has seen these scars, and also on his arms and ankles
where the chains cut into the flesh.

Seeing they would all die if too closely confined, they were carried out through the day to work.

Many Mexicans came in to look at Wallace while he was crazy,
to watch his actions, and hear him yell. One day after he had
about recovered two young Mexican women of the upper or
wealthy class desired to visit the prison and see the wild Texan.
They made this known to the padre of the city, and he came with
them to the prison. When they arrived at the entrance and the
guards threw back the prison door, the dusky damsels drew back
alarmed when they heard the clanking chains of the prisoners.
The good father assured them, however, that there was no danger; that trusty guards were at hand, and the "mucho grande
loco Americano" was unusually docile. In the meantime some
of the Texans who had seen the party enter, divining the import
of the visit, informed Wallace of the fact. He was lying on a
cot, but at once raised up to a sitting position with his feet on the
floor and enveloped himself completely in a sheet except the eyes,
and looked as much like a ghost as possible. When the party
came in front of Wallace and the shy maidens were tremblingly
viewing "el loco hombre" (the mad man), Wallace threw off his
sheet, and uttering a yell that would have made a Comanche Indian turn pale, sprang at them. With one long, wailing scream
of terror the two Mexican girls sank to the floor, and Wallace
caught one of them by the foot. Great excitement now prevailed.
The guards rushed in and seized Wallace and tried to loosen his
grip on the girl, but not being able to do so, dragged them both
about over the cell in a vain endeavor to pull him loose. The girl
still screamed, and Big Foot yelled and roared by turns. The

THE SURRENDER OF SANTA ANNA.

Mexican soldiers cursed, and drawing their sabers said they would cut him loose. To add to the excitement, the prisoners were rattling their chains and with upraised manacled hands were threatening to dash out the brains of the guards if they used their sabers on Wallace. The unfettered girl regained her feet, and went flying almost, out of the prison. The priest stood his ground, but called on all the saints he could think of to save them. Seeing the guards dare not use their sabers, he in sheer desperation threw himself upon Wallace himself, and then told the soldiers to pull. The strain was too great now when they did so, and he relaxed his grip. The girl sprang to her feet like a frightened deer, and with flying hair made a hasty exit, followed by the padre.

As soon as Wallace was able he was put out to work with the balance. Sometimes they were hitched twenty-five to a cart and made to haul rock from the mountains down to town. During this time the Texans let three carts get away from them on the side of the mountain (accidentally, of course), and they were smashed to pieces by running off a bluff. On one occasion they hitched Wallace to a cart alone to haul sand in town. A spirit of devilment came over him, and pretending to get scared at something, he gave a loud snort and ran away. He ran against things and tore the cart all to pieces before he could be stopped. It was a funny sight to the Mexicans to see a man run away with a cart and could not be stopped or headed off until it was demolished, and they gave way to loud peals of laughter.

During this long confinement a man named Joe Davis, one of the old rangers of Jack Hays, conceived the idea of digging under the dungeon wall. It was five feet in thickness, and twenty-two feet to get under the foundation. There were twenty-seven confined in this apartment, and all agreed to the plan and went to work. They dug at night and hid the dirt as best they could. Some of the dirt was carried out in their clothing as they went to work on the streets in the daytime, and scattered gradually so as to escape detection. In this way they succeeded in digging under and out. This made a hole of forty-four feet. Twenty-four of the number succeeded in getting out, but the plot was discovered before the others could go. Only one man could travel at a time in the excavation. Wallace heard that all the prisoners were escaping in that room and hurried in there, but found it

6

full of Mexican officers and soldiers, so hurried back to his own again. Four of those who got out were recaptured and brought back and chains put upon all of them again, which for a time had been taken off. They were compelled to work harder, and nearly starved. Many weary nights now passed away; and clanking chains could be heard at all hours of the night. Many rats invaded their prison den, and so near starved were the Texans that they were caught and eaten. The rats would come up the wall to a little cross-barred window where the sentinel stood, and going through would drop into the dungeon. When the sound of the rodent was heard hitting the floor chains would rattle all over the prison, as each man was on the alert to catch him.

The captain in command here was a wooden-legged fellow with a long Spanish name which the Texans could not remember, and the more irreverant of them called him "Limpin' Jesus." He would come limping in with a great splutter of official dignity to inspect the prison, and one of the men drew a picture of him on the wall. This made him very angry, and he had it defaced.

If all the minute particulars were written of the interesting incidents through which the captive Texans passed it would make a good-sized book. The main points have been given, and enough of minor details to give the reader a clear conception of the situation.

During all these tedious months of captivity friends in the United States were using their best endeavors to have the prisoners liberated. Texas alone was not able to send an invading army into Mexico and strike the chains from her citizens, but did all she could in conjunction with others to have it done by the Mexican authorities. The wife of Santa Anna, who was an invalid and a good woman, pleaded with the stern dictator for their release. He was greatly attached to her, and would grant almost anything she asked.

Not long after this four of the prisoners were released through the intervention of influential friends in the United States. These four were Big Foot Wallace, Thomas Tatum, James Armstrong, and William F. Wilson.

Thomas Tatum, who was a native of Tennessee, gained his liberty through the influence of Gen. Andrew Jackson.

William F. Wilson, a native of Virginia, was released through the influence of Governor McDowell.

The chains dropped from the manacled wrists of James Armstrong through the good offices of Thomas Benton, of Missouri.

Big Foot Wallace was liberated through his father and Governor McDowell of Virginia. Their plantations joined, and they were friends of long standing.

On the 5th day of August, 1844, the four men in question walked out from the dark dungeon of Perote free men, after a confinement of twenty-two months, and on the same day the wife of Santa Anna died, loved and regretted by every Texan who wore the chains in Mexico.

Soon after the death of the President's wife an order came for all the balance of the Texas prisoners to be released. Santa Anna had promised his wife on her deathbed that he would release them, and let it be said to his credit that once in life he kept his word.

When Big Foot and his three companions once more breathed free air they set out on foot for Vera Cruz, having one dollar each, which was given them for expenses out of the country. From Vera Cruz they took shipping for New Orleans.

Wallace at last found his way back to his old cabin on the Medina River. He soon found out that he had neighbors. The Germans were settling Castroville, ten miles above, having recently been brought there in a colony from Europe by Henry Castro.

The balance of the life of Wallace can not be given in a sketch like this for the want of space, and can only be noticed briefly. Some of his Indian battles will be given more in detail in the sketch of Ed. Westfall, who was with him on several expeditions.

After getting back to the Medina, Wallace spent his time in hunting and following Indians until the breaking out of the Mexican war of 1846. Part of this time he also served as a ranger again under Jack Hays. When the war broke out between the United States and Mexico on account of the boundary line of Texas, which had now become one of the Union of States, Jack Hays raised a regiment of rangers. Many of his old rangers were captains in this organization, among whom was Ad. Gillespie, Kit Ackland, Mike Chevalier, and Ben McCulloch. Samuel H. Walker, who figured in the Mier expedition, was lieutenant-colonel. Wallace joined the company of Gillespie and went out as second lieutenant.

This regiment of Texas troops did good service in Mexico.

Many of them had old scores to settle with the Mexicans. Only three years before some of them had drawn beans for their lives and worked on the streets in chains. Wallace recognized several places during the campaign where he had toiled along the dusty road in chains and nearly starved. He was in all of the fighting around Monterey, and in the desperate assault on the bishop's palace, where his captain was killed.

At the winding up of the battle, and while the bugles were sounding a parley and the Mexicans were surrendering, Wallace was seen to aim his gun at a Mexican who had a flag. Officers interfered and one of them said, "Lieutenant, don't you know a parley when you hear it sounded?" Wallace said, "No; not when I am in front of that man." The Mexican in question was the one who held the fatal bean-pot when the Texans were drawing for their lives at Salado, and called up others to look at the big hand of Wallace, and in many ways tantalized the wretched man. Wallace now accosted him angrily, and asked him if he had any bean lottery here. "Look at that hand. Do you know it? Ever see it before?" The Mexican said "No." "You have," said Wallace, "and called up others to look at it." The Mexican hung his head and Wallace cursed him for all the low-down Mexican cowards in the calendar, and then let him go.

During the storming of Monterey the Texas troops forced the upper part of the city and fought their way to the Hidalgo Hotel, and there made a halt. The Mexicans had all left except the cooks, and they were badly frightened when the Texans took possession and swarmed through the apartments looking for something to eat. The men, however, told them they had nothing to fear, but they must cook them something to eat. This seemed to be out of the question, as all the provisions had been carried away. Some of the men now went in search of something, and soon came back with thirteen sheep which they had found in a pen and killed. The cooks now went to work and soon had them well cooked, but there was no bread to eat with them.

A dried-up little Mexican, who did not seem to think anyone would want to hurt him, was hanging around, and said that for a dollar he would bring them a blanketful of bread. Wallace handed over the dollar and told him to skin out and get it. The Mexican soon returned with as much light bread as he could walk under, tied up in a blanket. One of the Texans said he was afraid to eat the bread, as it might be poisoned. Wallace said he would soon see whether it was or not, and calling up the Mexican picked up a loaf that had some cracks in it and told the fellow to sit down there and eat it. He refused to do so at first, but Wallace cocked his revolver on him and he took the dry loaf and went to work. It was hard work, but he finally got it all down. Wallace then selected another loaf and told him to try that one. The Mexican rolled his eyes and made signs that he was choking to death. A quart of water was handed him to wash it down with, and the bread placed in his hand. He took it and went quickly to work on it, but soon choked, and Wallace handed him more water. The Mexican again hesitated after swallowing the water, but Big Foot encouraged him to proceed by pointing the pistol at his right eye. This loaf was finished, and the Mexican looked glad and even smiled at the pleasant little joke of Big Foot. His countenance changed, however, when Wallace handed him another loaf and motioned for him to proceed. Before taking this loaf the Mexican made the cross and called on the saints. When he choked, Wallace would give him more water, and the Mexican would look in despair towards the pistol. When the third loaf was eaten, he was told to sit still awhile and see if it would kill him. As he did not show any signs of toppling over in two minutes, and the well cooked mutton was steaming hot before them, the hungry Texans pitched in.

While this dinner was being eaten, which was not on the bill of fare of the Hidalgo Hotel that day, the cannons were booming and soldiers cheering in the lower part of town, where General Taylor was slowly carrying one street after another towards the center. The little Mexican sat and rubbed his stomach while the Texans were eating, and once exclaimed, "Yo sentir, yo comer, no mas por semano" (I could eat no more in a week). When told he could go he went quickly.

After General Taylor's battles were over in Northern Mexico part of the rangers were sent back to Texas to protect the frontier. Among these was Wallace, and when his term of enlistment was out he returned to his old cabin on the Medina. The Indians made a raid in the Medina valley in 1848 and carried off a great many horses. Wallace went after Westfall, who lived on the Leona, west of Wallace, and they raised about thirty men and followed the Indians. Their camp was found at the "Frio waterhole," on the divide, and a battle ensued in which ten Indians were killed and some of the stock retaken.

Wallace had four dogs which he prized very highly. Their names were Rock, Ring, Speck, and Blas. Rock was his Indian dog. Wallace could always tell by his actions when Indians were around, and if it was night would take his blanket and gun and the dogs and stay in a thicket near by until morning. The dogs would lie down by him without making any noise. On one occasion Rock gave the sign of Indians just before daylight, and Wallace took his gun and watched until dawn. He then hissed the dogs out to see if they could find the trail, and soon heard them baying loudly. Coming to the spot, he saw an Indian down in a gulley, and the dogs around him. He was keeping the dogs from taking hold of him by throwing his blanket over their heads. Wallace raised his gun to shoot, but seeing the Indian was not armed, desisted, and calling the dogs off, made signs for the Indian to come out. A search revealed no weapon but a small knife, and it was broken. The Indian now told Wallace in Spanish that he had been a captive among other Indians, and had made his escape. Having no arms to kill game, he was nearly starved. He had broken his knife trying to open a terrapin. Wallace took him to his cabin, gave him all he could eat, and then, leaving his dogs to watch him, went and got his horse and carried the Indian to Castroville. This place by this time, about 1849, was building up fast and had county officers. Wallace carried his Indian around over town for people to look at, and would occasionally take a drink of whisky, until he got pretty full. A county officer now came and said he would take charge of the Indian. "No you won't," said Wallace. "This is my Indian; I caught him. If you want an Indian, go catch you an Indian." A large crowd had gathered around Big Foot and the Indian, and all laughed at the idea of the officer out trying to catch him an Indian. One of the party present that day and who heard Wallace say that is Mr. Chris Batot, of D'Hanis. Soon after this episode Wallace carried his Indian to San Antonio and turned him over to Major Neighbors, who was at that time Indian agent. About this time Wallace received a commission from Gov. P. H. Bell to raise a company of rangers. Ed. Westfall was his lieutenant.

The hardest fight they had with the Indians during this term

THE SPANISH DAGGER WHERE WALLACE'S STAGE GUARD WAS KILLED.
FROM PHOTO. BY MISS EDITH DILLARD.

of service was at the Black Hills, near the present town of Cotulla, in La Salle County. Wallace had nineteen men and defeated them, killing twenty-two of their number of eighty or
more. Wallace had several men badly wounded.

After his time was out in this service he obtained a contract
to drive the stage from San Antonio to El Paso. The distance
was about 600 miles, and frontier all the way. He and his six
guards had many encounters with Indians. Once on Devil's
River five Indians were killed and two guards wounded. On
another occasion the Indians attacked the stage at night, but were
beaten off. In 1861, with forty settlers, he defeated a large party
of Indians at the head of the Seco.

The writer had the pleasure of spending several weeks with
the old captain at the house of Mr. Doc Cochran, near Devine.
I never tired of listening to him talk. He was an intelligent and
educated man, and had read many books, but he loved the woods

best of all. He never married. He said he was engaged once while living at Austin, in 1839, but had a severe spell of sickness and his hair all come out. He left town as soon as he was able, and went into a cave in the mountains and lived there until his hair grew out, but in the meantime his girl married another man. Her name was Mary Jackson.

In October, 1898, the writer received a communication from Captain Wallace, that if I would come down and go with him and take care of him he would go to the Dallas fair and reunion of the old rangers. Accordingly I did so, and we had a fine time. Big Foot Wallace was as great a show as anything else on the grounds. All had heard of him, and wanted to talk to him and take him by the hand.

We got back about the 20th of October, and I bade him farewell at the home of Mr. Cochran and family, with whom he lived. That was the last time I ever saw him. Shortly after Christmas he took something like pneumonia, and on the 7th day of January he died, in his eighty-third year. He never wore spectacles, and could read any kind of print up to almost the day of his death. He never lost a tooth, but wore them off smooth to his gums. His remains were buried in the Devine graveyard, in Medina County, but did not rest there long. During a session of the Legislature shortly after a bill was introduced by Capt. E. R. Tarver, of Laredo, to have his remains taken up and deposited in the State cemetery at Austin. In the city he helped to build, and in which he dug the first well and ran the last herd of buffalo through town that ever made a track there, he lies, the last of the great ranger captains.

"BIG FOOT" WALLACE, AT 60 YEARS OF AGE.

MRS. SARAH J. KINCHALOE.

Born in Texas in 1838.

The lady whose name appears at the heading of this article is one of the true heroines of the west. She was born in Montgomery County, Texas, April 6, 1838, and was the daughter of Capt. William Ware, who commanded a company at the battle of San Jacinto. From Montgomery County she moved with her parents and family to Kaufman County, Texas, and from there to the Cibolo Creek, near the line of Bexar County. The next move from this place was the Sabinal Canyon, in 1852. Captain Ware was the first settler in the canyon, but he came at first without his family to look out a location in the west, and remained some time before returning for them. In the meantime Gideon Thompson came with his family, and his wife and children were the first white family to enter the lovely valley. Shortly after the arrival of the Ware family there came a young man named Robert Kinchaloe, whom Sarah J. Ware afterwards married.

Mr. Kinchaloe was a hardy frontiersman and Indian fighter, serving for a time as a ranger under Capt. H. E. McCulloch. They were stationed at the forks of the North and South Llano, where Junction City now is.

Mrs. Kinchaloe has passed through all of the horrors of a frontier life, and bears the scars of eleven wounds on her body inflicted by the hands of hostile Indians. She saw the bloody body of John Davenport after he was killed by Indians and then carried by friends to his home on Rancheros Creek. Mr. Davenport was killed on the spot where Sabinal station now is, and his ranch was a few miles east. She remembers how frightful his head looked where the scalp was taken off. The same Indians killed John Bowles on the Sabinal River, below where the station now is. Mr. Bowles had prior to that time killed three Indians one night near his ranch.

In 1866 Mr. Kinchaloe was living on Little Creek, three miles northeast from the present village of Utopia. His family at that time consisted of his wife and four children. The oldest was 8 years old and the youngest 8 months. Up to this time the Indians had killed but two people in the canyon, but others had been killed in the near vicinity. There was also at this time a man named Bowlin living near Mr. Kinchaloe. On the morning of the fearful frontier episode now to be narrated Mr. Kinchaloe, in company with Mr. Bowlin, went up the canyon about twelve miles to gather some corn which they had bought from a man who had moved away. During the absence of the two men Mrs. Bowlin and her family came to spend the night at the Kinchaloe ranch, as the husbands were not expected back until next day. That night the wily Indians were prowling about the premises and the dogs barked at them all night, and just before day some one entered the house. Mrs. Kinchaloe thought it was a Mexican herder whom Mr. Kinchaloe had in his employ, and who lived in his camp not far away. Getting up, she secured a gun, and told him if he did not leave she would kill him. The person then ran out, and was pursued by the dogs so closely that he took refuge from them on top of the smokehouse. Mrs. Bowlin was very much frightened, said she knew the Indians would kill her, and said her mother told Mr. Bowlin when they were preparing to move out west on the frontier that he was bringing her daughter out here to be killed by Indians. The next morning, Sunday, October 11, 1866, Mrs. Bowlin went back to her house to see about things, and on her return told Mrs. Kinchaloe that the Mexican herder was there and was tearing up the place, and that she believed he was a white man, as he was changed. Mrs. Kinchaloe, who was a fearless woman, at once returned with Mrs. Bowlin to see about the herder, and sure enough, when they arrived he was seen to be as white as any man. He was surly, and would neither speak to nor look at them. He was afraid of Mrs. Kinchaloe when she had a gun. The two women now returned to the Kinchaloe place, and soon after arriving there saw two Kickapoo Indians running after one of Mr. Kinchaloe's horses, which they finally roped. They now came galloping towards the house. Johnnie Kinchaloe, 6 years old, who was standing watching them as they came towards the house, said to his mother, "They are not white men; see how they throw their legs about." When the Indians got to the house they opened the gate and rode into the yard as unconcerned as if they were at home. The cowardly scoundrels knew none but women and children were there. The

woman now closed the door, and Mrs. Kinchaloe got the gun and
presented it as if about to fire, when the Indians ran around the
house, pursued by the dogs. Johnnie now wanted to take the gun,
but his mother would not let him have it. Poor Mrs. Bowlin was
so badly scared she could hardly move, but her two daughters,
Ella and Anna, dressed themselves in men's clothing and cursed
the Indians, thinking they could frighten them away. Mrs.
Kinchaloe told them to hush, as she could not stand that. The
heroic woman, with the fighting blood of the Wares now up, put
on a bold front and aimed the gun again at the Indians, who had
returned to the front of the house. Her attempt to fire failed,
for the gun snapped. At this the savages cried out, "No buena"
(not good), and dismounting from their horses again went to the
rear of the house. This frontier dwelling, where no lumber could
be had, was a long picket house, and the space between the upright pickets was open. There were two doors, but one of them
had no shutter and was partly nailed up, leaving a large opening.
One of the Indians now shot Mrs. Kinchaloe with an arrow
through this half-closed door, and the other one lanced her
through a crack between the pickets. The brave woman, however, continued at her post and vainly endeavored to fire the gun.
The weapon in question was a Spencer carbine, with a magazine
in the breech containing the cartridges, which were thrown into
the barrel with a lever. This Mrs. Kinchaloe did not know how
to work, as it was a gun she was not familiar with, and therefore
was unable to discharge it. She attempted to fire it as she would
a common rifle, by pulling the hammer back and pressing the
trigger. If an old-time shotgun or rifle had been in her hands
she would have won the battle, but, still unable to shoot and covered with wounds and blood, she stood between the savages and
her children, receiving the lance thrusts from the cowardly Kickapoos with a fortitude and heroism that would have done honor
to a veteran soldier of an hundred battlefields.

While this terrible scene was being enacted the children all
went under the bed except the baby. At last, covered with
wounds and almost exhausted from loss of blood, Mrs. Kinchaloe
handed the gun to Mrs. Bowlin, and told her to keep the Indians
back if she could and not let them carry off the children. As for
herself, she said she would not live five minutes longer, and sank
down upon the floor. When the Indians saw this fearless pioneer

woman fall they came into the house, one at each door, and stood near the fireplace, facing the helpless woman who now had the gun and was standing motionless in the center of the room gazing upon their hideous faces without making any effort at resistance. In this position they raised their bows and shot Mrs. Bowlin through the heart with two arrows. While she was falling to the floor one of the Indians took the gun from her hand and placed it in the quiver at his back. When Mrs. Bowlin sank down to the floor her two small children ran to her and commenced crying. She told them their mother was gone, and immediately expired. Mrs. Kinchaloe now exclaimed, "O, my God, the time has come now for me to die." She was lying in pools of blood upon the floor, well nigh exhausted. The Indians did not tarry long. They had consumed so much time in the fight with Mrs. Kinchaloe that they feared some settler might ride up. They made no further attempt to kill anyone, but hastily secured such things as they fancied, mounted their horses, and rode away, taking the one they had roped with them. They also took the trunks out into the yard, broke them open, pillaged the contents, tied up the articles in sheets, and carried them away.

Little Johnnie Kinchaloe now came to where his mother lay beside the dead body of Mrs. Bowlin, and said he must go and tell some one to come or she would bleed to death. She told him no, that the Indians might get him; but to pull the arrows out of her, especially the one in the shoulder, which was very painful. This the gallant little fellow did, and then brought camphor for his mother to drink, which revived her some. He then, in company with Anna Bowlin, left the house to give the alarm. Two more of the Kinchaloe children, Betty and Charley, now came out from under the bed crying, and asked their mother if she would live. She told the weeping children that she did not know, but there was little hope. Betty, 4 years old, said, "Mamma, will you go to the good man if you die?" "I hope so," was the reply. Betty then turned to Mollie Bowlin, who was sitting by the dead body of her mother, and said, "I know my mamma will go to the good man if she dies."

The nearest neighbor except the Bowlin place was Mr. Snow, two and a half miles distant, over on the Sabinal River, and thither the two children wended their way, the tall grass coming up almost to the top of little Johnnie Kinchaloe's head. The

family were eating dinner in company with several neighbors
when the two young messengers bearing the sad news of savage
barbarity arrived and told it. The neighbors present at Mr.
Snow's house were Messrs. Wish, Alexander, James O'Bryant,
and Jack Dillion. One of them remarked as they arose from the
table, "Now our troubles have commenced." The two last named
men at once mounted their horses and rode to the scene of the
tragedy. The little children were greatly rejoiced to see them.
When they came into the house Jack Dillion said, "Here is Mrs.
Bowlin, dead; let's take her up and take care of her." O'Bryant
said, "No; here lies Mrs. Kinchaloe nearly dead. Let's take care
of the living first, and then the dead." Mrs. Kinchaloe had become very cold, and they wrapped her up in a blanket and laid
her on the bed. The news was soon carried to other settlers, and
great excitement prevailed in the canyon.

On that day the Rev. John L. Harper was preaching at the
house of John C. Ware, brother of Mrs. Kinchaloe. The news
was rapidly carried to this place by Mr. Wilson O'Bryant, who
had arrived upon the scene. It was on the river about three miles
distant, and the old homestead of Capt. Wm. Ware, who died
soon after settling there. This was a short distance below the
present Utopia, and was known as Waresville. When the messenger arrived the men present at the service ran for their horses
and guns. John Ware was the first one on his horse, and calling
out, "Gentlemen, I am ready," galloped off, followed by the men
as fast as they could mount. Among those who went to the
scene of the killing were Rev. Harper, Mr. Simpson, B. F. Biggs,
and Judge James McCormick. Mr. Ware came to the bedside as
he thought of his dying sister, and weeping bitterly asked about
her wounds. "I am shot all to pieces," she said. "My God!"
said the brother. "O, that I could have been here to have saved
you." The wounded woman told her brother not to weep; that
she now believed she would get well. The country was thinly
settled, and most of the people soon got there. Jake O'Bryant
went after Mrs. Binion, the only doctor in the country, and made
a most remarkably quick trip. The good woman doctor said she
could revive and restore Mrs. Kinchaloe. Gideon Thompson and
James Snow went after Mr. Kinchaloe and Mr. Bowlin, who at
once mounted their horses and set out. The latter seemed dazed
and almost paralyzed by the news. He knew that his wife was

dead and that he could not succor her. With Mr. Kinchaloe it was different; his wife still lived. He rode furiously, urging his horse to his utmost speed, leaving his companion in distress far behind. Mrs. Thompson said when he passed their house he looked like a dead man, and on arriving home fell fainting at the door. After being revived he looked at his blood-covered wife and fainted again. He soon rallied again, however, and composing himself went to the bedside and promised her that as soon as she got well he would leave the frontier. The plucky woman told him no; she did not want to leave. On raising Mrs. Kinchaloe to dress the wounds where she had been deeply lanced in the body her sister, Mrs. Fenley, said, "She is bound to die." Some one said, "No she won't; she is a Ware, and you can not kill a Ware."

Who can describe the feelings of Mr. Bowlin when he arrived and stood by with his motherless children clinging around him? The body of his wife was buried near Waresville. Mrs. Kinchaloe was carried to the house of her brother, and after many days of suffering she recovered, with the scars of a dozen or more arrow and lance wounds on her body, one of which was a dangerous one in the neck. Although diligent search was made for the Indians they could not be found, and the sheep herder had also disappeared. No doubt he was in with the Indians and wanted to get a sum of money which Mr. Kinchaloe was supposed to have in the house from the sale of his wool. But he did not get it, the money being in San Antonio.

Mrs. Kinchaloe still survives at this writing, midnight, January 1, 1899, for the writer hears the bell at the church ringing in the new year. Part of this article was written in 1898 and the balance in the new year of 1899. The remark that Mrs. Kinchaloe would not die,—that you could not kill a Ware,—reminds the writer of some desperate wounds that others of this connection recovered from. William Ware, Jr., her nephew, on one occasion dropped a pistol from his hip pocket at the home of his father, John C. Ware, and it fell with the muzzle up, the hammer striking the floor with such force that it fired, the ball striking Ware in the lower part of the body and ranging up, going clear through and coming out in the right breast, penetrating the lung in its passage, and from this wound he recovered and still lives in the canyon. Last fall Mrs: Kinchaloe's son

Richard, while running a cow, was thrown from his horse and sustained such injuries about the head that he lay unconscious thirty days, without speaking, food being given him in a liquid state mostly by injection. Drs. Meer and Bowman were his physicians during the time, and kept sacks full of ice around him constantly. Twice he was pronounced dead, and one time the account of his death was written for the Galveston News by the writer of this, who was four miles away on his farm when the news of Richard's death was brought to him. The account was then written, and sent to the postoffice by Trueman Hill, who lost in on the way and it failed to be sent. Finally the doctors decided to take out part of the skull and relieve the brain on one side and see what effect it would have. The consequence was that he was soon able to be about. The portion of the skull cut out was placed carefully and scientifically back, and soon adhered and healed up.

Mrs. Kinchaloe now keeps the Utopia Hotel.

NICHALUS HABY..

Came to Texas in 1843.

Mr. Nichalus Haby, one of the pioneers of Castro's colony, was born in Alsace, Germany, in 1821, and started to Texas in company with his brother Joe and many other colonists in September, 1843. The ship in which they came was very old and came slowly, consuming 121 days in the passage from Europe to Galveston, Texas. The weather was good, and no accident happened on the trip. From Galveston they came to Port Lavaca, and there disembarked and made preparations for the long trip by land to San Antonio. Port Lavaca at that time consisted only of a few small houses. All of the colonists who came on the ship at that time with Mr. Haby are dead except his brother Joe and Mrs. Steinly, who now (1898) lives in Castroville.

Six wagon loads of the colonists came on to San Antonio and stayed about four months there, while Mr. Castro was getting ready to move his people to his grant of land west of the Medina River. When everything was ready the start was made, Castro himself taking the lead with his family in a buggy. Of this party also was Charles De Montel. The people enjoyed the beautiful scenery and herds of deer they saw while en route. The country was open then, and many miles of prairie could be seen covered with grass, and dotted about over this, some far and some near, were the herds of deer and wild horses, the latter called mustangs. Along the timbered streams were droves of wild turkeys. After the people became somewhat settled Mr. Haby became quite a hunter, and in one year killed more than 200 deer, ten bears, and some panthers. Mr. Castro, having his family with him and keeping house, paid Mr. Haby many dollars for venison and other wild meats, as he did not hunt any himself. Deer skins were very cheap, worth only 12½ cents apiece. Mr. Montel killed a great many deer. He had a fine rifle and was a good shot. At this time the famous pioneer Big Foot Wallace lived alone on the Medina River, ten miles below the Castro colony, and often came up to Castroville to spend a few days or hours, as the case might be, with his new neighbors. Mr. Haby

7

says he saw him many times, and that he was as fine a marksman with a rifle as he ever saw. One day when Mr. Haby was
out hunting he saw Capt. Jack Hays and twelve of his men
out scouting for hostile Indians, who had began to prey upon
the stock of the newly-arrived German settlers. Some of the
Indians at this time were friendly, and often came into Castroville to sell turkeys and deer hams. They would also run horse
races and show the whites how well they could ride, performing
some brilliant but daring and dangerous feats of horsemanship.
These were mostly Lipans, but sometimes the Comanches and
Kickapoos would come in, especially when a new treaty was to
be made with them. Mr. Haby says one reason the Indians became hostile was that they did not want to work, but loved to
steal horses and kill white people when they got a good chance,
and the settlers wanted them to leave the country.

Early in 1846 Mr. Haby went back to Germany after his
father and brothers and sisters. His mother had died in 1843.
His brothers were George, Jacob, Ambrose, and Andrew. There
were two sisters, Mary and Margarette. On the way back to
Europe the ship in which Mr. Haby sailed encountered a terrible storm which she could make no headway against, and was
driven backward twenty-five miles. The only accident was to
the kitchen, which was completely demolished. The weather
was good coming back, and they again landed at Galveston and
then came on to San Antonio, and from there to Castroville.

When the Indians became hostile Capt. John Conner raised a
company of rangers and was stationed at Castroville for the protection of the people. The Habys were good frontiersmen and
were not afraid of Indians. They were called by some the "fighting Habys."

In the winter of 1846, after the Comanches had again raised
the tomahawk and unsheathed the scalping-knife, M. F. H.
Golled, Joe Jonnes, Vincent Jonnes, and a boy 12 years old
named Joe Bassiel, went up the Medina above Castroville to open
up a farm. The first night in camp they were attacked by Indians and all killed. They went to sleep by their fire, leaving
their guns stacked against a tree several yards away. The
bodies lay where they were killed four days, and were then discovered by Mr. Nichalus Haby, who was out hunting. He first
saw the guns of the murdered men standing against a tree, and

thinking likely it was a camp of Indians, crept upon them very cautiously until he learned the situation. The mutilated remains of the three unfortunate men and the boy were covered with snow and ice. It was in December, and near Christmas. Mr. Haby only saw three of the bodies at this time—the boy and the two Jonnes brothers. Next day, when a party returned to the spot led by Mr. Haby, the body of Mr. Golled was found about 150 yards from the others. Mr. Golled, it seemed, had waked up when the onslaught was made and ran and fought them, breaking two lances in the fearful struggle. He was wounded in the back, and also in the hands, where he had grasped the lance points. Joe Jonnes, 17 years of age, had a lance wound in the neck which went downward and came out through the thigh. Vincent had several lance wounds through the body. Evidently he had turned quickly when the first lance thrust was made and broke the weapon, as part of it was still in the body. The boy, it seems, was held down, his breast cut open, and his heart pulled out and left hanging by his side. These three were killed on their pallets near the fire. Two of the bodies were placed in the same coffin and carried to Castroville, but were then placed in separate graves. When the coffins were made only three of the bodies had been found.

During the progress of the Mexican war of 1846 Mr. Haby enlisted in company D, Texas mounted volunteers, commanded by Captain Veach, and at once went to Mexico and did service until the war was over. After his return from Mexico the Habys settled on the Medina River, several miles above Castroville, and commenced farming, stock raising, and fighting Indians. Mr. Nic. Haby settled on the west bank of the river on a high bluff overlooking the surrounding country. Here he had many adventures with the Indians, but held his ground, still lives there, and gave the writer a cordial welcome when calling upon him for an interview. It was at this place that Mr. Haby killed one Indian that he caught stealing. It was in 1870, when the hostile Indians made their last raid on the Haby settlement. They made their first appearance below Mr. Nic. Haby's place and stole horses from his brothers Joe, Ambrose, and Andrew, and also from another settler named Monier. They then went to Mr. Wilmer's, who was a freighter, and stole his mules. Andrew Haby came up to his brother Nic's about midnight and told him

of the horses being stolen, and for him to look out for his, and
then returned home to protect and guard his family. Nic Haby
had two horses loose in a small pasture of about eight acres on
the north side of the house, and had trained them to come to
him when he whistled. So after the departure of his brother
he went out and gave the peculiar call and they at once came,.
and were tied up to a little log house in the yard. Mr. Haby
then got his shotgun, which was well charged with buckshot, and
went to a large liveoak tree standing near the pasture fence on
the north side of the house, and distant fifty yards from where
the horses were tied. The moon was shining brightly, and Mr.
Haby sat down in the shadow of the tree with his back against
it, facing west. The pasture fence ran north and south, and
thirteen paces in front of Mr. Haby was the west line, which ran
close to the house and only a few yards from where the horses
were tied. With his shotgun across his lap and finger on the
trigger the old pioneer watched and waited, knowing that the
Indians would have to pass near him to get his horses. The
fence was made of rails, and was what is called a straight fence.
Two pickets were placed in the ground close together and opposite each other, at regular distances apart, and then a short
piece of plank or board was nailed to each at the top to hold
them from spreading when the rails were filled in. When the
panels were filled in to the proper height a rail was then elevated
on top of the cross board, leaving a space of a foot or more
between this rider and the next rail in the panel.

After several hours of patient waiting the horses began to
snort and move about uneasily and look north up the pasture
fence. Mr. Haby knew the Indians were near, and cocked his
gun. The horses commenced to rear and to make frantic efforts
to break loose and get away. Mr. Haby at the same time saw
the Indians in the bright moonlight coming in a trot, stooped
over, and close to the fence on the outside, and making direct for
the terrified horses. Before reaching the horses they would have
to pass Mr. Haby. By the time he got his gun in position to
shoot the foremost Indian was opposite him, but suddenly
stopped and looked over the fence towards where Mr. Haby was
bringing his gun into position to shoot. The Indian was looking between the top rail and the rider, which was about his
height. At this time, and taking place quicker than it can be

told, the shotgun was fired and the Indian fell. Mr. Haby turned his gun quickly to fire at the other two, but they were gone,—vanished like a vision of the night. Mr. Haby remained for a short time in his position, listening and waiting, and watching the spot where he saw the Indian fall, but no sign or move came from there, so he ventured to the spot or fence and looked over, keeping his gun in position, ready to shoot at a moment's warning. The Indian was lying prone and motionless. Being satisfied he had killed him, Haby went to the house, got a pair of blankets, returned and spread them on the ground opposite the Indian, only the fence intervening between them. Then he lay down there and spent the balance of the night watching, thinking the other Indians would come back to see about their companion and he would get another one of them. They did not come, however, and when daylight came Mr. Haby crossed the fence and examined the dead hostile. Eight buckshot had struck him in the face and forehead, and two had struck him in the mouth, knocking out nearly all of his teeth. The Indian had fallen on his gun, a long flintlock rifle, and it was at full cock. It is evident that the Indian had discovered Mr. Haby and cocked his gun, but was uncertain what it was he saw, and before he could determine, the buckshot came and he was ushered quickly into the happy hunting grounds. He had on a shotpouch and a fancy powderhorn. He also had a bow and quiver of arrows at his back. A knife, rope, and blanket was around his waist. He was about 6 feet in height, strong, well made, and seemed to be about 25 years of age. His hair came nearly to the waist, thick and black. The news of the dead Indian at Nic. Haby's soon spread through the settlement, and many came to look at him.

There was an old gentleman stopping with Mr. Haby who had at one time lived in this settlement and had a horse stolen by the Indians, and in the pursuit which followed the horse was found dead on the trail and his entrails cut out. The old man was very mad, and said if he ever saw a dead Indian he was going to cut his entrails out; and as he was standing by the body on the morning after the killing he suddenly jerked out his knife and ripped it open. There was another man present who said he would like to have the hair of the Indian, but did not like to take it off. There was a boy also in the crowd named Frank

Haby, who had a sharp knife, and he proposed to cut it off for the man. This he did very neatly, close to the skull, but without cutting the skin, and presented the fine long hair to the man who wanted it. The distance from the oak tree to where the Indian lay was thirteen steps, and the writer sat at the root of the tree and took the notes from which this sketch was written. Mr. Haby also showed the writer the powderhorn, which was beautifully carved and finished. He does not know what became of the gun; he kept it and used it many years, and finally some one carried it away. The body of the Indian was dragged about 200 yards from the house and left for the hogs to eat. Mrs. Haby would eat no hog meat for several years after. In about eight days the Indians came back to see what became of their companion, but were afraid to come close to the house. Their tracks were seen in the field and the dogs barked all night. It is likely that they found fragments of the body and were satisfied as to his fate. Mr. Haby says the Indian was a Kickapoo. The boy Frank Haby, who cut off the Indian's hair, is now a well-to-do stockman, and one of Bandera County's most reliable citizens. He lives on Seco Creek, near the Bandera road, about twelve miles from Utopia.

Mr. Nichalus Haby draws a pension for services in the Mexican war, and exhibited to the writer a medal of which he is justly proud. The medal is bronze, heart-shaped, two and one-half inches in length by two inches in diameter. Between the medal and pin at the top is a thick piece of red, white, and blue cloth, which connects the medal and pin. The latter is for the purpose of fastening it on the front of the coat or vest in a parade or reunion of veterans. On the front side of the medal at the top is the cut of a ship, in the left hand corner on the right is a cannon unlimbered, as if ready for action. Between these are two guns crossed near the muzzles, one with and one without a bayonet. A sword then crosses both, and a large pistol is between the butts of the guns at the bottom. Below the guns is the name Mexico, and then comes a prickly pear and maguay plant. Below this is an old fort, and under it the date 1846. This is encircled by a wreath, with the name of Scott at the bottom. To the left and right of this name is that of Perry and Taylor, the whole then surrounded by stars. On the margin around the medal in raised letters are following names of battles: Tobasco,

Vera Cruz, Palo Alto, Buena Vista, Cerro Gordo, Cherubusco, Chapultepec. On the pin at the top is the following: "Patented March 7th, 1876." Below this is "National Association of Veterans." On the under side of the medal is the following: "Nichlas Haby, Ninth Texas Cavalry."

HENRY CASTRO.

HENRY CASTRO.

Came to Texas in 1843.

Henry Castro was born in France in July, 1786, of rich parents, and descended from one of the oldest Portuguese families, one of his ancestors, Zoas of Castro, having been the fourth viceroy of the Indies for the king of Portugal. In 1805, at the age of 19, he was selected by the prefect of his department (Landes) to welcome the Emperor Napoleon on the occasion of his visit to that department. In 1806 he was one of the guard of honor that accompanied Napoleon to Spain. In 1814, being an officer in the first legion of the National Guards of Paris, he fought with Marshal Moncey at the gate of Clichy. Having immigrated to the United States after the fall of Napoleon, in May, 1827, he was consul at the port of Providence for the king of Naples, having become an American citizen by choice the same year. He returned to France in 1838, was the partner of Mr. Lafitte, the banker, and took an active part in trying to negotiate a loan for the Republic of Texas at Paris. Having received large grants of land under certain conditions of colonization, he immediately proceeded to comply with his contract, and after great expense and labor succeeded in bringing to this State 485 families and 457 single men, in twenty-seven ships, from the year 1843 to 1847. He died at Monterey, Mexico, while on his way to visit the graves of his relatives in France.—[Thrall's History of Texas.

A. J. DAVENPORT.

Came to Texas in 1843.

One among the old-timers and Indian fighters of the West is
A. J. Davenport, familiarly called Jack by his many friends.
He has a fine farm and ranch near Sabinal Station, and a stock
ranch in Little Blanco Canyon. It was at the latter place the
writer found him busy salting cattle. Some of these old settlers
are very modest and loath to tell their experience, saying they had
done nothing worth recording. Their main business in the early
days was to raise cattle and trail and fight Indians, and one was
almost as commonplace as the other, and hence their view of the
insignificance of Indian raids, etc. People, however, who have
had no experience in such things take a different view altogether,
and look upon one of these old pioneers as being above the ordinary. The time has passed now for men to gain any notoriety as
Indian fighters, and when we look upon one of these men who
has trailed and faced and fought the wild, painted Comanche,
looked into his fierce, gleaming eyes, and heard his loud warwhoop; seen his matchless riding and lightning-like dexterity
with the bow as he sent his barbed and feathered arrows cutting
and hissing through the air, at the same time swinging from
side to side of his horse to avoid also the white man's rapid shots
from a revolver,—we stand before him and look at his gray locks
and sun-tanned face with great respect, akin to awe.

Mr. Davenport was born in Johnson County, Missouri, in
1843, and came to Texas the same year with his father, John
Davenport, and settled in Kaufman County. John Davenport
was a soldier under General Jackson in the wars with the Creek
Indians and the British war of 1812.

The subject of this sketch came to the Sabinal Canyon in 1853.
The following named men had already arrived and settled:
William Ware, Gideon Thompson, Aaron Anglin, John and
James Davenport, and Henry Robinson. His brother John was
killed by the Indians near where Sabinal station is now, not
long after Jack came to the canyon. His brother John, who
at that time lived below the mountains, had gone early on the

SCENE OF WOLFE AND HUFFMAN'S INDIAN BATTLE.

morning he was killed to Blanco Creek after a yoke of oxen, and was returning with them when attacked. Some Mexicans witnessed the fight, but were afraid to go to his assistance. They said that he shot two of the Indians with a sixshooter. When the Indians left the Mexicans went to Davenport, and he tried to talk to them but was not able to do so. He was badly shot and scalped, and soon died. When the news of his death reached the settlement his relatives came and carried the body to his home on Rancheros Creek and buried it. His young brother Jack said that if ever he had the opportunity he would take an Indian scalp and get even on that line for that of his brother John. This retaliation was accomplished in later years while a Texas ranger under Captain Montel.

The Indians who killed John Davenport were pursued by the settlers and a desperate battle fought with them. One of the Indians killed in the fight had been badly wounded by Davenport in their fight with him. His sixshooter was also recovered.

These same Indians also killed John Bowles lower down the country.

In 1860 Judge Davenport sent word from his ranch for all the men who lived on Rancheros Creek that could, to meet him at the Kinchaloe prairie, near D'Hanis, in Medina County. The Indians, he said, were on a raid in large force, and were now going out towards the mountains with a large drove of horses. The men who responded to this call were Jack Davenport, Ross Kennedy, John Kennedy, and Frank Hilburn, the latter a noted Indian fighter, who had already killed two Indians single-handed. When they arrived at the place designated they were joined by the Hondo settlers under the leadership of Big Foot Wallace. The trail of the Indians was soon taken up and went by the way of the Comanche waterhole, now a noted place for deer hunters to camp. From this place the trail went straight to the foot of the mountains and led up Big Seco Canyon. The Indians were overtaken at the head of the creek. The fight which followed has already been described, but each witness brings out new facts that were forgotten by others. Mr. Davenport says that their party stopped and ate their dinner in plain view of the Indians, who lay in ambush and had tied a horse on the side of the mountain in view as a decoy to bring the white men up that way. Several impetuous young men went ahead to be first to get hold of the horse, and received the first fire of the Indians, which wounded Bill Davenport, son of Judge Davenport, and drove the balance back to the main force of thirty or more men. In front, when the advance up the hill was made, were Jack Davenport, Lewis McCombs, and Jasper Kinchaloe. The Indians made their first fire with shotguns which they had taken from settlers killed in this raid. Firing down hill, they overshot the men in front and struck among those lower down. The attack from the Indians, however, was so fierce that all retreated back to the foot of the mountain, where they tied their horses and acted on the defensive. During the fight an Indian sat on a black mule a long distance off, on top of a mountain, intently watching the combat. Ross Kennedy, who had an Enfield rifle, said he could move him, and raising the sight of his gun took aim and fired. The Indian sat a few moments after the gun fired, then all of a sudden the mule jumped nearly from under him, and soon got out of sight in the rocks and bushes. Evidently the mule was hit. After the fight six shotguns were found on the mountain where the Indians left them, also the pistol of Murray, the assessor, who had been killed by them. The men went that night to Sabinal Canyon and next day followed the Indians again. There came up a terrible sleet, and the men spent the night about where Henry Taylor now lives. As before stated, they ambushed the Indians at Ranger Springs, and the whole plan was frustrated by Hilburn firing too soon. Jack Davenport says that Captain Wallace planned this ambush splendidly, and if order could have been kept, would have almost annihilated this band of red marauders.

In this same year Huffman and Wolfe, two young stockmen who lived on Seco, came out west of the Sabinal River, below the mountains, to hunt stock. When they arrived at a point on the prairie about where the hay farm of Mr. Ed Kelley now is, they came upon a band of mounted Indians. It was a mile or more east to the river, where there was some protection along the banks and in the rocks and scrubby brush and scattered timber. To this point the two men turned their cow ponies and made a desperate run for life. The Indians came on in swift pursuit, yelling loudly. At this time, just across a swell in the prairie at a place called the "rock pile," William Davenport was on his way to Uvalde with a two-horse wagon, and saw the dust rising and heard Indians yelling ahead of him. The road he was traveling ran southwest, and the Indians were running the cowmen in a northeast or east direction, and hid from view as before stated by rising ground. Mr. Davenport knew well what all this meant, and turning his horses around whipped them into a gallop and made his way back home at the Blue waterhole on the Sabinal river, at the mouth of the canyon. The distance was about three miles. Had the cowboys known that Davenport was over there and gone to him, the three might have stood off the Indians with the wagon for shelter. Not knowing this, however, they kept straight for the river, firing at the Indians as they ran. The Comanches finally ran around and in the midst of the boys, and they dismounted at a liveoak tree, turned their horses loose, and fought desperately for their lives. The tree was stuck full of arrows. The boys finally made another run on foot towards the Sabinal, but likely both were wounded by this time, as the Indians had circled the tree on their horses and shot arrows from

all sides, as those sticking in the tree indicated. In this run
they were soon surrounded and went down under numerous arrow wounds, firing their last shots at close quarters on the open
prairie. This spot is now just across the river from the home
of Mrs. Nancy Kelley and her son Robert. This same band of
Indians had the evening before killed the Mexican herder of Mr.
Ross Kennedy, first stripping and then torturing and scalping
him. Among the settlers who got together to pursue the Indians
were Jack Davenport, William Knox, Ross Kennedy, John Kennedy, Dock Lee, Ambrose Crane, and Albin Rankin. Knox was
chosen captain. They soon found the trail of the Indians and
commenced the pursuit. When they arrived in the prairie where
the old Uvalde road runs through the Kelley pasture the trail
of the Indians abruptly turned east towards the river, and they
knew from the signs of the torn-up earth that some one had been
pursued by them, but who they could not tell. It was here the
run was made on Huffman and Wolfe. Various articles were
picked up such as cowmen carry to their saddles—cups, coffee-
pots, wallets, etc. Out some distance from the river stood a liveoak tree in which the trailers noticed a large black object while
yet some distance away. They rode straight for that now, and on
coming to the spot discovered that the object in the tree was a
dead Indian. He was closely wrapped in a blanket, his eyes were
closed tightly with red paint, and his bow was hanging on a limb
by his head. His body was astride a limb and lashed to another
with a rope to keep it in an upright position. He had a bullet
hole in his neck, in what is usually called the sticking place.
The settlers had deviated from the trail by seeing the Indian in
the tree, and did not at this time discover the bodies of the slain
cowmen, which were lying in the grass about 150 yards away.
The trail of the Indians from the tree led northwest across the
prairie towards the mouth of Big Blanco Canyon, several miles
distant. As yet the trailers had no idea who had fought the
Indians or how they came out in the struggle. The trail was followed rapidly and the Indians overtaken before night in the
canyon, at a place called the "sinks of the water." Here the
Blanco River sinks and leaves the channel dry. The Indians
had ·dismounted and evidently intended camping there. They
were surprised by the sudden appearance and charge of the
whites and ran into the cedar brakes, leaving their horses, which

were all captured. Several shots were fired at the fleeing Indians, but none were killed on the ground that could be found. It was nearly night, and there was not much time to look around after the skirmish was over. Among the horses were found Huffman's mule, saddled and bridled, and his pistol hanging to the pommel of the saddle in the scabbard. One Indian tried to mount the mule, but he was fired at and ran off on foot. Jack Davenport knew the mule as one owned by Huffman, and told the men he was satisfied it was him that had been chased by the Indians and had killed one, and was evidently slain himself. The horses of the Indians were gathered, and the men returned that night to the settlement on Rancheros Creek. The place where they encountered the Indians, called "the sinks," is just below where the ranch of Mr. Charles Peters now is.

Next morning the men all started out again to search for the body of Huffman, not knowing as yet that Wolfe was with him and had also been killed. When they arrived at the scene of the fight they soon discovered the tree sticking full of arrows where they first dismounted to fight. A short search around soon discovered the bodies, mutilated and full of arrows. How many Indians they hit or killed besides the one found they could not tell. Huffman's pistol was empty, and the Indians had put it back in the scabbard, which was fastened to the horn of the saddle. Wolfe's pistol was not found. The bodies of the unfortunate young men were buried near where found, but were afterwards taken up and reinterred at D'Hanis. The Catholics took charge of the body of Huffman, as he had no relatives in this country.

In 1861 Jack Davenport joined a company of rangers commanded by Capt. Charles de Montel. They were stationed at Ranger Springs, on the Seco. While they were here the Indians made a raid below the mountains and were followed by settlers from below to the head of the salt marsh in Sabinal Canyon, about five miles west from the present village of Utopia. In the meantime a runner had been sent to the ranger camp, and a scout was sent out to intercept them. The rangers and settlers got together at the head of the salt marsh and continued the pursuit. Among the rangers were Lieut. Ben Patton, commanding; Jack Davenport, Ed Taylor, Cud Adams, Demp Forrest, Dan Malone, Charley Cole, Jasper Kinchaloe, Lon Moore, and John

Cook. The trail led in a northeast direction over a rough, mountainous country, towards the head of the Frio River. At length, arriving on a high mountain about three miles west of the present ranch of Mr. Sam Harper, in Sabinal Canyon, Lieutenant Patton discovered the Indians. They had camped in a valley, but on elevated ground, between two deep gullies, with a cedar brake in their rear. They were engaged in cooking horse meat, mending moccasins, etc. Without being seen by the Indians, Patton dismounted his men, left their horses, went down the mountain, and struck the creek about half a mile below the Indian camp, and came up keeping well concealed, until they approached the high banks of the gullies in less than fifty yards of the unsuspecting hostiles. Jack Davenport, having it on his mind to avenge his brother, kept his gun well in hand, and when the charge was ordered kept by the side of. Lieutenant Patton, who led. The men went up the banks in various places and with great rapidity, and were almost among the Indians and firing upon them before they were aware of the presence of an enemy. The onset was so fierce and the firing so fast and fatal that the Indians made a poor fight, and soon sought safety in the cedar brake near by. Davenport and Patton both fired their first shot at the same Indian, who fell near the fire. Another one fell fifty yards from the fire, and the third ran about 200 yards and fell. Many of the Indians were wounded but made their escape, leaving trails of blood behind them. One wounded Indian was found under the roots of a large cedar tree which had been blown down, and was pulled out and scalped alive by one of the white men. The Indian made a very wry face during the process of scalping, as if in much pain, and pointed towards the sky, as if threatening the man with the vengeance of God. In this fight John Cook shot twelve times at one Indian running, emptying two revolvers without bringing him down. Sometimes an Indian can carry off almost as much lead as a California grizzly bear. When the fight was over Jack Davenport went to the Indian whom he knew he had shot, and scalped him, saying as he did so that he was now even with them for his brother John. Be it said to his credit, however, his Indian was dead when he scalped him.

During the civil war Mr. Davenport belonged to Colonel Duff's regiment, Thirty-third Texas, company F, commanded by Captain Davis, from San Marcos, Hays County. He was in the fight at Powderhorn, where they fought the Union troops under General Ross. Was on picket duty, and saw the Union army land at Point Isabel. At the close of the war his command was in Arkansas, and was there disbanded.

Mr. Davenport is a successful stock raiser, and one of the solid citizens of Uvalde County, honored and respected by all who know him.

JOSEPH CONRADS.

Came to Texas in 1843.

Mr. Joseph Conrads, who lives in Castroville, is one of the original pioneers of Medina County, and has many interesting things to tell of the long ago, when times were not what they are now.

Mr. Conrads was born in Prussia, near Saar River, in 1832. His father, Nicholas Conrads, with his family set sail for America from Havre de Grace, France, in 1843. They came in the ship Obre as part of the colony of Henry Castro. They had a long, tedious trip of seventy-five days in crossing the ocean, and some of the passengers died at sea. The immigrants were all French except two families—Conrads and Wilkes. Many of them were really German, but all spoke French, being Alsatians. On New Year's day of 1843 the good ship landed at Galveston, and the tired and almost worn out colonists gladly set foot on Texas soil, although it was a strange and foreign country to them, thousands of miles from the place of their nativity. The elder Conrads started from Galveston with his family to Houston, but turned back at San Felipe and stopped on Buffalo Bayou and died there. Peter, the eldest brother of Joseph, went back to Galveston and the family became scattered. However, finding that a good living could be made in Galveston, he came back and got the family together and returned there with them.

In 1846 the family of Castro landed in Galveston direct from Europe, and the Conrads family came on out with them to Castroville, the future home of the colonists, part of whom had already arrived under the leadership of Castro and commenced erecting rude shelters. The Indians at that time were friendly to the newcomers and furnished them all the wild game they wanted, very cheap. The Indians were the Lipan tribe. The colonists were not possessed of suitable firearms to kill game with, and greatly appreciated the bountiful supply of fat turkey and venison. The writer will say here that the Lipans were a branch of the Comanche tribe. Some time previous to the advent of the American pioneers into Texas there were two powerful rival chiefs among the Comanches, one of whom was named Lipan. This chief finally quit the tribe and wandered far away from them, but was followed by a band of his friends and admirers, and in time a new tribe was formed which took the name of their chief and waged a constant and bitter war against the old tribe, and many desperate and cruel battles were fought with alternate success for both parties. Two of the colonists, Young and Kingle, hunted with the Indians and helped to keep their friends in town from starving. Hostilities commenced with the Indians by the latter having some trouble with Americans who were moving to the west. The Indians stole their horses, and they killed some of the Indians. Some ex-Texas rangers also had trouble with the Lipans, in which one of the latter was killed.

On one occasion Messrs. Conrads, Gerhardt, and Ihnukers went out on a horse hunt and also to see if there were Indians about. They camped for noon at the Mustang waterhole on the Francisco, and while there saw a band of Indians coming towards them. They at once ran away, leaving all of their things in camp. The chief of the party ran after them, and holding up a sack in which he had provisions told them to stop, "Indian no hurt." Seeing they could not easily get away, the three colonists stopped, and after some talk the Indians went on and the white men quickly returned home. These same Indians went on to the Quihi settlement and captured a woman and carried her way. (This was likely Mrs. Charobiny, who escaped from them on the same day she was captured.)

Some of the people in those days made a living making boards and shingles out of the cypress which grew along the Medina River. They found a market for such things in San Antonio. This was the only chance for people living there to get anything except grass with which to cover their houses. The people in and around Castroville lived on deer meat and corn meal. There were no cattle in the country at that time except as men would work in San Antonio, buy a cow with the money, and then bring her on out to the colony. In 1846-47 Mr. Conrads and his brother ran Mr. Castro's wagon to bring in colonists from Port Lavaca. The nearest place to get cornmeal was the Guadalupe River. One night when the Indians were hostile a Frenchman tied his horse to the bedpost to make sure of him until morning, but during the heavy hours of the night, while the Frenchman slumbered, a wily and very wideawake savage slipped up, cut the rope, and carried the horse away.

In 1848 Mr. Conrads moved to San Antonio, which by this time was improving very fast. In 1849, however, he moved back to Castroville. People were coming in all the time, and that place was improving fast. Mr. Conrads says people enjoyed themselves then better than they do now. They did not have much, but appreciated all they could get and make. There were but few wagons among the settlers in those days. Some of the people carried corn on their backs to the mill after one was built nine miles below San Antonio, a distance of thirty-five miles from the colony. The people dressed in a different way compared to this time. Their everyday clothes were their Sunday clothes, too, and some people would be ashamed to wear such now. Mr. Conrads knew Capt. Jack Hays and Big Foot Wallace well, and says both were good Indian fighters and were a great help to the people.

In 1852 Mr. Conrads and a party went out on a hunting expedition, and ate their dinner one day near where Mr. H. Rothe now lives. During the time a severe sleet began to fall, and they came upon a trail of Indians, which they followed, and came upon them near night while they were eating supper near a cedar brake. The white men dismounted, crawled near them, and fired upon them. The Indians scattered into the brush and the whites took possession of their camp, and while picking up such things as they wanted they heard groans in the brake not far away. On investigating they found a wounded Indian, who had his leg broken, besides a wound in the shoulder. He had tried to kill himself by sticking an arrow in his heart. He soon died and was scalped, and a strap taken from his back. Afterwards other Indians were found dead in the brake. This was between the Verde Creek and the Hondo, not far from the Peach Tree waterhole. The men who composed this party, besides Mr. Conrads, were Bob Harper, Tom Malone, William White, William Adams, Henry Adams, and the two Boones. There were some others, but their names are not remembered.

In 1857, Peter, brother of Joseph Conrads, went out to hunt a cow, and on ascending a liveoak hill saw something run into the brush. Not thinking it was an Indian, he went in there and soon came upon a dead mare belonging to his brother. Going back and giving the alarm, five or six men went back, among whom was Joseph Conrads. They soon met another mare of Joseph's running with a buffalo lariat on. The Indians were near by, and hearing the whites talking ran away about 300 yards. The chief was soon discovered, and was seen to fire a pistol in the air. Some Mexicans were out hunting oxen, and part of this band of Indians were running them, and the chief fired the pistol to recall them to help fight the white men, whom he had now discovered. The Indians had some horses, and instead of stopping to fight they ran away and carried the horses with them. The white men ran the Indians to the Mustang prairie, firing at them all the way, which was returned by the Indians. Here Mr. Joseph Conrads dismounted to load his gun, and his horse, being frightened, got loose from him and ran away. The balance of the men soon stopped the horse, and Peter Conrads ran between the horse and the Indians and tried to cut off the balance of the horses which the Indians had in their possession. His firearms consisted only of a pistol. The Indians were now very near the settlers, and Joseph Conrads, as soon as he got his gun loaded, shot one Indian, who dismounted from his horse and sat down by a tree. The white men now retreated and the Indians followed them. One man who had a loaded gun tried to shoot, but at the same time his horse fell with him and his gun went off in the air. Joseph Conrads, having again reloaded his gun, stooped down so as to get a good shot at another Indian, but the fellow at whom he was about to fire, seeing his actions, got behind a mesquite tree. He had a squaw with him who was armed with a bow, and she shot several arrows at Conrads. The latter now determined to shoot her, as she was in plain view, but when he made the attempt he could not pull the hammer of his rifle down. The Indians soon after gave up the fight and went off. When Conrads made an examination of his gun to ascertain the cause of its failure to shoot, he discovered that he had not pulled the hammer far enough back, and only had it on the half-cock.

These same Indians killed two men at Black Hill, not far from where Benton City now is, and on their return to the mountains killed Wolfe and Huffman on the Sabinal. The Indians were followed by another party farther west and a scalp taken from

them, which they supposed to be a woman's, but which proved
to be that of Bilhartz, one of the men who was killed at Black
Hill. He had long curly hair. The other man killed with him
was named Jungman.

On one occasion when Mr. Conrads went out to hunt a cow
four miles from Castroville he saw some horses coming towards
him, and soon discovered that they were being driven by Indians. He hurriedly ran into the brush, left his horse, and came
home on foot. The Indians did not see him and failed to find
the mare, which he had abandoned so as to be better able to
travel through the brush and cactus. A scout returned and
found the animal with coat and leggings still on the saddle. The
trail of the Indians was taken up, and the party soon came upon
two men who had been killed by them. The men killed were
old man Grace and his son. Their wagon was standing in the
road loaded with pickets. This took place near where Idlewild
is now, below La Coste station. Both of the men were shot in
the left side with bullets. Between Elm Creek and Medina
they killed a Mexican boy. The Indians were overtaken by another party and some of them killed.

CASTRO'S DIARY. PART I.

In getting together material for a history of this famous colony of southwest Texas I have spared no pains in getting the most reliable information, and have been very successful in finding old documents and papers among some of the old settlers, who have carefully preserved them through all these years, and willingly gave me all the information they were possessed of. They are justly proud of their achievement here in the wilderness, and they and their descendants will read with interest their history.

I am under many obligations to the citizens of Medina County for assistance in my work. Among these are Judge Herman E. Haas, of Hondo; Chris Batot, and the Kochs and Neys, of D'Hanis; August Kempf, district clerk of Medina County; Judge M. Charobiny, of New Fountain, and August Rothe, of the large ranch of the Rothe Brothers, on the Seco.

At the time of the incipiency of Henry Castro's immigration scheme in Europe, Texas offered rare inducements to the thousands of sturdy men in the old countries who had to labor for a living to get cheap homes and better their condition in life. Texas was new,—had just emerged from under the misrule of Mexico, and had set up housekeeping for herself as a Republic. She had rich lands by the millions of acres to give away to those who sought homes within her borders. Energetic men went to work to bring in people from some of the old countries to help settle up these vast regions which stretched away towards-the setting sun for many hundreds of miles, covered with rich grasses and cut through at almost regular intervals from San Antonio to the Rio Grande by clear, bold streams, as the Leon, Medio, Medina, Quihi, Verde, Hondo, Seco, Ranchero, Sabinal, Frio, Blanco, Leona, Nueces, Turkey, and so on.

Many people from Europe and from the States of the Union who had no part in bringing colonists here wrote to friends and relatives about this grand country and induced many to come. Henry Castro was a man of extraordinary ability and perseverance, or he could never have surmounted the many hindrances and obstacles which were thrown in his way for years before he could begin to see and taste any of the fruits of his labors.

From extracts of memoirs of Henry Castro, which were preserved by his son Lorenzo, we find that when General Henderson was in the city of Paris, France, to procure from Louis Philippe a recognition of the Republic of Texas, he visited the home of Henry Castro.

Castro in his memoirs says: "The Prince of Peace (Godoy), whom I had known after he was exiled from Spain, occasionally visited me. After having risen from a private in the bodyguards of the king to prime minister of Spain, and after having received all favors the king was able to confer upon him, he was reduced to poverty, and was then living in Paris on the income of 5000 francs a month, which he received as the recipient of the Grand Cross of the Legion of Honor, which had been conferred upon him by Napoleon the First. Among the many gifts made to Godoy by the king was the title to the province of Texas, and I then entered into negotiations with him to hunt up the original deed and execute a conveyance to the provisional government of Texas. But all of his property and papers had been declared confiscated by the Spanish government. Although he tried through some friends to procure that document he did not succeed in doing so. It would have been rather strange that Texas should have claimed her recognition through a deed of conveyance of the owner of the soil, the Prince of Peace.

"When I called to see Mr. J. Lafitte (banker) with General Hamilton, of South Carolina, to aid him in negotiating a loan of $7,000,000 for the Republic of Texas, after hearing me with a great deal of attention, he was pleased, and declared that the loan could be affected; but taking me to one side said to me in French, because he did not speak English and the general did not speak French, 'Mr. Castro, please tell me where Texas is situated.'

"On another occasion General Hamilton had an audience with Louis Philippe, who made him sit by his side and conversed with him in the most intimate manner, and having most solemnly promised his support to the projected loan, left the general perfectly delighted. He called upon me and expressed great hopes of success, and we then visited Mr. Lafitte, who, after hearing the general's report of his conversation with the king and his great promises, to our great astonishment he said to us confidentially that without any doubt the king would do exactly contrary to what he had promised the general. Hamilton was almost confounded at hearing Mr. Lafitte, but his prediction proved true, as afterward the king proved false to his word.

"When I first tried to charter a ship to carry immigrants to Texas I found great difficulty, as the coast of that portion of the gulf was hardly known. I could get ten vessels to go to New Orleans, but I could not find one to go to Galveston. I had maps of the coast of Texas, made according to the best data I could procure, which was from Captain Simpson, of Galveston, and circulated it in many parts of Europe. Among the pamphlets published by me, one particularly attracted attention. It was styled 'Coup d'Oeil Sur le Texas,' signed by Hr. Fournel, with a map by A. Bre, geographer to the king, dated 1840.

"For services rendered to the Republic of Texas I was allowed to enter into a contract of colonization to establish two colonies, one situated on the Rio Grande, commencing at a point nearly opposite Camargo and running to Salt Lake (Sol del Rey), thence in a parallel line to a point opposite Dolores, below Laredo. This colony I could not attempt to settle, as Mexican troops occupied in force that portion of the Rio Grande, and claimed all the territory between that river and the Nueces. The other west of San Antonio, including that portion of the country now comprising part of Medina, Uvalde, Frio, Atascosa, Bexar, McMullen, La Salle, and Zavalla counties, is the one I colonized. At the time that my first colonists arrived in San Antonio, in February, 1843, no settlement existed west of the San Pedro Creek to the Rio Grande. I met with great difficulties in procuring immigrants in France, because the government was trying to turn the tide of immigration toward Algiers. After great expense and arduous labor, I succeeded in sending my first ship, Ebro, Captain Perry, from the port of Havre to Galveston, Texas, with a load consisting entirely of French immigrants and a full cargo of merchandise subject to duties."

Henry Castro having landed one shipload of colonists in 1843, the following is his report to the President of the Republic of Texas in regard to his work of colonization:

"WASHINGTON, TEXAS, July 12, 1844.

"GENERAL: The period has arrived when I am bound to render you an account of the honorable mission confided to me, namely, the colonization by Europeans of a portion of the county of Bexar.

"At the time your excellency executed a grant in my favor, on the 15th of February, 1842, you were likewise pleased to appoint me consul-general of Texas for the kingdom of France. On that occasion the honorable Secretary of State wrote to me as follows: 'The President of the Republic has been pleased, in consideration of the services you have rendered to the cause of Texas, as well as from your known zeal for her interests and ability to protect and advance them, to appoint you consul-general of the Republic of Texas for the kingdom of France.'

"I lost not a moment's time, and on the 15th of May was in the city of Paris busily engaged in the execution of my contract by every means possible within my reach. My early efforts were in some measure frustrated by rumors of the invasion of the county of Bexar, which were widely and industriously circulated. These rumors were, however, contradicted by a letter addressed to me by your secretary, which read as follows: 'The President desires me to say to you that he hopes that recent occurrences may not incline you to defer the execution of your plan of settling your colony in our western confines. Its position for commanding internal trade and its capacities in points of soil and climate will make it a most desirable part of our country.'

"The encouragement given me by your excellency strengthened my determination to proceed in the work of colonization, and on the 3d of November, 1842, I was able to dispatch from Havre the ship Ebro, with 113 colonists. This first expedition was followed on the 10th of January, 1843, by the departure of the ship Lyons, and on the 27th of the same month the ship Louis Philippe sailed from Dunkirk with a number of colonists, accompanied by my agent, E. Martin, and by the Abbe Menetrier, chaplain to the royal chateau of Versailles. The voyage of Mr. Menetrier was undertaken with a view to examining the country, both on my account and that of his family, which had preceded him.

"These expeditions are authenticated by lists containing the names, ages, and professions of the colonists regularly transmitted by each vessel to the honorable Secretary of State.

"On the 14th of January that gentleman wrote me as follows: 'It affords to the Governor of Texas much satisfaction to be informed that you are carrying out your contract in good faith and with much apparent success, and I have great pleasure in assuring you that every proper facility will be extended to you by this government in the prosecution of an undertaking so manifestly adapted to promote the interest of the country. The President is fully aware of the obstacles of the late predatory incursions in Texas by Mexico and the various unfounded rumors of invasion by that power have thrown in your way, and he directs me to assure you that he will not fail to give to those circumstances a due consideration as connected with the fulfillment on your part of the conditions of the same.'

"This manifestation of kindness remunerated me for the innumerable difficulties by which I was surrounded in France and in Texas,—difficulties to dishearten and deter me from the execution of my arduous enterprise. I am fortunately so constituted that obstacles call forth my firmness and power of resistance, and impelled by these feelings I redoubled my exertions, trying to overcome all opposition and to justify the generous confidence you had reposed in me. I therefore continued boldly on the execution of my contract, and succeeded in forwarding from Antwerp the following vessels: October 25, 1843, the Jeane Key; December 11, 1843, the Henrich; April 12, 1844, the Ocean; May 4th, the Jeanette.

"The names of the persons composing each expedition are invariably entered upon a list regularly transmitted by each vessel to the honorable Secretary of State.

"These four expeditions, added to the three already mentioned, constitute altogether seven vessels transporting over 700 immigrants, of whom the great majority are tillers of the soil. In selecting colonists I have uniformly required certain conditions, such as good character, the necessary clothing and farming instruments, and means of subsistence for one year as near as possible.

"The difficulties inseparable from my first efforts, and erroneous statements of many of the immigrants may have affected to a great extent the rigid execution of this plan. The arduous and at the same time expensive exertions have incontestably laid the foundation in Germany and France of immigration to Texas.

It is beyond all question far more practicable at present to transport to Texas 7000 immigrants than it was to induce one-tenth of that number to engage in the enterprise at the time I commenced the fulfillment of my contract.

"A complete organization having been effected, will now secure a regular succession of expeditions, the first of which will leave the port of Antwerp in August and September next, so that taking it for granted that the last expedition arrived about July 15th, there has not been nor will there be any interruption in the process of settling the country.

"If I have been able to endow the country with vigorous arms for the cultivation of the soil, I have not been less instrumental in contributing to improve the financial condition of the Republic. The vessels already sent to this country brought full cargoes of goods subject to tariff duties, and those which may be expected during the winter will be loaded with large amounts of merchandise. The experience which I have acquired during more than two years of practical exertions in the undertaking intrusted to my care has convinced me that Texas can only be promptly settled by immigrants possessing the qualifications mentioned in a preceding paragraph. The poor, to whom money may be advanced on a promise of repayment in labor, are unsuitable persons for colonization, because the laws of this country refuse to recognize contracts by virtue of which the time and services of a party are engaged beforehand. The capitalist will naturally decline advancing funds on the sole guarantee of a promise.

"Farmers in easy circumstances rarely immigrate, and this remark applies to France more than any other country, hence the difficulty of obtaining settlers. By the terms of my contract I was to transport to Texas 200 families by the 15th of July, 1843. I believe that in spite of every obstacle I have.

"With regard to the occupation of the lands, that is a point which has not been under my control, and it has been retarded by various circumstances the existence of which was beyond my power to prevent. If required, I can quote the language of the honorable secretary in his letter of January 4th last, already alluded to: 'The president is fully aware of the obstacles thrown in your way, and he will not fail to give to those circumstances a due consideration as connected with the fulfillment on your part of the conditions of your contract.'

"My report would not be complete without I submit to your excellency a detailed statement of the expenses incurred, amounting already to $40,000, which are increasing the more rapidly because I am personally superintending the operations that could not be accomplished during my absence.

"I have laid before your excellency a statement of facts. I submit them for your consideration and for that of the government. What I have already accomplished under the most serious obstacles which could possibly be encountered will enable you to form an opinion as to my future success. I indulge in no vain boast or promises; they are valueless in an undertaking in which action alone is called for. I shall continue, therefore, my labors, with the courageous perseverance belonging to my character, and with incessant confidence in your justice and in that of the government. In 1841 you were pleased to acknowledge that I had rendered services to the country. I enjoy the conscientious conviction of having since that period pursued absolutely the same course, identifying myself with the cause of Texas and devoting to it my time, my fortune, and the future prospects of my family. I entreat your excellency to assist me in taking possession of the lands granted to me in organizing my colony and securing to every settler the protection he has a right to expect, by designating proper authorities in conformity with the laws of the country for the administration of the judiciary and the maintenance of order. HENRY CASTRO."

When Mr. Castro addressed these letters and statements to the which had been granted to him, and was in eastern Texas at old Washington on the Brazos, and it seems entertained some fears that he would have trouble in getting possession of the lands.

CASTRO'S DIARY. PART II.

Came to Texas in 1843.

After Henry Castro had sent his first colonists on to San Antonio he remained at Washington on the Brazos until he could communicate with some of the government officials in regard to taking possession of his land grant, and when this was all arranged he set out on the 13th of July, 1844, for San Antonio, in company with Mr. Louis Huth, and arrived there on the 18th of the same month. His arrival created quite a sensation when the fact was made known. In his memoirs he says he stopped with a native of Genoa named Antonio Lockmar, and that he kept the best house in the city. He says that in Don Antonio he found one of the best, most courageous and obliging men he had ever met with in his many travels. On the 19th he called his people around him, who had been anxiously awaiting his arrival, and thus addressed them:

"Henry Castro, to the colonists holding grants of land derived under his contract with the government of Texas: I have made you partake, within the limits assigned to me, with all the advantages that the government of Texas has made me by granting to me a large and fertile tract of land in the county of Bexar. Circumstances independent of my will have prevented until now the taking possession of these lands. To comply as much as possible with the terms of my contract with you, I have come among you to aid you in your labors and to constitute the colony where our hopes are to be realized. We live under the patronage of a liberal government, among the most hospitable and intelligent people of the earth, having at our disposal lands situated in a healthy locality and of notorious fertility. What have we to do in order to enjoy these advantages? We have only to labor with courage, unity, and perseverance. Let us then go to work at once without hesitation or loss of time. I have taken care that we should be in sufficient numbers to conquer all obstacles of locality. My incessant labors in Europe for the last three years have secured me numerous and good colonists, who will arrive here next fall. At this time the ship Jennette Marie, which left

Antwerp May 15th, and which has just arrived at Galveston, brings us reinforcements. Among all the concessions made by the government, the one to which you belong is the only one respected, on account of my efforts to fulfill the conditions of my contract. The land that you will acquire will in consequence of this exception be of more value. The Almighty has created us to work; let us fulfill our destiny if we desire to secure the welfare of our families. I will give you the example of courage, patience, and labor. You are associated in my enterprise. I will aid you with all my might and my resources. Actions and not empty words have always been and always shall be my rule of conduct."

The next few days were busy ones with Castro, making preparations to visit his lands and take a look at them for the first time. The famous Texas ranger, Capt. Jack Hays, was there and furnished Castro an escort of his men, which we see from his diary, which we quote now:

"July 20th, 21st, 22d, 23d, and 24th.—I received many visitors, explained my plans to my colonists, and made preparations to visit the colony lands.

"July 25th.—Left San Antonio with five men of Captain Hays' company of rangers. Our party consisted of seven, making in all twelve men, and well armed. Camped first night on Medio Creek, twelve miles west.

"July 26th.—Mr. John James, who accompanied us, killed three bears on the Potranco Creek; saw many wild horses. James Dunn, one of the rangers, ran them and killed a fine stallion Crossed the Medina River and killed two deer and one alligator and caught some trout; camped on the Medina.

"July 27th.—Recrossed the Medina. At 7 o'clock we had an alarm; one of the rangers reported having seen some mounted men, and not being able to make out who they were, six men left our camp to reconnoiter. They returned without any result. My grant begins four miles west of the Medina. The first thing I saw on my grant was a bee tree full of honey. Reached Quihi Lake, ten miles from the Medina. This point has water, timber, hills, and prairie. It is a good location for a settlement. Camped on the Hondo Creek; also another good place for a settlement.

"July 28th.—Reached the Rio Seco, twelve miles west of Hondo Creek, still on my grant; caught some trout and killed two deer.

Ascended the Seco to the foot of the hills and camped at a water hole below the hills.

"July 29th.—Rode across the country and again reached the Hondo, where we gathered some persimmons and wild grenadines. Camped three miles from Quihi Lake.

"July 30th.—Followed the banks of Quihi Lake, which valley possesses all the advantages for a colony; procured honey and fish in abundance. Camped on the Medina.

"July 31st.—Returned to San Antonio. Two of our rangers were taken sick with a fever.

"I have during this excursion of seven days seen 160 miles of country, which can only be compared to an English park, without meeting a single settlement. No dangerous wild animals were found, but herds of deer and wild horses. With coffee, sugar, and flour, we have lived well from the product of our hunting and fishing, and always had plenty of honey. I had left my colonists all quiet and full of hope, and on my return from this little exploration of part of the colony I found Prince Solms and his companions, with ten or twelve followers, had arrived at San Antonio a day or two after my departure, making a great noise and show, producing upon the modest people the same impressions as a circus troupe in their middle-age costumes. They did not have much trouble in gathering my colonists around them, as they spoke German and showed them certain liberality in the way of drink. Every one spoke of going and settling on the prince's land and following him wherever he should lead. Although the prince, acting as a gentleman, did not have anything to do with these maneuvers personally, still he manifestly sustained his agents in their course. He was much seconded by a desperate character by the name of Rump, who belonged to Captain Hays' company of rangers. Prince Solms having been informed that I intended to establish my first settlement on the Quihi Lake, ten miles from the Medina River, which was four miles east from my colony line, listened to certain propositions that were made to him regarding a seventeen-league tract of land belonging to a citizen of San Antonio known as John Mc-Mullen. He started with his party to explore said tract of land. I understood that if he negotiated for the occupation of such tract of land my enterprise would be ruined, and taking advantage of his absence, I entered into negotiations with McMullen, and with the assistance of one of our most able and honorable attorneys, Mr. Vanderlip, made a contract with the said John McMullen to colonize on certain conditions his grant. When the prince returned to San Antonio he certainly was disappointed. On the 12th of August I made my colonists the following address: President of the Republic of Texas he had never seen the land

"First. In order that each colonist remain in the true path that his interest commands him, it has become my duty to let him know what he would lose if he abandons it. You will have through me, first, a concession of 320 acres of land per family, and 160 acres for each of the single men, within thirty-five miles of San Antonio, in the vicinity of Quihi Lake, in a section of country where you will find good water, timber, prairies, and hills, the land being of the first quality.

"Second. A house gratis, for which you will have nothing to do but aid in its construction; during the occupation you will be fed at my expense.

"Third. A sufficient number of cows will be furnished to those who have not the means of purchasing stock; all the milk they may need the first year.

"Fourth. Work oxen, plows, and farming implements will be furnished by me free for the first year.

"Fifth. To those who have not sufficient means of subsistence, rations will be furnished until the first crop is gathered.

"Sixth. Labor will be given you in building up what buildings are necessary for the colony, for which labor salary proportioned to the ability of each will be paid you. I will also arrange the distribution of labor so that it will be equitably divided.

"The above is my profession of faith and my address to you. Should you ignore them, you will act contrary to the interest of your families.

"San Antonio, August 12, 1844.—I will only remark here that I had to contend with powerful enemies who were trying all their might to seduce my colonists, and that it took more than ordinary energy to fight against those enemies in a wild country far away from my associations. On August 20th I informed my colonists that in two former notices I had called their attention to their duties, that certain parties were trying to persuade them to ig-

9

nore by the meanest kind of proceedings. I defy those who direct these maneuvers to avow them. If they did so they would receive at my hands the chastisement that cowards deserve. To day I make known to you that in order to facilitate your settlement of our first establishment I have bought sixteen leagues of land on the Medina at certain conditions of colonization. We will settle there. I will grant to each colonist that will accompany me forty acres of land and one town lot on the same conditions that I have obtained for myself. The balance of the 320 acres granted to heads of families and of 160 acres granted to single men will be taken up on the lands of the colony grant. This new liberality on my part exceeds the promises of my contract with you. I hope that you will appreciate it to its just value. I gather you around me for a last communication.

"I wish to repeat to you that I have secured for you the following advantages. [The same already above mentioned.] Those advantages exceed the conditions of our contract, and are granted to you to accelerate our settlement and our prosperity.

"Aug. 23d.—Information reached Prince Solms that his confederates in Germany had entered into a contract with Fisher, and instructions received to abandon all projects of settling Bourgeois Dorvane colony. Yellow fever bad at Galveston and New Orleans."

CASTRO'S DIARY. PART III.

In writing the history of Castro's colony, I again quote from his diary:

"August 25th.—Some of my colonists who had left Galveston in the early part of July will not reach this place as soon as it was expected on account of sickness. At Santitas' ranch, forty miles from San Antonio, the Indians attacked a cart which had unfortunately remained behind the convoy. A young colonist aged 19 by the name of Z. Rhin was killed. The driver, who was an American, made his escape. The Indians burned the cart and all its contents. Afterwards in the ashes was found the gold and silver that was in the trunks. The silver had melted and the gold had only been blackened. The driver remained in the woods the following day, and although the Indians numbered twenty he kept them at bay with his long rifle. One of the hands of poor Rhin was found nailed to a tree. He was probably the first martyr of European emigration by Indian brutality in western Texas.

"August 26th.—To-day five or six Comanches came within two hundred yards of the house I occupy on Soledad Street and succeeded in capturing eleven mules that were grazing in the inclosure. Alarm was given in the town and the robbers were pursued, but without any result. The mules were lost. Such acts of audacity on the part of the Indians intimidate my colonists and tend to injure my enterprise.

"Four volunteers who were sent by Captain Hays to reconnoiter on the Nueces River ninety miles from San Antonio were surprised while bathing in the river by a large party of Indians. Two were reported killed. The other two reported that they had undressed themselves and with horses unsaddled they were bathing in the river when they were fired upon from the bank of the river. The attack was so sudden and unexpected that seeing their comrades fall and fearful of being surrounded, they fled, leaving their arms, clothing, saddles, and bridles in possession of the Indians. You Texans who read this may know what our friends suffered riding naked bareback a distance of nearly one hundred miles in the hot month of August, but they however reached this place in safety.

"The conduct of this scout sent as explorers in a portion of the country then full of Indians was certainly very imprudent."

(This surprise of the rangers which Mr. Castro has thus described occurred at the three forks of the Nueces, as the place was then called by the rangers, and was in Nueces Canyon. The men were Kit Ackland, Rufe Perry, James Dunn, and John Carlin. The two last named were in bathing when the attack was made on their camp and they went to San Antonio and reported Ackland and Perry killed, but they, although badly wounded, made their way back to San Antonio on foot.)

I quote again from Mr. Castro. He says:

"In the month of July last ,Captain Hays with twelve of his company encountered near Corpus Christi seventy-five Comanche warriors. A fight ensued which I am told lasted fifty minutes, nearly hand to hand. Thirty Indians were killed and many others wounded and routed. This victory was greatly due to the use of Colt's revolvers that the Texans used for the first time in this engagement, to the great astonishment of the Indians, who fought bravely."

There is a difference of opinion as to where the revolvers were first used in conflict with the Iidians. Capt. Mayne Reid, in his book, "Hays', Walker's and McCulloch's Rangers," says it was in the Pedernales battle. The writer had an uncle, Andrew Sowell, who was in the battle which Mr. Castro describes, and' says they used the revolvers (five-shooters) there, and he thinks for the first time. No doubt it was the first time this band was fought with them. Tom Galbreth, another old Hays ranger, says it was in Nueces Canyon; at least they used them on another bunch there for the first time.

Again Mr. Castro says:

"August 27th.—I hastened as much as possible the preparation necessary to my leaving this city, believing that I had the sympathy of the inhabitants of the place, but here again I met with a bitter deception. I had against me without my knowledge the merchants and large real estate owners. The first, because they feared that a new town started west of theirs would take away most of their trade with Mexico, and the others because they had received the services of many of my colonists at low rates, and because they found in them industrious and intelligent laboring men. As long as it was thought that my proposed settlement was all talk, no opposition was made, but when it was found out that my departure was certain, rumors were circulated by those interested that my people would all become an easy prey to the Indians; that they would not make a crop for a year to come; that the heavy rains that would set in about October would prevent them from constructing their houses. How could they live in that desert? They were going to leave a certainty for an uncertainty; they would certainly return, when they would find the situations they now filled occupied by others, and a most deplorable misery would be the reward of their removal. Those new enemies were not the least dangerous to encounter. However, I was inspired to give them a terrible blow by proclaiming that in my first attempt to settle the colony I would only accept men to accompany me; that the families should remain in the city until otherwise decided. That satisfied everybody.

"August 28th, 29th, 30th, and 31st.—These few days were employed in preparations for our expedition. On the 31st all the colonists who were to form part of the expedition, with their families and many of my American friends, were invited by me to participate in a farewell dinner, which went off exceedingly pleasant, and toward evening, owing to the great number of toasts drunk, became very enthusiastic. September 1, 1844, at 4 o'clock a. m., I had gathered carts numbering twenty-two. The farming utensils, baggage, and provisions being ready to be loaded in the town, some of my employes informed me that rumors had been maliciously circulated that we would not start on that day owing to the small number composing our expedition, and to give it more weight, it was said and reported that I had stated that we would be at least fifty men strong, but that I could not fulfill my promise, etc.

"I immediately sent ten men on horseback in all directions to contradict such rumors, assuring everyone that had enrolled his name to form part of my expedition; that nothing but death would prevent me from starting on the appointed day; that I would fulfill all of my promises at any cost and hazard, and that we would be fifty men anyhow at our departure. Although I made every effort in my power my adherents came in slowly, making many excuses under various pretenses, but always assuring me of their intended fidelity to their engagements.

"My position became critical, for in delaying my departure I encouraged the efforts of my enemies to discredit my promises and take away from me the colonists I had brought to this country at so much trouble and expense. Many unfortunately had allowed themselves to be persuaded. It was 2 o'clock in the afternoon, and rain was falling by torrents, as if to create me more embarrassments. It became necessary to supply the number of colonists missing with Mexicans paid by me. On this occasion my friend Don Antonio, with his numerous friends, secured me the number of men that I wanted, owing to the high pay granted them, and I must say to his credit that all of them were good men and behaved well in all circumstances. Although it was raining by torrents at 4 o'clock, having kept all day an open table well supplied with meat and drink, I managed to retain those who would take the trouble to come and inform themselves of what was going on. It appeared to me a proper time to call the roll of the colonists. Of those to be present only twenty-seven were there, but with my Mexicans we were fifty. The train of carts being then loaded, I ordered it to start. When we mustered I found thirty-five colonists and Mexicans well armed, who followed on foot. I accompanied them with about twenty men, all pretty well armed and mounted. This departure was fortunate, and was really one of the greatest triumphs that I obtained over the overwhelming difficulties I had to overcome in my enterprise of colonization. It entirely restored confidence in myself and my enterprise.

"September 2d.—On the Medina River. Started with a party to reconnoiter the point where we were to form our settlements. We only returned to camp at midnight. I caused my people to create an alarm by firing their guns and pistols, and was afterwards satisfied that the lesson was not entirely lost.

"September 3d.—Crossed the Medina River at about 8 a. m. at the actual crossing (now opposite Castroville), a beautiful location. Our camp was shaded by large pecan trees, at the foot of which ran a beautiful stream having plenty of game and fish. The improvised kitchen of my French colonists was soon filled with dishes which, aided by the drink I contributed, soon brought everybody in good humor, and the evening was spent in a gay manner.

"September 4th.—Built a shed in which to place our commissary. Arrival of Deputy Surveyor John James.

"September 5th.—A dispute arose between the French and German colonists, which I fortunately settled amicably.

"September 6th.—Labor more regularly organized.

"September 7th.—Messrs. Dr. Cupples and Charles de Montel leave for San Antonio to bring Bishop Odin.

"September 8th.—Storm during the night, which surprised us and gave us a good ducking. Drank twice a little brandy during the night and smoked a pipe, contrary to my habit.

"September 9th.—Arrival of three colonists. One of my mounted men reported having seen a trail of fifty Comanches. Information sent to Captain Hays and precautions taken against a surprise from the Indians. Built a guard house.

"September 10th.—Cut timber to construct a large shed to shelter every one temporarily. Discovered the kind of grass proper for roofing. Our camp abounds in game and fish. Arrival of Bishop Odin, Rev. Oge, Captains Hays and Chevalier.

"September 11th.—Departure of Captains Hays and Chevalier. To-day my table was set on the banks of the Medina, under the rich foliage of the pecan and walnut. Besides my customary guests we had the bishop and Rev. Oge, whom I did my best to please. Amongst the novelties we had for our fare we had several bottles of wine made from the mustang grape by one of the colonists from the Rhenish provinces. Without doubt it was the first wine manufactured on the Medina, and it was considered very fair.

"September 12th.—An election was held by the authority of the county judge for two justices of the peace and one constable to constitute the authorities of our new precinct. I acted as president of said election. Messrs. Louis Huth and G. S. Bourgeois were elected justices, and Louis Haas constable.

"On the morning of the same day we proceeded to the ceremony of laying the cornerstone of the church of Saint Louis (king) by the Rev. Bishop Odin, accompanied by his grand vicar and followed by all the little colony. Discharges of musketry, bonfires built, and the usual libations ended this well-occupied day.

"September 13th.—Departure of Bishop Odin, whom I accompanied part of the way. The bishop was pleased to deliver me the following certificate:

" 'I, the undersigned, bishop of Claudiopolis, affirm to whom it may concern, that upon the invitation of Mr. H. Castro, who has received from the government of Texas a large grant of land in the county of Bexar, I visited, accompanied by Abbe Oge, of my diocese, his settlement situated on the Medina River, twenty-five miles west of San Antonio de Bexar, to lay the cornerstone of the first Catholic church to be constructed in the first settlement of the said Castro, and that we placed the same under the invocation of Saint Louis. We have seen a good number of colonists at work building their houses with a view of forming a solid and permanent settlement.

" 'In faith of which I signed and affixed my seal to these presents.

" 'ODIN, Bishop of Claudiopolis.

" 'Castroville, Sep. 12, 1844.

" 'Seen for legalization of the signature of Odin, bishop of Claudiopolis.

" 'F. GUILBEAU,

" 'French Consular Agent at San Antonio de Bexar.' "

The document signed by Bishop Odin and dated Castroville, September 12, 1844, is no doubt the first time that the name Castroville was ever signed or printed, as it come into existence at that time.

CASTROVILLE FOUNDED.

1844.

After the colonists had become somewhat settled in their new habitations and their town named after its founder, the following document was drawn up and signed by those who had remained with him:

"Process verbal of the possession taken of the lands situated on the concession made to Mr. H. Castro by the Texan government, on the 15th day of February, 1842, situated in the county of Bexar, and of other lands belonging to him.

"We, the undersigned colonists engaged in France by Mr. H. Castro to participate in the advantages of the grant above mentioned within the limits assigned by the government of Texas, the terms of which are more particularly set forth in a contract passed between us and the said H. Castro, do declare:

"That the said Castro having assembled us at San Antonio de Bexar as our leader, conducted us on that which had been assigned and given us by him, in consequence of which we left San Antonio on the 1st of September to go to the Medina River, twenty-five miles west, which place we reached on the 2d instant. We declare that, independently of our contract and without any obligation on his part, Mr. H. Castro has made us the following advantages hereafter expressed, in order to facilitate to us our speedy settlement."

Here follow the advantages above mentioned:

"First. To each of us forty acres of land of his property on the Medina.

"Second. The necessary transportation and our rations secured until our houses shall be constructed.

"Third. Horses and oxen until next crop.

"Fourth. Bacon and corn to those who may want it until the next crop is gathered.

"Fifth. The use of his milch cows.

"We declare that Mr. John James, deputy surveyor of this district, came and surveyed the lots assigned to us. We declare since twelve days that we have reached our destination our labors, being well conducted, promise to give a comfortable shelter for ourselves and families within seven or eight weeks. We are satisfied, by the experience that we have acquired, that the climate of Bexar County is among the most salubrious, the water exceedingly good, timber sufficient, and the land appears to unite the qualities needed for a great fertility. Such is the protection under which we have established ourselves and which forms the base of our hopes. We have unanimously resolved to name the town of which we are the founders Castroville.

"Done at Castroville, on the Medina, in the county of Bexar, September the 12th, 1844.

"Signed: Jean Batiste Lecomte, Joseph Haguelin, N. Rosec, Theodore Gentil, Auguste Fretelliere, J. S. Bourgeois, Zavier Young, Louis Huth, George Cupples, Charles Gouibund, J. Fairue, N. Forgeaux, P. Boilot, C. Chapois, J. Macles, Leopold Menetrier, Michel Simon, Theophile Mercier, Antony Goly, Louis Grab, G. L. Haas, Joseph Bader, Bertold Bartz, Charles de Montel, Sax Gaspard, J. Ulrich Zurcher, George Spani.

"Certified to at Castroville, September the 12th, in the year 1844.

"G. L. HAAS, Constable.

"Louis Huth and J. S. Bourgeois, Justices of the Peace.

"Republic of Texas, County of Bexar.—I, the undersigned, do hereby certify that Louis Huth and J. Simon Bourgeois are justices of the peace and G. L. Hass constable for Castroville, in this county.

"Given under my hand and official seal at San Antonio de Bexar, this the 5th day of October, A. D. 1844.

"DAVID MORGAN,

"Chief Justice of Bexar County.

"Seen for the legalization of David Morgan's signature, the consular agent for France ad interim.

"FAUTREL AINE.

"Recorded by T. Hos. Addicks on the 7th day of October, A. D. 1844, in the records of Bexar County."

All of Castro's colony did not arrive until some time in 1847, but came as they could get ready and shipping.

The following are the names of the ships and the captains who commanded them, date of sailing, etc.:

1. Ebro, Captain E. Perry, from Havre to Galveston, 1842.
2. Lyons, Captain G. Parker, from Havre to New Orleans, 1843.
3. Louis Philippe, Captain Laborde, from Dunkirk to Galveston, 1843.
4. ——, —— ——, —— to Galveston, 1843.
5. John Key, Captain De Paw, from Antwerp to Galveston, 1843.
6. Henrich, Captain Andries, from Antwerp to Galveston, 1844.
7. Ocean, Captain Rochjen, from Antwerp to Galveston, 1844.
8. Jeannette Maria, Captain Perischke, from Antwerp to Galveston, 1844.
9. Probus, Captain Deonis, from Antwerp to Galveston, 1845.
10. Prince Oscar, Captain Azoerken, from Antwerp to Galveston, 1845.
11. Marcia Claves, Captain Caiborn, from Antwerp to Galveston, 1845.
12. Alberdina, Captain Matling, from Antwerp to Galveston, 1846.
13. Euprosina, —— ——, from Ghent to Galveston, 1846.
14. Talisman, Captain Loomis, —— to Galveston, 1846.
15. Diamant, Captain Baller, —— to Galveston, 1846.
16. Cronstadt, Captain Hatch, from Antwerp to Galveston, 1846.
17. Carl Wilhelm, Captain De Schelling, from Bremen to Galveston, 1846.
18. Louise Frederich, Captain Kniggs, from Bremen to Galveston, 1846.
19. Neptune, Captain Starsloppe, from Bremen to Galveston, 1846.
20. Leo, Captain Goerdes, from Bremen to Galveston, 1846.
21. Bangor, Captain Leighton, from Antwerp to Galveston, 1846.
22. Feyen, Captain Kruse, from Bremen to Galveston, ——.
23. Duc de Brabant, —— ——, from Antwerp to Galveston, ——.

24. Schanungza, Captain Patton, from Antwerp to Galveston, 1847.

25. ——, —— ——, from Bremen to Galveston, 1847.

26. Creole, Captain Wessels, from Bremen to Galveston, 1847.

27. Creole, Captain H. Hall, from Antwerp to Galveston, 1847.

There are but few of the original colonists now alive, but the writer has found and interviewed some of them, and will write biographical sketches of these. They have a very interesting tale to tell of the hardships and dangers they had to undergo, both in coming across the waters and from Indians on the frontier after they arrived at their destination. Some were lost at sea, others died en route after landing, and many were killed by Indians. Mr. Castro lived to enjoy the fruits of his labors. His wife and son Lorenzo died at Castroville, but himself in Mexico, and there is no relative in this country that bears his name.

I am indebted to Mr. Louis Haller, of Castroville, for a list of names of the ships, which he has preserved for many years.

JOSEPH BURRELL.

Came to Texas in 1844.

Mr. Joseph Burrell, who lives on the Medina River above Castroville at this date (1898), is one of the original colonists of Henry Castro. He was born in Aldorf, France, in 1829, and started to Texas in March, 1844.

The start was made from Antwerp to the promised land, and the trip was uneventful. The ship sailed fast, and made a much quicker trip than many others which came about the same time. The first landing was made on Texas soil at Galveston, but like nearly all the immigrants, those who were bound for west Texas re-embarked again for the port of Lavaca. Mr. Burrell says it took them a long time to arrive at the last mentioned port, and that a strange thing happened on the way. One day they landed on an island, and all of the officers on the ship went away and did not return for a week. The passengers could not tell where they went or what the meaning was. They could only wait and watch for their return. When the officers returned they gave no explanation of their conduct, but got under way again and arrived all right at their destination.

From Port Lavaca the Castro colonists went to Victoria, and there saw their first Indians. They were in large force, but seemed to be on good terms with the whites. The balance of the journey from here to San Antonio was made in ox wagons. Many of the immigrants by this time were sick from exposure, and two of them died on the way. Two oxen were lost on the San Antonio River, which caused some delay and extra expense to purchase more. Some friendly Indians had paid them a visit while in camp, and that circumstance likely accounts for the missing oxen. On the way out there was some talk of settling at Goliad. They had a surveyor along to lay off the land, but they abandoned this idea and moved on to their original designated place to settle. While in camp when the oxen were lost, most of the men scattered out to hunt them. The elder Burrell had one yoke of oxen, and with these he carried the women and children and those of the men who were sick to a Mexican ranch two miles

away. One man was left in camp with the other wagon, and
while here alone was attacked by the Indians and killed. These
pretended friendly savages then burned the wagon.

This first victim of the inoffensive German immigrants to
savage cruelty was named Rehen. On this same day the subject
of this sketch, then a boy 15 years of age, was out hunting the
lost oxen on horseback, and coming to the San Antonio River
started to ride down to the water's edge for his horse to drink,
but suddenly the animal wheeled back and tried to run away.
Young Burrell succeeded in checking him and looked back. The
cause of the fright of the horse was now apparent. A band of
Indians was on the opposite side of the river, and they at once
commenced crossing towards him. He now let the pony run and
made his escape from them. These same Indians went on to
camp and did the mischief before noted. The driver of the
wagon came in sight while the wagon was burning, but was
afraid to venture near, so ran away and gave the alarm.

The unfortunate colonists finally, by purchasing more oxen,
made their way to San Antonio. Henry Castro and quite a lot
of his people were at this place, not having as yet commenced his
settlement, which was to be on the Medina River, twenty-five
miles west from San Antonio, at the present site of Castroville.
The Burrell family was among the first to go out and help to
erect a shanty out of poles. It was a rude affair, but large and
capable of sheltering all the people until they could get their individual houses erected. This primitive shelter was covered
with grass, which made a good roof, turning water like shingles.
The people all stayed in it at night for fear of the Indians. Castro himself came out with them, but went back to San Antonio
and left Louis Huth in his place to see to the interest of the colony. His son now has a store in San Antonio.

Mr. Burrell knew Capt. Jack Hays, and says when he first
saw him he thought him quite young to be in command of a
company of rangers.

Mr. Burrell describes the country at that time as being very
beautiful. No brush, only scattered liveoak and mesquite trees
on the high ground, and large timber in the valleys. Many fine
pecan trees were on the river, and high grass everywhere. All
the streams were running high. The branch he now lives on was
fed by a large spring, and emptied into what was called the

Pecan waterhole, which was always full until the Spring branch quit running, a number of years ago. This place was the camping-ground of a large band of Indians when Mr. Burrell first came to the country. There is a well now on the original site of the spring, which affords plenty of water.

In 1846 Mr. Burrell joined a company of rangers commanded by Capt. John Conner. They moved their camp many times on the lookout for Indians, but had no fight with them. When a trail was struck the Indians would burn the grass behind them to cover it.

During this time the war with Mexico broke out, and Captain Conner carried his company to Mexico and joined General Taylor at Monterey. This was in 1847. On the way, and before they reached the city, they came upon the remains of a United States government train which had been captured and destroyed by the Mexicans. There were about 200 wagons, all of which were burned and the drivers all killed except one, who made his escape and carried the news of the disaster to General Taylor. Mr. Burrell knew a great many of the teamsters who lay dead beside the road. The Mexicans carried away the mules.

When the time of their enlistment had expired Captain Conner's men were discharged, and Mr. Burrell joined the company of Captain Veach and remained until the war was over. He was discharged at San Antonio, and now draws a pension for this service of $8 per month.

He next obtained a job as government teamster to assist in opening a road from San Antonio to El Paso. From the latter place he and others were sent seventy-five miles north to cut timber for the purpose of building forts. Beeves and goats were carried along to eat.

After arriving at the scene of their labors a place was selected in a secluded little valley in which to keep the beeves and goats. A heavy snow, however, soon fell, which covered the valley a foot deep, and which lasted several days. During this time the Indians succeeded in getting the beeves and goats out of the valley and carried them off. There were not sufficient horses in camp on which to pursue the marauders. The baggage wagon had been drawn to their present camp by oxen. These resolute fellows, however, determined to follow the Indians, and here commenced one of the most unique pursuits of Indians that has ever been recorded in frontier history. They hitched oxen to the baggage wagon and followed them in that. One reason which induced them to attempt a pursuit by this slow locomotion was the fact that the Indians would have to go slow with the goats and beef cattle. Not knowing the country, however, they soon got into a dry country and could find no water. The supply with which they started was soon exhausted. The oxen also gave out and lay down. They had one wagon, three yoke of oxen, and eight men in this strange expedition. The men now scattered in different directions on foot to hunt for water. In his rounds Mr. Burrell came to a clear lake, and being almost dead with thirst, lay down on his stomach and commenced to drink very fast. He soon sprang up in terror, for it was alkali, and came near killing him. He now found some prickly pears, and cutting out the inside, obtained some moisture by chewing them. On this same evening two of the other men found good water on the Sacramento Mountains, and came back to let the others know where it was. They all got together by firing pistols, and then lost no time in getting back to the water. Here they stayed three days, and were then loath to leave, as it was two days hard walking back to the wagon. The oxen had all been turned loose when the search for water commenced, but on the second day after the men had assembled on the mountain all of the oxen came up straight to the water. One man had started on the expedition on horseback, but had turned back when the water gave out. A man named Cotton, from San Antonio, was in charge of the timber cutting outfit, but had stayed in camp when the pursuit of the Indians was inaugurated, and he was informed of the situation by the man who returned on the horse. Cotton at once came with two men to hunt for them, and found them at the waterhole on the mountain. They now killed one of the oxen to eat and drove the balance back to the wagon, hitched two yoke to it, and drove the odd one along. The country was sandy, and the team could not well pull the wagon through it, so three men would push, one drive, and three rest until it came their time to push. Cotton and the men with him went on back to camp, taking the other wagon and some teams which had been left in camp, and went across to Donna Anna, thirty miles away.

The men came on with their slow and tedious way of moving.

If one ox gave out the odd one was put in until the other could rest, and so on. Finally, however, all of the oxen gave out, and they had to leave the wagon and oxen except one, on which they put their blankets and other things, and traveled that way until the ox gave out, and then the men had to make pack horses of themselves. Having no water was the cause of the oxen giving out. The men were without water on this return trip three days. Burrell had brought a five-gallon keg from the mountain, but it gave out three days before reaching their old camp from which they started in pursuit of the Indians. They stopped one day at the old camp and drank water. Next day one of the oxen which had been left arrived in camp. By this time the men were hungry again, and killed the ox for food. They remained one more day and ate beef.

Cotton went to a new camp where timber was better, and supposed the men would follow him when they returned. Some of them did so, but Mr. Burrell and two others went to El Paso, eighty miles distant. They had to make this journey on foot, and took some of the ox meat along to subsist upon by the way. It was thirty miles to the first water, and there they rested awhile. It was fifty miles to the next, El Paso. They were badly worn out. After resting awhile they built them a house, Mexican fashion, and went to farming by irrigation. Their crop, however, was never finished on account of the Indians stealing their teams. They now quit El Paso and started to California. There were fifteen wagons in the outfit, some of them containing whole families. This was in 1850. On the route the Indians stole part of their teams before they reached the Gila River. The Indians were pursued, and this time with success. The stock was all retaken and brought back. When the party arrived at the Gila a halt was made and Mr. Burrell went on alone. When he arrived at the Colorado River, on the line of New Mexico and California, he fell in with a friendly Indian who told him where to cross the river, as it was very dangerous. A party of white men now came along who seemed to know the fords, and Burrell crossed with them, but in doing so his horse was drowned. There was a train camped on the other side whose captain knew Burrell, and wanted him to remain and go with them. He stayed with them one night, but next day set out again alone. On the way he fell

10

in with another train which was going his way, and journeyed with them.

At Santiago he got on a boat and went to San Francisco, and from there to Sacramento. At the former place he again met Capt. Jack Hays, who had removed to California after the Mexican war and had been elected sheriff of San Francisco County. Burrell bought tools at Sacramento and went out to the mines and got into a job at $6 per day. It snowed here a great deal. There was at this time great excitement on Scott River, and Mr. Burrell went over there. On the way, however, his pack mule was stolen and he had to carry his pack on his own back. The snow was so deep he soon had to stop, and went to mining again at $8 per day. When the snow melted off he went on to the Trinity River and found better diggings there. There were six in his party now, and they soon heard news of a better place further on. Burrell and two others went on, but soon run short of means and had to return to the old camp. The other men by this time had gone and nothing was there. They went on down the country, and soon lost all they had in an Indian raid. Burrell then went back to Sacramento and from there to Oregon. He stayed here nearly a year and tried farming, but made nothing. Salt was $16 per sack, and flour could not be had at any price. He had to eat beef without bread. His partner was sent off on a horse with money to buy provisions, but he went on into California and did not return. He secured another partner and went into the mining business again. One day while at work there was a cave-in and he was partly covered with rocks, and had to remain in that condition until his partner could go half a mile and return with help. He thought Burrell was dead. After the rocks were removed he was not able to stand, nor could he see. He was carried to a shanty, and did not walk for many days. Nine other men were buried in like manner the same day, and most of them died. He quit mining then and went to building rock houses.

He came back to Texas by way of New Orleans, and again arrived at Castroville in 1855. Soon after getting back the Indians made a raid and stole some good horses from him, and also some from the ranch of Ed. Braden. The latter lived in San Antonio, but had a ranch on Calaveras Creek. Burrell and one of his brothers and a man named Huffman were up in the hills and saw the Indians with the horses, and Burrell wanted to make a charge and try to recover them. The others would not agree to this. He then said he would shoot and see if he could hit one at long range. The Indian's horse was hit, and he sprang on another and got away. It was one of Braden's horses that was wounded, and he was captured and brought back. Braden soon came and wanted Burrell to go with him on the trail of the Indians. The trail was taken up, and after circling about some went straight towards Westfall's ranch on the Leona. When they arrived at this place they found a dead man and a dead dog in the yard. They did not know who the man was, but knew it was not Westfall. The same Indians they were trailing had attacked the ranch. They quit the trail here, as the Indians were too far ahead to overtake them. They learned afterwards that the dead man was French Louie, and that Westfall himself was badly wounded, but had made his way to Fort Inge.

After this he joined a minute company commanded by Capt. George Haby. The Indians made one raid and stole horses all over the country. Captain Haby took twenty men and followed them. The trail was struck at a place called "Mescal camp," where some Mexican liquor had once been made. Here the Indians killed and ate a horse. They were overtaken at the head of the Hondo River, with 101 head of horses. Burrell tried to cut them off from the horses, but was prevented by a deep creek. The Indians left the horses they were riding and escaped into the brush. After a great deal of search and trouble the stolen horses were all rounded up and carried back to the owners.

Mr. Burrell used to live near the Medina River, but in 1871 was badly damaged by high water and wanted to move to the hills, but his wife's mother said no, it would never be this high again. Next year came a worse rise and he lost everything. He now lives on a high hill, a mile from the river. The wind took the roof off of his house here. Mrs. Burrell was a Haby, and came from Alsace.

INCIDENT OF RANGER LIFE.

1844.

The facts in the thrilling incident of ranger life now about to
be narrated were furnished the writer by the old Texas ranger,
Thomas Galbreath. While Mr. Galbreath was not a participant,
he was a member of Capt. Jack Hays' company of rangers at the
time, and well remembers all of the particulars of this frontier
episode.

In August, 1844, about a month after the fight in Nueces
Canyon, Captain Hays sent four of his men back to the canyon
to see if there was any fresh sign of Indians there. The men
sent on this rather hazardous mission so far from the settlements
were Kit Ackland, Rufus Perry, James Dunn, and John Carlin.
The four rangers went a westerly course until they arrived at a
point in the prairie north of where the town of Uvalde now is,
and then turned northwest towards the mouth of Nueces Canyon.

For some time no signs of Indians were seen, except the remains of some of those killed in the previous battle, until they
came to what the rangers called the three forks of the Nueces.
Here about noon, after a hard ride, the men dismounted, unsaddled their horses, put them out to graze, and prepared their
noonday meal. After dinner Ackland lay down to rest awhile
before continuing the scout, and Perry stood guard. Dunn and
Carlin took their horses down to the river to wash them and cool
them off, and to take a swim themselves. The rangers had not
stopped on the main river, but on a little creek with high banks
several hundred yards from the main Nueces. Dunn and Carlin
left their saddles in camp, and when they came to the river
stripped off their clothing and rode their horses into the stream.
Perry was a good and experienced ranger and Indian fighter, but
even his exeperienced eye failed to detect a band of Indians who
were concealed near by and intently watching every movement of
the scouts, and as soon as two of them went off the Indians
slipped down the bed of the small creek, keeping hid from view
by the banks, until they arrived opposite the camp of the rangers.
Their presence was not detected until they suddenly ascended the

bank and sent a flight of arrows at Perry, who fell with three wounds, two in the body and one in the face. Ackland at once sprang to his feet with his gun, but was fired on and hit in three places with bullets and arrows, one of which was in the mouth with an arrow, which knocked out some of his teeth and badly lacerated the flesh. He did not fall, however, but quickly aimed his gun at an Indian's face close by, who had his head above the bank of the creek, and fired. The charge hit the Comanche full in the face and he fell backward. The Indians had the advantage of the bank of the creek, which they could dodge back behind when they fired, but seeing the wounded condition of the two rangers, began to come out in large numbers and to charge them. Ackland, without backing, drew his revolver and fired on them with such deadly effect that they again sought cover. During this close combat the wounded Perry drew his pistol, and although unable to rise, turned on his side so that he could see the Indians, and by his shots helped to put them back in the ravine. Ackland now sprang to Perry, lifted him on his shoulder, and started in a run with him to the river, where Dunn and Carlin were. Ackland, although a powerful man physically, was nearly exhausted from loss of blood when he arrived at the place where his other two companions were and laid Perry down. Dunn and Carlin were brave men and had been in many fights with Indians, but failed to come to the assistance of their comrades in their terrible need, but sat on their horses and watched the battle at their noonday camp. Their plea was that it was useless to make an attempt against such a large band of Indians, many of whom they could see in the ravine from their position on the river, and knew they would be cut off before reaching their companions. They had stripped off their clothing and were in the water when they heard the fight commence at camp, and at once came out and mounted their horses without their clothing, ready for flight in case the Indians were too strong for them. By the time Ackland got to the bathers the Indians were yelling loudly and plundering the camp. Although the wounded rangers had pulled the arrows from their bodies they were bleeding profusely, and left a trail of blood from their camp to the river. The two unhurt and mounted rangers, seeing they could do no good, took Perry across the river at the suggestion of Ackland, and then waited until Ackland crossed. A brief consultation was now

held, and Perry asked Dunn to load his pistol for him. Dunn
took the pistol and ascended a tree to see what the Indians were
doing, but failed to load it, as he dropped it on descending, and
exclaimed: "The valley is full of Indians, and a large band of
them are coming this way." He and Carlin now set out for San
Antonio, naked as they were and bareback on their horses. We
will not judge the action of these two rangers too harshly. They
said it was useless for them all to get killed. They looked upon
Ackland and Perry as already dead,—badly wounded and no
horses to escape on,—and they would hasten on and inform Captain Hays of the situation. It indeed seemed that there was no
chance for the two wounded rangers, left alone on the banks of
the clear, beautiful river, with a horde of yelling savages on their
trail. Under the circumstances some men would have given up
in despair and met their fate without an effort, or, in the position
of Ackland, told his disabled friend good-bye and made his own
escape if possible. Not so in this case, however, with the lion-
hearted ranger. He determined to save his friend or die with
him. They had no chance to defend themselves except with
knives. The blood had dried and clotted around Perry's eyes so
that he could no longer see even his brave friend, who was now
bending over him and trying again to lift him on his shoulder.
"What are you going to do now, Kit?" asked the wounded Perry.
The loud yelling of the Indians denoted their near presence when
this question was asked, but they were on the opposite side of the
river tracking Ackland by his blood, like a hunter would a
wounded deer, and were not yet aware that the rangers had
crossed the river, and no doubt expected each moment to come
upon them and have an easy time taking their scalps. Ackland
was very weak from loss of blood, and his mouth was so badly
swollen that he could hardly talk, but managed to tell his friend
that he was going to secrete him somewhere and then hide himself, as that was the only chance. He succeeded in getting Perry
on his shoulder, but staggered to and fro as he went off with him
down the river. Ackland was careful in his flight to leave as
little sign as possible. The blood had quit flowing from their
wounds, and their saturated garments clung to their bodies.
When almost exhausted and ready to sink in his tracks, Ackland
came to a large drift that covered an acre or more of ground
which had been deposited there during some great rise in the

river, and this afforded a good hiding place. Crawling in under the drift he dragged Perry after him as far as he could go, and then explaining to him what kind of a place it was, said he would go and hide somewhere else, so that if one was found likely the other would escape. It was agreed that if either one recovered sufficiently and was not discovered by the Indians, to set out for San Antonio at once and bring help for the other. Ackland said he would not be far from the spot where he left Perry. The Indians could still be heard, and pressing the hand of his friend, the fearless Kit crawled away and was soon lost to hearing. After getting clear of the drift, he covered the trail he made going in and out by throwing leaves and sticks over it, and then stepping on stones, chunks, and logs as he went away from the place.

Ackland now went further down the river and secreted himself. Perry lay under cover where he was left and listened to the Indians. After a short time he could tell that they had crossed the river and were evidently on the trail of the rangers, and would soon be at his hiding place. For some time all was perfectly still, and then he was aware of their presence by low talking near by. The Indians had begun to hunt more cautiously, not knowing but that likely the other two rangers were also in hiding and had their guns and pistols. He could also hear the Indians walking over the brush, and finally they got onto the drift under which he lay and walked directly over him. O how he wished for his eyesight and gun and pistol well loaded; but he was helpless and lay still and listened, thinking that each minute would be his last. The drift covered so much ground and had so many openings in which a man could crawl that they failed to find the right one, and finally went on down the river.

Perry was now uneasy about Ackland, fearing the Indians would discover him. He listened intently, expecting each moment to hear the exultant whoop which they would utter in case they found him. He could tell this from the occasional yell of pursuit. His mind was greatly relieved as the hours passed by and he failed to hear the ominous sound come from the savages, who were anxious to avenge the braves who lay dead up the river, and one at least whose ugly face was badly mutilated by a rifle ball from Ackland's gun.

As the evening wore on Perry suffered much from his wounds and thirst. He could hear the river running near by, and was tempted to risk the Indians seeing him and try to get to it, but yet he waited and listened. He could tell by the birds singing that night was not yet approaching. After what seemed almost an age to him everything became still. He could no longer hear the birds, and all animal life seemed hushed except the hoot of an owl or the scream of a panther or wildcat. He now determined to leave his hiding place and make an attempt to crawl to the river. Slowly and in darkness he came forth, feeling his way and guided in the right direction after he got clear of the drift by the sound of running water. Many obstacles were encountered,—logs, tree tops, and large rocks,—so much so that many detours had to be made to get around them. Finally, however, he arrived at the edge of the water, and no one who has not experienced the same sensation can realize his sufferings or his pleasure while drinking the cold water, after dragging himself over rough stones and logs, guided by the rippling water to its brink. He now bathed his head and washed the clotted blood from his eyes so that he could open them and once more take a survey of the situation. It was indeed night. The dark mountains loomed up on both sides of the canyon, and the stars shone bright overhead and cast their reflection in the clear water at his feet. After his hot, fevered head had been cooled by frequent applications, and his thirst appeased, he felt strong, and for the first time since he felt the shock of the missiles which struck him that day at noon he was able to stand on his feet. One of the arrows had struck the lower part of his body and paralyzed it up to this time, except the use of one leg. He now thought of his wounded companion, whom he knew was not far away, but they dare not signal to each other for fear it might attract the Indians. Perry feared that when the reaction came upon Ackland, after his terrible efforts to save him, and the bad wounds he had received, it would prove fatal to him or render him incapable of making his way back to San Antonio, which was about 120 miles. The brave Perry now determined to make an effort to reach San Antonio himself and send back succor to his wounded friend. He was satisfied that Captain Hays would send men back to search for and bury their bodies, but as they had left the place where Dunn and Carlin had last seen them they would not know where to hunt. That night he set out on his painful, slow, and almost hopeless journey. We can not describe, but can only imagine, what he suffered from wounds, hunger, thirst, and the burning sun of August, impelled on by not only a desire to save his own life but that of his friend, if he yet had a chance for life. Suffice to say that in six days and nights of travel he arrived in San Antonio. Dunn and Carlin had arrived two or three days before in a most deplorable plight, being sunburned and badly worn out by riding so far without saddle or clothing. They reported Ackland and Perry both killed, as they thought it would be impossible for them to escape. Captain Hays at once sent back a scout of trusty men to rescue his two gallant boys if possible, and if not, to find the bodies and give them decent interment. Great excitement prevailed when Perry got in, and another scout was at once detailed to go and hunt for the other wounded ranger, as they had a better idea of where he might be found from a description of the place as given by Perry.

Where now was the gallant Ackland? All felt an interest in him, and men hurriedly made their preparations to start. Before this scout could get off, however, Ackland solved the problem of his fate by walking into town about two hours after Perry . He had left his place of concealment and started to San Antonio that night after he could no longer hear the Indians. They passed close to the place where he lay and went on down the river, but continued to circle and hunt until night. He and Perry started about the same time, and evidently were not far apart during the trip,—Ackland exerting himself the same as his companion to get to San Antonio to send succor back to the other. Both were in a horrible condition with wounds and starvation—three festering wounds apiece, and both their faces lacerated and badly swollen; even their messmates failed to recognize them on first sight. The best medical aid that San Antonio could furnish at that time was secured, and they were slowly nursed back to health and strength. The room in which they lay while under medical treatment was just north of where the large dry goods establishment of L. Wolfson now is, on the north side of Main Plaza.

The men who went back to look for the unfortunate rangers did their duty, but of course did not find them. They went to the battleground and saw plenty of blood on the ground where Perry fell and where Ackland stood over him with the blood streaming from his face, and could trace their flight by the blood where Ackland ran with Perry to the river. They could not track quite as well as the Indians, for it is evident they trailed to the drift where Perry was concealed, but were baffled there by the skill of Ackland. The rangers could not start the trail from where the two wounded men were left, but found Perry's pistol.

James Dunn was censured by Captain Hays and others of the company, but he was a good ranger, and had no chance in this affair. He was looked upon as one of the most daring men Hays had. He was in the fight at Bandera Pass, in which he and Ackland were both wounded, and also in the big fight in Nueces Canyon, and there did well. Kit Ackland and Rufe Perry had more scars on them than any other men who followed Jack Hays in Texas or Mexico. Ackland died in California and Perry in West Texas in 1898. The latter had more than twenty scars on his body made by bullets and arrows.

LOUIS HALLER.

Came to Texas in 1845.

.Mr. Louis Haller, one of the pioneers of Castro's colony, and who still lives at Castroville, was born in France, in Upper Alsace, in 1831, and started to Texas in 1845. He came in an English ship called the Queen Victoria, commanded by Captain Randle. His father was a soldier under Napoleon and saw a great deal of hard service, following the fortunes of this famous Corsican over the bloody fields of Europe. The Victoria was three months making the trip from the old country to the shores of the new. Her captain lost his bearings and sailed around the shores of Scotland and Ireland, then to the West Indies, from there to Mexico, and then to New Orleans by way of Key West, Fla. The sailors on board the ship bet young Haller $25 that he could not climb to the top of a mast, but when he had accomplished this feat they would not pay the bet. From New Orleans he went to Port Lavaca. He saw Galveston as he passed, but did not land. One lady died on shipboard while crossing the ocean. She had six children, one of them being born on board the ship.

From Port Lavaca Mr. Haller came to Seguin by way of Victoria and Gonzales, arriving there in 1845. A Swiss by the name of Hipp kept a store in Seguin at that time, and Haller could understand his language, but could not speak or understand English. Mr. Hipp hired young Haller to clerk in the store for him. Of the settlers living at Seguin at that time, Mr. Haller can remember the Johnsons, Calverts, Kings, Sowells, and Nichols. On one occasion he went down on the river fishing near town with the Johnsons, and left them for a short time to look at some hooks which had been put out lower down the river, and was chased by a band of Lipan Indians. He had no gun to shoot with and they gave him a good scare, but he dodged them very adroitly and made his escape. These Indians at that time were at peace with the whites, and did not intend to kill him. Next day they came to Johnson's and told about running the boy, and said he was the smartest young white man they had ever seen; that when he ran away from them he left no trail by which they could find him. Haller had ran upon the rocks, jumping from one to the other, and leaving no trace of his flight. When out of sight he hid, and the Indians came very close to him. They told Johnson that they did not want to kill him, but wanted to make a servant of him for a squaw of their party. These same Indians tried to get guns from the white men to go and fight the Mexicans when the war broke out in 1846. But there were no guns to spare, and General Taylor thereby lost a few volunteers.

In 1846 Mr. Haller left Seguin and went up to New Braunfels, and from there by the way of San Antonio to Castroville. At this time there were a good many people there and not much work to do, so he went back to San Antonio and clerked in a store for Nat Lewis. In 1850 he came back to Castroville and settled. His people had bought stock and he came out to attend to them. He spent many years in the woods and on the prairies and lost much stock by Indian depredations, and altogether had quite a hard time. He says the Indians were very bad around San Antonio while he stayed there, and one morning killed a Mexican boy near the plaza. The Comanches did this, and when they began their retreat back to the mountains they were followed by the friendly Delawares, and a severe battle took place in which the latter were the victors, killing many of the Comanches and taking their horses. The rangers under Hays had gone to Mexico, hence this daring raid. While in San Antonio Mr. Haller wanted to join the rangers who were commanded by Capt. Jack Hays. The captain told him he was brave enough and could ride a horse fairly well, but was afraid that he could not shoot straight. Haller then took the captain's rifle and showed him how he could shoot, and was complimented on his marksmanship by the great ranger captain. Soon after this Hays carried his men to Mexico, and young Haller went scouting on the frontier after Indians. He was on one scout with Big Foot Wallace, but his horse gave out at D'Hanis and he had to come back. Wallace went on and had a fight with the Indians at the head of the Big Seco Creek, in the mountains. This was about the commencement of the civil war. Soon after the war the Indians killed Valentine Guerly on the Francisco Creek. Mr. Haller helped to bring in and bury the dead man. Guerly was armed and fought the Indians. He was shot all over and scalped. They first buried the body at Castroville, but afterwards it was taken up and reinterred on the Francisco. These same Indians ran three men who were in an ambulance. There was also a wagon along,. and a fight ensued in which one Indian was killed. The men in the ambulance left it and ran to the brush and made their fight there. The men were Joe Meyer, Jack Bendeler, and Joe Kruest. The latter had a bullet shot through his hat. He had taken the horses out of the vehicle and was trying to make his escape with them, riding one and leading the other, but the led horse pulled back and broke his rope. The Indians tried hard to get the loose one and ran him very close, yelling loudly and shooting at Joe; but the horse was so badly scared at the yelling that he ran close behind the one ridden by Kruest, and the Indians could not cut him off. They all got safely to the brush without losing a horse or man, and there beat the Indians off, killing one of their number.

Mr. Haller's uncle, Valentine Haller, was killed on Lime Creek, or Clay Creek as some call it. This was seven miles south from Castroville. The old man was alone when killed, and the people hunted for him a long time before his remains were found. His bones were brought to Castroville and buried. The grass in those days grew very rank all over the country, and if a man was killed while alone his body was hard to find. The bones of Mr. Haller were not discovered until the grass burned off. His remains were identified by some bits of clothing which had escaped the fire. It was evident that he was lost at the time he was killed. His hearing was also defective.

A boy named Frank Gephart was stolen, or captured rather, on the Francisco by Indians, and was never heard from again by his people. His stepfather, Joe Murry, was with him, but fought the Indians and made his escape.

Mr. Haller was an old friend of Rube Smith, and remembers well when the Indians killed him on the Hondo. He also knew F. G. Tinsley, was an old-time friend of his, and said he was a justice of the peace in the frontier days of Medina County. He remembers the time when the man above Castroville beat the brass kettle all night during an Indian alarm.

In 1867 Joseph Meuret and Frank Gephart, who lived near Castroville, went out to hunt oxen between Black Creek and Francisco, and while on a cattle trail saw four or five men driving horses and coming towards them. These men had on hats, and it was supposed by the two ox-hunters that they were settlers. Their mistake was not discovered until the two parties came near together, and the Indians, for such they were, commenced yelling and shooting and charging upon them. Frank Gephart, who was but a boy 12 years of age, began to cry, but his elder companion told him not to be afraid; that they had good horses and could outrun the Indians. They ran about a mile, and the man told the boy to keep in the trail, and he rode behind and whipped his horse. In this way they got within 300 yards of the Moore ranch, when another trail crossed theirs, which was washed out to a ditch. The boy's horse would not jump this, but turned and ran to one side, while the man was turned and shooting at the Indians, thinking at the time that the people at the ranch would hear his shots and come to their assistance. No one came, and by this time the Indians were among them and seized the boy's horse by the bridle. Others were shooting many arrows at the man, but by dexterous dodging and wheeling his horse was not hit, but many arrows were picked up there afterwards. The hard-pressed man now went to the Moore ranch, but no one was there, and he went back home and raised the alarm. A party followed the Indians but they were not overtaken, and the boy was never seen or heard of again.

JUDGE BERNHARD BRUCKS.

Came to Texas in 1845.

Judge Bernhard Brucks, the subject of this sketch, was born
in Westphalia, Prussia, in the town of Cossfield, in 1835. He
started to Texas with his father, John Bernhard Brucks, and his
mother, in 1845.

They came on the ship Albertina from Antwerp by way of the
English coast, and lay up for some time at Brookhaven, which he
says was a great place for fish. At Brookhaven they took on
more passengers, and had a long trip of sixty-two days to the
coast of Texas, landing at Galveston. Here they stayed two
weeks, and then took shipping for Port Lavaca. The ship was
very old and leaked badly, necessitating a continual working of
the pumps. While in this condition a furious Texas norther
came from the land and blew them off from their course. It was
impossible to cook anything on account of the pitching of the
ship, so when they came close to St. Joseph's Island the passengers wanted to land and cook something to eat, but the captain
objected to it, and there was a mutiny on board. The commander was taken prisoner and guarded on the ship by part of
the men with guns, while others landed in boats and cooked.
They stayed here one day and then got under way again, all being satisfied, after their hunger was appeased, to proceed on
their journey.

The next landing place was at Corpus Christi, where they
stayed two months. The time was in 1846, and their destination
was Castro's colony. General Taylor was there with his army,
and the war was just commencing with Mexico. Before leaving
this place the colonists had to send to San Antonio for Mexicans
and carts to transport their effects to their destination. The
carts were of the old primitive type, with huge wooden axles that
could be heard creaking a mile when moving. They had no oil
for the carts, hence the fearful noise they made. While en route
they split open prickly pears and greased (?) with that. While
at Corpus Christi Mr. Brucks saw his first Indians—300 Comanches whom General Taylor had sent for and wanted to enlist

them to fight the Mexicans. This the Indians refused to do, and
went back to their hunting grounds. At that time they pretended to be at peace with the whites, but were ever treacherous,
as their name implies, which means "Snake-in-the-grass." The
immigrants had a hard trip to San Antonio. It rained a great
deal, and all the streams were overflowed. One cart was washed
away while crossing the Nueces River. It was recovered, but the
goods it contained were badly damaged. They had plenty of deer
meat and turkey on the trip, but had no bread, using boiled rice
instead.

When they arrived in San Antonio the Mexicans would go no
further, and ox teams had to be hired to carry themselves and
effects on to Castroville. The Brucks family stayed there one
month, and then went out with a party to settle Quihi, still further west, but on Castro's grant and under his jurisdiction. This
was on March 4, 1846. The town had already been laid off, and
ten families were the first installment. While at Castroville Mr.
Brucks saw Capt. Jack Hays and his company of rangers. They
were stationed for awhile on the Medina River above Castroville.

The people who settled at Quihi, on the creek of the same
name, had town lots in addition to their other land, and on these
they soon erected temporary shelters. The hostile Indians soon
found out this new settlement, and two families were killed by
them in one week after the settlement was begun. Mr. Brucks
heard the Indians howling in the night, and some heard the guns
when they were killing the families a mile away. A man named
Koch came to Quihi and told the news. The Indians took two
boys captive, and great confusion prevailed among the people
during the night. Mr. Brucks was a boy at the time, but can
distinctly remember hearing one of the captive boys crying and
calling for his father as the Indians passed near the Brucks tent,
but all at once he ceased his lamentations and they heard him
no more. The Indians had killed him.

The elder Brucks had brought a church bell from Europe, and
it was at this time hanging on the limb of a tree near his tent.
Here the men rallied to fight the Indians, and one man was appointed to ring the bell all the time. The bellringer became
badly frightened, and would ring a few jerks and then run to the
tall grass and lie down a few moments, and then run back and
ring the bell again, and then back to the grass, and so on.

Next morning the boy whose cries were heard the night before calling for his father, while in the hands of the savages, was found dead one-half mile from the Brucks tent. He had been killed by a lance thrust. The other boy, who did not cry, was carried on and was not killed. He stayed with the Indians six months and was then sold to a trader, who carried him to San Antonio, and he was sent from there home to Quihi. His people were all killed the night he was taken except his old grandfather, and he was badly wounded and died soon after. The boy could not or would not talk much in his own language when he came back, and being very young, could give no detailed account of his captivity. At first he said the Indians tied him behind an Indian on a horse that had long ears (mule), and also stripped and painted him. The boy did not like to have the paint on him, and the first opportunity that offered washed it off. The Indians whipped him for this, and then painted him again. This happened after they arrived at their far away retreat in the mountains. The squaws would take him out of camp, tie a rope loosely around his body, fill it full of wood, and make him carry it to camp. He said the Indians while traveling ate all of their meat raw, but when they stayed in camp they cooked it. They had plenty of deer meat and honey. The boy did not know where the camp was, but said it was a long distance towards the northwest. One morning the Indians tied their captive to a tree, and then all left camp. In the evening they came back and a white man was with them, who bought the boy and untied him from the tree, and then carried him to San Antonio. The name of this boy and the one killed was Brinkhoff.

On one occasion a boy named Henry Snyder, 12 years of age, who was herding cows one mile from his father's tent, was captured by Indians, carried off, and never heard from again. The cows were herded to keep them out of the crops, for as yet no fences had been made.

After the Indian raid in which the Brinkhoff families were killed the people all collected together and built a brush fort on the bank of the big waterhole in Quihi Creek. It was simply a high brush fence in a half circle, the deep, wide pool of water making the other side secure from attack. Inside of this rude fortress the people would sleep at night.

11

Mr. Brucks was at one time badly scared by friendly Indians when a boy and out after the cows. He was riding a mule, and had all of the cows in the trail ahead of him on the way home. Finally he took a fancy to walk, and let the mule follow the cows in front of him. During this time he heard the sound of an ax in the brush and scrubby timber near by, and at once left the trail to see who it was chopping out there so far from town. What was his surprise and terror, when he arrived at the spot from which the sound of the the ax proceeded, to walk directly into a camp of Indians. He was so close to them he was afraid to run, and stood and looked at them until an Indian came and took him by the arm and began to talk and motion all round in a circle with his other hand. Young Brucks could not understand what he said, and stood there in mortal terror. The Indians had plenty of deer meat, skins, and honey, and gave the boy some meat. Their honey was put up in deer skins. The old Indian chief took a piece of meat himself, and dipping it in the honey would put that end in his mouth and cut the piece off close to his lips. The boy thought he was a prisoner and had to follow suit, so he dipped his meat in the honey and ate like the Indian did. The chief then took Brucks out into the opening and showed him the way home, thinking he was lost. Young Brucks now made lively tracks and caught up with his mule, who seemed to be in no hurry, and was slowly making his way along the trail. Mounting now in hot haste, Brucks made his slow steed wake up, and as he expressed it, "made him git for home." These Indians were Lipans, and had a permit to hunt and carry skins to San Antonio.

The Indians all finally became hostile, and were so bad that the elder Brucks carried his family to San Antonio and boarded with an Italian named Locomer, who had once been a pirate under the famous Jean Lafitte. The Texas rangers were also quartered at this place, and one day in sport brought an Indian chief with them to dinner. They called the chief "Old Santa Anna," and had a good deal of sport with him, as he was very drunk. The landlord, as was his daily custom, was also drunk. The red chief was very awkward at dinner, and the rangers could not make him eat with knife and fork, but persisted in putting the meat and other edibles in his mouth with his fingers. Old Locomer did not like this, and hit the Indian over the head with a pistol, knocking him down. "Old Santa Anna," as the boys called him, was very mad at this treatment and went away, but soon came back with his bow and arrows and a big knife, and said he had come back to kill the white man that hit him. Locomer stood behind a half-open door, and as the Indian came in he grabbed him and held him against the wall, and took his bow and arrows and knife away from him. This Indian was one of the Lipans who came to San Antonio to sell skins under the treaty stipulation.

San Antonio at that time had no houses with a board or shingle roof. One house, called the "Plaza house," was being built by Mrs. Elliott and covered with shingles, but it was not finished. Mr. Brucks knew John Glanton, the famous gambler, and saw him cut a Mexican to pieces one day for spilling water on him. The Mexican, although badly hurt, got well.

After Mr. Brucks moved back to Quihi the Indians were still hostile, and he had many narrow escapes. On one occasion while out hunting on foot, three miles from home, he shot a deer, and when it fell his dog ran up and caught hold of it, but it got up and ran away, followed by the dog. This dog would never bark on a trail or when he caught anything, so Mr. Brucks ran through a thicket to see which way they went, as it was open beyond in the direction they were headed the last he saw of them. Before getting to the opening himself, however, he saw an Indian standing in the bushes watching the dog catch the deer. Brucks now secreted himself without being seen by his dusky foe, and reloaded his gun. Not knowing how many more might be near, he slipped away into a larger thicket and lay down and listened, intending to fight them there if they came upon him. While lying here he happened to think that his dog would trail him, and by following the dog the Indians would come upon his hiding place, so he crawled out and made tracks for home. About a mile from home the dog overtook him and was very bloody. At first Mr. Brucks thought the Indians had wounded him, but it proved to be the blood of the wounded deer which the dog had caught. The alarm of Indians was raised when Mr. Brucks arrived at the settlement, and a crowd of men went back to investigate. Only a portion of the deer could be found. The red hunter had taken the balance, but he could not be found. It was now evident that only one Indian was there, and if Mr. Brucks had known this he could easily have killed him.

In 1849 the elder Brucks died of cholera, during the prevalence of the great epidemic of that year. He had a hay contract with the government, and had established his camp between the Medio and Leon creeks. The contract was finished, and Mr. Brucks went to San Antonio to get his money and buy some goods. All this was accomplished and he started home, but had caught the dread plague and died on the road at Medio Creek. Another man with him, named Leinweber, also died. At this time young Bernard Brucks was county commissioner at Castroville, and had the cholera himself. Many people died.

In 1861 Mr. Brucks joined a company of rangers commanded by Capt. James Paul, and was stationed at Camp Verde. On one scout they got seventy-five head of horses from the Indians which these red thieves had stolen and driven off from the settlers. On another occasion Captain Paul lost his spectacles while on an Indian chase, and when it was over had the whole company looking for the lost glasses. A cedar limb had jerked them off, but a whole company of Texas rangers failed to find them. The famous Indian fighter and slayer of the "Big Foot" Indian, Ed Westfall, was their guide and trailer. Judge Brucks says that Westfall would follow Indians until his horse gave out, and then would abandon him and continue the pursuit on foot. In one camp they found seventy-five head of horses, but no Indians were around. They were off in the D'Hanis settlement stealing more horses. One shield was hanging on a limb in camp. These Indians were pursued from D'Hanis and the horses recovered which were stolen from that place.

In 1880 Mr. Brucks was appointed county judge of Medina County, and was then regularly elected to that office for fourteen years. He now lives at Dunlay, on the Southern Pacific road, and is strong and hearty.

Capt. James Paul was a lawyer and private secretary of Henry Castro. He lived to be quite old, and died at Castroville in 1897.

INCIDENT IN THE LIFE OF COL. J. C. CARR.

Came to Texas in 1845.

Around the old town of D'Hanis, situated two miles east of the Seco Creek, in Medina County, and on the line of the Southern Pacific railroad, cluster many historic incidents of the long ago, when these valleys and prairies were covered with rank grass, and herds of deer and antelope and wild horses called mustangs roamed over them instead of the domestic animals of civilization, as now.

At the time of which we write, a struggling little colony of German immigrants brought here from the old country by Henry Castro were fighting for existence and trying, it seemed almost in vain, to sustain themselves from incursions of hostile Indians and all the ills of an isolated frontier life, cut off as it were from the outside world. By pluck and perseverance, however, they weathered the storm, and now their children,—for there are very few of the old ones left,—enjoy the fruits of their labor and hardships in the possession of nice residences and beautiful and well laid out farms and ranches. Only a few of the low grass-covered huts remain to mark the footsteps of the pioneers.

In 1859, although the country had undergone a change and times were more prosperous, and a good deal of the hardships of frontier life had been overcome in the twelve years' existence of the colony, still it was the frontier, and Indians raided constantly upon them, killing the settlers, carrying some into captivity, and driving off many head of stock, especially mules and horses, to their strongholds in the mountains or on the "Staked Plains."

At the time of which we write (1859), Capt. Joe Ney, Sr., one of the first settlers, was still alive, and kept a hotel, store, and stage stand at old D'Hanis. In the fall of the above year the Indians made a raid on the town at night and succeeded in getting the stage horses and other stock which were in the corral, to the number of nearly thirty head. To illustrate with what sly and stealthy movements an Indian can work and not be detected, we will say that the inclosure from which the stock was taken adjoined the storehouse and hotel, and no one was disturbed or the presence of the Indians detected until the morning came and disclosed the fact that the corral was empty.

On the night of this daring raid there was a lone man camping on the Seco Creek, near D'Hanis, named James C. Carr, now known throughout the State as Colonel Carr, or "Locomotive," the noted depredation claim agent of the Alamo City. Early on the morning after the raid Colonel Carr, or "Buckskin" as he was then called by the settlers, on account of a suit he wore made out of that material, went to D'Hanis and there found Capt. Joe Ney, "Seco" Smith, Riley, and other citizens of D'Hanis preparing to go in pursuit of the red marauders. "Buckskin" was never too busy or in too great a hurry not to waive all other considerations and go in pursuit of Indians when they raided in the vicinity where he was, so he at once joined Captain Ney and set out after the hostiles. The trail led in a northwest direction to a point on the head waters and mountain creeks of the Medina and Guadalupe rivers. Here the trail suddenly turned towards the southeast, going in the direction of the little frontier town of Bandera, situated on the Medina River. These experienced frontiersmen from D'Hanis soon perceived, from the signs and general direction traveled, that the horses were now in the hands of white men, who were evidently making for Bandera. This surmise was correct, for when Ney and his party arrived at Bandera they found all of the horses in possession of a scout who had just arrived in town a little ahead of them. Captain Sauer and other citizens of the town and vicinity had struck a trail of Indians who had been raiding in their settlement, but abandoned it and were returning home when they struck this band of Indians who had raided D'Hanis, and gave them battle. The Indians failed to make much of a fight, and soon abandoned the horses and fled into a cedar brake. While considerable shooting was indulged in by Captain Saner and his men, it was not known if an Indian was killed or wounded, on account of the thick brush and rocks where the skirmish took place. The horses were all collected and driven to Bandera. This fight took place at the point where Ney's men noticed the acute turn the trail assumed, and at once surmised that here the Indians had met with white men and been defeated and the horses recaptured. Captain Saner said his men were tired, thirsty, and hungry when they met the Indians, and after routing them and rounding up

JAMES C. CARR (BUCKSKIN).
One of Capt. Joe Ney's scouts in the early 50's.

the horses, not only those which were taken from Medina County, but as many more which had been stolen elsewhere, came at once back home.

Captain Ney and party having cut out their horses, left Bandera in the evening, coursing their way without a road across the mountains in the direction of D'Hanis.

Late in the evening Colonel Carr, or "Buckskin," sighting a fine herd of deer, stopped behind to get a shot. The game was shy on account of the open country, and he had some trouble to get in good range. Finally, however, between sundown and dark, Carr took a shot at a fine buck. At the crack of the gun the stricken deer, which was standing about 100 yards away, came bounding towards him, and almost fell at his feet. His horse, which was being held by the bridle, took fright, jerked loose, bounded away, and was soon out of sight in the gloaming. The horse went in the direction Ney and party were going. "Buckskin" could have trailed his horse and followed the right course had daylight lasted, but night coming on this was impossible. He stood over the deer a few moments, loath to leave it, but as nothing could be done with it said to himself, "Good meat, adios." It was impossible to follow the trail, and it grew darker and darker. No direct course could be followed, and "Buckskin" soon realized that he was lost, and would have to spend the night alone in the trackless woods.

Captain Ney and his party camped a little after dark, and the horse ridden by Carr, true to the instinct of his animal nature, followed true on their trail and soon arrived in camp with saddle and bridle, but minus his rider. It was at once believed by all that J. C. Carr was killed by Indians, and falling from his horse, the animal had escaped. Thinking that a band of Indians was in their vicinty, like all prudent frontiersmen they built no fires or gave any signal to the missing man. Guided by a few dim stars, "Buckskin" wandered nearly all night in a vain endeavor to get the right course for the settlement at D'Hanis. At last, seeing all his efforts were futile, he lay down to rest but not to sleep. At daylight he ascended a mountain peak and got his course for D'Hanis, which was about ten miles distant. This was on Sunday morning. Captain Ney and his party had also made a daylight move and reached town early in the morning, ate breakfast, and then raised a large crowd for the purpose of hunting for the body of Carr, thinking they would find his mutilated remains and likely have to fight a band of Indians. Before they started,· however, they sighted a lone pedestrian in the distance, coming straight to town. By his garb they soon recognized him, and a wild shout went up as many galloped to meet him. They dismounted, took him on their shoulders, and came shooting and yelling back to town. He was carried to the hotel of Captain Ney, where was spent one Sunday never to be forgotten by those who were at that time citizens of the old town of D'Hanis. So much for this raid, fight, and loss of but one (buckskin) man. Col. Locomotive Carr came to Texas in 1845 from his native State, Tennessee, and has resided in the Rio Grande border counties ever since 1857.

JOHN L. MANN.

Came to Texas in 1846.

John L. Mann, the subject of this sketch, and one of Castro's colonists, was born in Upper Alsace. Mr. Mann, in company with the Habys, started to Texas in October, 1846, on the ship Duc de Braband, and made the trip in forty-eight days, which was considered fast time in those days. Other ships which started two weeks before the Duc de Braband were beaten two weeks in making the passage. In December the ship landed at Galveston. The immigrants went from there to Port Lavaca, arriving at the latter place on Christmas day. There were 200 passengers aboard, about one-half from Alsace and the others from Wittenburg. They did not celebrate Christmas, but spent the day unloading the ship. Mr. Mann had no relatives on the vessel, his parents having remained in Europe. Old man Joseph Haby helped to pay his passage from the old country to Texas, and he says was like a father to him. His father was taken sick in Germany the day he landed in Port Lavaca, and died on New Year's day. In 1851 his mother and brothers and sisters came to Texas and lived in the Haby settlement. Mrs. Mann, the aged mother of John L., lived to be 85 years old, dying in 1892. When Mr. Mann and the Habys arrived at Port Lavaca with other immigrants they had no way of coming to Castro's colony, and Nichalus Haby bought a horse and rode all the way to Castro's colony, a distance of nearly 300 miles, to procure wagons and teams, and then went back after his people and some others. The Habys had brought two wagons on the ship from Europe, and Nichalus procured oxen at Castroville to work to these wagons and drove them all the way to Port Lavaca for this purpose, and also carried one more wagon and team, and with these they came on out to the colony, arriving there on the 2d day of February, 1847. Mr. Mann's father told him when he went to sail for America to stay with the Habys, but 1847 was a very dry year, and the Habys not having much work to do, John left and went to San Antonio and there obtained work on the Alamo. After the Mexican war was over the people in San Antonio heard that Col. Jack

Hays was coming with his regiment of Texas rangers, who had so distinguished themselves in various battles in Mexico, and great preparations were made to receive him and his men, who were going to enter San Antonio from the east, coming by way of Seguin. When the news was spread through the town that the rangers were in sight, Mr. Mann and many others ascended to the top of the Alamo to see them pass through the Alamo Plaza. Thousands of people were present, and as the sunburned, warworn veterans entered the town cheer on cheer rent the air. A regular salute of twenty-one guns was to have been fired, but the cannon which they had ready for the occasion got out of order after a few shots, and this part of the program had to stop. Colonel Hays and his men marched on through the Alamo Square, crossed the river at the bridge, and passed up Main Street to the square in the central part of the city, followed by the shouting, cheering multitude all the way.

After night another cannon was procured, and Mr. Mann hitched two horses to it and proceeded to Main Plaza, followed by the men, who were going to try again to fire the salute to Colonel Hays and his men. Arriving in the center of the plaza, Mr. Mann unhitched the team and carried them away so that they would not be frightened when the big gun was fired. This time the salute was a success; boom after boom made the old town echo and re-echo again and again.

In 1849 Mr. Mann was employed by the government and sent to Port Lavaca after wagons. The government already had mules and oxen down there. Before arriving at the port, news was circulated that the cholera was there. Mr. Mann, however, did not believe this report, and proceeded on into town and found out that it was not true. When on the way back to San Antonio a rumor came that cholera was in that place, but this was also looked upon as a fake. While in camp, however, on the Salado Creek, four miles from the city, the report was confirmed. The dread epidemic was indeed there. Mr. Mann had started with a mule team, but had exchanged with another driver on the road for one of oxen, and as grass was good and water plenty, he remained here in camp until the dread disease had run its course. Many people died, and when he entered San Antonio he missed many faces of friends who had succumbed to the epidemic.

The wagons were now loaded with supplies for the post at El

Paso, which was under command of Maj. Martin Van Horn. A guard of soldiers went with the supplies, and also a party of engineers to work on the road, which was almost impassable in places, and which caused delays of many weeks. Two weeks were spent at Devil's River cutting down the bank before the wagons could go down into the channel. The mail at this time from San Antonio to El Paso was carried by Big Foot Wallace. He had guards with him, one of whom was Mr. C. Pingenot, who now lives at Kline, in Uvalde County.

On the way back from El Paso, and when about half way to the Pecos River, they met Howard's private train loaded with goods which were to be transferred to the government train and carried on. Mr. Mann's wagon was loaded with part of these goods and he went back to El Paso. The wagons were then sent up to Santa Fe and the teamsters discharged, but Mr. Mann got employment two months at the post. In May he came down on a pony in company with five teamsters who were driving government wagons to San Antonio. In June he was employed by Dr. Lyons of San Antonio to drive a wagon in his train up to El Paso. Mr. Nat Lewis of San Antonio also went up with a train about the same time, composed of wagons and carts. Mr. Mann knew all points well in regard to water, and was guide or general adviser in regard to travel and camps. The train arrived at El Paso all right, and started back on the return trip, arriving at "Dead Man's Pass" with five wagons and thirteen men. This is believed by a great many people to be an unlucky number. Eight other discharged men on horseback had been with the wagons, but had left them and went on, seven mounted and one on foot. At the pass the teamsters found one horse of this party which had given out, so this left two of them afoot. Three other wagons were behind, but had not arrived in sight yet. There was a long stretch of road ahead in view, and Mr. Mann saw some one on a hill in the road walking, and thought it was some of the party mentioned before. This person, however, was an Indian who had gone on the hill in the road to see how far the party of horsemen were ahead, for here the Indians had laid a trap to capture the train. Part of the Indians at this time were hid from view by the thick, tall bear grass on one side of the road, and the balance were behind a hill out of sight of the road on the opposite side, and mounted on their horses. The men in the

party of teamsters who were now about to experience one of those
fearful frontier tragedies so often enacted were John L. Mann,
Ben Sanford, Emory Givins, John Crowder, ———— McDonald,
Charley Hill, Jerry Priest, ———— Brown, Charles Blawinsky
(Polander), Nick Andres, and others whose names can not now
be recalled, among whom was a blacksmith.

John Mann's wagon was in the lead, and walking ahead of
him in the road about thirty steps was Jerry Priest and the
blacksmith. The latter had lost his mind while on this trip, and
at this time was perfectly crazy, but harmless. The wagons were
now inside of the ambuscade, and the Indians began to show
themselves on both sides of the road. Priest stopped and began
to look to the right and left, and Mann said to him, "What is
the matter there?" "Indians," said Priest, and at once ran back
to the wagons. The poor demented blacksmith made no attempt
to run, and was killed in his tracks by the first fire from the
Comanches.

The Indians kept firing, and soon killed the near wheel steer
in Mann's team, and also shot many arrows at him in a few moments. Thinking that his gun was in the rear end of the wagon,
he jumped out and ran back there and felt where he always kept
it, but it was gone, so he and Priest ran back to the next wagon.
Some confusion now ensued, but most of the men left their teams
and ran together, and the long, desperate battle commenced. The
man Brown was an old Indian fighter and took things very coolly,
standing near a wagon wheel and putting in his shots as fast as
he could load his rifle and take aim. The balance of the men
who had guns were doing the best they could against such odds.
The Indians would make close, daring runs, yelling loudly, and
on one of these occasions Brown killed one, and he fell from his
horse and lay on the ground within thirty yards.

The Indians were shooting both bullets and arrows, which
were almost continually striking the wagons, especially the one
at which the men had concentrated. A ball finally struck Brown,
and he fell. Some of the men who were inside of the wagon and
shooting from there saw Brown when he was hit, and knew from
the way he fell that he was killed. The Polander had stood by
Brown on the outside and was still fighting, but at length he was
hit and fell mortally wounded.

The situation now looked desperate, indeed; three of the men already killed and the Indians still numerous and exultant. Some of the men now proposed they make a sally from the wagon and bring the bodies of Brown and the Polander in; the latter they knew was not dead. This was at once and quickly done. Brown was dead, and his unfortunate comrade was writhing in agony. Nick Andres, who had been outside fighting near his own wagon, now got in the wagon with his gun and aimed it over the wagon-bed to shoot while the Indians were making a charge and were very close, but a ball struck him in the throat before he could pull his trigger, and he fell back and died in a few moments. It seemed now that there was no chance for the beleaguered men. One of their party lay dead in the road thirty steps away, two lay dead in the wagons, and another dying. An old man whose name is not now remembered, and who was in the wagon with Andres but had no gun, took the dead man's gun, jumped out of the wagon, and came to the other men during a charge by the Indians, and was wounded in the knee by a bullet. Besides him, Crowder and Givins were both wounded in the arm.

There were some squaws in the fight, and they used bows and shot arrows into the wagon time and again, sticking them into the wagon sheet and wagon bed. During the hottest part of the fight, when so many men were being killed and wounded, McDonald said he was wounded, but an examination of his person failed to find a scratch. The Indians captured the wagon in which the dead body of Andres lay, and carried it off and scalped the unfortunate man. Mr. Mann's wagon was also ransacked and a lot of beef taken out; also his gun, which he failed to get in his hurried search when the fight first commenced. It was a fine rifle, and cost $25. Mr. Mann had no gun during all this trying time, except as a comrade was shot and could no longer continue the fight. He made many narrow escapes from the balls which were constantly hitting the wagon. One rifle ball passed through his hair, but did not break the skin on his head. Mr. Mann had shot a beef with his gun the day before and had not loaded it, thinking he would do that when he got to camp, so the Indians had no chance to shoot his gun on account of their powder being too coarse. They loaded, however, and tried time and again that night to shoot it.

The fight commenced as the sun was setting, and the Indians stayed around and shot at the wagons at intervals until 2 o'clock in the morning. The brave Polander lived on through most of the night, but finally succumbed to the terrible wound which he had received. During the night Mr. Mann cut a hole through the wagon sheet, so he could tell something about the Indians and shoot when occasion offered. During these times he could hear the Indians popping caps on his gun, trying to fire it at the wagon, but could not do so on account of the coarse powder, which would not go down into the small tube of the rifle. Late in the night the Indians quit firing, and only occasionally shot arrows. Mr. Mann said to the men, "The Indians are out of ammunition for the guns and will soon quit and go off, and we will be saved."

Soon after this the Indians went into camp about 400 yards off, and building fires proceeded to cook and eat the beef which they had taken from Mann's wagon. It was a long and grewsome night the survivors of this fearful fight spent in the wagons among the dead men and hundreds of savages camped near, whose fires they could plainly see. When daylight came, however, not an Indian was in sight. The dead one who had lain near the wagon at dark was gone. Many other Indians were seen to fall during the fight, but had all been carried away during the night. Not seeing any Indians in sight, Charley Hill got out of the wagon, and taking his gun ascended a small hill near by to take a look. This was the hill behind which most of the Indians were concealed the evening before. As soon as Charley arrived at the crest of the ridge he saw some mounted Indians coming towards him, and at once ran back pursued by them, shouting as he came, "The Indians are coming again, boys!" He was fired at before reaching the wagons, and one ball just barely missed him.

Four of the Indians went up the road in the direction the wagons came from, and the others went back out of gunshot. Mr. Mann now left the wagon and went and turned his ox loose, which had stood there all night yoked to the dead one. The Indians had taken off the balance of the teams from the other wagons, and Mann said they could have this one, too. The ox commenced eating grass, like that was all he was thinking about during the night. As soon as he fed out of gunshot of the wagons the Indians got him. Some of the oxen had been turned loose from the wagons in which the men were fighting to prevent them from moving them, and all were taken by the Indians.

Besides the three wagons that were behind there was also a train of Mexican carts, and about 9 o'clock seven mounted Mexicans made their appearance, riding ahead of the carts. The Americans thought they were another band of Indians and almost gave up hope, but at once made preparations to fight another battle. They were greatly relieved and encouraged when the horsemen came up to them. They now explained the situation to the Mexicans, and they sent a runner back to hurry up the carts. The Indians had seen the Mexican train coming and had left. The Mexicans were not aware of this, and made ready to help the Americans to fight them. The white men during the night had brought two of the wagons up and had stopped them one on each side of the one they were fighting from, which afforded great protection and no doubt saved the lives of some of the men, as many balls and arrows struck these empty wagons. The Indians had got two, and carried them off a distance. The Mexicans moved the wagons around in a triangle and piled up rocks between the spokes, fixing for a regular seige. Jim Fisk was in charge of the Mexican train, and when he came sent a Mexican after the soldiers at Beaver Lake, but he met them coming this way and they got to the scene of the battle a little after dark. Next day the soldiers took the trail of the Indians, but never caught up with them. The teamsters were very much in hope they could get their own oxen back, and blamed the soldiers for not following faster and further.

The dead men were buried on the spot where the battle was fought. Brown and the blacksmith were both shot through the heart, and the Polander was hit lower down. Andres, as before stated, was struck in the throat. Dr. Lyons was behind with some other carts, and when he came up gave Mann a fine red blanket, as he was in his shirt sleeves and had nothing to sleep on. The Indians had pillaged his wagon and taken everything he had. The doctor took this blanket from around his own shoulders and gave it to Mann. When the other three wagons came up one man had a small one, and this was taken to pieces and placed in Mann's wagon and the team hitched to the latter, and his wagon carried along in that way. The balance of the wagons were left until Nat Lewis could send for them. Mr. Mann gave the teamster $25 to bring his wagon in the way described to Fort Inge, on the Leona, just below the present town of Uvalde, in Uvalde County. Mr. Mann tried to get pay from the government for the loss of his team, but failed.

He now went back to Haby's and made a crop, and selling his corn, bought another team and commenced freighting and made plenty of money. In 1853 he married Miss Magdalena Burrell and stayed one more year with the Habys, and then moved to where he lives now, on the Medina, above Castroville, and built a log house. He has a good residence now and a fine farm, and has plenty, although he has lost a great deal of stock from Indian depredations. He was with Mr. Charobiny the day his house was robbed and Mrs. Charobiny carried away captive. He says when they arrived at the house the yard was covered with feathers where the Indians had ripped the bedticks and scattered them and took the cloth along.

The writer received a hearty welcome at the house of Mr. Mann, and was entertained in the old-time frontier hospitality. May he live long to enjoy the fruits of his labors, and rest in peace at last.

12

ROBERT WATSON.

Came to Texas in 1846.

The subject of this sketch was born in Habersham County, Georgia, on the 23d of January, 1821. When 17 years of age he enlisted in the army under General Jesup to fight the Seminole Indians. They had made a break from the swamps of Florida and ravaged the lower part of Georgia. As soon as an organized force went against them they retreated back into the swamps and everglades of Florida, and thence the army followed them. In the Walklesassy swamp a hard battle was fought and an Indian town burnt. Mr. Watson was wounded in the left shoulder by a ball during the battle, and Sergeant Jennings of his company was killed. The ball struck him in the head, cutting his hat band. A negro man was captured who was with the Indians, and the soldiers sent him to the widow Jennings of Georgia as a gift. Seventy-five Indians were killed and wounded. Mr. Watson was in many skirmishes during the balance of the campaign.

He came to Texas in 1846 and first settled in eastern Texas, but moved from there to Llano County. He soon after joined Capt. John Williams' company of minute men for frontier protection. Dave Cowan was first lieutenant and his brother Gid was second. While this company was in service the Indians made a raid on the San Saba and killed a man named Jackson, his wife, and one daughter, and carried off two of the children— a girl and a boy—captives. The minute men got on the trail and followed it to near the Wichita Mountains, where they met the two little captives coming on the back track. They said the Indians left them in camp and ran off after some game which came near camp, and they left also and were trying to get back home. The party turned back here and carried the children home. They were entirely naked when discovered. Another band of Indians was also followed, supposed to be the same ones, and overtaken at the head of the Llano. In the fight which ensued the chief and his squaw were killed.

On one occasion, while Mr. Watson was in his field at work,

he was cut off from the house by a band of Indians. His only weapon was a sixshooter, but with it he stood them off until his son could come to his assistance with a Henry rifle, and a lively fight then took place. Several neighbors had penned cattle at his home the previous night, and were still there, and some of them came and helped him in the battle. These were Charley Roberts, Bud (his son), and William Higgins. Charley Roberts had his horse killed, and one of the Indians had his killed near the corner of the fence. William Higgins killed one Indian, and several were hit by Mr. Watson.

About the year 1873 a noted Indian fight took place at the Pack Saddle Mountain. Mr. Watson was not in the fight, but was near by and knew the men who participated in it. The Pack Saddle Mountain in Llano County derived its name from the peculiar shape it assumed at a distance, and which resembled a pack saddle. During a raid by Indians eighteen of them camped in the gap of the mountains and remained there to cook some meat of beef cattle they had killed. Five cow-hunters discovered them, and at once set about to give them battle. They were Robert Brown, Stephen Moss, William Moss, Eli Lloyd, and one whose name is not now remembered. The men were fearless, advanced boldly into the gap, and at once charged them. William Moss was in the lead when they ran in among the Indians, and was soon shot through with a bullet and was supposed to be mortally wounded. He moved back and dismounted from his horse, but the other men stayed with him and continued the battle. The Indians would charge them and fire, but always retired from the fire of the white men. This lasted for some time, until Lloyd and the man whose name is not known were both wounded with bullets. Only two men were now unhurt, but they were not dismayed and still held their position, the wounded men who were able assisting by loading guns or pistols. The Indians were badly hurt, too, and several of their braves lay dead on the mountain and others were sorely wounded. They finally gave up the fight and left the mountain, and the settlers made their way back home, carrying Moss, who was badly hurt. The ball had struck him in front and lodged in his back. A doctor named Smith cut it out, and he finally recovered after a close pull, as did also the other two wounded men.

Mr. Watson was in one fight at the head of the Little Llano

in which two Indians were killed. Captain Williams was in command. He was afterwards killed by Indians in Baby Head Gap, between Cherokee Creek and the Llano. He was on his way to Austin with a drove of cattle, and was cut off here and killed. One of his men also suffered the same fate. Before any settlements were made in Kimble County, where Junction City is now, Mr. Watson moved and settled just above the present town at a place called "The Boggs." On one occasion while here he was out bear hunting on the north prong in the rocks and cedar brakes, and suddenly came upon a camp of three Indians. They were camp-keepers for a larger party, and were engaged in making arrows. At the sight of the white man they sprang to their feet and ran before Mr. Watson could bring his rifle down on them. In a few jumps they were out of sight. Watson did not inspect the camp, but at once retraced his steps and soon after, in a few days at least, went to the nearest settlers and returned with reinforcements. The Indians had not returned, and the camp was as he had left it. In the camp were found three shields, three bridles, three lariats, a soldier's saber, cap, and cape, and also his scalp. There was also one woman's scalp. Her hair was long and black, while that of the soldier was short and light. There was the picture of a white boy painted in the center of one of the shields, with red garters on. On the head was fastened a bunch of hair taken from the scalp of the soldier. The writer remembers hearing Coon Taylor tell about finding the remains of a soldier in a cave on the North Llano while out there with a hunting party. This might have been the man. His comrades may have found his remains and placed them in the cave, as many such incidents happened during the frontier days. Not long after this incident Mr. Watson moved back to the settlements on account of the Indians. He now lives at Utopia, Sabinal Canyon, Uvalde County.

HERBERT WEYNAND.

Came to Texas in 1846.

The subject of this sketch was born in Bigenbach, Prussia, sixteen miles from the Belgian line, in 1822. In 1846, and also prior to that time, many immigrants from Alsace and other points near the Belgian frontier were coming to America and settling on the frontier of Texas, being led hither by Henry Castro.

In March, 1846, Mr. Weynand, in company with about 200 other colonists, started for the promised land, where they were told they could build up happy homes and have all the land they wanted. The colonists were delayed six weeks at Antwerp, and then set sail on the American ship Bangor. They were seventy-two days crossing the ocean. A boy was born on board the ship during the time, and was named after the ship. One of the party, Jacob Gold, was taken very sick and was left on the coast of the Belgian channel. A purse was made up for him to pay expenses during his sickness. He recovered and came on to the colony, and lived to be an old man and a veteran of the Mexican war, and died below San Antonio. The ship Bangor landed at Port Lavaca, on the coast of Texas, and the colonists scattered. Some came on west to the colonies, while others obtained work along the coast country. The mosquitoes were very numerous, and the travel-worn people presented a forlorn aspect as they stood grouped around the fires in the smoke, with blankets around them, when they were first put ashore.

Mr. Weynand obtained work from the government at $1 per day. Being a young man and without family, he did very well. On the first morning he presented himself for work after being employed the man in charge asked him if he had eaten breakfast. Not understanding the language well, at a venture he said no. He was then directed to the eating quarters, and was told to tell the cook to give him breakfast. Thinking this was something he had to bring to his employer, he delivered the message in the best English he could command. He was greatly surprised when he was told to sit down and eat. Not wishing to cause any more

confusion he did so, although it had not been many minutes since
he had eaten a hearty meal.

When his time was out he hired a man to bring his effects to
Castroville, then recently settled by colonists, twenty-five miles
west from San Antonio. The price charged for his freight by ox
team was $3 per hundred pounds. He worked here all winter
for a Frenchman, and in the following spring attempted to make
a crop, but failed, and was finally taken down sick. The people
gave him medicine made from some kind of leaves, and he recovered in fourteen days. Mr. Weynand now went below San
Antonio and hired to a man named Thomas to cut hay. This
work lasted forty-one days.

On the 3d day of March, 1847, Mr. Weynand and a man
named Rutinger arrived at D'Hanis, another colony still west of
Castroville, on Seco Creek. They worked one month clearing
off town lots, and then entered into a contract with a man to
make a crop on shares. They had no plows or team, and had to
plant corn with a hoe. The man Rutinger was still living in
1898, and was the oldest man in Medina County, being 92 years
of age. On one occasion seventy-three Comanche Indians rode
into town. They did not attempt to molest anyone, but took Mr.
Rutinger's horse and anything else they took a fancy to. At this
time the colonists only had meat and water to subsist upon. One
of the Indians came and sat down beside Mr. Weynand, and said
he was a Mexican, on account of the big wide hat he wore. The
Comanches were then at war with the Mexicans.

Not being successful in making any money farming, these
two primitive tillers of the soil went back to Castroville to get
work. Rutinger finally went to San Antonio and worked for a
man named Reese.

By this time the war was going on between the United States
and Mexico, and Mr. Weynand enlisted in the American army at
San Antonio. His command was the Twelfth infantry, Company
E, Captain Welsh. The lieutenant was named White, and Mr.
Weynand says he was a splendid man. The regiment was com-
manded by Colonel Bonham. The lieutenant-colonel was named
Seymore.

On June 2, 1847, the command started to New Orleans, and
from that place embarked for Vera Cruz. At the latter place
the regiment was kept for quite a while, and the men drilled and

practiced firing. Here also many of the men were taken sick, and only forty out of eighty of Welsh's men were fit for duty. General Scott was moving towards the City of Mexico, and 200 of the troops at Vera Cruz were ordered to follow in his rear as a rear guard. Mr. Weynand was with this guard, and says they suffered a great deal on the route. Besides having to fight almost daily with scattered bands of Mexican troops, rations were short, and the men had to subsist on crackers and berries. They finally turned and went back to Vera Cruz. Here they were met by 4000 American troops under General Lane, a very young man, Mr. Weynand said. These troops had 300 wagons and plenty of provisions, and all set out together after General Scott. At Jalapa they met Colonel Lawley and his men. Just before getting to the town, and not far from the national bridge, while in camp one night firing was heard in the direction of the bridge, and next morning when the command moved on a dead cavalryman was found on the bridge. He had been sent back by Colonel Lawley to see what delayed the troops in the rear, and was killed by some Mexicans who were ambushing the bridge to cut off small detachments of American troops. The clothing had been stripped from the body of the dead trooper. The troops moved on and came to the pass of Cerro Gordo, where General Scott had just fought a battle and lost many of his men. Many signs of the desperate struggle were seen. The entire command now went on to Perote, and from there to Puebla. All of the beeves had now been killed and consumed, and short rations prevailed again.

A German who could speak but very little English told General Lane that a Mexican army was close at hand. Firing was soon heard, and General Lane ordered the troops to move round a hill in the direction from whence it came. They did so, and came upon the town of Humantla. The advance guard was fighting, and the balance of the troops joined in and the battle soon became general. The troops went from house to house, breaking them open and routing the Mexicans on all sides, who soon abandoned the town and commenced a retreat. The dragoons pursued them, led by Lieut.-Col. Samuel H. Walker, the famous Texan. In this running fight out of town Colonel Walker was killed, and Mr. Weynand saw his body on a horse as it was being brought back to town by his men.

After the battle many of the soldiers went into the saloons and became so badly intoxicated and scattered about town that some were left when the army moved. The Mexicans captured these and kept them four months. On the march Mr. Weynand was in the rear guard behind the train. One day firing was heard ahead, and they soon came upon the wagon-master and one teamster badly wounded with buckshot, and a doctor attending to them. They were shot from ambush, but both recovered.

At Puebla quite a battle was fought, eighteen men being killed out of one company in a close fight on the plaza. Here part of the troops to which Mr. Weynand belonged stayed nine weeks, and were constantly harassed by the Mexicans. It was necessary to fire upon them every day with cannon to keep them at a distance. The main part of the army had joined General Scott. When the troops left here the man who shot the wagon-master and teamster was caught and swung to a limb. There were 2000 men on this march, and they made thirty miles in one day, which is far above the average for infantry. The roads were very good. One one occasion the Mexicans fired on the troops with cannon from a ridge. The cavalry charged up the ridge, and soon carbine firing was heard. Infantry was ordered to their support, but when they arrived the fight was over and threee dead Mexicans were on the ground. The cavalry went in advance of the train, and one day after a creek was crossed sharp firing was heard, and when the train and rear infantry came upon the scene forty dead Mexicans lay on a very small space of ground, where the cavalry had killed them.

When the command arrived at a small town in a valley at night about 9 o'clock they stopped on a hill and planted cannon, and the infantry lay down. Soon, however, the artillerymen commenced firing on the town, and before daylight an advance was ordered and the place captured. Some of the soldiers at once proceeded to rob it, and one of them went into a church and got a suit of clothing which belonged to the priest. It was very fine, trimmed with gold lace, etc. The captain of the company to which the soldier belonged dispossessed him of the fancy suit, and then placed him in jail.

Before the American army got into the City of Mexico they had to descend a very steep place with lakes on both sides, and the men had to keep the road in single file, which made a very extended line. Here the Mexicans had planted a cross, and said they would fight until all were killed; but they failed to do so on the approach of the United States troops. The city was taken by storm, and the army stayed four months. They were drilled every day on a prairie by General Smith. Mr. Weynand was under his command when the army left Mexico.

The writer will state here that in his interview with Mr. Weynand notes were taken, and the many stirring scenes he passed through during the compaign in Mexico are given as he now, at this late day, remembers them. At that time he could not understand much English, and fails to remember the given names of his officers, and also the names of many towns through which they passed.

When the war was over the troops came back 300 miles, and then broke up into detachments to take shipping for the United States. Mr. Weynand came on with 500 troops to New Orleans. They made the trip from Vera Cruz in nineteen days. Five men died on the way, and some in New Orleans. They were paid off here and discharged. Weynand and eleven other men hired a ship for $100 and came to Galveston. From here he and a companion came up to Houston in a boat, where they bought a wagon and yoke of oxen and set out for New Braunfels, in Comal County. The wagon had no bed on it, but his partner made a rough one that would answer their purpose. They were one month making the trip. They only rested here two days and then came on to San Antonio, arriving there the last day of August, 1848.

Mr. Weynand had a town lot and twenty acres of land at D'Hanis, and now told his companion, whose name was Charles Frederick, that he would go out to his land to make a crop, and for him to stay in San Antonio and work and send supplies out to him. He again failed to make anything farming, and had to go back to San Antonio to get work. His companion obtained a job working on the Alamo, but unfortunately fell from the walls one day and was killed.

Mr. Weynand now got a bounty of $100 in lieu of 160 acres of land which was due him, and with this cash he again tried farming, and again failed. In 1849 he went back to D'Hanis. In 1850 he once more tried his hand as a tiller of the soil, and this time made a good crop and times began to get better. The Indians were not so bad, as the Texas rangers had come, and were stationed near the town on Seco Creek, at a point now the home of Mr. Louis Rothe.

After the rangers left United States troops came and built Fort Lincoln, just below the old camp of the rangers.

Mr. Weynand now bought land and built a house upon it on the east bank of the Seco, just opposite Fort Lincoln. The troops at the fort were under the command of Major Longstreet, afterwards the famous Confederate general. Second in command was Lieutenant Dodge, for whom Dodge City, Kansas, was named. By this time Mr. Weynand had a family. In 1866 his son Herbert, George Miller, and August Rothe went out on a cow hunt and camped in Hondo Canyon, twenty miles from home, and stayed there several days. One morning ten Indians came upon them, killed George Miller, and took young Weynand captive. He was but 12 years of age. Rothe alone made his escape and told the news. Mr. Weynand made many trips in search of his boy, but of no avail; he never saw him again. He heard once there was a captive white boy among some Indians in Mexico at San Fernando, and at once set out for that place, paying large sums of money for guides. His horse became sick in Mexico so that he could not travel, and he had to delay several days, and as soon as the horse recovered a Mexican stole him and he had to buy another. Mr. Weynand could not find his son. The captive boy was not his, and he gave up the search. Before starting back home Mr. Weynand discovered that corn was cheap there, and bought ninety bushels for 33⅓ cents, and hired some Mexicans who were coming to San Antonio with wagons to transport it for him. For this he paid them $15, and sold the corn at home for $2 per bushel.

Mr. Weynand has been very unfortunate with his children. He had a large family, eleven boys and six girls. One of his boys died, another was stolen by Indians, one was accidentally killed by a friend when he was 19 years old, one of the same age was killed by a horse falling on him, another died a natural death, one had his arm shot off, and a daughter caught fire and burned to death.

Mrs. Weynand, who before marriage was Miss Angelina Ney, is a daughter of John Ney, whose father was a nephew of Napoleon's great field marshal, and fought under him at Waterloo. She was born in Prussia, six miles from the French line, at Dillingen, and came to San Antonio in 1846 as part of Castro's colony. When the remains of Col. Sam Walker were brought from Mexico for burial at San Antonio Miss Angelina was living there with the family of Mr. Geo. Paschal, father of Congressman Thomas Paschal, and helped to make the wreaths that were placed on the coffin of the hero of Humantla. Thomas J. Paschal at that time was two years of age.

JOHN W. PATTERSON.

Born in Texas in 1849,

On the Patterson irrigating ditch, near Rio Frio postoffice, in Frio Canyon, Bandera County, lives Mr. John W. Patterson, one of the early settlers of southwest Texas. He was born in Smith County, Texas, in 1849, and came west with his father, Mr. Newman Patterson, when quite young, and first settled on the Sabinal River, six miles below the present Sabinal station on the Sunset road. While Mr. Patterson has had quite an interesting experience on the frontier, the most important was the part he took in helping to rescue a little white girl who was a captive among the Indians. At the time of this Indian raid in which the little girl was captured Mr. Patterson was living in Frio Canyon, not far from the spot where he now resides. The Indians on this occasion, which was about 1876, had been down the Guadalupe River on a big raid, and when ten miles below Kerrville came upon Mr. W. R. Terry, who with his family had just settled on Verde Creek, not far from its confluence with the Guadalupe. The Indians came upon them suddenly and unexpectedly, and Mr. Terry was killed without any chance to defend himself. He was a short distance from their camp, making shingles to cover his house. Two of the children were also killed, and Mrs. Terry fled from the place and made her escape. She was repeatedly fired at, and both bullets and arrows cut her clothing. She avoided the savages by leaping down a bluff. One little girl 8 years of age was carried off by the savages. The Indians, after scalping and mutilating the body of Mr. Terry, continued their murderous journey and succeeded in capturing a negro boy further down the country, and then turned a southwest course towards the Frio and Sabinal canyons. The next place they were seen was on Little Blanco, between Sabinal and Frio canyons. Here they came upon Mr. Chris Kelley and came near getting him. He succeeded in escaping them by leaving his horse, which they captured. The next place they struck and made themselves known was at the mouth of Cherry Creek, where it empties into the Frio. Here they came upon the cow camp of Ed Meyers,

John Avant, and William Pruitt. The men were away on a cow hunt, and the Indians robbed the camp and took off all the horses that were there. They then turned and traveled northwest, crossing the Frio River about where Mr. Joseph Van Pelt now lives. The cowmen on their return to the pillaged camp took up the trail of the Indians and were joined on the route by other settlers, two of whom were Mr. Joe Van Pelt and a man named Martin. The Upper Frio men who lived on the Patterson ditch did not at this time get the news of the raid, but received it later in the day and began collecting to join in the pursuit. Before they got ready to start, the negro boy, who had made his escape from the Indians, came to where the Frio men were assembling. He said the Indians had traveled up Elm Creek, and then, ascending a high mountain overlooking the Frio valley, saw houses in the distance and stopped to look at them, neglecting to keep an eye on the negro boy, who was riding a pony up the mountain in their rear. Seeing their attention attracted to the white settlement, the sable captive slid off his horse and made his escape through the rocks and thick brush. He then told of the captive white girl, and said she was taken from the Guadalupe valley. He was going to mill, he said, when the Indians came upon him. The negro had many stripes on his person where his inhuman captors had whipped him; he was also nearly starved. This tale of the negro, and the little white girl still being a captive among the Comanches, lent new impetus to the movements of the men, and they mounted their horses with alacrity and set off, determined to rescue her or perish in the attempt. Night set in dark and foggy before the trail was reached, and the settlers had to camp to await the light of day to prosecute the pursuit. Next morning they found the trail on the divide at the head of Buffalo Creek, between Main and Dry Frio. The trail led one mile west and then turned north. The settlers could now see to their left into Dry Frio Canyon, and to their surprise and great joy discovered the Indians over there and traveling from them down Mare Creek towards the river. The men now quit the trail, and going down the mountain as best they could, took it up again where they saw the Indians, who by this time were out of sight again. One reason why they came so soon upon the Indians was the fact that the latter had traveled all night in the fog and had lost their bearings, and went round in a circle, which brought them back by daylight to within a mile of where they had passed out the evening before. This fortunate circumstance saved the settlers a long and tedious route of trailing, following the devious windings of the lost Indians in the fog the previous night. If the Indians could have kept a straight course that night it would have been a long chase, and they might have succeeded in escaping the pursuing party.

Five miles from where the trail was taken up in the valley of the Dry Frio they came upon the stolen horses which the Indians had dropped, seeing now that they had to make up for lost time. Half a mile further they came to a cedar brake, and also upon the Indians, who had stopped in the river and were letting their horses drink. The white men present now were only five in number, to wit: William Pruitt, John Avant, Lysander Avant, Jack Grigsby, and John Patterson. The other settlers from below had not joined this party, and were following the winding trail. At sight of the Indians the men all raised their guns at once and fired hurriedly, without taking a good aim. Not an Indian fell from his horse, but all dashed furiously out of the water to the opposite bank and disappeared amid the rocks and cedar. It was evident from the actions of some that they were badly hit. One reason, no doubt, of this bad firing was the fact that the little white captive was riding behind one of the Indians, and some fired high for fear of hitting her. The men dashed across the shallow mountain river after the Indians, and a wild and desperate chase commenced through the brush and over the rocks. The horse being ridden by the Indian and the little girl showed signs of weakening as the white men came in sight again and crowded close upon them, firing rapidly with their Winchesters. The Indian jumped off and mounted behind a comrade, and the little girl soon fell from her position to the ground. John Patterson was the first man to reach her. She was standing on her feet holding the horse by a rope in one hand, and in the other tightly clasping a small piece of blanket upon which she had been riding. She was badly scared when the men dashed up to her. The yelling, firing, desperate ride through the brakes, and the whistling bullets had completely unnerved her, and she stood shaking like an aspen leaf. The kind words of the men, however, who told her not to be afraid, and to stay where she was until they caught the Indians, had a soothing effect, and she said she would not leave. The Indians were again overtaken as they were ascending a hill and a rapid fire was opened upon them, and the rear one, who was the chief, had his horse killed. The chief himself seemed to bear a charmed life. Ten shots were fired at him as he was making off on foot, but he kept steadily on, carrying a long lance in his hand. He had part of a wagon sheet, which had been taken from the cow camp, wrapped about his body, and this he finally threw off. John Avant, to make sure of close shots, dismounted from his horse, and resting his elbow on his knee, fired twice as the chief arrived at the crest of the ridge; but he kept on and went out of sight. The men now crossed a gorge and went on up the mountain, hoping at least to find the Indian at whom so many shots had been fired. The covering which had been discarded by the Indian, and which the white men picked up, was found to be very bloody and had nine bullet holes in it. The Indians outnumbered the whites about two to one, but made scarcely any resistance, and seemed bent only on flight.

In going up the hill John Patterson's girth broke, but he let the saddle slide off without dismounting and continued the chase bareback. As they could see nothing more of the Indians, after going some distance and having things badly scattered, they took the back track to where the little girl was left. Another party of trailers were met on mules and played-out horses, and one of them had the girl behind him. She was where the first party had left her, and the second party had discovered her by being on the trail of the Indians. Both parties now camped together to rest and eat something. The little girl was nearly starved and ate ravenously, never taking a piece of bread from her mouth after the first bite until it was all gone. The last band of trailers had also brought the horses along which the Indians had abandoned on Mare Creek.

After resting their horses John Patterson and some others went back to see if they could find the wounded chief. Not far from the spot where they last shot him they heard a groan, which was shortly repeated, but the rocks and brush were so thick that it was impossible to find the spot that it emanated from, and they were again compelled to abandon the search, as night was coming on. Next morning Patterson and John Avant went back again and found where the Indian had lain on some cedar limbs which had been broken off and a bed made of them. These limbs were very bloody, but the body could not be found. It is evident the Indian died here and that some of his party had returned and carried him away, and likely made the bed of cedar boughs for him.

During the absence of Avant and Patterson, the man who picked up the little girl wanted to leave the crowd and take her on to the settlement, but was prevented by William Pruitt, who said they would all go back together. The little girl said that during the windings of the Indians in the foggy night the horse of one of them fell off a bluff and broke the Indian's leg. They then divided their force, one party going off with the crippled Indian. The negro boy said there were fifteen of them when all together. The white men afterwards found the place where the accident happened, and said the fall was twenty feet.

After the return to the settlement a messenger was dispatched to the Guadalupe to find out about the little girl, and her mother came after her. The captive girl lived to be nearly grown, and then died. Her mother and Joel Terry, her brother, now live in this country.

After this raid the Indians came again into Frio Canyon and stole two horses belonging to a man named Sawyer, who was afterwards killed in Dry Frio Canyon, some say by the noted Bill Longley.

The Indians then went down on the Sabinal below the mountains and killed a Mexican sheep herder. They then started back towards the mountains and came through Ross Kennedy's pasture and stole a horse from William Adams. Then they came on across to the Dry Frio. John Patterson and several others took the trail of the Indians and followed it over into Nueces Canyon. Here they came upon two men named Goodman and Wells, who had been chased and shot at by the Indians. They now joined the party in pursuit. Wells was a great bear hunter. The trail led up the Nueces and was very rough,—no roads or settlements in those days. Some of the men had to return on account of their horses giving out. Patterson and seven others were loath to give up the pursuit, and went on. Their provisions, however, soon played out, and left them in a bad fix. They were many miles from any settlement, and entirely unacquainted with the country. They knew that by going in a certain direction they would strike the Fort Clark road, and by taking either end get to some place where provisions could be procured. They could kill game and eat it without bread and keep from suffering, so there was no uneasiness on that score, and they continued the Indian hunt. Before coming to the Fort Clark road they came upon an Indian campfire which had been but a short time before abandoned. Five miles further on, in the draws of Devil's River, they came upon the Indians in camp in a large liveoak mott about 500 yards in extent and very brushy. The horses of the Indians were grazing in the edge of the thicket, and John Patterson called the attention of the men to something in a tree and smoke in the thicket. The men now circled around the mott to the left and saw an Indian coming, and Patterson at once shot at him. The Indian returned the fire and then ran into the thicket. The settlers kept on around, and soon saw two more Indians on foot running a horse with a pair of hobbles on his neck, which they were trying to catch hold of to stop him. They could run as fast as the pony, and likely would have caught him, but at this time were fired on and ran back to cover. The Indians, it seemed, wanted to get off as light as possible with the whites, and so after a time drove all the stolen horses out of the thicket and gave them a start towards the white men, as much as to say, "Take your horses, now, and leave."

The pioneers were not satisfied with this, and still guarded the covert by placing men on regular watch. John Avant went round on the south side of the thicket and set fire to the grass, trying to burn them out, but they would not come. One of the white men saw two persons coming up the creek and called Patterson's attention to them, who at once pronounced them Indians, and set about to cut them off from the thicket. They were Indian hunters, and had a pack horse loaded with buffalo meat. Some of the men followed Patterson, but the Indians, discovering them, dropped their pack horse and ran. Patterson pursued and got close enough to shoot, and was reaching to pull his Winchester out of the scabbard, when his horse stepped in a hole and fell. Patterson was thrown violently to the ground and his horse ran off. The Indians escaped, but the whites got the buffalo meat, which came to them very opportunely on account of their want of provisions.

13

The settlers now held a council to determine what to do. Half of the men wanted to go into the thicket and fight the Indians in there, but the balance objected. It was then agreed that those who did not want to go in were to hold the horses of the others, who would make an advance on the Indian encampment. The men went in shooting and making all the noise they could, and the Indians ran away in great alarm, so when the camp was reached it was deserted. The booty was considerable, and the men had to make several trips to bring it all out. It consisted of eighteen blankets, one buffalo robe, one saddle, four shields, two head-dresses, one microscope, and a pass from the Indian agent at Fort Sill for these Indians to go on a buffalo hunt. The pass was old, and here these fellows were down in South Texas, out of the buffalo range proper, killing people and stealing horses. The things were divided among the men, and the shield, which John Patetrson got, had a woman's scalp attached to it. They also got thirty-five head of horses and two mules.

Some of the stock belonged to the Allen brothers and some to Brown and Sawyer. They also found in the camp 500 smooth sticks for making arrows. These the men broke. There were nine Indians in this party, and the number of white men who routed them was eight. Their names are as follows: John Patterson, John Avant, Dick Humphreys, Lon Sawyer, L. L. Green, Dave Wells, Goodman, and A. Blackburn. The four first named are the ones who went into the thicket and captured the camp. Sawyer and Patterson got the head-dresses. They were gorgeous affairs, having a row of feathers reaching to the ground, somewhat like a Sioux war bonnet.

These men deserve a great deal of credit for this trip, and their perseverance and courage to penetrate a wild country, infested with savages, with so small a number, and then invest and rout the savages from their stronghold in the manner in which they did, and bring off the booty and recaptured stock.

They were gone fifteen days and were nine days without bread —three days on buffalo meat alone. A true frontiersman knows how to take care of himself and not starve when out.

JOHN REINHART.

Came to Texas in 1849.

Mr. John Reinhart, who has a fine ranch on Big Seco, in Medina County, is one of the pioneers of western Texas. He was born in Bavaria, town of Orb, in 1832. Came to New Orleans in 1848, and to New Braunfels, Comal County, Texas, in 1849. Moved from there to Cibolo River, and thence to the Seco Creek, near D'Hanis, in 1854. In those days the young German immigrants who had no families did not remain in the colonies long at a time, but sought work anywhere they could find it. Some worked for the government when Fort Lincoln was established on the Seco, and others drove teams or cattle, and in fact did whatever their hands could find to do.

About the time that Mr. Reinhart came to Seco, Mr. John Dunlap was in the country buying up a drove of cattle under a government contract, to be delivered at Fort Lancaster, which was situated at the mouth of Liveoak Creek, where it empties into the Pecos River. Mr. Dunlap lived at Fort Clark. As soon as the cattle were collected a start was made for the fort. Mr. Reinhart had been employed by Dunlap to help deliver the cattle at their destination. Situated as Fort Lancaster was then, far out on the extreme frontier, with no settlements between, and infested with hostile Indians, such an undertaking was extremely hazardous, but there are always found men who will brave any danger and start anywhere. There were but three men in the party to make this long, dangerous trip—Reinhart, Dunlap, and Capt. Joseph Richarz.

Nothing occurred to make the trip of more than normal interest until they reached Howard's Wells, out on the plains. Here, just before going down into the valley with the cattle, they discovered a man on a mountain, and at once began to proceed with great caution, fearing it was an Indian, and that they would lose the cattle. The man in question, however, was a white man, watching the road back towards the east for help. His party had camped the night before at the wells, and that present morning had been attacked by a large body of Indians, and all of their horses and mules taken off. There were nine white men and five wagons of this party. Their horses were out grazing with one man to watch them, when the Indians made a dash from cover to capture the horses. The Indians played a very smart trick to get the white men also, and came near being successful. Dividing their force, while still concealed from view behind the hills, one party charged upon the lone guard at the horses, and, as was expected by the savages, the men at the wagons seized their guns and rushed out into the prairie to save the horses and succor the guard. The other band of Indians now dashed across the open ground on their ponies to cut them off from the protection of the wagons. The white men saw this in time, however, and retreated back to their position. The guard, who was very well mounted, made a wide circle in the prairie, ran around the Indians, and joined his companions. The Indians secured the stock and drove them off, passing within long rifle range of the chagrined owners, who gave them one volley as a parting salute. One of these shots took effect on a horse ridden by one of the Indians, killing the animal in its tracks and throwing the Apache to the ground. He mounted behind another, however, and they all rode away. As the three cattlemen could do nothing for them, having no extra teams, they went on and reported the matter at Fort Lancaster, and the commander of that post sent out teams belonging to the government and brought the wagons in.

After delivering his cattle, Dunlap and his two men started back together, and when they arrived at the crossing of Devil's River met a drove of 150 head of horses. They thought at the time that only three Indians were with them. It seemed an easy job to rout these, and capture the horses, although they were only armed with pistols. They acted upon this impulse and charged, but what was their surprise when seven more Indians appeared on the other side of the horses. They had been concealed, and now dismounted and remounted on fresh horses to give the trio of white men a battle and chase. The horses ridden by the cattlemen were jaded, and the situation began to look serious. They at once reversed the matter, turning their charge into a retreat. The Indians, however, did not follow them, and the white men soon checked up. Dunlap now said: "Boys, I believe the guns of those Indians were wet (it had been raining), and that was the reason they did not fire or charge us, and we can go back and clean them up yet. That would be a good item for a newspaper, that three men whipped ten Indians and took 150 head of horses away from them." So it was agreed, and they turned back to have a fight. The Indians saw them coming back, and all left the horses and came yelling and charging upon them. Once more they beat a retreat, and continued their flight until they were safely ensconced in a big thicket where they could defend themselves, willing to let the Indians and horses go. The Apaches did not pursue far, but soon went back to their horses, and the white men continued their way home, where they arrived without further adventures.

So that the reader who has no experience in such things can more readily comprehend the dangers, seen and unseen, which beset the path of the pioneer, I will relate two incidents of this character.

In the spring of 1859 Mr. Reinhart went from his home on the Seco to the Comanche waterhole, several miles south from him, to look after stock and to kill a deer if chance offered. On the way he rode by a large thicket, and on looking back at it saw something move that looked like a deer, and at once raised his rifle so as to be ready to shoot if it came into plain view. It was an Indian, however, and thinking from the action of the white man that he was discovered, he dodged back from view. Mr. Reinhart was riding a horse which he did not often mount, and he was very sensitive to the spur. The settler knew that he saw one Indian, and not knowing how many more there were, put spurs to his horse in order to make a quick run to a mott of live-oak trees, where he could dismount and better stand them off. Besides his rifle he had a good revolver. This tender horse he rode now commenced to pitch instead of running when he felt the spur. This would have been the time for the Indians to have made their break for him, for it was all Mr. Reinhart could do to sit his horse, and he could not have used gun or pistol. He finally reached the timber and looked back. Quite a lot of Indians were in view on the edge of the thicket. The reason they did not pursue the settler was that they were all on foot, having just come in on a raid, and had not picked up any horses yet. As they did not follow, Mr. Reinhart rode off slowly from the trees and made a circle back home.

On the way back Reinhart met Jack Wolf, and advised him to

go home with him and spend the night. This Jack agreed to do, and next morning he and Reinhart went up to his brother's, Sebastian Wolf, on Huffman's ranch, which was on the Seco, a short distance above the present ranch of Mr. Reinhart. The three now went back to the thicket where Reinhart saw the Indians to see what discoveries they could make. The signs there showed the Indians to be about ten in number, and that they had been secreted while making arrows, and had killed a turkey, the feathers of which were profusely scattered around. The Indians from this place went down the Seco and stole many horses, among which was a very fine one belonging to Billy Doan. Being well mounted now, the Indians made themselves heard from in various places. The three white men went on down to D'Hanis and told the news of the raid. Huffman and his partner, Sebastian Wolf, went west and crossed the Sabinal River not far from the present station of the same name. They then made a circle west in the prairie. Here this same band of Indians came upon them and a desperate running fight took palce, in which the two ranchmen were killed.

It is supposed that the chief rode Billy Doan's horse and was killed off him in the fight by Wolf, as his throat was cut from ear to ear after he had been killed by arrows. The Indians were followed by citizens and defeated in their camp on Blanco Creek, and all the horses retaken.

When John Bowles killed three Indians on the Sabinal, Mr. Reinhart went over to the Bowles ranch and saw the three Indian scalps hanging on a clothesline in the yard.

On another occasion Mr. Reinhart went deer hunting to a noted place called the "cowlick," and while there saw something move which he thought might be a deer. On riding nearer to investigate, a dove flew up, and thinking this was the object which he had observed, rode on in another direction. At the cowlick, among other cattle he noticed one of his work oxen, called Tom, licking at the bank. It began to rain soon, and Mr. Reinhart went back home by way of the lick, and his steer was still there. When he arrived at home himself and gun were wet, and after putting on dry clothes he fired off the gun in order to dry and cleanse it. A man by the name of Webster was stopping at the Reinhart ranch, and came out to where he was working on his gun and told him the cattle had just run home and old Tom was shot with an arrow, which was still sticking in him. "Impossible!" said Mr. Reinhart; "I left him a few minutes ago at the lick, and nothing was the matter with him then." "Come and see," said Mr. Webster. It was even so; the cattle were at the cow lot badly frightened, and old Tom was running around trying to get rid of the arrow. He had to be driven into the pen and roped and tied before the feathered shaft could be extracted. It had penetrated one foot into the paunch. The question was, why did not the Indian shoot Reinhart? He evidently rode near him several times, and no doubt it was a glimpse of him he saw when he thought he saw a deer and the dove flew up, etc. The only solution that offers is that there was only one Indian, and he was afraid of the white man's gun and pistol in case he should fail to bring him down with his arrow.

Mr. Webster afterwards sold goods in Uvalde and was one night killed and robbed in his store.

In 1861 Mr. Reinhart joined a ranging company commanded by Capt. Chas. de Montel. Their station was at Ranger Springs, twelve miles above the present home of Mr. Reinhart, in the Seco Valley. On one occasion the Indians made a raid below the mountains, and runners were sent to D'Hanis to get men to follow them. Mr. Reinhart was in D'Hanis at the time, having been sent from the ranger camp to bring the mail for the company. However, he joined the expedition that was making up to follow the Indians. The trail led back to the northwest or west, in the direction of Sabinal Canyon. They went to the ranch of Ross Kennedy, and from there into the canyon, and took up the salt marsh. Near the head of this place the settlers camped on the trail about where Mr. Calvin Mitchell's ranch is now. Next morning they ascended to the top of the mountains, over which the trail led, and taking a look back into the valley saw a small squad of the rangers following them. They had been notified of the raid and in which direction the Indians were going out. The settlers waited until the rangers came up, and all went on together. The rangers were under the command of Lieut. Ben Patton, and among his men were Jack Davenport, John Kennedy, Pete Bowles, Lon Moore, and several others. The Indian trail led northwest through a very rough range of mountains. At length the trailers came to a cedar brake on the south side of the mountain, and Pete Bowles, one of the rangers, went slowly ahead until he could see into a valley beyond. He then pulled his horse back quickly and said, "There they are." The Indians had camped in the valley on the high ground, between a small creek with steep banks and a deep hollow. In their rear was a cedar brake. The white men now dismounted, and leaving two men with the horses, went round the mountains concealed from the view of the Indians, and then came up the creek through the brush, still hid from view. The Indians were close to a big spring, and there was about an acre of open ground around their camp. When the rangers and settlers came up under the bluff they were very close to the Indians, but could not see them, but could see their horses. The force was now divided and a party went round each way. Some of the men crept up the bank and peeped over, and could see the blankets of the Indians on the bushes. Another cautious step forward and the Indians themselves could be seen. Reinhart now motioned to the men who had not climbed up, and indicated with his finger the exact location of the Indians, and also signaled a charge. Both parties now leaped up the bank in plain view, and not over fifty yards from the astonished savages, and commenced a terrific fire from rifles, shotguns, and pistols. The Indians made but little attempt to fight, and at once scattered into the cedar brake, followed by a shower of bullets which cut the bushes on all sides. After the fusilade was over three dead Indians were on the ground, and one was trailed some distance by the blood, but could not be found. The reason no more Indians were killed was the fact that they had only a few jumps to make to get to cover. The Indians had cooked a quantity of meat, and were fixing to leave. They had their bows and quivers on their backs, and one of them was shoeing a horse with rawhide. This one looked over the horse's neck when the charge was made, and a ranger fired at his head, but hit too low and killed the horse. One man who did not live in this country, but who joined the scout and was in the fight, cut off the ears of the dead Indians and strung them on a string to carry back east with him.

The rangers and settlers now went back to their horses and took the back track for home and the ranger camp.

On one occasion Mr. Reinhart and others followed a band of Indians who had a lot of horses which they had stolen out of the settlement. After a long and hard chase they succeeded in retaking the horses without a fight, as the Indians left them and ran, and they returned with them to D'Hanis. The men were tired and worn out, and put the stock in the horse lot of John Ney, and proceeded to have a good night's rest. The Indians had followed the white men back, and that night got the horses again and carried them off, to the great surprise of the men when they woke up in the morning and realized the situation. They followed them again, but this time the Bandera men had taken up the trail when it passed through their country, and had overtaken the Indians and recaptured the horses. The D'Hanis men carried the stock back again, but this time kept better watch upon them.

CAPTAIN H. J. RICHARZ.

Came to Texas in 1849.

Among the pioneers of West Texas who deserve a place in Texas history is Capt. H. J. Richarz, one of the gallant men who led the famous Texas rangers against the savages on the frontier, and stood between these painted demons and the hearthstones of the pioneers. Captain Richarz was born in 1822 on his father's estate, near Cologne, on the Rhine, being at this writing (December, 1898) 76 years of age. His father was second burgomaster and head of the municipality of the town of Ella, having now a population of 4000 souls; also for a number of years head administrator of Castle House, Ella, the residence of the late Princess Louise of Prussia, and up to his death in 1886, at the age of 92 years, honorary president of the War Veterans' Volunteer Rifles of 1813 and 1815. He was also knight of the Order of the Crown of Prussia, an order for meritorious service from the king of Prussia and the duke of Saxe-Coburg.

Captain Richarz was the eldest son and received a liberal education, first in the town school, and until the age of 16 years at a private academy in the city of Dusseldorf.

At the age of 16 years Captain Richarz joined the same volunteer rifle legion in which his father served through the wars of the allies against Napoleon, and after serving his time out and being three times promoted, quit and took a confidential position as "commissar" of the chief engineer of the Prince Wilhelm Railroad, in the Prussian district of Berg and Mark.

In 1848 he took an active part in the revolution against the absolution and feudal system, having been elected and commissioned as captain of a camp of militia and twice as elector for the representative of the Frankfurt parliament and house of representants in Berlin. He also took an active part in the bloody struggles that followed, and in the meantime married. The merciless, reactionary monarchical side being victorious, Captain Richarz chose to go into voluntary exile, rather than to be fusiladed or imprisoned for years in a military fortress. He evaded the civil and military officers, had his property sold to a younger brother, and arrived safely in Rotterdam. He embarked at Havre, France, and arrived in New Orleans in the fall of 1849. The voyage across the ocean was disastrous, especially along the coast of Africa, and they were finally shipwrecked near St. Thomas, in the West Indies, and had to say there two months before they could again get shipping. From New Orleans Captain Richarz and his wife and two children went to Indianola, on the coast of Texas, and from there made their way to the San Antonio River and bought 500 acres of land opposite the mission of Espade, nine miles below the city of San Antonio. He brought with him some Saxon merino rams, which he was lucky enough to save, and commenced sheep-raising. He was the first man to import this kind of stock to Texas. In the sheep business he had a partner named John H. Herndon, of Velasco.

In 1853 he moved with sheep and cattle to Fort Lincoln, in Medina County, fifty miles west of San Antonio. The fort was situated on the Seco Creek, about two miles from the old town of D'Hanis. Captain Richarz here occupied for two years the quarters of the last commander of that station, Major Longstreet, afterwards the famous Confederate general. He purchased 500 acres of land near here, and established the first postoffice west of Castroville at the D'Hanis settlement, and acted up to the civil war as postmaster. He served one year as justice of the peace during the war, and after that as chief justice of Medina County. Up to the time of the war, Captain Richarz was the leader of the citizen scouts for protection from the bloody inroads of the savages.

In 1861 the brother-in-law of Captain Richarz was killed and scalped by the Indians.

In 1861 he was commissioned by the Governor as major cammanding the independent battalion of mounted home guards of Medina County. Part of this force was always placed in camp along the extreme frontier line, and kept scouts constantly out trailing and fighting the Indians wherever they could come upon them.

Captain Richarz succeeded in those times in checking to some extent the inroads of the savages and taking a good deal of spoils from them. This state of irregular warfare between the Indians and the volunteer organizations lasted until 1870. The country was really without aid from the government. The sparsely scattered garrisons of regular troops along the Rio Grande, mostly negro cavalry, were not adequate to the occasion. Captain Richarz says the Indians would drive off horses in sight of their camps.

In 1870 the State of Texas, under permit and authority from the Federal government, organized a frontier force of rangers, and Captain Richarz was given a commission as captain of E company, to be stationed at Fort Inge, on the Leona River, four miles below the town of Uvalde, and also an order from General Reynolds, of the United States army, to take the efficient warriors of the Seminole tribe of Indians under his command. The tribe at that time was under the control of United States agents, and encamped on the Rio Grande. The captain protested against this measure, and argued that he was well informed by personal observation of the unreliability of these savages and their moral degradation, and apprehending corrupting influence of his men. this plan was abandoned.

Captain Richarz placed his men, carefully selected, in various camps, and only retained enough at his headquarters to make an efficient scout, and kept scouts going constantly along the Rio Grande and various parts of the imperiled frontier, and had regular communications from Laredo to the Llano River. After having some successful expeditions and fights, one of which was near the Rio Grande, Captain Richarz received command of two more companies of rangers. The last bloody battle which the rangers under Captain Richarz had with the Indians was fought with the Kiowas and Comanches, near Carrizo Springs. The scout was commanded by Sergeant Eckford and Dr. Woodbridge. There were fourteen rangers and three citizens in the fight. The Indians numbered seventy, and fought in two lines. Eight Indians were killed, including their chief, who was fantastically adorned, and had four scalps of white women. The wounded of the Indians could not be ascertained. A ranger named Belleger, from Castroville, was killed, and Dr. Woodbridge was knocked from his horse by an Indian and severely injured. So hot was the fire the rangers ran out of cartridges and could not follow up the Indians, and had to return.

The Indians at this time had invaded the frontier in three strong parties, and Captain Richarz was following another band when this battle was fought. About this time Walter Richarz, son of the captain, and Joe Riff, both rangers, were killed on the Blanco by Indians. When the bodies were found, the signs of battle showed with what desperate valor the young rangers had sold their lives.

This was about the last of Indian raids on this part of the frontier. After Captain Richarz left the frontier service he served as justice and attended to his stock and farm. Served one term as representative of the Fifty-second district in the Legislature. His hearing becoming defective, he was incapacitated from further public service, and he spends a quiet life on the west bank of the Seco, in a romantic spot near the foot of the hills, where he attends to his irrigated garden and orchard. He reads the finest print without glasses, and never misses a rabbit or turkey at the distance of eighty yards with a rifle. He has a kind and friendly disposition, and has many friends. His judgment of men and things is astute, and he has a blunt way of talking and expressing himself, but his judgment is seldom at fault. He is a devoted Texan, and liberal in his views.

GIDEON THOMPSON.

Came to Texas in 1852.

Among the first settlers who came to Sabinal Canyon, but few
have had a more varied or interesting experience than Mr. Gideon
Thompson, who still survives at this date (1899) to tell the tale
of frontier days.

Mr. Thompson was born in Hawkins County, eastern Tennessee, on the 3d day of November, 1822. In 1842 we find him in
the State of Arkansas, where the same year he married Miss Margarette O'Bryant. He came to Texas in 1852, and in the fall
of the same year wended his way to Sabinal Canyon, the extreme
limit at that time of civilization in southwest Texas. Mr. Thompson made a short stop in San Antonio on his way out, and says at
that time he could have fired the town with a torch as fast as his
horse could run, on account of the houses being low and mostly
covered with grass.

Mr. Thompson's family was the first white one that came
west of the German settlement of old D'Hanis, in Medina County.
Capt. William Ware was the first white man to settle in Sabinal
Canyon, but he came without his family, and had to return to
East Texas for them, and in the meantime Mr. Thompson and
family came. About the same time came John Davenport, Lee
Sanders, Henry Robinson, and James Davenport. Mr. Aaron
Anglin, a young man, came with Mr. Thompson but soon re-
turned to Arkansas, where he married, and came back in 1853.
When Mr. Thompson first came to the canyon he had four chil-
dren in his family, namely, William, Hiram, Robert, and Mary
Ann. These were the first white children to cast their eyes over
the lovely valley.

The first winter after arriving the five families all lived together at Capt. William Ware's place. He was an old Indian
fighter, and said this would be best until they could find out what
the Indians were going to do.

In the summer of 1853, as no hostile Indians had put in an
appearance, Mr. Thompson moved to the place where he now resides and built a log cabin on the Anglin prong, as it is now

called, of the Sabinal River, six miles above Captain Ware's place
and five miles above the present town of Utopia. The first postoffice in the canyon was at Captain Ware's, and was called Waresville. Mr. Charles Durbin put up a store and sold goods there
until his death, which occurred in the early 80's.

Mr. Thompson built his house close to the creek, and says it
does not look now like it did then. It at that time was a clear,
bold, running stream, capable of running and operating machinery. The banks were steep and the water deep. There is no
water at all there now. He thinks the cause of this is that when
cattle were brought into the country they made trails down to
the water, and the banks commenced washing and caving in, and
filled up the channel gradually with soil and gravel. He says
where Mr. Dan Harper's place is now, when he (Mr. Thompson)
came here, there lay a large cedar tree top and roots, put there by
high water. This place is below Mr. Thompson's, and between
the Anglin prong and main river. Also on the George Murchi-
son place, below Utopia, lodged against a noted liveoak tree having large, peculiar knots on it, were three large cypress trees, also
put there by high water. If such overflows were to come now,
many houses would most likely wash away. In the same year Mr.
Thompson moved to his place the Tonkaway Indians came and
camped at the mouth of the canyon, under the bluffs at the Blue
waterhole. They were a friendly tribe, and assured the whites,
when Mr. Thompson and others went to interview them, that
they were only there for the purpose of hunting bear. They had
also camped before this below the mountains on the river about
where Mr. Bascom Lyell's place is now. Here they had planted
corn and watermelons.

About the same time the Lipan Indians camped and pitched
their tepees on the Frio River, near the "shut-in," where now are
the farms of Joe Richards and Ed Meyers. The government
moved these tribes the same year (before the watermelons of the
Tonkaways got ripe) to the Palo Pinto Creek, seven miles from
Fort Clark, and there established a reservation. Some of the
Lipans soon after left the reserve, and going into the vicinity
of San Antonio, killed some of the Foster family and carried
one of the girls into captivity. Mrs. Foster made her escape and
carried the news into San Antonio. This was the first Indian
raid Mr. Thompson heard of after coming to the country. Maj.

Robert Neighbors, Indian agent at that time, was in San Antonio, and learning of the Lipan raid procured a company of soldiers and went in pursuit of them. He had a German subagent named Linsell, who stayed at the Palo Pinto reserve, and who had just arrived in San Antonio, accompanied by four Lipan chiefs. These chiefs were compelled by Neighbors to go with the expedition and help to trail their own countrymen. The hostile trail led to the head of the Guadalupe River, and when it was taken up was followed rapidly by the trailers. After several days' hard ride over a rough country, the command stopped at the head springs of the Guadalupe to rest their horses a short time, and while so doing the Lipans went a short distance from camp to take observations, and were charged and run back by a squad of white men from Sabinal Canyon. Among these men was Mr. Thompson. They were out on a scout and looking at the country. As soon as matters were explained to them by Major Neighbors, they left and went back towards home and the soldiers continued the pursuit. The trail led around the head of the Nueces River. They next made a dry camp, but had water enough next morning to make coffee, and while it was being boiled the agent sent the Lipan chiefs and two soldiers to make note of the general course of the trail, who were soon to return and report. The two soldiers shortly came back and reported that the chiefs had suddenly left them and galloped away rapidly towards the Palo Pinto. The troops followed on, but when the reserve was reached the Lipans, having been warned of the approach of the soldiers by the chiefs, had hastily gathered up their belongings and decamped into Mexico. One of the chiefs carried off a horse belonging to Major Neighbors, and wanted to take the horses and tent of Linsell, but were prevented by the Tonkaways, who were always friends of the white man. Strange to say, the old Lipan chief sent the horse of Maj. Neighbors back, but the tribe always remained hostile to the whites and made many raids from Mexico into Texas.

Mr. Thompson does not know what became of the captured girl.

In 1856 the Indians made their first raid into Sabinal Canyon. They came in from the south, and entered the valley from the lower side. They first came upon the ranch of John Fenley, where W. B. Wright now lives, and stole two head of stock horses,

one mare belonging to the old man, or Uncle Johnnie as he was
called, and one belonging to his son Demp. Early that morning
Mr. Thompson discovered there was something wrong with his
cattle by their actions, and on investigating found a trail of
Indians not far from his house. This was the same band that
had raided Mr. Fenley nine miles below. Mr. Aaron Anglin lived
about 400 yards up the creek from Mr. Thompson's, and he was
at once notified of the presence of the Indians. John Brown, of
Tennessee, an old-time friend, with his family, was living with
Mr. Anglin. They had just come to the country a short time before. These three at once set out in pursuit of the Indians, who
had crossed the west prong of the Sabinal 250 yards below Mr.
Thompson's house and kept around the foot of a mountain northeast of his place until they struck a spur of the mountain which
extended west towards the river. On this spur was a thicket of
shinoak bushes, about the center of which was a sink hole. Here
in this depression they built a fire and spent the balance of the
night. This was near the spot where G. P. Wheeler afterwards
settled. After daylight the Indians came upon Mr. Thompson's
work oxen and shot several arrows into them. Mr. Thompson
heard his ox-bell rattling violently that morning soon after daylight, and was suspicious that all was not right. In trailing they
came upon the spot where the Indians ran the oxen, which
changed their course, and they went in a northeast direction.
They ran the oxen around the mountain and left them near where
Mr. Henry Taylor now lives. Prior to this raid of the Indians,
Leek Kelly, Laban Kelley, and Jasper Wish had settled on the
main prong of the river on the west bank, opposite to where Mr.
Bob Thompson now lives. This was two or three miles northeast
from Mr. Gideon Thompson's. These settlers, however, had
moved back to Williamson County, and left no one at their place.
Some of their effects had been left in the house, among which
were two spinning wheels and one room full of corn in the
ear. The trail of the Indians led to these deserted cabins,
and here they left plenty of sign of their presence. They had
fed their horses and left piles of corn in the yard, and broken
the two old-time spinning wheels all to pieces. An old sow that
had been left behind was killed, and many things broken to pieces
besides the wheels. The three settlers took hasty observations

14

of these things and continued on the trail, and coming to the spot where Mr. Nobe Green now lives, found in a thicket a bunch of cattle which had been chased by the Indians and arrows shot into some of them. A short distance further on Uncle Johnnie Fenley's mare was found badly used up, and had evidently been used in chasing the cattle. At this time the Indians were close by in camp, and would have been surprised but for an unfortunate circumstance. A dog had followed the white men, and at this critical moment jumped a rabbit. His yelps alarmed the Indians, who at once retreated with their horses into the mountains. In the camp was a large pile of cobs where the Indians had been shelling corn to carry along with them. Mr. Anglin now said he thought it of no use to go any further, as they could not catch them. Mr. Thompson said: "You two wait here while I look a little further." After going a short distance he discovered six Indians on foot coming towards him in a trot, on the opposite side of a deep gully, but out of rifle range. The other party was now signaled and told to "Come on; here are the Indians." The white men on getting together rode towards the Indians, who began to dance and to rub paint on their faces. They had their horses hid under a bluff, fifteen head in all, to the right of where they had displayed themselves, and three Indians left with them. This was just above where Mr. John Foster now lives. They had shown themselves on the opposite side of the deep gully to decoy the white men away from the horses. Mr. Brown had a long-range gun which was now handed over to Mr. Thompson, who said he could move them if the gun would hold up; but when he dismounted to make the attempt the Indians ran away up the mountain and hid themselves among the rocks and bushes. The white men now crossed the gully on foot and went to the base of the mountain. The Indians then commenced shooting arrows at them. They would rise up quickly and shoot, and then drop down again before a rifle could be aimed at them. These were the days of muzzle-loaders, and no ammunition was wasted by the pioneers without a chance of hitting something. The Indians discharged at least one hundred arrows, all black, but they had no spikes in them. The white men could easily dodge them at the distance they were shooting, and no one was hit. The arrows were finely made, sharpened to a fine point, and then hardened in the fire. A handful of them was picked up. Mr. Anglin finally got into some bushes where the Indians could not see him when he took aim, and awaited a good chance for a shot. One soon presented itself. First the head and then the shoulders of an Indian came up above the rock. A quick aim, and bang! The head went down instantly. The Indians now went further up the mountain, and were so hidden by rocks that they could not be hit by a rifle. Mr. Anglin could not tell if he hit his or not. Mr. Thompson now left the other two again and went on around the mountain to see what had become of the Indians, and saw them high up, but they soon disappeared from view. He kept on, however, and soon discovered an Indian sitting on a rock 150 yards above him. He took as good aim as he could under the circumstances, having to shoot almost straight up, and fired. The Indian never moved, but yelled and said something which was unintelligible to Mr. Thompson, but Mr. Anglin, who also heard him, said it sounded to him like the Indian said "Try again." The settler reloaded his gun and started up higher to try another shot, but the savage beat a hasty retreat. Three more Indians now came from where the horses had been secreted and joined the others. Mr. Thompson had passed the horses, and these three Indians tried to cut him off from his companions, but they warned him to look out. He had discovered them, however, and soon made his retreat back. He saw one of the Indians leading the roan mare which belonged to Demp Fenley. The white men now left and the Indians came back and got their horses, the former not knowing where they were. On the way back home they came upon the wounded oxen. One of them was shot behind the left shoulder, close to the work of the leg, with a spiked arrow, and was in very deep. The spike had become detached from the arrow and was still in the wound, but so deep it could not be extracted without cutting too much flesh. The spike remained in the ox two years, but the wound would not heal. About the expiration of this time the ox was loaned to Mr. Silas Webster to haul corn, but hurt his foot and became very lame. Mr. Thompson said now was a good time to cut the spike out, and it was accordingly done. It was four inches in length and shaped like a dirk, sharp and of good metal. A schoolteacher named Hutchinson put a handle on it and it made a good knife. The ox soon after died. Mr. Thompson went back to the place where he shot at the Indian on the rock, and saw that he had only struck four inches below him, and found the flattened ball where it fell.

Not long after this raid the Indians paid Sabinal Canyon another visit. This time they killed a big fat cow for Mr. Anglin, and were very bold about it. They slaughtered the animal in the night near the house, and in the cow lot. The meat was cut up, packed on an old gray horse, and carried away. Next morning Mr. Anglin raised the alarm and collected the following named men to pursue them: Gideon Thompson, Sebe Barrymore, William Barrymore, Henry Robinson and his son Frank, Silas Webster, Dud Richardson, and Henry Fuller. The last named was a negro man brought to the canyon by Capt. William Ware.

The trail of the Indians led west towards a range of high mountains two and a half miles distant. At the foot of these mountains the men dismounted, and leaving their horses in charge of William Barrymore and Henry Fuller, took the trail on foot up the mountain. It was a hot day and the mountain rough and steep. The men became greatly exhausted, and the trail was finally lost amid the rocks, tangled vines, and bushes. On arriving at the crest the trail could not be found after the most diligent search, and the hunt was about to be abandoned, when a great number of wild bees were discovered. Henry Robinson now proposed that the others sit down and rest while he descended into a gorge near by to hunt for a bee cave. While he was gone Mr. Thompson observed quite a number of buzzards sailing around over a cedar brake, coming close to the tops of the trees, but not alighting. When Robinson came back he called his attention to the peculiar action of the buzzards, and remarked that they were prevented from lighting by the presence of men or wild animals.

An investigation of the brake was now inaugurated, and a rude and freshly made brush fence discovered. Inside of this inclosure the Indians were encamped, and cooking the flesh of the slain cow of Mr. Anglin. They had built this brush screen on the night before, after they had carried the cow to the top of the mountain, so that the settlers in the valley could not see the fire while they barbecued the meat. Evidently they had packed the meat on the old gray horse, and were about to start when the white men came upon them. They became alarmed at some noise the settlers made as they came to the brush, and ran away. The brake was dense and the Indians could not be seen, although they heard them rattling the rocks as they ran. The trail of the old horse was easy to follow. His heavy tread left a great deal more sign than the light moccasined foot of the Indian. Besides this, he scattered chunks of meat as he went. After following some distance, however, and not being able to catch sight of an Indian or the pack horse, the white men halted and abandoned the pursuit, as they were all nearly exhausted by their exertions. While sitting to rest on a rock where they could see over into a valley, six Indians were discovered coming in a trot towards them, but low down on the mountain side, and out of gunshot. The white men all sprang to their feet and commenced to run down the mountain towards them. On coming near the spot where the Indians had been seen they were not visible anywhere, but signs were near by where they had pushed the old horse off a high bank into a gulley, down which they intended to continue their flight. The trail was taken up and soon three Indians were seen lying down, evidently exhausted by their exertions to get clear of the white men. Before a shot could be fired they sprang to their feet and were out of sight in a few moments in the rocks and bushes. The white men at this time were scattered, and the three Indians soon ran close to Henry Robinson and his son Frank, and stopped without seeing them. Henry Robinson carried a double-barreled gun, one for ball and the other for shot. Both father and son fired at the same Indian, and all three were out of sight again in an instant. On coming to the spot where the Indian who was fired at stood, plenty of blood was found, and also a belt which had been cut from his waist by a bullet. His trail was now taken up. It led down a gulley, and blood was profusely scattered and to be plainly seen on the rocks, and very black, indicating a liver wound. A pair of wet moccasins were found on a rock where the Indian pulled them off and left them after wading a small creek. They were heavy when wet, and retarded his flight. At last the white men were completely tired out, and yet the wounded Indian was not found. Dud Richardson had become very sick from exertion and overheat, and was vomiting. The chase was again abandoned. The old gray horse was finally found, however, lost in the shuffle, and taken in custody by the settlers. He came out of the chase with but very little of Mr. Anglin's big fat cow hanging to him. Besides the horse, there were captured one lance, one shield, two bows, one quiver of arrows, five bridles, and five lariats. Night was now approaching, and it was quite dark before they could descend the rough mountain to where they had left their horses. The animals were all right, tied up where they had left them, but the men left in charge were gone.

About one month after this raid the Indians came again, and no doubt for revenge, for it is almost certain that the Indian wounded by Henry Robinson died. As before, they first let their presence be known at the ranch of Mr. Anglin. They came at night and were discovered by the dogs. Mr. Anglin was gone to the Cibolo at the time to see Mr. Pancost about some horses. He lived at Selma, and afterwards sold goods in San Antonio under the firm name of Pancost & Son. One of Mr. Anglin's dogs was very much afraid of Indians, and as soon as he would get scent of one would rush into the house and go under the bed. On this occasion, when the dogs raised the alarm in the yard, this particularly nervous dog in regard to Indians made a break for the house, but as the door was closed he came near butting his brains out against the shutter. "Indians!" exclaimed Mrs. Anglin as soon as she heard the dog make such a frantic effort to get into the house. On this particular night Mr. John Leakey and wife were stopping with the family of Mr. Anglin, and he at once opened the door, pistol in hand, and went into the yard. The other dogs were still barking, but it was too dark to see anything. While Mr. Leakey was standing with his face in the direction of the Indians as indicated by the dogs, an arrow sped from out the darkness, barely missing Mr. Leakey. He now sent several bullets in the direction the arrow came from, and then went back in the house. Lights had been put out when the first alarm was raised, and Mr. Leakey now sat in darkness and kept watch until daylight. Mr. Leakey's home was below the mountains on the Sabinal, in the Patterson settlement. Next morning after the Indian alarm Mr. Leakey, while looking about for the signs of the Indians, found a cap of foxskin hanging to a blackjack limb about 100 yards from the house. It was evident that this was the cap of the Indian who shot the arrow at Mr. Leakey, and lost it in flight when the settler returned the fire. He might have been wounded. Mr. Leakey notified the nearest settlers of the raid, and five men soon collected at Mr. Anglin's house to go in pursuit of them. They were, besides Leakey, Gideon Thompson,

Henry Robinson, Silas Webster, and Sebe Barrymore. They decided to follow the Indians on foot, as the mountains were steep and rough for horses. The Indians were supposed to be some distance away by this time and the pursuit would last several days, but in the end they hoped to come upon them unawares in camp and get the best of them. Mrs. Anglin filled a pillowslip full of provisions, and Mr. Leakey fastened it across his shoulders back of the neck. The sequel will show that these daring pioneers were never to partake of the food which the good woman was so careful in preparing for them.

The trail led southwest to the mountains, two and one-half miles away, and the trailers soon arrived and commenced their ascent. The Indians were on top of the mountain in an ambuscade and watching all the maneuvers of the whites. They had made their trail plain, even cutting bushes with their tomahawks so that the white men would be certain to come into their trap. It was a hot day in August, and the men went up slowly. While ascending, Mr. Thompson, who was always on the lookout for signs, saw buzzards again, and said he believed the Indians were on the mountain. "Not an Indian in ten miles of here," said Mr. Leakey. When the top of the mountain was reached the men were hot and tired. It was a fine place for an ambush—rocks, low brush, and cedar trees. The lead men had penetrated the ambush, and their order as to position when the battle commenced was as follows: Robinson in front, Leakey next, Webster next, Barrymore next, and Thompson last. Mr. Thompson was incumbered with a large Spanish water gourd full of water which was strapped to his left arm. In addition to this he carried a heavy rifle, was very much fatigued, and had not quite reached the top. He had just called to the men to stop and rest awhile, when two shots were fired in front by the Indians at Robinson and Leakey. At the same time he saw an Indian running along a ledge in plain view waving a red blanket and yelling. He was trying to draw the fire of the men in the rear to him, so that, few and tired as the white men were, they would fall the easier victims. As before stated, the two foremost men had penetrated the ambuscade and had been fired on at close range, but without effect. Mr. Thompson thought at the time that these two first shots had been fired by Robinson and Leakey. The Indians now broke cover in many places, and showed themselves to be quite numerous. As the white men began to return the fire the Indians sprang from tree to tree and from rock to rock, and soon encompassed them on two sides. Mr. Thompson saw Mr. Leakey close among the Indians, and pointing his gun vigorously from one to another but failing to fire. The reason for this was the fact that Leakey had borrowed a rifle with set triggers, and he had been used to a single-triggered gun, so in this trying ordeal he had failed to spring the trigger and the hammer could not be pulled down. At this time Mr. Thompson was making frantic efforts to disengage the water gourd from his arm, but failing, was compelled to fire with this weight dangling at his left elbow. The Indian he aimed at was not more than twenty yards from him, but the smoke from his gun when he fired so obscured his view that he could not see the effects of the shot. He now heard Leakey firing, and looking in his direction saw him half bent, leaning towards the Indians, and shooting rapidly with a revolver. He had thrown his gun down. Robinson fired his gun and then retreated past Leakey, telling him to run—there was too many for them. Mr. Thompson made an attempt to reload his gun, but choked it, and was unable to do so. Calling now to Leakey to run, he started back down the mountain. Webster and Barrymore had passed him going back, after discharging their rifles. Robinson, brave as a lion, but seeing the utter futility of making a fight against twenty-five Indians under the circumstances, continued his retreat, after again calling to Leakey to come. Webster and Barrymore were going back the way they came up, Robinson further to the right, and all soon passed Thompson. In going down a limb caught in the strap of Webster's shotpouch, jerking it from his shoulder, and it was left dangling in the air. The Indians at this time were making the mountain gorges echo again and again with fearful warwhoops, and the shots from Leakey were no longer heard. An Indian now came out on a rock with a rifle in his hand where he could have a plain view of the retreating men, and taking aim fired it at Thompson. The ball passed through his hat brim on the right side, went between his ear and head, and passing on hit Barrymore in the hip, coming out at the thigh. This shot was fired from Leakey's gun. An Indian had picked it up where Leakey had discarded it, and knowing how to operate the set triggers, fired it with the result above narrated. The three men now retreated to an open ledge and halted, as Barrymore was continually falling. There was no doubt in their minds that Robinson and Leakey were both killed. All were silent for a short time, and then Leakey was seen staggering down the mountain towards them, and finally sank down. After emptying his pistol he had turned from the Indians and sprang down a ledge, covered with wounds, and made his way back more dead than alive. Mr. Thompson at once went to him and gave him water out of the gourd which he still carried on his arm. The water soon revived Leakey, and he began to talk. The first words he said were, "Damn the gun! I could not make it shoot. I must have broken it in some way. I pulled and pulled on the trigger." He was hit by arrows in nine places, and Mr. Thompson says he was the bloodiest man he ever saw. One arrow had struck near the wrist as he had his arm extended towards the Indians, firing with a pistol, and it penetrated lengthwise of the arm nearly to the shoulder, and was still transfixed. Other wounds were in the neck, face, head, thigh, and body.

Robinson had also sprang from a ledge and stopped in the brush and reloaded his gun. He then rejoined his companions, who thought him killed. After he came an Indian was discovered on a rock looking for them. Robinson at once prepared to shoot him, but Mr. Thompson said, "No, Henry, don't shoot. It will bring all of them on us again, and no loaded guns. Mine is choked; Leakey's is gone; Barrymore is wounded, and his gun not loaded, and Webster has lost his ammunition and his gun is empty." Robinson then desisted and all went down the mountain, Barrymore having to be supported. Thus they got clear out of this most desperate situation without losing a man. Leakey still had the provisions strapped to his shoulders. They were saturated with blood, and were taken off and thrown away. After arriving at the Anglin ranch again Dud Richardson was sent to the Patterson settlement after men, and an expedition was organized to go in pursuit of the Indians. When the reinforcements arrived they at once repaired to the battleground and took the trail of the Indians. How many were killed in the fight could not be ascertained. There was blood on the ground in places, but no doubt some of this came from Leakey's wounds.

The trail led a southwest course towards the town of Uvalde, about forty miles distant. On Bear Creek some dead grass had been burned off, leaving the ground covered with ashes, and in this twenty-two trails of foot Indians were counted. Mr. Thompson thinks they fought twenty-five on the mountain. Besides the trails of the Indians there were fifteen trails of horses. The Indians made one camp on Bear Creek. Here they took Leakey's gun to pieces and scattered the parts around. All of it was found except those parts which had holes through them for screws, etc. The trail was continued on from here in the general direction until they came to the "yellow banks" on the dry Frio, at the foot of the mountains. Here the Indians separated into two parties, and it was afterwards ascertained that the largest party went down the main Frio. The trail here was hard to keep, and the Indians scattered considerably on purpose to retard the pursuit of the whites, whom no doubt they had seen from some mountain top. The smallest trail was finally located, and it tended in the direction of Pilot Knob, at Fort Inge, four miles below Uvalde, on the Leona River. The soldiers had been removed from the fort, and no one was there at this time except old man Griner and his family. The Indians passed around to the left of the fort and kept south. For two days the men trailed through dense brush and pears, and finally lost the trail. It had been put out by numerous wild cattle that had passed over it. The men were now without food and water, and were compelled to quit searching for the lost trail and go to the Leona for water. Some of the men were in favor of giving up the pursuit and returning, but Mr. Thompson and "Butch" Dilliard persuaded them to try one more day. This was finally agreed to, and the trail was found again. The Indians on their way up to Sabinal Canyon on this raid had traversed this part of the country and had roped and tied up three head of wild cattle, no doubt intending to eat them on their return, but failed to do anything with them, likely passing the spot in the night and not being able to find them. When the white men passed two of the cattle were dead, and the other had got loose and made his escape. The trailers also found where the Indians had killed one old male of the wild cattle and cooked the meat. They took the bones along with them until they came to where there was some rocks, and there cracked them to get the marrow. They passed near Westfall's ranch, and when the settlers came to a point on the river about a mile below they heard the Indians singing and making a noise like a gang of Mexicans. The men all dismounted now, and leaving three of their party with the horses, advanced cautiously toward the banks of the Leona, from whence the sounds emanated, led by Henry Robinson and Newman Patterson. The Indians were all in bathing, except two bucks and one squaw. Some were yelling and some singing and making a great splashing in the water. It seems they were of the opinion that the white men had abandoned the pursuit. The surprise was complete. The first intimation they had of danger was the sight of white men standing on the bank shooting at them. The men in front fired first and killed the squaw and one buck. The balance of the men scattered along the bank and poured a perfect storm of bullets at those in the water. The buck who was on the bank and was not killed at the first fire ran to an elm tree, and was shot by Jesse Lewis, a half Cherokee Indian. The hostile then left the tree and ran a short distance and fell, with his bow in one hand and three arrows in the other. Some of the Indians in the water tried to come out and secure their arms, but the fire from the white men was so severe that only one got out on the bank, and he caught up his quiver by the wrong end and his arrows all dropped out as he attempted to run back in the water with it. Mr. Thompson saw one Indian in the water who had been shot, and with his back half exposed was watching to see who was going to shoot at him again. Mr. Thompson shot him again, and he turned over and over in the water, like a snake with his back broken, until he got to the opposite bank, and then got out and went about 200 yards on the opposite side of the river and lay down. Some of the men stripped off their clothing and followed him and killed him. He had on a big sixshooter, two of the chambers of which were loaded. It is somewhat strange that he had it on in the water. Two guns were picked up and were found to be badly overloaded, the charges measuring four inches. An Indian believes in making all the noise he can when in a fight. One Indian made his escape without being hit. He was afterwards seen on a reservation at Fort Belknap by Mr. Black, who was in the fight. Eight Indians were killed on the spot. Mr. Black was afterwards killed in Uvalde. On one of the shields captured was found the missing parts of Leakey's gun— the pieces that had holes in them. This gun belonged to John Richards, and he had but recently purchased it in San Antonio from Mr. Charles Hummell, who dealt in firearms, and is still in that business under the firm name of Charles Hummell & Son. All parts of the gun were finally collected and sent back to San Antonio, and Mr. Hummell put it together again. Besides Mr. Thompson and the others already mentioned, there were in this Indian killing scrape Judge McCormick, John Ware, John Davenport, John Bowles, Joel Fenley, and others. None of the white men were hurt, and all returned safely home.

In 1861 Big Foot Wallace fought the Indians on the head of the Seco, about twelve miles from Sabinal Canyon, and that night came with his men into the canyon with some wounded men, one of whom was William Davenport. He left the Indians in possession of the battleground and about 200 head of horses. He wanted more men to help to pursue and fight them again, and if possible to retake the horses which were stolen below. This band of Indians had penetrated into the settlements as far as Atascosa County and killed many people. Around the little village of Pleasanton they had killed a man named Herndon, wounded Anderson and O'Bryant, and chased several others. On the way back they were fought by a small party of settlers, in which James Winters was killed and others wounded. Further on they killed "Mustang" Moore, near where Moore's station is, and Peter Ketchum, on the Hondo. They also killed Mr. Murray, tax assessor of Bandera County. Others were also killed and wounded by them, and horses gathered up all over the country. Captain Wallace stayed that night at John C. Ware's place, near where Utopia now is. Jasper Kinchaloe was sent up the canyon to notify the settlers who lived above. Late at night he came to Mr. Thompson's house and told the news of the battle and the need of more men. Jack Kelley lived still above, about where Mr. Sam Harper now lives, and Mr. Thompson went to notify him. His horse was out, but they hunted him up in the dark and came on down to Mr. Anglin's house. Here they tried to shoe their horses in his shop, but the wind blew the light out and they could not do it. Next morning seven of the canyon men went to the Cypress spring, where the Bob Harper place is now, and there intended to wait for Big Foot Wallace and his men from below, and in the meantime shoe their horses, as Mr. Thompson had brought his tools along. By the time the shoeing was over a cold rain had set in, and as Wallace and his party had not as yet put in an appearance, Thompson and his men mounted their horses and started back home. After crossing the river, however, and coming to a point about where Mr. Henry Taylor now resides, they came upon the trail of Wallace and his men, who had crossed below and came up the west bank of the river. The Thompson party at once turned and followed their trail, and came up with them at the old Kelley ranch, which has been previously mentioned as the place where the Indians broke up the spinning wheels. Here the whole party stayed until morning, as by this time the weather had become fearfully cold, the rain turning to sleet. Most of the men were not prepared for such a change, some of the Atascosa County men not even having their coats with them. They did very well, however, at the deserted ranch during the night. The following morning was clear and not so cold, and the Indian hunt was resumed with vigor. The intention of Captain Wallace was to get ahead of the Indians and lay an ambush for them. His party was traveling north and the late battleground was east, but the general course of the Indians was northwest, and would intersect that of the whites. The Indians traveled slowly with so many horses and over a very rough country, and no doubt also laid up for the sleet in some cedar brake. Wallace got ahead of them on the divide and placed his men in ambush for them. The impatience of the men, however, and their want of discipline, caused them to fail in their object. Many of them left their places of concealment to look, and when the Indians did come and before they were in gunshot a man named Hilburn fired his rifle and the Indians ran and scattered. Some of the men had left their horses too far, and could not get them quick enough to do any good in the pursuit. The horses, however, were all captured and carried back to the owners by Wallace and his men.

In 1866 the Indians attacked the ranch of Mr. R. H. Kinchaloe in his absence and killed Mrs. Bowlin, a neighbor lady, who was there at the time. They also wounded Mrs. Kinchaloe in a dozen places, and left her for dead on the floor.

Mr. Thompson took an active part in the pursuit of the Indians, but was unsuccessful in getting them. He had the misfortune to get his leg broken after he got to be an old man, but is hearty and carries his years well. He still lives on the place he first settled over forty years ago, but has made many improvements and is well to do. His wife died a few years ago. Mr. Aaron Anglin died at his home on May 15, 1884. His wife, Mrs. Jennie Anglin, died in November, 1894, on Thanksgiving day.

Mr. Anglin was one of the commissioners who helped to lay off the town of Uvalde. His son, Job Anglin, still lives at the old home on the Anglin prong of the river.

CAPTAIN MALCOLM VAN PELT.

Came to Texas in 1853.

Fifteen miles west of Sabinal Canyon, running nearly south, is Frio Canyon, a long, wide, beautiful valley, with the Frio (pronounced Freo) River running through its center. There are many clear creeks flowing into it on both sides, and each of these streams has small canyons containing many acres of rich land which is now (1897) being rapidly settled and small farms opened.

One of the early settlers here is Capt. T. M. G. Van Pelt, who has a fine ranch and farm fronting the river. Mr. Van Pelt was born in the town of Charlotte, Mecklenburg County, North Carolina, in July, 1831. His great-grandfather was a soldier in the war of the revolution, and was killed by the tories and Indians. He was at home at the time when the Van Pelt house was attacked by the red and white savages. His grandfather first discovered the enemy and ran to the house. As he was getting over the yard fence the tories commenced shooting but missed him, and hit the top rails of the fence. In the fight that ensued at the house the elder Van Pelt (the soldier) was killed, but the son made his escape. In the war of 1812 his grandfather was on his way to join General Jackson's army when the battle of New Orleans was fought.

Mr. Van Pelt came to Texas in 1853 and first settled at Gonzales, but soon moved from there and settled at Prairie Lea, in Caldwell County, in 1854. He bought cattle there and drove them to the Hondo River just below where Hondo City now is, the county seat of Medina County. That was in 1855. In 1860 he moved and settled in Frio Canyon, Uvalde County. Among those who were there at the time was E. V. Dale, Richard Ware, and Capt. Theophilus Watkins. The latter was captain of the frontier guards. Mr. John Leakey was the first settler, but had moved his family and was running some freight wagons below. In 1861 Mr. Van Pelt went back to the Hondo to gather his hogs, and while doing so stayed at the ranch of Widow Dean and her son Joe. During that time the Indians made a raid and killed several settlers, among whom was Mr. Pete Ketchum. Mr. Van Pelt helped to bury Ketchum, and also saw nine head of horses the Indians had killed. The hostiles were in large force, and nearly all of the men in the country rallied under Big Foot Wallace to pursue and fight them. The Indians were overtaken at the head of the Seco (Saco) Creek, where they had selected a strong position and had halted to give the settlers battle. Mr. Van Pelt had joined the expedition. Near their ambush the Indians had tied a horse on the side of the mountain near their trail, and in plain view of anyone approaching from the valley. It seemed to be an abandoned horse. Judge Davenport was the first one to see the animal and exclaimed, "To first sight belongs the property," and started up the mountain, followed by several others. Captain Wallace said, "Look out, boys; that is a trick of the Indians," but they kept on and were soon fired upon by the Indians at close range with shotguns and other arms. Some of the men were hit, among whom was a son of Judge Davenport, William. There was a general stampede back down the mountain, and some confusion prevailed amid the yelling of Indians. Mr. Van Pelt says the first sight he saw of the Indians was one rise up on his knee and fire a shotgun. Captain Wallace ordered all to dismount at the foot of the mountain and tie their horses to the cedar trees which grew thick on the bank of the ravine. He also requested some of them who had long range guns to ascend a hill in the rear and fire from there, as they could better see the Indiians, who had now taken refuge from the rifle shots in the rocks, and could not be seen from below, where most of the men were posted. During one charge Mr. Van Pelt had his gun up to his face and was taking aim at the chief when a man named Hilburn fired first and killed him. The Indian fell forward on his face with an arrow in his hand, which he was about to adjust to the bowstring to shoot. The other Indians carried his body up the mountain. He was very brave, and continually charged the whites until he was killed. One Indian was observed with a shotgun which he laid down after discharging it, and commenced shooting arrows very fast. He had on a hat and shirt which reached down nearly to his knees. George Robins fired at him with a shotgun, but he caught the load on his shield and ran, leaving the shotgun. This gun belonged to "Mustang" Moore, whom the Indians had killed on this raid near the place where

Moore's station now is on the International Railroad, and which was named for him. Moore had camped on a return trip from San Antonio. William Davenport, who was wounded and lying under a cedar tree during the hottest of the firing, wanted to get up and join in, but Judge Davenport stopped him, and said, "Lay still, Bill; there are a thousand of them here yet." When the fight was over and the Indians had all gone back on top of the mountain, Mr. Van Pelt asked if there was any man in the crowd that had on a linen shirt. No one had, but there was one found who had linen wristbands on his shirt sleeves. These were taken off and picked to pieces very fine by Mr. Van Pelt, and twisted into a cord and carefully inserted into the wound of Davenport and drawn through, but left there. The wound was in the leg above the knee, and was made by a large ball that went through. The cord afterward was turned frequently until it began to get well. This was to keep the wound cleansed. Judge Davenport wanted to cut the leg of the pantaloons off, but Mr. Van Pelt objected to that, saying the leg would freeze before they could get to the settlement in Sabinal Canyon. By this time it was nearly night, cold and sleeting. The Indian chief killed in the fight was afterwards found in a cave. He was finely dressed, having many beads on his clothing and a magnificent headdress and shield. These things were sold, and the shield alone brought $30. When coming on the trail of the Indians up Seco valley the settlers crossed the bridle road that led from Bandera over to Sabinal Canyon. Captain Wallace said the Indians had run some one along the trail, as the tracks of running horses indicated. This was correct, and the man pursued was Mr. Murray, the tax assessor of Bandera County, who was coming over to Sabinal Canyon to assess, as part of the valley was in Bandera County. Murray was killed, and his body, at the time Wallace and his men passed, was lying not far away on the side of the mountain. The Indians who killed him got back to their companions in time for the battle, in which they lost Murray's pistol, and it was recovered by the white men.

After the fight Wallace and his men went to Sabinal Canyon and spent the night. Additions were made to his force by canyon men, and the pursuit of the Indians commenced again. Mr. Van Pelt says they ambushed the Indians at Ranger Springs, but, as

15

has already been written, Frank Hilburn fired too soon and spoiled it all. Mr. Van Pelt says that Hilburn badly wounded the Indian at whom he fired, although at long range, and that he died and his body was found afterwards. The Indians had many horses, and when the stampede commenced after Hilburn fired a bell was heard on one of the loose horses rattling loudly. Mr. Van Pelt exclaimed, "My bell!" meaning he would have the horse that wore the bell. An Indian had mounted this belled horse, and Mr. Van Pelt gave him a close chase and was about to fire his rifle at him when the Indian looked back to see if the white man was going to shoot, and a limb knocked him off. He made his escape to the brush, but Mr. Van Pelt got the horse and also one of his own, which the Indians had held for more than a year. Nearly 200 head of horses were taken and carried back to their owners.

While Mr. Van Pelt lived on the Hondo, in 1859, the Indians made a raid, and after killing a Mexican herder, chased and killed two cowboys, one Huffman and Sebastian Wolfe. Van Pelt, Mike Whiff, George Johnson, and Jack Wolfe, brother to the one killed, followed the Indians, but were met by Jack Davenport and others who had followed the Indians and whipped them and taken their horses. They had Huffman's mule, saddle, and pistol. The bodies of the men had not as yet been found, but it was very evident that they had been killed. All now went to look for the missing men, and soon found their dead and mangled bodies and buried them. Wolfe's throat was cut from ear to ear. The dead Indian in the tree was also taken down by them.

In 1862 Malcolm Van Pelt, Frank Hilburn, Jasper Wish, Gid Thompson, Joel Fenley, Chris Kelley, Ezekiel Tucker, and James Davenport followed a band of Indians from the Frio to the head of East Nueces, near the head of Ash Creek. There they found a mare killed, with the back skinned where the Indians had cut out the sinews to make bowstrings. Some said the animal had been killed several days, but Mr. Van Pelt knew the mare and said that she belonged to Joe Harrison, and was at his ranch only a few days before. He was confident the Indians were near who killed her. In scouting around through the hills seventy-five wigwams were discovered, and near them a horse belonging to Mr. Van Pelt. He, however, declined to go to him, and said he did not need that particular horse in his business just at that time. The men now went back and camped, as they could not make a fight if all those wigwams had tenants. Next morning in going back to the spot where the dead mare lay it was discovered that the meat had been taken away, only the skeleton remaining. It was afterwards learned that nearly all of the Indians at this time were below on a raid, and those in camp kept hid from the white men, and when they left followed them and tried to ambush them on Patterson's Creek, but the white men passed the danger spot ahead of them. Another party of white men returned to the wigwams, but they were deserted. The Indians anticipated a return of the whites and left. While the men were looking about the camps a smooth, flat pecan stick was found, and on it was drawn the Frio River, nine white men, and four Indians, the white men going down the river and the Indians to the northwest. This was for the information of the war party when they should return from the raid. The pictures of the Indians were drawn with red paint. They also drew a picture of the moon, showing how old it was when the white men were there.

Mr. E. V. Dale, an old San Jacinto veteran, who lived many years in Guadalupe County and died there, was a neighbor of Mr. Van Pelt. They were good friends but entirely different in their temperaments. Mr. Dale was always in earnest and serious on all subjects, and was never known to get off a joke on anyone. Mr. Van Pelt was exactly the opposite, always running over with fun and practical jokes, and when no one else was around would perpetrate them on his friend Dale. On one occasion Dale was invited by Van to take a hunt with him and another neighbor. He consented, and came at the specified time with gun, blankets, and provisions. Van Pelt was to furnish the wagon and team. The wagon had no bed on it, and the things were strapped to the coupling pole. Mr. Dale did not like these arrangements, and wanted a wagon bed put on so a sheet could be stretched over it at night to sleep under, as he was solicitous about his health. This was overruled, however, and they started, Mr. Dale perched astride of the coupling on the bedding. Mr. Van Pelt was on the rocking bolster, where he could control and guide the oxen. The other man was on a horse carried along to pack game to camp on. Everything went on all right until they went to cross the Frio River. It was shallow at the crossing, but deep above. The

spirit of mischief now came upon Mr. Van Pelt, and it was almost irresistible to give Mr. Dale a ducking. He had one ox that,
if he jumped out beside him and talked quick and loud to him,
would swerve sharply in the opposite direction and was hard to
control. Just as they were entering the stream Mr. Van did that
trick, and the oxen turned sharply up stream into deep water,
submerging Mr. Dale and all the bedding. Van Pelt held on to
the rope and yelled "Whoa!" with all his might, and of course
was wet himself, to make Dale think it was accidental. When
they got out Van told his wet friend how it all happened, and
when he got through Dale said, "Yes, and you are an old fool."
The balance of the day was spent drying clothing and bedding
around large fires. Mr. Dale said it would be the death of him.
No bad effects, however, occurred from the wetting, and they
killed plenty of game and had a good time.

When Mr. Dale was loaded up and ready to move east he drove
by Van Pelt's, and calling him out, extended his hand, saying,
"Van, I am going to do something for you now that the devil
has never yet done for you,—tell you good-bye." Van laughed
heartily at this, shook his hand, and they parted friends.

JACK MILLER.

Came to Texas in 1854.

Among the pioneers of Southwest Texas who has endured the perils and hardships, met the dangers unflinchingly, and suffered loss of loved ones at the hands of the savages, is Mr. J. W. Miller, better known as "Jack" among his friends. Mr. Miller was born in Pulaski County, Missouri, near Waynesville, which was the county seat at that time. His grandfather was a soldier under Washington. Jack Miller came to Texas in 1854 and settled in Sabinal Canyon, near the present village of Utopia. He moved from this place and settled at Fort Lincoln, on the Seco, below the mountains near old D'Hanis. While living at this place, on the 29th of January, 1867, his brother George, in company with August Rothe and Herbert Weynand, went up into Hondo Canyon on a cow hunt and camped out several nights below where the Bandera road now crosses the valley. Early one morning the Indians came upon them and the boys ran from camp on foot, not having time to untie and mount their horses. There were no guns in the crowd and but one pistol, and it only partly loaded, carried by August Rothe. Rothe and Miller were about 17 years of age and Weynand about 13. Miller was killed and Weynand carried off a captive. Rothe made his escape to a mountain, and kept the Indians off by aiming the pistol at them when they ran close to him. Keeping his few loads in reserve was all that saved him, the Indians not knowing how badly loaded his pistol was. Young Rothe came to a settler named McCay and told the news, and a party came and carried away the body of Miller in McCay's wagon. A runner was then sent to notify the Miller and Weynand families at Fort Lincoln. The father of the murdered George came and brought the body of his son home and buried it there. (See a more detailed account of this affair in the sketch of August Rothe.)

On one occasion Jack Miller, Ambrose Crane, "Seco" Smith, George Johnson, Charles Richter, and William Wagener were camped on the Seco cow-hunting below where the railroad now

crosses the creek. The elder Miller, father of Jack, came down
to see about the cattle, and on his return home was run onto by
Indians in Seco bottom, but succeeded in getting away from
them and back to the boys, and gave the alarm. The cowboys at
once mounted and put out after the Indians and soon came upon
them. The Indians had forty head of horses belonging to Judge
George Harper, who had a ranch on the Hondo River some miles
east of the Seco. The Indians ran when they saw the cowmen
and a long chase commenced. In about one and a half miles run
one Indian was overhauled with a worn-out horse, which he deserted, took to a thicket, and there prepared to fight the white
men. All of the cowboys now stopped, as no more Indians were
likely to be caught, and concentrated around the thicket where
the lone Comanche had made his stand to fight his pale-faced
foes, who greatly outnumbered him. Even with only one Indian
to fight the men had to approach him with great caution to keep
any of their party from being killed. As soon as the Indian
would get a glimpse of a man as they circled around trying to see
him an arrow would come in quick flight, and some narrow
escapes were made. Ambrose Crane, who was a very tall man
and could see over bushes and tall grass, obtained a view of the
Indian and shot at him with a pistol. Many shots were now
fired, the men charging in and firing with sixshooters, their only
weapons. The Comanche was badly wounded, having his elbow
shot off so that he could not use his bow, and becoming desperate,
left his cover and charged the crowd. The pistol balls met him
on every side, and he soon sank down and died, with a butcher-
knife clenched in his only hand that he could use. Mr. Rolly
Miller, father of Jack, and a very old man, who had followed the
boys, scalped the dead brave, and his body was left where it fell.
Jack Miller gave the Indian one stab with a knife when he left
the thicket, and the white men closed around him. The Millers
had in mind the dead and mutilated body of a son and brother.
Years after some one found the skull of the Indian and carried
it away. Judge Harper got all of his horses back. The Indian
had selected a bad one on which to make his escape, and lost his
life in consequence. There were many horses in the herd that
would have carried him away safely. The Indian looked to be
about 30 years of age, and was tall and slim.

Jack Miller is one of the successful stock men of Medina County, and has a fine ranch on the Seco. About 300 yards from his house, and nearly opposite, on the west side of the creek, is the site of the old house built by Mr. Myrick, in which Richard Ware and Charles Durbin made their stand and kept off a large body of Indians in the early settlement of the country.

AUGUST ROTHE.

AUGUST ROTHE.

Came to Texas in 1854.

Among the pioneers of the west who have seen wild Indians, fought them, and been chased by them, is Mr. A. C. Rothe, who now lives on his ranch on the west bank of the Seco, about six miles north from the town of D'Hanis.

Mr. Rothe was born in the northern part of Bavaria in 1847, and came to Castroville, Texas, with his father, Henry Rothe, in 1854. They sailed from the old country in the ship Salucia, and landed at Galveston. From this point they came by ox teams to Castroville. Mrs. Rothe was sick on the way, and died in fourteen days after arriving at their new home in this far away, strange, and frontier country. It is always sad to think of a death under these circumstances. These people, cutting loose from all ties of relationship, friends, home, and country; braving the dangers of the deep in a small vessel; landing on a foreign soil among people whose language they could not speak; the long and tedious trip to the west by slow moving ox wagons, and at last reaching the place of long expectation, and then not live to enjoy the fruits of the sacrifices which they have made in order to reach the place where they expected to rest from their toils and build up pleasant, happy homes in the beautiful new country.

The Rothe family first settled on the Medina River, six miles above Castroville, and then moved up near the Haby settlement, six miles further. The Rothe boys were Fritz, Henry, Louis, and August, and one daughter. The Rothes had a hard time of it at first. The boys had gone to school most of their time while in Europe, and had not as yet learned how to work on a farm or handle cattle, which was all that young men could do at that time in the west, except probably freighting or working for the government on forts, etc. The elder Rothe was also unused to this kind of work, being a man of some means, and an office-holder in the old country. However, they soon learned how to manage and raise stock, and farmed until 1862. They then moved to the Seco, near Fort Lincoln, and took charge of the Riley stock of cattle under contract to keep them three years.

In the meantime the civil war had broken out, and the two oldest boys, Fritz and Henry, joined the company of Captain Kampmann and went to the Confederate army and served the cause of the South until the break-up.

August and Louis had to fill the contract with Riley's cattle, and they had a hard time of it. The Indians constantly depredated upon them and kept stealing their horses, so that they could hardly keep ponies enough to handle the cattle. Horses were high and hard to get. In the three years they were engaged in handling the Riley cattle they lost $3000 worth of horses. After this contract was finished, and the other boys coming back from the war, the Rothes brought their cattle from the Medina and commenced to raise cattle on an extensive scale, and were very successful. August saw his first wild Indian in 1863. In that year he and his brother Louis and Charles Richter, all boys, went on a cow-hunt to the Cedar waterhole, on Seco, some distance above the settlement. On the way they came upon three head of cattle which had been killed by Indians. Two of the stock had arrows in them, and the boys dismounted and pulled these out and carried them along with them.

At this time Jacob Sauter, Tobe Sauter, and Mike Schreiber had gone up to the Cedar waterhole to cut grass. The boys went up there and told them to look out, "the Indians were in." The grass-cutters said they had seen a man running horses, and Tobe Sauter said it was an Indian, but the others thought not; that the Indians would not run horses in daylight that close to camp, and then kept on with their work. It seems that the Indians had not as yet discovered the presence of white men, so that when one of them commenced to whet a scythe blade he looked towards them quickly, and then left the horses and ran across the creek out of sight. The three boys now made a circle in the prairie not far from the present residences of August and Fritz Rothe, and then came back towards the waterhole. When near there they saw four saddled horses in a liveoak grove. Not knowing for certain that it was Indians, they rode on and came near them. An Indian now jumped up from among the horses and gave a keen whistle. He had heard the noise of the horses' feet on the rocks. When he whistled, three other Indians came from cover near the waterhole and advanced rapidly towards their horses. Two of these Indians had guns. One mounted and sat on his horse and the others stood on the ground, the one with his gun ready to shoot, all four intently watching the young cowboys as they slowly rode around them. The boys only had two six-shooters in their party, and some of the loads of these had been fired at a fox before they knew that Indians were around. The Indians all mounted now and rode off across the creek, and the boys went back to the grass-cutters and told them of the Indians. One man was just preparing to start with a keg to the waterhole for water, and would have been killed by the Indians if the boys had not come upon them and caused the Indians to leave their ambush and go away. The hay camp was not at the water, but near enough to get their supply there. The Indians were watching for some one to come after water.

The Indian alarm was raised in the country, and a scout made up which followed the trail into the mountains, but the hostiles made their escape.

In the spring of 1865 August Rothe, George Miller, Herbert Weynand, and Jacob Sauter left the settlement on Seco, near Fort Lincoln, and went to hunt oxen on the Hondo at a place called "sink of the water." These places are at or near the mouth of all the canyons through which these mountain streams flow. The water sinks here in the accumulation of heaps of gravel that for ages has been piling up. Sometimes the water will break out again many miles below.

The boys were all young. Weynand was about 12 years of age, and the youngest. The others were some years older. They made their camp at the sinks, and then commenced to hunt their oxen. Sauter found his oxen the first day, and went home.

The same day, while August Rothe was hunting his oxen in the mountains, about 2 o'clock in the evening, he found old man Ludwig Mummie, who had been lost part of two days and a night. He was very hungry, and almost delirious. He had lost his way trying to come through the mountains from Bandera to D'Hanis. Rothe took him to their camp, and when he had been refreshed with food and coffee he mounted his horse and went on home, although the boys begged him to stay. He had a good gun, pistol, and plenty of cartridges, and had he stayed would no doubt have averted the terrible tragedy which was enacted the next morning at this camp, in which one of the boys lost his life and another was carried off into captivity, never more to return, and which caused two families to mourn the loss of loved ones. After Mummie left, Rothe went to see about the horses, and soon heard firing in camp. He at once hastened back, and found that George Miller had nearly emptied Rothe's pistol at a tree. The pistol was the only weapon in camp. August said, "George, you should not have done that. I have no more loads, and now suppose the Indians should come upon us." Weynand spoke up and said he had a little powder and two buckshot in his pocket. There was one load left in the pistol, and August took the two buckshot, and by patching them like loading a rifle, charged two more chambers of the pistol, making three in all. Next morning after breakfast Rothe and Weynand went to get the horses, which had gotten a mile and a half from camp with hobbles on, which was an unusual thing for them to do. It consumed about two hours to find the horses. Rothe tied his horse and Miller's together and led them back. Weynand had his bridle with him, so he mounted his horse and rode back. The camp was situated on the bluff bank of the Hondo, and in the rear was a small rocky hill. Four hundred yards further was a high, rocky mountain. When Rothe and Weynand got near the small rocky hill in the hear of the camp, and before they could see the latter, they met George Miller coming in a run with a scared look upon his face, who said that a lot of Indians were under the bluff watering their horses. At first Rothe thought that Miller was trying to fool them, and stood a few moments, but soon saw by his pale face that it was no joke. Miller said he was lying down smoking a pipe and heard the rattle of the rocks as the Indians came up the bed of the creek to the water, and not knowing what it was, walked to the bluff and looked over, and was very close to them. Up to this time the Indians had not seen the camp, but saw Miller when he looked over the bluff at them, and then turned to run.

The Indians had to run down the creek bed a short distance before they could find a place where they could ascend the steep bank. While Miller was telling this, they heard the rattling of the rocks as the Indians were coming out of the bed of the creek to chase Miller, not having as yet discovered the other two boys. In a very short time the Indians were close upon them, eight in number and all mounted. Rothe had no time to untie the two horses so that he and Miller could make their escape on them, and said to George, "We must run for the mountain. If we get to it before they kill us we may get away." He then told young Weynand to run up the road as fast as he could to McCay's ranch, several miles distant. The boy did so, and he and Miller set off at full speed to the mountain, pursued by five of the Indians. Three ran after Weynand. The Indians came close, yelling, and Rothe drew his pistol and waved it as he ran. When near the base of the mountain Miller gave out and said he could go no further. "Run! run!" said Rothe, as he pointed his pistol back at the Indians, who were close upon them, and still continued himself to make desperate efforts to reach cover. The Indians were afraid of Rothe's pistol, and would dodge when he aimed at them, and this would give him a chance to make another spurt ahead, and in this way he succeeded in getting a short distance up the mountain. He then stopped, nearly exhausted, and looked back. The Indians saw Miller was not armed, and one of them caught hold of him just as Rothe looked back. The boy jerked loose, and again ran towards the mountain. An Indian then ran up to him and struck him over the head with a lance. George staggered from side to side, but still continued to try to run. An Indian then ran ahead of him and aimed a lance at his breast, and Miller stopped. Rothe thought that Weynand had made his escape, but at this time heard him scream, and looking in that direction saw an Indian have him by the hair and pulling him out of some bushes. Whether the boy fell off the horse or jumped off could not be told. This was the last Rothe ever saw of him, for he himself was compelled again to run. Two of the Indians had carried Miller back to camp, and the other three were coming up the mountain on their horses after him. The Indians were all on sorry horses but one, and he came so close to Rothe that he recognized the horse as belonging to Cosgrove, who had a ranch on Seco where John Reinhart now lives. This fellow, whom Rothe thinks was a Mexican, had on a hickory shirt. His face was brown, nose flat, and he said in fair English that he was going to have the white man's scalp. The others he knew were all Indians; they wore the garb, and had long black hair. The other two flanked the hard-pressed youth and tried hard to get around him, but the way was steep and rough and difficult for horses to ascend. The one on the Cosgrove pony came so close that Rothe concluded to risk one shot at him, and stopped and aimed his pistol. The fellow, however, wheeled his horse quickly behind some liveoak bushes, but at the same time sent an arrow which hit the muzzle of Rothe's pistol, glanced down, and went through his pants leg, just grazing the skin. The other two now commenced shooting, and the arrows came from both ways, but their aim was bad, owing to the strained position they were in on the steep hillside. Rothe could hear the arrows pass him, and once more made an effort to reach the top of the mountain, pointing his pistol as if about to fire when they came close, and thus gaining a little time and pushing on. The Indians seemed to be very much afraid of the pistol, but if they had konwn the true condition it was in would have crowded upon him and no doubt have succeeded in getting his scalp, for on examination afterwards it was discovered that one of the loose-fitting buckshot had dropped out in his flight, and the good load, as he supposed, failed to fire when tried. The only shot he had was the other buckshot that still remained in the chamber. Two Indians now went back down the mountain, and the one on the brown pony tried to pass around Mr. Rothe and turn him back. The hard-pressed man, although nearly exhausted, managed to keep ahead of him. The Indian when he discovered that his two companions had quit the chase and gone back beat a hasty retreat himself. When Mr. Rothe finally succeeded in reaching the top of the mountain, which was quite elevated and steep, he stopped and looked back into the valley below, but could see nothing of the Indians. He now continued his flight and went down the mountain on the other side, and finally laid down in a dense thicket, and there came near dying from over-exertion. When sufficiently recovered to travel he went to McCay's ranch and also to that of Miller, to tell them the news. McCay got four men together, and led by Rothe went back to the camp. The first thing they saw when they arrived there was Miller's shoes, close together, like a man would place them in retiring for the night. A short search, and Miller's dead body was found under the bluff near the water, where the unfortunate young man had first seen the Indians. He was stripped except as to one sock, and his hands were tied behind him with a pair of hobbles so tightly drawn that the flesh was cut to the bone. He was lanced in the left side and the jugular vein in the neck was cut. He was not scalped or in any other way mutilated, except the bruise on the head where he was hit with a lance at the time of the capture. Mr. Rothe said that when he went to tell the Miller family of the death of George, he would rather have faced the Indians again that have done so. Young Miller was well liked by all who knew him. Before they got to the camp McCay said he did not believe the boys were killed, as he thought they could have killed August and George both before they got to the mountain if they had wanted to. They never shot at Rothe until they saw he was about to make his escape. The body of Miller was taken to Fort Lincoln and buried. A scout followed the Indians from D'Hanis under Captain Joe Ney, and they were overtaken, but they scattered into the mountains and nothing could be done with them. Some horses which they had stolen at Quihi were recovered, and also the horse, saddle, and bridle of Herbert Weynand, but the captive boy was never heard of again by anyone in this country.

August Rothe was several days recovering from his over-exertion, and drank water almost constantly for three days. These were the same Indians who killed Buchaloe on the Sabinal, and then came on down and got Cosgrove's horses.

It seems that everything worked against the two unfortunate boys, Miller and Weynand, and that they were doomed. In the first place, had Mummie remained with them, well armed as he was, they might have kept the Indians off. If the horses had not been so far from camp that morning the Indians would only have found a deserted camp, as they intended going home as soon as the horses could be caught up and saddled. There was a place below called the Mustang waterhole, and to this place the Indians went first to water their horses, but it had dried up, and they moved on to the next at the camp. This was ascertained by following their trail. Had not Miller looked over the bluff when he heard the rocks rattle the Indians might not have discovered the camp, etc.

August Rothe saw Dr. Woodbridge three days after the fight at Carrizo, and said the back of his neck was badly swollen and bruised, the effect of the blow from the Indian which knocked the doctor from his horse. Dr. Woodbridge said the Indian hit him with a bow, which came near breaking his neck. In 1872 the father of the Rothe boys died. In this same year August and his brother Fritz started to Bandera, and at Quihi Pass came upon five Indians and a sharp fight ensued, in which fifteen shots were fired. The Rothes were armed with Winchesters, and by some means so were the Indians. Fritz was riding a young horse, and he became so badly frightened at the yelling and firing as to be unmanageable, and his rider was not able to work his gun properly. The Indians had twenty-five head of horses, and were first seen by the white men. Fritz said, "Who are those over yonder?" August said, "Indians!" his brother thought not. About this time the Indians discovered the white men and dropped back behind their horses so as to get together. They now made a charge, and the Rothes ran up a bare hill where there was no protection, but stopped to make a fight. One Indian came very close and August shot at him, but the Indian was keen-sighted, dodged behind his horse, and avoided being hit. Another shot was fired quickly, which struck under the horse and caused the Indian to straighten up very suddenly, as he was hanging low down on the opposite side of his horse. The Indians now divided, and some went around the hill so as to cut them off if they attempted to come down. All of this time the Indians were firing rapidly. August saw one whose body was exposed sitting upright on his horse with his gun in the act of shooting, and both fired at each other about the same time. The ball from the Indian's gun almost grazed Rothe's head, and the Indian fell to the ground, bringing his saddle with him. He succeeded in crawling to a tree, but left his gun where he fell. The other Indians now came back to this one, and the white men left the hill and continued their course to Bandera. They had not gone far before they discovered two Indians in ambush ahead of them. August held up his gun and advanced upon them, and they gave way without a fight.

In 1873 August had one more bout with Indians near the Medina River. They tried hard to ambush him and cut him off into a trap, but he outgeneraled them and got clear. These were the last wild Indians he ever saw.

The Rothe brothers, by strict attention to stock, have been very successful, now having 100,000 acres of land, 85,000 of which is fenced. They have had at times 16,000 head of cattle and many hundred head of horses. While the writer was at the house of Mr. Fritz Rothe he related a circumstance of early times out west, which shows what kind of a country it was at that time as to game and wild animals. Mr. Jack Davenport was out hunting one day, he said, near the Sabinal River, and killed a deer. There was a large mesquite tree near, and to this he dragged the deer and proceeded to skin it. Two more deer now came up and snorted at him. Jack reloaded and fired until he killed both of them, and brought them to the same tree. While stooping over at work he suddenly felt something clutch at his shirt collar behind. Turning quickly, he saw a large panther reared up behind him. His gun was not loaded, and he backed off, loading as he went, the panther following. He killed this one, and happening to glance up the tree saw another, which he also killed. Three deer and two panthers under one tree, you might say, killed in a pile.

J. W. GARDNER.

Came to Texas in 1855.

J. W. Gardner, who lives near Big Foot postoffice, in Frio County, is one of the many Texans who bear scars on their bodies, relics of wounds put there by the heavy hand of the red man as he retreated, delivering his blows against the pale face in a desperate but futile effort to stay the advance of civilization toward the great west.

Joseph G. Gardner, father of the subject of this sketch, was a native of middle Tennessee, but moved from there to Lousiana, where his son J. W. Gardner was born in 1851. The family came to Texas in 1855 and settled in Atascosa County, but again moved in 1861 and settled near "Old Frio Town," in Frio County. They stayed at that place four years and then moved to Guadalupe County, settling fifteen miles south from Seguin, in the Sandies country. Here, in 1869, the elder Gardner died, and was buried at the "Sandies Chapel Church." The widow Gardner with her children now moved back to Frio County and settled where Mr. J. W. Gardner now lives, seven miles south from Devine and three miles from Big Foot postoffice. Here, in 1871, young Gardner hired to Mr. Simpson McCoy to drive cattle out to the Nueces River near where Cotulla now is, or to be more exact, seven miles above, at the Lago Cochina, or Hog Lake. About one week after arriving at this place the Indians made a raid in the vicinity of the ranch. This was about the middle of the summer. The people here were not aware of the presence of Indians in the country, and were not as much on the alert as they would have been otherwise. On the morning that this frontier episode which we are now about to narrate took place, J. W. Gardner went out very early in the morning on foot to hunt some horses which were to be used that day in their business of handling stock. The men at the ranch at this time were Simpson McCoy, A. F. Gardner, J. C. Gardner (brothers of J. W.), W. M. Wilkins, John De Spain, Joe Culp, Howell, and Burk—two last given names not remembered. Besides the men above mentioned, there were the families of McCoy, A. F. Gardner, John

De Spain, and Duncan Lemons, the latter being absent at the time. When young Gardner had left the ranch house about half a mile he discovered a man on horseback ahead of him and coming in his direction. He was a curious looking fellow, and Gardner, thinking it was an Indian, turned to run, but the man said in a loud voice in the Spanish language, "Parity! parity!" (stop! stop!). Thinking now by his language that it was a Mexican, and from having on a hat, Gardner stopped and looked back, but discovered that the supposed greaser was drawing an arrow from the quiver at his back, and had a bow in his other hand. Being now thoroughly frightened, the youth turned and fled, pursued by the Indian, who adjusted an arrow to the string as he ran, and on coming within range let it fly at the boy, who had gotten about seventy-five yards from the starting point. This first arrow wounded him in the left arm, and passing through also inflicted a wound in the side.

By this time twelve more Indians had shown themselves, all on horseback, and commenced closing around Gardner in a circle. Seeing there was no chance to get through them, he ran into a thick clump of persimmon bushes and stopped. One Indian rode up close to him and by signs demanded his hat. This was promptly obeyed, and then signs were made for him to run and the direction to go. Looking that way, the boy saw an Indian sitting on his horse whom he supposed was the chief from his head dress, which was profuse with feathers.

Up to this time the Indians had been very quiet, not wishing to alarm the men at the ranch, for no doubt they had investigated and knew the situation and were looking for the ranch horses, and also expecting to catch some settler alone and kill him, which now seemed to be the fate of Gardner. The young man had called several times for help, but was made to hush by the Indians after he was wounded and they caught up with him. The rest of the Indians stopped a short distance off, some with their horses' heads turned one way and some the other, leaving an open space between them of ten yards or more. Gardner, although badly wounded and bleeding, fully took in the situation at a glance, and made up his mind to make a desperate run through the open space between the Indians and try to gain the ranch.

In an attempt to carry out this plan he darted forth, at the same time calling loudly for help. The Indians followed on horseback and one of them shot him with an arrow, striking the right side under the shoulder blade, and then ran his horse over him, knocking him down. The boy arose and still attempted to flee, calling at the top of his voice for help. The men at the ranch heard the cries and soon McCoy, Culp, Howell, De Spain, and A. F. Gardner came to his assistance. The Indians, seeing the white men coming, no longer tried to conceal their presence, but commenced to yell and fire pistols at Gardner, and the one who ran over him with his horse came close and aiming a pistol at the back of his head at close range fired. The ball struck on the right side of the neck, barely missing the neck bone, and came out under the jaw. Many other shots were fired, but this was the only bullet that hit him. By this time the ranchmen were on the scene, and taking trees on the Indians commenced firing on them. When struck by the pistol ball young Gardner fell to his knees, but regained his feet and ran about thirty yards further, and then commenced staggering—the earth, trees, everything faded from sight, and he felt that he was going down. Deafness to some extent came on. The yelling of the Indians and firing of guns sounded far away, although they were so near. About this time he was jerked clear off the ground and he felt that he was going through space, tightly grasped by a strong arm. His brother, older than himself, had made his way to him in among the Indians, and taking him up under one arm and holding his gun in the other hand, made his way back, amid a shower of bullets and arrows, to the men who were fighting the battle. The nearest Indians to A. F. Gardner when he picked up his brother were within thirty steps, and although fired at repeatedly, he was not touched except in his clothing. He had no time to stop and shoot until he gained the position of McCoy, who was the leader of the frontiersmen.

The Indians soon gave up the fight and left, and the white men went back to the ranch with the wounded boy, who, besides the three wounds on the body, had seventeen holes in his clothing made by bullets and arrows. Seven of the settlers soon obtained horses and went in pursuit of the Indians and overtook them twenty miles from there on the Nueces River, and another fight took place, which wound up in a standoff. The guns and pistols of the white men were in poor condition, and some of them could not be made to shoot at all. During the fight Mr. Burk, before mentioned and given name not known, was hit in the top of the shoulder by a bullet, which penetrated the neck and lodged against the neck bone. The ball was cut out by J. A. Gardner with a pocket knife.

After the Indians left the place where they wounded Gardner they crossed the Nueces River and killed a Mexican who was herding horses for Jesse Laxson. The body was not found for some time after, as the Mexican made a run and was killed in the brush.

It took young Gardner six weeks to recover sufficiently to be carried home. A runner was sent at once to notify his mother when he was first wounded, and she started at once to go to him, but in the meantime there had been a great rain, and when she arrived at the Nueces River it was one and a half miles wide and her son was on the opposite side. Here she stayed several days and nights, but as it continued to rain there was no chance to cross. Men, however, swam back and forth every short while to let her know how her boy was, and when he was on the road to recovery and out of danger she went back home to take care of the smaller children. As this was below the mountains the country was low and flat and the waters ran off very slowly, sometimes remaining overflowed for several weeks at a time.

Mrs. Gardner died in 1882. Mr. Gardner still lives on the old homestead place, and has a good farm. He has been married twice. His first wife was Miss Jennie Holmes, sister to Mr. Sam Holmes, who was killed in his store at Utopia by a burglar several years ago. His second and present wife was a Miss Lucy Wingate.

JESSE LAWHON KILLED BY INDIANS.

1855.

The following detailed account of an Indian raid in Comal
County and the killing of Jesse Lawhon I get from an old
copy of the Seguin Mercury, published by R. W. Rainey, and
bearing date of July 21, 1855. The account is furnished by the
Hon. William E. Jones, and is as follows:

"Mr. Editor: It is a painful duty devolving upon me to communicate to you the particulars of an Indian outrage just committed in this neighborhood. On Saturday morning last Mr.
Jesse Lawhon, who has been living with me for nearly two years
in the capacity of overseer and manager of my farm and stock,
went out accompanied by one of my negro men to drive up some
oxen. About 11 o'clock the negro boy ran home afoot and bare-
footed and wet to the hips, and told me he feared that Mr. Lawhon had been killed by the Indians; that Mr. Lawhon and himself were riding together in search of cattle, and when descending a hill into the valley of one of the branches of Curry's Creek,
near the foot of the mountains, they were attacked by five Indians who emerged from the bed of the creek and rushed upon
them at full speed. They did not discover the Indians until
within forty or fifty feet yards of them. Mr. Lawhon wheeled
and ran in the opposite direction, while the boy dashed towards
home. A large Indian, mounted on an American horse, pursued
the boy. On arriving at the creek his horse plunged into it and
fell. He jumped off and ran up the bank, when the Indian fired
at him, the ball striking the ground beyond him. He then saw
the other four pursuing Mr. Lawhon very closely on the hill, and
then jumping into the channel of the creek, made his escape, and
saw no more.

"He stated from the beginning that one of the party was a
white man and the other four Indians, naked and armed with
guns. The white man was dressed in dark clothes with a white
hat. He saw most distinctly the one that pursued him. After
he had shot at him, and being not more than twenty steps from
him, he thinks he can not be mistaken in saying that he was

an Indian and not a Mexican. The boy has often seen Indians in Texas and has mixed a good deal with Mexicans, and as his statement is thus far the only evidence of the character of the party which we have, I thought it more proper to give them more fully than I should have done under other circumstances.

"In the meantime the alarm had been given in the settlement and a party of men repaired to the scene, taking the boy along with them. On arriving there the Indians had left and Mr. Lawhon could not be seen, but the statements of the boy being all substantially confirmed by the horse tracks and other signs on the ground, they proceeded to search for him. His hat was found near the starting point; his saddle, with the skirts and stirrups cut off, was found on the trail of the retreating savages about one mile off. Then they found the trail of his horse from the place where he was attacked, and followed it until they found the dead body in a thicket. He had been shot through the heart with a large ball, and his body and face otherwise bruised and cut. A blunt arrow was found by his side. He was wholly unarmed and compelled to trust to his horse for safety, and the horse he rode, although large and strong, was not fleet. He had evidently made a desperate struggle to save his life.

"From the point at which he first discovered the Indians, he had turned westward in the direction opposite to that which they came, but soon being overtaken by his pursuers he wheeled by a short circuit, and leaping a large ravine, passed the place from which he had started, crossed the creek at the point from which the Indians had first issued, and ran up the hill on that side in the direction of home. Being overtaken again by his savage pursuers, he dashed back again into the creek valley lower down, and there, among the small thickets and brush, he seemed to have been surrounded and hemmed in in an angle made by the creek impassable here, it being a perpendicular bluff. Wheeling again, he burst through the Indians and regained the elevated ground, followed by the whole pack, and once more faced home. After running 400 or 500 yards across the heads of ravines he appeared to have been again overtaken, when in utter desperation he plunged down a bluff thirty feet high and nearly perpendicular, part of the distance his horse tearing up the rocks and crushing the brushwood in his downward course. At the foot of this bluff he landed in one end of a long thicket, and possibly might have escaped if he had abandoned his horse. None of the Indians followed him down the bluff, but the horse tracks indicated that a portion of them turned the point of the bluff and met him as he emerged from the point of the thicket and shot him.

"Mr. Lawhon was an industrious and most worthy citizen, sober, moral, and of unimpeachable integrity, universally esteemed by all neighbors and acquaintances. He was about 25 years of age, of manly person, and gave the highest promise of usefulness to his country and honor to his family. He left a wife and two small children, who were in his lifetime dependent on him for their maintenance."

The writer will say here that Judge Jones was a prominent man in West Texas in his time, was a good lawyer, and held the position of district judge with dignity and ability. He presided at the first term of district court ever held in Seguin, and the house is still standing where it convened. It is now known as the Rust property. When the grand jury was impaneled on this occasion, there being no jury room, they assembled under a live-oak tree north of where the court was being held, and there proceeded to business. The first bill they found was against one of the petit jurymen. This spot is now the property of G. W. L. Baker.

The Jones family were brave, patriotic people, and did their part when Texas needed brave men on her border, where Mexican and Indian depredations were so frequent.

When Capt. James H. Callahan organized an expedition into Mexico in 1855 to chastise a band of Indians who had taken refuge there after a raid in Texas, one of Judge Jones' sons (Willis) went with Callahan and was killed in the fight with Indians and Mexicans near Piedras Negras.

Capt. Frank Jones, a brave and gallant ranger captain, was also a son of Judge Jones, and was killed a few years ago in a desperate fight with Mexican robbers near the Rio Grande. Capt. Frank Jones was once a citizen of Uvalde.

1. Charles Meadows.   2. James Finch.   3. Walter Franks.   4. Albert Finch.

A GROUP OF TEXAS COWBOYS.   ATASCOSA COUNTY.

EARLY SETTLERS OF ATASCOSA COUNTY.

Created in 1856.

During the days of Indian raids in the west and southwest, Atascosa County did not escape, and has her bloody chapter in the frontier history of Texas.

The county was created from Bexar in 1856, and named for the Atascosa Creek. The Navarros, Salinas, and others established stock ranches inside the present limits of the county at an early day, but were broken up during the Texas revolution and the Navarros moved further east and established ranches near the present town of Seguin, in Guadalupe County.

In 1853 permanent settlements began to be made, and by the time the county was organized quite a number of settlers were located, among whom were Justo Rodrigues, Judge J. S. Fern, Calvin Horton, the Askins, Yarbers, Tumlinsons, Brights, Slaughter, "Scotch" Jim Brown, Franks, Spears, James Lowe, Charles Hood, old man Terry, McCoys, and Dan Arnold.

The first county seat was called Navatasco, and located twelve miles above the present one of Pleasanton. The land on which it was built was donated by Col. Antonio Navarro and named by him. The first half, it will be observed, was part of his own name, and the last the middle half of the name of the county of Atascosa. The first court was held here in the spring of 1857. Jose Antonio Navarro was a grand and noble man. He was born in San Antonio in 1795. His father was from Corsica. In 1834-35 Antonio was land commissioner for Bexar district and De Witt's colony, a member of the convention of 1836, and one of the signers of the declaration of Texas independence. He loved Texas and her institutions, and was always ready to take up arms in her defense. He was in the unfortunate Santa Fe expedition as one of the commissioners, and was carried a captive with the balance of the Texans to Mexico, and there confined for years. Santa Anna hated him because he was of Spanish origin and a friend to Texas, and when the Americans of the expedition were released, kept him in chains in the strong castle of San Juan d'Ulloa. While he was chained down to a stone floor in the dark, damp dungeon, Santa Anna offered to release him if he would renounce all allegiance to Texas and become a citizen of Mexico. The grand old man, with his gray locks damp with dungeon mold, scornfully rejected it and taunted Santa Anna with his perfidy, saying: "I am a Navarro. No traitor's blood runs in my veins. You can only do your worst with me. I will die chained on this prison floor before I will for a moment entertain a thought of accepting your insulting proposition." When Herrera became President he released Colonel Navarro and allowed him to return to Texas. He died in San Antonio in 1870, loved and respected by all who knew him.

In 1858 a new county seat was laid off on the west bank of the Atascosa Creek and named Pleasanton, after General Pleasanton. John Bowen donated the land and named it. He was an intimate friend of the general. It is situated thirty-five miles south of San Antonio. Many settlers soon began to come in. The first one to settle and build a house was E. B. Thomas, who also put up the first store in the prospective town.

Soon after the town was laid off came Tobias Kelly, Calvin S. Turner, Judge Ferryman, J. H. Dorsey, Capt. John Tom, Rev. W. W. Whitley (Methodist preacher), John W. Stayton, and V. Weldon. The two last named were brothers-in-law and partners in the blacksmith business, and also young law practitioners. This same V. Weldon came prominently before the people a few years ago in the congressional race against W. H. Crain in the Eleventh District. Dr. Pyrtle came soon after, and also another blacksmith named Garlinghouse and a German named Slickum. The latter put up a saloon and grocery store, backed by his partner, Louis Zork, a capitalist of San Antonio. The first county officers were: County judge, or chief justice, as it was then called, Marcellus French; sheriff, James H. French; county and district clerk, Daniel I. Tobin, brother of Capt. William Tobin, of San Antonio; assessor and collector, Ed Walker. W. H. Long was elected to the last named position, but for some cause did not serve. The first commissioners were Eli J. O'Brien, Levi English, James Lowe, and J. A. Durand. The first district attorney was James Paul, and the first district judge E. F. Buckner. The first grand jury were William N. Gates, James McDonald, Jacob Ryman, Sexto Navarro, Gil Rodrigues, James Brown, Jesus Hernandez, James Feeder, Rich Hilburn, Isaac Cavender, Drake Gil-

lelland, Thomas R. Bright, Tryon Fuller, Cullen Benson, and
Calvin Horton. As far as is known, none of this first grand jury
are now living. Calvin Horton died in February, 1898, at a very
advanced age.

About 1859 the Rev. Uzzel came and settled, and also a mechanic named Carter.

In the Somerset settlement, near the Bexar County line, were
the Ducks, Klemkes, Millers, and Louis families. At Gates Valley were the families of Rutledge, Gardner, Gates, and Williams.
Of the Spanish families were the Navarros, Flores, and Tiriens.
The Musgroves, Barksdales, and O'Briens lived in town. Below
town, on Laparita Creek, lived Juan Palacia, Captain Fountain,
Jesse Lott, the Cook boys, and Dan Brister. On the Laguilinas
were the Marshalls, Odens, Newtons, Lease Harris, and Tom
Kerr. On Galvan Creek were R. G. Long and the Cavenders.

Mr. Eli Johnson, one of the early settlers, and who still survives, came from Montgomery County, Alabama, to Texas in
1856, and first stopped in Guadalupe County, near Seguin, with
the Sheffields and Olivers, but the same year came on out to
Atascosa County with Ed Lyons and Jake Young. They settled
on Salt Branch, seven miles from Pleasanton.

In 1860 Mr. Johnson joined a company of rangers commanded
by Capt. Peter Tumlinson. They were stationed on the Sabinal
River below the mountains. Their camp was attacked one night
by Indians, who were beaten off without loss.

On the 22d of May, 1861, he was married to Miss Melissa
Tucker. She died on the 16th of March, 1865. In 1869, on the
22d day of February, he married the widow Mary Adams, whose
maiden name was Lawhon. She died April 22, 1892. He again
married, and his present wife was Miss Mildred E. J. Hurley.

Mr. Johnson passed through all the exciting times when the
country was raided by hostile Indians, and now lives on the Atascosa Creek three miles below town, where he is engaged in farming and stock raising. He has 200 acres of land in cultivation,
and a fine artesian well near his residence flowing fifty gallons
of water per minute; also a fine orchard of ten acres. No man
stands higher in the estimation of the people who know him.

Mrs. Amanda Turner, also one of the early settlers, and widow
of Calvin S. Turner, still lives in Pleasanton, near where they
settled in 1858. She was the daughter of Ezekiel Tucker, and a

native Texan. She was also one of the first settlers of Hays County, living there on the Little Blanco when very young. She was married to Calvin S. Turner in 1851, and moved to Guadalupe County, near Seguin. In 1858 she came to Pleasanton. Mrs. Turner had four brothers—Columbus, George, Napoleon, and Marion. The latter went off with the Walker expedition, and never returned. There were three sisters of them: Polly Ann married James C. Carr, now the rustling agent for the San Antonio *Express;* Melissa married Eli M. Johnson, of Pleasanton. Mrs. Turner kept hotel for many years and is known far and near. She has eight living children, four boys (Gilbert, Robert, Thomas, and Albert) and four girls (Sarah, Dallas, Anna, and Dora). Sarah married William Franks, who died at Eagle Pass; Dallas married William A. Purgason, now merchant at Amphion; Anna married Gus Clark, merchant of Pleasanton. Two have remained single—Gilbert and Dora.

Calvin S. Turner was the son of Maj. Wiliam Turner, who came to Texas in the early 40's. He was a soldier under General Jackson, and participated in the battles of Talladega, Tallahassee, Horseshoe Bend, and New Orleans. He was twice severely wounded. Calvin was a ranger under Jack Hays, and took part in the battle of Salado in 1842. In this fight he was wounded in the head by a musket ball. He served through the Mexican war of 1846 in the famous regiment of rangers commanded by Col. Jack Hays, his old captain. He took part in the battles of Monterey and Buena Vista.

After returning from Mexico he received a commission from Gov. P. H. Bell as second lieutenant in the ranger company commanded by Capt. Henry E. McCulloch. He engaged in stockraising after coming to Pleasanton, and also opened up a hotel. He served under Capt. John Tom part of the time as minuteman to repel Indian incursions, and participated in the Indian battle on San Miguel Creek. During one raid near town his Mexican herder was killed by Indians. During the civil war he was a lieutenant in Captain Maverick's company, Wood's regiment. He died in 1872, honored and respected by all who knew him.

In 1861 the Indians made one of the most daring and extensive raids ever known in Atascosa County. They were in large force and scattered all over the country, killed fourteen people, wounded many more, and carried off a large lot of horses. They did not confine this raid to Atascosa alone, but spread death and destruction on their trail as they went back to the mountains. They killed "Mustang" Moore where the station of that name is now, on the International Railroad; James Winters on Black Creek, and Murray the tax assessor of Bandera County. At Pleasanton they killed William Herndon and a negro belonging to Marcellus French, and wounded Alexander Anderson and Eli O'Brien. These last named were all out from one to two miles from town, hunting stock, etc. Napoleon Tucker was with Herndon, and being on a fast horse made his escape, at the earnest solicitation of Herndon, and brought the news of the presence of the Indians to the people in town. They first made their appearance in the settlement above, and Ed Lyons sent Alex Anderson on a fast horse to notify the people at Pleasanton. The Indians came upon him a mile from town and ran him in, shooting an arrow into his back. News now came fast, and there was great excitement. One of French's negroes was killed and another captured. Men continued to run in wounded, or their faces badly torn by limbs in their desperate flight from the Comanches.

One of the most remarkable escapes was that of Eli O'Brien. He had gone out on that morning to hunt stock without gun or pistol, and had been warned by a neighbor, William Dillard, that it was not safe to go unarmed. His reply was, "There are no Indians in the country," and he went on. When about two miles from town he came upon a band of Indians in a blackjack and postoak timbered country. The Indians were sitting on their horses under the trees, and as some of them had on hats which they had procured from men they had killed or chased, O'Brien thought they were cowmen. When they started towards him yelling he cried with a loud voice, "No use, boys; you can't scare me." When they came out from among the trees so that he could see them plainly and began to string their bows, the settler at once realized who they were and the great danger which now confronted him. Wheeling his horse, he started at once towards home with them in pursuit. His horse was a good one and they failed to run on him at once, and so divided their forces, running parallel with and to the right and left of him. He watched both sides closely and saw that he was gaining some on them, but failed to look behind until he felt the wind of an arrow near his head. Turning, he saw an Indian close behind him, and at the same time got an arrow in the back. His only weapon was a butcher knife, which he now drew when he saw that the Indian was going to get up beside him. Two more arrows, however, came in quick succession and fastened in his back. The Comanche now yelled loud, and making a sudden spurt came alongside of him and reached to pull the stricken man from his horse. O'Brien, with the strength of despair, made a stab at the Indian with his knife, who barely interposed his shield in time to catch the blow, and then stopped. The town was near, but the other Indians still tried to ride around the white man and turn him back. A most serious difficulty now came in the way, which caused the white man's heart to sink within him, and the Indians to yell loudly and urge their horses to greater speed. The cause of this was a deep and wide gully directly in front, ten feet across and the same in depth. There was no way to turn to avoid it without being cut off. I will say here that this is the reason that Indians in chasing a man run to the right and left of him, so if any obstruction comes in the way and he is bound to turn, they can get him either way he may turn. One or more on good horses run straight behind so that he can not double on his track and dodge them or gain time. In this case the only chance for O'Brien was for his horse to safely leap the gully. If he fell the man was gone. It will be understood that all of this was done very quickly. There was no intermission in the speed of the horses; all were doing their utmost, and the two miles from the place where the chase commenced had been passed over in a few minutes.

When the Indians perceived that the white man was going to attempt the leap they yelled louder and fiercer, so as to terrify the horse and make him overdo himself or stumble or leap too quick, or anything which would be in their favor. When the brink was reached and the spring had to be made that meant life or death to him, O'Brien held his bridle lightly and let his horse jump naturally making no extra motions with hands or feet, and the gallant animal passed safely over and had several feet to spare. No Indian attempted to follow, and all went back and gave up the chase. O'Brien was hardly able to sit on his horse, and was swaying to and fro in the saddle when his horse dashed into the assembled and excited crowd in town. When he passed William Dillard's house, who had given him the advice that morning, and who knew from his speed that Indians had been after him, he exclaimed, "What's your hurry, O'Brien?" There are no Indians in the country." The arrows were removed, the spikes cut out, and the wounded man recovered. The horse was kept in the O'Brien family as long as he lived, and tenderly cared for.

Eli Johnson and others went out and brought in the body of Herndon. The citizens, not thinking they were able to cope with such a body of Indians alone, sent a runner east for help, and 200 men came from Gonzales and Guadalupe counties, under command of Captain Rabb. Eli Johnson with a minute company, aided in scouting, and it was perceived that the Indians had left the country and gone back to the mountains, kiling people and capturing stock as they went. They were not to get back, however, without a battle. Big Foot Wallace, with the Hondo and Sabinal settlers, defeated them in a battle in the mountains and recaptured 200 head of horses from them.

Judge A. G. Martin, who still lives at Pleasanton, was one of the early settlers of Atascosa County. He came to San Antonio in 1849, and was with the first train that ever went through to El Paso. The same year he went to Seguin and located there. When he arrived at Seguin a big Methodist meeting was in progress, and this fact was the real cause of his settling there. He stopped to attend it, and liked the people and country so well he concluded to make his home there. For a while he worked in the county clerk's office under Paris Smith, and in 1854 was elected district clerk over John F. Gordon. He came to Atascosa County in 1856, built a house, and then went back for his family and returned in 1857.

In 1864 he was elected county clerk, but during the days of reconstruction he was removed and another put in his place. He was disfranchised, not allowed a vote, and as the judge expressed it, "Not given a negro's chance." When restored to citizenship, he was elected district and county clerk in 1873. He held this office seventeen years, and was elected county judge and held one term, refusing to be a candidate for office any more. The present county jail was built during his term of county judge and under his supervision. It is one of the best jails in the west. It is built of red sandstone and brick, the stone being on the inside. It is two stories, commodious, and with strong iron cages. The first jail here was a hole in the ground, with some roofing overhead to keep the rain out. It was twelve feet deep, and was covered with a raised trap door and fastened with a padlock. The writer was here in 1872, and saw the sheriff put a man in this hole.

Judge Martin has four sons. The eldest, J. L. Martin, was born at Seguin. By profession he is a lawyer, and at one time was county judge of Kinney County. He served in the Twenty-fourth Legislature, and in 1897 was appointed district judge of the Thirty-eighth Judicial District on the death of Judge Eugene Archer, who held that position at the time of his death. When the next election came off he was elected to that position, and is the present incumbent.

The second son, H. G., was elected district clerk of Atascosa County. The third son, John B., is a printer by trade. The youngest, J. R. G., at this time is in Louisville, Ky., studying medicine.

A. M. Avant, present sheriff of the county, was born and raised in Gonzales County. He came here in 1886, and is now serving his second term as sheriff.

The present county judge, N. R. Wallace, better known to his friends as Jack Wallace, came to Seguin, Guadalupe County, in 1876, and did a banking business there. Here he married Miss John Irvin, niece of the old San Jacinto veteran, Capt. John Tom. She has a sister named Tom, so you see their two names make that of their beloved uncle, John Tom, for whom they were named. They are called Johnnie and Tommy by their intimate friends. Judge Wallace came to Pleasanton in 1880, and was elected sheriff in 1883. He was elected county judge in 1894, and still holds that position.

Judge W. H. Smith came to Pleasanton in 1867, and was elected to the office of presiding justice. He was then elected county judge, and held that position eight years. Was then tax assessor for one term. Held the office then of treasurer. Is now practicing law, and is the oldest male resident of the city.

MRS. R. D. KENNEDY.

Born in 1856.

At this writing (1889), in Sabinal Canyon, Bandera County, there lives the daughter of a famous Texas ranger who followed the fortunes of Jack Hays on the Texas border and stood by his side during many bloody encounters, both with hostile Indians and treacherous Mexicans. This daughter is Mrs. R. D. Kennedy, wife of Mr. Houston J. Kennedy, and daughter of George Jefferson Neill, who died in Travis County a few years back. Her grandfather was the Colonel Neill who commanded the artillery at the storming of San Antonio in 1835. He bombarded the Alamo to draw the attention of the Mexicans from Col. Ben Milam, who was entering the town on the other side with a storming party. Mrs. Kennedy was born in Comal County, Texas, in 1856, on York's Creek, near the Guadalupe and Hays County line. She was married to Mr. Kennedy at Seguin, Guadalupe County, in 1875, Rev. Buck Harris performing the ceremony.

Her father, George Neill, while a member of a ranging company commanded by Jack Hays, participated in the famous Indian fight at Bandera Pass. The rangers on that occasion were ambushed in the pass, and a most desperate fight took place, in which five of the rangers were killed and some wounded. Among the latter was Uncle Ben Highsmith, the old San Jacinto veteran who still survives, and now lives in Blanket Creek Canyon, Bandera County. A more detailed account of this fight is given in the sketch of Mr. Highsmith. Mr. Neill was also in the charge on the battery at the Hondo, when the Mexicans halted to fight the pursuing Texans after their disastrous defeat at Salado. It was Jack Hays and his rangers who made this charge and captured the cannon, shooting the gunners down with their pistols.

Mr. Houston Kennedy, while not being a noted Indian fighter, was a cowboy in his young days, and made four trips with cattle up the Chisholm trail to Kansas, when that route was infested with hostile Indians, and has had many narrow escapes.

17

While on one of these trips, after they had crossed the Texas line and entered the Indian Territory, ten cattle herds were encamped near each other on Pond Creek. This traveling of the herds close together on the trail was for mutual protection, and accounts for so many herds getting through to Kansas without being captured by the hostiles. This number of herds generally had more than 100 cowboys with them, most all of them being brave and good Indian fighters. The bands of roving Comanches and Kiowas would not dare face a band of Texas cowboys like this, but would wait for an opportunity to catch two or three together on the back track after lost horses, or ahead hunting water, or anything else that would carry them away from the protection of their comrades. In charge of one of these herds at Pond Creek was Mr. Ed Chambers, an old cattle boss. The trail forked here where his herd had stopped, and he in company with two cowboys went a considerable distance ahead to see which trail the majority of the herds were following. The country was mostly prairie, with depressions here and there deep enough for men to conceal themselves on horseback. Suddenly out of one of these draws in front of them rode ten Indians. The two cowboys wheeled their horses and started back rapidly, pulling their sixshooters as they ran. Chambers, thinking they were friendly Creeks or Caddoes on a buffalo hunt, galloped slow, telling the boys to stop, the Indians would not hurt them. In a short time the Comanches, for such they were, came close upon them, yelling and shooting. These Comanches were on a buffalo hunt, and had long-range and large bore guns. Chambers fell from his horse the first fire, shot through the body, and some of the band stopped and soon finished him and scalped him. The other two men, seeing they could not assist their dead companion, put their horses to their utmost speed to make their own escape. One Indian came up with the hindmost of the fleeing men and almost yelled in his face. The cowboy had his pistol ready and promptly shot him from his horse, and the balance turned back. When the two cowboys arrived in camp and told the news a detail of one man from each herd was sent back after the body of the unfortunate boss. From the Perkins herd, the one to which Mr. Kennedy belonged, they sent J. C. Neill, brother-in-law of Mr. Kennedy. When the party arrived at the scene of the chase the Indians were gone, and had carried off the body of the one the cowboy had shot. It seems that the Indian was not quite dead, as a place was found where the others had rolled him around on the ground and had probed his wound with coarse straws of prairie grass, the blood on the straws showing they had probed six inches. On examining the body of Chambers it as found that the Indians had taken neither his watch nor money. The body was taken back and buried on Pond Creek, where the herds were camped. This was about twenty-five miles from Caldwell, on the Kansas line.

Mr. Kennedy also tells of many exciting buffalo chases on these trips.

The writer has had some experience on the frontier as a ranger, and learned that it is best when a few men have to fight a superior force of Indians, unless they can get to a good cover, to make as long a run as possible, in order to scatter the Indians in pursuit and fight them in detail, as they do not all ride horses of the same speed. In this way they only fight the Indians on the fastest horses. If a stand is made without cover, they all get around him.

Mr. Kennedy was born in Jackson Parish, La., in 1847, and came to Texas in 1869. He is on his mother's side, who was a Perkins, related to Gen. Joseph Warren, who was killed at the battle of Bunker Hill at the commencement of the revolutionary war. It may not be generally known to Masons that General Warren was at the time of his death grand master of all Masons in America. In regard to this I quote from "History of Freemasonry in America," by Z. A. Davis, page 284, published in 1846:

"In the year 1773 a commission was received from the right honorable and most worshipful Patrick, earl of Dumfries, grand master of Masons in Scotland, dated March 3, 1772, appointing the right worshipful Joseph Warren, Esq., grand master of Masons for the continent of America.

"In 1775 the meetings of the Grand Lodge were suspended by the town of Boston becoming a garrison.

"At the battle of Bunker Hill, on the 27th of June, this year, Masonry and the Grand Lodge met with a heavy loss in the death of Grand Master Warren, who was slain contending for the liberation of his country.

"Soon after the evacuation of Boston by the British army, and previous to any regular communication, the brethren, influenced by a pious regard to the memory of the late grand master, were induced to search for his body, which had been rudely and indiscriminately buried on the field of slaughter. They accordingly repaired to the place, and by the direction of a person who was on the ground at the time of the burial, a spot was found where the earth had been recently turned up. Upon moving the turf and opening the grave, which was on the brow of a hill and adjacent to a small cluster of sprigs, the remains were discovered in a mangled condition, but were easily ascertained by an artificial tooth, and being decently raised, were conveyed to the State house in Boston, from whence, by a large and respectable number of brethren, with the late grand officers attending in procession, they were carried to the stone chapel, where an animated eulogy was delivered by Brother Perez Morton. The body was then deposited in the silent vault without a sculptured stone to mark the spot, but as the whole earth is the sepulchre of illustrious men, his fame, his glorious actions, are engraven on the tablet of universal remembrance, and will survive marble monuments or local inscriptions.

"In 1777, March 8th, the brethren, who had been dispersed in consequence of the war, being now generally collected, they assembled to take into consideration the state of Masonry. Being deprived of their chief by the melancholy death of their grand master, as before mentioned, after due consideration they proceeded to the formation of a Grand Lodge, and elected and installed the Most Worshipful Joseph Webb their grand master."

JOSEPH M. VAN PELT.

Born in Texas in 1857.

Although not an old man when the writer interviewed Mr. Van Pelt in 1897, still he was one of the early settlers and pioneers of Frio Canyon. He was born at Pririe Lea, Caldwell County, Texas, on the last day of May, 1857. This is a noted year to old Texans, and is still called by some of them the "starving year." This was the year of the great drought, when no crops were made, and many families went without bread for weeks at a time. The writer well remembers that hard year, and what a struggle it was to get bread. To get meal was out of the question after the supply which was on hand at the first part of that year was exhausted. There was no flour or wheat in the country, and there were no railroads in Texas to bring supplies. Ox teams had to be sent to Port Lavaca after flour, and it took a long time to make the round trip of 500 miles or more. The struggle was to keep from starving until the wagons could get back. This has reference to the upper San Marcos and Guadalupe country. People living further east did not have quite as hard a time.

One can imagine what rejoicing there was in the settlement when the flour wagons, as we called them, arrived. The flour came high, $18 per barrel. The neighbors in a settlement would raise money enough to load several wagons with flour at the port, and some of those who had large wagons and five or six yoke of oxen would make the trip, and they were paid so much per barrel for hauling. If my memory is not at fault, it quit raining about the last days of February, and none fell again until the 5th day of August. Creeks dried up, there was no grass, and cattle died by the thousands all over the country. We could not even get beef to eat or milk to drink.

The Van Pelts moved to Frio Canyon in August, 1860, when Joe was about 3 years old. That was at the time of the great flood in the Frio River, and the house in which the Van Pelts spent their first night in the canyon was surrounded by water. When morning came there was no chance to get out to high ground, and they were compelled to remain until the water fell. Fortunately the house was not carried away. One of the first things Joe became familiar with as he grew up was moccasin tracks and the almost constant alarm of Indians in the settlement. He went on many scouts after Indians when quite young, and grazed danger many times. Indian tracks were often seen in the field where they stole potatoes and roasting ears.

In 1878 Joe went to Uvalde with his father, Capt. Malcom Van Pelt, and on their return had quite an exciting time with a band of Indians. They first passed a drove of sheep belonging to W. B. Knox, being controlled by Davy Brown and herded by a Mexican. The Van Pelts stopped and got a drink of water from the herder, who gave it to them out of his canteen. About one mile from where they got the water was a dense thicket with mesquite brush around it. When opposite the thicket, but out of gunshot of it, three Indians showed themselves in the open brush on the opposite side to them and commenced yelling. Now, Joe was young and not much afraid of Indians, as he had said many times, and really wanted to have a fight with them. As soon as he saw the painted and feather-bedecked hostiles he jumped from his horse and pulled his Winchester to make his threat good of being change for any reasonable number of Comanches. The old captain, however, had fought Indians before, so pulling his gun and making ready to shoot, told his son to get back on his horse. One of the Indians, who rode a bald-face horse, was very conspicuous in his endeavors by yelling and other demonstrations to induce the white men to run to the thicket. To run was the very thing the captain intended to do as soon as he got Joe mounted again, but not to the thicket. He feared more Indians were around, and being on good horses, thought best to make a run for it down the road and see what it would develop. When Joe got on his horse he made for the thicket near by, but his father told him not to go in there, but to hit the road and warm up that pony behind with his quirt. The young frontiersman acted on this advice and soon a lively chase commenced, the old man bringing up the rear with his carbine ready to shoot if crowded too close. The captain told his son to dismount in the big thicket about a mile ahead. When Joe arrived at the place designated to make a stand he rushed in, but could not find a place that looked thick enough to stop in. In fact it seemed to him at the time that a jack jabbit could not find cover there. It seemed to Joe that he could hear a score of Indians coming at full speed and yelling at his heels, but in fact the hostiles had turned back, yelling defiance, and no one but the old man was crowding him. Not finding a place suitable in the thicket to dismount, he kept on, and he and the captain arrived at home safely. It was found out afterwards that the Indians were ten in number, and seeing the two white men coming down the road, seven of them went into the thicket first mentioned in ambush, and the three were to give them a scare from the opposite side of the road and run them into the ambuscade. Shortly after the chase the Indians all got together and went to where the Mexican herder was who a few minutes before had given the Van Pelts water, and killed him. They were seen shortly after by another man, and there were ten of them together, and the tracks of the seven were found in the thicket.

This same night Silas Webster, a merchant of Uvalde, was killed in his store for his money, but no clew to the murderers could be found.

Shortly after this incident the Indians crossed Frio Canyon not far from where Joe Van Pelt now lives, and went on towards Dry Frio west, having a negro boy and a little white girl captive. Joe was one of the men who followed these Indians, but his horse gave out and he and several others had to return. The Indians were overtaken by another party and the captives rescued.

About 1880 the Indians made their last raid in the vicinity of the Van Pelt settlement. They were followed by men from Frio and Sabinal under command of Henry Patterson. The Indians made a wide circle back to the Rio Grande and killed sixteen people. They killed a Mexican herder in the employ of Joe Ney shortly after leaving Sabinal Canyon. He made a desperate fight with them, and killed one Indian. They scalped him, pulled off one shoe, left him face downward. The body was warm when Patterson's men arrived on the scene. Both arms of the unfortunate man were also broken.

Two men were killed at Crouch's ranch a short time before the trailers came. One of the slain men had bled a great deal. They had six fine sheep tied in a hack, which the Indians also killed and cut the tongue out of one of them. Another man was

killed on the Nueces River near Westfall's ranch. He had made
a fight and also killed one Indian, and they did the same to him
as they did to Ney's herder,—they pulled off both his boots and
one sock, and left him on his face, scalped. The trailers were
out of provisions, and coming upon a herd of sheep the captain
told Joe Van Pelt to shoot one of them for the men to eat. Here
Joe made quite a remarkable shot. His ball hit one sheep behind
the ear, and then it went on fifty yards and struck another behind the shoulder, and killed both of them. Most of the people
killed on this raid were Mexicans.

The pursuit was kept up to the Rio Grande, the boundary line
of Texas and Mexico, and Captain Patterson intended crossing
and continuing the pursuit, as he had been joined by some
United States soldiers, but there was a heavy rise in the river,
and they had to return without sighting the Indians.

Mrs. Melod Van Pelt, wife of Joseph M. Van Pelt, was born
in Taylor County, Virginia, and was the daughter of Richard
Johnston, who was a cousin to the famous confederate leader,
Gen. Joseph E. Johnston. She is also a niece of Dr. Johnston
of San Antonio, and by marriage of some of her family connections related to Gen. U. S. Grant. Mrs. Van Pelt has literary
talent, and is now completing a book entitled "Truth Stranger
and Sadder Than Fiction," which will no doubt be very interesting when completed. Mr. Van Pelt has a beautiful home,
situated on the high bluff of the Frio River, whose sparkling
and leaping waters are a relief to the eye by day and music to
the ear at night. East and west are the mountains clothed in
living green by the dense cedar brakes which start from the valley and climb the rugged, rocky heights to the crest of the highest
peaks. Here for fifteen years Mrs. Van Pelt has lived and
gathered many curiosities from the hills and caves around, and
with them beautified and bedecked her home with artistic eye
and hand. It was here in this far-away frontier valley, so unlike
the old Virginia home, with these strange surroundings that the
outlines of her book developed, which under other circumstances
might never have been created or written.

INDIAN FIGHT ON DOVE CREEK.

1865.

In the winter of 1864 a large band of Kickapoo Indians left their reservation on the Kaw River in Kansas, and with all of their women, children, and worldly possessions started for Old Mexico. The reason of their exodus from Kansas was the fact that they had been called on to take sides in the great civil war which had been raging for some time between the Northern and Southern States. It seems that some of them had enlisted and done some service for the cause of the Union, for they were well armed and munitioned with government guns and knew how to use them, as the sequel will show, in their desperate battle with the Texans at Dove Creek. They crossed the Indian Territory all right, but when the border of Texas was reached their large force of several hundred warriors, besides their women and children, caused uneasiness among the scattered frontiersmen on the Texas side of Red River. Runners were sent far and near to notify the settlers of their approach, and men were collected to dispute their passage through Texas. The Kickapoos, not wishing a collision with the Texans, kept far out on the border after crossing the line, intending to skirt along the edge of the "Staked Plains," and thus make their way safely into Mexico. They crossed Red River about where Clay County now is, and pushed on through the "Panhandle," crossing the Clear fork and main Brazos above all forts and settlements. Texas scouts, however, followed their trail, while men were collecting further east. The place where the different companies formed a junction was at the head of Yellow Wolf Creek, under the following captains: From Bosque County, Capt. Sam Barnes; Hamilton County, Capt. ————; Comanche County, Capt. James Cunningham; Erath County, Capt. Gullentine; Brown County, Capt. Matron; Palo Pinto County, Capt. Totton. Capt. Henry Fossett also commanded a company, and some say he was in command of the whole force of near 500 men, part of whom were Confederate soldiers. Others say that Totton was in command. James Mulkey and Brooks Lee were the main scouts.

The trail of the Indians was taken up at Yellow Wolf by the main force, and as it was large and plain, was followed rapidly.

The Indians were overtaken at the mouth of Dove Creek, near its confluence with the Concho River, in the present limits of Tom Green County, Fort Concho at that time being not located or an abandoned post, on account of the civil war. The Texans halted about three miles from the Indian encampment and sent scouts to find out the situation. The scouts returned and reported the Indians well posted in the timber and thickets bordering Dove Creek and just above its mouth. They also said it would cost the lives of many men to rout them, and they believed also that they were friendly Indians. The officers in command, however, seemed determined to hazard a battle, come what might. The looked upon the Kickapoos as armed invaders and enemies, even if they were from a Kansas reservation, but they likely did not know of this fact at the time, for some thought they were Sioux under old Red Cloud. Be that as it may, on the 8th of January, 1865, the whites moved forward to the attack, some no doubt thinking the day was a good omen, as it was the anniversary of General Jackson's great victory at New Orleans. The Indians were watching all the movements, and remained perfectly quiet until the Texans began to enter their position, when the warwhoop was raised and a deadly fire opened upon them. A fierce charge was now made on the part of the whites, many of whom dismounted and tied their horses so as to better get at the Indians through the brush. After a short and sharp struggle the Indians gave way and retreated with great loss. The camp and all loose horses were captured. But at this moment the Texans made a sad and fatal mistake, the same that Captain Bryant made many years before, and which has gone down in history as "Bryant's defeat." Those that were still mounted left their horses and all commenced to pillage the camp, thinking the Indians were utterly routed and scattered. The Kickapoos rallied, however, and seeing the unorganized condition of their enemies, turned back and fiercely charged them, aiming their rifles with fatal precision. The white men were now at great disadvantage,—dismounted, badly scattered, and many with empty guns. The Indians came among them in great numbers and a panic ensued. Frightened and wounded horses were running in every direction, and many of the men were unable to mount. Ropes and bridle reins snapped on all sides, and the liberated horses galloped over friend and foe. In vain brave men tried to stay the tide and bring order out of chaos and confusion, but in vain; all were carried along by the impact of the general stampede. Those who could mount their horses as a general thing put spurs to them and left the field. But many brave and heroic deeds were performed—friends stayed with wounded friends and helped them to mount horses, or died with them in the bloody fight. The Kickapoos mounted all the horses they could lay hands upon and pursued the white men for some distance, and many were killed and wounded. The loss of the white men can not be accurately ascertained. The following names of some of the slain have been obtained: Don Cox and Tom Parker of Comanche County; Capt. Sam Barnes of Brown County; and from other counties, Albert Everett, Noah Gibbs, John Stein, James Mabry, Joseph Byars, William Epps, Capt. Gullentine and his son. Among the wounded were, W. W. Pierce, Captain Maton, John Brown, and Emms Adams. After the pursuit was over the white men scattered back to their various homes and the Indians went on to Mexico. It is a pity that all the long-haired, painted scoundrels could not have been killed before they crossed the Rio Grande, for the writer knows that these same Kickapoos raided Texas from their secure retreat in the Santa Rosa mountains in Mexico, and caused untold suffering along our border for many years.

A FRONTIER TRAGEDY.

1865.

In 1865 occurred one of those sad frontier tragedies, where the settlers were unable to sustain themselves in an Indian battle, and wives and mothers were made to mourn for loved ones who never returned except as mangled or inanimate bodies. This noted fight occurred on the 4th day of July in the above named year, near the mouth of the Leona River, in Frio County. The settlers in the vicinity at that time were the Martins, Odens, Franks, Bennetts, Hays, Parks, Levi English, and Ed Burleson. These were all in what was known as the Martin settlement.

On the morning in question Ed. Burleson went out a short distance from his ranch to drive up some horses. He was unarmed and riding a slow horse. Suddenly and very unexpectedly to him he was attacked by two Indians who ran him very close, one on foot and the other mounted. The one on foot outran the horseman and came near catching Burleson, but he ran through a thicket, and coming out on the side next his ranch arrived there safely. Quite a lot of people had collected at his house—men, women and children—to celebrate the Fourth and wind up with a dance at night. Ere the sun went down on that day, however, the festivities were changed to mourning. Instead of the gay tramp and joyous laughter of the dancers, wailing and the slow tread of a funeral procession were heard. Excitement ran high when Burleson dashed in and gave the alarm. Most of the men present mounted in hot haste to go in pursuit, and others were notified.

When all the men had congregated who could be gotten together on short notice they numbered eleven, and were as follows: Levi English, L. A. Franks, G. W. Daugherty, Ed. Burleson, W. C. Bell, Frank Williams, Dean Oden, Bud English, Dan Williams, John Berry, and — Aikens. Levi English being the oldest man in the party, and experienced to some extent in fighting Indians, was chosen captain.

When the main trail was struck the Indians were found to be

in large force and going down the Leona River. They crossed this stream near Bennett's ranch, four miles from Burleson's. They then went out into the open prairie in front of Martin's ranch, ten miles further on. The settlers first came in sight of them two miles off, but they went down into a valley and were lost to sight for some time. Suddenly, however, they came in view again, not more than 200 yards away. They were thirty-six in number and mounted two and two on a horse. The Indians now discovered the white men for the first time, and at once commenced a retreat. The white men were all brave frontiersmen, and made a reckless and impetuous charge and commenced firing too soon. The Indians ran nearly a mile, and thinking likely they had well nigh drawn the fire of the settlers, checked their flight at a lone tree at a signal from their chief, and each Indian who was mounted behind another jumped to the ground and came back at a charge, and for the first time commenced shooting. The mounted ones circled to right and left and sent a shower of arrows and bullets. Some of the Indians went entirely around the white men, and a desperate battle at close quarters ensued. The red men had the advantage of the whites in point of numbers and shots. The latter having nearly exhausted their shots at long range, had no time to reload a cap and ball pistol or gun in such a fight as was now being inaugurated. Captain English in vain gave orders during the mad charge, trying to hold the boys back and keep them out of the deadly circle in which they finally went. Dan Williams was the first man killed, and when he fell from his horse was at once surrounded by the Indians. English now rallied the men together and charged to the body of Williams, and after a hot fight drove them back, but in so doing fired their last loads. The Indians were quick to see this, and came back at them again, and a retreat was ordered. Frank Williams, brother to Dan, now dismounted by the side of his dying brother and asked if there was anything he could do for him, and expressed a willingness to stay with him. "No," said the stricken man, handing Frank his pistol; "take this and do the best you can. I am killed—can not live ten minutes. Save yourself." The men were even now wheeling their horses and leaving the ground, and Frank only mounted and left when the Indians were close upon him. The Comanches came after them, yelling furiously, and a panic ensued. Dean Oden was the next one to fall a victim. His horse was wounded and began to pitch, and the Indians were soon upon him. He dismounted and was wounded in the leg, and attempted to remount again, but was wounded six times more in the breast and back, as the Indians were on all sides of him. Aus. Franks was near him trying to force his way out, and the last he saw of Oden he was down to his knees and his horse gone. The next and last man killed was Bud English, son of the captain. His father stayed by his body until all hope was gone and all the men scattering away. The Indians pursued with a fierce vengeance, mixing in with the whites, and many personal combats took place, the settlers striking at the Indians with their unloaded guns and pistols. In this wild flight all the balance of the men were wounded except Franks, Berry, and Frank Williams. Captain English was badly wounded in the side with an arrow; G. W. Daugherty was hit in the leg with an arrow; Ed. Burleson in the leg with an arrow; Aikens in the breast with an arrow, and W. C. Bell in the side with an arrow.

In this wounded and scattered condition the men went back to the ranch and told the news of their sad defeat, and the long, piercing wail of women was again heard on this far-away frontier. Other men were collected and returned to the battleground to bring away the dead, led by those who participated but escaped unhurt. The three bodies lay within 100 yards of each other and were badly mutilated. The Indians carried away their dead, how many was not known, but supposed to be but few, on account of the reckless firing of the men at the commencement of the fight. Bud English was killed by a bullet in the breast, and there was also one arrow or lance wound in the breast. The head of Dan Williams was nearly severed from the body, necessitating a close wrapping in a blanket to keep the members together while being carried back. Oden and Williams were brothers-in-law, and were both buried in the same box. Eight out of the eleven men were either killed or wounded.

Aus. Franks, who gave the writer the particulars of this fight, now lives in Atascosa County.

Dean Oden was born on Mill Creek, in Guadalupe County, and was known to the writer years ago, but he never knew what became of him until getting the particulars of this Indian battle.

FIGHT WITH INDIANS AND RANGERS.

1870.

In 1897, in Frio Canyon the writer interviewed Mr. B. F. Payne, an ex-ranger, who had some interesting experience while serving on the frontier. Mr. Payne is a native Texas boy, and was raised near Austin, Travis County, being born there in the early 50's.

In 1866 he, in company with his father and several others, among whom was William Rutledge, went out on a cow hunt. At this time the Indians still raided the western portion of the counties bordering Travis on the west and northwest, and cow-hunters going in that direction generally went armed, especially with revolvers. One day about noon, before the cow-hunt terminated, the party came upon a band of Indians who had stopped in the bed of a dry ravine and were eating dinner. The white men, who were on the high ground above the Indians, were not discovered by them, and they kept on with their repast, which consisted of meat of some animal, wild or domestic, slaughtered by them. The white men at once made preparations to attack them, and drew back under cover and held a council. They did not wish to let the Indians escape without a fight, but Mr. Payne was concerned about his young son Frank, for fear that he would get hurt. The boy was about 12 years of age, and was not carrying any arms. The elder Payne finally told his son to remain where he was and not to leave the spot until the fight was over and some of them came back to him.

These arrangements being now agreed upon, the white men advanced and charged upon the Indians, who at once mounted their horses and fled. The whole party of whites and Indians were soon lost to sight of Frank across a low range of hills. The cowmen, being on good horses, soon came within pistol range and the fight commenced, the Indians giving shot for shot and warwhooping as they went. Young Payne, from his position in the rear, heard all this commotion and became very anxious to witness the combat. Accordingly he put spurs to his pony and galloped to the top of the ridge where he could have a plain view, not intending to go any further. When he arrived at the crest of the elevation, however, he met a loose and terror-stricken horse coming out of the fight, and the boy's horse took fright at him and ran away, and instead of going back the way he came, ran straight ahead and followed in the wake of the Indians. The white men were scattered and one of them unhorsed, and the boy soon passed all of them and ran into the Indians. Mr. Payne saw the peril his son was in, and when he passed called out, "Hold up, Frank; hold up!" That was what the boy was trying to do with all of his strength, but the pony had the bit in his mouth and was beyond control. The Indians evidently thought this a daring and intentional charge on the part of the young white brave, and, yelling loudly, prepared to fight him. The boy passed some of the Indians, who shot at him and threw lances from all sides. Finally a bullet, arrow or lance cut his bridle rein in two. His horse then increased his speed and soon got clear of all the Indians. Frank now took the rope from the horn of his saddle, and making a loop leaned forward and secured it over the nose of his horse, finally stopping him.

In the meantime the elder Payne had followed his son as fast as he could in order to try and save him, and fought his way through the Indians, assisted by some of his companions. He succeeded in killing some of the Indians and scattering the balance. Young Frank made a circle and came back. Besides having his bridle reins severed, two arrows were sticking in his saddle. Only one of the cow-hunters was wounded. He was able to ride, and when his horse was brought back he mounted, and the party arrived at home without further incident.

In 1870 Frank Payne, although still young, joined a company of rangers commanded by Capt. Rufus Perry. The captain was an old Jack Hays ranger, and was the same who had such a fearful experience in Nueces Canyon when he and Kit Ackland were so severely wounded. Captain Perry's company was stationed at a place called Little Red River, near Camp San Saba Springs. While there the rangers received information that a large body of Indians were raiding below and had carried off a drove of horses near Dripping Springs, in Hays County. The rangers lost no time, and were soon at the scene of the raid and on the trail of the redskins. The trail was discovered near Shovel Mountain, and was so plain and fresh the rangers knew the Indians could not be far ahead, and dashed on as rapidly as the nature of the ground would admit, all eager for the battle. When nearing the base of the mountain a white man was discovered running at full speed and being pursued by Indians. The latter stopped on seeing the rangers and turned back, and the hard pressed settler made his escape to the ranger boys. The Indians had 100 head of horses, and were going slow on account of the rough country. The rangers now made a flank movement to the right, kept under cover of the brush until near the horses, and then making a sudden dash cut them off from the Indians in a narrow place. They ran them back south against the foot of Shovel Mountain, and left three men to hold them there until the battle was over. The rangers knew they would have to fight the Indians, as they were in large force and yelling loudly. It seems that during the excitement of running the settler the Indians and horses had become scattered, and the rangers, taking cover and coming out in an unexpected place, by a bold, quick dash had secured the horses. ·The Indians collected in plain view of the rangers and began to divest themselves of blankets and outrigging, and to pile them up on the ground. The rangers now advanced and dismounted in a post oak ravine, tied their horses, and filled the magazines of their Winchesters full of cartridges, and awaited the charge which they saw the Comanches were about to make. The Indians numbered 125, as near as could be ascertained, and the rangers 28, besides the three who were holding the herd of horses against the mountain. The Indians when they did charge made a turn and tried to recapture the horses, but the rangers charged in turn and opened such a rapid fire that the savage warriors retreated back to their position. The three plucky fellows who were with the horses remained at their post and also opended fire. The Indians could not get to the horses without passing within gunshot of the position occupied by the main body of the rangers. The next charge of the Indians came close to the rangers, and a short but desperate fight took place. The Comanches, however, soon gave back before the galling fire of the Winchesters. They fought with muzzle-loading guns, bows and lances. Captain Perry was a good Indian fighter and handled his men well. The Indians killed in this charge were carried off by daring fellows

18

on horseback, who would lean from the saddle, and taking them by their long hair drag them back to cover. In the third charge the Indian chief was killed and his horse ran in among the rangers with the dead body, which was held to the saddle by a strong strap of leather. If the horse had gone back the other way the body of the chief would not have been captured. The Indians evidently overrated the force of rangers on account of the number of shots fired. The Comanches finally left after suffering heavy loss. The dress and rigging of the dead chief were taken to Austin and placed in the capitol building. Of the men in the fight the writer can only get the names of Captain Perry, B. F. Payne, Frank Enoch, the three Bird brothers, Griffin from Austin, Page from Blanco, and a man named Cox.

The three Bird brothers displayed great bravery and exposed themselves in every charge to the enemy's fire. One of them was killed and the other two wounded, one in the nose and the other in the ear, with arrows. Other rangers and horses were wounded. The dead ranger was carried to Birdtown and buried. The stolen horses numbered 100 head, and were carried back and turned over to the owners. The rangers in this fight were all young men, none being over 25 years of age.

INCIDENTS OF FRONTIER LIFE.

Desperate Indian Battle, 1870.

Among the many interesting incidents connected with the early settlement of Old D'Hanis, the following facts were collected from Mr. Chris Batot, one of the original first settlers:

In 1861 a band of Indians came in near D'Hanis and stole a lot of horses. Before the people knew they were in the country an old man named John Schreiber went out one morning on a mule to hunt a yoke of oxen. Some time in the day the mule came back without his rider and an arrow sticking in him. Great excitement prevailed in the settlement, as all were satisfied that the old man was killed. A large crowd assembled at D'Hanis to organize a search for the body and to fight the Indians if they should come in contact with them. These people were very particular to comply with and adhere strictly to the formalities of the law, and therefore made arrangements to hold an inquest over the body when found. They had no justice of the peace to act in the capacity of coroner, but Mr. Schalkhausen, their school teacher, was an educated man, and they supposed he could hold an inquest as good as anyone. He agreed to go with them, and soon all things were ready. A wagon and team had been procured, and in this the teacher rode with the driver. The balance of the party went ahead on horseback to search for the body. When they arrived about the place where they supposed the old man had been killed the mounted men separated to hunt, and it was understood that the one who should first find the body of the unfortunate settler would make it known by a loud call to the others. A man named Deckard first came upon the body, and gave the signal. The searchers soon collected together on the spot, and Mr. Chris. Batot was sent to inform Mr. Sauter, son-in-law of the man killed, who was in company with the teacher coming with the wagon. When Mr. Batot met the wagon and told the news of the finding of the body to Mr. Sauter, and how he should drive to reach the spot, he rode back to the assembled crowd. The wagon had passed the spot where the body lay, and

had to turn back and go up a ravine to get there. This was back
towards D'Hanis, and Mr. Batot said as he rode off, "You can
see us when you get up the ravine opposite the body." Mr. Batot
says the driver had only to put on the bridles of the horses, as
they had not been unhitched while Mr. Sauter was waiting for
the dead man to be found and informed where to drive to. Now
a strange and most unaccountable thing occurred. While Mr.
Sauter was adjusting the bridles to the horses the teacher got
out of the wagon and followed Mr. Batot on foot, while the
driver carried the wagon up the ravine as instructed. When the
wagon arrived the men were around the body ready to hold the
inquest, but the teacher had not as yet arrived. After a short
time waiting, two men went to see what was delaying the pro-
fessor. They were gone about twenty minutes, and then came
back and reported that they could not find him. Fifteen men
now set out on horseback and scattered in various directions to
search for the man of letters, shouting and shooting for six hours,
but no response came from the missing man. He had disappeared
as completely as if the earth had opened and swallowed him up.
By this time a cold norther had come upon them, and as the men
were without coats the search had to be abandoned. The dead
man was placed in the wagon and carried back to D'Hanis and
buried without the inquest being held. The body was lanced
and scalped, but had not been shot with either bullet or arrow.
The wounded mule must have dodged into a thicket and eluded
the Indians. The old man evidently fell from him or was
dragged off by a limb. The mule came in with saddle and
bridle on.

After returning home the men got their coats and some provisions and returned to the scene of the killing, and there
searched in wide circles for three days without success. The
missing man was never seen or heard of again by them. It was
surmised that the Indians who killed Mr. Schreiber were concealed near by watching the searching party, whom they were
afraid to fight, and seeing this man alone and on foot and not
armed, he was captured and carried off. It is all shrouded in
mystery, however, as it does seem that so many men scattering
in various directions would some of them have come upon the
Indians, even in their ambush. The teacher was a man of 60

years of age, well educated, had a good school, and would have
had no occasion to voluntarily absent himself without letting
some one know it.

Six months after this startling frontier episode, Mr. Deckard,
the man who found the body of Mr. Schreiber, was himself killed
by Indians under like circumstances. He was not found until
the body was reduced to a skeleton by wolves and vultures, and
the bones were put in a sack and carried to D'Hanis and buried.
The remains could only be identified by the shoes and some camp
outfit.

Mr. Batot says that in the year 1870 the Indians invaded the
west as if they were going to take the whole country. There
were Indians everywhere. At this time Mr. Batot belonged to
the ranging company commanded by Capt. Joseph Richarz, and
they were stationed at Fort Inge, four miles below Uvalde, on the
Leona River. At this time news came to the rangers that a large
body of Indians were stealing horses on Turkey Creek, twenty
miles west of Uvalde, beyond the Nueces River. There were but
sixteen men in camp, two scouts already being gone, one under
Captain Richarz and the other under his lieutenant, Sevier
Vance. The only officers in camp were Dr. Woodbridge, company physician and surgeon, and Sergeant Eckford. The doctor
took command and at once set out to hunt for the Indians, leaving only one man in camp. Court was going on in Uvalde at the
time, and Mr. Batot, being a witness in a case there pending,
and could not go with the scout, and therefore missed being in
the desperate battle near Carrizo Springs which followed. The
rangers took up the trail of the Indians on Turkey Creek and
followed its tortuous and scattered windings through the chaparral and thorny catclaw brush for two days, and then made the
discovery that they had lost a man. It was useless to hunt for
him in this brushy and uninhabited country, so the scout pushed
on to Carrizo Springs. There was one lone ranchman near this
place named English, and he said the scout was a long ways behind the Indians, as they had passed there two days before. This
man said that if the doctor and rangers would take his advice
he might tell them of a plan by which they could get a chance to
fight them. This was agreed to, and English took the men
eight miles west, entirely leaving the Indian trail, which was
going south. Here about dark English told the men to stop and

camp. The idea of English was that the Indians would again turn north when their raid was over and pass near this place.

Next morning English took two of the rangers and went out to see if there was any sign of the Indians having passed in the night. This left Dr. Woodbridge with twelve men. One hour later he sent two men out on a hill as spies, and in a valley to the south they discovered a large band of Indians coming towards them and driving a herd of horses which they had stolen. The two spies at once put back to camp and informed the doctor of the situation, and he gave orders to saddle and mount. The rangers soon came in sight of the Indians going over a ridge, and a charge was ordered. The rangers at this time were armed with Winchesters, and thinking they could sustain themselves, boldly advanced with twelve men against the Indians' sixty. The Comanches had discovered the approach of the rangers, and as soon as they got over the ridge they turned and formed for a fight in two lines and came back at a charge and met the white men on the crest of the ridge. The looks of the Indians and their fearful warwhoops were appalling, and two of the rangers ran. Ten stood their ground, however, and met the onset. The fight was fierce and at close quarters. A gallant ranger named Bedinger, who was in the thickest of the fight, was seen to reel and fall from his horse, and Dr. Woodbridge was struck and knocked from his horse by the Indian chief. The fight seemed hopeless against such odds and the rangers retreated, firing as they went. Dr. Woodbridge at this juncture was seen standing behind a prickly pear shooting at the chief, who was securing the doctor's horse. Two of the rangers, Blakeny and Whitney, went back to the assistance of the doctor and charged the Indians. The other rangers also made a stand and continued to fire. The two rangers above mentioned were in a perfect Vesuvius of fire. No two men, it is thought, ever fired so many shots in so short a space of time. Blakeny's gun became so hot that he could not touch the barrel without getting burned, and all the time during this conflict he and Whitney returned yell for yell with the Indians.

The Comanches had never met such a fire before, and did some most dexterous riding and dodging, but nine were seen to fall from their horses to the ground. Whitney's horse was wounded, but still he advanced to the side of the doctor, who was dazed from the blow he had received, and was slowly retreating and firing. He succeeded in mounting behind the ranger, who bore him safely back to the other men, the retreat being covered by Blakeny, who still continued to yell and fire. The other rangers had formed near and still continued a brisk fire, and the Indians went back, not daring to risk another charge in the face of such a fire. The Winchesters were all that saved the rangers; they would have been crushed if muzzle-loaders had been their arms. The Indians scalped the dead ranger while the fight was going on, as he fell in the hand-to-hand fight, and his body remained in their possession when the rangers fell back. The men had nearly exhausted their supply of cartridges, especially Whitney and Blakeney. The former was short eighty after the fight. The rangers went back to their camp, and next morning a party went back to the scene of the battle and buried the dead ranger. He was hit three times in the breast by bullets. The Indians got his horse and saddle, Winchester, pistol, and belt of cartridges. They also got the doctor's horse, saddle, and bridle, but the chief's horse was found dead on the ground. The Indians had carried off their dead, but the bloody ground where they fought told the tale of what they suffered.

These same Indians after the fight continued their course, and came upon English and the two men who went to look for the trail, and a long running fight took place with them, but the rangers, being on good horses, made their escape to camp. Joe Brierly was behind in the chase and fired repeatedly at the Indians, who also fired many times at him, but appeared afraid to come closer.

The chief's horse which was killed in the fight was a gray, and well known to the rangers as belonging to a ranchman below. One shield was picked up on the ground with a bullet mark on it and a woman's scalp attached. The shield and scalp were sent to Austin. The ranger who got lost while trailing found his way back safely to the camp below Uvalde.

The ranchman English, who was with the rangers on this occasion, afterwards commanded the settlers in a disastrous battle with Indians near old Frio town, in which his son and two other men, Oden and Williams, were killed, besides a number wounded.

FIFTIETH ANNIVERSARY OF THE SETTLEMENT OF D'HANIS.

1897.

The morning of May 1, 1897, was a grand day for the people of D'Hanis and surrounding country. The sun rose clear, ushering in the fiftieth anniversary of the settling of Old D'Hanis, one mile east of the new town of the same name on the Sunset Railroad. Here at the former place the pioneers of fifty years ago unloaded their wagons on the prairie by the side of a clear-running little creek. In the early morning of this present occasion of the celebration a cool wind blew from the north, and everything was propitious for a nice day. At an early hour busy preparations were being made for the day's festivities.

In company with John Gersdorff of San Antonio the writer at an early hour repaired to the barbecue grounds, which were in the rear of the two-story rock store house of Mr. John Fohn. The entrance was through a wide gate which fronted on the main road to Hondo City. Already many people had arrived, but still the horsemen, footmen, and vehicles continued to pass through the entrance from the country, Hondo City, and other points until a vast multitude had assembled within the grounds. During the gathering of the people, Dr. Bradley of Hondo City brought the news of the death of Dr. Cummings of Uvalde, who was well known here, and many regrets and much sorrow was expressed at his sudden demise. Last year he was elected county judge of Uvalde County, and was very popular among the people.

The barbecue grounds was about 300 yards from the spot where fifty years ago the travel-worn pioneers unloaded their wagons and said, "Here we rest." The country was more pleasant to look upon then, as far as scenery is concerned, on account of the thick undergrowth which has since sprung up all over the country. Then towards the west were no settlers. The country was rolling prairie, covered with grass. Along the Seco Creek were small hills and some timber. Towards the north, ten miles of open country and the blue mountain ranges of Seco, Sabinal,

and Hondo could be seen. In other things, however, the contrast is just as great. The settlers then had poor teams and
clumsy wagons, with no houses and no material at hand to build
with, except short pickets and prairie grass for roof. Now we
see fine teams and costly carriages, nice houses, and good farms.

On this day the old settlers group together and talk over old
times, while the young ladies and gentlemen are in high glee
over the anticipated pleasures of the day. There was nothing
stronger than beer to drink, and that popular beverage was partaken of freely but not to excess by anyone. Lighter drinks,
such as lemonade and soda water, were on hand to be dispensed
to those who preferred that kind of refreshment.

When the hour for the parade arrived, the marshals formed
the people in line and the start was made from the gate in front
of the Fohn building. The line of march was south. First
came Mr. Chris. Batot, one of the first settlers, bearing a Texas
flag of the days of the Republic, with the legend inscribed on the
blue ground: "D'Hanis' Fiftieth Anniversary." Next came a
wagon containing a string band, which discoursed sweet music
as they went marching along. Next in order were forty little
girls bearing flags; then old setttlers, citizens, and visitors of
all ages and sizes. In the procession also was an old settler
named John Rudinger, bearing a United States flag. The procession was quite extended, the objective point being the old
town, where the grass-covered shanties were first erected, some
of which were still to be seen. Along the route they passed the
residence of Mrs. Fohn, one of the first settlers, who at this
time was dangerously ill in San Antonio. The procession returned by a circuitous route, and again entered the grounds.
The Texas flag was furled and laid away, and the stars and
stripes planted at the gate, where it flapped in the breeze the balance of the day. Trains coming from both ways continued to
bring visitors from points along the railroad. Among the people
present on the ground was a son of Capt. Charles de Montel, who
commanded a company of Texas rangers in the early days and
did good service with his men along the border. The younger
Montel is a lawyer by profession, and resides at Hondo City,
county seat of Medina County.

Dinner was announced at noon, and all repaired to the long
tables near the meat pits, and ample justice was done to the

fat beef, bread, coffee, and pickles. This feast was quite in contrast with fifty years ago. The old settlers were not possessed of guns sufficient to kill large game, and often suffered with hunger, subsisting many days at times on meal and water made into mush. It will be remembered that these early settlers came direct from Europe, and had never lived in a new country. Their firearms mostly were small bird guns, and not all had them. Sometimes the Indians, who at this time professed to be friends, would come and take what meal they had.

The number of people present today was estimated to be between 1200 and 1500, and 200 vehicles. At 3 o'clock speaking commenced, Judge S. B. Easly first occupying the stand, which was on the balcony at the head of the stairs on the outside of the Fohn building. Judge Easly, in his remarks, paid a glowing tribute to the people of D'Hanis as brave pioneers, honest, law-abiding citizens, and said that no D'Hanis boy had ever been sent to the penitentiary. Mr. Easly was loudly cheered on leaving the stand.

Mr. Chris. Batot, one of the first settlers, now came before the people and rehearsed the history of the colony from the start in Europe up to the time when the country had passed out of the wilderness state into an epoch of more prosperous times. The people listened with great interest and with many cheers, interspersed with peals of laughter at some of his humorous sallies. It seemed almost to make the contrast more perfect, while Mr. Batot was telling of the slow, toilsome march with weary teams across the prairie following the trail of the surveyor's wagon through the high grass, that a fast train dashed by not more than 300 yards from where the speaker stood, and the scream of the locomotive would have drowned the yell of the Comanche of whom he had just been telling. This closed the speaking, and was followed by music from the string band, baseball in the evening, supper at sundown, and dancing in Fohn's hall at night. During the dance Miss Ida Durban of Utopia met with a painful accident by a splinter penetrating her shoe and going deeply into her foot. The young lady was at once conveyed to the depot, where the services of Dr. Patterson, also of Utopia, were secured and attempt made to remove the splinter, but without success, as the doctor was in attendance at the celebration and had no instruments with him. Dr. Bradley of Hondo was now sent for and the splinter removed. It was large, being two inches in length. Miss Durban suffered great agony for more than two hours.

Below are the names of the first settlers who are still alive, and who were of all ages at the time the colony came here. Some were very young: Joseph Finger, Joseph Wipf, Chris Batot, John Reiderman, John Deckert, L. Essen (92 years old), John Batot, John Rudinger, Mrs. F. A. Lutz, Mrs. L. Zurcher, Mrs. Jos. Wolf, Mrs. H. Weynand, and H. Weynand. There were twenty-nine families originally, and numbered about 100 persons. But few of those who were grown at the time of arrival are now alive.

D'Hanis is in the western part of Medina County, on the east bank of Seco Creek.

RICHARD M. WARE.

Came to Texas in 1829.

Mr. Richard Ware was born in Arkansas on the 20th of October, 1828,. while the family were en route to Texas. His father, Capt. William Ware, settled in Montgomery County, Texas, in 1829. In 1835, when the war between Texas and Mexico broke out, his father raised a company and went to San Antonio with Gen. Ed. Burleson. When Col. Ben Milam called for volunteers to storm the city, Captain Ware and his men went in and materially aided in capturing General Cos and his army. During the fighting around the Veramendi house, on Soledad Street, Captain Ware was severely wounded in the hand. After the fall of the Alamo and the setttlers commenced their retreat from the Mexicans the Ware family went to Natchitoches, on Red River, ready to cross if the Mexicans were successful. Captain Ware and his company was with Houston's army and fought at the battle of San Jacinto, which gave peace for a time to Texas, which was now organized into an independent Republic.

In 1842, after San Antonio was captured by General Wall, Captain Ware joined the Somervell expedition for the invasion of Mexico, but turned back on the Rio Grande with a great many others.
,
In 1851 the Wares started west with a drove of cattle. Winter came on when they were in the vicinity of San Marcos, Hays County, and they concluded to stop and hold their stock until spring opened. Some one informed them that if they would go south to the Yorks Creek country, in the Sowell and Turner settlement, they would find some vacant houses which they could occupy and it would be a fine place to spend the winter. This they did. Grass was fine and the stock did well, but many of them were lost on account of their mixing with wild cattle in the big thickets. These wild cattle were not domestic gone astray, but original wild cattle, smaller than the common breeds or home cattle, and all one color—brown. The writer remembers

when a boy and living in Hays County, on the Blanco, of seeing a great many of them. They were wilder than the deer.

In the spring of 1852 Captain Ware moved his cattle on west and settled in Sabinal Canyon. The old cabin is still standing, built by himself and his boys, and should be preserved. The elder Ware did not long enjoy the new home, dying the following year.

In 1856 Richard Ware had his first experience with Indians. On that occasion the Indians made a raid into Sabinal Canyon and were fought by John Leaky, Gid Thompson, and others, the particulars of which have been described elsewhere. Mr. Ware joined the force that pursued these same Indians, who were overtaken on the Leona River while in bathing and all killed but one. They had no chance to make a fight, as the settlers were on the bank right over them before they knew it, and they had to dive in trying to avoid the shots. Mr. Ware says when it was over the water was very bloody. This affair has also been described more fully in another article.

In 1859 Mr. Ware was living in Frio Canyon when a raiding band of Comanches came through, having a lot of stolen horses which they had taken in the Guadalupe valley. A party of twelve was made up and pursued them. Of this number were John Daugherty, captain; Wm. Russell, Geo. Patterson, John Williams, Dan Turner, Henry Courtney, Richard Ware, and — Lambert. The trail of the Indians led west to the Nueces Canyon, and the first night the settlers camped without water. They were on the trail again early next morning, and when they came to the Nueces found themselves on a high bluff. It was level on the opposite side of the river and open country for some distance, and the Indians were discovered going across the valley towards the foot of the mountains. The only chance to continue the pursuit was to go on foot. It was decided to do this, and Lambert and Courtney were left with the horses. The other men had some difficulty in getting down the bluff themselves, but finally succeeded and crossed the river without being discovered by the Indians. They went on about two miles and discovered a smoke coming out of a cedar brake, and knew the Indians had camped. Their plan now was to creep upon them and make an attack. They advanced to a water hole not far from the Indians and discovered some one coming towards them after water. All lay close in the brush, and as the Indian, as they supposed, came in range two rifles cracked and he fell in his tracks. A rush was now made for the camp, but the alarm had been given and the Indians were scattering through the brake without attempting to make any fight, and none of them were killed. Eight head of horses were taken, and the men went back to the waterhole and examined the dead body there. They now discovered what a sad mistake had been made. It was a captive white boy they had slain. Who he was or where he was captured they could not tell. Evidently he had been with the Indians some time. He was badly sunburned and his hair very long. Around his waist was a belt and knife, and he had two bullet wounds in the breast. By his side lay a water vessel made from the paunch of a cow or horse, and the Indians had sent him to the pool for water. Even if he had been an Indian the settlers made a mistake in killing him at this time, as the fire of the rifles alarmed those in camp and spoiled their plans. Being nearly night and some distance from their horses, and nothing to dig a grave with, the poor unfortunate, whoever he was, had no burial, and was left where he fell by the white men, food for vultures and coyotes. He seemed to be about 14 years of age. With some difficulty a place was found by going below and the recaptured stock brought out of the valley to where the two men and horses were. The return back was made without incident, and the stolen horses returned to their owners on the Guadalupe.

In 1858 a stockman named I. C. Isbel, who lived on the Frio at the foot of the mountains, had eighty head of horses stolen by a band of Indians. The alarm was given and twenty-one men assembled at the Isbel ranch to go in pusuit of them. In the party were six United States soldiers from Fort Inge, under the command of a sergeant. The settlers were commanded by Capt. Henry Robinson. The trail of the Indians led in a northerly direction toward the divide at the head of the Sabinal and Frio rivers. The country there was open postoak and blackjack. The Indians ket a spy back to watch for pursuers, and Captain Robinson, knowing they were in the habit of doing this, made a wide circle to the left so as not to be seen, and came upon the Indians between two noted watering places called the Postoak and Frio waterholes. The white men outnumbered the Indians, but in their first onset made a mistake by all firing their guns at once. The Indians took notice of this, and turning, boldly charged the settlers. The writer has heard men say that Indians in the early days had a poor chance in fighting men who were armed with rifles and they only using bows. This is a mistake, and until repeating arms were invented the Indian had the advantage. A brave when on the warpath carried from forty to sixty arrows in his quiver, and if he could by dodging and the use of his shield avoid the shot which the white man fired at him from a muzzle-loading gun, would then boldly charge him. If the settler did not happen to have a brace of pistols, he was bound to run or be stuck full of arrows unless he could take shelter somewhere until he could reload. This was the situation in this case. The settlers ran and took shelter among the trees until they could reload their rifles. A crisis was avoided by John Leaky and some others who had revolvers and met the charge with a rapid fire. Two Indians were killed on the spot at this place, and John Cook was wounded with an arrow. He was on horseback when hit, and the arrow went through his thigh and pinned him to the saddle. Two of the Indians' horses were also killed. One Indian was shot through both hips and fell in a sitting position on the ground, but pulled an arrow and was about to shoot when a soldier fired at him with an army gun carrying a buck-and-ball paper cartridge. The shot struck the Indian high up on the forehead, tearing off the top of his skull and exposing the entire brain. During the battle the loose horses were badly scattered, and some of the men who dismounted to fight let their horses get away from them. One Indian displayed great bravery and a tenacity of life that was remarkable. He came close to the white men and was twice shot down, but regained his feet each time and continued to battle until the other Indians ran off and left him. He was shot six times by John Leakey with a revolver, and as he went off on foot to follow his comrades was fired at by every man who had a loaded gun. He was very active, and could dodge many shots aimed at him. Henry Courtney followed him on horseback and fired a load of buckshot at him from a shotgun, but the Indian kept on. John Daugherty now mounted a horse, and with a loaded revolver in his hand once more caught up with the brave to give him battle. The badly wounded Indian was still game, and turned back on Daugherty, uttering a warwhoop and sending his arrows with such precision that the settler dismounted behind his horse to avoid them. An exciting and strange battle now took place. The Indian advanced until nothing but the horse separated him from his foe, and both used the animal for a breastwork. Daugherty tried in vain to bring the Comanche down with repeated shots from the pistol until the chambers were empty. He had thus far avoided being hit himself, but was now at such a disadvantage without a load left, and the Indian with arrows yet in his quiver, that he turned and ran to some trees for better shelter, and the redskin mounted the horse and rode off. This Indian had on during the most part of the fight a large piece of cloth, like sail duck, closely wrapped around his body, which he now threw off, and it was picked up by the white men. It was covered with blood and had many bullet holes through it. He also lost his shield, which was spattered with blood.

Richard Ware was in this fight, and came near killing one of his comrades while they were at close quarters and men hurrying here and there and passing in front of one another. He aimed at an Indian, and when about to pull the trigger saw a white man's head through the sights of his gun, but lowered it in time to save him. The man had stepped directly in front of him. The Indian who got off with the horse and saddle also got a good overcoat and a canteen full of water. Several Indians were killed on the ground and most of the balance went off wounded. The horses stampeded badly during the fight, but were collected and driven back to the settlement.

In 1866 Mr. Ware was again living in Sabinal Canyon, but in the meantime had married Miss Slaver, stepdaughter of Mr. Gideon Thompson. Mrs. Thompson and she were the first white women that saw Sabinal Canyon. Captain Ware's family were the first here, but his girls were small, and Mrs. Ware died in eastern Texas. Mrs. Richard Ware saw Mrs. Bowlin after she was killed by the Indians, and helped to wait upon Mrs. Kinchaloe, who was wounded at the time.

In the above named year Mr. Ware was living on Onion Creek, in the canyon, and was engaged in opening a ditch to irrigate a small piece of land situated some distance below the house. While here alone he was attacked by six Indians. He heard the Indians coming through the brush, but thought it was cattle, as they watered near here. When he looked around the Indians were in ten feet of him, and one was aiming his gun to shoot. Mr. Ware had no gun with him, but had his pistol, and being quick to draw and fire, got in his shot with the Indian, who missed Ware, but was himself badly wounded. He then started for the house, shooting as he went, followed by the Indians, who yelled a good deal but did not crowd him close. There were several men living near Mr. Ware, and some at his house at the time, and all heard the yelling and shooting, but no one got to him except his brave wife and John Ware. The wife met him with his gun, knowing he had only a pistol. The Indians got five head of horses and took their departure. At this time there was a boy named Buckaloo captive among the Indians, who was taken from this country, and knew the horses when they were brought in. They said they lost one man in the fight when they got the horses. This was the first one Ware shot. Mrs. Ware saw the Indians when she came to her husband with the gun, and said the hair on their heads, which was very long, "flopped up and down when they galloped their horses."

In this same year Mr. Ware and Charles Durbin went to Bandera after meal. The distance was forty miles, and it was the nearest mill from this canyon. On the way back, and when nearly home, in the lower part of Seco Canyon they saw a drove of horses coming up the valley towards them, driven by a band of Indians. Just ahead of them, about where the old Bandera road crosses Seco, a man named Myrick had built a house, but it was now vacant. To get to this house for shelter was the best thing to do, and the horses were whipped into a run to reach it. The Indians saw them and came yelling to cut them off. The white men beat the race and got inside. Mr. Ware could not find a crack inside the house that he could see through, and after waiting awhile ventured outside to take a view of the situation. Now the Indians were sharp and thought that one of the white men would do this very thing, so posted one of their men behind a tree near by with a gun to shoot anyone that ventured out, while the others drew back and kept silent. After Ware got outside he looked cautiously around the corner of the house trying to see what had become of the Indians, and was startled by the loud report of a gun very near and a ball passed just over his
19

head. Smoke from a liveoak told where the shot came from.
The Indian was lying behind it waiting for this opportunity.
Ware came to the corner of the house handling his gun as if
about to shoot, and the Indian shot too quick, thinking likely
he was discovered. The tree stood on the brink of a ravine, and
just the glimpse of the Indian's black head was seen as he went
over into it after shooting. Mr. Durban, who could not see very
well and remained in the house, was under the impression when
he heard the loud report of the gun that it was Ware who shot
at an Indian, and exclaimed, "Did you hit him, Richard?"

The Indians kept them here all night but did not venture near
enough to get the horses, which were tied near the door; but they
got the sheet from the wagon, which was left further away.
The besieged men left next day, without seeing any more of the
Indians.

On one occasion Mr. Ware and some others were in Nueces
Canyon looking for some white men who had killed another and
were hiding out. At this time there were scarcely any settlers
in this far western valley. A few daring men had brought their
families there and were living in camps preparatory to forming a settlement. Among these were the Cox family, on West-
prong. Ware and his party went to the Cox camp, and found
everything torn up and the people gone. To the practiced eye
of these frontiersmen it was soon apparent there had been a
battle here. Among other things they found a newly made
grave, and digging into it with their knives found the body of a
little girl, one of the Cox children, who had been killed in the
fight. In a waterhole near by they found the dead body of an
Indian. Blood and many other signs of the fight were there.

Mr. Ware has had many reverses in life, but he and his wife
at this writing (January, 1900) still live in Sabinal Canyon.

Mrs. Ware was born in Shawneetown, Ill., in 1839. Her
father's name was David Slaver, and he died when she was quite
young. Her mother then married Mr. Gideon Thompson, with
whom she came to Sabinal Canyon in 1852.

AUNT MARY DAVENPORT.

Came to Texas in 1830.

Among the many pioneer women of Texas but few have passed through a more varied experience than "Aunt Mary" Davenport, as she is generally called by all that know her. The writer found the good lady at the house of Mr. Monroe Fenley, her son-in-law, who lives two miles east of Sabinal Station. Mrs. Mary J. Davenport was the daughter of Capt. John Crane, and was born in Hardeman County, Mo., in 1823. Her father was a companion and playmate of Sam Houston, and both enlisted in General Jackson's army in Tennessee when the war broke out with the Creek Indians. The two took part in the famous Indian battle of the Horshoe Bend. Houston was a lieutenant, and was severely wounded. After the battle was over Mr. Crane and another young man came upon the body of a dead squaw with a live babe beside her, and they were at a loss to know what to do with it. At this time another soldier came up, named Nick Baker, and they asked him what would be best to do with the Indian baby. "Kill it," said he. This they declared they would not do. "I will, then," said Baker, and thereupon he snatched up the swarthy infant and dashed its brains out against a tree. This man had suffered many things at the hands of the Indians. He had seen them do his little brothers and sisters the same way, and also kill his mother and father. He alone made his escape during the terrible slaughter, and had declared war against all Indians, regardless of age or sex.

John Crane came to Texas with his family in 1830 and settled in Nacogdoches. From there he moved in 1834 and settled about where Huntsville is now. A friend came with him, named Pleasant Grey, and they agreed to lay off their land adjoining and build close together, so they could be near neighbors.

In 1835, when the Texas revolution broke out in a war with Mexico, Mr. Crane raised a company and went to San Antonio, and was one of the captains with his men who entered the town under Ben Milam and helped to capture General Cos and his army. Captain Crane was a relative of Capt. William Ware,

who also commanded a company. After the fall of the Alamo
and General Houston was retreating before the exultant Mexicans and settlers were fleeing, Captain Crane stayed with his
and Captain Ware's families, and the latter went on to San Jacinto and led a company in the battle.

Captain Crane carried the families from near Montgomery
and crossed over the Sabine at Natchitoches, La., and remained
there until the battle was fought, and then came back with the
families to Montgomery, where Captain Ware joined them.
Captain Crane then stayed three months in the service, until
times were settled and all the troops discharged. He then
moved to Walker County and settled about ten miles from
Huntsville. While living here a war broke out with the Cherokee Indians, and Captain Crane went out under General Rusk
against them. In the battle which ensued he was killed—shot
just under the heart by rifle ball. His body and that of a neighbor who was killed at the same time and fell with him were
buried on the field by John Robbins and Ben Highsmith. The
Indian chiefs who led the Cherokees were Bowles and Big Mush,
both of whom were killed.

In 1839 Miss Mary J. Crane married James Elkins, of Walker
County. He died in 1844, and in 1848 she married John M.
Davenport, in Kaufman County. They moved from there to
Sabinal Canyon in 1852 with Capt. William Ware. In 1854
they moved below the mountains and settled at the German
settlement of D'Hanis, and from there to Ranchero Creek and
engaged in stock raising. In 1858 Mr. Davenport was captain
of a minute company and had a fight with the Indians on the
Leona River, below the town of Uvalde. The Indians were surprised in camp and all killed but one.

Shortly after this Captain Davenport started early one morning to make a trip of several miles west to Blanco Creek to see
some parties about cutting hay for him. When he started Mrs.
Davenport cautioned him to keep a sharp lookout and to not
let anyone get near him before he found out who it was. "All
right," he said. "You take care of yourself and the children,
and watch good when you go to the creek after water." This
was the last time "Aunt Mary" saw her husband alive. He
was killed that evening by Indians near where Sabinal Station
is now. Mrs. Davenport pointed out the spot to the writer as

THIS ROCK MARKS THE PLACE WHERE JOHN DAVENPORT WAS
KILLED BY INDIANS.

we sat on Mr. Fenley's gallery. The country then was mostly
open prairie, with here and there motts of timber and thickets.
Now it is covered with mesquite. Mr. Davenport was in three
miles of home when the Indians came upon him, and the desperate fight he had with them was witnessed by some Mexicans,
but they were afraid to venture to his assistance. When the Indians left they went to the spot and found Mr. Davenport just
dying, and not able to speak. They pulled some arrows out of
him, and one of them carried an arrow to Mrs. Davenport and
told her the sad and startling news. Another Mexican carried
an arrow to Mr. John Kennedy, and told him the news. Runners were now sent to alarm the scattered settlers, and Mr. Kennedy came to the Davenport ranch. Mrs. Davenport wanted to
go at once to where the dead body of her husband lay, and was
about to start in company with, Mr. John Kennedy, when Ross,
his brother, came up and prevailed upon the bereaved wife to

desist, as she might also be killed by the Indians, who in this short time could not be far away. The two Kennedy brothers now rode off together, and John assured Mrs. Davenport that he would go and stay with the body of her slain husband until the settlers who lived below could get together. He took a lantern with him, and when night came lighted it and sat by the body with gun and pistol. When enough came an inquest was held by the dim lantern light, and before day the body was moved home. This was the first inquest held over a person killed by Indians.

As soon as daylight came John Kennedy took some of the assembled men, and going back to the scene of the killing took the trail of the Indians. The others dug a grave and buried the dead man. The trailing party was joined by citizens of Uvalde and soldiers from Fort Inge. They overtook the Indians and had a fight with them, and obtained the pistol of Mr. Davenport. It was learned afterwards from a boy who was a captive at that time in Mexico that Davenport shot one Indian in the arm, one in the body, one in the hip and shoulder, and that one of them died of his wounds on their retreat. This was told by an Indian to the boy. This Indian also said that they killed one white man in the morning that had no gun or pistol, but the one they killed in the evening fought like the devil. The man they killed in the morning was John Bowles. He was a brave man, but not being armed had no chance to fight.

Davenport was killed about 4 o'clock in the evening of the same day. He was riding a mule that day, something he seldom did. He wanted to trade the mule; that was why he was riding him. The Mexicans who witnessed the fight said the Indians rode furiously around Davenport in a circle, yelling, lying low on their horses and shooting arrows. It was with difficulty he could hit them with his pistol, but fought them until he sank down full of arrows.

Mrs. Davenport has spent many sleepless nights on account of Indians. She saw a band near the house once running horses. She remembers well how General Houston looked, and at one time made coffee for him.

J. A. BOALES.

Came to Texas in 1834.

Mr. James A. Boales, one of the early settlers of Texas, was born in Christian County, Ky., August 17, 1829, and came to Texas with his father, Capt. Calvin Boales, in 1834, and settled on the Brazos River at a place afterwards known as Old Nashville. This place was named by the immigrants from Tennessee who settled there. The Boales family started to Texas from Lawrence County, Mississippi, in company with the Tandy family, their relatives. There was also of this party Billy Smith and Billy Moore. On the way they fell in with Jerry and John Bailey, and they all came on together. There also came about this time the Powers and McCanlis families. When the party arrived at their destination only two settlers had preceded them, and they were living in a camp. One of these was James Mc-Laughlin. When the Boales party arrived at the Brazos, opposite the place where they wished to settle, they had to stop and build a boat before they could cross their effects to the prairie and bluff on the other side. Like all Texas at that time, it looked wild and romantic. High grass covered the country in all directions, game was gentle and plentiful, and there was no lack of fresh meat at all times. Bread to these daring settlers was the greatest object in regard to food supply, and they soon learned to do without that without any great inconvenience when they could not obtain it. The soil was very rich, and small patches of corn were planted at the proper season. Before they could get plows and other farm utensils, these primitive Brazos farmers cleared off the high weeds and cane in the bottoms and planted their corn with handspikes, and then without much cultivation fair crops were made. When the corn was matured and well dried they made mortars to pound it in. Although the meal thus made was coarse and rough these people were happy and contented, and really saw more pleasure and enjoyed life better than most people do at this day and time. One great trouble they had to contend with while their crops were growing was the game. They had to guard against bear, deer ,and turkeys to keep them from destroying the growing products before time to harvest.

Among others with whom Mr. Boales came to Texas was Rev. Mr. Smith, a man who became noted in religious and educational work in Texas, and who died mourned by all with whom he came in contact during his long and active life upon the wild frontiers of Texas. At the time of his appearance in Texas he was young, irreligious, and had no education, and for some time worked as a striker in a blacksmith shop at Old Nashville. During a revival meeting he was converted, and showed so much zeal for the cause of Christ that he was taken in charge by two Baptist preachers, Garrett and Fisher, and educated. He it was who founded the famous college at Independence, which was afterwards moved to Belton. He was also a relative of the Boales family.

When these first settlers pitched their camps and built their cabins along the banks of the Brazos they had no trouble with the Indians, who were quite numerous and often visited and traded with the whites. Peace and quiet, however, did not long remain. Mexico had trouble with her American colonies, which soon burst forth into open hostilities. After the fall of the Alamo the settlers all had to retreat before Santa Anna's army until the famous battle of San Jacinto was fought and won. The old settlers called this flight the "Runaway scrape." The party with whom Mr. Boales, then a boy, made his escape was composed of about seventy-five persons. They went into camp on the west side of the Trinity River at Clapp's ferry. There had been a great deal of rain during the flight, and the river was very high. Here, in anxious expectation, the settlers who had stayed with the women and children for their protection awaited news of the battle which they knew General Houston and the brave men with him would fight before they turned their backs on the soil of Texas. While in this condition of anxious solicitude a man named Love came in hot haste with the astounding news that Houston's army had been cut to pieces and almost totally annihilated, and that they had better cross the Trinity at once and continue their flight. What could the wretched people do under such circumstances? The impassable river was in front and the fierce Mexican army in the rear. After some consultation the few men of the party concluded to fight, and commenced the erection of breastworks. On the heels of this messenger, however, came an express from Houston telling the people he had Santa Anna a prisoner and had killed and captured most of his army, and for them to return to their homes. Despair was now changed to joy, and shout after shout went up from the camp. Some say that the man Love was only in sight of the battle, and saw Houston's men prostrate themselves to avoid a discharge from cannon in the charge and thought they were all killed, and reported accordingly as he made his way east. The people at once commenced their westward march, and those that lived at Old Nashville arrived in due time.

Shortly after these events Indian troubles commenced. A man and his brother named Riley moved further up the country with his family, intending to settle on the Gabriel, but were attacked by the Indians. In the fight that ensued one of the Rileys was killed, but his brother bravely continued the fight and succeeded in keeping off the savages and bringing away the body of his brother. While the fight was in progress the family made their escape into the brush and succeeded in getting back to Nashville on foot. There was also one man in the party who ran off when the fight commenced and made his escape. He reported that all of the party were killed.

In 1837 Captain Erath with a small company of men had a desperate fight with the Indians on Elm Creek. Among others of the settlers who were killed in this fight was Frank Childress, with whom Mr. Boales was well acquainted. Erath County was named after this famous Capt. George B. Erath. He often stopped with the Boales family when down in that country.

In 1838 a family named McLelland lived in a camp on Little River and were attacked by Indians. McLelland was gone, and the Indians took possession of the place, killed an infant child by dashing its brains out, and treated Mrs. McLellan with the most monstrous indignities. During the plundering of the camp the Indians found a quantity of whisky and all got drunk. When the effects of the liquor died out they all went to sleep and the woman made her escape in the night with three remaining children of the Folk family, whom she had taken to raise. Their names were John, Charley, and Elizabeth. Mrs. McLelland hid herself and these three children in a drift near the bank of the river. When the father came home he found the dead infant, his only child, and feathers were scattered where the Indians had ripped the beds and poured them out. They were gone, however, and McLelland, not knowing where his wife and the other children were, went down to the settlement and gave the alarm. A party came back with him, and his wife and the children were found nearly dead with hunger and exposure through several nights in the drift, fearing to come out.

In this same year an election of some kind was to be held at Old Nashville, and McLelland and his neighbors who had moved up around him concluded to go down and vote. The men with him were Sam Jones and his two sons, Eli and Wiley, Isaac Standifer, and Solomon Long. McLelland went ahead of the others, against their advice, for they cautioned him to stay back with them, as the Indians might attack him if alone. He said: "No; I will go on; the Indians will not kill a Scotchman." (It seems he had a faster horse than the others.) About ten miles on the road above Old Nashville there are some peculiar shaped mounds called "sugar-loaf hills." Here the Indians attacked McLelland and killed him, and his body was found by the other men when they came along, who took it on to town and buried it.

Mr. Boales was acquainted with most of the men who took part in the famous Indian fight called "Bird's Victory." This was fought on Little River, about three miles from the present town of Belton, county seat of Bell County. The settlers far and near would occasionally get together and fort up at Old Nashville during some extensive Indian raid or series of raids. The ladies of Nashville, Tenn., had taken up a subscription and bought a small cannon and sent it to the settlers at this place to help defend themselves. It is thought that the presence of this little cannon saved the town from being attacked. The settlers would fire it occasionally at sunset or on holidays, and no doubt the Indians were near enough at times to hear it, and knew it was there.

In 1838 or 1839 five of Captain Erath's rangers were killed at a place called Postoak Island, or grove. This was a dense mott of postoak timber surrounded by open prairie, not far from the road which led from the upper settlement to the town. The Indians had been making raids incessantly for some time, and Captain Erath thought it was best for the people to move down to town until something could be done to check the Indians. Some of them were not prepared with teams and wagons to go, and the captain sent five of his men to Nashville to procure wagons and teams for these people. After having accomplished what they went for, the rangers started back up the country, and were attacked by a large force of Indians in the open prairie near this grove. The particulars of this struggle can not be given, as none were left of the white men to tell the tale, but from the signs of the fight it must have been desperate. The names of the rangers were Dave Farmer, Clabe Neill, Jesse Bailey, Aaron Cullins, and Sterett Smith. The delay of these men in returning caused Captain Erath to send more men to see what the cause was. This scout came upon the scene of the battle and found the bodies. The bodies of Cullins and Smith were found in one of the wagons, and the other three were scattered on the prairie between the wagons and mott of timber. It is likely the Indians discovered them some distance off and hid their force in or behind the mott, and when they charged out and cut the rangers off from this protection, they had made a desperate effort to fight their way through the Indians to it. It is likely also that some confusion reigned and there was no concert of action, as the scattered position of the bodies would show. The rangers either went down in one wagon and then each drove one back, or else they rode their horses down and worked them back thus far in the wagons, or some of them. The Indians got all the teams, guns, pistols, etc.

About this time old "Grandpa" Neill was killed by the Indians within 300 yards of the house of Mr. Boales. The morning was foggy, but when the report of the gun was heard that killed him, the neighbors seized their weapons and went to his aid. They found his dead body, but his slayers were gone in the fog and could not be found. One of the sons of the old man named William was killed by Indians on Battle Creek while out with surveyors. Dr. Hill was also in this fight, but made his escape. James Shaw, a representative man of the people, was wounded, and a negro man belonging to Holtsclaugh was killed while out on another surveying expedition. This negro's master and others made their escape.

About 1840 a mail route was started between Old Nashville and Washington and Independence. A man named Joe Taylor

carried the mail, and often had narrow escapes from the Indians. On one occasion they pursued him so close to town that
the citizens heard his calls for help and came to his aid in time
to save him. His old flint-lock gun had failed to fire, and the
Indians ran on both sides of him and tried to catch his horse by
the bridle. They also shot him in the shoulder with an escopet,
and he shot one of the Indians with a large holster pistol he
carried. They were not likely aware he had this pistol, and ran
close upon him when his gun failed to fire. In the chase the
mail bag was lost.

In 1841 three families lived on Walker Creek, where Cameron is now. They were Capt. Dan Walker, Billy Smith, and a
man named Monroe. The Indians being very bad, they concluded to move down to the big settlement on the Brazos, and
were all fixing to start from the same house when they were
attacked by the Indians. The men had just commenced to lift
a big box into a wagon when the savages made their appearance,
and dropping it ran into the house and a battle commenced.
Now, it seems that all the money wealth of the Smiths was in
the box, and when the Indians advanced toward the wagons to
take shelter behind them Grandma Smith ran out under fire
and lifting the lid off the box secured the money and ran back
without getting hurt, leaving the box lid standing up. An Indian had a curiosity to know what was in the box and crawled
up behind the standing lid and reached his hand around to feel
in the box, but at this moment a ball from the rifle of Uncle
Billy Smith put an end to his existence. He made the calcula-
tion as to the position of his body, and shot him through the
box lid. The Indians had enough of the battle now, and left,
dragging their dead companion away, and the settlers finished
loading and came on down to town. The Smiths were related to
the Boales family.

Mr. Boales knew the old pioneer Baptist preacher, Z. N. Morrell, and attended a camp meeting held by him once, and during a service, while the people were thick under the arbor, a
band of mounted Indians dashed by and fired into the crowd,
killing two men. Some of the white men had guns and returned the fire, but no Indian was killed. Mr. Boales' father,
Calvin Boales, was captain of a company of rangers and did
good service on the frontier. Mr. Boales says he used to camp

with his wagon where Hearne is now, and no one lived there except Billy McGrew. He knew Fort Sulivan when there was no one there except Sulivan, his negro man Dennis, and a man named Poole. He voted in Bee County the first election held there, and after moving further west voted in Edwards County at the first election held there. He was in Milam County when Burleson was cut off.

When the Civil War broke out Mr. Boales joined the Confederate army and served on the Texas coast in Hobby's regiment. P. H. Breeden was his captain, commanding company C. He was in the fight at Corpus Christi and Fort Esperanza. After this the regiment went to Galveston, and was quartered at Bolivar Point until ordered from there to Virginia Point to guard the bridge to keep deserters from crossing. This was about the wind-up of the war, and soon after the regiment was disbanded.

He was made a Mason in 1864, while stationed at Bolivar Point. The lodge was called Hobby Lodge.

In 1881 he moved westward and settled in Frio Canyon, Edwards County, 120 miles west of San Antonio. He arrived in August, a few months after Mrs. McLauren and Allen Lease were killed by the Indians. He has made several short moves around, once to Uvalde and then to Dry Frio, and is now back in Main Frio Canyon.

The writer has spent several nights with "Uncle Jimmy" and his good lady. They are old-time Texans, and one can sit and listen for hours to "Uncle Jimmy" without tiring of his truthful statements of the pioneer days.

F. G. TINSLEY.

F. G. TINSLEY.

Came to Texas in 1834.

Fountain Gillespie Tinsley was born in Barren County, Kentucky, November 23, 1832, and came to Texas with his parents in 1834. His father, Dr. John Turner Tinsley, was in the battle at Gonzales in 1835, when the Mexicans came there to take the cannon, an account of which is elsewhere mentioned.

In 1836, after the Mexicans had stormed the Alamo and Gen. Sam Houston was at Gonzales with his army, he made the Tinsley house his headquarters. Mr. F. G. Tinsley could remember seeing General Houston and sitting in his lap. When the army left Gonzales on the approach of the Mexican army under Santa Anna, Dr. Tinsley materially aided the cause of independence by making a trip to the coast after ammunition and intercepting the army of Houston on their line of march with the powder and lead in time to be used in the famous battle of San Jacinto, which was fought soon after. Dr. Tinsley and his wife Nancy both died at Gonzales at a very advanced age.

The subject of our sketch was in the famous flight before the victorious Mexicans after the massacre of the heroes of the Alamo, and rather indistinctly remembers the terrible hardships endured by the fleeing families from Gonzales towards the Sabine, in the rain, mud, and water of that wet month of April.

After the victory at San Jacinto the Tinsley family, among many others, came back to Gonzales and erected new homes over the ashes of their former ones, which had been burned. When General Houston left Gonzales with his men, and all the families were gone, he left two men with instructions to burn the town on the approach of the Mexicans, which they did.

Mr. Tinsley grew up to manhood at Gonzales. He was of a lively disposition, fond of music and dancing, and was a fine performer on the violin. He was much liked and a general favorite among all the young people. He had three sisters — Mary, Amanda, and Virginia—and one brother, John. The eldest sister, Mary, married a Mr. Sweeny; Amanda married Crockett Jones, and Virginia married Andrew Moore. John married

Miss Dora Houston of Gonzales, and still lives there, as does also Amanda. The others are dead. F. G. Tinsley married Miss Sarah Almedia Davis, at Gonzales, on the 29th of June, 1854. The ceremony was performed by Justice of the Peace John Goss. Just prior to the Civil War Mr. Tinsley moved westward and settled on the Hondo River, in Medina County. Here he raised stock, taught school, and for some time served Medina County in the capacity of justice of the peace.

This was a frontier country, and Mr. Tinsley with his young family passed through all of the exciting times of Indian raids, murders, and alarms, and forting-up of the scattered settlers for protection. In one Indian battle his brother-in-law, Nathan Davis, was severely wounded with an arrow. Wild animals were numerous, and their roars and screams could be heard at night as they came out of the jungles of chaparral and prickly pear down to the Hondo River on the opposite side from the house to quench their thirst. There were wildcats, panthers, tigers, and Mexican lions. These larger ones were shy in daylight and could seldom be seen. They depredated constantly on young stock and were very annoying to the stockmen. One of these, Gip Tilley, conceived the idea of having a large steel trap made, with which to catch a lion or any other of the larger animals. With this purpose in view he went to San Antonio and succeeded in getting one which weighed about seventy-five pounds. The animals had a regular beaten trail from the thickets to the water, and in this trail Mr. Tilley set his trap, but failed to drive a stout stake near to fasten the chain to. A Mexican lion got caught, but ran away with the trap on his foot. Next morning Mr. Tinsley and Mr. Tilley trailed him for several miles where he ran, and in places where the ground was soft holes were made several inches deep where he shoved the trap into it. He ran over prickly pears and tore them down as if a cart had passed over them. The trail was finally abandoned at a place where the pears and brush were so dense that a person could not advance any further without crawling. The time will come, perhaps, when these thickets will be cleared up, and some farmer will plow up a steel trap with the skeleton of a foot in it.

On one occasion Mr. Tinsley and others were out on a cow-hunt and camped in a draw with low brushy hills around and hobbled out their horses. One of the men killed a deer near by, and the hams were cut off for use and the balance left. Next morning Mr. Tinsley went to get his horse, and passing by the spot where the remains of the deer were left discovered that they were gone. Not seeing his horse in the draw, he started through the brush and Spanish daggers which covered a small hill to look in a little valley on the other side. He had proceeded but a few yards, pressing through the undergrowth, when a fierce growl, deep and guttural, came from about the densest portion of the jungle in front of him. He had on a revolver, but backed out the way he came and went on around and got his horse. This was no doubt a lion, and it had the remains of the deer in there. When the other men were informed of the fact it was at first decided to make an assault on the thicket and route the animal, but some of the older men said it was best to leave him alone, not that they had any fear of the beast, but in those days only cap and ball arms were used, and the men only had their sixshooters along, and ammunition was scarce, and a battle with a lion with navies would exhaust all of their shots, and afterwards the party might be attacked by a band of Indians. So the monarch of the jungle was left alone with his prey.

On another occasion Mr. Tinsley was out alone hunting stock, and as frontiersmen sometimes will do, left his firearms at home. He saw no Indians, but found a big black bear up a low tree, and conceived the idea of roping him and pulling him out and then trying to kill him with a pocket knife. The bear was fat and lazy and made no attempt to get down and try to escape, and the noose was thrown nicely over his head and he was pulled out. Mr. Tinsley was riding a trained cow pony, and now circled rapidly around the struggling bear and soon so entangled him in the coils of the rope that he was helpless, and lay panting and growling on the ground. Mr. Tinsley now dismounted and opened his knife, and while his cow pony held the rope taut, cut bruin's throat. The animal would weigh several hundred pounds, and a pack horse had to be brought to carry it all away. In the meantime, however, a great alarm had been raised in the country. A man on his horse on the top of a hill a long distance off had witnessed the roping and killing of the bear by Mr. Tinsley, and reported Indians in the country, and that he had seen them kill one man in the valley of Black Creek. Runners were

20

sent all over the country, and men gathered at different ranches to organize a scout. A messenger came to Mr. Tinsley and informed him of the raid, and when he learned about the man seen killed at a certain place on Black Creek, told his informer to go back and counteract the alarm, as it was himself killing a bear, and he had just brought it in.

In 1861, when the Indians made the big raid, penetrating the settlements as far as Pleasanton, in Atascosa County, men gathered from all over the country to fight them, and Mr. Tinsley and his brother-in-law, Nathan Davis, and other Hondo settlers rallied to the call and joined the men from Sabinal and Seco, and all to the number of thirty or more went under command of Big Foot Wallace in pursuit of them. The account of the trailing and battle at the head of Seco has been fully described elsewhere. Mr. Tinsley was with the main body when the fight commenced in front on the side of the mountain, and when the boys were hurled back on the second squad, went back in the retreat and dismounted and tied his horse with others at the foot of the mountain on the bank of a cedar-timbered ravine. Captain Wallace and others took shelter under cedar trees and a rock ledge to the left, but a more advanced position. The Indians were firing continually at them both with firearms and bows. Mr. Tinsley took shelter behind a cedar tree, but soon perceived that some one had picked him out and was firing at him especially. He soon located his man, who was about 200 yards away, half up the mountain, and firing with a rifle. He would conceal himself to load and then step between the rocks to shoot. He had on a hat and a white shirt. They had killed many people on this trip and had stripped them of their arms and clothing, and were using the weapons now in this battle, and some had invested themselves in the shirts and hats of the slain settlers. Mr. Tinsley had a short, heavy rifle, and fired two shots at the fellow, but perceived that his bullets were falling short. The Indian cut off one limb an inch thick with one of his shots, within a foot of Mr. Tinsley's head. He now poured two full charges of powder in his gun, and when loaded and capped laid the rifle in a fork of the tree and awaited for another opportunity to shoot at his man. When the Indian again appeared to fire, the white man fired first, aiming high at the white shirt front. The double-charged rifle made a loud report, and kicked back under the arm of Mr. Tinsley, and the breech struck the ground a yard in his rear, making the small gravel fly in various directions, and the hammer going back at a full cock. The white-shirted man was seen no more. A few days after the fight a party of Sabinal men went over the battleground, and among other things picked up a hat near the spot where he stood to shoot.

When the fight was over Wallace and his men went to Sabinal Canyon. It was cold and sleeting, and before morning Mr. Tinsley had a very sore throat, and did not go on the trip to cut the Indians off at the head of the Sabinal, but loaned his pistol to Mr. Bob Kinchaloe, who went.

Soon after this Mr. Tinsley enlisted in the Confederate army and served in the regiment of Colonel Woods and in the company of Capt. Josiah Taylor. He removed his family to Gonzales, and they remained there until the close of the war. Mr. Tinsley was in most of the fighting in Louisiana, including the big battle of Mansfield. Before this engagement closed quite a number of Federals were captured and sent into the city of Mansfield near by, with a strong guard to hold them until the battle was over. Among this detail of guards was Mr. Tinsley. The prisoners were held in the courtyard, and during the time a citizen of Mansfield came riding up on a fine horse to look at them. He was very fleshy, and sat back in his saddle with a very important and pompous look on his face, for he was very wealthy, and commenced cursing and abusing the captured soldiers. He shook his fist at them, and said he had a good mind to get down there and cut every one of their throats. Mr. Tinsley walked up close to his horse and said: "Look here, my friend; these are prisoners. Do you hear those cannons down there? Go down there and you can get accommodated. Where those guns are firing men are in that business—cutting throats. Go down there and take a hand, or truck back the way you came." The fellow looked for a moment at the little black-eyed man who thus addressed him, and then, wheeling his horse, went back up the street in the opposite direction to the sound of rifles and cannon. After he was gone one of the prisoners who was standing near, and who wore the shoulder-straps of a colonel in the Union army, asked Mr. Tinsley his name and what State he was from, and on

being given the information took out a notebook and pencil and
made an entry of it.

When the war was over Mr. Tinsley came back to Gonzales
and moved to his old home on the Hondo, but did not remain
long. His stock were mostly gone or badly scattered and wild,
and he again returned to Gonzales County. From here he removed to Guadalupe County and remained several years, and
again moved west, settling near Benton City, in Atascosa County.
During the last eight or ten years of his life he preached the gos-
pel of Christ under the auspices of the Methodist church. He
died at his home, twenty miles south of San Antonio, on the 13th
of February, 1896. He was long afflicted and confined to his bed
the last six months of his life, but accepted the chastening hand
of God as a child of God, thanking his Creator for the many
manifestations of his mercy and love.

Mr. Tinsley was the father of nine children, all girls. Their
names were as follows, according to age: Mary, Almedia, Nannie,
Emma, Betty, Cordelia, Sopha, Mattie, Eddie. Mrs. Tinsley still
survives and lives with a married daughter, Cordelia, near the
old home. Those that survive of the children are all married.
The eldest, Mary Lillian, married the writer; Almedia married
a brother, Leroy P. Sowell, who lives in San Antonio; Nannie
married Andrew Wildman, son of a Baptist preacher who lives
near Devine, Medina County; Emma married David Calk, and
they live in San Antonio. Betty died when she was about eighteen years of age, unmarried; Cordelia married Pearl Briggs, son
of a Baptist preacher; he kept the store and postoffice at Segler,
and died there in 1898; Sopha married William Pue, son of a
Baptist preacher, and they live in San Antonio; Mattie married
Emmett Huett, and they live in San Antonio; Eddie died when
she was two years of age.

Mary Lillian Sowell, wife of the author, was small when her
parents lived on the Hondo, but can remember when one of their
neighbors, Rube Smith, was killed by Indians, and the settlers
forted-up at his house, while part of the men followed the Indians and fought a battle with them. One of her uncles, Nathan
Davis, was badly wounded in the fight. She can remember how
the dead man looked. She and some other little girls were afraid
to go close to him. He was scapled and very bloody.

THOMAS GALBREATH.

Came to Texas in 1837.

In Medina County, three miles north of Devine, lives one of Jack Hays' old rangers, Thomas Galbreath. When we find one of the old-time rangers who followed Ed Burleson, Jack Hays, and other border leaders in the 30's, 40's, and 50's, we get information that is of more than passing interest. They tell of the time when they used flintlock rifles and heavy single-shot pistols. During some of these years percussion locks had come in use, but still many used the old-time flint which their fathers carried in the last British war.

Mr. Galbreath was born in Macon County, North Carolina, on the 22d day of March, 1823, and came to Texas in March, 1837. In the fall of the same year the Galbreath family settled at Bastrop, on the Colorado River, which was then the outside settlement. The Indians were so hostile and made such frequent raids that these isolated settlers at times almost despaired of sustaining themselves. Gen. Edward Burleson, who had already distinguished himself in the Texas revolution, lived seven miles below Bastrop, and to him the people looked for protection and advice in these perilous times. Burleson said, "We must defeat the Indians in a general engagement, or else leave the country." It was decided by the settlers to endeavor to give the Indians a battle, and to do this they must invade their stronghold, which was in the mountains far up the Colorado. General Burleson was asked to lead the force, which was soon raised, of men and boys who could load and shoot a gun and had a horse.

About one hundred settlers assembled at Bastrop for the expedition. Among this number was Thomas Galbreath, then a boy of 15 years of age, and carrying his father's old flintlock rifle. He had only that year come to Texas, and had never seen a wild Indian.

General Burleson led his men up the Colorado to the mouth of the Llano, and there came upon the Indians in their village in large force. Besides the warriors there were many squaws and children. The Comanches were aware of the approach of the white men, and met them half a mile from their village to give them battle. Burleson formed his men in one line, and the Indians came at a full running charge and yelling loudly. They presented a formidable appearance, riding good horses, their shields on their left arms, and a quiver full of arrows protruding above the left shoulder. All had on the fierce-looking war paint, and many of them had buffalo horns on their head. Their long black hair waved in the breeze like streamers behind them. Their looks, loud yells, and impetuous charge was enough to strike terror to the hearts of men who had never met them before. Young Galbreath felt uneasy, and said if he had seen anyone else run he would have followed suit. He looked at the men around him. Some had fought Indians before, and seemed in nowise put out by this demonstration on the part of the Comanches. General Burleson passed close to Galbreath with fire in his eye and giving his commands short and quick, in about these words: "Dismount now, men, and stand to them. They are not going to run over us. Hold your rifles ready and don't shoot too quick. Take good aim. We will scatter them the first fire." Many of the Indians were nearly naked. They came as if they were going to run over the settlers without making any halt. The loud, clear voice of Burleson was heard, "Fire, boys, fire!" There was a rattling, cracking volley all along the line, and the Indians divided, circling right and left all around the white men. They lay low on the opposite side of their horses and shot arrows as they went. The effect of the fire from Burleson's men could be seen in front. Horses were down and struggling amidst dead and crippled Indians, while others were running riderless with the charge. Others turned back, bullet stricken, and galloped in terror from the field. Some of the Indians who had been fatally hit were falling from their horses as they passed around the settlers. "Load quick, men; they will come again," said the commander. The fight lasted some time, the Comanches making four charges in all. When the quick eye of Burleson perceived that they had begun to weaken, he ordered his men to mount with loaded guns and charge them. The Indians gave way and began their retreat across the open prairie towards the mountains, not even stopping at their village. The running fight lasted two miles, and then the pursuit was called off. The settlers came back by way of the village and took possession of a number of

horses, eighty head in all. The squaws looked sullen and would
not talk. They were mad because the warriors had been whipped
and had run away. The horses which were taken belonged to the
settlers around Bastrop. None of Burleson's men were killed on
the ground, but many were hit with arrows and some died afterwards. The Indians had no firearms. Many of the settlers' horses
were wounded. Mr. Galbreath says this battle caused the settlement to start where Austin is now, but it was then called Waterloo. During the fight he fired his rifle four times. The Indians
moved further west.

Living near Bastrop was a man named Manlove, who was the
owner of a fine pair of gray horses which were stolen by the Indians. He was greatly distressed about his buggy team, and
called on his neighbors to help recover them. Mr. Galbreath and
several others responded and at once set out on the trail. They
had Tonkaway John with them, who was a good trailer and also
fighter. He was a Tonkaway Indian, and lived with General
Burleson. The trail of the Comanches was followed rapidly by
John, and on the evening of the same day the party started the
hostiles were discovered. They were camped in a ravine cooking
meat, and the smoke from their fire betrayed them. The white
men charged into the ravine, but the Indians discovered them in
time to make their escape and carry one of Manlove's horses
with them, but leaving the other. The men had ridden all day
without anything to eat, and at once proceeded to appease their
hunger upon the roasted meat left by the Indians. While engaged in this they heard an Indian yell, and soon discovered him
on a hill mounted on Manlove's horse. When he perceived that
the white men were looking at him he yelled again and began
to wheel the horse in a circle. There was a man of the party
named Hutch Reed, who was riding a very fast horse, and Tonkaway John said if Reed would let him have this horse he would
catch the Comanche and bring his scalp and Manlove's horse
back. Reed said, "All right; but don't you loose my horse."
The Tonkaway mounted the fast horse with a sardonic grin on
his face and set out, only carrying in the way of arms his bow
and arrows. When the Comanche saw John coming to chase him
he left the hill and galloped off across the valley, yelling defiance, thinking he could easily get away. When John got clear
of some ravines and rocky places and turned his horse loose the

Comanche began to get uneasy and kicked and whipped very energetically. It was no use, however; the gray was no match for Reed's horse. The hostile Indian, seeing that he could not save himself by flight, strung his bow, and a battle with arrows commenced between the two red men. It was evident the Comanche was rattled and shot wild, while John soon filled him full of arrows in spite of his artful dodging and dextrous use of shield. When the Tonkaway finally came up alongside of him the Comanche threw away his bow and begged for life. John paid no attention to this, but taking him by the hair pulled him from his horse, and dismounting, repeatedly stabbed him with a long knife and then scalped him. Remounting now and catching the gray, he came galloping and yelling back to his white companions, leading Manlove's horse with one hand and waving the bloody scalp with the other. Manlove was profuse in his thanks, and dilated on the bravery and prowess of John.

From Bastrop Mr. Galbreath moved to Cedar Creek, ten miles from town, and there hunted and farmed until the

BATTLE OF PLUM CREEK.

This was in 1840. In this year the Comanches, smarting under the defeats inflicted on them by General Burleson and by Col. John H. Moore, made a raid on a large scale through Texas. They penetrated to the coast, sacked and burned the town of Linnville, partly destroyed Victoria, killed and captured some of the settlers, and then commenced their retreat back to the mountains with a great deal of plunder. There were about 600 warriors, besides squaws, and as the settlements were scattering in those days and chiefly confined to the watercourses, it was some time before men enough could assemble at any given point to successfully fight them. In going down from the mountains the Indians had kept between the rivers, where there were no settlements, and consequently were not discovered until a short time before their attack upon Linnville. Runners were sent to the various settlements, and men began to cut across the country in small squads from the valleys of the Colorado, Guadalupe, and San Marcos. Mr. Galbreath heard the news at his home on Cedar Creek, and mounting his horse dashed away to the Colorado, where he found General Burleson at the head of a large company and just starting for the scene of action. Joining him, the command started across the country towards the San Marcos and Guadalupe country, hoping to intercept or cross the trail of the Comanches, who were said to be traveling between the San Marcos and Colorado, going west. On this route they intercepted Guadalupe and San Marcos men, who were already on the trail of the Indians. Among these men were Matthew Caldwell, Jack Hays, Ben McCulloch, Henry McCulloch, Dr. Switzer, Aulcy Miller, French Smith, Ezekiel Smith, Andrew Sowell, John Sowell, James Nichols, Wilson Randle, Barney Randle, and others.

Among the Colorado men were Z. N. Morrell, the Baptist preacher, and Ben Highsmith, the San Jacinto veteran.

The combined forces now numbered more than one hundred men. Nine miles from where the Colorado and Guadalupe men consolidated they caught up with the Indians. This place was at Plum Creek, within the present limits of Caldwell County, and about three miles from Lockhart, the present county seat. Two Indians had been left on a ridge as spies, and sat on their horses and watched the approach of the white men until they were almost within gunshot of them. Both of these fellows had on plug hats which they had obtained at the looting of Linnville, and presented a most comical appearance. A hat never becomes a wild Indian. With his thick, long hair it never fits, and he looks as if he was masquerading with one on. Among the front men of the whites was George Neill, who had a long-range gun. Dismounting, he said he would move them, and aiming high, fired. At the crack of the gun the Indians wheeled their horses quick to run, and both lost their plug hats. An Indian's head is not shaped right to wear a hat, and it is hard for him to keep it in place. The writer, while a ranger in 1870, remembers seeing the friendly Indians who were in the government service as scouts at Fort Griffin wearing hats, but they had to tie them on, otherwise every time their horses jumped or a puff of wind came off they would go. Before the battle came off many more men came, until about two hundred were following the Indians. A large company came from down towards the coast, under the command of Gen. Felix Huston. The Indians made one general stand, but soon broke before the terrible fire of the rifles, and the balance of the battle and pursuit was quite extended, covering several miles of country. Many of the Indians had on fine coats and boots, and some of them carried umbrellas over them. They had many horses and mules packed with goods, and these were rushed on ahead by the squaws, while the warriors fought the battle. At a mott of timber the Comanches rallied in large force and a sharp fight ensued, but they again fled and scattered. Mr. Galbreath says that here he saw a white woman and a negro girl who had been killed by the Indians when they began to retreat from the place. He says another woman was shot with an arrow, but was not killed. He does not remember their names. (These were Mrs. Watt, Mrs. Crosby, and a servant girl captured at Linnville.) It was Mrs. Watt that was killed. Many of the pack animals gave out in the long run and were abandoned and fell into the hands of the Texans. After the Indians left this place they came to a boggy branch, and many of the horses of the Indians stuck fast, and here they left all of the pack animals, with probably a few exceptions, and most of the saddle horses. Some of the hindmost Indians used some of the poor bogged animals as pontoons, and passed over the place on their bodies. The white men ran around the head of the boggy branch and cut off some of the Indians who were on foot and killed them.

The pursuit lasted to the foot of the mountains, between where the towns of San Marcos and Kyle are now, and was there abandoned, as all of the horses were run down, having passed over fifteen miles of country in the chase. The men collected where the fight was severest and most Indians killed, and there camped for the night. Some of the white men were wounded, but none killed. James Nichols, one of the Guadalupe men, received a peculiar wound. He was in the act of firing, when a bullet from the Indians struck him between the middle and forefinger of the right hand and lodged in the wrist. His gun fell without being discharged.

There were ten Tonkaway Indians with Burleson's men, and that night after camp was made they cut off the hands and feet of the dead Comanches who lay near, and roasted and ate them. They also cut one big fat fellow into strips and hung the pieces on a rope.

Many narrow escapes were made by men crowding the Indians too closely when the main body of whites was too far behind and the Comanches turning back on them. Ben McCulloch had an-

experience of this character. Some were hurt by their horses falling with them.

Soon after the battle of Plum Creek the Galbreaths moved and
settled near where the first fight commenced, a few miles from
the present town of Lockhart.

In 1842, when San Antonio was captured by the Mexicans,
Mr. Galbreath went with other citizens to fight them. Among
those he went in company with were the Buntons and Capt.
Jesse Billingsly. This party joined the other Texans on the
Salado, seven miles northeast of San Antonio. All were under
the command of Gen. Matthew Caldwell of Gonzales. Capt.
Jack Hays was also there with a company of rangers, having
been commissioned by General Houston to raise a force for frontier protection soon after the battle of Plum Creek. General
Wall had possession of San Antonio with about 1500 men. Captain Hays with his mounted rangers drew him out to Caldwell's
position. Wall crossed his army to the east side of the creek
facing the Texans, planted cannon, and the battle commenced.
The Texans, 200 in number, acted on the defensive, dodging the
pecan limbs which were cut off by the cannon balls and were
falling among them. The Mexican commander thought to rout
the Texans with this artillery fire, but failing, made preparations to charge them. Cavalry was sent across the creek to
cut off their escape on that side, and Cherokee Indians posted
on the creek below, and both infantry and cavalry sent above to
head off any fugitives in that direction. The Mexicans little
knew what kind of men they had to deal with. All were good
shots and frontier men, with such Indian fighters as Hays,
McCulloch, Walker, Gillespie, Lucky, Dunn, Ackland, Chevalier,
Neill, Wallace, Galbreath, Highsmith, and many others equally
as good. When the bugles sounded the charge the Mexicans
came in fine style and in such dense masses that for a while the
situation looked critical. They came almost in among the Texans and fired their escopets. The latter, protected by the creek
bank and pecan trees, poured such a volley of death and destruction into their ranks that their formation was broken up and
they went back in confusion and disorder to the battery on the
elevated ground. A company of cavalry also charged close, but
the horses recoiled at the fire, and those who lost their riders
went back in confusion, knocking down some of the infantry as

they did so. Loud and continuous cheering went up from the Texans. The cannons now opened again, but Caldwell's men only yelled the louder. Several more charges were made, but without success, on the part of the Mexicans, and many were killed and wounded.

Mr. Galbreath said the Mexican cavalrymen had on the largest spurs he ever saw, and when any of their horses were shot down the troopers could not run with their spurs on, and were invariably killed if they happened to be near the riflemen. The rowels were several inches in diameter and dragged on the ground. They would try to run on their toes so as to lift the rowels from the ground. The ground there after the battle looked as if a garden rake had been used over the ground. The Mexicans were badly defeated by Caldwell, but they cut off the force under Capt. Nicholas Dawson of fifty men from Fayette County and almost annihilated them. They were coming to the sound of the firing, thinking the Mexicans were on the west side of the creek, but discovered their mistake when too late. They fought Wall's whole army until nearly all were killed. Two made their escape—Aulsy Miller and Gonzalvo Woods. About twelve were captured. One of these was the young son of Rev. Z. N. Morrell, who was with Caldwell, not knowing at the time that his boy was with Dawson. The following are some of the men who were killed: Captain Dawson, First Lieutenant Dickerson, Zodack Woods, David Berry, John Slack, John Cummins, — Church, Harvey Hall, Robert Barclay, Wesley Scallorn, Eliam Scallorn, Asa Jones, Robert Eastland, Frank Brookfield, George Hill, John W. Pendleton, J. B. Alexander, Edmond Timble, Charles Field, Thomas Simms, — Butler, John Dancer, and a negro belonging to the Mavericks. He had been sent out by Mrs. Maverick to try and communicate with his master, who had been captured while attending court in San Antonio when the place was taken by the Mexicans. The Mavericks were then living on the Colorado, near Ed Manton's. They had sent this trusty slave with Dawson, hoping he might be able to learn something of Mr. Maverick. Poor fellow! Faithful to his trust, he died by the side of Dawson, fighting to the last.

Mr. Galbreath says these were not all the men who were killed that day trying to get to the position of Dawson. They were found killed all over the prairie on both sides of the creek.

He says a man named Butler with eight men heard the firing of the rangers and Mexicans on the west side of the creek during the running fight from town, and thinking it was the main body of Texans, and that they were engaged, crossed over there and were cut off by the cavalry and killed.

The loss of the Texans during the various engagements of the day was less than one hundred killed and wounded, the heaviest being that of Dawson. The Mexicans went back to San Antonio, and becoming alarmed at the result of the battle, hastily decamped for Mexico. They were followed by the Texans, and the rangers under Hays fought the rear guard at the Hondo, but there the pursuit was abandoned and the men returned to their homes.

After the return of Captain Hays from the Somervell expedition in 1843, Mr. Galbreath joined his company of rangers, which was stationed on the Leon Creek west of San Antonio. Not long after joining the company he went on a scout and participated in the famous

BATTLE OF BANDERA PASS.

When Captain Hays went on this scout, his intention was to go out to the head of the Guadalupe River, and then down some of the canyons below the mountains and then back to camp. The scout numbered between thirty and forty men, among whom were Ben McCulloch, Sam Walker, Kit Ackland, Ad Gillespie, George Neill, Sam Lucky, James Dunn, P. H. Bell, Mike Chevalier, Ben Highsmith, Lee Jackson, and Tom Galbreath. The others can not now be remembered. Sam Walker had just returned from Mexico, having made his escape from the Mexicans after the capture at the ill-fated battle of Mier. Some of the old Hays rangers who were also captured at Mier were still in prison, among whom was Big Foot Wallace.

The course of the rangers after leaving camp was northwest. They struck the Medina River above where Castroville is now, and kept up that stream to where the town of Bandera is now. The last camp of the rangers before the fight was made here. Next morning they turned north towards the Bandera Pass, which they entered about 10 o'clock in the morning.

The Comanches had discovered the approach of the rangers

as they came through the open country south towards the Medina, and laid an ambush for them in the pass. They had all of the advantage for the first onset, being concealed among the rocks and short gullies on both sides of the pass, which is about 500 yards in length by 125 in width. This pass runs through a range of mountains which divides the Verde Creek valley from the Medina. The Indians let the rangers get about one-third of the way through, and then commenced firing from both sides at once. The rangers were coming two and three together, and the sudden and unexpected fire threw the front men into a momentary confusion, mostly, however, on account of frightened and wounded horses, which tried to wheel and run back. The Comanches greatly outnumbered the rangers, and for some time the battle was hotly contested. The Indians had guns among them, besides bows and arrows, and men were killed and wounded on every side. Captain Hays was cool and collected, and gave orders as if everything was all right. "Steady there, boys," he exclaimed. "Get down and tie those horses. We can whip them." Many of the Indians came down the pass and engaged the rangers at close quarters. Pistols were freely used, and some hand to hand conflicts took place, in one of which the Comanche chief was killed by Kit Ackland, who was himself wounded by the daring chief. Before the fight was over nearly one-third of the rangers were killed and wounded. The Indians had many killed, and some were carrying them back towards the north end of the pass during the fight. Mr. Galbreath was wounded with an arrow during the severest part of the conflict. He was on the ground facing towards the north, and the arrow came from the right and struck him just above the pistol belt on the left side. The arrow came quartering and went shallow until near the hip bone, when the penetration was deeper, striking the bone and making a severe wound. The hardy ranger made no complaint, but at once drew the arrow and finished loading his gun, which he was engaged in when hit. No one knew he was wounded until the worst part of the fight was over. Lee Jackson was killed at the first fire. Sam Lucky was shot through the body with a ball and was assisted from his horse by Ben Highsmith, who was himself soon after wounded with an arrow.

The Indians, finally seeing they could not drive the rangers

THE BANDERA PASS FIGHT.
From Photo by Steve Surber, Center Point, Texas.

back, withdrew to the north end of the pass, and the rangers went back the other way, carrying their dead and wounded, and encamped at a waterhole near the south end of the pass. Here they buried the dead rangers and attended to those who were wounded until morning. The Indians remained at the north end of the pass and there buried their chief and killed all of their crippled horses and those that belonged to the chief, whether hurt or not. The first settlers in this part of the country will remember seeing these bones. The badly wounded and dead horses of the rangers were left near the south end. There were five rangers killed and six wounded. Mr. Galbreath does not remember their names, as he had not been in the company long enough to become as familiar with them as he did others later. Mr. Highsmith says Jackson was killed there. The wounded were Sam Lucky, Kit Ackland, James Dunn, Ben Highsmith, Tom Galbreath, and some others whose names can not now be recalled. Galbreath and Lucky were carried to San Antonio to have their wounds attended to.

In the following year Captain Hays took fourteen men and went on a scout to the Nueces Canyon. Of these were Sergeant Kit Ackland, Mike Chevalier, Creed Taylor, Sam Cherry, Noah Cherry, Tom Galbreath, and an Irishman called Paddy. The others can not now be remembered. After a long trip out to the head of the river without seeing any fresh signs of Indians, Hays turned back down the canyon and camped one night, and next day traveled until about noon, when some one discovered a bee-tree, and the captain told the men to pull the bridles off, take their ropes down, and let their horses graze, and they would rest awhile there and get the honey. Noah Cherry secured a small ax that was in the luggage on a pack mule, and ascended the tree for the purpose of chopping into the honey without cutting the tree down.

Now it happened that about this time a large band of Comanches were coming down the canyon on a raid, and seeing the trail of the rangers they followed it, and were at this time close upon Hays and his men. The man in the tree, having a good view of the valley, saw the Indians coming and sang out, "Jerusalem, captain, yonder comes a thousand Indians!" They were approaching rapidly on the trail and made a good deal of dust, hence the rather exaggerated statement of the ranger as to their number. Hays had sat down and was watching Cherry chop. He had a listless, tired look on his face, but at the name of Indians he sprang to his feet as quick as a cat and the whole expression of his countenance changed, his eyes flashed, and he gave his orders quick and to the point; first to the man up the tree: "Come down from there, then, quick! Men, put on your bridles! Take up your ropes! Be ready for them! Be ready for them!"

The rangers on this occasion were armed with Colt's five-shooters, besides rifles and a brace of holster single-shot pistols. This made nine shots to the man. When the Comanches came in full view it seemed that the rangers could not sustain themselves against such odds. Mr. Galbreath says that they seemed to be 200 or more. It was characteristic of Jack Hays that he never ran from Indians and was never defeated by them. The Indians came at a full charge, yelling loudly, and thinking no doubt that it would be an easy matter to run over and rout the small squad of white men who were drawn up around the tree and facing them. Some of the men began to raise their guns, and Hays said, "Now, boys, don't shoot too quick. Let them come closer. Hit something when you shoot and stand your ground. We can whip them; there is no doubt about that." When the rangers fired the Indians were close and many fell from their horses, and several horses fell, so much so that quite a gap was made in their front, and the balance divided and ran to the right and left of the rangers, discharging arrows as they went. Captain Hays now sprang into his saddle and shouted, "After them, men! Give them no chance to turn on us! Crowd them! Powder-burn them!" Never was a band of Indians more surprised than at this charge. They expected the rangers to remain on the defensive, and to finally wear them out and exhaust their ammunition. The rangers ran close beside them and kept up a perfect fusilade with pistols. In vain the Comanches tried to turn their horses and make a stand, but such was the wild confusion of running horses, popping pistols, and yelling rangers, that they abandoned the idea of a rally and sought safety in flight. Some dropped their bows and shields in trying to dodge the flashing pistols. The pursuit lasted three miles, and many Indians were killed and wounded. Some of them kept the rangers from powder-burning them by the dangerous thrusts of their long lances. Conspicuous in the chase was Kit Ackland, who ran so close among the Indians trying to carry out the captain's orders that he was lanced three times. He chased one Indian on a blue mule, but it outran his horse. When the fight was over the rangers rode back, and Mr. Galbreath says he never saw as many dead Indians before or since. The Irishman, Paddy, said he saw a wounded Indian go in a certain thicket, and he was going in there after him. Captain Hays said: "If there is a wounded Indian in there you had better let him alone. If you go in where he is, he will kill you before you see him." Paddy hesitated, but concluded to give the Indian a trial anyway. He said the Indian had his leg broken and was not able to do much, and he was not afraid of a crippled Indian, no way. Soon after disappearing from sight he was heard to make a noise or cry out as if in pain, and then all was still. Three or four rangers now dismounted and advanced cautiously in single file and soon perceived a slight rustling in the underbrush, and all fired towards the spot. A squall like a wildcat from the Indian told the tale that he was badly hit, and the four rangers went to the spot with pistols presented. The Indian was dying, having been hit by all four rifle balls. Sixteen feet from the Indian lay the dead body of the ranger with an arrow through his heart and body, the point coming through the skin on the opposite side. The Indian was a large fellow, and had strong arms. He was lying flat on the ground, almost covered up with leaves, and had all the advantage of the unfortunate ranger, who no doubt received the fatal arrow without seeing the Indian. Paddy was taken out of the thicket and buried, and Captain Hays returned to his camp on the Leona.

Many years after this a friendly Delaware Indian named Bob saw the Comanche chief who led his warriors in this fight, and asked the Delaware who it was he fought on that occasion. Bob told him Jack Hays and his rangers. The chief shook his head and said he never wanted to fight him again; that his men had a shot for every finger on the hand, and that he lost half of his warriors. They died, he said, for a hundred miles back towards Devil's River.

Mr. Galbreath can not locate this battleground, but says it was before they got out of the mountains. Mr. Galbreath also says that this was the first time the rangers used the five-shooters

21

in an Indian fight, but some say the Pedernales battle was the place. It was, however, the first time this band of Indians ever had five-shooters used on them.

When the time of enlistment of this company commanded by Hays expired, Mr. Galbreath enlisted in Gillette's company.

During his service with Hays and other captains he remembers the following names of men who from time to time served in the same company with him: Kit Ackland, Shapley Woolfork, Joe Tivey, Mark Rapier, James Galbreath, Big Foot Wallace, Tom Buchanan, Coho Jones, Peter Poe, Mike Chevalier, James Dunn, Ad Gillespie, P. H. Bell, Jeff Bond, James Gocher, William Powell, Leander Herrill, Ed Lofton, Bill Chism, Calvin Turner, James Roberts, Jack Johnson, Sam Holland, Dick Hilburn, William Jett, — Spain, Charles Donoho, Tom McCannon, Ben McCulloch, Henry McCulloch, Sam Walker, Sam Lucky, George Neill, Ben Highsmith, Creed Taylor, Pipkin Taylor, Josiah Taylor, James Taylor, Rufus Taylor, Andrew Sowell, John Sowell, Asa Sowell, Sam Cherry, Noah Cherry, John Carlin, Rufus Perry, John Williams, Joe Davis, Lee Jackson, Leo Huffman, John Saddler, Wesley Deer, Nat Mangum, Stoke Holmes, Heck, Knox, Kaisey, and many others not now remembered.

Gillette's company was stationed in this year, 1845, on the Seco, near D'Hanis, to defend the German settlement there. The first captain being promoted, Captain Warfield was put in command, with William Knox as first lieutenant, Kaisey second, and Lee third. While the company was stationed here Lieutenant Knox went on a scout into Sabinal Canyon and had a fight with the Indians, in which Wesley Deer was killed and John Saddler was wounded. Eight Indians were killed. Mr. Galbreath was not on this scout, but told Wesley Deer in a joking way that the Indians would kill him this trip. Deer was very young, and this was one reason the old ranger spoke to him in this way.

From Seco the camp was moved to the Leona River, about thirty miles further west. The location was three miles below the present town of Uvalde, seven years before it was laid off. Soon after arriving here the captain sent five men to San Antonio after supplies. Of these were Lee, Golsten, Heck, and Huffman. The other one can not be remembered. While in San Antonio a man named Ben Pettit and a negro man were there with corn from Peach Creek, which they sold to the government. The corn was sent out to the rangers' camp, and Pettit and his negro were employed to bring it out in their wagons. The rangers had three wagons containing other supplies. When the five wagons arrived at the crossing of the Sabinal River, where the Sunset Railroad now crosses it, Heck and Huffman went on ahead for the purpose of killing a deer. One mile west of the river they were ambushed by the Lipan Indians and Heck was killed. Huffman, not being hit by the volley that killed his companion, wheeled his horse and ran back toward the wagons. Fifty mounted Indians followed him, and spreading out tried to cut him off from the river. A desperate hard race now commenced. The loose horse of the dead ranger followed close in the rear of Huffman. The Indians shot many arrows at long range, and finally stuck one in the ranger's thigh. He pulled it out and used it for a switch on his horse, wearing it out to the feather. The wagons were at the river, and the men with them seeing the Indians running Huffman, made ready to fight them. The Lipans turned back when they saw the wagons, and the hard-pressed ranger arrived safely. All night the men stood guard. When the Indians went back they picked up Huffman's hat and mutilated the body of Heck. After night came on one of the rangers named Lee volunteered to take chances and go to the ranger camp after help. He made it all right, and Captain Warfield sent thirteen men to their assistance. Of this number was Tom Galbreath. When the rangers got into the prairie between the Blanco and Sabinal the grass was burning for many miles around. The Indians had fired it to cover their trail. It had burned over the body of the dead ranger, badly disfiguring it. The smoke was so dense it was some time before the rangers could find the body, but it was finally recovered and carried to the wagons at the river. It was near day, and the men had spent an anxious night. One of their comrades lay dead on the prairie, another one wounded, and a third in great danger trying to bring succor to them. Besides this, the grass was burning in every direction, and the whole country was lit up. When morning came the body of Heck was buried, and here is a strange story. His grave was already dug and had been for six months. This is the history of the grave: Six months previous to this time a party of surveyors had camped there and one of their number, becoming very sick, apparently died. He was laid out and his grave dug in a small hackberry grove near by. The tent where the body lay was closed up for the night, and the interment of the dead man was to take place next morning. No one stayed inside the tent, but remained until morning just on the outside. When daylight came one of the men looked into the tent, and was almost scared out of his senses by seeing the supposed dead man standing on his feet and gazing about him like a man who had just waked up out of a sound sleep and did not know exactly where he was. The man who made the discovery turned and ran away, but a bolder fellow went in and asked him how he felt. "Very well," he said, "but very weak." He was then taken to San Antonio, and recovered. The grave had remained there open ever since, and in it Heck was buried. No doubt but he had ridden up and looked into this grave while on scouts.

After the last sad rites to their comrade was performed the rangers guarded the wagons past what they thought was the danger line, and then went to hunt the trail of the Indians. They had tried to baffle pursuit by starting north, but had turned back to within half a mile of where they had killed Heck and then went south, burning the grass behind them. The rangers got on their trail all the same and came upon them that evening in the edge of the Leona bottom, on the east side of the river, ten miles below the present town of Uvalde. The rangers at once charged and the Indians ran, but stopped in the bottom and fired on them with guns. The Lipans numbered about forty and the white men thirteen. The latter fired when they charged, and were very close when the Indians fired on them. The rangers being scattered in the charge, the bullets aimed at them did not find many victims, but hit the trees quite lively. One gallant ranger, however, named Nat. Mangum, received a mortal wound from a large bullet. The rangers went back from the charge away from the bottom, dismounted, and tied their horses. Mangum rode his horse back, and was then helped off and laid on a blanket under a tree. It was a drawn battle now. The Indians would not risk the fire of the rangers in the open ground, and the latter could not afford to charge their position with the force they had. Each fired as opportunity offered. The chief had buffalo horns on his head, and could occasionally be seen in the edge of the thicket with a gun in his hand, which he would fire quickly and then disappear again. The sergeant in command of the rangers finally told his men to reserve some loaded guns especially for that chief, and kill him if possible. The next time he appeared nearly all of the rangers fired at him, and he fell.

The wounded Mangum suffered a great deal, being shot through the bowels, and begged the boys to shoot him out of his misery. As he lay under the tree during the fight he called one of his particular friends to sit down by him and asked if he would do him a favor. Thinking he wanted to send some message home to loved ones, he promised. But no; that was not it. He wanted his best friend to shoot him. The other ranger began to cry, and said, "O no; O no. I can not; I can not." Mangum looked straight at him, and said, "Remember, now, you promised to grant any favor I asked you. I can not get over this shot, and I am suffering death over and over again." His friend continued to weep and say, "I can not." "I'll give you my horse and saddle and pistol, and all the wages due me," continued the wounded ranger. "Take your pistol now, my friend, and do what I tell you, or give me mine." Mangum's belt and pistol had been taken off and laid aside. Of course no persuasion could induce the friend to comply. He leaned over him and almost bathed his face and forehead in tears.

About this time another brave ranger named William Lowe came to them badly wounded with a bullet, but laughed and said, "I'll get over this shot all right." It was at this time that some one said, "Look, boys, there he is!" as the chief with the buffalo horns again came into view. A dozen rifles cracked at once and he was seen to fall. Not long after this the Indians were heard crossing the Leona River, and the battle was over. The rangers now entered the bottom lately occupied by the Indians and found plenty of blood, but the dead had been moved. Near where the chief was seen to fall was a pool of blood and a loaded gun, cocked. Heck's gun and hat were also found, and Huffmann's hat. Some one making a close search along the bank of the river discovered the body of the chief in the water wrapped up in blankets, they being lashed close to his body with ropes. When it was taken out and unwrapped the horns were still on his head, and there were seven bullet holes in his breast. The

wounded rangers were tenderly conveyed to camp that night, and
Mangum died next day and was buried on the banks of the Leona,
near Uvalde, and rocks piled over the grave.   Lowe got well.

The next fight the rangers had was with the Comanches.   The
trail of this band was discovered at the foot of the mountains on
the Frio River.   There were fifteen of the rangers together at the
time, and the Indians numbered sixteen.   The trail led south
across an open country for some distance and the rangers gained
rapidly on the Comanches, as they were riding very tired horses.
They kept under cover as much as possible, riding in ravines
which had bushes and prickly pears around them, whenever they
could do so.   When the rangers arrived at a dry little creek called
Cibolo (buffalo), just above the Laredo road, they came upon the
Indians, who were traveling in a ravine but hid from view.   The
rangers could hear their leggings scraping against the brush.
For some distance they rode parallel with them, waiting for a
good place to charge.   The Indians could also be heard talking.
Suddenly they left the ravine and rode out in open view, not
more than thirty yards away, and were not aware of the presence
of their white foes until fired on.   A man named John Saddler
fired the first shot, and an Indian fell from his horse.   The
others attempted to run back to cover, yelling and shooting at
the rangers, who charged and cut them off from the ravine.
One, however, seemed determined to go back into the ravine at
all hazards.   Tom Galbreath dismounted, and running to the
edge of the thicket and gulley after the Indian had got into it,
and getting a view of him, fired and killed him from his horse.

After the Indians had been cut off from the brush they tried
to make their escape across the open country—open except scattered bunches of prickly pear (cactus) and catclaw bushes.
Some of them were on mules and others on jaded horses, and all
were killed, one here and one there as they were overtaken.   None
of them got more than half a mile from where the fight commenced.   One was riding a paint horse, and to him Mr. Galbreath gave chase.   The Indian galloped slow and the ranger
soon came alongside of him, but kept about forty steps to one
side until he could take aim and fire.   One shot was sufficient,
and the Comanche fell heavily to the ground.   The Indians only
shot with arrows, and did but little damage.   They were more
on the run than fight.   One young ranger named Stoke Holmes,

who rode a fast little pony, singled out an Indian and said he was going to rope him. While he was running and swinging his rope the pony attempted to jump a large bunch of prickly pears, but reared so high his rider lost his seat in the saddle and fell backwards into the terrible cactus. Some of his comrades, seeing the mishap, killed the Indian and then came to his rescue, as he was unable to extricate himself. His horse had galloped off, but was caught and brought back. The ranger was in a sad plight. His body had thousands of pear thorns in it, and his clothing was pinned to him on all sides. He was almost in agonies with pain. The rangers stripped off all his clothing and extracted all the large thorns, but it was impossible to get out the thousands of needle-like small ones, but with a sharp knife they shaved them close to the skin, so the clothing would not irritate by rubbing against them. He was hardly able to ride for several days.

When the time of enlistment had expired the rangers were ordered back to their old camp on the Seco, and were there mustered out of the service.

Early in 1846 Capt. Henry E. McCulloch raised a company of rangers and Mr. Galbreath joined them. Their station was at the head of the San Marcos River. The officers, besides the captain, were First Lieutenant Story, his son Fred, second, and Asa J. L. Sowell orderly sergeant. The latter was father of the writer.

During this enlistment no important Indian battles were fought, and when the time was out Mr. Galbreath joined Capt. Sam Highsmith's company, which was stationed at Fredericksburg, in Gillespie County. Kijah Highsmith, son of the captain, was first lieutenant and George Gamble second. In three months this company was disbanded.

About this time the war with Mexico had broken out, and Capt. Jack Hays was raising a regiment of rangers for service in Mexico. Many of the old rangers raised companies for the regiment. Among these were Ben McCulloch, Sam Walker, Ad. Gillespie, Kit Ackland, and Mike Chevalier. Mr. Galbreath joined the spy company of Ben McCulloch, and went through many stirring scenes during the war. Being always in advance of the main army, a spy company is exposed all the time to ambuscades, and fight many small battles, besides being in the gen-

eral engagements. Mr. Galbreath was at the storming of Monterey and the battle of Buena Vista.

After the war he served again as a ranger, and was stationed
at San Lucas Springs, between Castroville and San Antonio.
Soon after this all of the rangers were mustered out, seven companies being disbanded at San Antonio in one day.

In 1848 Mr. Galbreath married Miss Nancy Jane Wining, and
in 1852 settled on Chicon Creek. The next move was where he
lives now, near Devine, in Medina County. He was still on
the frontier, and had many more scraps with the Indians until
they left, never more to return.

In 1875, while living at this place, his son Isaac, a youth of
17 years, was killed by Indians. He went out one morning to
drive up the horses, and Mr. Galbreath heard the shots that
killed him. He was not sure it was Indians until the horse his
son rode came running back to the house. He at once armed
and repaired to the spot, but too late to do any good except to
bring the dead body of Isaac in. He was shot with firearms
and one arrow. There were about fifteen of the Indians. They
committed other depredations as they went on, but were not overtaken. Young Galbreath was buried in the Devine graveyard,
one mile from town, and was the second person put there. Three
others are also buried there who were killed by Indians. George
Wheat, brother-in-law to Mr. Galbreath, was killed by Indians.
His son Ira was for a long time sheriff of Edwards County.

Mrs. Galbreath died in 1879, and in 1890 he married Miss
Mary Shores, his present wife.

Mr. Galbreath relates this rather humorous episode which occurred during the perilous frontier times. On one occasion
when several men were out together, among whom was a Mr.
Avant, a tolerably old man, and another named Woodward, they
came upon a party of Indians, who sprang up out of the grass
and commenced shooting at them. Mr. Avant's horse threw
him, and he made an attempt to save himself on foot, not being
able to get hold of his horse again. All the men ran away except Mr. Woodward, and he stayed with Mr. Avant and pointed
his gun at the Indians when they came near, and they would
stop and dodge, thereby giving the footman a chance to sprint
ahead. This was done several times, and again the Indians
came close, and Mr. Avant, who was nearly out of breath, said,

"Aim your gun at them, Mr. Woodward; aim your gun at them. I see it has a good effect." Both made their escape.

Mr. Galbreath was in the ranging service with Big Foot Wallace, and said he could stand more cold than any man he ever saw. He would scout all day in a cold norther without a coat, and then lie down at night on his saddle blanket without cover and sleep soundly all night if not disturbed.

Mr. Galbreath has a good ranch and 300-acre farm.

JACK HAYS.

JACK HAYS.

Came to Texas in 1837.

John Coffee Hays, better known in Texas as Jack Hays, the famous ranger captain, was born in Wilson County, Tennessee, in 1818. He was named for General Coffee, who commanded a brigade in the army of General Jackson at the battle of New Orleans. He came to Texas in 1837, when but 19 years of age, and located at San Antonio. He was a surveyor by profession, and was employed to survey lands on the frontier. His long life on the frontier gave him a hardy constitution, and none were able to stand more hardships and endure more privations than he. His talent as a commander and leader of border men early developed, and he was soon among the chosen leaders of the pioneers in southwest Texas. His reputation as a fighter arose so rapidly he was given the command of the frontier with the rank of major in 1840. This was in part owing to his gallantry at the great Indian battle of Plum Creek, fought the same year, and which has been described elsewhere. If an account was given in detail of all his exploits and battles on the frontier it would make a book within itself.

His two famous battles of Bandera Pass and in the Nueces Canyon have already been given, as also the part he took in the battle of Salado when San Antonio was captured by Wall. He fought one battle west of the Nueces with the Comanches and badly defeated them, and also one near the head of Seco and Sabinal. He was surrounded here for some time, and finally sent one of his men, who slipped out in the night and went to Seguin to notify Captain James H. Calahan, who commanded another company of rangers, to come to his assistance. The messenger rode day and night, as did also the rangers who came back, and the reinforcement soon arrived on the scene, but Hays and his men were gone. Signs of a fierce fight were there, and the dead bodies of sixteen Indians were found. Calahan took the trail and soon discovered that the Indians were in retreat, and that Hays and his men were following them. At the head waters of Sabinal River rangers and Indians were overtaken. The

Comanches were on a mountain and Hays and his men were in the valley, watching them. When Calahan and his men arrived an assault was made on the position of the Indians, and after some firing, in which one of Calahan's men was wounded, the Indians left the mountain and scattered in the roughs and the rangers returned, Hays to San Antonio and Calahan to Seguin.

On another occasion Hays was close upon a band of Indians and located them by his scouts in a cedar brake. The rangers had eaten nothing all day, so hot was the pursuit, and the captain now told them to dismount for a few minutes and partake of some cold bread and beef they had in their wallets, but by no means to raise a smoke. Hays always had a few Mexicans with him, as they were good guides and trailers, but on this occasion, in lighting their cigarettes after eating, they let a pile of leaves get afire, and soon smoke was curling above the tree tops. Hays was furious, and the Mexicans were badly scared and made frantic endeavors to stamp out the fire, he striking some of them with his quirt during the time. An order to mount was now given and a furious run made towards the Indian camp, which was a mile away. It was as Hays had anticipated. The Indians saw the smoke and knew the rangers were on their trail, and had fled, leaving many things in camp, which were taken.

One of the hardest fights Captain Hays had was on the Pedernales in 1844. On this occasion he had gone out with fourteen men about eighty miles from San Antonio northwest in the Pedernales country, now within the limits of Gillespie County, for the purpose of ascertaining the position of the Indians and their probable location.

On arriving near the river about fifteen Indians were discovered well mounted, and they seemed to want a fight. When the rangers advanced upon them, however, they retreated and endeavored to lead them towards a ridge of thick underbrush. Captain Hays was too well acquainted with the Indian character to be caught by their snares, for he suspected an ambush. It was hard to keep his boys from advancing to the attack, among whom was Ad. Gillespie, Sam Walker, and Mike Chevalier. Hays went around the thicket and posted his men on another ridge separated from their position by a deep ravine. This position was occupied but a short time when the Indians discovered who he was, and knowing their man, gave up trying to catch him by stratagem and showed themselves to the number of seventy-five and challenged him to the combat. Hays accepted the challenge and signified to them that he would meet them, and immediately started down the hill with his men toward the Indians, moving, however, very slowly, until reaching the bottom of the ravine, where he was hid from the view of the Comanches by the brow of the hill upon which they had formed. Then turning at full speed down the ravine he turned the point of the ridge and came up in the rear of the Indians and charged them while they were watching for him to come up in front of their position. The first fire of the rangers with rifles threw them into confusion.

The yells, warwhoops, and imprecations that filled the air were enough to blanch the cheeks of the bravest, but Hays and his men had heard such sounds before, and stood their ground unmoved. The Indians, seeing their superior force, soon rallied. Hays now told his men to draw their five-shooters to meet the charge that he saw was coming. In order to resist attack on all sides, as the Comanches were surrounding them, Hays formed his men in a circle fronting outwards, being still mounted on their horses, and for several minutes maintained that position without firing a shot, until the Indians almost came within throwing distance of their lances of them. Their aim was now sure when they fired, and nearly every shot took effect. Twenty-one Indians were killed here before they desisted from hurling themselves on the muzzles of the revolvers. When the Comanches fell back the rangers changed their ground and charged in turn. The fight lasted nearly an hour, each party charging and recharging in turn. By this time the rangers had exhausted the loads in their revolvers, and the chief was again rallying his warriors for one more desperate struggle.

The number of the rangers was by this time reduced, some killed and others badly wounded, and the situation was critical. Captain Hays saw that their only chance was to kill the Indian chief, and asked of his men if any of them had a loaded rifle. Gillespie replied that he had. "Dismount, then," said the captain, "and make sure work of that chief."

The ranger addressed had been badly wounded — speared through the body—and was hardly able to sit his horse, but slipping to the ground took careful aim and fired, and the chief fell

ENCHANTED ROCK.

headlong from his horse. The Comanches now left the field, pursued by a portion of the men, and a complete victory was gained. When all was over on this battleground lay thirty dead Indians, and of the rangers two were killed and five wounded. Sam Walker was one of the wounded, and was also speared through the body.

On another occasion Hays was on a scout with about twenty of his men near the head of the Pedernales at a place called then the "Enchanted Rock." It was of large, conical shape, with a depression at the apex something like the crater of an extinct volcano. A dozen or more men can lie in this place and make a strong defense against largely superior numbers, as the ascent is steep and rugged.

Not far from the base of this hill, at the time of which we write, the rangers were attacked by a large force of Indians. When the fight commenced Captain Hays was some distance from his men, looking about, and attempted to return and was cut off and closely pursued by quite a number of warriors, and made his retreat to the top of the "Enchanted Rock." Here he entrenched himself, determined to make the best fight he could and, as the border men say, "sell out" as dearly as possible. The Indians who were in pursuit upon arriving near the summit set up a most hideous howl, and after surrounding the spot prepared for a charge on the position of the ranger captain. They were determined to get him at all hazards, for no doubt there were warriors along who knew him. For some time as they would see the muzzle of the rifle come over the rim of the crater they would dodge back, knowing it was death to one to face it, and each thought that one might be him. Becoming bolder, however, it was necessary for Hays to fire, and one fell at the rifle shot, and then the revolver went to work, and as they were close, each discharge from the five-shooter found a victim. In those days there were no six-shooters, but these were made soon after. The Indians fell back before this fire, which gave Hays a chance to reload. This was kept up for some time. The rangers heard the battle on the hill and knew it was their captain, and gradually fought their way to him. The Indians below were defeated, and those after Hays fled down on the opposite side when they saw the battle had gone against them in the valley and that the rangers had commenced the ascent of the hill of the "Enchanted Rock."

Captain Hays was glad to see his boys, as the case had become desperate with him. The Indians, maddened at their loss, were drawing closer around him, becoming reckless of life, and would in the end have overpowered him. Five or six dead lay around the spot where Hays fought, and twice as many below. Three or four rangers were wounded but none killed.

When the war of 1846 broke out with Mexico Captain Hays raised a regiment of Texas rangers and fought in nearly all of the desperate battles in Mexico, in which many of the regiment were killed, including Ad. Gillespie, who was captain of a company, and Sam Walker, who was lieutenant-colonel of the regiment. After the war was over Colonel Hays went to California, and was elected sheriff of San Francisco County, and as a matter of course made a brave and efficient officer. He married a daughter of Major Calvert of Seguin, and was brother-in-law to John Twohig of San Antonio, and Colonel Thos. D. Johnson and Alfred Shelby of Seguin, these having married his wife's sisters.

Colonel Hays had his last Indian fight in Nevada in 1860. At that time Virginia City was a mining town, and many Texans, Californians, and others had gathered there. The Piute Indians declared war against the whites and committed many depredations, among others massacred Major Ormsby and his men. There was at this time at the mines an old Texas ranger, Capt. Edward Storey, a man of great courage and very popular among the people. He had fought Indians in Texas under Colonel Hays and Gen. Henry E. McCulloch. Captain Storey at once raised a company, called the Virginia City Rifles, and proceeded against the Indians. Col. Jack Hays heard of the war which his old comrade Captain Storey was engaged in, and came over from California with several companies to help him, and together they attacked the Indians at Pyramid Lake, about twenty-five miles from Virginia City. The Indians were about 1000 strong and well armed, and flushed with their victory over Major Ormsby and his men. They had the advantage of position in the mountains and more than doubled the number of the whites. A complete victory was won by Hays and Storey, but at fearful loss, and among the slain was the brave Captain Storey. This was on the 2d of June, 1860. The dead captain was rolled up in a blanket and conveyed to Virginia City on a pack horse.

Colonel Hays became very wealthy. He never made Texas his home again, but occasionally came on visits to see old friends and relatives. He died at his home near Piedmont, Cal., in 1883.

MRS. M. A. BINNION.

Came to Texas in 1838.

Among the many interesting characters of Southwest Texas
was Mrs. M. A. Binnion. While the writer was traveling, hunting up the old settlers, and gathering information from them,
he found Mrs. Binnion at the ranch of her son-in-law, Mr. A. J.
Davenport, in Little Blanco Canyon. She was then very old and
feeble, and on account of failing memory was not able to tell
much of the many stirring events through which she has passed
—of Indian alarms, massacres, and sleepless nights on the border
long before the prairies were dotted with ranches, and when the
beautiful canyons were only inhabited by bears, panthers, Mexican lions, and other vicious animals.

Mrs. Binnion was born in Alabama, near Tuscaloosa, in 1818.
She was the daughter of Benjamin Phillips, and came to Texas
with her husband in 1838, first settling in Titus County. She
lived in Burnet County quite a number of years when that was a
frontier, and Mr. Binnion was engaged in stock raising. He
and the family came to Uvalde County in 1865. Their son Samuel was sent back to the old home in Burnet County to gather
and bring the cattle to Uvalde County. That was the last the
mother and father saw of the son. He was killed by the Indians
while engaged in gathering the cattle. The unfortunate young
man was riding a mule at the time, and had no chance to make
his escape. The Indians ran all around him and threw their
ropes over his head and pulled him from his saddle to the
ground, and then ran and dragged him across the prairie.
While some were engaged in this others were following and
throwing lances into his body. When life was extinct and they
were satiated with their savage pastime, the ropes were taken
off and the mangled body left.

In 1866, when the Indians made a raid in Sabinal Canyon and
killed Mrs. Bowlin and badly wounded Mrs. Kinchaloe in many
places, Mrs. Binnion, who was a good doctor and really the only
one in the settlement, was sent for. She at once mounted a horse

22

and made a most remarkably quick ride to the scene, and remained fifteen days by the bedside of the wounded woman, attending on her, and she recovered.

In 1870 the Indians made a raid on the settlements and appeared at the Binnion ranch. Mr. Binnion was in bed sick, and could scarcely walk when up. The Indians remained off a distance and watched the house a while, and then one of their number came towards it. Mrs. Binnion now dressed herself in male attire, and getting a rifle sallied from the house to fight the Indian who was approaching. The Comanche acted cowardly and retreated back to his companions. The Indians then rode off down the river toward the other settlement. Mrs. Binnion and her husband now became uneasy about their children, who had gone down to a neighbor's below, and taking their guns followed after on foot. Mr. Binnion being very weak, his wife carried both guns, and still having on a man's clothing. They soon discovered three Mexicans coming around a thicket, and at first glance supposing them to be Indians, sprang to one side and leveled their guns at them. Mrs. Binnion in the excitement of the moment failed to cock her gun, which likely saved the life of a Mexican, for she aimed at one and pulled the trigger trying to shoot. The Mexicans knew Mr. Binnion and called loudly to him not to shoot. They had not seen the Indians, but stayed with Mr. Binnion and his wife to help them fight. One of their sons made a narrow escape. He met the Indians, who chased him, but being on a good horse made his escape. They also ran a Mexican into the thicket, but failed to get him. At another time Mrs. Binnion and another lady kept off a band of Indians by arming themselves with long stalks of the soto plant and aiming them as if about to shoot when the Indians advanced. They dreaded the long rifles of the Texas pioneers and would retreat, not being near enough to detect the deception. In this way the two women who were alone and away from the ranch made their way safely back to it. This sketch is only a faint outline of what this brave heroine of the West passed through, but alas never to be told by her.

CAPTURE OF MATILDA LOCKHART AND THE PUTNAM CHILDREN BY INDIANS.

1838.

In the early pioneer days of southwest Texas Mitchell Putnam and another settler named Lockhart lived on the Guadalupe River below the town of Gonzales. They were industrious, thrifty men, and soon had good homes, and were also blessed with a family of nice, healthy boys and girls. Life ahead of them looked bright and cheerful, but, alas for human hopes and aspirations, how soon was their cup of sorrow to be filled to overflowing and they compelled to drink to the bitter dregs.

One bright day in the fall of 1838 Matilda Lockhart, James Putnam, and his two sisters, one older than he, went to the river bottom to gather pecans. For some time they picked up the nuts, which were in abundance, and their merry laugh continually rang out through the forest. At last it was time to go home; their vessels were full of the rich pecan nuts, and their exertions had given them a keen appetite for their dinner, the time for which had now long passed. The baskets, bonnets, and buckets were gathered up, and the merry group emerged from the bottom to the edge of the prairie. But what a sight now met the eyes of those merry ones! The laughing voices were hushed, and the cheeks which but a moment before had glowed with health and gay spirits, now blanched and paled with terror. There, in a few rods of them, rode a band of wild, painted Comanche Indians, the scourge of the Texas frontier. Escape was impossible. With a wild shout the Indians circled around them, and without dismounting reached from the saddle and secured the screaming victims, and holding them in front dashed away up the valley towards the wilds of the great West.

When the children failed to come home at the proper time the parents became uneasy and a search was instituted in the pecan bottom, whither they knew the children had gone. Their ages ranged from six to thirteen years. Matilda Lockhart was the eldest and one of the Putnam girls was the youngest. Can pen describe the agony of those parents when they come to the spot where the children were captured? It can not. A bonnet here; a bonnet there; an overturned bucket or basket and pecans scattered promiscuously about. A short distance out in the open ground lay little Jimmy's hat. The ground was torn up by horse tracks, and too well these pioneers knew what had become of their loved ones. No time was to be lost. They rushed back and alarmed a few neighbors, who were soon on the trail of the daring red men. Lockhart was furious, vowed vengeance of the most direful nature, and galloped madly on the trail. Putnam was more composed and wanted to be cautious, but he was not lacking in courage, for he fought at San Jacinto in Captain Heard's company, and was one among the foremost in that terrible charge. Among the few men who followed Putnam and Lockhart on the trail of the Indians was Andrew J. Sowell, Sr., uncle of the writer.

The trail led up the Guadalupe River and was hard to keep, as the country became rougher towards the foot of the mountains. The last place that any signs of the Indians could be seen was at the mouth of the Comal River on a sandbar. Here the Indians had halted, and the tracks of the children could be seen in the loose soil. This place is where the German city of New Braunfels now is. Here the Indians entered the mountains and the pursuit had to be abandoned, as the force of the settlers did not justify further advance into the stronghold of the savages. They returned, but only to get a larger force, and this time penetrated the mountains far west of the Comal into the head waters of the Guadalupe, now covered by Kerr County. Here, in a secluded valley, the scouts discovered a large Indian encampment, and that night a daring settler penetrated the Indian village and found out the captive children were there. When the faithful spy came back and reported, Lockhart was for an immediate advance, and it was difficult for his friends and neighbors to restrain him until some plan of action could be agred upon. After some deliberations the plan was to assault the Indian camp at daybreak, as soon as it was light enough for the men to see how to shoot. Lockhart knew no fear, and when the time came led the advance. The loud yell of an Indian announced the fact that the white men were discovered. The time for battle had come, and the settlers made a rush, intending to fight their way to the center of the camp where the children were. The white men were greatly outnumbered, but fought with desperation almost amounting to madness or frenzy. Lockhart led with clubbed rifle trying to fight his way with physical force to his children. Putnam was beside him. The settlers soon saw that the conflict was going against them. Lockhart was wounded in several places, covered with blood, and getting weak. There seemed to be no end to the forces of the Indians, fresh swarms of them continually coming into the battle from the village, only the outskirts of which the white men had reached. Never had such a noise been heard in that valley before. Loud yells rent the air, tomahawks glanced against rifle barrels, and whizzing missiles flew on every side. The settlers could not sustain themselves; the contest was too unequal; valor must to numbers yield. They slowly retreated, fighting as they went, and carrying their dead and wounded comrades with them. Lockhart was loth to give up the fight, but weak, wounded, and bleeding, he allowed his friends to carry him away, seeing all of his hopes of recovering his daughter and the children of his neighbor fade away. After getting clear of the Indians the dead, five or six in number, were buried and the wounded carried back down the valley of the Guadalupe.

In 1840 a treaty was held with the Comanches in San Antonio, in which Matilda Lockhart was recovered, but the Indians failed to bring in other prisoners as they had promised, and the council wound up in a fight in which many of the Indians were killed.

James Putnam after several years' captivity was finally through treaties recovered, but his eldest sister by this time had become the wife of a chief and would not leave, saying that society would not receive her among white people and she would have to spend the balance of her life as an Indian. The other sister had been carried away among a different band of the tribe.

About thirty years after the capture of the children a gentleman named Chenault, who had been an Indian agent, bought a middle-aged white woman during that time and carried her to his home in Missouri. Afterwards he moved to Gonzales, Texas, and brought her along as a member of his family. She was so young when captured by the Indians that she could not remember her name or where she was taken from by them. When, however, she saw the Guadalupe valley in the region of Gonzales she

had a dim recollection of seeing the country before, and thus expressed herself. It was now believed that it was the youngest
girl of the Putnam children. James Putnam, who lived up the
river fifteen miles above the town of Gonzales, was sent for to see
if he could by any means ascertain if this was his sister. When
he came the fact was established beyond a doubt that it was his
sister, by a scar caused by a burn on one of her arms.

How strange that she should be brought back almost to the
very spot where she was captured thirty years before, and there
spend the balance of her days. The writer was well acquainted
with James Putnam, and was at his house many times. He married the widow Nash, and lived on Nash's Creek near the confluence with the Guadalupe. He said the Indians carried him
all over Texas, Arizona, New Mexico, and California. Often
when he had been left with the squaws and children on some high
mountain he could see the warriors fighting with immigrants or
Santa Fe traders in the valley below. If they were successful in
the fight they came back gleeful and had scalp dances; but if they
were defeated, especially with much loss, they beat the prisoners
and otherwise maltreated them. He saw many bloody reeking
scalps brought in by them of men, women, and children.

Mr. Putnam died near the line of Hays and Travis counties
several years after the civil war. His stepdaughter, Louise Nash,
married Granville Nicholson, but she died soon after. Mr. Nicholson now lives on the Verde Creek, in Kerr County.

REV. E. A. BRIGGS.

Came to Texas in 1841.

One of the old-time frontiersmen, rangers, and preachers is Rev. E. A. Briggs, who at this writing lives near Seglar post-office, near the line of Bexar and Atascosa counties. He was born in Amherst, Mass., in 1819, and came to Texas in 1841. His ancestors were in the war of the revolution, and among them were some noted divines and scholars. Mr. Briggs upon first arriving in Texas went to Houston, where he had an uncle, T. P. Andrews, minister to Europe from the Republic of Texas. In 1842 Mr. Briggs was teaching school at Richmond, Fort Bend County, when the news come of the Vasquez raid. There was a good deal of excitement in the country in regard to this invasion of the Mexicans, and a company was at once raised in and around Richmond to go and fight the Mexicans who had captured San Antonio. The school of Mr. Briggs was composed chiefly of young men, and the majority of them joined the company. Their teacher said, "Well, boys, if you are all going to the war I had as well go, too," and he also joined the volunteer company.

These men lived so far from the scene of hostilities that when they arrived at San Antonio the war scare was over. General Vasquez and his men had gone back to Mexico after holding the city only a few days. This raid was nothing more than a plundering expedition, the Mexicans only holding the town long enough to rob it. Here Mr. Briggs first saw Capt. Jack Hays, the famous Texas ranger, and talked with him.

While the settlers were moving west of San Antonio Mr. Briggs was commissioned to raise men for the protection of a German colony which was settling at Quihi in 1846. The war with Mexico, however, broke out at this time, and the rangers were sent to Mexico to assist General Taylor. Mr. Briggs went out under Maj. Sam Highsmith. Out near the Rio Grande, on this side of the river, the rangers come upon a lot of Mexicans who had been attacked and whipped out by the Indians and some of them killed. They had been in camp catching mustangs, and when they were driven out came to the rangers for protection, who at this time were passing near on their way to Mexico. They had lost all of their provisions and the rangers were also out, but all went on together. When the party went into camp some of the rangers were complaining of being hungry, whereupon one of the Mexican women who was with the party of mustang catchers went to the chaparral and soon returned with her apron full of mesquite beans and prickly pear apples, and said, "No starve; plenty to eat." Mr. Briggs said, "How long can a man live on such grub as that?" One of the Mexican men said, "Live on pear all right alone; mix pear and beans, get fat;" and continuing, said, "A man should not want anything better to eat than that."

The Mexicans were protected across the river and the rangers went on to Taylor's army, but arrived too late for the battle of Buena Vista, which had been fought and won. Some of the rangers were sent back to protect the Texas frontier, and Mr. Briggs came with them. There were a great many rangers in Mexico under Hays and Walker. They remained and participated in many battles. Colonel Walker was killed, as was one of Hays' captains, Ad Gillespie. Big Foot Wallace was in this expedition. But a few years before he had been one of the prisoners after the disastrous battle of Mier (Meer), when they had to draw beans for their lives.

Mr. Briggs was altogether three years in the Texas service, part of the time in Captain Cady's company, stationed at Austin to keep the Indians and buffalo out of town.

On one scout the rangers, only a few in number, were sent out to take some observations in regard to a body of Indians that was over on Little River. These Indians were supposed to be friendly at the time, but the people were suspicious of them and wished to keep a watch on their movements. The rangers camped on the same river near the Indians fifty miles from Austin, but did not know of their presence until attracted by the smoke of their camp fires, and even then supposed it was grass burning. Next morning the Indians also discovered the rangers, and two young fellows come out of the timber across the prairie towards them. They made many circles around the rangers lying low on their horses to see if they were going to shoot. They finally straightened up and came to them when they saw no demonstrations were made towards them. They were fierce, devilish-looking rascals, and demanded of the rangers what they were doing there. They thought discretion the better part of valor on this occasion, and replied, "Buffalo hunting." One who could speak a little English said, "Maby so you lie." John Herral, who was in command, said, "Boys, that's hard to take, but we will have to stand it. If we kill these we will never get away from the balance in camp." The whole band numbered about 500. The two young bucks galloped back to their camp and the rangers saddled up and went back to Austin. Of this party, besides Mr. Briggs, was William Winin, who has a brother Edward who lives near the Bexar postoffice, in Atascosa County.

During the civil war Mr. Briggs sold goods in San Antonio with Pancost. The firm name was Ward, Pancost & Co. Mr. Briggs was a member of the firm, the largest at that time in San Antonio. The goods were sold in the Jones building, southeast corner of the plaza. They had extensive stables where the new courthouse now stands. When the business broke up considerable loss was experienced, and Mr. Briggs moved out of town and settled where he now resides, twenty-two miles south of San Antonio, near a noted place called Black Hill. Two young Germans were killed near there after he settled, but he does not remember their names. (See account of this elsewhere.)

He has been in the Baptist ministry now more than twenty years. It was almost a necessity, he said, that he became a preacher out in this frontier country. A frontier preacher named L. S. Cox came and organized a little Baptist church and Mr. Briggs helped him to conduct the services; and finally the people prevailed on him to preach for them. He was ordained, and has been doing the best he could ever since. He has been a member of the Baptist church since he was 16 years of age, and has spent all of his life in a new country in the woods and along the border. He has eight grown sons, four married, one of whom has since died—Pearl, who married Miss Cordelia Tinsley. He kept the Segler store and postoffice near the residence of the Rev. Briggs until a short time before his death. This postoffice was named after James Segler, an old Texas ranger who lives near, and with whom the writer served in the Wichita campaign in 1870-71. Rev. Briggs has one son, Bevy, who is also in the Baptist ministry.

RUDOLPH CHAROBINY.

RUDOLPH CHAROBINY.

MEXICAN WAR VETERAN.

Came to Texas in 1845.

Among the first settlers of Quihi, in Castro's colony, and who still survives, is Mr. Rudolph Charobiny, now living about two miles from the Quihi store south on Quihi Creek.

Mr. Charobiny was born in Zips Comitat, Hungary, in January, 1817, and set sail from Havre, France, in September, 1845, for Texas, as part of Castro's colony. He came over in the ship Deaucalion, which was an American vessel and commanded by an American captain. They were eight weeks on the ocean and had a very good trip, without incident except one fire on shipboard, which originated in the kitchen, but was soon extinguished without much damage being done. The Deaucalion landed at New Orleans and the passengers got aboard the ship Galveston, bound for the city of Galveston, Texas, at which place they landed in November. From Galveston Mr. Charobiny and another young man went on board a steamboat and came up Buffalo Bayou to Houston. It was very cold and the two young immigrants got near the boiler to warm themselves. Now at this time Gen. Sam Houston was on board, and noticing the two young fellows warming themselves at the boiler, took one by each arm and said, "Come, I will warm you up," and leading them into the saloon treated them to a drink of whisky. The general had some fine horses on the boat which he was carrying up the country.

The boys stayed in Houston fourteen days, and in the meantime became acquainted with Dr. Acke, who purchased some drugs with the intention of coming west to practice medicine. Mr. Charobiny and two other young men named Korn hired a man named Alexander to bring them to San Antonio, and they and Dr. Acke journeyed together. The young immigrants intended to join Castro's colony and go to farming. One of the young men, Louis Korn, lives at Kline in Uvalde County at this time, at a very advanced age. The trip from Houston to San

Antonio was with ox teams and very slow and tedious. It rained a great deal; creeks were up and they had to watch constantly for Indians. One of the colonists had already been killed by them while en route from Port Lavaca to San Antonio. The young men had to unload the wagon many times so that the team could pull out of bogholes. They arrived in San Antonio in April, 1846, and at Castroville in May of that year. Mr. Charobiny lived six months in the Republic of Texas before annexation. Henry Castro was planting colonies still further west on his grant of land, and Mr. Charobiny concluded to settle at Quihi, ten miles west of Castroville. The town of Quihi (pronounced Qeehe) being laid off, one lot and twenty acres of land was donated by James Brown, Castro's agent, to the settlers. This was within the town limits. Single men received 320 acres and married men 640 outside of the town. Mr. Charobiny received his 320 acres but did not at once settle, from the fact that about this time he joined a company of Texas rangers, commanded by Capt. John Conner. Dr. Acke, who came up with them from Houston, was also a member of the company as surgeon and physician. He did not, however, serve long in this capacity, from the fact that he was killed in a difficulty at Castroville by a ranger. The company scouted for Indians about two months, and then, the war breaking out between the United States and Mexico, Mr. Charobiny and other rangers enlisted in Bell's regiment of mounted riflemen to aid General Taylor, who had crossed the Rio Grande with an invading army. Texas at this time had been annexed to the United States, and a dispute over her boundary brought on the war.

Captain Conner commanded a company in Bell's regiment, and it was with him as captain that Mr. Charobiny served in the Mexican war. The regiment joined General Taylor at Buena Vista, but too late for the battle there, which had been fought and won. The enlistment was for twelve months, and the time was served out in Mexico. They then returned to Texas and were disbanded at San Antonio. Mr. Charobiny did a great deal of scouting around Monterey while in service in Mexico to keep the Mexicans back from General Taylor's headquarters. The riflemen under Jeff Davis aided in this scouting.

After being disbanded Mr. Charobiny came back to Quihi and

settled on his headright on Quihi Creek, and commenced farming and stock raising. Grass and water were plentiful, with no brush then, but open, lovely valleys. Game and wild honey were in abundance and living cheap. The seasons were good and splendid crops made, and the hardy pioneers began to enjoy the fruits of their labor and sacrifices.

In November, 1847, Mr. Charobiny married Miss Francisco Meyer, and in three months after a band of Kickapoo and Lipan Indians came through on a raid and robbed the house in Mr. Charobiny's absence, who was out on a cow-hunt, and carried off his wife a captive. The same band killed her brother, Mr. Blas Meyer, at his house before they came to the Charobiny ranch. After taking and destroying everything they could, the Indians placed Mrs. Charobiny on a horse and started up towards the Quihi settlement north, about two miles distant. After keeping this course a short while the Indians bore to the left, going a northwest course, and left the settlement to the right. The captive woman had it in her mind to escape if possible, and thought she would try even if killed by them for so doing, dreading captivity among these savages more than death. So when the party arrived at a pecan grove Mrs. Charobiny sprang from the pony and fled, followed by several Indians, who shot arrows at her and succeeded in wounding her badly in two places, so much so that she fell and was unable to rise. The Indians, thinking she was dead and fearing pursuit, rode back and continued their course, without getting off their horses to scalp her or see if she was dead. When Mr. Charobiny came home and found his place torn up and his wife gone he knew it was Indians, and at once ran his horse to the settlement, gave the alarm, and raised men to follow them, and also sent a runner to the ranger camp on the Seco to notify them of the raid. In the meantime Mrs. Charobiny recovered sufficiently to drag herself to the settlement and have the arrows extracted, and by careful nursing finally recovered. The Indians were not overtaken. Major Neighbors, Indian agent, who was then in San Antonio, was also notified of the raid. When Henry Castro heard of this misfortune of the Charobiny family he donated a house and lot in town for them to live in. Castro did all he could to aid his colonists while they were contending with the savages and subduing the wilderness.

The following is a list of the first settlers at Quihi, as given to
the writer by Mr. Charobiny: Baptiste Schmidt, John Rieden,
Amb. Reitzer, Jac. Ribf, Blas Meyer, K. Bonekamp, H. Gersting,
H. Wilpert, H. Gerdes, Jans Sievers, B. Brucks, — Bickmann,
F. Bauer, — Boinkhoff, — Opus, — Deuters, John Toucher, H.
Schneider, — Rensing, — Gasper, — Eisenhauer, Louis Korn,
and Dr. Acke.

Mr. Charobiny draws a pension as a Mexican war veteran, and
has lived under five flags. Born under the Hungarian, then under the Republic of Texas, then under the Lone Star, then the
Confederate, and also the United States stars and stripes.

He holds commissions as justice of the peace of precinct No.
2, Medina County, signed by three governors of Texas.

The first was by P. H. Bell (his old colonel in the Mexican
war), dated on the 6th day of September, 1851. This document
winds up thus: "In testimony whereof, I have hereunto set my
hand and caused the great seal of the State to be affixed, at the
city of Austin, in the year of our Lord one thousand eight hundred and fifty-one, and in the year of the independence of the
United States of America the seventy-sixth, and of Texas the
sixteenth."

The second commission was signed by Gov. H. R. Runnels, 9th
day of July, 1859, and twenty-fourth year of Texas independence.

The third was signed by Gov. Sam Houston, 12th day of November, 1860, and twenty-fourth year of Texas independence.

Mr. Charobiny's pension certificate is No. 14,600, and was issued on the 6th of November, 1894. It states that Rudolph
Charobiny was a private in Bell's regiment of volunteer mounted
riflemen.

Mr. Charobiny still resides on his headright grant of land donated to him over fifty years ago. His house is on a high elevation on the east bank of Quihi Creek, and commands a fine view
of the surrounding country and the range of mountains to the
north. He selected this place so that he could have a view of the
mountains, which reminded him of his native land. When the
writer visited him in 1897 he was then 80 years of age, and was
living quietly and pleasantly with his wife and unmarried son,
Judge M. Charobiny. The good lady was afflicted with rheum-

atism which almost bent her body double, and it was with great difficulty that she could get about. A great change has come over her since that trying day when, in the hands of painted savages, she bounded from her horse and ran almost with the fleetness of a deer to make her escape from them. May these good people live long yet to enjoy the evening of life and rest from their labors.

ED. WESTFALL.

E. D. WESTFALL.

Came to Texas in 1845.

Edward Dixon Westfall was born in Knox County, Indiana, on the 22d day of December, 1820. His father, Abraham, was a Virginian by birth, but went to Indiana with his parents when quite young. His grandfather, Isaac, was a surveyor, and followed that profession for several years in the new State. When the Indian war broke out and General Harrison fought the battle of Tippecanoe young Abraham wanted to go with the soldiers and take part in the battle, but his father made him stay at home and went himself.

In 1841 Abraham Westfall moved with his family to Jasper County, Illinois.

In 1843 Edward Dixon left Illinois and came over into Missouri, but being of a roving disposition soon moved on, and arrived in Hopkins County, Texas, in 1845. In the following year he came on to San Antonio.

By this time the Mexican war had broken out and he joined the company of Capt. John Conner, Bell's regiment of mounted riflemen. The lieutenants in the company were — Jett and — Patterson. Col. P. H. Bell, who commanded the regiment, was afterwards Governor of Texas. As to the service of Mr. Westfall in Mexico, suffice it to say he made a brave and gallant soldier, never shirking duty or danger at any time.

After the war was over the regiment returned to Texas and was discharged at San Antonio.

Mr. Westfall, although educated and a well-informed man, had a natural love for the solitude and romance of the wild woods, and like his erstwhile boon companion, Big Foot Wallace, delighted to roam over a new country, shoot game, and camp out. At this time no country afforded a more inviting field for a man of that turn than Texas, and he soon cut loose from the companionship and habitation of civilized man and built a cabin on the banks of the Leona River, in the dense solitude of the great southwest, distant more than 100 miles from San Antonio. The

23

only settlement then west of San Antonio was the colony of Henry Castro, and he was far in advance of them. Soon after Westfall settled on the Leona, Fort Inge was built on the same stream about thirty miles above. This induced others to come, and in a few years a settlement was made at the present town of Uvalde, four miles above the fort. This was about 1852.

Westfall soon became familiar with the surrounding country and the ways and customs of the Indians, who then held sway in all this vast country. He became a noted man on the frontier as Indian fighter, guide, and trailer for soldiers, rangers, and settlers. Hardly an expedition went out without him or the two other famous guides in the west, Big Foot Wallace and Henry Robinson, being along. They looked to either of these three men to pilot them through mountains, canyons, and cedar brakes, or the devious windings through chaparral and prickly pear.

Just before Fort Inge was built the Lipan Indians came down from the mountains and raided the country east in the vicinity of where Big Foot Wallace lived, and carried off some of his horse stock and others of the settlement. Wallace waited until the Indians thought no one was going to follow them, as he conjectured, and then came after Westfall. These two hardy leaders came back to the Wallace ranch, and gathering about thirty men went on a hunt for the Lipans, who were found in camp at a place now called the Frio waterhole, on the divide at the head draws of the Frio River. A battle ensued in which ten of the Indians were killed, and about 200 mules and horses taken which had been carried off from the settlements. The Indians were completely surprised and made a poor fight, none of the settlers being killed. Wallace was riding a fine mare, and she fell with him just as they were charging into the Indian camp, and he went over her head but lit on his feet. Wallace killed one Indian with the only shot he got with his rifle. He had a flintlock, and the flint in the holder burst. One old squaw and a daughter of the chief were left in camp. The old squaw had nails on her fingers an inch long. She tried to scratch Wallace in the eyes when he stooped to look in her face after the fight. Some one wanted to shoot her, but Big Foot prevented them.

Westfall and Wallace were conspicuous figures in the fight. Wallace had black curly hair, dark eyes, 6 feet 2 inches in height, and weighed 240 pounds. Westfall had nut-brown hair, blue eyes, 6 feet 3¾ inches in height, and weighed 190 pounds. From the battleground it was a long, tedious route over the rough country, without roads, to drive the horses back to the settlements, but it was finally accomplished, and Westfall, bidding farewell to his friends, went back to his ranch.

As the country began to settle stock was brought in, and Westfall, having located a considerable tract of land and having plenty free grass and water, also commenced raising stock. To do this successfully he needed neighbors for mutual protection for stock, especially horses, as they drew raiding bands of Indians around a ranch. Having this in mind, he went to San Antonio and made an offer to anyone who wished to come that he would give each 100 acres of land. Several accepted and went, but the majority soon tired of frontier life and went back. Two, however, remained—James Hammock and a man named Blanchard. They opened up a farm and lived in the house with Westfall. In 1850 they planted a crop of corn. There was no provisions to be had except wild meat, and deer at this season of the year were poor. Thinking this was not substantial enough to make a crop on, Hammock got Blanchard and another man who was there to go with pack mules to San Antonio and bring back some bacon, flour, and salt, and he would cultivate the crop. Three months passed away, and nothing was seen or heard of the two grub-hunters. Hammock made the crop, living on deer meat, and as farmers say, "laid it by." Westfall, who took all of these things philosophically and never complained at anything, now proposed to Hammock that they take a hunt to the Espantosa Lake and get a supply of venison and honey. This was very agreeable to the despondent farmer, who had complained a great deal and would have said hard things about his long-absent partner if he had been certain he was not killed by Indians.

They arrived at the lake all right and found everything to their hands—fat deer and plenty of wild honey. Hammock was in high spirits and enjoyed himself. He had made a crop on poor venison without salt, and said now he did not care if they never come back from San Antonio. Soon after the return to the ranch, however, their absent friends also arrived. They had a tale of woe to tell of incessant rains, high water in creeks and rivers, which caused many delays. All they returned with was a little bacon and coffee. The flour and salt had all been spoiled by the rain.

Long and impatiently they now waited for the corn to get hard enough to grit or grind. When the shucks began to dry they gathered some, and by exposing it to the hot sun soon had it dry enough to shell and grind on a steel mill which Westfall had. Some was ground that looked sufficient for four men to eat at one meal, but Jim Hammock said grind some more; that he wanted a good bait while he was at it. When the corndodgers were cooked and put on the table the men were mistaken in how much they could eat. There was plenty left. They had done without bread so long it did not taste natural, and they soon got enough of it.

Westfall now proposed to take another hunt with Hammock. Jim, however, objected this time, saying it would turn out disastrously. He was always predicting dire calamities, and said he had been warned not to go on this trip. Westfall laughed at these things, and said he thought it was a fine time to go. Hammock finally, with a long and sad face, began to get ready and said he would go and risk it. They intended to stop this time on the Nueces River, not quite so far out as before, and where there was also plenty of honey. Deer were everywhere. On the way out they stopped to noon in a shady elm grove, not far from a lake. Hammock was to get dinner, while Westfall went to kill a deer for the purpose of casing the skin to put the honey in. No sooner had Jim raised a smoke than it attracted a large band of Indians passing, who at once came and attacked him. Hammock saw them in time to make a run and fired at them as he went. At the lake he threw his rifle down and sprang in, with the Indians in pursuit, yelling and shooting at him. He had no time to mount a horse, as they were both staked out. By diving almost continually as he swam he avoided the arrows which cut the water around him, and arrived safely on the opposite bank. The Indians did not attempt to follow him, but went back to plunder the camp. He continued his flight through the brush for some distance until he got out of the valley and ascended rising ground. Then he looked back to see if the Indians were following. He was very uneasy about Westfall, and what was his consternation now to see his friend running at full speed almost into the Indians to succor him, thinking he was being killed by the

Indians in camp. The distance was too great for his voice to reach him in assurance of his safety, and with a heavy heart he sped on, not wanting to see the horrible sight of his noble companion butchered. His purpose was to get to the ranch somehow, and get help and come back after his body.

Westfall was a quarter of a mile or more from camp when he heard the rifle shot, but at first supposed Jim had shot a deer or turkey. He had stopped for an instant and was about to resume his walk when the loud yelling of Indians suddenly burst upon his hearing. "Indians!" he exclaimed. "My God, they will kill Jim; I must go to him," and wheeling with his gun in his right hand he sped back towards camp. He ran about 600 yards before stopping, and was getting somewhat winded when he approached the camp. The grove was literally swarming with Indians, but he could nowhere see his friend. While stopped in plain view getting his wind back the Indians discovered him, and they came yelling in crowds, on foot. They were coming in on a raid and had no horses. Westfall was willing to risk his life to save his friend, but not to throw it away if it was too late to help him. He now yelled and called the name of his companion, but getting no response, and thinking and almost knowing it was all over with him, turned and ran, followed by a flight of arrows and the Indians who were shooting them. There was an open flat around the grove of several hundred yards in extent, and across this he had to run to cover. The Indians saw he was fast, and sent one of their number who was on a mule to cut him off from the chaparral. Westfall watched him, intending to kill him if he came too close or was about to run around him, but he beat the mule to the brush too far to talk about. He also left the foot ones far in the rear. Almost exhausted, he made his way to about the center of the thicket and lay down. Besides the load in the rifle he had a large single-shot pistol. He knew Indian nature well—that they dreaded a concealed foe. Here he was, besieged by the whole band, it seemed from the noise they made, until night. They whooped and yelled, beat the brush, and shot arrows into it. At times they would come part of the way in, making the brush rattle as much as possible, like they were going to charge over the spot where he was, hoping he would get scared and run out. He stood all this, however, and kept his rifle ready, knowing if they did come he would get one or two, and he had just as soon be killed in the brush as out in open ground. This was not the first time he had been in a thicket from Indians.

On this occasion, when the Indians finally hushed their jargon and demoniac yells, and the dark mantle of night closed down on hill, dale, and chaparral, Westfall came forth slowly and cautiously, stopping and listening at the slightest sound, sometimes with one foot raised and bated breath, as the distant bark of a coyote was heard or the bushes rustled by some prowling nocturnal animal gliding away from his presence. In this way, step by step and many halts, he approached their noonday camp, determined not to leave until he found out the fate of his companion if possible. Poor Hammock! Where was he now, at whom he laughed only that morning about his warnings and bad omens? All of these things passed through Westfall's mind as he passed among the trees. Every dark object on the ground was examined or touched. A white something appeared at his feet. His heart sank within him. It might be the body stripped and mutilated. He slowly stooped and touched it, and a breath of relief came. It was the ashes where the fire had burned out that Jim had made that day at noon to boil their coffee and roast their meat. His search was of course fruitless, as at this time Jim was tearing through the brush and pear, lacerating himself at every step, trying to get to the ranch in the dark.

Horses, saddles and everything were gone. With noiseless tread of his moccasined feet he searched the open ground around the mott. He might have ran a distance before being killed. Finally, however, he gave it up and was about to start on his journey to the ranch, when he thought of his spurs. Surely the Indians did not find them hung up as high as he could reach among the thick leaves of an elm tree. When he felt for them they were gone, too. There was nothing left now for him to do but to return to the ranch and report Jim killed and get Blanchard to come back with him after the body. With shouldered rifle and long, steady strides he commenced his dark and lonely journey through the pathless woods.

Long after the turn of the night, when the cock had crowed twice, Jim Hammock, torn by thorns, wet and full of prickly pears, startled the inmates of the Westfall ranch by knocking at the cabin door and announcing his name. Explanations soon followed after he entered. He told of the attack by the Indians and flight of himself across the lake, and then from elevated ground beheld his noble companion going in a run to his rescue. Being almost in among the Indians when he last saw him, it was almost certain that he had perished. Winding up, he said, "Yes, boys, Westfall is gone. The Indians got him this time, and no mistake."

"No they haven't, Jim. , Here I am!" came a voice from out the darkness near the cabin door, which at that instant opened and the tall form of Westfall stood before them. The reader can imagine the joy and explanations that followed. Westfall was just about to announce his presence and the death of Jim when he saw a light in the house and heard the voice of his companion telling the others of his death.

Although Hammock had nearly half a day the start of Westfall, the latter came near beating him to the ranch on account of his better knowledge of the country and coming straight.

Soon after this the men all left Westfall, and he was alone once more except for the companionship of his dogs and horses. He was greatly attached to one of his dogs, whom he called George Washington. Jim Hammock wanted to see some of the country still further west, and when Big Foot Wallace obtained the contract to carry the mail to El Paso he got in as one of the stage guards. Before starting on his first trip, however, he again predicted evil and said he would never come back. This time, as before, his words seemed prophetic, for he was killed at a fandango in El Paso by a Mexican.

The Indians learned to know and dread Westfall, and tried many times to kill him. On one occasion he went on foot to take a short hunt, and the Indians came in his absence and laid an ambush for him. They saw his trail where he had left the cabin and crossed the river on a foot log which he had placed there by chopping a tall tree across it for convenience when wishing to pass to the opposite side on foot. Here at this log the Indians waited concealed. One, however, exposed himself, and the keen eye of the settler discovered him when he returned, and he hastily went back, knowing there was an ambush there. The Indians left cover and followed, and he took the brush on them in a dense thicket and stopped, lying flat on his stomach, so that he could see to some extent under the brush. Here he awaited developments. Presently the Indians commenced a great yelling all on one side of the thicket, like they were coming in. Westfall turned a little and listened at them, but without getting up. Soon a stick cracked in the other direction, and his attention was directed there. With his face almost to the ground and rifle ready he waited. A bush moved. A dark object was seen, which finally developed into the face and black head of an Indian as he slowly, inch at a time, moved into view looking for the white man. Only a moment it was seen there and the crack of a rifle was heard. The brush around Westfall for a few moments was enveloped in smoke and he lay still in the position he occupied, with his pistol ready for an emergency if any others were close behind. All was still, and he hastily reloaded his rifle. The Indians outside of the thicket quit yelling. When the smoke cleared away Westfall saw that he had got his Indian. He could see his hair spread out on the leaves. All the balance of the evening he stayed here, but could hear nothing more of the other Indians. About sundown he crawled to where his dead Indian was and looked at him. He was shot between the eyes. His hair was about two feet in length and very thick. His bow was strung and one arrow in his hand ready to shoot. The Indians evidently sent this fellow in there to crawl up on Westfall and shoot him while they attracted his attention by their yelling in the other direction. When their man did not return after the report of the rifle they knew what his fate was, and left without any further investigation. When night come Westfall cautiously left the thicket and made his way back to his cabin, but not by way of the foot log; he avoided that and crossed lower down. When he did not wish his dogs to follow he left them in the cabin, and they were there on his return. Although the Indians had been near they had not approached the house.

Westfall went several trips with Wallace as stage guard, but not liking this business soon quit.

One of the relay stations for Big Foot Wallace was at Fort Inge, and on one occasion just before arriving there he discovered the track of the Big Foot Indian where he and six of his followers had crossed the road. Wallace had often trailed this Indian on the Colorado, had seen him three times, but never fired at him. His track was fourteen inches in length as measured by Wallace on one occasion near Austin. On arriving at the fort Westfall was there, and Wallace told him of the presence of Big Foot and his band, and furthermore, if the Indians made a raid in the vicinity and cleaned up the horse stock, that he would leave his relay of mules on the Frio, and if he needed them to follow Big Foot with, to go and get them. As Wallace expected, all of the horses were taken and the mules were sent for, and three or four men and one boy mounted and set out on the trail, led by Westfall. The Indians went up Nueces Canyon to its source, and then crossed over into the head draws of South Llano. Here they went into camp in a dense cedar brake and proceeded to rest and cook a small bear which they had killed. Thinking they had got all the horses, they did not fear pursuit. The soldiers at the fort had gone on a scout.

About sundown of the second day of the pursuit the camp of the Indians was located by their smoke. Westfall now camped, but without building any fire, and awaited morning for the attack. At daybreak he went to reconnoiter their position, taking the boy, whose name was Preston Polly, with him. The other men were told if they heard his gun to come quickly. At first he descended into the bed of a gorge which skirted the foot of a hill to the right of Big Foot's camp, which was on this elevation, but back in a cedar brake, as before stated. Following up the gorge to a point opposite the place where smoke was seen the evening before, a trail was discovered which led down the hill to a pool of water fed by seep springs, and below it was very rank, coarse grass. Westfall had halted in this grass for a few moments looking at the trail and was about to follow it, when he saw the legs of a horse and an Indian under the bushes following the trail coming towards the pool of water. He now instantly cocked his gun and stood in readiness, and when the Indian came into full view the heart of the pioneer beat quickly, for Big Foot, the scourge of the southwest frontier, was before him. Silently motioning for the boy to be still who stood behind him, he slowly and steadily raised his gun. At this time the horse discovered the presence of the ambushed marksman and snorted. Big Foot turned quickly to look at him and was for a moment stationary, presenting a fair side view, and—bang! Night came down on the burly chief. He fell in his tracks, shot through the heart. The last object his eyes rested on was a white man's horse. He belonged to Adolf Fry, and was taken near Fort Inge. The other men now came quickly and a charge was made up the hill, past the body of the dead chief, into the camp. The other Indians, however, were gone, being alarmed by Westfall's gun, which no doubt they thought boded no good for their chief, as no shout or call came from him. The stolen horses were all in camp except those ridden off by the fleeing Indians. It was evident they were about to leave, and the chief was going to water his horse. The hungry men ate a good portion of the bear meat, which was fat and well roasted. Among other things left in camp was a shield and quiver of arrows. The big chief was 7 feet in height and would weigh about 300 pounds. He had such a grip on the halter by which he was leading the horse that the animal could not pull away from him or move him out of his position as he lay. He made several efforts to do so, when the gun fired and the Indian fell. Also in one hand the chief clutched a bow and some arrows, and his fingers had to be opened with force to release them, as was also the halter in the other hand. He had a broad, rough face and powerful arms and legs, and his hair was about a yard in length. It was not in the nature of Westfall and Wallace to scalp their victims, as many did. Westfall had promised Wallace to bring him the moccasins of Big Foot if he killed him, so these were taken off for that purpose. One of the men wished to wear them back and pulled them on over a heavy pair of boots, and then they were too large. On the Indian's right knee was the sign of Tom Green's bullet, where he wounded him near Austin in 1839. This was Gen. Tom Green in the civil war, and he was killed at the battle of Blair's Landing, La., in 1863.

When Westfall and his men returned to Fort Inge the moccasins were left there for Wallace, but he never goth them. A man there obtained possession of them with a promise to deliver them to Wallace at San Antonio, but he never did, and went on to the States with them.

When Big Foot Wallace quit the mail service he was commissioned by Gov. P. H. Bell to raise a company of rangers for frontier defense. The company was raised, with Westfall as lieutenant.

The hardest fight they had during this service was on the Todas Santos (All Saints) Creek, at a place called the Black Hills, sixteen miles from the present town of Cotulla, in La Salle County. There were eighty Indians and nineteen rangers, and one of them named Jackson was very sick, and had to lie on a blanket under a mesquite tree during the combat. It was hot, dry weather, and the rangers had been three days without water. It was in August, 1854, and the rangers were fighting to get at a waterhole which was in the possession of the Comanches. Captain Wallace knew where all the waterholes were, and had led his men over the hot, desolate hills and valleys, through prickly pear and catclaw bushes, to this watering place, and found the Indians there, and a desperate battle ensued of an hour or more. The Indians were finally driven away, leaving twenty-two of their number dead on the ground, among whom was the chief. Captain Wallace killed him with a large rifle which once belonged to Col. James Bowie. The mesquite tree behind which Wallace stood was struck by many bullets. Westfall did some splendid shooting, and more than one Indian went down under his fire. Several of the rangers were wounded, some severely, and they were carried on stretchers to Fort Inge. None were killed.

After the company was disbanded Westfall returned to his ranch and once more took up his hermit life. The Indians still tried to get him, but were foiled many times.

In 1855 a Frenchman named Louie came down from Fort Inge and wanted to live with Westfall. This was agreeable, and a day was set to return to the fort to bring his effects down to the ranch. When the time arrived Westfall said it was best to wait until night to make the trip, as there were Indians in the country. He had been out to kill a deer and saw their signs. This was the 30th day of June, 1855. At 3 o'clock Westfall went out to the hand mill and ground some corn. Everything looked quiet and serene, but at this moment a band of Indians were secreted near by and watching his every movement. When his back was turned and he started back to the house with the meal on his shoulder, an Indian left cover, and making a quick run gained a position behind the corn crib near the cabin. When Westfall arrived at the door of his house he turned, as was his custom before entering, and took a look around. At this moment the Indian behind the crib, who had his gun in position, fired and badly wounded him in the right breast. The ball entered high up near the collar bone and ranged a little down, going through the upper part of the right lung and passing on out through the body. He did not fall, but carried the meal in the house, and getting his gun and pistol started to go out to fight the Indians, who by this time were yelling and shooting at the house. Thinking he could not recover from the wound, his intention was to try and get as many of them as they did of him, or more if he could.

The Frenchman held Westfall back, and said that he would fight the Indians. Being now very weak from loss of blood, he yielded and fell back on the bed, but protruded the muzzle of his rifle through a crack between the logs of the cabin, from which he had torn a board for that purpose. The brave Louie kept his word. He took up a shotgun loaded with buckshot, and throwing open the door fired one barrel and killed the Indian at the crib. A great shout was now set up by the Comanches, and many balls hit the house, mostly coming from across the open ground.

The Frenchman was greatly excited and raved and swore, going to the door again to get another shot, against the advice of Westfall, who admonished him to keep still and watch a chance to shoot. As he presented himself in the open door he was struck by a ball that went through his body and fell in a tin pan sitting on a table behind him. He turned quickly and looked at the ball as it rattled in the pan, and then put his gun down and told the almost unconscious Westfall that he was killed, too. He then sat down in a chair, pulled off his boots, called for water, and fell over dead on the floor. The door was still open and Westfall was not able to get up and shut it. The dog, George Washington, who was in the house, now sallied forth when Louie fell, and attacked an Indian who was approaching the house. He pulled the rigging off the Comanche, even the quiver from his back, and bit him badly, but was mortally wounded by a lance, and returning to the house went in and died beside the Frenchman. Westfall now gave up all hope. He was too weak to make a fight, and expected every moment his foes would be in upon him, who would have paid any price almost for his scalp. This was the only time they ever had him in their power and unable to defend himself, and would have got him if they had known the situation. Not knowing this, they finally took their departure and left him alone.

The wounded man stayed all night in the cabin on the blood-covered bed, part of the time unconscious. When daylight came his head, neck, and eyes were so badly swollen he could not see, and only knew when daylight came by the birds singing. He had been expecting some men down from Fort Inge to fish and hunt, and now looked to them to help him, expecting them to come that

day. The day passed off and they did not come, and he passed another night alone and in darkness on the bed, aud his dead companion and dead dog on the floor. The only chance to get help
was for him to go to the fort himself. He was a man of powerful
strength, courage, and will power, and on the third day determined to make the effort. The swelling in his eyes had abated to
some extent, so that he could see his way. Not wishing for the
dead man and dog to decay in the house, he had a hard time in
getting them out, but was finally successful. He was not able to
carry his rifle, and hid it in the weeds. A pistol, gourd of water,
and some ground coffee and tin can to make it in was carried
along. He also aided locomotion with a stick. The first day only
five miles were made. When he became exhausted he would make
a little very strong coffee and drink it. On the third night, as he
was slowly and painfully making his way along the Fort Inge
road, he was met by the party whom he had been expecting at his
ranch to hunt. They were traveling at night to avoid Indians.
One of the party, named William Luckey, came near shooting him
for an Indian. They helped him to get on to the fort, and he was
put under the post surgeon there.

About three days after Westfall left his ranch Big Foot Wallace and two other men come on the scene. At first sight of the
dead man in the yard Wallace said, "Hello! the Indians have
killed Westfall." On coming nearer and seeing the discolored
face and black hair of the Frenchman, he again exclaimed, "No;
Westfall has killed an Indian." Further inspection revealed the
truth of the situation, and Wallace then went to look for his
friend, believing he was either dead or wounded somewhere near
by. By his knowledge of woodcraft he soon found the trail of
Westfall, and came back and told his companions, who had never
been on a frontier before, that Westfall was wounded and gone to
Fort Inge, and described all the circumstances of his having his
pistol and gourd, walking with a stick, and had no gun, etc.

Wallace now took the trail, expecting to find the wounded man
on the road, but late in the night met a party who were coming
down to bury Louie. They went back to the fort together, and
told Wallace the particulars as they went along. After staying
a while with Westfall, Wallace went back with a party and buried
the Frenchman and also the dog. Westfall had two horses tied
in the brush when he was wounded, and thought the Indians

had got them, but they were found by Wallace and taken care
of. They were nearly starved. The two men who came with
Wallace first to the ranch were planters from the Colorado, hunting for runaway negroes. They went back to San Antonio from
the fort. Westfall had a hard pull for his life. Big Foot Wallace
came often to see him, and brought books and papers for him to
read while convalescing.

This episode in the life of Westfall caused him to think of laying up something for a "rainy day." After his recovery and return to the ranch his brother Abel, who had been informed of his
situation, came from the States and lived several years with him,
and assisted in the management of the stock. During the civil
war the stock was removed to Nueces Canyon and located near
Camp Wood, another military post which had been established.
Here he stayed nine years, and during that time acted as guide
and trailer for citizens, rangers, and soldiers. The Indians knew
him and Henry Robinson so well they painted their pictures on a
rock—Robinson with his shotgun and Westfall with his rifle.

In 1874 he sold all of his cattle, and in 1877 moved to Bexar
county and settled fifteen and one-half miles southeast from San
Antonio, on the west bank of Calaveras Creek. In 1881 he sold
his Leona ranch and went farming. In the same year, June 5th,
he married Miss Josephine Susan Dillon. He lived on the farm
here until his death, which occurred on the 12th day of June,
1897. He had been in bad health for some time, and on Thurs-
day, the 10th, before his death, was taken in the middle of the
afternoon with cholera morbus, which terminated fatally on Saturday. He died easy and without a struggle. Those who stood
around his bedside in his last hours besides his wife were his
brother, Abel Westfall, William Boykin, Lemuel Mays, and D. H.
Dillon, a brother of Mrs. Westfall. In the cemetery at Elmen-
dorf, on the Aransas Pass road, the great frontiersman was
buried. He left no family except his wife. He had a brother-
in-law, John Reinbold, who lives in San Antonio. Had also
two neices and one nephew there. One brother, Isaac, died in
Grayson County, Texas. Henry, another brother, died near
Mumfordville, Ky., during the civil war. Mrs. Westfall has a
knife which her husband carried for many years, and which
originally belonged to his old friend and companion, Henry
Robinson. It has "H. R." cut on the handle, done by Robinson

himself. The following is the will of Westfall, as copied by the writer from the San Antonio *Express,* bearing date of June 26, 1897:

"The last will and testament of the late Edward Dixon Westfall, who died June 12th, 1897, has been filed for probate. All of the deceased's property, valued at $5000, is bequeathed to his wife, Josephine Susan Westfall. The will provides that after her death the property shall be invested in the city of San Antonio in trust to be converted into cash and applied to the establishment of a free public library, to which whites and blacks shall have access on equal terms, but separate reading rooms."

At the request of many friends of Mr. Westfall in the West, the writer made a journey of more than 100 miles in February of 1897 to interview him and write a sketch of his eventful life, not knowing he had passed away. His wife and brother furnished most of the data for this sketch. He thought a great deal of Big Foot Wallace, and said that while he was the most cautious man he ever saw, that when the test came his courage never failed him, nor his presence of mind, and that his judgment was never at fault.

HENRY BRUCKS.

Came to Texas in 1846.

Mr. Henry Brucks, the subject of this sketch, and one of the pioneers of Southwest Texas, was born on the 16th of February, 1838, in Westphalen, on the Rhine, and came to Texas with his parents and brother in 1846 as a Castro colonist. The ship in which they sailed was the Medina, and the first port touched was Galveston, Texas. The objective point, however, from which to make their start on the overland route to the Castro settlement was Port Lavaca, but in attempting to land at this place the ship was blown off by a norther and had to land at Corpus Christi.

In writing up the early history of the West there is bound to be more or less repetition and the same ground gone over again to some extent, where different individuals are interviewed who participated in the same events described, but in getting the statements of more than one, new facts are brought out. Every one does not have the same experience, and often in giving the details of battles or settlements one will remember an incident that escaped the recollection of another who was present.

From Corpus Christi the Brucks family after many hardships arrived at Castroville. Other colonists who had preceded them had already commenced a settlement under the management of Henry Castro, and their future town named. This was on the Medina River, twenty-five miles west from San Antonio. After staying a month at this place the Brucks family, with others, went further west about ten miles and commenced a settlement on the Quihi Creek, at the famous lake of the same name. Quihi means eagle in Spanish, or one certain kind which Americans call a Mexican eagle, or buzzard. They are not a buzzard, however, but an eagle. They have white heads, brown bodies, white tails, and tips of wings white. They were quite numerous in this country at an early day.

A town had been laid off at this place by Castro, and each settler received a town lot besides his regular grant of farming land. There were no roads out to this place, and the journey with women and children and heavily loaded carts and wagons was slow and tedious. The start was made on the 2d day of March, 1846, and at sunset of the same day they arrived on the ground. Each man's lot was numbered on a stake driven in the ground. John B. Brucks, father of Henry, had a lot near the lake and succeeded in finding his number before dark, and camped the first night on his possession. Night came on so soon after arriving that many could not find their numbers, and they camped as convenience suited them for the night, building many bright and cheerful looking fires up and down the creek. Mr. Brucks distinctly remembers how the bright fires looked on that first night. Next day the people all found their lots and occupied them. As there was no chance to build houses for some time to come, the people had to live in tents. The colonists divided, part of them settling one mile below the lake. Of this party was the old man Boinkhoff, his wife, one married son and his wife, one single son about 10 years of age, and a grand-son about the same age. All of these were living in one tent. About 12 o'clock at night of the eighth day of the new settlement, a man who had been a cook on board the ship in which they sailed for America came up from the lower settlement, where he lived, and told the elder Brucks that the Indians were in the lower settlement and were killing all the people down there. On being awakened and told this startling news Mr. Brucks hastily arose, and, donning his garments, went and aroused every man in the colony who had been a soldier in Europe, and organized them into a squad to fight the Indians. Those who had not been soldiers were not allowed to go with this crowd, but were left with the women and children. A man named Deides was detailed to ring a bell which hung on a mes-quite tree near Mr. Brucks' tent. This bell had been sold at auction on board the ship and bought by Mr. Brucks. Captain Brucks now formed his men and ordered them to fire off their guns and reload them, so as to be sure they were in good con-dition. They now marched down to the scene of the trouble. They were not used to Indian warfare, and talked loud as they marched along. On arriving at a point about half way to the lower settlement a voice came out of the brush and darkness

24

asking if Mr. Brucks was in the crowd. On being answered in the affirmative, the voice said, "Come out here to me and pull these sticks out of my head." Mr. Brucks at once went to the man, and found it was old man Boinkhoff with two arrows in his forehead. With some difficulty they were extracted, and the wounded man went on up to the upper settlement. Brucks and his men went to the tent and found that the two women were dead and scalped in front of it. Another voice now came out of the darkness about thirty yards away, calling for Mr. Brucks. On going out there young Boinkhoff was found to be mortally wounded, shot through the bowels with a bullet. He begged the men to kill him, and died before daylight. He told them before he died that they heard wolves, as they supposed, that night close by, but paid no attention to it. After a while a shot was fired, and the ball came through the tent and struck him. He knew nothing about Indians, and supposed it was a man named Bruckman shooting turkeys, which he had been doing several nights. The turkeys roosted in the timber on the creek not far from the tents. He told his wife to go and tell Bruckman not to shoot any more, as he had already hit him. Both of the women went out of the tent to do so and were met by the Indians almost in the door of the tent, who at once began to lance them. They screamed and tried to escape, but soon fell and expired under the terrible thrusts. The old man now went out under the tent and got behind a tree and looked around it to see what was going on, and received two arrows in the forehead. Young Boinkhoff also crawled under the tent and went to the brush while the Indians were killing his wife and mother. The man Bruckman, who was supposed to be shooting the turkeys, lived in a tent near by.

After the two unfortunate women were slain the Indians went into the tent and began to plunder it. In the tent was a large box which had been brought from Europe, and which contained clothing and guns, the latter being at the bottom and hard to get at, and had never been taken out. By this time the alarm had been raised above, bell ringing, guns firing, etc. The Indians only took a few things, not getting down to the guns, which were left, and they commenced their retreat, carrying the two boys with them. The wounded man in the brush could hear his son calling, "Help me, father; help me!" but his cries soon ceased, and the father thought that they had gone out of hearing; but the Indians had killed him to stop his cries. His body was found next morning not far away. It was lying inside of what is now the yard of Lienber Boele. Next day the news of the raid was carried to Castroville, and men came and followed the Indians, but could not find them.

In about six months news came that the boy who had been carried off was in Fredericksburg, having been brought there by an Indian agent, and old man Boinkhoff went there on foot to bring him home. Mr. Henry Brucks was with the boy a good deal after he was brought back, but he would not talk much, and very little could be learned about his captivity. He said, however, that the Indians traveled three days after the raid before they would stop and make a fire. They then camped on a bold, running stream, where were many pecan trees. This must have been the South Llano. They stayed here some time, and the Indians painted the boy. As soon as he got a chance he washed it off, and was whipped by the squaws for it. The boy and the old grandpa both died in less than a year after the boy's return.

Not long after this first rude shock of the western savage the settlers built a large brush fence near the lake and fronting on it. Here the people lived inside of the inclosure and called it "the yard." Many of them took the fever, however, and here old man Boinkhoff and the captive boy died.

The next thing to happen was the capture of a boy named Henry Snyder by the Indians. He and Baptiste Nuspaum, a grown man, were herding cattle to keep them out of the crops, as they had no fences at that time. Baptiste and the boy separated, and no one saw the Indians when they captured him. He was never recovered. In 1847 the elder Brucks went to hunt cows for Baptiste Nuspaum, who had no horse. Mr. Brucks went down the Quihi Creek beyond where 'Squire Charobiny now lives, and ascending a hill so as to see over into the valley, discovered six Indians dismounted and standing by their horses. At sight of the white man the Indians mounted to chase him. Brucks, having no gun, turned and fled towards the settlement, followed by the yelling savages. The chase led through what is now the yard of 'Squire Charobiny, down the steep hill, then into Quihi Creek, and across the open flat now inclosed in the Charobiny farm. The Indians, seeing they could not catch him, stopped on the bluff and fired their guns at him as he ran north of the creek. The faithful horse who was carrying his master safely away was struck by a ball and mortally wounded. He held up, however, and kept his speed until out of sight of the Indians, and then fell dead in a liveoak grove. After the death of his horse Brucks continued his flight on foot and safely reached the settlement. Next morning he and others went back to the dead horse and removed the saddle. The bullet had passed through him. Nothing was seen of the Indians.

After Meyer was killed and Mrs. Charobiny captured, an Indian was taken in a fight out west and was brought to Quihi by Tom Rife and a man named Allen, and some others. They wanted to see if Mrs. Charobiny could identify him as one of those who had captured and badly wounded her. All Indians, she said, looked alike to her, and she could not tell. There was a family who kept a barroom or a barrel of whisky at Quihi, and would sell to anyone who wanted it. To this place the men who had the Indian went and stayed all night and drank whisky, and during the time some of them killed the Indian. Next morning a man put a rope around the dead Indian and dragged the body half a mile, and left it for the hogs to eat. A field covers the place now. The Indian was killed where Rolhf's blacksmith shop is now, or was. Some of the old settlers that live at Bandera think the Indian that was killed here was "Old Delaware Bob," a friendly Indian, or had been at least.

On the 14th of March, 1867, the Indians killed old man Hiram Gerdes, about two and a half miles southeast of Quihi. At this time Henry Brucks was a guard for the United States mail from Fort Clark to Fort Stockton. Holiday was boss of this part of the line, and Cook of the other. One would start from Stockton and the other from Clark and pass on the route. At this time the Indians had captured and robbed the Cook outfit. They went into camp on Liveoak Creek, above Fort Lancaster, intending to rest the mules three hours and then go on. A man was sent with the mules to water a short distance from camp, and the Indians made a rush and got them. The men stayed in camp all night, and next morning saw the Indians coming in all directions to attack them. There were only ten men in Cook's party, but they fought the Indians for some time and then began a retreat through the roughest part of the country, fighting as they went.

There was a Mexican in the crowd called Big Joe, who got into a hole in the side of a hill and watched the Indians rob the mail and burn the stage. When Brucks and his party came on they met Big Joe just beyond the Painted Cave, on Devil's River, and he told the men not to go on, as they would all be killed. The party, however, said they must go on with the mail, and would do so and deliver it or die in the attempt, and told Joe he had better go with them. He got in the stage and rode a short distance, but then jumped out, and said, "I can't go; you will all be killed, boys; they have done killed our men." Near Camp Hutson a halt was made to rest and feed the mules. Mr. Brucks, who had just been relieved from guard duty, heard someone talking on the road in English, and it was soon discovered that it was Cook's men. They were glad to get with the others, and were hungry and tired. They told about the fight, and said they tried hard to save the stage but were compelled to abandon it, not, however, until their ammunition was nearly all gone. They retreated into a gorge full of cedar, and the Indians did not follow them any further. The Mexican, Joe, they also said, left before they did and watched the Indians burn the stage, and supposed they were all killed, as he did not see them when they commenced their retreat. The Cook party were all on foot and went on to Fort Clark, and the Brucks party to Lancaster. There were two roads. One went down a steep hill, but cut off eight miles. The Cook party went the long route by Liveoak Creek, but Holiday's men went down the steep hill so as to get to the fort as soon as possible. At 12 o'clock in the night they saw fires and were almost sure there were Indians, but saw none. Passed the Pecos and stopped two hours at Pecos Springs. They got to the fort all right and stayed there three days, so as to give Cook's party time to go down. The Indians thought the stage was coming back at once, and laid a trap to capture it at Howard's Wells, but left when they saw it was not coming. When the men did come on with the stage they saw signs of a large crowd of Indians at the wells. They went by and examined the place where Cook's stage had been burned. The ironwork of the coach was seen in the ashes, and portions of the mail scattered around. These Indians went on down to Bear Lake on Devil's River, and then went towards the head of the Nueces and Frio rivers and raided below the mountains. Mr. Brucks thinks these were some of the Indians who killed old man Gerdes, as it was done about the same time.

Mr. Brucks was a member of Captain Richarz's company of rangers, and did good service on the frontier. He now lives in Quihi, near the place where he settled with his father fifty-four years ago. In regard to the bell which was rung that night during the Indian raid, it was carried to D'Hanis and used for a church bell. A sister of Mr. Brucks married Mr. Nick Ney and moved to D'Hanis, and that is the reason why the bell was carried there. This was the first bell brought to that country. When a new church was built and they wanted a better bell they sent the old bell to the foundry and used it in the construction of the new one with the other material. The people thought a great deal of the old bell, and this one, composed of the old and the new material, is still at D'Hanis.

HERMAN HUEHNER.

Came to Texas in 1846.

Five miles east of Castroville, on the San Antonio road, lives a quiet, unassuming farmer named Herman Huehner, and anyone seeing him at his daily labors as he toils for an honest living on his farm, and hears him speak in his soft, low voice, never alluding to what he has done as frontiersman or soldier, would be led to infer that he had never been fifty miles from his little farm since coming to this country and settling, and that nothing of passing interest had occurred in his quiet home life to ruffle the even tenor of his way. On the contrary, however, this pleasant, sociable old gentleman has passed through some stormy scenes in his life—fought Indians on the Texas frontier, Mexicans in Mexico, and on several occasions followed the fortunes of the famous "Mustang" Grey.

Mr. Huehner was born in Switzerland, but his parents were German. His father was of delicate constitution and went to the mountains of Switzerland for his health, spent several years there, and finally died there. Herman was born there in 1825. His mother also died there, and then he made his way back to Germany. In 1846 he come to Texas with one of his uncles, sailing from Bremen. The ship on which they sailed was the Louise Fredericke, commanded by Captain Knigge. On board were 103 immigrants, sixteen crew, and two mates. The vessel was one of the fastest on the line, and made the trip without incident in forty days. One ship left two weeks before this one, but was seven days behind when the Louise arrived at Galveston. The names of some of the colonists who came on the ship were Louis Moehnig, George Leisburg, John Leisburg, Keiser, Esanhauer, and Frederick. The uncle of young Huehner was named Herman Fernan. When the ship landed at Galveston our subject obtained a job of helping to unload it, which took several days. The final start for the west was made from Port Lavaca, and they came direct to Castroville. Supplies were short in the colony, and cornmeal had to be brought from Austin, the capital of the State, distant about 100 miles.

On one occasion Mr. Keiser and Mr. Keller went to Austin in
an ox cart after meal, and stayed so long fears were entertained
for their safety. The delay, however, was caused by an overflow
in the Guadalupe River. They remained a long time on its
banks, but as it went down slowly and they were consuming their
meal, finally gathered logs and made a raft, on which they crossed
their cart and oxen. It was a long, slow, and tedious trip through
the black prairie mud to Castroville, and when they finally arrived there they only had a pint of meal apiece for each member
of the two families.

After arriving in Castroville Mr. Huehner only remained there
ten days, and going to San Antonio in search of work found a
job of cutting pickets for Mr. Nat Lewis on the Leona, ten miles
west of San Antonio. He worked at this ten days, making money
enough to buy a horse, when he joined a company of Texas
rangers commanded by Capt. John Conner. They were stationed at the San Lucas Springs, between San Antonio and
Castroville. Their lieutenant was William Jett, and Mr. Huehner says he was a splendid man. A great deal of scouting was
done by this company, but not many encounters were had with
the Indians. On one occasion, however, Mr. Huehner participated in his first fight while in this service. The rangers were
scouting on the Seco, and late in the evening were just preparing to camp two miles above the present town of D'Hanis, when
they were attacked by the Lipan Indians. The rangers had all
dismounted, but their horses were still saddled. Taken by surprise, but not dismayed, the rangers met the charge on horseback, having mounted at the first yell. The numbers were equal,
being twenty-five on each side, and the combat did not last long.
The Indians went back after the first charge and scattered,
leaving two dead near the rangers, and some went off wounded.
Old Castro, the Lipan chief, led· the Indians. The rangers
camped on the ground and kept vigilant guard through the
night, but nothing further transpired. Next morning the
rangers took the bows and shields of the dead Indians and a
pistol which one had in a belt around his waist, and left, but did
not scalp them.

The war with Mexico now being on hand, Captain Conner's
company was mustered into the service of the United States on
the 23d day of September, 1846, and joined General Taylor's

army at Monterey. They were placed in the regiment of rangers commanded by Col. Jack Hays, and did picket duty outside of the city, and the regulars stayed inside. Many Mexicans were killed here and there by the pickets. Captain Conner had four Indian scouts in his company. One, a Choctaw, was called Captain Williams; Bill Chism, another, was a Cherokee, and Merrell was a Tonkaway. The other's name is not remembered. The Tonk was the best runner; no horse could catch him in the brush. The road into the city of Monterey was lined on each side with brush and Spanish daggers, and the Mexican cavalry would conceal themselves here near the road and rope any of the regular infantry who happened to be caught out and drag them in. The rangers were always mounted, and the Mexicans never tried to rope any of them.

During the movement of supplies for the army up from Camargo a large train was attacked by the Mexicans between Monterey and Seralvo, near a large ranch called Santa Maria. The Mexicans ambushed them beside the road in the brush, and a terrible massacre of teamsters ensued. The escort was small and soon put to flight, and most of them were killed. Behind this train four days was another large one of 300 wagons and 400 men as an escort. Two companies of regular infantry, with two cannon and two companies of mounted Texas rangers composed the force. The rangers were commanded by Capt. John Conner and Mustang Grey. Mr. Huehner was still with the former command. They heard of the capture of the train at Camargo, and Captain Grey called for volunteers to go on ahead and bury the dead teamsters. Sixty volunteered, among whom was Mr. Huehner, and they set out rapidly for the scene of the massacre. When they arrived at the place they first began to find the dead teamsters scattered along the road in a little valley, and then on both sides of the road. Towards the last they were badly scattered, where they attempted to escape. Many were found in the brush some distance from the road, where they were overtaken singly and killed by the Mexican cavalry. Some were lying in the road where they were shot dead from their mules when first fired on. The bodies were badly mangled on account of the wagons in the rear running over them during the terrible panic of yelling Mexicans and running mules as they dashed along the road with the wagons and without drivers. Wild animals and buzzards had torn the bodies of the Americans badly but had not touched the body of a Mexican, twenty-two of whom were killed in the fight and had also been left where they had fallen. The teamsters and escort were greatly outnumbered, but put up a good fight, as the dead bodies of the greasers that lay among them attested. Forty Americans were found and buried. Mustang Grey was furious, and when the last sad rites to the dead were finished, took his men and captured the village of Pana Maria and burned it, killing twenty-five Mexicans there. He was satisfied, he said, that Mexicans from this place helped to capture the train.

Mr. Huehner went on to Monterey with Captain Grey, and his men came later. A lot of Mexican women came on from Pana Maria and reported to General Taylor of the raid on their village, and pointed out Mustang Grey as the captain who with his men did it. Grey sat very unconcerned and said nothing while the women were pointing their fingers at him in accusation. General Taylor looked at the ranger captain a few moments, and then, laughing, turned away. The Mexican women had to return without seeing the "mucho diablo Tehanas" shot, as they foudly hoped to see.

Another train was now coming up from Camargo on a new road which ran by the town of Catarina, and General Taylor was told that a body of 500 Mexican lancers were going to attack it. One hundred and fifty rangers and two companies of regulars were at once sent to protect it. Conner's and Grey's companies composed the ranger force, and they were very anxious to proceed in a hurry. Catarina was the place where the attack was supposed to be made. The line of march was taken up at 10 o'clock p. m., with Grey's men in the lead. Next came the regulars, and Conner's men brought up the rear. The regulars went slowly, and Grey, who was anxious to reach Catarina by 4 o'clock in the morning, became very impatient at the slow progress. The officer in command of the regulars gave orders through the night in a loud voice to "Slow up in front." Grey finally said he would go on with his men, and if the rangers in the rear wanted to go with him to come on, and if the regulars did not get out of their way to run over them. Conner's men now divided and ran on both sides of the regulars until they got ahead of the line and went on with Gréy. At daybreak the rangers arrived at the town and saw Mexicans running from it in all directions. Grey would not go in at once for fear of a large force there, but he had accomplished what he intended—to arrive in time to succor the train if necessary at this place. The sun was high up when the regulars got there, and the officer in command wanted to enter the town in regular battle order, with the rangers in the rear. Mustang Grey said, "No, sir; I was here first, and I am going into the town first." A quarrel now ensued, and Grey cursed the officer in fierce language, and said that he and his men would go into the town as they d——d please, and wound up by drawing his pistol and threatening to shoot. Lieutenant Jett, of Conner's company, now went to Grey and persuaded him to come away. When the start was made into town the rangers took the lead. A great disappointment, however, met them—no Mexican soldiers were there. The Americans were very hungry, and soon found plenty to eat, and took everything they wanted. Some of the Mexicans treated them well, and Grey put guards around their houses and would not allow anything of theirs to be molested. They went on from here and met the train and escorted it safely through.

After the return to headquarters there were so many complaints made to General Taylor of the insubordination of the rangers he thought best to send the most of them back to the Texas frontier, as the fighting was now about over in Mexico. The general liked Grey for his vim and unquestionable courage, but thought he should keep his men under better control. He sent for him when it was decided to send the rangers back, and said: "Grey, your rangers are rough, ready, and rugged, and you can take them back to Texas to fight Indians."

Most all of the rangers were sent back at this time except the spy company of Ben McCulloch. Many of them, however, went back to Mexico again and participated in some battles under General Scott. Grey's and Conner's men separated on the Rio Grande, the former going to Corpus Christi. Mr. Huehner was mustered out of the service in November, 1847. He intended to join the company of Big Foot Wallace, whose captain, Ad. Gillespie, was killed at Monterey, and he was raising a company to go back, but at this time was taken sick and did not get off. Mustang Grey and his men had a fight on the Nueces with the Comanche Indians before they got to Corpus Christi, and were badly used up, but not whipped. Grey was wounded and his horse killed, besides quite a lot of his men. Mr. Huehner heard that Grey was killed in the fight, and never knew any better until he met him one day in San Antonio. He says Grey was tall, handsome, well made, and had light hair and blue eyes. His given name was Mabry, and he was a native of Tennessee.

While in Mexico one of Conner's men named Adolph Gusman owned a fine gray horse, which took the fancy of General Taylor, who wanted him to match one he had, and a trade was made. This horse lived to be very old, and died near Baton Rouge, La., during the civil war.

On one occasion Mr. Huehner and Jim Brown followed some Indians who had stolen horses, and came upon their camp ten miles above Castroville. Only two Indians were in camp with the horses, and they crept within eighty yards of them, each selecting an Indian, and fired at once. The Indian Brown shot yelled once, although hit in the head. Mr. Huehner shot his in the breast, and he fell over without uttering a sound. The horses were gathered up and brought back to the settlement.

When Nat Lewis built a mill in San Antonio in 1850 Mr. Huehner was married and living there, and boarded the hands that built the mill.

To give an idea how many rattlesnakes there were in southwest Texas in the early days, Mr. Huehner said that on one occasion he and Bill Adams came out from Castroville on the San Antonio road and stopped to camp about sundown, two miles from Castroville, at the first creek, near where Fisher's farm is now. They dismounted under a mesquite tree and took off their saddles, but had to kill seven rattlers before they could spread their blankets for the night.

INDIAN FIGHT IN SABINAL CANYON.

1848.

In the above named year a company of rangers were stationed on the Seco two miles above D'Hanis, in Medina County. Gillette was first captain of this company, but he being promoted, Captain Warfield was in command at the time of which we write.

The time of enlistment for this company was about to expire, but one more scout was made up for a trip into the Sabinal Canyon, then unsettled, and distant from the ranger camp about twenty-five miles. The rangers anticipated a fine time killing bear if no Indians were found. The scout was composed of thirteen men as follows:

First Lieutenant Knox, in command; Second Lieutenant Kaisey, John Saddler, Doc Saddler, Jim Fell, Doc Huffmann, Rothe, Heynard, John Wesley Deer, Josiah Cass, Rothe Reinhard, John Eastwood, and Harrison Daugherty. Also one visitor who accompanied the scout.

The men passed out through what is now the pastures of the Rothe brothers, John Reinhart, and Mrs. Donoho. They went into camp in a pecan grove somewhere not far from the present village of Utopia, and had fine sport for several days. It was in the fall of the year; pecans were plentiful, as were also bear, and very fat. One evening Indians were seen on a mountain some distance off, and that night the usual guards were placed, but as the weather was cold a fire was made and some of the men lay down near it. After the turn of the night Wesley Deer was put on guard and he stood his time nearly out, but being very cold came to the fire and kicked together the smouldering chunks and made a blaze. Now at this time a band of Indians, having located the ranger camp by the light of their fire, were cautiously creeping upon them as young Deer stirred up the fire. A single shot was fired from the darkness, and the young ranger fell backward shot through the heart. His head struck the pallet of Lieutenant Knox and Josiah Cass. The Indians at once charged after the shot with loud yells, thinking to put the balance to

flight, but the rangers met them bravely and a fierce fight commenced. John Saddler received an arrow in the breast as he
sprang up and fired his gun at an Indian near the fire and killed
him, supposed to be the one who killed Deer. The fight was not
of long duration. The rangers poured in such a deadly volley
from rifles and pistols that the Indians were beaten back and disappeared in the darkness. The arrow was taken out of Saddler,
and a strict watch was kept until morning, but no more Indians
appeared. Daylight revealed eight Indians dead around the
camp. Doc Huffmann had an arrow shot through his hat, which
was hanging up in camp or on the horn of his saddle. Deer was
the youngest of the party, and had never seen an Indian. He
was lashed to his horse and conveyed to camp and buried. Saddler recovered.

Lieutenant Knox was afterwards sheriff of Bexar County.

Josiah Cass is the only one known to be alive now of the men
who were in this fight. He now lives at Somerset, Atascosa
County.

"DOKE" BOWLES.

Came to Texas in 1849.

Among the early settlers of Uvalde County were the Bowles family. They were bold, fearless men, and aided materially in settling up the country and fighting the numerous bands of Indians who made desperate efforts to drive the border men back on the settlements east.

W. B. Bowles, better known as "Doke," was born in Allewamby County, Tennessee, October 22, 1835, and came to Texas with his father, John Bowles, in the winter of 1849, and settled on the Lampasas River, in Bell County, four miles from Belton. John Bowles helped to organize Bell County in 1851. He was born in Virginia in 1802, and went to Tennessee with his parents when quite young. When the war of 1812 was in progress and General Jackson was raising volunteers, his father joined and was killed at the battle of New Orleans. He was hit twice, and died of the wounds. There were thirteen children in the family of John Bowles—seven girls and six boys. At the time the Bowles family lived in Bell County a large band of Kiowa Indians were in the country and camped three miles from the Bowles home, on the spot where the beautiful little town of Salado is now. There were but few settlers in Bell County at that time, and they had been on friendly terms with these Indians, and let their horses, which were few in number, run on the prairie, which was covered with fine grass and nothing fenced. Game was abundant, and the Indians spent most of their time in the chase. Things went on this way for some time, but finally the settlers began to miss horses off the prairie, which by the most diligent search could not be found, and suspicion pointed to the Indians as having something to do with their disappearance. A consultation was held among the white settlers, and it was determined to drive the Indians away. So accordingly eight men went to their camp and gave them orders to leave at once, or a strong force would be brought against them. These men were John Bowles and some of his sons, Doke being one, and a man named Blair and his sons. The Indians, when they heard the demand of the white men, stood in silence a few moments and then commenced singing and preparing to leave,—saddling horses, packing others, until all were ready,—men, squaws, and children. Five or six of them would leave, and when they were fairly on the way another band would go, until all were gone, stretched out across the prairie, headed north. The settlers went home relieved, as the presence of the Kiowas had been a menace to the whites ever since they pitched their camp on the banks of the Salado.

About ten days after the departure of the Indians every horse on the prairie and the forks of Little River was stolen, supposed to have been done by them in revenge for having to leave. About four months after this some of the settlers were at a trading post up the country, and saw some of the horses, which had been brought in by the Kiowas and traded off.

John Bowles came to Uvalde County with his family in 1855, and settled on the Sabinal River, in the Patterson settlement, six miles below the present Sabinal station. At this time the Indians were numerous and hostile, and it was only by constant watching that a horse could be kept. Mr. Bowles had brought some good horses to the country, and in 1856 established a ranch on the west side of the river and built a house. This place was below the settlement, and was somewhat more exposed to Indian raids. Mr. Bowles built a strong pen in front of his house, and one of the boys or himself stood guard almost every night, especially during light moons. The horses were put in this pen and a blind made for the guard to stand behind, so that he could not be seen and make a target for an Indian. Some one has said that "eternal vigilance is the price of safety," and it seems to hold good under all dangerous circumstances; but men will get careless even on an exposed frontier, and it always happens that at that time the savages strike their blow. One night they failed to mount guard at the Bowles ranch, and the first thing anyone knew the horses were all out of the corral and in a dead run. All arose, grabbed their guns, and went in pursuit. The course of the horses could be followed by the rattling of a bell on one of them. Mr. Bowles and his sons followed in their night clothes and without their shoes, and soon became scattered. The old man caught up with the horses first and saw one Indian leave them, but fearing it was one of the boys did not fire at the moment, and soon it was too late. The horses were now driven back and put in the pen, and Doke got in the blind to stand guard the balance of the night. The father said he would go and sit under a hackberry tree on the east bank of the river, near a trail, with his shotgun and six-shooter, and watch there. The moon was just up, and Doke had not been long on guard when he heard the report of his father's gun, and the boys all started in a run towards the spot, but before getting there heard the old man fire six shots from his revolver. Thinking he was having a close fight, the boys ran with the utmost speed, and when they arrived at the scene saw their father rising up from a prostrate Indian with a scalp in his hand, and remarked to them, "Hog my cats, if I haven't got one of them." This was about the only byword Mr. Bowles ever used. He never swore or allowed his boys to do so if he could prevent it, especially in the presence of himself or their mother. Mr. Bowles said there were three Indians, and he first discovered them about fifty feet off in the trail, one behind the other, and when they came close, not more than thirty feet distant, he fired one barrel of his gun, and one of the Indians fell and the other two disappeared. The one who fell raised up to a sitting position and attempted to shoot an arrow at Bowles, but he fired the other barrel at him and then emptied his pistol before he fell over. While Bowles was scalping him he raised one hand feebly three times towards the knife. There was a gray horse standing not far from the Indians, and he was hit in the shoulder by some of the buckshot. While looking around a groan was heard near by, and the men bunched together and commenced a cautious search, and a dog that was along struck a trail. They soon heard him baying and started to him, but met the dog coming back with an arrow in him. The party now all went back to the house and a runner was sent to the settlement to give notice of the raid, and several got to the Bowles ranch before day and had a jolly time over the dead Comanche. By daylight next morning a party went to the spot where the dead Indian was, and about thirty steps from him lay another dead one, shot through the bowels with three buckshot. The first one had an arrow grasped in his hand with which he was about to shoot Bowles when he received the second shot. His bow also lay near him.

25

Another bloody trail was found leading from the spot where the Indians were fired on. This Indian was followed four miles but not found at that time. It was he who shot the dog when overtaken. The groans and strange noise heard came from the one found dead next morning. The Indian who made his escape at the time was afterwards found one mile from where his trail was lost or abandoned. All three of the Indians received mortal wounds from the first shot from the gun. Doke Bowles was a quick, wiry man in those days, a good shot with rifle or pistol, and was guide and trailer on many occasions after Indians.

In 1856, after the fight in Sabinal Canyon in which Leakey and Barrymore were wounded, old man Bowles joined the scouts who went in pursuit and was in the massacre of Indians on the Leona, an account of which is given elsewhere. In 1859 John Bowles moved and settled on the Leona, near where they had this fight. This was a very exposed place, no one else living near. Westfall had lived down there but was gone. At this time Doke, who was married, had a ranch on the Blanco where the Wish ranch is now, and no other settlers were near.

On the 28th day of October, 1859, happened one of those sad frontier tragedies which so often threw the settlers into great excitement. This was the killing of John Bowles and John Davenport by the Indians. On the day before Doke Bowles and his wife took a horseback trip to the mountains, several miles away to the north, and returned late in the evening. On the way home they passed their herd of horses, which were quietly feeding, and they passed on to the house. The horses they had ridden were hobbled out, and they went jumping up the creek to join the others, about 300 yards or more away. About sundown Mr. Bowles picked up a rope and started to get a horse near by to go after the others, but changed his notion and came back. This surprised his wife and she asked the cause, and he said he did not know, but it seemed his legs refused to go any further, and that he was very uneasy from some cause, he could not tell what. About this time he looked up the road towards the settlement and saw a man coming on horseback. He was glad to see the man, and started to intercept him and have a talk, but the horseman turned himself and come towards the house. It was Tom Wall, who lived in Frio Canyon, and was on his way home from San Antonio by way of Uvalde. He told Doke he was sick, and wanted to stay all night. "All right," said Bowles, "I am glad to have you stay, for I feel greatly depressed about something." By the time Wall's horse was staked out it was getting dark, and in a few minutes the stock horses came running in and the two saddle horses were not with them. The others stood about the yard the balance of the night. About daylight John Davenport rode up driving a yoke of oxen. He lived on the road at Rancheros Creek. This was the main road that ran from San Antonio towards Mexico. Davenport said to Bowles as soon as he came, "There are Indians around here. Did you know it?" Bowles replied, "I thought so." There was a large train encamped about 300 yards from the house on the way to Mexico, and some of these men had just told Bowles that the Indians had been around all night trying to get their mules, and succeeded in getting one horse and one mule which had strayed off with drag ropes on. Davenport had started before day to get his oxen, as he knew where they ranged, and was now starting home with them and soon proceeded on his way. After sunup twelve men come from the Frio on the trail of the Indians. This was October 28th. These men said the Indians had come near getting some one on the Blanco, near the foot of the mountains, the evening before, but they had left their camp before the Indians got there. This was Doke and his wife, where they ate their noonday meal on their trip to the mountains. The Indians had followed them and caught their two hobbled horses after they returned.

Mr. Bowles joined the Frio scout and took the trail of the Indians, leaving a guard at his house. About 11 o'clock the scout rode to a hill between the Blanco and Sabinal and looked over towards the Patterson settlement. Doke was in the lead on the trail and saw a man running his horse in their direction, and when in speaking distance he said the Indians had made a raid in the Patterson settlement and killed John Bowles, Doke's father, but the body could not be found. This was a severe blow to Doke, and a surprise, too, as he supposed his father was at his ranch on the Leona, many miles away to the southwest. This news was hardly told before another man was seen running his horse on the San Antonio road. He was signaled by the waving of hats, and when he came he said the Indians had killed John Davenport between the Sabinal River and Rancheros Creek. He was on his way from Doke's ranch, and was still driving his

THIS STONE MARKS THE SPOT WHERE JOHN BOWLES WAS KILLED
BY INDIANS.
FROM A PHOTO BY MISS EDITH DILLARD.

oxen. This man said the Indians had gone northwest towards
the mountains after killing Davenport, and that John Bowles
was missing and all were satisfied he was killed. Doke told him
to go back and tell all of the connection to look for the body of
his father, and he would follow the Indians. He led the scout,
and went to John Kennedy's, on the Sabinal, where there was a
little store, and laid in a supply of provisions, which were packed
on a mule, and then sent a runner to Lieut. W. B. Hazen, who
was in command of Fort Inge, asking him to come with all the
men he could spare and meet his scout at the mouth of Frio Canyon. Doke and his party took the trail of the Indians where
they killed Davenport, and followed it to the foot of the mountains on the Blanco, and here the Indians had made a halt, and
here also Doke made the discovery that beyond a doubt his father
was killed, and also aroused a spirit of revenge which made him
furious to overtake the Indians and give them battle. This cer-

tain proof of his father's death was the finding of his shoes, covered with blood. When dark came the settlers lay down on the prairie and spent the night without water. On the 29th the trail was again taken up and followed to the Frio road, and kept that on out through the pass. On the way they come across some men who had seen the Indians in the distance, but thought they were the scouts. Lieutenant Hazen and his men now got with them, and also part of a minute company of citizens from Uvalde numbering ten men. Hazen had thirteen, and these combined with the force under Bowles made forty-two in all. Among the settlers there were John Q. Daugherty, John Kennedy, James McCormick, Ben Pulliam, Clabe Davenport, William Thomas, Frank Isbell, Nobe Griner, Arnold, Arnette, Everette, Williams, and others whose names are not now recalled. Daugherty was in command of the minute men, with Everette as second, and Lieutenant Hazen was in command of the whole. He told Daugherty to take the lead on the trail and follow it to the jumping-off place, and when they came upon the Indians he would take command and lead. Williams was selected as trailer, and all moved forward at a good speed. Doke Bowles asked permission to consult with Williams and help trail, and it being granted, these two took the lead. The trail led across the canyons and sides of the mountains until the settlements were passed, and then it kept the beds of the creeks. They camped that night on the river, and on the 30th the trail lead out to the head of the Main Frio. Here the Indians had left a bunch of horses as they came down on the raid, and which they now collected and carried along with them. They had been hobbled and left in a little valley, rough on all sides, so they could not get out. From the signs there were about fifty head of these, and this accession made the trail much plainer. Noon was made at the Frio waterhole, and a dry camp that night on the plains.

The trail now led across the prairie. Being plain, it was followed fast, and seventy-five miles were covered that day, no halt being made at noon, and the horses a good deal of the time in a gallop. Passed two fires where the Indians had stopped and cooked meat, the first since they commenced their retreat from the settlement. This day's trailing was very exciting. The prairie was in rolling swells, and as each crest was crossed all were eager to get to the next to look over, expecting each time to sight the Comanches. This long stretch of prairie was finally crossed, and they came to low hills and cedar brakes. Daugherty said halt. The water had given out, and had been for half the day. The men lay down and made a dry camp, too thirsty to eat. Daugherty said, "Boys, we are close upon them, and they have not discovered us yet." Bowles asked permission for himself and Williams to take a scout and see what was ahead. This was granted, and the two trailers went about two miles in the direction the trail pointed at dark, and then climbed a cedar tree, hoping to see their fire, but could see nothing and returned.

At daybreak the trail was again taken up, and when they arrived at a point half a mile beyond where the trailers had climbed the tree the Indians were discovered in camp nearly a mile away, in a glade near a small cedar brake, and were saddling their horses. Williams suddenly exclaimed, "Yonder they are, boys." The citizens were in front and the soldiers next, led by Hazen; they traveled in this manner during the pursuit. When the alarm of Indians was raised in front Hazen came forward and at once ordered a charge, himself leading the way. It was a wild and disordered charge. Soldiers, settlers, and pack mules all went together with a terrible clatter, and everything was soon badly scattered and making the rocks and brush fly. The Indians were taken by surprise and ran, but tried to carry the horses along with them. Being pressed for time, all were not able to mount a separate steed, and sprang behind others. One Indian tried to rope horses for those afoot, and another went off with just a loop over the nose of his horse. During all of this time the terrible charge was sweeping towards them and the Texans had begun to yell. The foremost ones soon closed in on the rear of the Indians. Bowles came close to one and jumped down so as to get a good shot at him, but before he could do so the Indian tumbled from his horse, hit by a volley fired from the left. At this time Arnette came up to Doke, riding a race horse called "Fuzzy Buck," and proposed to exchange with him, as Bowles' horse was not as fast as his. He had agreed to do this if it was a running fight, so Doke could have a chance to kill an Indian.

Bowles now mounted "Fuzzy Buck" and set out again after the Indians, who were now 200 yards ahead. Lieutenant Hazen was ahead now on a fast horse, holding his pistol in his hand, and came close to an Indian, who turned with pistol also in hand and charged the lieutenant. Both fired together and at close range. The ball from the Indian's pistol struck Hazen in the right hand, knocked the pistol from his grasp, and then penetrated his breast and lodged against the backbone. His horse reared and fell backward, and then sprung to his feet and ran off, leaving his rider on the ground. The white men were badly scattered, and only those who rode the fastest horses could get into the fight. The Indians, although outnumbered by the whites, were game, and knew how to scatter their enemies and fight them in detail. A part of the Indians had left this bunch and gone another way. Bowles was coming up behind Hazen when he was shot from his horse, and as the Indian turned his horse to run again saw where the lieutenant hit him, but it was too low down, and he went on waving his pistol and yelling. The Indian who rode the horse without bridle or saddle ran to the left, and was pursued by John Kennedy and William Thomas. Kennedy fired and hit the Indian in the back of the head, and he came tumbling from his horse. In the meantime Bowles had dismounted by Hazen and turned him over, and feeling the bullet in his back, said, "There is one dead man, sure," and remounting went on in the chase and soon came to the front again, and saw four Indians in sight. The second lieutenant of the minute men, Everette, was ahead of Bowles, and attacked the Indian who had just shot Lieutenant Hazen. Both had pistols, and when the Indian turned to face him the muzzles of the revolvers almost touched and both fired at once. Everette fell from his horse, with the hammer of his pistol shot off and wounded in the hand and mouth, all done with the same bullet. Two of his teeth were knocked out, and the ball lodged in his left temple. The Indian wheeled his horse, waved his pistol, and went on yelling. Bowles halted at the body of this second fallen man, and seeing blood running from his mouth again exclaimed, "Another dead man!" The horse of Everette went on in the charge.

There were now ahead of Bowles Ben Pulliam, William Thomas, and Arnold, and just ahead of them were two Indians on the same horse and all going at a breakneck speed. In crossing a deep ravine the hindmost Indian fell off in it, and as Ben Pulliam, who was in the lead, dashed in the Indian shot him in the back with an arrow after he passed. Pulliam fell from his horse and the Indian was killed by Arnold, who was coming close at hand, with a shotgun. The Indian died with his bow and another arrow in his hand. This was the finest-looking Indian in the lot. He was young, nearly white, and had fine, soft, black hair, and was profusely ornamented with beads, rings, and silver plates. He had John Davenport's pistol belt on, fastened to which hung the scalp of John Bowles.

When Pulliam fell and Arnold shot the Indian, Thomas, who came next, dashed up the bank in pursuit of the mounted one and soon came alongside of him, and both commenced firing with pistols hand to hand. Thomas fired once and the Indian twice in quick succession, his balls glancing the thigh of Thomas and going into the front of his saddle not more than two inches apart. Thomas went out of sight in another gulley, and the Indian went on yelling and waving his pistol. "Another dead man," said Bowles, who saw it all as he came charging on. The Indian who shot the two lieutenants covered the retreat of the balance. He did the most of his bloody work that day with Davenport's pistol. When it was empty he threw it away and used arrows, and it was recovered. This Indian had been fired at more than a hundred times, and was now stripped completely naked and was bloody from head to foot, as was also his horse, but he continued to yell defiance to his foes and wave his pistol. He still carried his shield and had three pistols, all of which he emptied. When his pursuers would come close he would wheel his horse and make many motions with his pistol before firing, and keep the men dodging. The white men in the chase would only come up with the Indians two or three at a time, and so the fighting that was done was evenly matched. The horses of the settlers at this time were nearly all run down, and there were three Indians still in sight. Bowles now got a shotgun from Arnette, and leaving all behind chased the Indians alone, thinking he could run up close and kill two of them. He had emptied and reloaded and emptied his revolver several times, firing many shots at the noted Indian in the rear. When he came up close to the rear Indian with the shotgun all three were in line. Attempting now to fire, the gun snapped. There were no caps on the gun, and having to stop now to adjust some the Indians made a good spurt ahead. "Fuzzy Buck," however, soon overhauled them again, and the Indians in sheer desperation plunged down a steep bluff. Bowles came up and looked over and saw that it was about fourteen feet down, but not exactly perpendicular. He waited until some more of the men came up and they said it was too steep to go down on horses, and fired their guns at the Indians across the valley, but they were out of range.

Bowles said where the Indians could go white men could, and plunged down, landing safely. Frank Isbell, Nobe Griner, and Williams followed, and these four went on after the Indians. In three miles Doke overtook and once more commenced the battle with them, firing both barrels of the shotgun. The Indians stayed together and sent arrows back, and yelled continually. The other men could not catch up. Bowles would stop and wait for them and get loaded pistols, and then on the racehorse come up with them again. In this way he fought them many miles. Williams had a very long-winded horse, and finally caught up and they both charged together. Doke fired the last load from the shotgun, and only had one in his pistol. The bloody Indian now turned back and charged Williams, who was coming towards him, and he dismounted to fight him with a pistol. The Indian also dismounted and faced him with bow and arrows, no longer having any loaded pistols. The fight commenced at six yards. Williams only fired one shot and received an arrow in the breast. He turned towards Bowles, and the Indian continued to drive them into him. "I'm killed, Doke," he said as he passed, and Bowles saw arrows sticking in his back. The Indian now charged Bowles, who leveled his pistol at him and fired his last load, and then had to turn back and commence dodging arrows, as the Comanche still advanced. The Indian himself was in a terrible plight. He was covered with wounds, and the strap shot from his shield which held it in place, and it was gone. When he left Bowles and went back he mounted the horse of Williams and rode off yelling. Doke counted nine bullet holes in his body as he rode away, and his horse and saddle looked as if they had been dipped in blood. Fourteen bullets had hit the horse on the side that Bowles rode on and fired during the long chase. The Indian lay low on his horse while being fired at, and that accounts for the animal being hit so much. On this horse, which the Indian left standing nearly ready to sink to the ground when he mounted that of Williams, were the saddle rope and bridle of Doke's father, but his horse was still ahead, ridden by another Indian.

The Indians could tell when Doke's loads were out, and would then turn and run him back, but being on a fast horse they could not catch him. Williams lost one of his pistols, which was on the horn of the saddle, when the Indian got his horse.

Bowles watched the three Indians until they got to the top of a hill, where two of them dismounted and laid down, and it was afterwards learned from an Indian on a reservation that they died there, and the third one had a broken arm. Williams was put on a horse and carried slowly back. It was twenty miles back to where the fight commenced, and men were scattered all the way,—here and there a dead Indian and wounded white men. Most of the soldiers stopped with Lieutenant Hazen. The heavy cavalry horses of those who went on soon gave out, and none but the toughest Texas ponies could keep in sight of the Indians. No one had any water, and the wounded men nearly perished for it, but were finally relieved on the way back by men who were met on the trail with some. It was 12 o'clock when Bowles and the others started back with Williams. The bullet was cut out of the temple of Lieutenant Everette with a pocket knife. All the men hit were badly hurt, but none died. Judge James McCormick, who was in the fight and took a conspicuous part, volunteered to go to Fort Clark, a distance of eighty miles, after surgical assistance for Lieutenant Hazen. In the meantime a camp was established and a guard left with Hazen, and the balance of the men drifted back home. McCormick made the trip all right with the surgeon, but had a race with Indians before arriving at the post. It took three days and nights to get back to the spot with a hack. He pulled spikes out of some of the men with his bullet moulds. It was found on examination of Lieutenant Hazen that the ball did not go directly through his body, but struck the breast bone and ranged round. He was first carried to Brackett, and then in about three weeks back to Fort Inge.

During the chase Mr. Bowles noticed an Indian throw something under a cedar tree which he thought was his father's scalp, not knowing at the time that the fancy Indian killed at the ravine had it. Doke hunted for it on the way back, and found that it was an old-fashioned reticule with a drawstring to close it up, that women used in those days, and that it contained four children's scalps, paint, poison, etc.

On the way back, ten miles from where the battle commenced, a bunch of horses was discovered in a cove, standing still, about a mile away. Williams being wounded, Bowles was in charge as guide, and said they were Indians, and at once made preparations to charge them. About this time also a large bear put in an appearance, and four of the men were detailed to charge the bear and the balance to charge the Indians. The men were very hungry, and did not want the bear to escape. The bear was fat and large, and was ample to last the men all the way back, they eating it without bread or salt. The horses taken to be Indians were brought back by Captain Daugherty and his crowd, who charged the supposed Indians. They were some of their own that had broken away from the battle. The paint horse which was ridden by one of the Indians, and which was wounded so many times, belonged to a man named Wheat, of Medina County, who was killed off of him by Indians on Black Creek. The settlers also got Wheat's coat, and the holes in it showed where the Indians shot him. His sons came to Uvalde when the men returned and claimed the property. One of them, Ira, was for long time sheriff of Edwards County.

The body of John Bowles was found at a place called Guide Hill, six miles below where Sabinal station now is. He had come over the day before from his ranch on the Leona to hunt stock, and that night his horse was taken out of an inclosure by Indians. Thinking the horse had got out himself, he procured another at the place where he was stopping in the Patterson settlement, and went to hunt him without his gun. The trail of the horse led toward Guide Hill. During part of this time he rode in company with a frontier preacher named H. G. Horton, who was going up the country, and he was the last white man that saw Mr. Bowles alive or talked to him. After parting company with Rev. Horton Mr. Bowles went to Guide Hill, and from close observation of signs afterwards seen, the Indians had tied the horse in the brush on the side of the hill, but where he could be seen from the valley below, and secreted themselves near him and awaited for some one to come after him. They shot Mr. Bowles at ten steps distant with three arrows at once, which all struck near the left nipple, not more than an inch apart. This fact was ascertained by Doke finding his father's vest in the chase after the Indians, and the holes in it showed where the arrows struck.

The Indians got his horse after he fell from him. A stone now
marks the spot where he fell, with date of birth, death, manner of
death, etc.

Doke was an inveterate Indian hater, and trailed and scouted
and fought them until 1879, when they made their last raids on
this part of the frontier. The fight above described took place
in the head draws of North Llano, in the edge of the plains, 200
miles from Uvalde.

This fight caused the rapid promotion of Lieutenant Hazen in
the army, and he wore the shoulder straps of a general in the
Union army during the civil war, and was connected with the
signal service department after its close. He died in the early
90's, and in the fall of 1899 his widow married Admiral George
Dewey, while the laurel was still green on his brow after his
famous victory over the Spanish fleet in Manila Bay.

W. M. BRAMLETT.

MEXICAN WAR VETERAN.

Mr. Bramlett has been in southwest Texas ever since 1849, and has had the experience of all other frontiersmen—Indian fights, alarms, trailing, and scouting.

In 1846, when the war with Mexico broke out, Mr. Bramlett was at his home in Virginia, and there enlisted for the war in the company of Capt. Montgomery Coarse, Company B, First Virginia Volunteers. Colonel Hamtinmoch commanded the regiment. Lieut.-Col. Thomas Randolph, of Virginia, was sec- ond in command. He was related to the noted John Randolph, of Virginia. The command went round by water, and Mr. Bram- lett says they sailed by the coast of Cuba, and it was the greenest looking country he ever saw. The grass came down to the water's edge, and beautiful green hills and prairies could be seen far back from the coast. The portion he saw was unsettled, no houses being seen.

In Mexico they went to the army of General Taylor, and Mr. Bramlett participated in the battle of Buena Vista, being under the command of Col. Jefferson Davis, and was in many desperate charges during the all-day battle, and saw many men killed and wounded. During one severe fire Colonel Davis ordered the men into a ravine and came in himself on horseback. Mr. Bramlett noticed that one of the colonel's feet was partly shot off, and some of the men called his attention to it, but he said it was only a scratch, and then dismounted. He could hardly stand, and suffered a good deal with it. Colonels Clay, of Kentucky, and Yell, of Arkansas, were both killed, and after the battle Mr. Bramlett helped to bury them. They were buried in one grave. Both had gray hair, and wore the same kind of uniforms, and were buried in them, wrapped up close together. When they were taken up to be carried to their respective States to be rein- terred, Mr. Bramlett helped to take them up, and thinks it likely a mistake was made. He is certain that Clay was put on the north side and Yell on the south. There was a controversy as to which body was on the north side, and he thinks it might be possible that Clay was sent to Arkansas and Yell to Kentucky. Both were shot and lanced.

Mr. Bramlett passed over the ground where the train was captured by Mexicans and nearly all of the escort and teamsters killed. Many signs of the conflict were there. Here his command killed the largest rattlesnake he ever saw. It was lying across the road, and its body was as large around as a man's leg and about seven feet in length.

On one occasion, while himself, Calvin S. Turner, and others were on a scout they discovered six Indians camped in open ground, and charged and killed all of them before they could get to cover. Two got into the edge of a thicket.

Mr. Bramlett came from Mexico after the war and settled in southwest Texas, and has been there ever since. After Big Foot Wallace got too old to live alone he lived with Mr. Bramlett in Frio County, near Big Foot postoffice.

TWO FIGHTS BETWEEN RANGERS AND INDIANS.

1851.

Some time in the month of March, 1851, While Lieutenant Walker, of Capt. John S. Ford's company of rangers was scouting with a few men on the Arroyo Gatto (Cat Creek), about sixty miles southeast from Laredo, they came upon a band of hostile Indians fifteen in number. The rangers at once charged them, and in the first onset four of the Indians were killed and the others ran and were pursued for some distance, and two more killed. The Indians made a poor fight, and the rangers suffered no loss. They captured sixty-nine head of mules and one pony. Among the men along were Robert Rankin, Vol. Roundtree, David Steele, John Walker, Andrew Gatliff, Marvin E. McNeill, Albert Gallatin, — Brown, and others not now remembered.

Now, about this time Lieut. Ed Burleson was on his way from San Antonio with a scout of rangers going to Laredo, and came upon this same band of defeated Indians on the following day and had another fight with them about twenty-five miles from Laredo. This time, however, the Indians made a most desperate fight, and the rangers had all on their hands that they could manage. They were evenly matched as to numbers—nine Indians and nine rangers. The names of some of the rangers besides the commander were Baker Barton, William Lackey, James Carr, Alf. Tom, Warren Lyons, and a German whose name was something like Mille.

The Indians were on the open prairie, and when the rangers charged them they did not run, and a hand-to-hand fight commenced. Pistols, rifles, arrows, and lances got in their deadly work at close quarters, and for a time it seemed as if the rangers would be defeated. The Indians would yell and charge the rangers whenever they would get scattered in the fight by their horses running or rearing in fright. The terrible conflict ended in a drawn battle. The rangers held the ground, but all of their men were killed or wounded except two. The Indians finally rode away, leaving four of their warriors dead on the ground and all the others wounded.   Of the rangers, Baker Barton was killed, William Lackey was killed, and Lieutenant Burleson, Alf. Tom, James Carr, Warren Lyons, and the German were wounded. Lyons had once been a prisoner among the Indians.   He was captured near Lyonsville, in Lavaca County, at an early day. The rangers who were able to do anything had a hard time getting their dead and wounded to Laredo.

Alf. Tom was wounded in the leg by an arrow, and when it was withdrawn the spike remained, but was not noticed at the time, as the man who pulled it out threw it down without looking at it.   The wound would never heal, and two years after it was sore and running corruption.   He got his brother, Capt. John Tom, to examine it, and the spike was discovered and cut out.   The wound then healed all right.

CAÑON DE UVALDE.

The above was the original name of the beautiful valley now known as Sabinal (Cypress) Canyon. It is situated about ninety miles a little north of west from San Antonio and is partly in Uvalde and Bandera counties, the northern half being in the latter. It is about twenty-five miles in length and from three to eight miles in width. The Sabinal River runs through its center, skirted on both sides with pecan, cypress, cedar, and other timbers. The land is black and very productive, yielding fine crops of corn, cotton, oats, wheat, potatoes, etc. Occasional severe droughts is one great drawback to farming. Utopia, the principal village, is situated about midway of the valley, twenty-two miles from Sabinal station, its nearest railroad point, and forty miles from Uvalde, the county seat.

This beautiful valley was once the home of the Comanche Indians. Long before the white man made his appearance they lived here, had numerous villages, and roamed at will over the mountains in pursuit of game, or fished and bathed in the clear waters of the river. Numerous mounds and stone arrow-heads tell the tale of their presence.

The question has often been asked how the county of Uvalde obtained her pretty musical name. I will say that it was named for Colonel Uvalde of the Mexican army, who defeated the Comanche Indians in a great battle in this valley. Long before the white man came near enough from the east to meet the rude shock of the western Indians the Mexican pioneers along the Rio Grande had to contend with them. The town of Laredo was founded in 1757, and ranches were extended between that place and the Nueces, and during the last quarter of the century above mentioned many herds of cattle, horses, and sheep grazed there. The first ranch on the Rio Grande was that of Barrego, at a place called Dolores, twenty-five miles below Laredo. These settlements and fat stock attracted the attention of the roving bands of Comanches, and numerous raids were made from these mountain strongholds and the stock driven off. To check these raids and to punish the Indians, Colonel Uvalde of the Mexican army

26

was ordered by his government to take a large force and follow
these marauding bands to their strongholds and drive them out
with fire and sword. Uvalde was a brave and energetic officer,
and at once set out to carry his orders into effect. With expert
scouts and trailers a band was pursued across the country towards the Sabinal mountains, and it is likely that Uvalde and
his men passed over the spot on which is now situated the town
of Uvalde, then across the Frio and Uvalde prairie to the mouth
of what is now Sabinal Canyon, where is situated a dense cedar
brake. Here information was received that the Indians were in
large force in the canyon and had many villages and much stock.
Uvalde's force consisted of about 600 or 700 men, and the
Indians were capable of bringing 1000 warriors into the fight.
The Mexican commander pushed on, and instead of trying to
conceal his movements began to fire the villages which he first
found on passing the cedar brake and entering the canyon.
These, however, had been deserted. The first one was at a place
now called the Blue waterhole, on the west bank of the river, at
the extreme entrance of the south end of the canyon. No Indians were as yet in sight, but they were concentrating further
up the valley, where the greatest confusion prevailed. Crowds of
squaws and children were fleeing north up the canyon, and warriors were coming south from the upper villages to meet and fight
the invaders. There has been some doubt as to where the final
battle was fought. There was a tradition among the early settlers
of the valley that it occurred below the present site of Utopia,
along the brakes of the river, across the land now owned by Mr.
Tampke. On one occasion a young man named Harly Martin
told the writer he believed he had found a place where a battle
had been fought. I asked him why so, and he said on account of
the numerous bullets he had found there. I examined the balls
and found there two sizes—the large ounce ball and buckshot.
This was the kind of ammunition used in those days by the Mexican soldiers, and they fired them out of a short musket called an
escopet. They were done up in paper cartridges, and called "buck
and ball" by the Americans. The ounce ball was in front and
three buckshot behind it. The Mexicans used the same kind of
cartridges when they fought the Texans at the battle of San
Jacinto. Also a few copper balls were found. I at once asso-

ciated this place with Uvalde's battleground. It is situated four miles below Utopia on the west bank of the river, several hundred yards from the stream, on a low hill which is the extreme south ·end of the divide between Salt marsh and the river. It is now in the pasture of Mr. John Kincaid, of Uvalde. Five hundred yards north of this ridge is another higher hill, part of the same divide, with a timbered valley between. Here also bullets were found, but not so many as on the first hill mentioned. On towards the river and across the field of Mr. Tampke other signs of the battle were seen—bullets, arrow-heads, etc. I made a close examination of these places in company with my brother, Mr. P. S. Sowell, of Seguin, and concluded beyond a doubt that this was the famous field of strife. My son, Lee, who was also along, found a human tooth.

Here then the fierce, painted warriors assembled to try issues with their no less dusky foes. It was a fine position to make a stand, for the view to the south was unobstructed to the mouth of the canyon, six miles away. The Indians could see the smoke of the burning villages below and the advancing Mexicans. When Uvalde's men arrived at the point of the hill and commenced the assault the battle must have been long and fierce. Thousands of musket balls must have fallen like hail on the hill, from the amount of them found there at this late day. Of course those that fell in the flats have long since been covered up by decaying vegetation. After a hard rain is the best time to find the balls on the hill, for they are moved out of place and sometimes are found lying clearly exposed on flat rocks. This first hill was finally carried, and the Comanches retreated across the flat and made a stand on the next ridge, but evidently not of long duration, for not many bullets are found here. The rout of the Indians being now complete, they broke away from here and went down the steep bluff on the north side of the hill and scattered along the banks of the river.

Uvalde pursued the Indians relentlessly for twenty miles, in fact until he drove them out of the canyon and on to the rocky divide along the brakes of the Llano, burning all of the villages and taking all the stock that could be secured. The squaws and papooses were scattered for many miles through the brakes and gorges.

At this time the Apaches lived in the Medina valley and their stronghold was around the Bandera Pass, as it is now called. A force sent out from San Antonio under General Bandera defeated and drove them away.

After Uvalde's fight the canyon was called by his name. I saw a deed to some property in Utopia which read, "Being and situated in the Canyon de Uvalde, in the town of Montania." Montania was the name of the place until changed to the one it now bears. When the country settled the name of the valley was changed, but the county and county seat retained it.

JAMES BOWIE'S OLD FORT.

Attacked by a Band of Comanche Warriors—"Nigger" Jim's Perilous Trip for Water—A Texan's Deadly Rifle Shot.

There is a place on the divide between Dry and Main Frio where is a circular pile of rocks resembling an old fortification. These rocks had been placed there at an early day by the hand of man. The fort, which I call this rude structure, was built on the south side of the hill which slopes towards the Main Frio. It makes a complete circle except a gap at the lower end which had been left for a place of entrance. Some of the stones are very large and would have required the united efforts of a dozen men to put them in place. The height of the rock wall when first built would have covered a man to the neck, and would have been an admirable place to stand off a band of Indians, which no doubt was the purpose for which it was constructed.

When the writer first discovered this place many years ago, although it was known to the old settlers years before that, I made a critical examination of the surroundings to see if I could determine the cause for building this rude fort in such an out of the way place. I half suspected it had been done by gold or silver hunters, and soon this fact was verified. I noticed the entrance to the fortification was on the lower side toward the foot of the hill and opposite a small cedar brake, as if men would come from that point to enter it in case of danger. As soon as I entered the cedar brake above mentioned the problem was solved at once. I saw an immense pile of soil banked up, and near it a shaft. It was near the base of the hill, not a hundred yards from the fort, near the head of a ravine. It was an old mine, either of gold, silver, or lead, and had been worked many years before. The entrance into the shaft was down a flight of ten steps cut in the soil, which time and the action of water pouring into it during heavy rains had not effaced. At the bottom of the steps the excavations extended west under the hill upon which the fort was built. I did not penetrate it far, on account of having no light. A great deal of the soil which had been taken out had washed into the ravine, which run east towards the Main Frio. On the

mound of soil near the entrance to the shaft grew cedar trees as
large as a man's body, indicating a period prior to the advent of
the Texas pioneers into these mountains, when the country was
full of hostile Indians. The fort on the side of the hill commanded all approaches to the mine, and a signal from the lookout
which I suppose was kept there would bring the workmen into the
inclosure in a short time.

BOWIE'S BATTLE.

In surmising in regard to who worked this mine I at first concluded it was Spaniards or Mexicans, but finally connected this
place to my own satisfaction with the famous Texan, Col. James
Bowie, and the time about 1831. I recollected hearing my father
tell of a circumstance which he heard Colonel Bowie relate in
Gonzales, in substance as follows: That on one occasion about
the time of the above date, while prospecting for gold or silver in
the mountains west of San Antonio, he had sunk a shaft where
there were indications of silver. He had about thirty men with
him, and anticipating attacks from Indians, they fortified their
camp by piling up large rocks. Their position commanded every
approach to their camp and shaft, and also a spring of water
something more than a hundred yards distant at the foot of the
hill. While engaged here working in this shaft they were suddenly attacked one morning by a large body of Comanches.
Bowie and his men at once took refuge in their fortification, and
the battle commenced with great fury. The Indians, however,
were soon driven to cover in the ravines and among the rocks by
the deadly fire of Bowie's men. The fight lasted all day, each
party firing as opportunity offered. During the day, however,
Bowie's men drank up all their water, and began to suffer very
much with thirst. The Indians, from their position in the ravines and rocks, commanded the spring, and it was almost as
much as a man's life was worth for anyone to venture near it.
If the men all sallied from the fort they would be overpowered
by the superior force of the savages; but something must be done
to relieve their thirst, if possible.

A NARROW ESCAPE.

Now, Colonel Bowie owned a strong young negro man named Jim, who was now with him.

"Jim," says Bowie, turning to the negro, who was keeping his head below the level of the fortress, "I want you to take, the canteens and bring us some water from the spring."

"No, sar, Mars Jim; couldn't think of sech a ting. Dem ole Injuns is a layin' dar in dem rocks and bushes an' dey can git up from dar an' kill dis nigger fo' you could say scat twice, and befo' I could half fill dem canteens. No, sar; can't go."

Bowie looked at the negro with his keen, piercing eye, and said: "Jim, which are you the most afraid of, me or those Indians?"

"Well, now," says Jim as he caught the meaning of the eye and question, "if you 'sist on me goin', ob cose I'll go, if de boys is bound to have some water befo' dey can whip de Injuns, an' you 'sist on me goin' den I'll voluntare my service. Hunt up dem canteens. I'm off."

Bowie now told Jim he need not fear, as they could protect him with their rifles from the fort while he was getting the water. It seems the Indians were not expecting anyone to make an attempt to get to the water, and evidently did not see him when he left the inclosure; in fact, they had to keep well hid themselves, as the least exposure of their person brought a whizzing rifle ball from the fort. The negro advanced to the spring, filled the canteens, and was starting back before the Indians discovered him. They now, however, set up a terrible yelling and commenced shooting at him, which also drew the fire from the fort, as several of the Indians had shown themselves. Jim now commenced running as best he could with the canteens dangling about him and several Indians in pursuit, notwithstanding several of their number fell before the deadly aim of Bowie's rifles. All ran back except one burly savage, who dropped his empty gun and pulling his tomahawk ran close to Jim, intending to strike him down with that.

Jim now began to get thoroughly frightened and sang out, "O Mars Jim, shoot dis Injun here! He gwine to hurt somebody here d'rectly."

A DEAD SHOT.

Bowie's gun was empty, but he was rapidly ramming a ball, when a rifle cracked from the lower edge of the inclosure and the Indian fell back so suddenly his feet flew up in the air. Jim, who was running and watching the Indian at the same time, again shouted out, "Never mind now, Mars Jim. Mars Bob done knock his heels higher'n his head."

The negro soon arrived safe in the fort, puffing and blowing, but unhurt, and bringing all the canteens with him.

"Now, Mars Jim," he said between breaths, "make dis water go fur as possible. It won't take much mo' dis kind a work to be one nigger less in dis big wide world. De wool lacked a flew dat time. All dat kept dat big, ugly debbil frum puttin' dat hatchet on my head cause Mars Bob hold him load back and make de bullet cum straight. Ha! ha! ha! You orter hear him grunt when dat piece lead took him kerchug."

The "Mars Bob" to whom Jim here alludes was Robert Armstrong, one among the bravest and best rifle shots of the men that followed the fortunes of Bowie. The negro either knew the crack of his gun or saw him when about to fire, as he kept turning his head alternately from the fort to the Indian as he ran and called for help. It was Armstrong who shot the Indian through the head as he was attempting to fire the grass around them during Bowie's terrible fight in the San Saba hills while in search of a gold mine up there in the following year.

This negro lived for many years after the death of Colonel Bowie in the Alamo, and went by name of "Black Jim Bowie."

On this present occasion the Indians withdrew when night came, and nothing more was seen of them. This place is 100 miles west of San Antonio.

Since the writer visited this old mine parties have been at work there opening up the old shaft, which had been greatly filled up by the washing in of soil and small rocks. They brought to light twelve more of those steps alluded to, and then come to the top of a cedar ladder. When the bottom of this was reached it was found to be twenty feet long, and at its foot lay a pick. It was short and heavy and was made on an anvil, as the hammered spots indicated. It is not known if any thing in the way of paying ore was found.

EARLY HISTORY OF GUADALUPE COUNTY.

Guadalupe County was originally a part of Gonzales, which latter was settled by colonists from the United States under Green De Witt, who contracted among others with the Mexican government, who then owned the country, to bring and settle a given number of families at various places which were assigned them.

These contractors were called empresarios, or emperors on a small scale, and the magistrates of the towns were called alcaldes. For their services in bringing and settling the families the contractors received fifteen leagues and two labors (labores) each, or 66,774 acres of land. Each immigrant who was the head of a family received one league and a labor of land, which was called his headright. A league of land contains 4428 acres, and a labor contains 177 acres. Each head of a family could make his own selection for a place to locate his headright.

De Witt selected a spot on the Guadalupe River one mile below its confluence with the San Marcos River to plant his first colonists and build a town. In 1825 the first colonists arrived with the surveyor James Kerr, and went to work. Among these were — Berry, Edward Morehouse, Henry S. Brown, Elijah Stapp, John Wightman, — Durbin, and Erastus Smith, afterwards known as "Deaf" Smith, the famous spy and scout of the Texas army. This first installment was broken up by the Indians, and Wightman killed and Durbin severely wounded. By the year 1830 the settlement was firmly established, and in 1832 the town named Gonzales, for Raphael Gonzales, Provisional Governor of Texas, as was also the county, which at that time extended to the line of Bexar, including all of the territory of what is now Guadalupe County.

Among the families which came in 1829 were those of John Sowell, grandfather of the writer, and his son-in-law, Humphrey Branch. As most of the best land in the vicinity of Gonzales had been taken up, these two came on up the Guadalupe River in search of a location, and passed over the spot where Seguin is now in 1831. At the mouth of the Comal River they turned back.

Branch located his league and labor on the spot where Seguin is now situated, and John Sowell located his league in the bend of the river below, now known as the Stuart Bend, but reserved his labor and located it at the mouth of what is now called Sowell's Creek, where it empties into the Guadalupe, six miles below town.

The next fall or winter they both moved from Gonzales and settled on Sowell's Creek and commenced clearing land. Their nearest neighbors were at Gonzales, and no white family lived west of them.

In 1833 the Sowell boys—Andrew, William, Louis, John, and Asa—raised the first corn ever raised by white men within the present limits of Guadalupe County. It was planted between the creek bottom and the river, in what is now the Lay farm, and about forty bushels per acre were gathered.

Other colonists came in during the year and settled on the river above the mouth of Mill Creek, among whom were Dickinson, Baker, Tomlinson, Montgomery, and others. In this year also Humphrey Branch moved up and settled on his league. His house stood on the spot now known as the Neill place, but was called by him "Elm Spring Hill."

At this time the prairie stretched away from the river without a bush to obstruct the view as far almost as the eye could reach, dotted here and there with small motts of liveoaks. At times vast herds of buffalo could be seen crossing the prairie north and coming towards the river. At times they would stampede, and the noise of their running resembled an approaching hurricane. Walnut branch at that time was a rushing torrent fed by a large spring at its head, which sent a perfect sluice of water to the river.

The settlers in the meantime at the mouth of the two creeks were doing well and thought they were settled in permanent homes. Some had milk cows, game was in abundance, and living cheap. The country also abounded in dangerous wild animals, such as bears, panthers, Mexican lions, and tigers. Often on moonlight nights grandfather's family could see bears crossing the open flats between the creek and river bottom. On one occasion Mrs. Baker was coming up the river to a neighbor's house when she was suddenly confronted in the trail by a ferocious-looking animal. The woman was badly frightened, and after setting the dogs upon it which were following her, turned and ran back. The dogs were badly whipped, and one of them killed. The next morning James Tomlinson killed a large tiger near the carcass of the slain dog. On another occasion a large bear ran through grandfather's yard in daylight, but did no harm except to give the small children and women a scare, the boys being gone. A panther also came one night and took a pig out of a pen in the rear of the house, but the boys and dogs gave him such a hot chase he was compelled to drop it and take to a tree in the creek bottom, where he was killed. One morning a settler went out to hunt and was never seen or heard of again. His dog come back on the following day, badly torn and mangled. About this time two of the Moore children were lost, girls eight and ten years of age. They went out in the evening to drive up the cows, but never returned. Diligent search was made for them many days but without success. Andrew Sowell hunted sixteen days for them. On York's Creek he found a small bit of the dress worn by one of the girls, which had been torn off by a thorny bush. At the time the little girls disappeared an old blind horse on the place was also missing, and it was believed the children had managed to mount this horse to search for the cows and had lost their way. This old horse was also found by Andrew Sowell on York's Creek, near the "Big Thicket." Whether they were carried off by Indians or perished in the woods no one could ever tell.

For some time after the settlement commenced at Sowell's Creek no signs of Indians were seen, but one day a hunter came in and reported that Indians were in the vicinity, for that day he had crossed the trail of a red man. This news caused some uneasiness, and the settlers were ever on the alert. Things went on in this way for some days, when suddenly a band of Indians boldly entered the settlement. They professed friendship and camped and hunted several days on the river, but when they departed two horses were missing out of the neighborhood. It was believed that the Indians got them, and Andrew Sowell, James Tomlinson, Montgomery, and two others armed themselves and went in search of the missing horses. At the mouth of Mill Creek in the river bottom they found the horses in the possession of two Indians. They were disarmed and taken into custody and carried to the house of Dickinson, near the spot where the farm house of Thomas D. Johnson afterwards stood, on the west bank of Mill Creek. Here the settlers who had captured the Indians proposed to try the Indians and come to some understanding as to what disposition to make of them. Dickinson was not at home, and after some consultation these men passed a law among themselves that the punishment of all horse-thieves, whether white or red, should be death, and at once carried the Indians off to execute them. Mrs. Dickinson implored them not to kill them near her house. It was then decided to carry them across a ravine to a grove of timber on elevated ground. As they walked along Montgomery was on the right of the largest Indian. They knew what was in store for them, and commenced conversing in a low tone in the Indian dialect. Andrew Sowell was closely watching them as they talked, and was satisfied from their actions that they were going to make a desperate attempt to escape, and although disarmed, warned Montgomery not to walk too near the big Indian. By this time they were nearing the place of execution.

"All right," said Montgomery, in answer to the warning; "I am watching him, and if he makes a move I will plug him." These words had scarcely left his lips when the Indian, with a motion almost as quick as lightning, drew a long knife from somewhere about his person and plunged it to the hilt in Montgomery's breast, who sank to the earth without a groan, and expired in a few moments. Both Indians now made a quick leap and ran. Three shots were fired almost together, and the big Indian, the one who killed Montgomery, fell dead before he had gone a dozen yards; but the men in their hurry and confusion shot one of their own number, wounding him severely in the leg. The other Indian was not hit and was about to escape, when one of the men snatched up the dead man's gun and at a distance of more than one hundred yards shot the Indian dead in his tracks. This occurred in the timber south of the widow Patterson's farm.

After this occurrence the Indians did not show themselves, but prowled about the country and their tracks were frequently seen. One evening as two of the youngest Sowell boys, John and Asa, the latter being the youngest and father of the writer, were out after the cows they saw an Indian secrete himself ahead of them, evidently with the intention of killing or capturing them. Terror lent wings to their feet, and they soon arrived at home and told the news. Search was made for the Indian, but he could not be found.

There were no mills of any kind in the settlement, and John Sowell made a mortar to pestle corn in. This was a heavy liveoak log (short) with a cavity chiseled in the end of it sufficient to hold several quarts of corn. It was set on end and the corn beaten into coarse meal with a wooden pestle, having nails driven thickly in the end of it. Years afterwards, when this property came into the possession of Mr. Wilson Lay, this old mortar was still to be seen there. Mr. Mitty Lay told the writer that he remembered seeing it many times. An attempt was made by some of the younger Sowells to recover it in after years as a relic, but it could not be found.

On account of Indians and trouble brewing with the Mexicans this settlement was broken up, and by the year 1835 they were all back at Gonzales. Branch left his place and came to Sowell's Creek and they went back together, and for several years no human being crossed the spot where Seguin now stands except it were Indians or fugitive Mexicans from the battlefield of San Jacinto.

The Mexicans commenced the trouble by sending a company of men to demand a small cannon which was in the possession of the settlers at Gonzales. They refused to give it up, with the excuse that their alcalde was absent, and the matter would be referred to him on his return. This was done to gain time, although the chief magistrate was absent. That evening eighteen men assembled under arms, runners were sent to other settlements for reinforcements, and a boy named John Gaston ascended a tall tree to watch the Mexicans. This gallant boy was killed the following year in the Alamo when it was stormed by the Mexican army, as was also Almon Dickinson, one of the first settlers in the present limit of Guadalupe County.

We will not go into the details of the war for Texas independence, the flight of the settlers before Santa Anna, and the great victory at San Jacinto, which is a matter of Texas history, and is mentioned incidentally in some of the sketches of old veterans in other parts of this work. I will here, however, give the names of those who had gotten back to Gonzales up to 1838, many of whom were citizens of Guadalupe County after it was made such, to wit: Judge McClure, Mr. Havens, the Lockharts, the De

Witts, Simon Bateman, Ben Duncan, the Hodges, Colonel King, J. D. Clements, Widow Rowe (husband killed in Alamo), — Fraiser, Geo. W. Davis, Almon Cottle, the Berrys, Daniel Davis, John Clark, I. J. Good, Eli Mitchell, Matthew Caldwell, James Patrick, Adam Zumwalt, Ezekiel Williams, E. Bellinger, Miles Dikes, the Sowells, the Darst and Nichols families, Wm. A. Matthews, Dr. John T. Tinsley, Widow Fuqua (husband killed in the Alamo), Maj. V. Bennett, Henry and Ben McCulloch (brothers), John McCoy, Wilson and Barney Randle (brothers), Arthur Swift, the Smiths, Kings, Days, V. Henderson, James H. Calahan (escaped from Fannin's massacre), John S. Saump, Baskes and Rhodes, Mitchell Putnam, — Kinkennon, William Morrison, Aulcy Miller, Kit Ackland, Clem Hines, Eli Hankins, Nathan Burkett, Simon Cockerell, — Wolfin, — Cooksey, — Hoskins, George Edwards, Arch Gibson, John Archer, Arch Jones, Josh Threadgill, W. B. Hargess, — Grubbs, — Baker, R. Miller, John Miller, — Killin, C. C. Colley, — Fraiser, Pony Hall, and Robert Hall. All of these did not live in the town of Gonzales, but in the colony in and around the town, and many of them were in the battle of San Jacinto.

By this time the settlers had again pushed out towards the west, and the smoke from the white man's cabin once more floated over the green liveoaks on the spot where Seguin now stands. As we have before stated, Humphrey Branch built a house here in 1833. The next one was built by Robert Hall six years after. It stood on Walnut branch, not far from the spot where Judge Doc Douglas afterwards settled. Humphrey Branch sold his league of land here and never returned any more. In 1838 three Mexican families lived in the vicinity of Seguin. Manuel Flores and Jose M. Cardinus lived on the south side of the river and had large ranches on the property afterwards owned by Gen. William Saffold. Antonio Navarro and Luciano Navarro had ranches north of town on the San Geronimo Creek, where Ewing Springs is now. Before any settlements were made here Ben McCulloch was in command of a company of rangers and stationed at Walnut Springs, now almost in the heart of the city of Seguin, for the defense of Gonzales County against Indians.

Guadalupe County takes its name from the Guadalupe River, which derived its name from a shrine in Mexico, "Maestro Dona de Guadalupe" ("Our Lady of Waurloopa"). Most of the early

settlers called the river "The Warloop." The county was not
organized until 1846, and was up to that time known as Gonzales
County. It is bounded on the north by Comal, Hays, and Cald-
well; Wilson on the south, Gonzales on the east, and Bexar on the
west. The first Americans who settled in the county after the
battle of San Jacinto were Henry and Ben McCulloch, Andrew
Neill, Colonel Young, Andrew Sowell, John Sowell, Asa Sowell,
John Nichols, James Nichols, Tom Nichols, Soloman Nichols,
Milford Day, Soloman Brill, James H. Calahan, William S.
Turner and his sons, William, Calvin, Hardin, and John. Then
there were the Mays, Johnsons, Smiths, Olivers, Toms, Jones,
Wilson Randle, Hopple, T. N. Menter, Boyds, Kings, Henderson, and others. The first families were few in number, and
drawn closer together by their isolation. They were sociable,
free-hearted, and respected, and were ever ready to aid and assist
those who needed it. They depended on each other in time of
danger. Soon after the first settlers many others came and occupied the rich bottom prairie lands.

The county seat of Guadalupe County was laid out in 1838.
Its first document is dated "the 12th of August, 1838, Gonzales
County, Republic of Texas." Henry and Ben McCulloch, Arthur
Swift, J. A. Martin, Matthew Caldwell, and James Campbell
were instrumental in laying out the town on the eastern half of
the Humphrey Branch league, situated on the north side of the
river, half way between the town of Gonzales and the city of San
Antonio, being thirty-six miles to each. This tract of land was
divided into four classes of lots, which were located in the center
of the tract from east to west. It was first laid off into fifty-six
blocks two hundred feet square, with a seventy-foot street between each block; the second center blocks were designated as a
public and market square, and the blocks fronting this square
were divided into ten lots, the remainder of the blocks were divided into eight lots. Outside of these blocks was a tier of blocks
of one-acre lots, and that portion of the tract fronting the river
was laid off into five-acre lots. The northern being much the
largest portion of the tract, it was laid off into twelve-acre lots
and called farm lots, and the said lots were then divided in forty-
four shares. J. S. Martin, then being the owner of the land, reserved ten shares, and the remainder were sold to the following
parties: Arthur Swift, W. W. Killen, H. P. King, Barney Ran-

dle, John R. King, Wilson Randle, P. E. Beall, Abe Roberts, P. Martin, W. Clinton, J. Roberts, J. A. Swift, Milford Day, Andrew Neill, W. A. Hall, Matthew Caldwell, M. Cody, W. Cody, A. S. Emmett, John Russell, Miles Dikes, G. W. Nichols, J. W. Nichols, Cyrus Crosby, French Smith, H. G. Henderson, R. St. Clair, Andrew Sowell, W. S. Beebe, Kelley Matthews, and Robert Hall.

On the 22d of September, 1838, the shareholders met, and after arranging the preliminaries, proceeded to draw their lots, which was done by placing the number of shares on slips of paper, and the lots were arranged in the same manner, and these were placed in a hat and drawn out by Asa J. L. Sowell, then a youth 17 years of age. The names of the shareholders were then called out after the drawing. The town was then named Walnut Springs, taking its name from the many walnut trees which grew along the margin of the spring branches.

The lots were to be sold for $50, and each shareholder was to build a house in the town and settle either in person or by proxy. Some of the shareholders failing to comply with the terms of contract, their shares were sold to others on the 23d of February, 1839.

On the 25th of February, 1839, another council was held, at which they changed the name of the town. Seven voted it be called Tuscumbia and eighteen Seguin, in honor of Col. Juan N. Seguin, a Mexican, who was at that time a fast friend of the Americans and fought with them for the independence of Texas, and commanded a small company of his countrymen at the battle of San Jacinto. Some years later, for some fancied or real grievance, he turned traitor to Texas and moved with his family to Mexico, and returned with the invading army of General Wall and fought against the Texans at the battle of Salado.

As soon as the settlement commenced at Seguin it attracted the attention of the hostile bands of Indians who roamed in the wilds of the great West. The leading Indian fighters at that time were Ed. Burleson, Jack Hays, Henry and Ben McCulloch, Matthew Caldwell, and James H. Callahan.

Grandfather John Sowell died at Gonzales soon after returning at the close of the war with the Mexicans. William was killed there in a difficulty, Louis died there, and Andrew, John, and Asa, his boys, came and settled on their league below Seguin.

Soon after the settlement was made at Seguin Capt. Matthew Caldwell raised a company of minute men for its protection and kept scouts out, especially west of the setltement. About this time Gen. Vincent Cordova, a disaffected Mexican who lived at Nacogdoches, left there with a motley crowd of Mexicans, runaway negroes, and Biloxi Indians, and started to Mexico, stealing horses as they went and committing other depredations. Their trail was discovered at the crossing of the Colorado by the scouts of Gen. Ed. Burleson, and he went in pursuit with his rangers. Cordova was overtaken in Guadalupe County, five miles east of Seguin, on Mill Creek, at a place now called Battle Ground Prairie. The impetuous charge of the rangers soon broke the formation of the enemy and they ran, firing as they went. Night put an end to the pursuit two miles south, in the edge of the Guadalupe bottom. How many were killed could not be ascertained. Three rangers were wounded, but none killed. Citizens of Seguin, among whom was the father of the writer, came out to the battleground next morning. The grass had been set on fire by paper wads from shotguns of some of Burleson's men, and had burned all over the country, exposing plainly to view several dead bodies. The fight commenced at the head of a ravine around which the Seguin road now runs near the Handley place. Here were the bodies of two dead Mexicans. About one hundred yards from these further south in the prairie lay two negroes, and an Indian with his head cut off was under a mesquite tree on the rising ground south of the road. The Mexicans and others of the band in their flight passed over the spot where now is the farm of Mr. Clay Butler. One old negro was captured and carried to Seguin, but was there shot on account of statements he made of killing white women and children. A young wounded negro was also taken.

Cordova's band traveled up the west bank of the river after crossing, and at daylight came upon the Seguin scouts, members of Captain Caldwell's minute company. They were Milford Day, Tom Nichols, and David Runnels. This was near Young's ford. The scouts made a fight, but were forced to leave their camp, losing everything, including horses and saddles, and Milford Day

27

was badly wounded. His comrades, however, bore him to the river and secreted him under a bluff, and Tom Nichols then swam the river and went to Seguin after assistance. A cart was sent back strongly guarded, and Day brought in. Cordova was pursued to the Nueces River by citizens and rangers, but was not again overtaken.

In 1840 the Comanche Indians, about 500 in number, made a raid through Texas and burned the town of Linnville, on the coast, a trading point on Lavaca Bay. Among the victims of this raid were Dr. Gray, Mr. McNuner, Vartland Richardson, Pinkney Caldwell, Major Watts, Mr. O'Neill, Dr. Bell, one Mexican, four negroes, and the infant of Mrs. Crosby. Besides those slain they carried off Mrs. Crosby, Mrs. Watts, and a negro girl as prisoners. Men rallied from every point to fight them on their return, and the battle took place at Plum Creek, now in Caldwell County. Among the Guadalupe (present limits) County men who helped to win the victory were James Nichols, Ben and Henry McCulloch, Ezekiel Smith, French Smith, Andrew Sowell, and Milford Day. James Nichols was wounded. During the battle Henry McCulloch and others rescued Dr. Switzer, who was surrounded by Indians and was helpless, on account of having one arm pinned to his side with an arrow.

Among the men in the fight from other places were Gen. Ed. Burleson, Gen. Felix Houston, Jack Hays, Gen. Matthew Caldwell, Clark L. Owens, Thos. W. Ward, W. B. Dewees, Col. John H. Moore, Monroe Hardeman, W. J. E. Wallace, Dr. Brown, Judge Clint C. De Witt, Aulcy Miller, Maj. A. S. Miller, Judge Bellinger, Dr. Switzer, Rev. Z. N. Morrell, Rev. R. E. B. Baylor, Rev. T. W. Cox, Ben Highsmith, Tom Galbreath, John Jenkins, and many others.

At the commencement of the fight the Indians attempted to kill their prisoners. Mrs. Crosby was shot in the breast and soon expired, but not before her husband had dismounted by her side and soothed her last moments. Mrs. Watts was also shot in the breast, but the arrow, striking a steel corset which she wore, glanced and gave her a painful but not fatal wound. Her screams attracted Z. N. Morrell, the pioneer Baptist preacher, to the spot, who dismounted and attempted to withdraw the arrow, but was at first unsuccessful on account of the wounded lady holding on to it as if not being able to withstand the pain of having it withdrawn. About this time Dr. Brown of Gonzales came upon the scene, and while the preacher held the hands of Mrs. Watts the doctor removed the shaft. The Rev. Morrell then spread his blanket under a liveoak tree for her to recline upon, and she soon became composed. Near by was the body of the negro woman, who had also been killed.

On one occasion, while Seguin was in the incipiency of its settlement, a band of Indians were running buffalo on the prairie north of town. The herd became scattered and one turned towards the river, pursued by several Indians. Now, Seguin was a small place at this time, and almost obscured from view under the liveoak trees along the spring branches, and probably the Indians or buffalo were not aware of its existence. Be this as it may, however, they ran the buffalo into town, and one of them shot it with such force with an arrow that the spike came through the hide on the opposite side, having passed between the ribs. The Indians made no halt, but dashed on and crossed the river south of town. At this time there were no houses around the square, but the noise of the running brought several citizens out where they could see what caused the commotion, and beheld the Indian when he bent his bow, and with the spike almost touching the side of the buffalo sent the arrow into him. Before a pursuit could be organized the Indians made their escape into the sandhills. The wounded buffalo ran around in a circle a few times, and then fell and died near where the courthouse now stands, and was cut up and divided among the citizens.

On September 11, 1842, the Mexicans under Gen. Adrian Wall very unexpectedly to the Texans advanced from Mexico and captured San Antonio. The district court was in session, and the members were taken prisoners, among whom were Col. Andrew Neill, of Seguin, and Rev. Gustav Elly, the latter a resident of the county for many years, and who died at Seguin at a very advanced age. The news was carried swiftly from settlement to settlement, and once more the call to arms was sounded along the border to repel Mexican invasion. This call was, as ever, promptly obeyed by the brave pioneers of the Guadalupe, San Marcos, and Colorado valleys. Once more the gallant Hays, Caldwell, and others rallied their chosen scouts and rangers around them. Seguin was the place of rendezvous, and all night long before the start on the following morning men were busy making preparations to meet once more the dusky sons of Mexico on the field of battle. There was a scarcity of horses among the citizens of Seguin on account of a recent Indian raid, and men gave high prices for common Spanish ponies that would carry them to San Antonio. All through the night men were coming from the east. Rifles were cleaned and bullets moulded. Those that had no horses were trying to make trades for them, offering land or anything else almost three times the value of them. Two men fought over a stray horse which happened to be in town, until neither one was able to go. Enough of Guadalupe County men, however, got off to count in the news of the battle, which, as has been stated in other places, was fought on the Salado near San Antonio. The following men from Guadalupe County participated: Henry E. McCulloch, James H. Calahan, Ezekiel Smith, French Smith, Soloman Brill, Calvin Turner, William Turner, Hardin Turner, Andrew Sowell, T. N. Menter, Wilson Randle, Andrew Erskine, John P. Erskine, William King, John King, Milford Day, and probably some others who can not now be recalled. After the departure of Caldwell and his 200 men, when a sufficient time had elapsed the people at Seguin began to look anxiously for messengers from the scene of action. Only six years had elapsed since nearly that many had perished in the Alamo, and they had left home as light-hearted and as confident as those now under Caldwell. Once more the mothers and wives of the Guadalupe valley had to watch and wait, every minute expecting the messenger of death to dash in upon them bringing the sad news of defeat and slaughter like that which befell Travis and Fannin. They thought these fears were realized when Aulcy Miller rode into town, bareheaded, his horse covered with foam, a fugitive from Dawson's battlefield, and bringing the news of a most desperate fight, that nearly all of Dawson's men were killed, and that he and one other alone made their escape by hard and desperate riding. He knew nothing of Caldwell's men. They heard heavy firing in the direction of the creek, and were hurrying rapidly to their assistance, when they were surrounded by the whole Mexican army and cut to pieces.

The father of the writer stood by Miller's panting horse and heard him tell the sad tale of Dawson's defeat. The Indians had stolen father's horse, and he could not go. Miller was badly

MASSACRE OF DAWSON'S MEN.

sunburned, and father took a fine Mexican hat from his own head and placed it on that of Miller as a present.

Nicholas Dawson was a lieutenant in the battle of San Jacinto, and fought in the front where men fell thick, and rejoiced with his comrades over the victory and the independence of Texas, and when the messenger came announcing another invasion, he rallied his neighbors around him and met his fate at the hands of his old enemies. On the way from Fayette County to join Caldwell, Dawson made his last camp on Nash's Creek, in what is now the lower edge of Guadalupe County. Here he met Caldwell's messenger urging every one forward, and hastened on, making an all-night ride.

Here are the names of those who fell with him: Lieutenant Dickinson, Zodack Woods (80 years of age), — Church, Harvey Hall, Robert Barclay, Wesley Scallorn, Eliam Scallorn, Asa Jones, Robert Eastland, Frank Brookfield, George Hill, John W. Pendelton, J. B. Alexander, Edmond Timble, Charles Field, Thomas Simms, — Butler, John Dancer, and a negro man belonging to the Mavericks. This negro was sent out by Mrs. Maverick to communicate with his master, who had been captured while attending court at San Antonio. He was faithful to his trust and fought bravely in the battle, dying by the side of Captain Dawson.

The bones of these brave men now rest on Monument Hill, opposite La Grange, in Fayette County. The gallant patriots from the Colorado valley were ever ready to peril their lives in defense of their country, and there was hardly a battle fought in Texas where their blood did not stain the soil, and on this occasion, when the fiery Dawson came among them calling on them to rally to the defense of the "Lone Star," they seized their rifles and told him to lead the way, and rushed day and night to their death.

Wilson Randle, of Seguin, killed General Cordova in the battle on the Salado. Cordova had returned from Mexico with the army of General Wall to help chastise the Texans for his defeat at Mill Creek. Calvin Turner was the only man hurt from Seguin in the battle. He had a glancing shot from a musket ball on the side of the head.

In 1843 Captain James H. Calahan raised a company of minute men for the protection of Guadalupe County, which was constantly harassed by Indians and Mexican horsethieves. Now, before this time a Mexican named Flores had raised a band of robbers, and after committing some depredations between Seguin and San Antonio went on towards northern Texas to incite all the Indian tribes to make war on the Texans. The career of this freebooter, however, was short. He was pursued by Lieut. James O. Rice, of the rangers, and overtaken on the San Gabriel, about twenty miles from Austin.

In the battle which ensued the Mexicans were defeated and Flores killed. Rice captured 300 pounds of powder, a quantity of lead, shot, and balls, and about 100 head of mules and horses.

On the person of Flores were found papers and letters showing the grand scheme of the Mexicans of arousing and inciting all the border Indians to aid them in the war with Texas.

Flores had messages from General Canalizo, of Matamoros, to the chiefs of the Caddoes, Seminoles, Biloxis, Cherokees, Kickapoos, Brazos, Tehuacanas, and others. By concert of action, at the same time the Mexican army marched into San Antonio, the Indians were to light up the whole frontier with the flames of Texas dwellings and cause the very air to resound with cries of women and children. It was well for Texas at this time that she had a Hays, a McCulloch, a Burleson, a Caldwell, a Calahan, and a James O. Rice on her borders to hurl defiance to her thousands of foes, and who dared to lead where any dared follow.

While Calahan was operating in Guadalupe County with his company, Jack Hays was on a scout in the Sabinal and Seco mountains with his men, and finding a large force of Comanches, sent for Captain Calahan to come and help him to fight them. Calahan took a portion of his men and went at once. He found Hays in the mountains at the head of the Sabinal River, and the Indians strongly posted on a high, rough mountain. Captain Hays and his men had one fight with them in the valley, in which sixteen of the Indians were killed, and they had retreated up the mountain. The combined force of the rangers assaulted their position and drove them off. The only casualties on the side of the white men was one of Hays' men wounded. Calahan, Ben McCulloch, and Andrew Sowell from Seguin were in the fight. McCulloch had a very long range gun, and did good service in picking off Indians from the crags and high places that others could not reach.

Mr. H. G. Henderson, a resident of Guadalupe County, while in San Antonio soon after this learned that a band of horse-thieves had a hiding place near Seguin. He lost no time in communicating the same to the ranger captain. The best scouts were sent out from time to time to get trace of them, but for some time were unsuccessful, but finally Milford Day, who was a good trailer, located them in a dense thicket on York's Creek, about eight miles northeast from Seguin. This thicket was cut through by a deep gully near which was the camp of the robbers.

Captain Calahan and a portion of his men approached on foot through the underbrush, often crawling upon their hands and knees, and succeeded in surprising them. The Mexicans, after hastily firing their escopets, scattered into the brush, and most of them escaped, the rangers only getting one fire at them. Two or three were killed and several wounded. The rangers returned to Seguin, but in a few days came back again to look around, and found a wounded Mexican at a spring. He was killed by one of Calahan's men. Near the place was a round, rocky hill, with a grove of liveoaks growing on its crest, and there the Mexican was buried by the rangers, and to this day it goes by the name of the "Rogue's Grave," and the place where they fought is called "Rogue's Hollow."

Soon after this two more Mexican horse-thieves were caught and brought in. By a vote they were condemned to be shot. They

MILFORD DAY, ONE OF THE FIRST SETTLERS OF
GUADALUPE COUNTY.

were executed and buried under some liveoak trees in the western
portion of town, near the General Jefferson place. The members
of Calahan's company who were present besides himself were Milford Day, Calvin Turner, Andrew Sowell, John Sowell, Asa Sowell, John Nichols, and some others, likely. Calvin Turner was
one of the four who did the firing. The Mexicans were made to
dig their own graves by Captain Calahan. This fearless ranger
captain saw the fearful butchery of Texans at Goliad, saw his
comrades shot down right and left after they had surrendered,—
men who had stood shoulder to shoulder with him and had fought
as men seldom fight, and for nine long hours in an open prairie
held an army at bay.

During these years the Lipan Indians, then friendly, came

from the Colorado valley and made their camp at the Walnut Springs by permission of the settlers. They went on many hunting trips and often came in contact with the Comanches, their bitter enemies. On one occasion, while the tribe was camped here, one of their hunting parties had a fight with the Comanches up the river near where New Braunfels is, and defeated them, killing four. They returned with the scalps, and that night had a scalp dance in their camp at the springs, and invited the citizens of Seguin to witness it, which many of them did.

At the time of which we write Castro was head chief of the Lipans and Flacco was second chief. The latter delighted to accompany Jack Hays (one of the most famous Texas rangers that ever lit a camp fire on the frontier of Texas) against the Comanches, and fought bravely by his side on several occasions.

Captain Hays was early identified with the people of Seguin, marrying a daughter of Major Calvert of this place, and was brother-in-law to Col. Thomas D. Johnson and Alfred Shelby of this place, who also married daughters of Major Calvert. One night in 1844, while a dance was in progress at the house of Milford Day, near the Walnut Springs, a band of hostile Indians made a raid in the vicinity and attempted to carry off some horses. They were discovered by John R. King, who was on guard, and he fired on them. One of the Indians returned the fire, and then they all retreated. The alarm was soon given, and the dance came to an abrupt termination. The men at the dance all had their guns, and a party was soon mounted and in pursuit. They were William King, Henry King, John R. King, Andrew Sowell, Anderson Smith, Paris Smith, and Milford Day. The night was dark, and the settlers, after riding through the prairie for some time, and finding no clew to the whereabouts of the Indians, repaired to the Three-mile waterhole. By this time a drizzling rain had set in, and they sat under the liveoak trees and held their horses by the bridles until morning. As soon as it was light enough they again set out in quest of the Indians, and found their trail near Plum Ridge. It led up the river, and the men followed rapidly and soon came upon them, as the Indians were on foot and twelve in number. The place was near Twelve-mile Spring in the prairie. Only one of the Indians carried a gun, and he dropped down in the grass and attempted to fire at William King and Anderson Smith, who were riding close to-

gether. His gun failed to fire, and he was instantly killed, shot
through the head by William King. A curious fight now commenced. When the balance of the settlers attempted to fire all of
their guns failed, and the Indians commenced yelling and shooting arrows, but they fell harmless, having no force. The trouble
was that the rain during the night had spoiled the caps on the
guns of the white men, and had also wet the bowstrings of the
Indians and they had relaxed, being made of sinews, and an arrow could not be sent with any force. It was not far to the river,
and the Indians soon ran in that direction, followed by the settlers, who put on fresh caps as they ran, and tried in vain to fire
on them, but the tubes were stopped up from the damp friction
of the inferior caps of those days, and it was no go. The Indians would turn and make a weak discharge of arrows when the
white men came too close, but no one was hurt. They could be
warded off with arm, hat, or gun barrel. When the Comanches
came to the river they plunged in and commenced swimming
across, and the whack, whack, whack of snapping locks could be
heard on every side as the settlers still continued to try their
pieces. Presently bang went one gun, and an Indian sank, shot
in the back of the head. William King had reloaded his gun, and
coming up at this time had fired and killed another. The balance all got over safely and soon disappeared in the bottom. The
dead Indian in the prairie was scalped and his gun taken, and a
return to Seguin was made.

In 1845 Prince Solms Braunfels arrived at Seguin with German immigrants for Fisher and Miller's colony, but the Indians
being so numerous and hostile in the country where the first intention was to settle (within present limits of Gillespie County),
a large tract of land was purchased on the west bank of the Guadalupe River, at the mouth of the Comal, at the foot of the mountains, and here the colony was settled and their town named New
Braunfels. This colony was not harassed as much by Indians
as those further west, but they suffered all the privations and dis-
comforts of subduing the wilderness and building up homes.
Many of them were poor and had a hard struggle to succeed, but
did so. Some became wealthy and all prospered, and there are
no more thrifty people now than those of Comal County.

From Seguin there was no road leading to the place of destination of the colony, it being northwest from the San Antonio road

up the river. All was prairie and grass. It was necessary to have a guide from there on, and Asa Sowell and Calvin Turner were employed by Prince Solms to pilot them through. They were acquainted with the fords of the Guadalupe, and could go straight across the prairie to the mouth of the Comal. Ferdnand Weyel, who lives on the Santa Clara, is one of the pioneers of that colony, his father having built one of the first houses in New Braunfels.

Guadalupe County was organized in 1846. The first officers were H. G. Henderson, chief justice; Thomas H. Duggan, county clerk; Asa J. L. Sowell, district clerk; Milton Osborne, sheriff, and William G. King, assessor and collector of taxes.

The first term of the district court was held in September, 1846, at the residence of Mr. Paris Smith, afterwards known as the Rust place. Hon. William E. Jones was judge, Asa J. L. Sowell district clerk, John A. Green district attorney, Milton Osborne sheriff. The sitting of the grand jury was in the live-oak grove now inclosed in the yard of G. W. L. Baker. The following are the names of the first grand jury: Paris Smith, foreman; Sam Towner, John F. Tom, S. R. Miller, Col. French Smith, G. W. Lonis, John W. Nichols, C. A. Smith, John Sheffield, Soloman G. Nichols, I. H. Turner, John N. Sowell, John R. King, Matthew A. Doyle, and Andrew J. Sowell, Sr.

The first bill found was State v. William Baker, charged with theft of a hair brush. His sentence was to be publicly whipped in the square. This sentence was only partly carried out, so some of the old settlers say, by Col. French Smith coming on the scene when about five licks were struck, and picking up a rock, told the man who was laying them on to desist.

One of the grand jury, George Washington Lonis, was a veteran of San Jacinto, and was severely wounded in the breast on that occasion, as was also John F. Tom, who had a leg broken by a musket ball there. John Sowell, another one, was also in the battle of San Jacinto, and loaned a pistol to a man to shoot Santa Anna. Matthew Doyle was one of James Bowie's men in his terrible Indian battle near the San Saba gold mines.

The first petit jury was as follows: Solomon W. Brill, foreman; Joseph Zorn, Jacob Eckstein, John Lowe, P. Medlin, W. B. Pinchard, William C. Winters, E. P. Forest, — Baker, William Turner and W. Clark.

In March of the previous year the Indians made a raid in the
vicinity of Seguin and killed a Mexican named Verimendi near
Ewing Springs. Most of the citizens were in Gonzales attending
court. A severe norther and sleet came up soon after the killing
and the settlers followed the trail of the Indians but a short distance, as they were forced to return on account of the cold.

Cottonwood Creek, which empties into the Guadalupe about
three miles below Seguin, on the south side of the river, was
known to the first settlers as "Shawnee Creek." It received this
name from a circumstance which happened there before the white
settlers came into the country. At that time the Comanches were
very numerous in the Guadalupe valley above the forks, and the
Shawnee Indians, a friendly tribe, lived in the white settlement
near Gonzales. They often came up the river on hunting expeditions, and on one occasion encountered the Comanches, their bitter enemies, on the little creek now known as Cottonwood, about
three miles above its mouth. A battle ensued, in which the Shaw-
nees were defeated and two of their chiefs killed. In their retreat
they carried off the bodies of the chiefs and buried them on a
point that fronts on the river, a little below the mouth of the
creek. White hunters from the settlement below also came up
in here hunting and knew of the circumstance above mentioned,
and called the place "Shawnee Creek."

In 1847 a contract for building the first courthouse was let to
Thomas D. Spain. It was a two-story frame building 30x50 feet.
The upper room was to be used as a courtroom; the lower part
was divided into four rooms, for the chief justice, county and
district clerks, and sheriff.

Mrs. Mildred P. King was one of the noble pioneer women of
Guadalupe County, and lost a son (William) at the storming of
the Alamo. When General Wall captured San Antonio and the
settlers there were hurrying to the front to repel the invaders,
Lieut. H. E. McCulloch, of Hays' rangers, was riding night and
day through the settlements notifying the settlers and urging
everyone forward that was able to go. When he came to the
house of Mr. King he said to him, "I know you are too old to go,
but is there not some one on the place who could go?"

His only son old enough to bear arms was standing by impatient for the answer, as the father hung his head in deep emotion. Mrs. King spoke up: "John might be spared from home a

few days very well." The old man's eyes filled with tears as he said, "We lost William in the Alamo. Can we see John go, too?" The mother said with a firm voice: " 'Tis true, William died in the Alamo, and we have no son to spare, but we had better lose them all than our country." He went, and like a true son of the noble mother who had offered him, if need be, upon the altar of her country, he stood amidst the clash of arms and din of battle side by side with the descendants of the heroes of the Alamo and other citizens of the country, till victory perched upon the banner of the Lone Star on the bloody field of Salado.

In 1855 the Indians made their last raid into Guadalupe County. They came along the western edge down the Cibolo valley and first stole some horses near the residence of James F. McKee. From there they went to the ranch of Mr. Robert Hellmann, passing around his field near where New Berlin is now. The first victim at their hands was a negro belonging to Mr. Elam. Next they came across Mr. Pendleton Rector and Doc McGee, a young son of the Rev. John S. McGee, a Methodist preacher. They attempted to save themselves by flight, but the animal Mr. Rector rode fell with him and he narrowly made his escape into a thicket, the Indians getting his mare and saddle. Young McGee was riding a mule and fell an easy prey. He was roped, dragged to the ground, lanced and scalped. Mr. Rector got to the setlements and gave the alarm, and a runner was sent to Seguin. Capt. H. E. McCulloch called for volunteers to follow the Indians, and a general panic ensued among the people. Twenty-eight men rallied to McCulloch, among whom were John Ireland (afterwards Governor of the State), Rus. Hudson, D. C. Bledsoe, Sam Calvert, Frank Marshall, Nat Benton, and others. The Indians had a long start ahead, and were not overtaken.

Not long after this raid Capt. James H. Calahan got up an expedition into Mexico to chastise Indians over there who depredated on Texas. They had a hard battle and were compelled to cross the river. (See full account of this in another place.) Among those who went from Guadalupe County were Capt. Nat Benton, his son Eustus, Wesley Harris, Hughes Tom, John King, Henry King, and others. Captain Benton, Eustus Benton, and Henry King, Seguin men, were wounded.

Some time after Calahan's expedition a freebooter named Cortinas invaded Texas with several hundred men and committed depredations along the Rio Grande. Captains Herron (from Seguin), Tobin (from San Antonio), and others raised companies and marched against him. Among the Guadalupe men along were De Witt Petty, Luke Mayfield, John Mayfield, Hez. Williams, and others. Cortinas was defeated near the Rio Grande and driven back into Mexico. At one point where the Mexicans had planted a cannon a sharp fight ensued. When the cannon was captured, De Witt Petty, from Seguin, mounted it, and, standing erect, clapped his arms to his side and crowed.

Guadalupe County has had her statesmen. Arthur Swift and Ben McCulloch were in the Congress of the Republic in 1839 and in the Legislature of 1845; Henry E. McCulloch in the Legislature of 1853 and in the senate from 1855 to 1859; Thomas H. Duggan in the senate previous to this; John R. King in the Legislature in 1855; I. V. Harris in 1857; W. H. Burges in the senate in 1882; M. D. Anderson of prior date; Middleton Dunn in the Legislature in 1866, as was also Captain Wm. M. Rust.

At a later date P. S. Sowell was in the Legislature and Joseph B. Dibrell in the senate; James Greenwood, also in the Legislature; John Ireland, twice elected Governor of the State—1882 and 1884.

Guadalupe County has had her military men. Ben and Henry McCulloch were both generals in the Confederate army. William P. Hardeman, known in the army as "Old Goch," lived in this county for many years. He commanded a company, and greatly distinguished himself at the battle of Val Verde, in New Mexico, and arose to rank of general in the Louisiana campaign. Capt. Nat Burton raised a company, arose to the rank of colonel, and lost an arm at the battle of Blair's Landing, in Louisiana. John P. Bane raised a company and arose to rank of colonel. John Ireland commanded a regiment, and John P. White a company.

LIST OF MEN KILLED, WOUNDED, AND DIED FROM GUADALUPE
COUNTY DURING THE GREAT CIVIL WAR.

Col. John P. Bane, severely wounded at Gaines Mill.
Thomas Cox, wounded at the second battle of Manassas.
Andrew Herron, killed at Gettysburg.
George Buttler, killed at Gettysburg.

Levi Maddox, captured at Missionary Ridge, and died in the Rock Island prison.

Dolf Allen, died in a hospital on the Potomac.

James Buttler, killed at Sharpsburg.

Paris Smith, wounded at Gaines Mill.

Julius Glazier, severely wounded with a ball and bayoneted at Chickamauga.

Fritz Glazier (brother), killed at Chickamauga.

R. J. Burges, desperately wounded with a grape shot at Manassas; same discharge killed Lieut. Ig. Johnson; R. A. Burges, wounded at the battle of the Wilderness.

W. H. Burges, wounded at Sharpsburg.

Lot Calvert, wounded at Gaines Mill, and died.

James Campbell, died in service near Richmond, Va.

John Davidson, killed at Gaines Mill.

Tom Ewing, wounded at Gaines Mill, and died.

Hat Franks, wounded at Chickamauga.

Isham Fennell, killed at Gaines Mill.

William Erringhaus, wounded at Gaines Mill.

Middleton Dunn, wounded at Gaines Mill.

Alonzo Gordon, wounded at Gaines Mill, and died.

Scott Green, wounded at Gaines Mill and killed at Gettysburg.

Andrew Erskine, killed at Sharpsburg.

Albert Green, wounded at Gaines Mill.

Fred Glazier, killed at Gettysburg.

Austin Jones, wounded at Gaines Mill. (He was the man that turned General Lee's horse around and led him back from the front at the Wilderness.)

R. H. Jones, wounded at Manassas.

John R. Jefferson, Jr., wounded at Manassas.

James King, died in service.

William Davis, killed at Sharpsburg.

James Whitehead, killed at Manassas.

Lieut. Tom Holoman, killed at Gaines Mill.

Napoleon Dimmit, wounded at Gaines Mill.

James Dimmit, wounded at Gaines Mill.

John Young, killed at Gaines Mill.

James White, wounded at Gaines Mill and in several other engagements.

William Harris, wounded at Cold Harbor.

Nelson Mays, killed at Gettysburg.

Lieut. Henry McClaugherty, severely wounded at the Wilderness and at Chickamauga.

Frank Saunders, wounded at Gettysburg.

Steward Sanders, died in the hospital at Fredericksburg.

James Herron, died on the Potomac.

John Smith, died on the Potomac.

John Dibrell, died on the Potomac.

John Miller, died in service.

Ben Terrell, wounded at Sharpsburg.

Reason Lackey, killed at Gaines Mill.

John Baker, wounded at the Wilderness.

Rainey Brooks, died in prison at Springfield, Ill.

Lewis and William Smith, brothers, died in prison in Springfield, Ill.

Abe White, killed at Chickamauga.

Alex. Ochiltree, killed at Chickamauga.

William Moltz, wounded in Georgia.

John Donegan, wounded at Franklin, Tenn.

—— Hale, wounded at Jonesborough.

Adam Saunders, wounded at Chickamauga.

Capt. Ed Thompson, killed at Franklin, Tenn.

Zeke Smith, died at Richmond, Va.

Tom Smith, died in service.

Capt. Dudley Jeffries, wounded at Manassas.

Lieutenant Richards, killed at Gaines Mill.

Leonidas Millett, killed at Gaines Mill.

Alex. Wilson, wounded at Gettysburg, the Wilderness, and at Chickamauga.

W. W. Wilson, wounded at Gaines Mill.

Mike Rogers, died at Fredericksburg, Va.

John King, wounded at ———.

Henry King, wounded at ———.

Frank Newton, wounded at Chickamauga.

——Glawson, killed at Chickamauga.

Tom Watson, killed at Chickamauga.

A. J. Cody, killed at Chickamauga.

—— Dovie, killed at Chickamauga.

George White, wounded at Val Verde, N. M.

Henry Many, wounded at Val Verde.

Colyer Allen, died and was buried at "Dead Man's Hole," in the edge of the Staked Plains.

George Turner, died at Albuquerque, N. M.

Pendleton Francis, killed at Franklin, La.

Aaron Ferguson, wounded at Cheyneville, La.

Martin Rogers, wounded at Franklin, La.

William Ferguson, wounded at Val Verde, N. M.

Robert Ferguson, killed at Mansfield, La.

Austin Ferguson, wounded at Mansfield, La.

James Sowell, accidentally wounded after Yellow Bayou fight, in Louisiana.

Bud Pearman, died near Fort Thorn, N. M.

Col. Nat Benton, severely wounded at Blair's Landing, La.

Fritz Suchart, leg torn off at Atlanta or Peach Tree Creek, Ga.; same shell killed Bates, Pace, and Alfred Alexander.

Henry Roemel, died in prison at Springfield, Ill.

——Swan, died in prison at Springfield, Ill.

Sawney Calvert, killed at Blair's Landing, La.

Lochard Arbuckle, wounded at Saline Creek, Ark. Marlin Heflin passed by where he was lying wounded with others under a tree, and gave him his blanket and $5 in money.

Lieut. Norvel Cartwright, killed in Louisiana.

Henry Nicholson, died at Ringgold Barracks, on the Rio Grande.

Dr. George Francis, died at Galveston.

George Sanders, died in Virginia.

Victor Stein, wounded at Corpus Christi, Texas.

Joe Francis, killed at Gaines Mill.

Sam Herron, wounded at Stone River.

Gustav Werner, killed at Blair's Landing.

Henry Brands, died at Jones' Bayou, La.

William Scull, killed at Murfreesboro, Tenn.

Most of these men belonged to the famous Fourth Texas, and followed Hood in all of his battles. They were the flower of the country and the bravest of the brave.

28

MASSACRE OF THE PEDDLERS AND BATTLE OF EL BLANCO.

From the year 1832 to 1835, while numerous disturbances were going on in eastern Texas, and collisions taking place between Mexican and American settlers, especially around Velasco and Nacogdoches, and the war cloud just then visible in the east, but which was soon to spread from the Sabine to the Rio Grande, or vice versa, leaving desolation in its path, De Witt's colony at Gonzales on the Guadalupe River had just begun to flourish. Numerous accessions of settlers had arrived and the population largely increased in and around the town. Indians were hostile and numerous in the west, and committed many depredations. Some of the colonists had settled a considerable distance west of Gonzales, and bore the same relation to people in town as the advance guard to an army. As the Indians generally came in from the west, these isolated settlers received the first blow, and then on swift horses alarmed the people further east of the approaching raid. Some had settled as far west as the present town of Seguin, but had returned, not being able to sustain themselves so far out. In the spring of 1835, or about that time, as near as we can get the record now, there lived an outside settler named John Castleman. His ranch was fifteen miles west from Gonzales in the Guadalupe valley, on the south side of the river.

One evening just before sundown there stopped at his house a French merchant or peddler named Greser, accompanied by ten Mexicans as guards. He had a large lot of costly goods which he was going east to sell, probably having purchased them in Mexico. Castleman lived on what was called the "Old San Antonio road," the main traveled route from San Antonio to eastern Texas. The merchant in question inquired of the settler as to a good camping place for the night, where there was wood and water. Castleman informed him that there was a large pool of water not far from the house, and pointed towards it, but at the same time remarking, "You had better camp here by my yard. I have plenty of wood and water, and you can get all you want. The Indians are very hostile now, and they might attack you before morning; there is no telling. You will be safe here, for my house is surrounded by strong palisades, and in case of danger you can come inside, and I will help to defend yourself and property." The Frenchman thanked him very politely for his proffered hospitality and protection, but declined, saying his men were well armed, and would go down and camp by the pool of water.

Castleman made everything secure for the night and retired. Just before daylight next morning he was awakened by the firing of guns and the yelling of Indians in the direction of the Frenchman's camp. He instantly sprang out of bed, hastily clothing himself, unbarred a small window, and looked out. Day was just beginning to dawn, and by this time the fight was raging at the peddler's camp. The Mexicans seemed to be making a stout defense. The loud reports of their escopets continually ringing out on the morning air mingled with the yelling of the Comanches. The sun arose, but still the Mexicans kept them at bay. Castleman stood at the window with his long rifle and several times expressed an intention of trying to get to them and aid in the battle, but it was too hazardous, and he could only watch and wait and see how it would terminate. The Indians would make a charge, but being repulsed each time with loss, would fall back and wait some time before renewing the contest. The Mexicans had made breastworks of their carts, saddles, bales of goods, etc. This accounts for the length and obstinacy of the battle, considering the numbers engaged, for the Comanches had seven to one of the Mexicans. At this time there had been no rupture between the Mexicans and De Witt's colonists, and Castleman would have risked his life in their defense, as the Comanches were the foes of both Mexican and Texan. The latter was hid from view during the fight, but the Indians could be plainly seen, being between the house and the encampment. The fight was going on at the base of the elevated ground on which the settler's cabin stood. The pool of water was near a mott of timber, in which the Mexicans were posted. The Indians often changed their position, and were very numerous.

About one hundred and fifty yards from the house, at the foot of the hill, there stood a large tree upon which Castleman had tacked a piece of white paper to serve as a target when he felt disposed to rifle practice. This paper caught the eye of an Indian as he was scouting around, and he came to the tree for the purpose of seeing what it was. The settler saw him and at once raised his rifle, as this was too good a chance to lose of killing an Indian. His prudent wife, however, laid her hand on the gun and begged him to desist, saying the Indians might go away and not molest them if he would not take a hand. The Indian did not long remain a target for the pioneer, for as soon as he discovered several bullet holes in and around the paper on the tree a revelation came to him, and he turned and looked towards the house, and seeing Castleman at his window beat a hasty retreat, using the tree for cover as he went.

The fight lasted until about 10 o'clock, and by that time the Mexican force seemed to be greatly reduced or else their ammunition was failing. Only an occasional shot could be heard. The Indians now assembled their whole force and charged on three sides at once and entered their position. Castleman could tell this from their great yelling and the direction their voices came from. The position the Mexicans occupied could be located by the smoke from their guns, which drifted above the treetops. Evidently a short hand-to-hand conflict took place, then all was still for an hour or more. The Indians were then discovered in long single file coming towards the house. It was a trying time for the lone pioneer, not knowing what their intentions were, but he consoled himself, like many had done before him and since, with the grim satisfaction of knowing that if they attacked him he would get as many of them as they did of him. The Comanches, however, had enough fighting for that day, and rode slowly past the house and shook their lances at it. There were eighty of them, and they had their own horses and those of the Mexicans which had not been killed or crippled in the battle, laden with the Frenchman's goods. The bloody scalps of the slain men were also visible. They had no firearms, it seemed, except those taken from the Mexicans, and likely no ammunition for them, as none of these were used in the battle which followed with the settlers from De Witt's colony. They had bows and lances.

As soon as Castleman was satisfied they were gone he went and examined the battleground. The Mexicans had arranged their carts in a circle and piled up goods and saddles and chunks of wood in the spaces between carts and wheels and spokes, and here in a small compass the eleven bodies lay horribly mutilated and drenched in blood. Many arrows were in the trees and carts, and several broken guns were there. The Indians evidently lost heavily, as the blood stains on the ground away from the carts indicated, but they had thrown their dead in the waterhole.

When Castleman returned to his house he mounted himself and family on ponies and hastened to Gonzales with the news. It spread rapidly, and before morning twenty-seven men were in their saddles and on their way to the Castleman ranch. From Mr. David Darst, of Gonzales, who was a boy at the time and saw them start, I obtained the following names of the men whom he remembered were present: Gen. Matthew Caldwell ("Old Paint"), James C. Darst, Dan McCoy, Ezekiel Williams, B. D. McClure, John Davis, Tom Malone, — White, Jesse McCoy, Washington Cottle, Almon Dickinson, Dr. James Miller, Andrew J. Sowell, Sr., and John Castleman. The balance of the names can not now be ascertained.

B. D. McClure was elected captain, and the party, pushing rapidly forward, soon arrived at the scene of the massacre. Only a short halt was made here and the trail taken up, which led up the Guadalupe valley on the south side of the river. Ten miles west the Indians turned north and crossed the Guadalupe River at a place afterwards known as "Erskine's Ford," in the present limits of Guadalupe County, and distant about twelve miles below the present town of Seguin. After crossing Darst Creek about twenty-six miles from Gonzales, just below where the ranch of Col. French Smith afterwards was, the Indians amused themselves by unwinding spools of thread across the level flats, likely tying the ends to their horses' tails. They did not seem to apprehend pursuit.

After passing through this part of the country they bore to the northwest, passing out near the head of Mill Creek and crossing the York's Creek divide. The pursuing party would camp as soon as night came, and then be off again as soon as it was light enough to see the trail. The Indians were traveling slower than the white men on account of their heavily loaded horses, but they moved on sometimes in the night, and thus had the advantage, as the settlers could only trail in daylight. Two ravens followed in the wake of the Indians, picking up the offal from their camps, and would fly up and follow on at the approach of the white men.

One night when the trailers were camped near the York's Creek divide Andrew Sowell, who was a good scout and trailer, left the camp and went some distance and remained alone on a ridge, listening, and while doing so his quick ear caught a far-off sound like Indians singing. The captain was informed of this fact and went out and listened, but could hear nothing, and supposed it was coyotes.

By daylight next morning they were again on the trail, and in about two miles came to the Indian camp, in the midst of which stood a pole. The camp was on a high ridge, south of and overlooking the present town of San Marcos, in Hays County. The grass was tramped down around the pole in a circle where the Indians had performed the scalp dance the night before. As they always sing when engaged in this merry-making, it proved beyond a doubt that the scout was right in his assertions that he heard Indians singing. The sound of the voice in their frenzied screechings would float a long distance on the still night air.

From here the Indians went to the foot of the mountains and entered them, and the pursuit was still continued. The trailing was now more difficult, and that night Captain McClure and his men camped in the brakes of the Blanco River. Next morning was foggy, and they moved with great caution. The signs indicated that they were close upon the Indians. As they were going down into the valley of the Blanco the fog lifted, and soon the yelling of an Indian was heard on a mountain across the river. He had been placed there as a spy, and was giving the alarm of the approach of the white men to his comrades in the valley below. Captain McClure, knowing that he was now discovered, ordered a rapid advance, but they soon entered such a dense cedarbrake that they were compelled to abandon their horses and proceed on foot. Almon Dickinson and James Darst were sent ahead to locate the Indians, and the others slowly followed in single file, stooping and crawling as they went. Finally they came out into an opening near the river where three or four could walk abreast, and at this instant bang! bang! came the sharp report of two rifles and the yelling of Indians near at hand. "Charge up, boys!" shouted McClure, as he sprang in front. "Here they are!" The two scouts were now seen running back, closely pursued by several Indians, who were pulling arrows and adjusting them to their bowstrings. The captain and others raised their rifles, but could not shoot without endangering the lives of Darst and Dickinson, who were directly between them and the Indians. They saw this, and sprang to one side, and gave them a chance to fire. Captain McClure shot first and killed the foremost Indian. John Castleman shot the next one and he fell across the body of the first, being directly behind him. Several shots were fired, and a third Indian had his bow stick shot in two while in the act of discharging an arrow. Andrew Sowell attempted to fire with a flintlock rifle, but it flashed in the pan. He had stopped up the touch-hole to keep the powder dry in the fog, and had forgotten to take it out. The other Indians now ran back towards the river, yelling loudly. By this time most of the men had gotten clear of the brush and charged with McClure across the open ground.

Near the river they met about fifty Indians, and the fight became general. The yelling of the Comanches almost drowned the report of the firearms, and echoed far up and down the Blanco valley. The Indians soon gave way and commenced crossing the river. Some had been engaged trying to cross the goods over while the fight was going on, and partly succeeded. They had camped here near the water on the east or south bank the previous night. Another fight took place at the river, some of the Indians stopping in the water to shoot, but they soon retired before the rifles, and all went across and disappeared in the brake beyond. Andrew Sowell killed one after they got over. He tried to cross lower down than the balance, and came in contact with a steep bank on the opposite side which he could not hastily climb, and was discovered and shot. He rolled back to the edge of the water. None of the white men crossed the river.

None of the settlers were killed, and those wounded with arrows were not badly hurt. The Indians made a very poor fight and seemed badly rattled at the very commencement, shooting wild and running at every volley from the whites. They had evidently exhausted most of their arrows in the fight with the Mexicans. Those killed had but very few in their quivers, and some even had none.

A return was now made by the settlers back to their horses, which were found all right, except one which had gotten away and gone on the back track out of the valley, but was recovered. One man was also missing, and a search was made for him, thinking he was killed somewhere, but without success. Finally he came to them, as one of them afterwards expressed it, "looking as wild as a buck." He had neither hat, gun, nor shoes, and seemed to be perfectly bewildered, and could give no rational account of himself. He said he could not stand the firing and yelling, and ran and kept running until it was all over. He could give no account of his gun or shoes. The latter were found at the river, almost in the edge of the water, below the battle-ground. The gun or hat could not be found.

The settlers carried their horses back to the river and loaded them with goods, but could not take them all, and left the remainder piled up on the bank of the river, with bows, shields, blankets, and buffalo skins. The return to Gonzales was made without further incident. A party afterwards went back to bring away the balance of the goods, but they were badly damaged by rain.

Matthew Caldwell took part in many battles. He was a member of the Santa Fe expedition in 1843, and was captured with his son Curtis and others and carried to Mexico and confined with the Mier prisoners. Caldwell County was named for him. He was called "Old Paint" on account of his having gray spots in his black hair. Almon Dickinson was the Lieutenant Dickinson that perished in the Alamo with Travis, and father of the famous character known in Texas history as the "Babe of the Alamo." She was an infant in her mother's arms in the fort during the terrible conflict.

OLD SETTLERS OF D'HANIS.

In 1897 the writer, while circulating around the old historic place of D'Hanis, found many interesting old settlers. Among these were the Kochs, Saatoff, Enderle, Wolf, Richarz, Judge, Miller, Neys, Rothes, Fingers, and many others.

The Ney family, who came here at an early day, are related to Napoleon's great field marshal of that name. John Ney, grandfather of the younger ones here, was present at the battle of Waterloo. On the morning of that famous battle Marshal Ney was sitting on his horse listening to the roll call and heard the name of Ney, and a man answered to it in the ranks. He at once rode up and asked the man where he was from and who his people were. On the information being given, the marshal said, "You are my nephew." This was John Ney, ancestor of the Neys who now reside in Medina County. John Ney was in all the desperate fighting that day at Waterloo, and charged repeatedly with the troops led by the marshal. Of the large company to which Mr. Ney belonged, and with whom he fought that day, only seventeen came out alive. They were engaged from early in the morning until about 3 o'clock in the evening, when Marshal Blucher came upon the scene with 50,000 fresh troops to the aid of the English commander, Lord Wellington. The French army then went to pieces, and the rout commenced.

The Waterloo veteran, John Ney, had three sons—Joseph, John, and Nicholas—and two daughters, Elizabeth and Angelina. Elizabeth married Mr. Zurcher, and Angelina Mr. Herbert Weynand. Of the boys, John was killed by Indians on Black Creek, in Medina County, and Nicholas died at Fort Lincoln, on Seco, two miles from D'Hanis. Joseph Ney had four sons—Joseph, John, Antone, and Henry. Joseph is now and has been for many years sheriff of Medina County, and lives at Hondo City, the county seat. John lives at New D'Hanis, and Henry at the old town of the same name. The writer was shown a bronze medal by Johnnie Ney which was given to their grandfather, John Ney, by the French government on account of his relationship to their great field marshal, and for services at Waterloo. On one side of the medal is an image of Napoleon, and the date of his death on the other. This medal is prized very highly by the Ney family. The Ney boys, except the sheriff, are engaged in farming, stock raising, etc. John has a gin at D'Hanis, and Antone is on a ranch in the mountains on Parker's Creek.

Another old pioneer of D'Hanis is Mrs. Caroline Brotze. She was born in Wurtemburg, Germany, and came to America, landing at New York in 1849. The trip across the ocean was very slow, consuming six weeks. She came to Texas in 1850, and first lived on the Cibolo and then on the Salado, coming to the Seco in 1856 and settling where she now lives, about a mile north of New D'Hanis. Mrs. Brotze has had some interesting experiences on the frontier. Many times has she moulded bullets for her husband and other men to fight the Indians, and prepared narrow strips of greased cloth to patch the bullets with. Her husband was a ranger, and on one occasion captured an Indian girl and brought her to Fort Lincoln and gave her to the commander, Captain Oakes. Many times the people suffered for bread, and her husband, who died several years ago, went to Mexico after flour. The flour was high-priced, dark, and hardly fit to eat, and Mrs. Brotze does not believe it was made from wheat. It tasted, she says, like it had cinnamon bark in it.

On one occasion the men caught up with a band of Indians who had stolen a lot of horses, and recaptured them and returned to D'Hanis, putting the stock in a pen in the rear of Ney's saloon for the night. The Indians followed the settlers, and during the night succeeded in getting the horses again and carrying them off. They were again pursued, stock retaken, and brought back; but this time a stricter watch was kept over them.

Old Fort Lincoln, which has been referred to several times in these sketches of the pioneers, was not named for President Abraham Lincoln, as many might suppose, but for General Lincoln, of Revolutionary fame, who took a prominent part in the battle of Monmouth and many other engagements. He was an able officer and had the respect and confidence of General Washington. The fort was erected long before Abraham Lincoln came into any prominence. It is built of rock, and is still standing. Many young officers have been inside its walls while on duty in the Southwest, who espoused different sides when the great civil war burst upon the land, and fought each other.

HISTORY OF THE SETTLEMENT OF D'HANIS.

Settled in 1846.

There is in Medina County, near the line of the Sunset, or Southern Pacific Railroad, fifty miles west from San Antonio, a very interesting and historical place called "Old D'Hanis," settled in 1846 by German colonists. Among the very few nqw left of the first settlers is Mr. Christian Batot (pronounced Bah-do), who was young at the time and can tell many stirring incidents of that time, being well informed and having a bright and retentive memory. He was born in Alsace, near the town of Colmer, capital of Upper or Northern Alsace, in 1838. This country at that time belonged to France.

In 1846 Henry Castro came through that country representing an immigration company for America. The land upon which the colony was to be planted was in the wilds of western Texas. Each immigrant who was head of a family was to receive 320 acres of land, and each single man was to receive 160 acres. The conditions were that each colonist was to pay 260 francs from fifteen years and upwards, and those under that age half price. For this sum per head the company agreed to deliver them at their destination, food, etc., furnished. To these hardy Germans who dwelt in Alsace and other parts of the adjacent country this seemed to be a fine opening to secure good homes at small cost. That amount of land in the country where they lived would be a small fortune, and it was worth the attempt to brave the dangers of the ocean and all other hardships to obtain it. Castro was very successful in his mission, and soon obtained three shiploads of colonists, amounting to about 1000 persons of all ages. The vessels set sail from Antwerp on the 1st day of August, 1846, and many long and last looks were cast back at the fast receding shores of the old country. The time consumed in crossing the ocean was ninety-two days, and on the 10th of December they landed at Galveston, Texas. The ship in which Mr. Batot came was the Herratzes.

The colonists had paid their fare to Castroville, another colony of Henry Castro which had preceded them and had made their settlement on the Medina River, twenty-five miles west from San Antonio.

The land of this second colony had not yet been surveyed or their town of D'Hanis laid off, so they had to remain at Castroville until a surveying party could go out and do the work. When the time came for the lots in town to be drawn, old man Batot, father of Chris, went out, and being satisfied with the situation, drew his lots, which consisted of one building lot and one twenty-acre farming lot. When Mr. Batot came back to Castroville he said to his family, "Well, I am going out to our land now to fix a home, and will take Chris along to cook." When everything was ready the old man took his provisions, bedding, and tools on his back, and Chris took a pick, and they walked from Castroville out to the new town, the distance being about thirty miles, with no road except the trail of the surveyor's wagon through the high grass. The town was laid off on a high prairie about two miles east of the Seco Creek, on a bold-running but small creek. The land was black, very rich, and covered with rank sedge grass. One drawback which confronted the men who were trying to build homes for their families was the want of building material. The only chance was short mesquite pickets, which grew in the valley near the Seco. Some of these were six feet long and some only four feet. These were set in an upright position, making a pen, and others tied together at the top and slanting both ways, so as to make the frame for a roof, and then covered with the long grass of the prairie. For a door a kind of framework was made of small poles, and then the grass worked in and out to close up the spaces, and then fastened to one end of the shanty. In constructing these rude shelters it was all done without a nail or any kind of metallic substance in its structure. Some only slanted the roof one way, letting the ends of the poles rest on the ground, and then digging a hole inside to make the roof high enough so that a man could stand erect inside of it.

Of all the vast throng who started from the old country to obtain a home here, only twenty-nine families succeeded in arriving and finally settling. They were scattered from the coast to Castroville, some stopping in San Antonio and various other towns and settlements. When the families came out they had poor transportation, and came out slowly from Castroville. They came by the surveyor's trail through the high grass across the prairie, and saw many deer and wild mustang horses. The families did not all come out at once from Castroville, and up to the 19th of March six families were still behind. The lack of provisions was keenly felt in this far-away frontier country, and the colonists had no money. On the day of the above date the colonists were surprised and somewhat frightened to see seventy-two painted Comanche Indians ride into the settlement. They carried a white flag, however, and the little German children and women stood and looked in wonder and astonishment at the strange, painted men. The Indians all carried shields, bows, and arrows, and each one had two horses, making quite a formidable appearance. These Indians brought a letter from the Indian agent at Fredericksburg, stating that they were not enemies to white people. They also said if they were Mexicans they would not let them settle here. These Indians showed their friendship and good will to the white men by taking all the provisions the poor colonists had, which was not much, and then taking their departure.

After they had gone old man Batot said to his son, "Chris, here is a little meal left; make some mush and we will eat it up." While the mush was making the Indians came back, and some of them stood around Batot's fire and watched the mush cook. Finally one of them took out a little sugar which he had robbed a settler of, and putting it into the mush stirred it up. Mr. Batot thought the Indian was going to fix it up good for him and Chris, but when it was cooked sufficient, the Indians lifted it from the fire and ate it all themselves. The colonists had placed a white flag on the D'Hanis hill to the south, near the settlement, to guide any lost settler back home, and the Indians finally all went up there to look at it. From this elevated position they discovered some immigrant wagons coming containing six families, the last of the original twenty-nine families which composed the first settlers. The Indians now turned east down the hill and met the wagons and stopped them, but did not molest anyone. In this party was Mrs. Batot, who up to this time had remained in Castroville. When the Indians rode up to the wagons there was a young woman in one of them named Josie Rutinger, who was dying, having been taken sick by the way. This family had a hard time of it. One of their horses gave out, and they had to unload their wagon at a place now called "Finger

Hill." The load which they had to leave consisted of trunks containing all their earthly possessions of value, and they left one of the Rutinger girls only 14 years old to watch them. The wagons then slowly moved on, trying to get to the setlement with the dying girl. Three miles further the team gave out entirely, and they had to send to the settlement and get the Castro oxen, as they were called, as they had been furnished by him for their use. When the oxen were brought and hitched in, the wagon moved on again, and about midnight arrived at their destination, and just as they did so the sick young lady died, and was the first one buried at D'Hanis.

Can anyone imagine the feelings of the little sister left alone six miles back on the prairie with the trunks? Night soon closed down around her. The range of mountains to the north faded from sight. One by one the stars came out and commenced their ceaseless twinkling. The night wind stirred the tall grass around her, and anon the distant bark of the coyote was heard. Alone on the prairie, far in advance of civilization, with roving bands of Comanches not far away! No doubt her mind as she kept the solitary vigils of the night went back to the old home across the ocean,—the preparations to embark; the talk of the new home in the far distant country; the long, tedious voyage, and the joy at sight of land, the place where they were to find a beautiful home; the disappointment on landing; the long distance yet to go by land towards the setting sun, most of the way on foot, following the slow, heavy-laden wagons, and on and on to the present night,—nearly there, but left alone, and her sister dying in the wagon ahead. This is no overdrawn picture. Next morning a party came back with a wagon and got the trunks and little girl and brought them on to the settlement, and that evening the dead sister was buried.

The place where the little girl was left, called "Finger Hill," was named for Mr. Joseph Finger, who camped there and cut grass to cover his house. It is near the present town of Hondo City. The little girl lived to be an old lady, and died at D'Hanis in 1893.

We can hardly realize now what these early settlers had to endure while trying to subdue the wilderness and build up and provide homes for their families. They had no money, and here they stayed six months alone, cut off from the rest of civilization, not a house west of them in Texas, and none for many miles east. Corn was $6 per bushel, and no mills to grind it on except by hand. The turfy soil was hard to subdue with insufficient plows and teams. Game was plenty, but these people were not hunters. They had no guns suitable to kill large game. Some few brought small bird guns from the old country, and those that had guns that they could kill a deer with soon exhausted their ammunition, which was high, and they had no money to buy any more. They deserve more credit than the American pioneers. The latter came from States where they were used to hunting game, brought good rifles with them, and were at home in the forest or on the plains. On the other hand, the Germans came from towns and thickly settled districts, and knew nothing about camp life or living in the woods and shooting wild game.

At last, however, relief came. One evening a band of Texas rangers arrived in the settlement and went into camp on the Seco two miles from town. They were commanded by Capt. Tom Rife, and were sent here to protect these isolated settlers, as Indian friendship did not last long. The rangers had good guns and plenty of ammunition, and not only gave them ample protection, but killed game of various kinds and brought to them. The Delaware and Lipan Indians also came and traded with them until the latter became hostile. The Delawares lived over in the Guadalupe valley, near where Comfort is now, but there were no settlers there then. The Lipans were on the Francisco. One day a discharged ranger named Sam West came to D'Hanis from below and got some men from the rangers and went to the Lipan camp and arrested some of them, stating that they had killed a man in Quihi, a new settlement of Germans fifteen miles below, and had robbed him and carried off a girl 16 years old. The girl got away before they carried her far, and that night got back home. West found one camp of the Lipans at the Comanche waterhole and carried them to Quihi to see if the young woman could identify any of them, which some say she did, a pointed out one, and the men killed the Indian and carried the balance to San Antonio and turned them over to the authorities. This young girl, as the ranger West called her, was Mrs. Charobiny, and she had been married three months. The man killed was her brother, Blas Meyer.

In 1849 a company of United States regular troops came and

went into camp in tents two miles from D'Hanis, and good times began to come to the colonists. The rangers had been ordered elsewhere or disbanded before the regulars came. Mr. Batot speaks highly of the Texas rangers, and says if it had not been for their timely assistance he believes the colony would have broken up. With the soldiers came employment for the men of D'Hanis. They could get $1 per day for cutting tender grass to furnish hay for the cavalry horses and many other things they required to be done.

In 1850 Fort Lincoln was built and Captain Oaks put in command of it. The building of the fort, barracks, hospital, quartermaster department, and many other things gave employment to the D'Hanis men at $1.50 per day and board. By the time the government contracts were all finished crops began to be raised in the settlement and times were good. In 1857, however, crops began to fail and the Indians became hostile, especially when settlers began to go further west, and the D'Hanis people saw hard times again.

These people were so completely cut off from the outside world that they could only get their mail once a month. Big Foot Wallace had a contract to carry the mail from San Antonio to El Paso, and it was only when he stopped at their settlement going west that they obtained their mail.

On one occasion Mr. John Grocenbacher and his daughter Barbara became lost while out from the settlement, and wandered about fourteen days. During this time they lived on bird eggs and a young fawn which they caught. They first sucked the blood of the young deer and then carried the body along, which they partook of from time to time, even eating the hide. They were found by a band of friendly Indians and brought to the settlement. This girl, Barbara Grocenbacher, lived many years, and was the mother of the Leinweber boys, who now live at Hondo City.

Mr. Batot relates an incident of one of his escapades at D'Hanis when a boy. A stray steer came into the settlement, having both horns sawed off, and he gave the people a great deal of trouble by depredating upon their crop. He was also a fighting steer, and would run anyone who would come to put him out of a field. These honest people finally concluded to kill the steer and cut out the brand on the hide and take care of it, so that if anyone came there making inquiries about stock in that brand they would pay him for the slain animal. When the steer was killed a square piece of hide was cut out, containing the brand, and placed in the care of old man Batot for him to keep secure in case it was ever needed. Now this brand and piece of hide on which it was imprinted was the prime factor in getting Chris into trouble and causing him to run away from home. The old man placed the piece of hide in the roof of the house between the grass cover and a rafter over the bed upon which Chris reposed at night. In time the piece of hide became full of hairy worms, and often would fall upon Chris at night. This made the boy mad, and he arose in his wrath one night, and seizing the offending thing hurled it out into the darkness. The old man had all this time kept an eye on it, and when it was missed asked Chris what had become of it. He denied any knowledge of it whatever, but the old man had an idea that he was concerned some way about its disappearance and sprang at him to chastise him, but Chris ran, followed by his father, who threw things at him, but could not catch him. The old man was very much afraid of the law. The boy was afraid to come back home, so he took the road and traveled east until he came to Sutherland Springs. He was now footsore and nearly starved. He was afraid to stop at any of the settlements further west, for fear his father would find him. This place was a new settlement, and the property owned by Dr. Sutherland, who had a hotel. Here Chris stopped and applied for something to eat, which was given. and then the doctor employed him. His business was to wait on table, and his compensation was $2 per month and board. Chris thought this was fine, living at a hotel, and enjoying himself very much. For fear he might be found out, he told the doctor his name was Joseph. One night the Indians came into the settlement and stole some horses, and next morning the doctor and some of his neighbors followed and had a fight with them about thirteen miles from there, over in Karnes County. They killed three of the Indians and brought their scalps and shields back. Chris finally went back to D'Hanis and got on good terms with the old man again.

In 1858 they had their first trial at D'Hanis. A bachelor who lived in the lower part of town stole a pumpkin from Mr. Strausser, and he was tried for the offense before Justice Marrell,

29

who found him guilty and assessed his punishment as follows:
He was to have the pumpkin strapped securely between his shoulders on Sunday, and march from one end of the town to the
other, followed by the jeering populace. Mr. Herbert Weynand,
an old settler, and who still lives, was at one time justice of the
peace in the early days.

In 1861 a band of hostile Indians came in near D'Hanis and
stole a lot of horses. Before the people knew they were in the
country an old man named John Schreiber went out in the morning on a mule to hunt a yoke of oxen. Some time in the day the
mule came back with an arrow in him. Great excitement prevailed in the settlement, as all were satisfied the old man was
killed. A large crowd assembled at D'Hanis to search for the
body and fight the Indians if they came upon them. These people were very particular about adhering strictly to the letter of
the law in all of their proceedings, and thought best to hold an
inquest over the body when found. At this time they were without a peace officer, but their school teacher was an educated man
and they thought he could hold the inquest as good as anyone.
His name was Schalkhausen. When all this was agreed upon a
wagon and team were procured. The teacher was placed in the
wagon with the driver, and the balance of the men went on horseback in search of the missing man. When they arrived near the
place where they supposed the old man had been killed they separated to hunt for the remains, and it was understood that the
successful one should let it be known by hallooing. A man named
Decker first came upon the body of the unfortunate settler and
gave the signal. The searchers came together on the spot, and
Mr. Batot was sent to inform Mr. Sauter, son-in-law of the dead
man, of the fact of the finding and how to come with the wagon,
as he was the driver. The wagon had passed the spot where the
body lay and had been stopped to await developments. They had
now to turn back and go up a ravine, near which the dead man
lay, in order to cross the gully. This was back towards D'Hanis,
and Mr. Batot told Mr. Sauter how to go, and said "You can
see us when you get opposite the place" (where the crowd had
now assembled awaiting the wagon and school teacher). Mr.
Batot now rode back, crossing the ravine and going a nearer
route, and told the men the wagon would soon be there. The
horses had not been unhitched, only the bridles removed, and

when these were adjusted the wagon was turned up the ravine. In the meantime, however, the teacher had left the wagon and followed Mr. Batot, saying he too would go the near way on foot. Mr. Batot looked back and saw him leave the wagon and follow on after him, but as the distance was not great paid no attention to it and hurried on, thinking he would come in a few minutes. When the wagon arrived the men were around the body ready to hold the inquest, but the teacher had not yet arrived. After waiting a short time two men were sent to see what had become of him. They were gone about twenty minutes, then returned, and reported that they could not find him. Fifteen men now set out on horseback and scattered in various directions, shouting and shooting for six hours, but no response came. By this time a cold norther had sprung up, and the men, being without coats, were compelled to abandon the search and return to D'Hanis. The dead body was placed in the wagon and carried back, where it was buried without the inquest being held. The body was lanced and scalped, but had neither been shot with bullet nor arrow. The wounded mule must have dodged into a thicket and the limbs and brush dragged the old man off, and he fell an easy prey to the lances without being shot. The mule came in with the saddle and bridle on.

After returning home the men got their coats and some provisions and returned to the scene of the killing to look for the lost man, and there searched in wide circles for three days, but without success. It is surmised that the Indians who killed Mr. Schreiber were concealed near by and watching the party, whom they were afraid to attack, and seeing this man alone and on foot captured and carried him off, as he was not armed and could make no resistance. If he had been killed some remains of some kind would certainly have been found of clothing, etc. He was a man 60 years of age, had a good school, and it was not reasonable that he would absent himself without letting some one know it. There were plenty of Indian signs in the vicinity, but these could have been made by those that killed the other man. Be this as it may, he was never heard of again by the people of D'Hanis.

Six months after this the man Deckard, who found the body of Mr. Schreiber, was killed by Indians under almost similar circumstances six miles below. He was also out ox-hunting and

was not armed. A searching party went after him and hunted
several days before he was found. He was killed on a ridge, in
some liveoak timber, and the coyotes dragged the body down into
an open flat, and there it was discovered. Only the skeleton remained, and it was put in a sack and brought to D'Hanis and
buried. It could only be identified by shoes and some other
things.

Mr. Batot was in Castroville one day when Big Foot Wallace
brought an Indian in there whom he had captured. A crowd
gathered around Wallace and the Indian, among them being a
county officer who proposed to take charge of the Indian. Big
Foot refused to give him up, and said to the man, "If you want
an Indian, go and catch one. This is my Indian; I caught him."
There was a general laugh over this—the idea of the officer out
trying to catch an Indian. Wallace took the captive to San Antonio and turned him over to the agent there.

In 1870 Mr. Batot joined a company of rangers commanded
by Captain Richarz. They were stationed at Fort Inge. During
this year the Indians invaded the west like they were going to
take the whole country, and part of Captain Richarz's company
had a desperate battle with them, the particulars of which are
given elsewhere.

There is a vast difference now in the looks of the country
around "Old D'Hanis" and when the first settlers came there.
It is grown up in mesquite and other kinds of brush, and the
little creek which ran so clear and bold is now dried up. There
are still many of the grass-covered houses standing, but they are
used for outhouses, cribs, stables, etc. There are but few of the
original picket shanties left. These grass-covered ones here now,
though old, were once comfortable, being built of rock at a later
day. The old grass covers still shed the water as good as shingles. The old town is one mile east of the new.

Mr. Batot furnishes the names of all he can remember of the
original settlers, as follows: Old man Finger, — Hagemueller,
Donnel French, Whipf, Batot, Carr, John Ney, John Riedde-
mann, John Schreiber, Antone Ludwig, Joseph Wollehker, Antone Strausser, Frank Biell, John Nehr, Joseph Rudinger, J. B.
Deckard, Dr. Marrell, John Schumaker, Ben. Grocenbacher, Riss-
mann, Kaufmann, and Joseph Echtile. Frank Biell was killed
by Indians on the Medina, above Castroville.

OLD SETTLERS.

Thirty-three miles southwest from San Antonio is the flourishing little city of Devine, in Medina County. It was named for Judge Devine, of San Antonio, long before the whistle of a locomotive was heard in this country. The pioneers had erected their cabins here and commenced that long and desperate struggle with the savages for the mastery, in which civilization in the end was destined to triumph.

Now, instead of the yell of the Comanche, Lipan or Kickapoo, is heard the scream of the steam engine, and the trail of the redman is covered along the graded track by the right of way. In a radius of twelve miles of this place, covered by portions of Frio and Medina counties, many bloody encounters took place. Nearly every hill, valley, branch, creek, or mott of timber is historic; and many graves are shown here and there, and the traveler is told "they were killed by Indians." Many of these old settlers still survive who escaped the arrow, bullet, lance, or tomahawk, and among these at the time of which I write (1897) were Tom Galbreth, Lon Moore, Sam McCombs, Gip Tilley, Bee Tilley, J. W. Winters, Big Foot Wallace, Thomas A. James, John Craig, Tobias Long, James Long, West Davidson, Holly Laxon, George Crawford, James Crawford, Mrs. Amanda Long, Aunt Peggy Halsel, Mrs. Minerva Laxon, Rev. Newton, Reese Moore, W. M. Bramlett, Mrs. Anna Burch, Mrs. Sarah Smith, George McCombs, and many others. Nearly all of these have been here from thirty-five to fifty years; the first one to come being Big Foot Wallace.

The writer, in company with an old friend, Tobias Long, set out from Devine in April, 1897, about the 20th, to his ranch and farm twelve miles south of Devine. The country is very sandy in places, which makes locomotion slow, but the soil is very good for corn, cotton, melons, and potatoes. We arrived at Mr. Long's place about sundown, and the writer received a hearty welcome from Mrs. Long, who was an old acquaintance of other days in Guadalupe County, but she could not see me, having been blind for many years. Her first husband, James Winters, was killed by Indians, and during my stay I was shown the three arrows which were pulled from his body, and which she had carefully preserved for nearly forty years. The Indians in scalping him had taken the hair off so close but little was left on the head, and the grief-stricken wife could only procure a small bit just above the ear to keep as a memento. The opposing forces consisted of six white men and twenty-five Indians, and a full description of the battle is given elsewhere. Mrs. Long, before her first marriage, was Amanda Davidson, and the daughter of "Aunt Peggy" Halsel, by Mrs. Halsel's first husband.

In this settlement the writer met two old schoolmates of forty odd years ago, Mr. West Davidson and Mrs. Minerva Laxon, son and daughter of "Aunt Peggy" Halsel. This old pioneer mother, who still lives, was born in Alabama in 1812. Her father, Tobias Long, was a soldier under General Jackson, and was in the battle of "Horse Shoe Bend."

While taking a drive through the country with the family, consisting of Mrs. Halsel, Mrs. Laxon and her husband, Holly Laxon, the writer was shown an old road which was washed out into gullies where it emptied into Cesquadara Creek, at the mouth of Elm, and was told that here a boy's horse fell with him while he was making a desperate run from the Indians. The name of the boy was Simon Fraiser. He was out in the woods near Sand branch when he discovered a band of Indians. The horse young Fraiser was riding was a mustang, which had been caught when a colt and was a rather awkward pacer and not noted for speed. It was two miles home, and the boy turned for the nearest house, only half a smile away on Cesquadara, and made the best time he could, with the Indians in pursuit, three of them on good horses. So confident were they of their little victim that one of them fixed his rope as he ran to throw over Simon's head when he came up beside him. The boy used every effort to urge his mustang to his utmost speed in this run for life, but at first the pony only went in an ungainly pacing gallop. The three Indians were mounted on races horses which they had stolen from settlers, and soon shortened the distance between them and the seemingly doomed boy. Two of these fast horses belonged to Than. Terry, and one noted for speed was called Cornet. The other one belonged to Lon Moore. When the Indians came near they began to utter loud, keen whistles to terrify the lad, but this likely saved his life, as the mustang became badly frightened and at once began to get his legs under him in proper shape and to run level and at a terrific speed. In vain the Indians tried to flank him, two running on each side and one in the rear. When the bank of the Cesquadara Creek was reached the boy's horse plunged down and fell, throwing his rider over his head, and then rising dashed away, leaving Simon to take care of himself as best he could. Near by, however, was a family living at the old James Winters place, and thither he made his way in safety. The horse passed this place and went on to Mr. Trout's and was there caught by Miss Louisa Trout. They had been listening to the noise of the running horses across the creek, but were not aware of the presence of Indians in the country, but now realizing the situation, thought sure young Frasier was killed. The Indians came close to the house, trying to get the horse after he threw the boy, for they saw he had wonderful speed, and they wanted him very much, but were prevented by Miss Trout catching and tying him near the door, and the Indians would not come within gunshot of the house.

The boy Simon Fraiser had a brother killed by Indians. His name was Henry McCulloch Fraiser, and he was named for Gen. Henry McCulloch. This boy was out near the house hobbling a horse, and as he raised up an Indian grabbed him around the waist, and pulled a knife from Henry's belt and stabbed him with it, and then stripped him of his clothing. The boy succeeded in getting to the house in this bloody and naked condition and lived long enough to tell how it was done. The Indian who did this was supposed to have put on the boy's shirt, as one was killed shortly afterwards by Montel's rangers who had on a hickory shirt, the sleeves of which were very much too short for him. This killing of Henry Fraiser was a short time before the Indians gave his brother Simon such a chase.

While being shown several places of interest by Mr. West. Davidson, we came upon a small elevated place near Sand branch, where was a lone grave in a mott of liveoak trees. The man buried here was a Texas ranger and had been killed near this place in a battle with the Indians in 1845. The rangers on this occasion, twenty in number, were coming back from a scout to their camp, which was at the Garcia crossing on the Medina. It was nearly night, and the rangers were going up Sand branch to

a spring, where they intended camping for the night. Eighty
Indians were already encamped at the water, and their spies had
discovered the rangers approaching. The Comanches met them
near this grove and a battle ensued. The rangers took advantage
of the liveoak timber along the branch and opened a severe fire
from their rifles. The Indians did the same, and many shots
were exchanged, during which one of the rangers was killed,
and night coming on the Indians went back to the spring, carrying away their dead, and the rangers camped on the battleground,
and that night buried their dead comrade and attended to others
who were wounded. Next morning the Indians attacked them
again, but soon drew off. The rangers went on to their camp,
and getting additional force returned and trailed up the Indians
and completely routed them and captured many head of horses
and other property. On the way back from the scout the rangers
stopped and built a pen of poles around the grave of the dead
ranger. When the settlers began to come into this part of the
country the grave attracted their attention, and a Mr. Woodward who lived near Pleasanton gave Mr. Davidson the history
of it, for he was one of the rangers in the fight. The grave is
now marked by a mesquite stake about four inches in diameter
driven into the ground. The pen first placed around it by the
rangers in time rotted away, and this stake was put here by
"Aunt Peggy" Halsel many years ago, and has thus far preserved the site of the grave from being lost. Mr. Davidson
could not tell me the name of the ranger or his captain, but
thinks the latter was Walker. The old ranger who gave the
account is now dead. If the writer could learn the name of this
dead defender of the Texas frontier who has now lain for fifty-
four years in this lonely liveoak grove, a stone suitably inscribed
should be placed over it. The spring mentioned is now filled
with sand and used to be known as the "Toola waterhole."

Mr. Tobias Long was one of Montel's rangers, and also served
under Capt. Ed. Burleson, and has had much experience on
the frontier, and has eaten horse meat with Big Foot Wallace
while nearly starving on the plains.

Byrd Smith, an old Texan near Devine, was born in Gonzales
County in 1845. One of his ancestors, after whom he was
named, was a soldier under General Jackson in the Indian wars

and fought in the command of General Cocke. Just before one battle he told General Cocke that he would be killed in the fight, and while it was raging came up to the side of the general and was killed by a rifle ball in the forehead. After the war General Cocke named one of his sons Byrd Smith Cocke.

Y. P. OUTLAW.

Came to Texas in 1848.

In the summer of 1898, while the writer was hunting for old settlers in the vicinity of Moore's station, between Pearsall and Devine, he was fortunate enough to find an old friend from Guadalupe County, Mr. Y. P. Outlaw, who lives near Moore, with whom a most agreeable night was spent, as he is an old Texan and has many interesting things to relate. He was born in Manuel County, Georgia, in 1817, and when quite young served against the Creek Indians, in which he experienced a great deal of hard service during the bloody war with this fierce tribe. He was in many battles with small bands, but passed through them all without receiving a wound. In 1836 he entered the service in the war with the Seminoles in Florida, and carried arms for the troops from middle Georgia to where the army was operating in the Everglades. This service lasted until 1837 and was marked with many hardships for the soldiers in that swampy and brush-covered country.

In 1848 Mr. Outlaw came to Guadalupe County, Texas, and settled near Seguin and successfully farmed and raised fruit for many years.

When the Civil war broke out he served the Confederacy in the regiment of Colonel P. C. Wood, Company D, Capt. W. L. Foster. He was in the battles of Blair's Landing, Yellow Bayou, Marksville, and many others. At the battle of Blair's Landing he was near Gen. Tom Green when he was killed. They were in plain view of the Federal gunboats and in a very exposed position. General Green was anxious to make an attack, and remarked that he thought the gunboats had grounded. Colonel Majors, who was present, said: "No, that is a trick; they are only anchored." General Green said he would make the attack anyhow, if he got the top of his head shot off. The charge was made all along the bayou, and General Green rode his horse close to the gunboats under a terrific fire and dismounted, holding his bridle on one arm. Many of the men by this time were being hit by the rifle fire and grapeshot from the boats, and one of the latter struck General Green on top of the head and he fell to the ground. Mr. Outlaw was so near that blood flew all over him, but he at once went to the prostrate general, and with the assistance of Nathan Busby and Schram tried to carry their slain commander off the field under a heavy fire. General Green kicked a good deal while they were trying to carry him away. Mr. Outlaw received several severe kicks from him. The grape shot which struck the general carried off the top of the skull, exposing the brain, but without breaking the membrane that inclosed it. The fire became so severe that the brave men were compelled to abandon their commander for the time being and seek shelter in the brush and cane further back. Busby caught the general's horse and mounted him, and Mr. Outlaw got on behind him, and thus they left the field. The blood of the slain general remained on the clothing of Mr. Outlaw until it wore off. During this short time of attempting to carry off the body of General Green, Mr. Outlaw was wounded three times, but none of the wounds were severe, and two balls passed through his hat. Capt. Eugene Millett went back with a squad of men and succeeded in bringing off the body. In 1867 Mr. Outlaw married Mrs. Celes Little, widow of Mr. W. W. Little. The maiden name of Mrs. Little was Grinage, one of the old settlers of Guadalupe County.

In 1882 Mr. Outlaw moved from Guadalupe County and settled at Moore's station in Frio County. He has a nice home there and carries his eighty-three years well, and takes a lively interest in all of the main issues of the day.

MRS. NANCY KELLEY.

Came to Texas in 1850.

While we record the deeds of the heroes of the frontier and tell of their prowess in verse and prose, we must not forget our heroines. In following the tracks of the pioneers in later years when the country is no longer a frontier, we only see the signs which they have made. Here and there are decaying log cabins with a few acres around them which were once cultivated but now grown up in brush, and the picket or brush fence rotted down. Old roads are seen which were cut through the brakes; lone chimneys rudely built of rock standing like sentinels, the cabin gone, crumbled into dust, and many other things tell of their presence in the long ago and which mark the footsteps of the pioneers. Scattered through the country, and often in close proximity to these old ruins, stand nice ranch houses, strong pasture fences, schoolhouses, churches, and farms. Where are the pioneers,—the first white settlers of this fair land? We ask ourselves this question as we gaze around. How did they live and die; where and when and under what circumstances? What were their names and where did they come from? Perchance we ask a man who lives here now and has for many years, and he willingly gives us all of the information that he is possessed of. He might tell you that the man who built that cabin which is now crumbling to decay was killed by the Indians—went out one morning to get his horse or oxen, and not coming back search was made and his body found full of arrows and scalped. He is buried in that grave over there. "Come and I will show you his grave." Almost covered by weeds and briars we see a sunken mound; a rude stone marks the head, and by pulling the shrubbery back can make out the date of his death some thirty, forty, or fifty years ago. Some of the first settlers moved on when crowded, as they called it, and no one here knows what became of them. Some met death in violent ways, and some naturally. Many stopped in the country and settled permanently and now live in good houses near the old cabins where they unloaded their wagons under the trees fifty years ago and made their first rude shelters. Many of these places and graves were shown to the writer while traveling over the counties of the southwest.

During all of these exciting frontier times frail women were there and nobly did their part in the desperate struggle for the mastery in the west. While nearly every State in the Union has had experience with Indians in settling up the country, none has equaled Texas in combats with the savages. Kentucky, the "dark and bloody ground," can not compare with the Lone Star State in the number of her battles with Indians. Boone, Kenton, and Logan with their men fought some bloody and most sanguinary battles, such as "Blue Lick" and Point Pleasant, but Texas fought four to their one. One reason of this was the extent of the Texas frontier—600 miles across—and the numerous tribes of Indians which infested the border and roamed across the vast plains,—Comanches, Apaches. Lipans, Kickapoos, Cheyennes and others, besides Mexicans, who for years invaded Texas with large armies.

Among the pioneer women of Southwest Texas who deserve a chapter in the history of early settlers is Mrs. Nancy Kelley, wife of Mr. Chris. Kelley, an early settler of Uvalde County, who died some years ago. Mrs. Nancy Kelley was the daughter of Milton Williams and was born in Perry County, Illinois, in 1833. Her grandfather, Robert Williams, was a soldier under General Washington and took an active part in the War of the Revolution.

When quite young Mrs. Kelley came to Arkansas and was married there to Mr. L. C. Kelley in 1847, in White County, near Siercy. She came to Texas in 1850 and lived two years in Kaufman County, and then in 1852 moved to Sabinal Canyon, Uvalde County. Mr. Kelley built his house in a beautiful and romantic valley on the west prong of the Sabinal River, now called the Anglin prong after Mr. Aaron Anglin, another early settler, now deceased. This house was near the present ranch of Mr. Sam Harper. Here they lived in peace and quiet for more than a year before any trouble with Indians was experienced. It was not long, however, before these painted and feathered nomads discovered the new settlement in the mountains, and then the trouble commenced.

To the question asked by the writer if she had ever seen an

Indian, Mrs. Kelley said: "Oh, yes, and heard them yell, too." When the Indians commenced raiding they killed and carried off Mr. Kelley's horses and cattle, and it was very dangerous to hunt stock or even do the work about the house away from shelter. Mrs. Kelley often went with her husband to the field and held her baby and his gun while he pulled fodder or did other work.

On one occasion Mr. Kelley and other settlers followed the Indians, and the women and children of the settlement congregated and all stayed at one place until the return of the men. Some of the women were timid and fearful, but Mrs. Kelley was calm and serene, telling the others to trust in a higher power and all would be well. The Indians often came near Mr. Kelley's house, and one one occasion went through his field.

Mr. Kelley finally concluded to go to California with his stock, and moved his family to Uvalde for safety. Uvalde was a small place then, just starting, but had the protection to some extent of soldiers and sometimes rangers who were stationed at Fort Inge, three miles below.

In the winter Mrs. Kelley went back to the canyon, forty miles distant, to kill her hogs, which had been left on the range at the ranch, but before arriving there had a narrow escape from Indians. Her party consisted of her two boys, Robert and Joseph, and three smaller children. George Spencer and Jesse O'Bryant, two young lads, were mounted on horses, and Mrs. Thompson, who lived in the canyon, was in the wagon with Mrs. Kelley and the children. The wagon was drawn by two horses. When near Nolton Creek in the Uvalde prairie they came upon a fresh trail of Indians going west. Mrs. Kelley was traveling northeast. A mounted Indian spy was now discovered on a hill, watching the wagon. He had one led horse, which he tied and then came towards the wagon as if about to make an attack upon it. A less courageous woman than Mrs. Kelley would likely have turned back and been pursued by the Indian, whose yells would have brought others, and the whole party would have been massacred. She, however, put on a bold front and resorted to a frontier strategy in order to fool the Indian, who was too far off to make out exactly what they were doing. She told her two boys, Robert and Joseph, to get out of the wagon and get a stick each, and then mount the horses hitched to the wagon and put the sticks on their shoulders. The two other boys, Spencer and O'Bryant, were told to tie their lariats to the tongue of the wagon in front of the other horses, and then to proceed at a fast gait along the road. The Indian had stopped and was watching all of these proceedings, and no doubt was under the impression that the sticks were guns which had been taken out of the wagon and that there were four men ready to fight. He came no nearer and the party made their trip in safety.

Mr. Kelley stayed two years in California with his cattle, and Mrs. Kelley managed as best she could under the circumstances, aided by her boys, and they had many experiences with Indians. She moved to Frio Canyon to get the benefit of a school there, and had another frontier experience while making the journey. She saw some white men over a hill with a wagon, and not being able to see them distinctly thought they were Indians, as they were out of the wagon, moving about loading wood, and she could only see their heads. Not wishing to turn back she again resorted to strategy. There was one man along whose daughter was in the wagon going over to attend the school, and the girls all had new hats but did not have them on, but were now requested to put them on and sit up straight so they could be seen good. Her two boys were in the wagon with hats on, and the man on horseback rode up where he could be seen, and altogether they presented a rather formidable appearance. Five men at least, it seemed, and they now awaited developments. The other party soon discovered them and the identity of each was soon realized, and they made the trip without further incident. The children in the wagon were very much frightened, but Mrs. Kelley told them to trust the Lord and all would be right.

When Mr. Kelley came back from California he made a trip with his family to Sabinal Canyon, but camped on the way at a place called the Blue waterhole. That night the Indians got his horses and he had to leave his family there in the mountains near a cedarbrake in dangerous proximity to the Indians, and go on foot to the settlement ten miles above to get a team to bring his wagon and family on.

Mr. Kelley afterwards settled at this place, and one morning he mounted his horse and went to look for his oxen. Not finding them at the place expected he kept on around the foot of the mountains until coming to the mouth of Blanco Canyon, he turned up that. He soon discovered where some horses had passed along, but thought they were ridden by cowmen, who he knew intended to camp over there. The men, however, had not as yet arrived, and the trail he saw was made by a band of Indians who had come over from the Guadalupe valley and were at this time encamped on a mountain overlooking the valley. This place is now called Lone Tree Mountain, and John Davenport has a ranch at its base.

The Indians had two captives, a little white girl 8 years of age and a negro boy about 12. One Indian came down the mountain to get water and saw Mr. Kelley coming, and at once gave a peculiar howl to inform the others of the fact. Mr. Kelley heard this, but thought it was a wolf. The negro boy afterwards said that as soon as the other Indians heard this howl they grabbed their guns, seven of them, and went down the mountain to where the one was who gave the signal. It was Mr. Kelley's intention to go to a spring he knew of and get a drink of water, and that was where he was making for when the Indians came down, and placed seven of their men near the spring in ambush and awaited him, while the eighth was stationed close to the trail beyond to get him if the others failed. Mr. Kelley changed his mind and kept on by the spring on the high ground, thinking he would soon come to the camp of the cowmen and get water there without dismounting and having to go into the ravine after it. As soon as the Indians discovered by the noise of the horse's feet that the white man had passed the spring they went up on the bank and all aimed their guns at him and fired, he being only thirty steps away with his back towards them. Not a ball touched him, and he thought it was the cowmen firing to scare him, which it did, coming so sudden and close, and he turned his head towards them quickly and exclaimed, "What in the hell are you doing?" In making this quick move his hat fell off, and at the same moment he made the discovery that it was Indians, and at once put the quirt to his horse and dashed up the trail, but ran upon the Indian who had been placed there to kill him and had his gun up ready to shoot.

Mr. Kelley had pulled his Winchester from the scabbard, but the Indian was on the wrong side to shoot him easy and he had to bring his gun around with a swing, and as he did so, fired, and the Indian did the same, but both missed. When Mr. Kelley again looked ahead his horse was about to run under a low limb with him, and he was compelled to abandon the horse to keep from being knocked off. He now turned towards the mountain on the east side of the creek on foot and succeeded in eluding the Indians in the thick brush and rocks, and made his way on up the mountain towards home. The balance of the Indians came on the scene, and he heard them yell loudly when they caught his horse, thinking he was near by badly wounded or killed. The first fire the Indians made at him at the spring the balls cut the limbs and twigs all around him. He had killed a deer and had the hams and hide tied to the saddle. On the way up the mountain Mr. Kelley began to suffer very much with thirst and stopped in the head of a little gorge and raked up snow and ate it to quench the thirst. There had been quite a snowfall a few days before, and there was still some in the gorges where it was protected from the sun. While here, looking to the west across the valley, he saw the Indians on the mountain beyond, packing up to leave camp. He thought there were eleven Indians and some pack horses. What he took to be packs on some of the horses were the captives, no doubt. Mr. Kelley was very much exhausted, but after resting and quenching his thirst his strength returned and he succeeded in getting home about sundown. Mrs. Kelley was expecting him back at dinner time, not knowing he had extended his ox hunt over into the Little Blanco country, and when he failed to arrive at the time expected the children began to express their fears as to his safety. Mrs. Kelley felt distressed but prayed all evening for his deliverance. Mr. George Dillard, his future son-in-law, was at his house when he returned, and saw Mr. Kelley before he got to the house. Being on foot and his hat gone, Mr. Dillard knew something was wrong, and said to Mrs. Kelley: "Here comes your old man and the Indians have been after him." She ran to meet him and could hardly be convinced that he was not wounded as he was very tired and was bracing one hip with his hand as he walked.

Next morning Mr. Kelley and Mr. Dillard went back to the scene of the ambuscade and found the deer hams where they fell from the saddle, but of course the horse and hat were gone. The distance where Mr. Kelley and the Indian exchanged shots when he abandoned his horse was found to be ten steps. The account

30

of the fight which the Frio men had with these Indians, in which they recovered the captives and Mr. Kelley's horse and hat and gun scabbard, has been given elsewhere.

At one time Mr. Kelley owned a very fine horse, which he kept for his own use, and which was very fast and long winded. He loaned this horse, however, on one occasion to a man who lived on the Medina to ride home, and he started the horse back in the care of two boys, or young men, named Alf and James Watson. They camped on the road, and that night the Indians stole all of their horses and the young men had to walk to Sabinal Canyon. Mr. Kelley was very much distressed at the loss of his favorite horse, and at once raised a squad of men and went in pursuit of the Indians, who went west. The trail was closely followed, and in the Frio Canyon the settlers came upon the body of Young Henry Robinson, whom the Indians had just killed. They caught up with Indians, who had stopped and dismounted, but at the sight of the white men they again mounted and made off. The chief was mounted on Mr. Kelley's horse, but was thrown as soon as they started, but he held on to him and mounted again, and this time stayed with him and made his escape. Mr. Kelley ran after him for some distance, but knew it was hopeless, for he was familiar with the speed of both horses. The Indian actually played along ahead of them, out of gun shot, and made the horse prance, and would sometimes turn him around in a circle. He had on a fine bridle, with silver ornaments, which would glisten in the sun very brightly when making the turns. The men finally gave up the chase and came back home.

In 1880 Mrs. Kelley lost her eyesight and has been hopelessly blind ever since. Mr. Kelley died in 1888.

Mrs. Kelley was the mother of twelve children, four of whom died in infancy. The oldest of those alive (Sarah) married Mr. George Dillard. Joseph married Miss Ida Crank. Robert is unmarried and lives with his mother. Emma married Mr. John Davenport and lives on Little Blanco, near the spot where her father made such a narrow escape from the Indians. Zeno was killed by a horse falling on him. He had been married six months. Edward married Miss Lela Martin, daughter of Judge William Martin, of Kerrville. Florence married Mr. Henry McBride, merchant of Sabinal. Albert is unmarried.

Mrs. Kelley is a member of the Christian church and bears her affliction with calm patience and has a kind word and gentle greeting for all with whom she comes in contact. She has great faith in the Lord and looks earnestly to the time when somewhere in the great heavenly kingdom of God she will see the Savior whom she has trusted all her life.

MRS. MAHALA JONES.

Came to Texas in 1850.

Mrs. Mahala Jones, one of the early pioneers of Bandera County, was born in Granger County, Tennessee, in 1825, and came to Texas from Missouri in 1850. Her grandfather, Joseph Yaden, was a revolutionary soldier and was present at the battle of Bunker Hill as a drummer boy, and lustily beat his drum while the British troops were advancing to assault the American works. Mrs. Jones now lives at Indian Spring, on Myrtle Creek, six miles north of the town of Bandera, coming to this place in 1863 with her husband, John A. Jones. About three years after settling here, one day at noon, just as the family were sitting down to dinner, Mr. Tom Click dashed up to the yard fence and called for Mr. Jones. He was bare headed, and his horse was breathing heavily and panting. Mr. Jones thought that Mr. Click had been on a bear chase from all appearances, but soon discovered that he had been chased by Indians and was badly wounded. He was coming from the Guadalupe valley and was ambushed at the Bandera pass and had a desperate run for his life, leaving the main road and taking the road to Jones' ranch, three miles away. The Indians shot many arrows at him, one of which struck him in the back. One Indian came so close that he tried to catch the bridle, but the fleetness of the nag he rode eluded the grasp of the savage, and to this fact Mr. Click owed his life, as he was not armed. He pulled the arrow out of his back as he ran, and had it in one hand and a sycamore switch in the other when he arrived at the yard gate of Mr. Jones. During all of this long, exciting chase the dog kept close to his master, and was not hurt. After Mr. Click was assisted into the house he was unable to remain still on account of the great misery he was in, and walked the floor incessantly, and finally took a severe chill. He called for a pipe to smoke, but when it was prepared for him was deathly sick and unable to smoke it. A negro was placed on Mr. Click's horse and sent to Bandera after Dr. Fitz Gibbons. In the meantime Mrs. Jones with a pair of scissors clipped the shirt from around the wound, stopped the flow of blood, and put hartshorn on it. Mr.

Click was not frightened and remembered everything distinctly in regard to the chase, and said that a hackberry limb had torn a piece out of his shirt, and that there were twelve Indians. He also said that he could find the last arrow they shot at him, as he saw where it struck in a bunch of bushes, a little to one side and ahead of him. All this was found to be the case afterwards, the bit of shirt on the hackberry limb and the arrow in the bunch of bushes. When the doctor came and made an examination of the wound it was discovered that Mr. Click had been wounded with a poisoned arrow, which was the direct cause of his intense suffering. The pain was like that which ensues after being bitten by a rattlesnake, for the spike was poisoned by venom from one of these most deadly reptiles. The doctor gave strychnine until the water in which he gave it was colored like milk, to counteract the poison. Mr. Click finally, after months of suffering, recovered, but a large piece of the flesh rotted out around the wound.

Soon after the Civil war Mr. Joseph Moore was living near where Medina City is now, and one Sunday he went visiting in a wagon drawn by a yoke of oxen, having his wife and four children with him. One of his children, a boy, had been left at a neighbor's house. In the evening, while returning and near home, Mr. Jones got out of the wagon in order to drive carefully down a steep hill into the bed of a deep ravine or small creek. A band of Indians was lying in wait here, aware that some one was coming by the noise of the wagon coming over the rocks. The first intimation that Mr. Jones had of the presence of the Indians was the exclamation from one of his little girls, "Papa! Papa! There is some men!" The Indians had just raised up from their concealment near the wagon, and one of them aimed a gun quickly and fired, and gave Mr. Jones a fatal wound. The stricken father attempted to get back into the wagon, but was not able to do so, and after holding onto the wagonbed a few moments sank down and died. The Indians now fired again and killed Mrs. Moore, who was in the wagon with the children. One Indian then got into the wagon and began to lance the terror-stricken and screaming littles ones. One little boy jumped out and succeeded in making his escape to the house of John Walker. The other three children left in the wagon were all wounded, but none of them died. One little girl had the baby in

her lap and displayed great presence of mind and courage. Instead of throwing the child down and trying to make her own
escape she held on to it and jerked it first one way and then the
other to keep the Indian from getting his lance through it, which
he would have done but for her quick movements of the child
when he would make his thrusts, and it only received glancing
wounds. One circumstance, however, which saved the lives of
the children finally was the fact that during this time the oxen
were running away with the wagon towards Mr. Walker's house,
and when nearing that place the Indian jumped out and ran
back.

One of Mr. Moore's boys, the one who had been left at Mr.
Walker's, was in the cowpen at the time, helping to milk, and
when he heard the guns remarked: "I expect that is Indians
killing papa and mamma." As soon as the situation was known
Mr. Walker armed himself and went to the place of the killing,
but the Indians were gone. The bodies of the dead pioneers were
buried, and Mr. Walker took the orphan children to his house
and cared for them.

A brother of Mrs. Moore lived at Boerne, in Kendall County,
and he came and carried the wounded children to his home as
soon as they were able to travel. On the way back the uncle
camped for noon with the children near Mrs. Jones' house, and
she carried some milk to them. She tried to get him to come
to the house with them and eat dinner there, but he said they
had plenty to eat and that he only wanted milk for them. The
children looked pale and thin.

Not long after the Indians killed Mr. Moore and his wife they
made another raid and killed his mother. The old lady was
going to see Mrs. Curtis, who was sick, and she was killed near
the house of Mr. Walker. Mr. Walker armed himself when he
heard her screaming, and ran to the spot, but the Indians were
gone and Mrs. Moore was lying on her face, lanced to death.

On another occasion, above where Medina City is now, about
where the Crockett place is, Mr. Joe Sheppard was riding along
alone, and was shot by an Indian with a gun, who was hiding behind a big cypress stump. Sheppard saw the Indian just before he fired and thought it was a bear. When the ball struck
him he sprang from his horse and ran behind a drift near the
river and waited with his gun ready to shoot, not knowing how

many Indians there were, and supposing they would follow him. No Indians came, however, but soon a man named John Henning came upon the scene in a wagon and helped Sheppard to get into it and lie down. The ball hit him in the side, and he was badly hurt. Henning carried him to a doctor called the French doctor by the people, but he could not find the ball and said it must have dropped out while jolting in the wagon, or else dropped inside of him, as he was unable to find it. After a hard struggle Sheppard recovered.

In 1867 the Indians made another raid into Bandera County and were followed with a small squad of men by Capt. Bob Valentine. One of the trailers in this chase was Andy Jones, son of Mrs. Mahala Jones. During the time that Captain Valentine and his men were on the trail of the Indians John Scott and one of his boys were at work in the field, and the Indians were just preparing to kill them when the trailers came upon them and they rapidly stampeded, leaving some of their paint sacks and one horse. These same Indians got together again and killed a Mexican on Pipe Creek. The scouts kept after them and found the body of the Mexican. He was at work on a fence, and when shot ran and took refuge in an old chimney, which was standing alone where a cabin had stood, and there squatting down presented his pistol and died in that position. The Indians, not knowing he was killed, did not assault his position and went on, but Captain Valentine could never bring them to battle, and finally had to abandon the chase.

Mrs. Jones has a fine ranch and a good deal of stock and lives with her brother, Mr. Capps, and some of her children, her husband having died some years ago. The brother, Mr. Delaney Capps, has no family. He came to Texas in 1850, and in 1851 cut hay near Seguin, Guadalupe County. The first work he did in Texas was for Gen. Ed Burleson. He put up a house for his son-in-law, Felix Kyle, at Sink Springs. He knew Gen. Sam Houston and heard him make two speeches. During the Civil war he served the Confederacy under Gen. H. E. McCulloch. He also knew Capt. Jesse Billingsly and heard him say that when he was a member of the Legislature he furnished his own grub, slept on his own blanket, and wore a buckskin suit that he took from a Comanche Indian whom he killed in a battle.

L. C. DAVENPORT.

Mr. L. C. Davenport (Clabe) came to Texas at an early day from Missouri, and in 1853 settled in Sabinal Canyon, Uvalde County. In 1856 he lived on Ranchero Creek, when the Indians made the raid, in which they killed his half brother, John Davenport, and also John Bowles. At the time of this raid Mr. Clabe Davenport was at work on the ranch of Dr. Isbell, which was situated on the Frio at the foot of the mountains. This ranch is now called the Annadale, and is owned by Judge Florea. The Indians came near this ranch and were followed by Mr. Davenport and three others, one of whom was Frank Isbell. The trail was followed south down Blanco Creek, through the prairie to the Eagle Pass crossing, on the main road from San Antonio to Mexico, and then it turned towards the Patterson settlement on the Sabinal. The settlers continued to follow, and during the day learned from other settlers who had discovered the presence of the Indians and were gathering, that they had killed John Bowles near Pilot Knob, and John Davenport six miles north towards the mountains. The scout now went to where Davenport was killed, and getting more men took up the trail of the Indians, which led back in a northwest course. Some citizens from Uvalde and soldiers from Fort Inge joined them the next day. Among the citizens from Uvalde were James McCormick, Doke Bowles, Ben Pulliam, and others. The Indians made several halts and had a wounded one with them evidently, from the bloody rags which were found where they dressed his wounds. They also found where grass had been pulled for this one to lay on. It was also supposed that the Indian died in camp, but his body could not be found. They could smell it, but it was in a cave or under rocks, and not a great deal of time was spent in searching for it.

The Indians were overtaken in a hilly country, near the head of North Llano. The men were badly scattered and could only ride in single file on account of the nature of the country. Word was passed back to the rear that the Indians were in front and to keep still. The Indians, however, soon discovered the white men and commenced hastily leaving their camp, two of them mounting on one horse. A charge was ordered, and shooting soon commenced. In the pursuit the Indian who rode behind the other one on the same horse was killed and fell off into a ravine. At this time Ben Pulliam, Clabe Davenport, and two others were in front. Pulliam dashed into the ravine and was shot by the wounded Indian, who was not yet dead, but had a mortal wound. The arrow struck Pulliam in the back as he passed the Indian. The Comanches did not remain together and many shots were fired in the long running fight. One Indian did splendid riding and shooting. He shot Lieutenant Hazen from his horse and also a man named Williams, and got his horse, which he was riding the last seen of him. Mr. Davenport got some close shots and thinks he hit several Indians. Three Indians were killed and all of the balance wounded, and among the killed was the one who had John Davenport's pistol. Another one of the dead Indians had John Bowles' scalp. It had been stretched around a hoop made of a switch and nicely dressed. The scalp of Davenport could not be found and was no doubt carried away by one of those who made their escape. The Indians killed had been hit many times.

After the chase was over the men went into camp and stayed several days with the wounded men, and a messenger was sent to Brackett for surgical aid. Some of them came on with Ben Pullium, but when they arrived at the head of the Frio River he requested the men to stop and make an examination of his wound, as it was paining him very much and something was wrong with it. On examination it was found that the spike had struck the backbone and twisted around it like a fishhook. He had pulled the arrow out himself when it struck him and threw it down, but the spike remained, hence the trouble. He was now placed on his stomach on the ground, the wound pressed open until the spike was revealed, and then a man with a pair of bullet moulds caught it and pulled it out. The wounded man suffered excruciating pain, but it had to be done. Mr. Davenport also thinks a man named Everette was wounded.

On another occasion the Indians made a raid and stole about fifty head of horses belonging to Dr. Isbell and drove them along the divide between the Frio and Sabinal, the roughest place they could find, and many colts were killed by having to jump down bluffs and steep rocky places. Mr. Davenport and other citizens

and a few soldiers from Inge followed them to the head of the
rivers and overtook them on the divide in an open postoak country with small cedarbrakes interspersed. The Indians ran, but
were pursued so closely they dismounted and made breastworks
of their horses, and the fight commenced. There was a good
deal of shooting done, and two horses were soon killed. The
Indians had large guns of some kind, and one of them was aimed
at Mr. Davenport and fired, but the ball struck the ground at
his feet and went skipping and bouncing beyond him. The Indians, seeing the whites about to surround them, once more ran
and made another stand in a small cedarbrake. The white men
now dismounted and commenced shooting into the brake, and
the Indians saw their only chance was to charge, which they did,
coming close to the white men, and a hard fight ensued. One
Indian especially was very brave and was hit many times, and
finally couched down on his knees, and a soldier, taking good aim
at him, shot him through the head. Mr. Davenport was so close
to him he saw the smoke from the hot brains as they flew out of
the top of his head. The Indians now ran back into the brake
and went on through in a desperate attempt to escape. The
men followed and fought them for several miles. John Leakey
followed one and shot at him many times, and got close enough
to him once to strike at him with his gun, but could not bring
him from his horse. It was now nearly night, and the Indian
getting into the cedarbrake, Leakey left him and went back. One
Indian turned on a man, who dismounted and aiming his gun
fired, but missed, and the Comanche crowded him so close he left
the horse, not having time to mount, and the Indian mounted
him himself and rode away, carrying a pistol, overcoat, and other
things which were on the saddle. The stolen horses were all
retaken except a few and carried back to the ranch. Years after
the skeleton of an Indian and a horse were found under a tree
near where Leakey left his wounded Indian. It is supposed the
Indian, when clear of his pursuer, dismounted and tying his
horse to the tree lay down and died and his horse starved to
death.

On one occasion in 1862, when Mr. Davenport was living on
Ranchero Creek, he and Ambrose Crane went out towards the
Comanche waterhole to look for some horses and came upon the
trail of a shod horse, and wishing to ascertain who it was, went

on the trail at a gallop and found that it was John Ware coming back home from the war on a furlough. Crane went home from there, but Davenport went on towards the waterhole, although his horse was well jaded by the long gallop. Arriving at the place he ascended a hill to see if he could discover the horses he was looking for, and saw six men coming around the brush towards the water, driving some horses, but they stayed partly in the brush so that he could not make out who they were until they came close, and he then perceived that they were Indians, and they charged him. A desperate race now commenced, and Davenport had to make a circle to get home, as the Indians were coming from that direction. He ran over one hill and then made for another which had brush and liveoak on it, and which was about half a mile away. In making the run across the flat between the two hills he passed through a bunch of sheep and looked for the herder, thinking he would make a stand with him and fight them, but not being able to see him anywhere he kept on to the hill, which he ascended, and then stopped as his horse was nearly run down, being tired when the chase commenced. While halted here he heard a terrible yelling among the Indians and knew they were killing the herder, whose name was Shockhouse, and was a brother-in-law of Captain Richarz of D'Hanis, who owned the herd of sheep. Mr. Davenport, being uneasy about his family at home, six miles away, again ran. When he arrived at home he found his people all right, but he had killed his horse, the faithful animal dying soon after the saddle was pulled off. Next morning Mr. Davenport went back and met some men, who told him that Shockhouse was killed. There was a little house at the sheep camp, and two of Captain Richarz's children were at it at the time, but their uncle not coming back they went to D'Hanis in the night, five miles distant, and informed their father.

When the Indian raid was made in which Wolf and Huffman was killed, Mr. Davenport was in the cowpen milking, and heard Indians yelling at Ross Kennedy's ranch, and at once went to the house and told the family that the Indians were killing some one at Kennedy's ranch. The ranchman himself soon came and said the Indians had run his Mexican herder to the house and killed him. Men were raised and the pursuit commenced, Mr. Davenport being one of the number. The Indians were heard of on the Sabinal, and some more men being raised the pursuit was continued, and on the river not far from the present home of Mrs. Nancy Kelley a gray horse was found shot in the hip with an arrow. The trail was here scattered a good deal, showing a fight had occurred, and soon a dead Indian was found under a tree with his shield, bow, and quiver hanging near him. Not knowing who had the fight, the party went on and came upon the Indians camped in the edge of a cedarbrake on the Big Blanco. They had killed a muley cow, and setting a brush pile on fire were cooking the meat while their horses stood tied near by. When they saw the white men close upon them they ran and left their horses. Mr. Davenport had a good shot at two Indians running close together, but was prevented from shooting by General Knox, who said: "Let the Indians go and save the horses." He had charge of a train, and his mules being stolen, thought these were the ones and wanted to save them. The horses and saddles of the Indians were all captured, and the men went back home that night, arriving there when it was nearly day. Next morning they went back and found the bodies of Huffman and Wolf near where they saw the dead Indian in the tree. The two white men had made a stand at a liveoak tree which was full of arrows, but had run from there and were killed in the flat one hundred yards away. The Indian was also killed there, for the blood' was on the ground where he fell, and also the sign where the other Indians had dragged him to the tree.

Mr. Davenport had lost many head of stock from Indian raids, but still has plenty and lives on a fine ranch at the mouth of Dry Frio Canyon.

His son Sidney also had a narrow escape from Indians when a small boy. He had been sent down the road to notify the people of an Indian raid, and the Indians crossed the road just ahead of him, and his horse reared and wanted to run back when he smelled the trail across the road.

Mrs. Della Davenport, wife of Sidney, is the daughter of Mr. Joe Kelley, of Sabinal Canyon, and has been raised on the frontier. She can remember seeing the Indians running off their horses and her father getting on his horse with his gun and following the Indians to get his horses back.

SECO SMITH.

Came to Texas in 1856.

There is no name along the Texas border, comprising the counties of Uvalde, Medina, Bandera, and others, that is better known than that of Seco Smith. While not in as many Indian battles as some others, he was a splendid scout and trailer and knew all of the country for hundreds of miles around. He could lead a band of frontiersmen through all of the dense brakes and dangerous defiles in the mountains, and was never at fault as to his bearings. He was strong and wiry, of a jovial disposition, and had many friends, even among the police of San Antonio, although he handled them very rough at times when they interfered in his little games of sport when on a trip with the boys down there. He would yell when the spirit moved him, and no two of them could carry him to the calaboose. They finally got so that when they heard his warwhoop they would smile and say "That is Seco Smith; he won't do any harm if they will let him alone."

W. D. Smith (Seco) was born in Mississippi in Copiah County, October 24, 1836. In 1849 he took a trip to California by way of Salt Lake City, Utah, arriving there in 1850. He stayed there six months and then came overland to Texas by way of El Paso, Fort Thorn, and Quitman, and arrived in San Antonio, June 26, 1856. They had no trouble with the Indians on the trip until near Fort Davis, and there one night the Indians stampeded the horses and ran them over the guards, but the men followed and rounded them up in a cove and put out guards again, and held them there until morning, so the Indians failed to get any of them. Seco was one of the guards, and before day was certain he saw an Indian. He leveled his gun and fired, but it proved to be a Spanish dagger. His aim, however, was good, and he put a hole through it, as daylight revealed.

From San Antonio he moved out to Olmos Creek, six miles from town, and commenced ranching. The Indians, however, soon found him out here and stole all of his mules and horses. A crowd of men were gathered to follow them, among whom were John Jones, Henderson McCoy, Grant Bennett, Dave Bennett, Jim Bennett, Amos Jones, Robert M. Smith (father of Seco), and Oliver Bacon. The Indian trail led out towards the head of the Cibolo, and thither it was followed by the trailers, and when arriving at the head of the creek the trail led directly through a large patch of wild plums, and it being in season for them the fruit almost covered the ground where the ripe ones had fallen off. Here a rather strange thing happened, somewhat out of the ordinary. The trail of the Indians was lost on account of bear tracks. It seems that all of the bear in the country had been there after the Indians passed, eating plums, and completely obliterated the trail, and the settlers turned back after a fruitless effort to locate it again.

In 1859 Seco moved further west and settled on Seco Creek, and hence his familiar nickname. Stock-raising was the main pursuit, from a financial standpoint, of the settlers, and many cow hunts and Indian scouts were participated in by Mr. Smith.

On one occasion, while out on a cow hunt, George Redus won thirty yearlings from Lon Moore shooting with a pistol. Seco then bantered Redus to shoot with him for yearlings, and the challenge being accepted, he won all of the yearlings back and returned them to his friend and boon companion, Moore.

In 1862 Mr. Smith joined the Confederate army and served in the Louisiana campaign against General Banks, and was in many battles and skirmishes. The hottest place was in the fight at Cheneyville, where they fought in a lane almost hand to hand, and fought with revolvers, both Federals and Confederates.

In 1866, while Seco and John Elam were building a house at some stockpens on Seco Creek, old man Miller, father of Jack Miller, a well known settler, came down there with provisions for his son Jack and other hands, who were engaged in branding cattle. Mr. Charles Richter started to go back home with the elder Miller, but in a short time they came running back and said the Indians were up the creek with a large drove of horses. The men at the pens mounted their horses in hot haste and went after them, the party being composed of George Johnson, Ambrose Crane, Seco Smith, Isaac Elam, Charles Richter, and William Fritz. The Indians were soon overtaken and found to have forty head of horses belonging to Judge George Harper, who lived on the Hondo. The Indians scattered, as was supposed, for a great dust arose and objects could not be seen very plainly. Seco Smith says that he did not see but one Indian and took after him. Others said they saw another one, but he fled at great speed when the charge was made. Seco soon ran close to the Indian he was after, who was poorly mounted on a mare belonging to Judge Harper. During the chase the Indian ran into a thicket and Seco closely followed, shooting at him with a revolver. When the Indian got through the thicket he dismounted and crawled on all fours to a mott of liveoak timber. By this time Smith had fired eleven shots at him and the other men were also shooting and made quick work of the lone warrior. Seco wounded him the first few shots in the arm and he dropped his bow, not being able to shoot it, and threw rocks at Seco. After he was dead an examination of the body was made, and five bullet wounds were discovered in the back and one in the arm. He was a very fine, stout looking Indian, and appeared to be about forty-five years of age. During these troublesome times a family named Long lived on Blanco Creek, east of the Frio, and the Indians made a raid in that vicinity, and killed Sam Long, who was out herding cattle. One of his sisters who had been to a neighbor's house that day was seen by the same Indians as she was returning home and they galloped around her in a circle and one of them taking her by the hair pulled her from her horse, at the same time pulling a good deal of her hair out. They now lanced and scalped the unfortunate girl and left her for dead on the prairie. Life, however, was not extinct, and she was found and conveyed home, and by careful attention recovered and afterwards married Seco Smith. She died a number of years ago, leaving a family of several children. Seco Smith still survives and lives at Medina City, in Bandera County.

JACOB HABY.

Came to Texas in 1844.

Mr. Jacob Haby, who now lives on the Medina River above
Castroville, is one of the old pioneers of southwest Texas and
one of those large connection of Habys who made a record as
brave men and Indian fighters on the frontier. He was born
in Alsace on the 16th of October, 1833, and started to Texas
with his parents the 19th of March, 1844. Of his family on
the ship was his father, Jacob Haby, one brother, Louis, a sister
named Paris, and his mother. His mother was a Kempf, and
some of the connections are still in Medina County. August
Kempf is clerk of Medina County and lives at Hondo City, the
county seat. One brother, Nichalus, had preceded the balance
of the family to Texas. One other brother was named George.
He served as a captain on the frontier.

The ship the Habys were on first landed at Galveston, but
went from there to Port Lavaca and made the start for Castro's
colony. They were one month on the road from the coast and
arrived in San Antonio in July, but did not go on to the settlement of the present town of Castroville until October of 1844.
They first settled in the town and stayed there four years and
then moved up to what is now now called the Haby settlement,
and where Jacob and others still reside.

The Lipans and Delaware Indians lived along the Medina
River at that time and were friendly. The Comanches, he said,
were not so good and would not come about the settlement much,
remaining further west. On one occasion, however, a large body
of them came close to town and the people were very uneasy.
Capt. Jack Hays was in town, and he was informed of the proximity of the Comanches. Captain Hays at once mounted his
horse and set out for San Antonio, distant twenty-five miles,
where his company of rangers were stationed, and when daylight
came next morning the people were surprised to see his men
camped in the edge of town and their guards scattered around
it. These tireless guardians of the frontier, on being notified by
their captain of the danger to the settlement by the presence in

the near vicinity of the Comanches, mounted their horses and sped away in the darkness, and while the inhabitants of the little village slept, silently placed their guards around them and watched and waited, ready to risk their lives in their defense.

No wonder that these old men of Castro's colony revere the name of Jack Hays and his rangers and never tire of sounding their praise. The Comanches no doubt had their spies out, and knowing the situation dared not attack the place while their dreaded foes, the rangers, who had so often defeated them, were there. Captain Hays said he believed the intention of the Indians was to burn Castroville and kill and drive the people away. Mr. Haby told the writer that Jack Hays was one of the best Indian fighters that was ever in the west, and that the people always felt safe when he was around. Haby and others were in the Bandera Pass in 1856 and saw many signs of the battle there fought by Hays and his men some years before. There were graves of rangers and bones of horses and Indians killed in the fight. He says that in a fight which Captain Hays and the rangers had with Indians, one Alsace man was killed who was a ranger under Hays. His name was Peter Fore and he was from Strasburg.

While Mr. Haby was in San Antonio in the summer of 1844 he saw two of Jack Hays' rangers who were badly wounded by Indians in a fight on the Nueces. He says they were both shot in the face and were under the doctor's care when he saw them; that they lay in a room back of the large mercantile establishment now run by Mr. L. Wolfson. No buildings, however, were there then except the small house in which the wounded rangers lay. He does not remember their names, but the writer will say that they were Kit Ackland and Rufe Perry.

Mr. Haby has not been in any Indian fights, but saw four men once who had been killed by Indians, the account of which and the names are given in the sketch of Mr. Nichalus Haby.

Mr. Jacob Haby did not travel about the country much, but stayed at home and helped his father work. His father died in 1853. One night when all of the Indians had become hostile and left the country a band of them came back on a raid, and first struck the Haby settlement above town. The alarm was given and all kept a sharp lookout that night for their horses.

31

Mr. Haby chained his horse close in front of his open door and lay on a bed where he could watch the horse, with a new six-shooter in his hand. The moon was full and shining brightly. Late in the night the horse became uneasy, snorted, reared, plunged, and stood on his hind feet. Mr. Haby knew an Indian was near, and expected every moment to see him approach the horse, when he was sure he could kill him. While intently watching he saw a curious thing close to the door facing, and at first could not imagine what it was, but as it came a little further into view and grew larger and more distinct he discovered that it was the feathered end of a quiver of arrows on an Indian's back. The Indian was inching slowly so as to get one eye around the door facing and see if Mr. Haby was asleep, being afraid to approach the horse until assured of that fact. The wide awake settler at once cocked the pistol to shoot him, but the new weapon clicked loudly and the Indian vanished like a ghost and nothing more was seen of him. Mr. Haby said he made a mistake in not having the pistol ready to fire, and could then have got him. The writer was shown the old cabin near Mr. Haby's more substantial residence where this occurred.

HENRY SHANE.

Came to Texas in the 40's.

Six miles south of Sabinal station, on the east bank of the Sabinal River, lives Henry J. Shane, one of the old pioneers and Indian fighters of Uvalde County.

Mr. Shane was born in Berlin, Germany, in 1836, and came to America with his mother and other members of the family in the late forties. They first landed in New York City. The father had preceded them and sent back for the family. They stayed some time in New York, not knowing where the elder Shane was, as he had gone from there to Texas. During this time he was with the American army in Mexico and knew not of the arrival of his family.

After the war with Mexico was over the family learned from returning soldiers that Mr. Shane was at Laredo, Texas, on the Rio Grande. Thither the family started by way of San Antonio, Texas, and joined him in 1850. He still belonged to the army, and his regiment was ordered to Arizona soon after the arrival of Mrs. Shane. The family now went back to San Antonio. From here Henry went back to Laredo and took a trip with Colonel Ruggles to El Paso as a soldier. Here he quit the command on account of a severe affliction of the knee, which rendered him unfit for the service. He then went to Fort Clark with David Vanderburg and hired to Major Baredon to take charge of a sheep camp. The major was quartermaster for the troops at the fort and also owned a sheep and goat ranch on Pinto Creek, twelve miles from the fort. To this place young Shane was sent to oversee the Mexicans there and to keep supplies, etc. Deer were plentiful, and being fond of hunting he killed a great many of them for use at the ranch. One day while out he killed a deer and laid his gun down to skin it without reloading. He was soon after surrounded by Indians who had been attracted to the spot by the report of his gun.

It was no use to make any resistance, and as they did not seem disposed to kill him, he surrendered. The first thing they did was to give him a severe whipping with a pair of hobbles.

They then placed him on a mule and started off briskly towards the northwest. They had not proceeded far, however, when they were joined by nine more Indians, making fifteen in all. They traveled all that day and part of the night and then stopped to rest and eat something. Here they whipped their captive again, but for what cause he could not tell, as he had given them no trouble whatever. For his repast they gave him a small piece of burnt meat with the hair on it. The Indians then lay down and rested until nearly morning, and then started again, moving rapidly until 9 o'clock in the forenoon, when they again halted to eat and rest.

In the meantime the Mexican herders had raised an alarm about the Indian raid. They heard Shane's gun when he killed the deer, and when he failed to put in an appearance at the expected time they went in search, finding the slain deer and the trail of the Indians. They knew he was killed or captured; the latter they supposed, as his body could not be found. News was at once carried to the fort, and a squad of soldiers was ordered out to follow the Indians, guided by "Old Roka," a Mexican who had been with the Indians many years and was a good guide and trailer. The camp of the hostiles was near a cedarbrake, and the soldiers came upon them while they were eating. The Mexican guide had taken advantage of the cedarbrake when the camp was discovered and led the soldiers upon them unawares. Shane was not aware of the presence of the soldiers until they were among them and firing.

The Indians, although taken by surprise, made a fight with the soldiers, and things were lively for a few minutes. Bullets and arrows were both flying, and Shane concluded he would run out of it into the cedarbrake near by. It is a custom with Indians when they have captives to kill them when attacked, so when Shane started an Indian shot at him with an arrow, which went through his arm and remained fixed there. After getting into the brake he stopped, and breaking the arrow below the spike so he could pull it out, threw it down and listened. The fight was still going on, the Indians yelling and the carbines in the hands of the soldiers still continuing to pop. Some of the Indians seemed to be trying to make their escape into the same brake where Shane was, and he continued his flight, intending now to make his way back to the fort without waiting for the soldiers.

He saw four Indians fall before he left the scene of the battle. He came to a creek, which he followed all of that day and saw many wild animals, tigers, bears, panthers and Mexican lions. When night came he was nearly exhausted and climbed into a tree to spend the night for fear of wild animals. He obtained some sleep by getting into the fork of a tree so that he could not easily fall out when he could no longer keep awake. When daylight came he resumed his journey and arrived at the fort that day. He was forty-eight hours without food except the little piece of burnt meat the Indians gave him. After the fight the soldiers looked for Shane, but not being able to find him, returned.

Mr. Shane remained here at this fort until the Civil war broke out, and then joined Captain Gibson's command, Company B of the Eighth Texas Cavalry, Col. Rip Ford's regiment. He was in several fights with the bands of Cortenas and had to guard the river all the time. At one ranch, about thirty miles above Brownsville, the troops had a sharp fight, and many of the Mexicans jumped off the bluff into the river and were drowned. Captain Dunn of the Confederate force was killed and several others were killed or wounded. The fight took place in a very brushy place and some of the men killed were not found. Mr. Shane was in the last battle of the war between the North and South. It commenced, as near as he can remember, near the old Palo Alto battleground and lasted all the way to the Federal ships, ten miles away. About 100 prisoners were taken, and among this number was a man called Paddy, who had been with Shane on the frontier, but had joined the Union forces when the war broke out. He recognized Shane when brought in a prisoner, and ran to shake hands with him, but was stopped by a soldier, who raised his gun to strike him. Shane now interfered and prevented him from getting hurt.

After the war Mr. Shane settled on the Chicon creek, thirty miles east from Eagle Pass and sixty miles west from Uvalde, at the foot of the Anna Catchi mountains. While living here on one occasion he started to the Cameo ranch, but on the way had to pass the San Miguel ranch. This was an old-time Mexican ranch with a rock wall all around it, with an entrance through a gate. When he arrived at this place he could see no one stirring and the gate was open. He dismounted and went in, but could see no signs of life except a little dog, which barked at him. On a smooth piece of sheet iron which lay upon two rocks were several cakes of bread which had not been turned and were burned on the under side, and the fire still burning under them. Shane thought there was something wrong, but as he could see no one, proceeded on his way. About 300 yards from the ranch he had to cross Sauce Creek, and here he found a dead Mexican. That he had been killed by Indians was evident, as the body was full of arrows, and near by was his horse, which had also been killed. It could be seen that the Mexican was trying to get to the ranch, pursued by the Indians, who first killed his horse and then killed him. When Shane got out of the Sauce bottom and up on a ridge he discovered a horse tied some distance off. By this time he had learned enough about Indians not to approach the horse, but went around him and continued his journey. Before he lost sight of the tied horse he saw an Indian near him and soon five others came into view and came in pursuit of Shane, but he was on a good horse and made his escape from them. He now came to a ranch where there was a crowd of excited Mexicans, some of whom were from the ranch where lay the dead Mexican. This man, they said, was away from the ranch when it was attacked, and they cut him off and killed him when he made a run to get inside the walls. After the Indians left these people also left and came to this ranch.

In 1866 Mr. Shane moved from the ranch on the Chicon and settled at the Presidio crossing of the Frio. Next year he moved up the Frio to the Adams ranch. In March of the next year he had a sheep camp half a mile from Adams, and there he had another experience with the Indians. There was no house of any kind at the camp, but the tent was surrounded by a brush fence. One night Shane was sitting with his back to this fence, parching coffee, and was not aware that the Indians were in the country, but at this time they were prowling around his camp, and even noticed his position while roasting the coffee. One of them slipped up on the opposite side of the fence with the intention of poking his gun through the brush and shooting Shane in the back. In getting the muzzle of the gun through, however, the Indian made too much noise breaking twigs, and Shane heard him. Turning to his Mexican herder, Felipe Flores, he said: "What is that?" The Mexican replied: "It is a rat; I saw one go in there." About this time the Indian attempted to shoot, but his gun snapped and hung fire, and Shane jumped, but the gun went off as the Indian attempted to jerk it back through the brush, and the ball went through the rim of Shane's hat. The Indian ran before a gun could be got to shoot him, but was seen as he ran off and went into a thicket. Next morning Shane went up to the Adams ranch and found that the Indians had been there and carried off twenty-five horses. A few men were raised to follow them, and by the time they got to Rhiner's ranch on the Blanco the force had increased by accessions on the route to thirteen men, and the Indians were overtaken on the west prong of the Nueces. They were in camp, but saw the white men as they came up a mountain, and ran away, carrying the horses with them. The trailers saw the Indians going through a gap in the mountains, and at once charged and crowded them so close they dropped seven head of the Adams horses. These were recovered, but they got no shots at the Indians. The men were very hungry and went back to the Indian camp and did justice to the fat beef which was on the fire cooking. The camp was on a mountain a mile from water, and the Indians had two beef paunches up there filled with water. The horses were down in the valley. So sudden was their flight they left some shields and headdresses. The settlers had water along with them and did not sample any of that in the cow paunches.

After leaving the Indian camp the men came back to the chalk bluff on the river and camped for the night. Next morning Mr. Shane, being anxious to get back, saddled up first and started back home, as the scout was now over. A Mexican named Leal, who was boss at the Knox ranch, also went, and they traveled on together about two miles, when suddenly and very unexpectedly they met a band of Indians in the road driving a bunch of horses. When the Indians saw Shane and Leal, they turned the horses away from the road and kept on. Shane said to his Mexican companion: "We should go back and tell the other men here is a chance to fight Indians." Leal said no, he was going home, and continued on his way, while Shane hurried back to the other party, who were still in camp at the bluff, but had their horses saddled and were about to start when Shane returned. On hearing the news some of them mounted quickly and set out, anxious for a fight. These men were Ben Pullium, Nubb Pullium, Capt.

Bill Adams, Ed Downs, Henry Shane and a Mexican named
Antonio Lopez. When the men overtook them the Indians ran
and waved their blankets and fired on the white men, who ran
among them and passed a few shots at close quarters. During
this close firing Shane had a piece shot out of the horn of his
saddle, and two Indians were killed, but their horses carried
them into the brush. The Indians finally made a stand on a
round top mountain, but ran again when the white men charged
them, and left three saddled horses. There were nine of the Indians when the chase commenced, and when last seen going up a
mountain there were but seven, and some of these were wounded.
The white men got thirty head of horses and seven mules belonging to Chapman, who lived on the Frio. All the men on
this trip were not in the fight, but only those whose names are
given. The others were slow in getting off from camp, and only
came up as the pursuit ended. They followed and picked up
shields, blankets, etc.

In 1870 Mr. Shane still lived near the Adams ranch, engaged
in the sheep business, and one of his brothers, named Constance,
lived with him and helped with the sheep. One morning Constance was about 200 yards from the house with a bunch of sheep,
near the creek bank, and heard horses' feet knocking the rocks
under the bluff. He stepped up to look over, thinking it was
cowmen coming, but it was a band of nine Indians with the chief
in the lead. Just as Constance looked over at them they rode up
the creek bank in a cow trail. It was steep and they came
rapidly, almost running against young Shane as they came out.
The chief had a heavy quirt in his hand, with which he struck
Shane a stunning blow over the head which knocked him down,
and then dismounted and stripped him. The Indians now all
collected around the naked and stunned captive. Henry Shane
saw the Indians from the sheep camp, and getting his gun went
to the corner of a fence and stood and watched them, not knowing they had his brother there. When the Indians saw Shane
with the gun they shot Constance with an arrow and then went
off. Henry followed on after them to see which course they took,
and then came back to the camp, still not aware that anything
had happened to his brother. Not long afterwards Constance
came in covered with blood and the arrow still in him, which he
he was unable to extract. It had struck below the left shoulder

blade and ranged downward, nine inches of the deadly weapon being hid in his body, and it was with great difficulty that Henry, who was a powerful man physically, could withdraw it. The Indian who shot him was on horseback, and that gave the shaft the downward tendency. Constance said there were eight bucks and one squaw, and that it was the squaw that shot him. It was evident the arrow penetrated part of the left lung, for he spit blood for six months, but finally recovered. Every one who looked at him said he was bound to die and would not live past the ninth day.

In 1871 Mr. Shane married a daugher of "Butch" Dillard, and they all lived on the Sabinal at the present ranch of Mr. Shane.

In January of the above mentioned date Henry early one morning went up the river, about one and a half miles, to the ranch of Joe Brown, who had a sheep vat and furnace. The ranch was vacant, Mr. Brown having moved to Uvalde. He had told Shane he could have the use of his vat and furnace for dipping sheep, and also his pens, etc. Shane intended to start a fire in the furnace for the purpose of boiling tobacco, which was used in dipping the sheep to cure them of scab or preventing them from taking it. A Mexican named Bernaldo, who was in the employ of Mr. Dillard, went with Shane to bring back some horses which were in a small pasture up there. Soon, however, the Mexican was seen running back from the pasture, whipping his horse with his hat. When Shane asked what the trouble was the Mexican was so excited he passed on without seeing or hearing him, although close by. Shane was not armed, something that seldom happened with him, as he rarely ever left the house without his gun, even for a short distance. Not wishing to raise a false alarm he went to the pasture on that side where he heard a commotion among the horses, bells rattling, horses running, etc. He soon discovered seven Indians in the pasture after the horses. When they saw him coming three of them left the inclosure and gave chase to him. Shane carried a long stick in his hand, which he used to punch up the fire in the furnace. He turned and ran, but the Indians, being mounted, soon came close upon him, and he pointed the stick at them as if about to shoot. Every Indian dodged and hunted the other side of his horse. This gave him a chance to make another run, and he now made for the ranch of John Patterson, who lived just above

Shane and nearer than to his own house. The Indians soon
caught up with him again, but again he fooled them with the
stick, and gaining a little more time finally reached Patterson's
and jumped over the fence into the cowpen. The Indians shot
some arrows at him and then turned backed and helped to get
the horses out of the pasture. Shane told Patterson if he would
go with him they would have the horses. This was agreed, and
the two men sallied forth. Patterson gave Shane a rifle and he
himself took a six-shooter. They soon met the Indians coming
down the D'Hanis road, driving the horses, and the two men
stepped to one side to ambush them. Shane got behind a large
Spanish dagger, and as the foremost Indian came near took good
aim at him through the dagger top and the gun snapped. The Indians had not as yet discovered the white men, and Shane turned
to ask Patterson for the pistol, but he was not near enough to
hand it to him. The Indians now discovered them and turned
the horses out of the road and went south. About the time Shane
got back to Patterson's, Mr. Dillard rode up on the horse which
the Mexican had ridden when he gave the alarm of Indians, and
having a shotgun said he would follow the Indians. Patterson and Shane had no horse and could not go with him. Dillard soon overtook the Indians, but they turned and chased him
back, shooting at him, and he fired both barrels of his gun at
them. They did not quit him until they came close to the
house, and then turned back and went on with the horses. A
party was now made up and mounted to follow them, consisting
of the following names: Henry Shane, "Butch" Dillard, William Brown, and two Mexicans. They overtook the Indians
where Pearsall now is, in Frio County, but the Indians had received accessions to their number and showed up about twenty-
five. The attack was not made on them, and the settlers hurried
across to Blackally's ranch and got him and his hands, and once
more took the trail of the Indians, but so much time had been
lost they could not come in sight of them any more, and the pursuit was reluctantly abandoned.

In 1872 Mr. Shane commenced a sheep camp about two and
one-half miles from where he lived, and was down there one
morning with a wagon, fixing it up, his Mexican herder being
out with the sheep. The camp was under a forked liveoak tree,
and Shane was adjusting a plank between the forks to serve as a

shelf to place things on. His wagon was a dozen yards away from where he was at work, and in which was two guns. This was the situation when he was attacked by the Indians. At first only one Indian showed himself, and he came up behind the wagon on horseback and shot at Shane with a six-shooter, the ball striking the right hand fork of the tree and knocking bark into his face and eyes. The guns being in the wagon between him and the Indian, Shane had to face the leveled revolver of the savage to get to them. Being a cool and composed man under all circumstances, he went for his gun and received two more shots from the Indian before he could get to the wagon. He avoided these by stooping low as he went, and the balls passed over his head, the Indian having to fire over the wagon. The Comanche realized what the white man was after, and when he saw that his shots had failed to take effect wheeled his horse and ran off. Shane having secured a gun, fired a shot at him as he went and killed his horse, which ran some distance before falling. Eight more Indians now showed themselves and commenced yelling and charging, to fight the lone ranchman. The gun which he had just fired was a Mississippi yager, and he had no more balls for it. The other gun was a new, single-shot Ballard rifle, and he had only two cartridges for it, one in the gun and one in his pocket. In getting away from home that morning he had left his belt, which was full of cartridges for the Ballard gun. He now found himself in a very close place, but determined to make the best fight he could and not waste a shot. Using the wagon for a breastwork he awaited the onset of the Indians, and when they came near he raised his gun and aimed at them. They soon realized what kind of a man they had to deal with, and not knowing but what he had a repeating gun and plenty of cartridges, dodged and took shelter behind prickly pears and chaparral and mesquite bushes. From this cover they opened fire, hitting the wagon and the ground around it repeatedly. Several times Shane had fair opportunities to shoot, but held his fire. The wagon had been brought down the day before with camp equipage and provisions, and the herder had remained there with the sheep, and on this morning Shane had ridden a mule down there to arrange camp fixtures, as before stated. He had tied the mule ninety-four steps from the wagon, where he could eat grass. During the progress of the fight a daring Indian concluded to risk his chances and get the mule, and leaving cover advanced across open ground for that purpose. When Shane saw the Indian coming with his knife ready to cut the rope, he determined to risk one of his shots at him. He was a good shot, and knew he could kill the Indian if he did not dodge too quick. He took a quick but good aim and fired. The Comanche jumped three times high and then fell in a sheep trail and lay there. The other Indians set up a terrible howling when they saw this one was killed, and several of them ran quickly, and taking him by the hair dragged him out of sight behind the pears and bushes. The Indians did not show themselves any more, dreading to expose themselves to such marksmanship. The pioneer still remained and watched for them with but one shot left.

The Mexican herder heard the fight, and from the number of shots fired supposed his employer was killed and ran to the ranch on foot to inform Mrs. Shane of the fact. He knew it was Indians making the attack by their yelling. Mrs. Shane now sent two other Mexicans to the camp to see what was the fate of her husband. The Indians left before they arrived on the scene, and they met them on the way, but the Mexicans hid themselves and were not discovered. After the Comanches passed them they came on to where Shane was and found him still on the lookout, not knowing the Indians were gone. They informed him now of this fact, and also said the Indians had a dead one with them on a horse, wrapped up in a blanket. For the first time now Shane left the wagon and went to the spot where the Indian fell. There was plenty of blood there, so much so that it had run four feet in the sheep trail, the ground there being slanting or undulating. It seems the Indian was not dead when they carried him away from the place where he fell, and they had tried to doctor him. The ball went through the Indian and they had made a poultice for each bullet hole out of mashed prickly pears and bound them in place by a belt around the body. When the Indian died and they were fixing to leave they cut the belt and left it and the two bloody poultices lying on the ground.

These same Indians went in near where Sabinal station is now and stole horses from John Kennedy. They were followed by George Johnson, C. Pingenot, John Kennedy, several other white men and one negro. They overtook them and a fight ensued, in which the negro was killed, and the Indians getting the best of the fight went on with the horses. John Kennedy said the Indians still had the dead one with them which Shane killed.

When Shane returned home from the scene of his fight he found that his shepherd was in a very bad condition from over-exertion while carrying the news of his supposed death. His body and stomach were badly swollen and he was in great pain. Mr. Shane, wishing to do all in his power for the poor fellow, placed him in a wagon and carried him to San Antonio, a distance of eighty miles, and employed the best physicians there to attend him, but all of no avail; he died.

In January, 1874, Mr. Shane had a sheep camp three miles from his house at a place called Long Hollow. He had his old Mexican herder, Felipe Flores, with him. Early one morning Shane heard rocks rattling in the hollow, and he and Flores walked out a short distance from the tent to investigate. The Mexican said it was Mr. Dilliard, whom they were expecting to come and help hunt for some lost sheep. It was ten Indians, however, and they were up the bank on horseback, and after them before they knew what it was. Shane turned and ran to the tent after his gun, but Felipe was crowded so closely he ran backward with an Indian close upon him trying to thrust a lance into his body, and fell into the fire, which was away from the mouth of the tent. The balance of the Indians were all firing, trying to hit Shane before he could get his gun, and many balls hit the tent. Shane got in one shot at them and they retreated, but if he killed one the others carried him away. It was very brushy and they all soon disappeared. The fact of old Felipe falling over the fire likely saved his life, as the Indian nearly had the point of the lance against him when he went over. One saddled horse was left close by. Two Indians on the same horse were seen to ride behind a thick bunch of prickly pears, and only one was seen to pass on. Flores said the other Indian was still behind the pears, and was left there to shoot any one who should come out to look around. Shane aimed and fired at this bunch of pears, and sure enough routed an Indian, who ran off. When the spot was afterwards examined a bullet hole was seen in the pears and the Indian made a narrow escape when he stood behind them. At 9 o'clock Mr. George Dilliard came, and he and Shane followed the Indians, but did not overtake them.

In 1876 Mr. Shane and two Mexicans, Antonio Guerril and

Salizar, went down the river less than a mile from the ranch to
a place called by some the "Weed Patch" and by others "Indian
Crossing." They had with them a wagon and pair of mules and
were out for the purpose of sawing up cypress logs to make boards
or shingles. These logs had been left by an overflow against an
elevated place in the river channel, and it was around this place
where there were so many weeds, mostly cockleburrs, that gave
rise to the name. They managed to get the wagon to this place,
the bluffs being high on both sides. There was a crossing above,
and they came down the hill there and drove the team to where
the logs were deposited. They finished their work and loaded the
wagon with cypress blocks and were about to start back home
when Shane got into one of the closest places with Indians that
he had as yet experienced. One of the Mexicans (Antonio) had
a gun which had been resighted, and he wanted Shane to try it
at a certain tree upon the bluff on the west side of the river before they started. Shane fired two shots, and then the Mexican
went to see where he had hit. About this time there were forty
Indians coming to the old crossing of the Sabinal above, as before mentioned, and heard Shane firing at the tree. Upon investigation they learned the situation and invested themselves in
such a way that it seemed impossible for Shane and his party to
escape. Half of the Indians came up on the bluff on the east
side, opposite Shane and his men, and the balance went to the old
crossing above so as to come around opposite them on the west
side, having them between the two fires and their retreat cut off
both ways. The first intimation they had of the presence of the
Indians was the rattling of the rocks at the crossing. Antonio
was still on his errand of investigation in regard to the accuracy
of his gun and the marksmanship of Shane. The other Mexican
mounted a stump so he could see the crossing, and said it was soldiers coming across the river. Shane now got on the stump to
look, and said: "Soldiers, thunder! Those are Indians." The
first Indians to get out of the channel of the river had only to
turn down a short distance to be opposite Shane, and in doing
this encountered Antonio and opened fire on him. He had discovered them and was trying to get back to Shane, but was hit by
a bullet and badly wounded. He fell in the high weeds and
lay there. The Indians on the east side now appeared and
opened fire, and the brave settler saw that once more he had des-

perate chances against him and had to fight the battle alone. One of his men was already down, wounded, and was even now calling to him for help, and the other had crawled under a tree top until nothing but his feet were visible. The Indians dismounted and commenced a rapid fire with Spencer carbines. Shane took shelter behind a large cypress log and commenced the unequal battle, firing with unerring aim as opportunity offered, and the savages soon learned what manner of foe they had to deal with. The bullets came from both sides of the creek and kept a continual spattering on every side, hitting the logs, wagon, etc. Shane lay close and refrained from firing much, and it was evident the Indians were uncertain as to the force they were fighting and were afraid to come down into the bed of the river and fight at close quarters, for at this time on the border many of the settlers had cartridge guns. I will state here that the Sabinal River only stood in pools below the mountains, and there were long stretches without any water at times, but the channel was covered with rocks. The bluffs also were high. During the fight the wounded Mexican crawled to where Shane was, but left his gun, being too weak to bring it along. The fire from the Indians' guns made it smoky on both sides of the river like a regular battle, and must have nearly exhausted their ammunition. Finally they sent a warrior on horseback below where Shane was to come up the river channel through the high weeds to investigate and see if the white man's party were all killed, which they thought must be the case from the amount of lead they had fired into their position. Shane was on the alert, with watchful eyes, and caught the first motion of the weeds as the Indian approached. The balance of the Indians on both sides of the river had ceased firing and were all under cover and still. Shane held a large revolver in his hand as he lay close to the ground, watching around the end of a log as the fellow came in view, and at once aimed at his breast and fired. The Indian reeled and fell to one side of his horse, but clutched the mane of the animal, and he ran up the bluff with him, where he was headed by some of the other Indians. The horse ran around in a circle with the Indian still hanging to his mane. Shane could see all this from where he lay. This wound up the fight. The Indians held a short council and then mounted and rode off, both parties getting together before starting. They had to pass through some open country after starting and getting away from the brush along the river, and Shane left his position and got up on the bluff where he could watch them. He counted forty, but how many he hit besides the last one he could not tell. He took no time to investigate, but made preparations to leave. The signs of the battle which he noticed at the time was his Mexican with a broken hip, one bullet hole through his own bootleg, one through the top of his hat, two through his shirt, three in the wagonbed, and one of the mules wounded, besides many marks on the ground and in the cypress log where they struck. The side of the mound which had formed the drift where the logs had caught was also perforated in many places and balls were dug out of these afterwards. These balls flew high and came from the crowd on the east bank. The wounded mule was able to help pull the wagon home, so Shane placed Antonio in it with the help of the other Mexican, who crawled out of his hiding place when the battle was over. Bullets were found in the blocks when the shingles were made. Shane acted as surgeon for his wounded Mexican, cutting the bullet out and dressing the wound. The ball had gone in a little below the hip and ranged down, and was cut out below the kneecap. It took this course on account of the Indian who was on the bluff firing down at Antonio as he was running back. He recovered after many weeks of suffering. Shane raised a party and went back to the battleground and found one moccasin full of blood and one buckskin hunting shirt with two holes in it, one on each side, and very bloody. In the high weeds where he shot the Indian a six-shooter was found, and the distance from there to where Shane lay was sixty steps.

Mr. Shane was out one time with a wagonload of water barrels, hauling water to one of his camps, and was attacked by a band of Indians. It was in an open country, and he took refuge under the wagon after locking the wheels so that his team could not easily run away. His sharp fire soon drove the Indians off, and he suffered no inconvenience, except the shots from the Indians perforated his water barrels and let all of the water run out, and it almost drowned him as he lay under the wagon.

In the same year of 1876 Mr. Shane saw his last wild Indians. One evening in the winter he went down to a place called "Griner's bottom" to listen for turkeys to fly up to roost. He was not long there when he heard the sound of horses' feet, and looking around saw five Indians riding towards him, but unaware of his presence. There was no time to run, so he stood close behind the large liveoak tree, against which he was leaning, and the Indians passed on both sides of him, two on one side and three on the other. It was getting dusk, but had they looked back after they passed the tree they would have discovered him. He was not fixed for a fight, only having a muzzle-loading shotgun loaded with shot, and it sometimes missed fire. He stood very straight behind the tree while the Indians were passing.

Mr. Shane had two Mexican shepherds killed by Indians at different times, but as he was not with them could tell nothing about the circumstances, except that he found them and pulled the arrows out of them and buried them. One was killed with lances and bullets, and the other with arrows.

Mr. Shane once hunted twenty-four hours for a little girl that was lost. He passed her twice, but the child was afraid of him and hid. He finally came across a Mexican and told him he could trail the child to a certain place, but there always lost it and could not find it any more when it had passed a certain point, and she must be near there somewhere. The Mexican went with Shane to the spot, and the little girl came out of the brush to them. Her father had employed the Mexican at one time, and the child knew him and was not afraid of him.

Henry J. Shane is one of the solid citizens of Uvalde County, has many friends, and can be relied upon for any statements made of frontier days. He has a good ranch and is doing well.

KILLING OF JAMES WINTERS BY INDIANS.

1861.

In connection with the killing of Mr. James Winters by Indians, briefly mentioned in a previous article, the following by Dr. Thos. Speed is taken from an old copy of the San Antonio Herald, bearing date of November 2, 1861, and the article being as follows:

"INDIAN NEWS.

"FRIO COUNTY, October 24, 1861.—Messrs. Editors: Having partially recovered from my wounds, received in an encounter with Indians on Saturday, the 19th instant, at about 11 o'clock, and thinking a few lines from myself and comrades in defeat may be of interest to your readers, I endeavor to give you some of the incidents of the fight:

"At about 8 o'clock on the morning of this fateful day Mr. N. Kennard came to Mr. Hood's, near my ranch, and informed me that the Indians had passed near my house with a large caballado of horses, and that some of the neighbors were on the trail in pursuit. I instantly mounted my mule, then almost exhausted, I having been on his back some eight or ten days almost constantly, and the last four days riding in deep sand. I started home for my gun. I then happened to fall in with Mr. T. L. Ward, James Bishop, James Craig, and N. Kennard. We all started off on a long gallop to find the trail, which we came across near the divide between the south fork of Cesquadara and the waters of the San Maguel. We followed it as rapidly as we could in a gallop nearly all the time until we reached a high eminence overlooking the San Maguel valley, at which place I loaded my gun, not having taken time to do so up to that time. We then started on, and in a few jumps we saw Mr. James M. Winters and W. W. Davidson about one mile across the San Maguel on the high ground waiting for us. The boys broke off at a rapid rate, leaving me greatly in the rear, their horses being much fleeter than my mule. Upon coming up with them they informed us that the Indians

were not more than two miles ahead. We all immediately started
in pursuit, but did not go but a short distance before Mr. Davidson's horse gave out, being a 2-year-old colt, and he with much
regret was compelled to turn back, which left but six of us. We
did not delay. We had no organization or understanding, and
at this time I mentioned to the boys that we must stay together,
but upon the run I can not say whether they all heard me or
not. We there struck the blackjack timber between the Maguel
and Black Creek, in which Mr. Winters and I were thrown near
together, when I again said we must all stay together. His reply I did not distinctly understand, but thought he said 'Certainly.' About four or five miles from where we overtook Winters and Davidson, and just as we came out of the thick black-
jacks to the valley of Black Creek, Bishop said, 'Boys, there they
are.' At this instant Winters and Kennard changed horses, Kennard's horse being the fleetest in the company. Again I said we
must all stay together, and without anything further being said
the boys pushed on as fast as their several horses could carry them
without ascertaining the number of the Indians, and leaving me
greatly in the rear, having to make a run of about a mile from
where we first saw them. The Indians on discovering us began
to assemble together and to string their bows. They stabbed a
little negro boy they had with them, belonging to Mr. Marcellus
French, in two places, and gave him some external bruises, none
of which were fatal, and left him and also the horses in a large
mott of timber, and ran up a hill. When overtaken by the boys
they were out in open ground covered with tall grass and scrubby
mesquite bushes, and then the fight opened. At this time they
were all behind the liveoak mott. I could not see them. I must
have been 150 or 200 yards behind, pressing on as hard as my
mule could carry me. When I rounded the point of timber all
the Indian warriors were on foot and their horses stampeding.
Their number was about twenty-five, and they were yelling
'Charge,' as I understand the meaning of the word they used in
English. They had been at this for some time before I came in
sight of them from behind the timber. I then saw our boys in
a state of confusion and disorder. Mr. Winters was down on
one knee surrounded by the Indians. At about this stage Winters said to Ward, 'Come to me,' which Ward attempted to do
until he had exhausted his shots and had to retreat. I, seeing

his condition, made the charge to his relief, and when near enough fired a volley upon the Indians from a double-barreled shotgun which I had got from Mr. Davidson when he turned back. Not being in the habit of shooting such a gun I caught the wrong trigger, and before I could touch the other one an Indian shot my mule in the neck, which caused her to wheel around and commence pitching. This she continued to do for some twenty or thirty steps. The Indians, seeing me come up, commenced their charge on me. At this time I did not know where the other boys were, but when my mule stopped pitching saw all four on the retreat together, two on horseback and two on foot. Craig and Bishop were on horseback, going off the way we came. My mule again commenced pitching, turning to the right, and an Indian shot me in the back with an arrow, a glancing shot three or four inches deep, and I then went to the boys. Ward was wounded in the back. He had lost his gun and his pistol was empty. Kennard had also lost his gun and was wounded in the shoulder. Bishop and Craig were unhurt. Bishop had no pistol and only a single-barreled gun. Kennard's and Craig's pistols proved inefficient and were of no use. The four had but two guns and one pistol, and all empty. When I came up I gave Ward my shotgun, and Bishop got him up behind him, and Kennard mounted behind Craig. After traveling 150 or 200 yards to a clump of trees they got down to load their guns. I then discovered that Ward did not have the gun that I gave him. I asked him what he had done with it, and he said I did not hand it to him. Some of the boys now told him that I had done so. His wound had so paralyzed him that he was not cognizant of what had transpired for a time. His wound, though painful, was not dangerous. Kennard's wounds were slight. The Indians having left the horses and stabbed the little negro, and leaving behind them the large mott of timber of which they had complete possession, proves to me that they were willing to make their escape, but seeing the confused state of our boys in the charge they dismounted and commenced themselves to charge, the horses all stampeding except a few on which were squaws. Their whole number must have been from twenty-five to thirty. By not attempting to pursue us in our unarmed and disabled condition proves to me that the boys did good service with their shots, and when they went back after Winters there were five or six different pools of blood near where Winters lay dead. Ward says he shot one who fell from his horse and his horse kicked him. Their wounded and dead was the cause of their not following us. Had I been up in the charge and missed my shots, all would have been killed, for they quit the other boys and came after me and came near cutting me off from the others, of which I was entirely unconscious until my mule stopped pitching. At this point I looked back to see if I could be of any service to Winters. He was falling over, having made his last effort. My comrades no doubt did all in their power to save our unfortunate companion, but of no avail. None knew him but to admire him. He was in every sense of the word a gentleman, and as a neighbor, citizen, and frontiersman was all that he should have been. His bereaved companion has lost a kind husband, and his small children a faithful father. This was the second time he had pursued and overtaken the Indians. The first time he and his comrades did not charge them, their number being too small for the attack. After this time he had been heard to say the next time he saw the Indians he would make the charge and get some of them anyhow, and now I have no doubt he kept his word, for he never looked back after he commenced the charge to see where the rest of us were. The Indians must have had 200 horses or more, as they covered a large space of ground. We could not see them all for the bushes in the valley. About the same time of day five of our neighbors—Major A. Allen, Nathaniel Terry, D. Yarboe, J. W. Bennett, and R. Coode— coming on after us over the same trail, discovered a band of Indians going up the Chicon near the mouth of the Francisco and near where our trail had crossed the Maguel, those streams uniting to form the Maguel. As soon as they could assemble they made the run after the Indians, and who, when discovered, commenced to charge. The major and company dismounted, fastened their horses, and made a stand. The Indians before coming within range of the guns turned off. The number of the Indians was from fifteen to eighteen, but they finally left and the major and his party went on westward, riding in the direction where we had the engagement, distant about five miles. We learned at Mrs. Tomlin's that about twelve men from the Hondo were close on the trail, not more than two or three hours after us, where we were in the battle with the Indians, so if we had all kept together and kept them off from the horses, we had got all of the animals, or so engaged them until we had been reinforced by those twelve men. Monday morning twenty men started in pursuit six miles beyond D'Hanis, about eight or ten hours behind them, intending to keep the trail until they found out where they went or overtake them. That they were Indians of small stature there is no mistake. The little negro said they were all Indians except one, and he was a Mexican and had curly hair, and that there were three squaws among them. They also killed two grown negroes of Mr. French. They killed a man by the name of Herndon, wounded O'Brien and Anderson, and pursued another named Tucker in sight of Pleasanton, all below here. This is the fourth time they have been in this season, always going out near where we had the fight with them. There must have been fifty Indians in a space of five miles at the time we fought them. Respectfully yours,

"THOS. SPEED.

"We the undersigned corroborate the foregoing statement.

"L. T. WARD,

"JAS. BISHOP,

"JAS. CRAIG.

"NORVILL KENNARD."

[I will say that Dr. Speed was well and favorably known in the community where he lived, that he died a few years after the fight, and some think caused by the wound received there. Kennard was also a long time in recovering. Ward was wounded in another fight after this. The men he mentions as being on the trail at the time he wrote were led by Big Foot Wallace. They fought the Indians at the head of Seco in the mountains and captured 190 head of horses from them. Just before the fight the Indians killed the tax assessor of Bandera County.—AUTHOR.]

TRAILING INDIANS.

For quite a number of years after the Civil war the Indians continued to raid the settlers in West Texas. In the fall of 1876 they made their last raid through Sabinal Canyon. They first struck the settlers on Main Frio, and then came like a wave of destruction through this valley, and then made a circuit of many miles back towards the Rio Grande, sixteen persons meeting death at their hands during the raid. They came into Sabinal Canyon on the 10th of September, and stole quite a lot of horses, and then turned southeast below the foot of the mountains, palying havoc as they went.

The Sabinal men gathered quickly and were soon joined by the scouts from Frio Canyon, who were coming rapidly on the trail. The following are the names of the men from both canyons: From Sabinal were James Thigpen, Phil Hodges, Albert Harper, C. S. Jones, J. H. Simpson, James Watson, Jack Kelly, and a German schoolteacher named Lirch. From Frio were Henry Patterson, John Patterson, Riley Patterson, Joe Van Pelt, James Highsaw, Jack Grigsby, William Wall, John Kittenger, William Nichols, and Joe Richarz. Seeing the necessity of having a leader, the settlers elected Henry Patterson to fill that position, and they soon set out briskly on the trail, Phil Hodges and John Patterson being the trailers, taking alternate turns. For the first day and night the trail led southeast, and in this route the Indians killed a Mexican who was herding sheep for Henry Shane. He was literally shot to pieces and horribly mangled and scalped. He had made a desperate fight for his life and killed one of the Indians and wounded others; this was supposed from signs on the trail. On Squirrel Creek they killed and scalped another Mexican herder.

From the place where the Indians killed the herder they turned a south course for sixty miles, and while on this route killed six men in the lower part of Frio County—two white men and four Mexicans. The white men were out in a buggy looking for sheep when attacked, and as to the fight they made no one could tell, Their mangled bodies lay on the prairie; their buggy was torn to pieces, horses gone, and the harness cut into small bits. From

this place back to the Rio Grande they completed the list of sixteen victims.

When the pursuit first commenced the schoolteacher, who had
not been long in this country and knew nothing about trailing
and fighting Indians, took quite a lot of provisions with him,
and when the balance of the men run short divided with them,
saying he would buy some more when they got to town, which he
thought would be the next day. The boys helped to clean up
what he had and then commenced joking him, saying he would
do well to get back alive, as there were no towns. He then
wanted to know how the Indians lived on these raids if they did
not pass through any towns where they could get some provisions. The boys said they would show him how Indians lived
before they got back.

By 3 o'clock the next day the men were very hungry, and also
about this time they struck a flock of sheep. Captain Patterson told some of the men to go and get two or more muttons for
the men to eat. Phil. Hodges and Joe Van Pelt went and asked
the herder for the sheep, stating their business, how long they
had followed the Indians, the hunger of the men, etc. The man
informed them that they could not get them. It was generally understood on the frontier that men who were following
Indians were welcome to kill stock of any kind to subsist on
when in this business, and if the parties owning the stock refused
to let it go the trailers played "old soldier" on them and con-
scripted it. The two men on being refused the sheep pulled
their guns and killed three and dragged them to where the captain and the balance of the men were. Joe Van Pelt killed two
of these sheep at one shot; the ball went through the first one
and killed another thirty yards away. The horses were now unsaddled, so their backs could cool while they fed on the luxuriant
grass. The hungry men built fires and commenced cooking and
eating, calling the attention of the schoolteacher as they did so
to take notice how Indians got something to eat on a raid. After
the repast the horses were again saddled and the trail taken up,
the men tying what meat was left to their saddles, which was
very little.

After the trailers left this camp and kept on after the Indians
it was found that they had turned in a northwest direction, and
in two miles came upon the dead bodies of two white men who

had been slain with bullets, no arrows being used. They were both lying together and had evidently been ambushed as they were traveling a road and met their death without warning or any chance to defend themselves. From here the trail led to Westfall's ranch on the Leona, and the Indians had been fought and defeated here by Henry Courtney and his hands who occupied the ranch attending to stock, Westfall at the time being absent. By this time, as the route had been long and tedious, the men were hungry again, and at once began to hunt for something to eat, Courtney telling them to help themselves to anything they could find that was eatable. A pot of cooked turkey and dumplings was soon found and the men went for it with forks, soon taking out all of the meat and leaving the soup and some of the dough condiments. Harper Simpson, being fond of thick turkey soup and having no spoon readily at hand, turned up the pot and proceeded to drink some of it out, but unfortunately the bail of the little pot dropped down over his head and around his neck, and he could not get it off. But the boys with shouts of laughter continued to fish in the pot with their forks for the dumplings on both sides of his head, despite his protest, and for a minute he presented quite a humorous spectacle, they not giving him any assistance in relieving him from the pot until the contents were all out.

From here the trail turned west to the Nueces River.

Captain Patterson now concluded that the Indians were a good distance ahead, and he would have to change his tactics to overhaul them before they reached the Rio Grande. Indians when being pursued had a great advantage over the pursuing party. When night came the trailers had to stop, while the Indians could keep on. This was one reason why so many raiding bands got out of the country without being brought to a battle. The captain now decided to try a night ride, thinking that if he would go straight west, guided by a bright star in that direction, it would throw him south of the trail, and then when daylight came turn north and intercept the trail of the Indians again. One reason why he thought this plan would work was because the Indians generally turned up the country and crossed into Mexico at the mouth of Devil's River. This time, however, the Indians acted the reverse and turned south, and the settlers failed to find the trail as they anticipated when daylight came. Finding the marauders had eluded them, the party now turned and went to Uvalde to procure fresh horses and more provisions, intending to strike the trail again and follow it into Mexico. Here eight of the men left and went home, including the schoolteacher in the party.

The company was now reduced to twelve men, and it was thought advisable to telegraph to Fort Clark for United States soldiers to meet them at some point west of the Nueces River. The soldiers were allowed to cross into Mexico after Indians, but citizens were not. There was at this time a frontier telegraph line from San Antonio to the Rio Grande. The place designated for the soldiers to meet them was the "Anna Catchi" mountains, twenty-five miles or more west of the Nueces. The men who remained to go in pursuit were Capt. Henry Patterson, John Patterson, Riley Patterson, Joe Van Pelt, Jim Highsaw, Jack Grigsby, William Wall, John Kittinger, William Nichols, Jim Thigpen, Albert Harper, and Phil Hodges. The commanding officer at Fort Clark responded to the call and sent Lieutenant Boyd with a detachment of soldiers, and they all got together at the place designated. Lieutenant Boyd had strict orders from General McKenzie about crossing the Rio Grande, and all had to act accordingly; but it was agreed that the citizens should cross as United States soldiers, but still be under the command of Henry Patterson. Everything being arranged, the party, forty-nine in all, set out for the Santa Rosa mountains in Mexico, as that was supposed to be the stopping place for all Indians when they crossed the river to avoid a battle with the Texans.

The soldiers had a Seminole Indian along for a guide and trailer, but the first night out he lost his horse and the men lost his services. The trailing then devolved on some of Patterson's men. The day before the command got to the river another large Indian trail came into the one they were following. A consultation was held, and it was decided to halt there, and Lieutenant Boyd would send down to Fort Duncan after more men, as the Indians now greatly outnumbered them and they would have to follow them into Mexico to chastise them. About twenty men came from Duncan, and it is supposed brought whisky along, for that night the soldiers got on a spree and one of their number was badly wounded by the accidental discharge of a gun. The man who did the shooting was tied up all night by the thumbs

by order of the commanding officer, Boyd. The wounded man
had to be sent back for treatment, and the balance went on to
the river. Here, however, an insurmountable difficulty confronted them. The Rio Grande was badly swollen by recent
rains and could not be crossed. Some of the men were so anxious
to go over they made an attempt to swim it, but came near being
drowned and had to desist. Among those who made the attempt
was a daring man and good Indian fighter, Jim Thigpen.

The Indians had not long crossed over before the rise. Their
place of crossing was opposite "La Villa Nueva" (new town), and
they carried 200 head of horses into Mexico. Some of the men
wanted to shoot across the river at some Mexicans who were
standing over there watching them, but the officers said it would
not do. A few shots, however, were fired by some of Patterson's
men and the Mexicans beat a hasty retreat. The citizens went
back as far as Fort Clark with the soldiers and from there home.

I have given rather a lengthy detailed account of this scout,
that those who are not familiar with such things can form a clear
conception of the difficulties which had to be encountered in the
efforts of the settlers of southwest Texas to chastise the Indians
who were continually depredating upon them and killing the
citizens.

Henry Patterson, who led the settlers, was at one time sheriff
of Uvalde County, and later tax assessor. Newman McCollum
Patterson, father of Henry Patterson, was born in Alabama in
1825, came to Texas in 1845, and first settled in Smith County.
In 1853 he came to Uvalde County, then very sparsely settled,
and on the extreme frontier, and was in many fights with the Indians in the early days. He served Uvalde County as sheriff in
1860 and as tax collector in 1865, and as county judge two terms
in the 80's. Before leaving Smith County he married Miss Lucy
Dollihite. Judge Patterson still survives and lives on the Patterson ditch farm, in Frio Canyon, where he has a mill and cotton gin. He has three other sons living, William, Riley, and
John.

M. C. CLICK.

Came to Texas in 1863.

While traveling through the mountain country of Bandera County hunting for frontier incidents, the writer had the pleasure of spending a night under the hospitable roof of Mr. M. C. Click, who lived at that time in the Hondo Canyon, about two miles south of the Bandera and Utopia road.

While Mr. Click is not one of the earliest settlers of this country, he came here before all of the Indians were gone, and has many true and interesting tales to tell of their daring raids and bloody deeds. He came from Arkansas to Texas in 1863, and to Bandera County shortly after. In 1875 he moved to Hondo Canyon, but there were already some settlers here and had been for some time. The following incident, which took place before he came here, is a fact which he was familiar with:

In 1866 David Cryer and a Mr. Foster, who lived in the canyon north of the Bandera road, went to the town of Bandera in a two-horse wagon, purchased supplies, and came back across the mountains through the pass, and saw no signs of Indians until arriving near a noted mountain called the Sugar Loaf, from its peculiar shape, which was near their homes, and distant from Bandera about ten miles. Here at the head of a ravine around which the road ran they were ambushed by five Indians who were on foot, and likely saw the white men when they came through the pass. The Indians were not more than thirty feet from the two settlers when they showed themselves and drew their arrows back to shoot. Mr. Cryer saw the Indians just as they were in the act of shooting, and hit the horses a sharp blow, which caused them to spring forward quickly, and at the same time the arrows came, one of which struck Cryer in the small of the back and he fell from the seat backward into the wagon bed. Foster was not hit, and at once took the lines and whipped the team into a fast run, followed by the Indians, who commenced yelling and still continued to shoot arrows. There was a gun in the wagon which Foster now secured and aimed back at his pursuers, but they sprang to one side and he would not fire for fear of a miss, and waited for a better chance. During this flight over a rocky road the wagonbed jolted up over a wheel, and the horses, not being able to run with it in that condition, began to slacken their speed. Although it was a most critical time, Foster stopped them, and getting out with great effort, lifted the bed back in place and then resumed his flight. The wounded man suffered untold agony during the wild ride, bouncing from one side to the other in the wagon with the arrow still in his body. It was not more than two miles home, and at the rate of speed the horses were forced into they soon arrived there. The Indians had long since abandoned the chase and went back. There was no doctor near to attend Mr. Cryer and he suffered great pain, as the arrow was deeply imbedded and could not be withdrawn by ordinary force or means. A man at Bandera named O. B. Miles had been a hospital steward and generally attended men who were shot by Indians or any other way, and he was at once sent for and came, but Cryer had received a mortal wound and died in three days. Miles did all he could for him, extracted the arrow and dressed the wound, but of no avail. Three or four men went back to the place of the ambuscade, but could see nothing of the Indians. Many arrows were picked up along the road.

The writer drove around the foot of Sugar Loaf Mountain, inspecting it, and indeed it is of peculiar shape and location, rising abruptly and alone out of the valley and towering high in a conical shape, and being almost perfect in symmetrical formation, except near the base, where it terminates in rough spurs and small gullies. The place of the ambush was also visited. The road is the same as at that time, coming round in a curve as it crosses the ravine near its head. There is a fall here of about six feet, over which the water pours during a freshet, but dry at other times. It is all solid rock, and the action of the water in time has scooped out a basin underneath in which a dozen men could secrete themselves and not be seen by any one traveling the road unless they stepped out into view. In the few moments the writer spent here recalling and pondering over this sad frontier tragedy and gazing down on the very spot where the savages stood and sent the fatal shaft into Cryer, he could almost, it seemed, see their upturned, painted faces, and hear the twang of the bowstrings as with brawny and sinewy arms they drew the

arrows almost to the head and let them fly on their mission of
death to a pioneer.

In the fall of 1866 Thomas B. Click, brother to M. C., was
killed by Indians on the Medina River. He lived in Bandera, and
was on his way up the river to see a man named Huffmann, who
lived six miles west of town, and who was going to move away.
Mr. Click started in the early part of the night and was riding
a mule. When arriving at a point three miles from town at the
fork of the road the Indians attacked him. He had no gun, and
it was supposed from the sign that he turned and attempted to
make to the Medina River, 300 yards away. An Indian on a
big horse (from the tracks) cut him off from there and turned
him back to the road, where he was killed by a lance thrust, done
evidently by the Indian, who ran around him, as the mule and
horse track indicated they were close together. The slain man
fell in the road, but the Indians dragged him out and left the
body about fifteen steps away. Mr. Click had on a fine pair of
buckskin breeches, which the Indians stripped him of and carried away with them. Next morning M. C. Click and D. A.
Weaver started to Bandera, from about where Medina City is
now, to attend to some business, and came upon the spot where
the unfortunate man lost his life the night before. Mr. Click
saw his brother's blood in the road, and stopping his horse said
to Weaver, "Some one has killed a maverick here." About that
time, however, his eyes rested on a small butcher knife in the
road, and he dismounted and picked it up, recognizing it as belonging to his brother. This discovery made him feel uneasy,
and a short search, for the grass was high, revealed the body by
following the trail where it had been dragged. Officers in town
were notified and an inquest held over the body, after which it
was taken back and buried in the cemetery at Bandera. A party
took the trail of the Indians, but they scattered and nothing
could be done with them. The Indians also got the mule and
saddle.

In 1867 Rufus Click, another brother, while coming from
Kerrville to Bandera, was ambushed by Indians at the Bandera
Pass. He had a dog with him, and when they got into the pass
the dog raised his hair and got behind Mr. Click. This looked
suspicious, but being on a fast horse he rode on, and was soon fired
on both with bullets and arrows. The frontiersman leaned for-

ward on the horse's neck and the race for life commenced. There were two parties of the Indians, some on both sides of the road, and he had to run the gauntlet between them. A bullet hit his mare in the neck above the windpipe, and an arrow struck him below the shoulder blade and ranged up as he was leaning forward. The speed of his nag saved him, and he made it to the ranch of Mr. John A. Jones, three miles distant. He had to be assisted into the house, and a negro was sent to Bandera after Dr. Fitz Gibbon. He came and said Mr. Click was shot with a poisoned arrow, and he would have to give strychnine to counteract it, as it was the only chance to save him. He got well, but was never stout again. The poison was that of a rattlesnake. The Indians afterwards made a raid and stole the mare that Mr. Click rode that day and killed her below Bandera, stretched her hide on the ground and cut lariats out of it, commencing in the center.

In the winter of 1875 Jack Phillips, who lived six miles above Bandera on Winin's Creek, started to Sabinal Canyon on business for his brother-in-law, Buck Hamilton, who was sheriff of Bandera County. There was no wagon road over the mountains then to the canyon after leaving the settlement in Hondo Canyon; only a horse trail from there on. Phillips ate dinner with Mr. Click, then living in Hondo Canyon, and then went on his way. When he arrived at the pass which leads into Seco Canyon he was attacked and killed by Indians. This trail was above where the main road now runs. Mr. F. L. Hicks had made a pasture fence across the trail, and in lieu of a gate had common draw bars through which to pass. Phillips got through this and the Indians came down a point to the right and made their attack upon him. He ran back the way he came and succeeded in getting through the bars again, but was closely pursued. It was a long chase of half a mile, the Indians firing, and the horse was finally shot through the shoulder with a ball and fell into a ravine. The doomed man now took down the ravine on foot, but was soon overtaken and killed. If he made any fight with them it could not be told.

At this time Mr. William Felts and Miss Josephine E. Durban were on their way from Sabinal Canyon to Bandera to get married, and came upon the body shortly after the Indians left. They first saw the horse, which was lying in sight of the trail, and went to him.   Here they discovered the tracks of Phillips, where he ran down the ravine, and following these about fifty yards came to him lying face downward.   They now hurried to the ranch of Mr. Click, told him the news, and stayed at his house that night.   Next morning Click, Weaver and others went after the body, and Felts and Miss Durban went on to Bandera and carried the news over there.   When Mr. Click and his party arrived at the scene of the killing the horse was still alive but unable to get up, and was shot by Dave Weaver.   The body of Phillips lay face downward, stripped and mutilated.   The Indians took the saddle off the horse and carried it away.   The body was brought to Joel Casey's, the nearest Hondo settler, but off the main road, and Mr. Click went to Bandera that night and had a coffin made.   Mr. Phillips was a Mason and was buried by them at Bandera.   Mr. Click is also a Mason of long standing.

The Indians were followed by Hondo men, but not overtaken. The shoes of Phillips were found on the trail.   A scout of Texas rangers was on the trail of these same Indians, but their horses gave out and they were just turning back on Wallace Creek, fifteen miles away north, at the time the Indians were killing Jack Phillips, as it was afterwards learned.   Dr. J. C. Nowlin, of the Guadalupe valley, was with the rangers on this occasion, and said they followed the Indians from North Llano, about where Junction City is now.

Mr. Click was a Confederate soldier, and was in many battles during the Civil war.

LAST INDIAN RAID IN FRIO CANYON.

1882.

In 1882 the Indians struck their last blow at the settlers in Main Frio Canyon. For more than thirty years they had made constant raids and many whites were slain, and in this last two more victims fell,—Mrs. Kate McLauren and Allen Lease, a youth who lived with the McLauren family.

John M. McLauren, husband of the murdered woman, was born in North Carolina and came to Texas in 1857. In 1871 he married Miss Kate Ringer, at Lockhart, Caldwell County, Texas. They soon after came to Frio Canyon and first settled below the town of Leakey, but moved in 1880 seven miles above, and were the outside settlers at that time. Here they lived two years without being molested.

On April 19, 1882, Mr. McLauren left home and went down to Cherry Creek, below the Leakey settlement. It was a wild, gloomy looking place where the McLauren family lived. The canyon was narrow, and just below the house was almost a shut-in. The sides of the mountains next to the river were high rock bluffs, and in time many huge boulders had become detached and went plunging into the river below. Just above this narrow place is an elevated spot on which the house stood. There was a garden spot between the house and the river east. Above, north and west, the valley widened and the mountains curved around and terminated in the huge cliff fronting the river. At the time McLauren left home that morning a band of Indians came around on top of the mountains and stopped on the cliff which overlooked all the valley and house, and no doubt saw the settler when he left home. The family at home consisted, besides the mother and boy Allen, of Maud, 6 years old; Alonzo, 3 years, and Frank, the baby in arms. The eldest daughter, Mary, was away boarding with the family of Richard Humphreys, near Leakey, and going to school.

After dinner Mrs. McLauren took the children and went down to the garden to work. During this time Mr. John Thompson,

33

who had been up the river horse-hunting, passed back and saw the woman in the garden; but no signs of Indians at that time. He carried a Winchester, and no doubt the Indians saw him from their elevated position. They could keep concealed from view by the rocks and cedar with which the mountain top was covered. About 2 o'clock the Indians came down the mountain north of the bluff where it was not so abrupt, and going to the cabin commenced to plunder it. Mrs. McLauren had sat down on a blanket to rest and nurse her baby, and the balance of the children were sitting down around her. The Indians made a noise at the house, which was not more than sixty yards away, but back from the brow of the hill at the base of which the garden was situated. Thinking hogs were doing some mischief there, Mrs. McLauren told Allen Lease to run up there and scare them off. The boy did so, and almost ran into a crowd of Indians in the yard. Uttering a cry of fright he ran back, pursued by an Indian with a Winchester, who fired at him just as he reached the foot of the little hill. The ball hit Allen in the back of the head and came out at the nose, and without uttering a sound he fell forward on his face dead. By this time Mrs. McLauren had sprang to her feet and the Indian fired a shot at her, hitting her in the breast. She fell to the ground, but at once arose and started to run, with the baby still in her arms. The Indian now fired again, and she was wounded in the right arm, but kept on towards the garden fence next to the river. The murderous rascal kept on shooting, and before getting to the fence the poor woman was wounded three times more, twice in the right leg and once in the hip. Before this time she had told the children to run, and Maude was over the fence. The now badly wounded woman handed Maud the baby, which she still clung to despite the fearful shots she was receiving, and tried to get over herself, but another whizzing ball came and struck her again in the hip, and she fell to the ground on the outside of the fence and was unable to rise. The Indians did not follow them and continued to rob and pillage the house, and now occurred an incident that has but few equals in frontier annals. Mrs. McLauren was lying with her head on the bare ground and rocks, writhing and moaning, covered with blood, and little Maud was weeping beside her. The child conceived the idea that her mother could rest better with a pillow under her head, and in her

devotion and solicitude lost all fear, and crossing the fence ran
swiftly across the garden, past the dead body of Allen and through
a crowd of Indians into the house, seized a pillow, and running
back tenderly placed it under the dying mother's head. Strange
to say the Indians made no attempt to molest her. Did not this
innocence and devotion call forth the Divine power which stayed
the bloody hand of the savage?

The mother now told her daughter that if she could get help
she might live, and the brave little Maud set off at her utmost
speed down the river towards the settlements. Now, at this time
Mr. George Fisher was not far down the river fishing, and the
child soon came upon him. He heard her breathing hard on the
bank just above him, and looked up and said, "Is that you,
Maud?" "Yes," she said, excitedly; "is that you, Mr. Fisher?"
and at once sprang down the bank to where he was. In broken
accents she told him that the Indians had killed Allen and shot
her mother, and wound up by saying, "Mamma says for you to
come quick." Mr. Fisher lived a mile below, and Mrs. McLauren
had told Maud to go to his house first, as it was the nearest place.
He, not believing that he was able to cope with the Indians alone,
carried the child to his house and then informed his neighbors—
James Hicks, Henry Wall, and Mrs. Goodman—of the fearful
tragedy. Mrs. Goodman wanted to go back to the wounded
woman at once, but no one would accompany her, the men scattering with the news and gathering a force to fight. Before doing this, however, they carried Little Maud and Mrs. Goodman
to the house of another neighbor, named David Thompson.
James Hicks came on down the river to John Leakey's, who as
soon as he learned the news took two Mexicans who were in his
employ and set out rapidly on foot for the McLauren place. Before he went far he saw McLauren coming behind him in the
road, and stopping told him the news. He had, however, already
ran his horse down going back home, having a presentiment that
all was not well. At J. B. Johnson's he found Mr. Fisher and
they went together, having obtained a fresh horse from Mr. Johnson. Mrs. McLauren was still lying where she fell when they
came to the spot—alive, it is true, but that was all; the last spark
of life was flickering. She faintly asked for water. McLauren
went to the river a few yards away and brought some in his hat
brim. This she drank, and died in three minutes after. The

baby was lying on the ground by her side, and little 3-year-old Alonzo was sitting beside it.

It was now sundown, and who can tell what that poor woman suffered from 2 o'clock until this time with wounds and thirst, expecting each moment when sufficient time had elapsed for some one to come and assist her. Then likely the thought would occur that something had happened to 6-year-old little Maud, and that she had never reached her destination, and still no one knew of their direful distress. Allen Lease was still lying at the foot of the hill where he fell, but the hogs had eaten his face off. The bodies were taken down to the lower settlement and buried in the Leakey cemetery. Great excitement prevailed. It had been a long time since an Indian raid, and the people had begun to think that the days of Indian alarms were over. Twenty men assembled to follow and fight the Indians, if possible to overtake them. The trail was taken up at the McLauren ranch, and it led back up the mountain the way they had come down. Among the pursuers were W. J. McLauren, captain; Tobe Edwards, James Hicks, — Coryell, H. T. Coston, Henry Wall (better known as "Boy" Wall), Frank Pollard, George Leakey, M. V. Pruitt, John Thompson, and Frank Sanders. John McLauren, husband of the slain woman, was not .of the party, the reason of which he says was his horse running into a stooping tree the day of the killing and nearly putting his eyes out, so that he could hardly see for several days. The trail led a western course, and was followed with such vigor and over such a rocky country that many of the horses gave out, and at Kickapoo Springs all turned back except W. J. McLauren, Tobe Edwards, H. T. Coston, and Coryell. These went on to the last slope that turns into the Rio Grande valley, and then they turned back. Coryell left them where the trial crosses the road that runs from Brackett or Fort Clark to Howard's Well, and went to Fort Clark and informed Lieutenant Bullis, who commanded the Seminole scouts, of the raid, and where they last saw the trail, which he was satisfied led into Mexico. Bullis at once took his scouts, and getting on the trail followed it out of Texas and five days into Old Mexico to a place called by the Seminoles "Horseshoe Bend." Here the Indians were in camp in a little valley on a creek, thinking they were now safe from the vengeance of the Texas settlers. Bullis had two guides—one Seminole buck and a Lipan squaw. The

Indians being followed were Lipans, and when the squaw learned from something found on the trail that it was her people they were following, she tried to decoy Lieutenant Bullis and his party off another way on a cold trail, where some Indians had passed some time before. The Seminole guide, however, said she was wrong, and that they were on the right track. When the squaw perceived that her directions were not to be followed she got on the warpath and had to be tied on her horse. She was the wife of one of the Seminole scouts.

Lieutenant Bullis located the hostile camp with the aid of a spyglass three miles away, from a hill top. Dividing his men, he left half with the horses and belligerent squaw, and taking the others surrounded the camp at night and awaited the dawn. At daybreak the chief came into view, smoking a pipe, and was instantly killed by some shots from the ambushed scouts. A general charge was now made on the camp, and some were killed before they got up from where they were lying, and others as they ran. When the fight was over five Indians were dead on the ground—four bucks and one squaw. One buck ran off, pursued and fired at many times, but jumped off a bluff twenty feet high, and the last three men to shoot at him after he jumped off said streams of blood were running from his wounds. That he survived these shots is not likely. One wounded squaw with a hand shot off was captured and brought back.

John McLauren met Bullis at Fort Clark on his return and identified several things that were taken from his house, and there is no doubt that the right Indians were punished. The wounded squaw acknowledged they were the ones, but claimed leniency from her captors, stating that she kept the bucks from killing the children. Some might say now that it was the Indian squaw that saved the little girl's life when she went after the pillow, instead of Providence, but God makes wicked and bloody men sometimes the instruments to carry out his behest. The heart and mind of the wild, painted Indian squaw could be used the same way. The wounded squaw was sent to the Fort Sill reservation.

About two weeks before the killing of Mrs. McLauren and Allen Lease one morning McLauren was telling a dream he had the night before of something horrible, and could see streams of blood running, etc. His wife said, "O, don't tell those scary dreams; I don't like to hear them." Allen then put in and said, "Don't tell it before breakfast; it might come to pass." Mrs. McLauren had an uncle killed in the Alamo. His name was Galbreath Fuqua. McLauren's father was a gunsmith, and he showed the writer a gun barrel which he made and which was used in the Seminole war in Florida. He also had an Indian tomahawk which was washed up out of a ravine. It had a long, thin blade.

Mr. John Thompson showed the writer over the ground where Mrs. McLauren and Allen Lease were killed. Some remains of the house are still to be seen. Young Lease only lacked one day of being 15 years old.

AMASA CLARK.

VETERAN OF THE MEXICAN WAR.

Came to Bandera County in 1852.

Mr. Amasa Clark was born in Schoharie County, on a creek of the same name, in the State of New York, in 1828. In 1846, when the war with Mexico broke out, Mr. Clark was in Albany, and volunteered from that place. He enlisted for the war in company I, commanded by Captain Chandler, Third United States infantry, Major Alexander commanding the regiment, Twigg's division. The first lieutenant was named Whistler. The regiment joined General Scott at Vera Cruz, and here Mr. Clark, then a youth, saw his first battle when the city was bombarded. The troops landed in surfboats before the war vessels opened fire. The Mexicans would not surrender, and General Scott gave permission for all those who wished to abandon the place before a shot was fired. The troops on land had a good view of all that was transpiring on the war vessels in front of the city. There were three foreign warships there, and the men on them watched the American vessels with great interest. These ships were British, French, and Spanish. The officers were on deck and the men in the rigging. The American army landed in three divisions some distance from the city. Just before the bombardment commenced, and while the American army was landing, the bands of the different regiments played "Yankee Doodle," "Hail Columbia," and the "Star-Spangled Banner." After the firing commenced it was kept up at intervals for three weeks. Seven thousand shells were sent into the city. The troops on land watched the shells with great interest, especially at night, when they made a grand display, looking like meteors as they flew up and then dropped into the city. After three weeks of this kind of work the Mexicans surrendered.

Mr. Clark went on with the army and participated in the battles of Cerro Gordo, Contreras, Cherubusco, Molino del Rey, Chapultepec, and the street fight in the City of Mexico. At the entrance of the gate of the city the American troops lay down at night to await daylight to resume operations. The men were very hungry, and many of them had nothing with which to appease it. Mr. Clark had a piece of coarse barley bread in his haversack, which he began to munch at as soon as they were settled for the night. Near him was Captain Van Horn, who, seeing the young soldier had something to eat, came close and asked for a piece, which was readily given, and the two sat there in the dark and consumed the barley bread together. The famous "Van Horn Wells," on the plains of Texas, were afterwards dug at his instigation, while on frontier duty in that desert and almost waterless country, and named for him.

Mr. Clark said that at the battle of Cerro Gordo many Mexican women, wives of the soldiers, were killed, greatly to the regret of the Americans, but it could not be helped. They would come in among the Mexican troops while under heavy fire.

The American army entered the City of Mexico on September 14, 1847. Mr. Clark helped to raise the Stars and Stripes over the palace.

At the battle of Contreras Mr. Clark said he saw a young soldier fall as if struck a dead shot, and when the battle was over he and several others went to see about him. He was dead, and no mark of a wound was on his person. Blood was coming from his mouth, nose, and ears. It was supposed that a large cannon ball came so near his head that he died from concussion.

In this battle Mr. Clark gave many wounded Mexicans water. Their cries and appeals to the American soldiers was touching as they writhed on the ground with shattered legs and arms from grapeshot, cannon ball, musket ball, saber and bayonet wounds, calling in their native tongue "Water, water," and when the cooling fluid was placed to the parched lips they called down the blessings of the Virgin and all of the saints upon the heads of the strangers from the north whose language they could not understand, but whose deed of kindness they could, exclaiming "Amigo! Amigo!" (Friend! friend!)

At the battle of Chapultepec, while charging down an aqueduct the command was halted. While bullets were whistling in every direction and cannon balls raking their position, Mr. Clark noticed a young man drop into a sitting position behind a pepper tree to avoid the shots, laughing as he did so, but had hardly got down before a cannon ball cut a hole through the tree just above his head. He vacated the position quickly, but still laughing.

At the close of the war Mr. Clark was discharged from the service at San Elizario, twenty-five miles below El Paso. Some of the officers signed a paper and gave it to Mr. Clark, stating that Amasa Clark had distinguished himself for bravery and good conduct at Vera Cruz, Cerro Gordo, Chapultepec, Molino del Rey, Contreras, and the City of Mexico. This was signed by Major Henry, commanding the post, Lieutenants McFersen and Whistler, and Orderly Sergeant Davidson.

After being discharged from the service, Mr. Clark came to San Antonio, and from there went to the Fredericksburg crossing on the Guadalupe, and soon after came from that place to the present site of the town of Bandera, in 1852. At that time there were but three families there, and all in camp making shingles. They were Judge Saner, now of Boerne, Kendall County, and the families of Milstead and Odum. The latter was afterwards sent to the Legislature. At the time of which we write the county was not organized, but attached to Bexar County. Game of all kinds was in abundance, plenty of wild bees and honey, and the streams full of fish. At that time the Delaware Indians lived on the Guadalupe River, north of the Medina, where Mr. Clark settled, about twenty miles. He camped and hunted with them a great deal, as they were a friendly tribe and remained so. One night he camped where Kerrville is now, with an Indian named Jim. He loaned Jim a horse to go on a hunt with him, and when the hunt was over sold the horse to another Indian and took his pay in bear grease and honey. This commodity he carried to San Antonio and sold for cash.

Among other settlers who came later on was one named Richard Davis. He went eight miles up the river, above the present Bandera, and camped with his family. His occupation was making shingles. Early one morning Mr. Clark started up there, but had not proceeded more than a mile and a half when he met Davis bringing the dead body of one of his little girls to the settlement. She had been killed by Indians. The circumstance was this: Three of his daughters—Amanda, the one killed, and Susan and Lucy—went to the spring after water, and while there Lucy saw three Indians rise out of the grass close by, and at once screamed out "Indians!" and ran, followed by the other two girls. The Indians shot arrows at them and hit Amanda, who ran about eighty yards and then fell dead on a large flat rock. She was shot through the heart. Mr. Davis and a man named Kit Stanford followed the Indians on foot, but did not catch them.

In 1856 Mr. Clark made one of the most remarkable escapes from death almost ever recorded. Himself, Dr. Thompson, and a Polander named Kendall went with two wagons to San Antonio and on their return trip camped on the road five or six miles from town. It was dark, raining, and cold, and they went to sleep around their fire. Robbers had followed them, as was supposed, from San Antonio, and coming upon them while asleep knocked all three in the head and robbed them and pillaged the wagons of what things they wanted or could conveniently carry off. Dr. Thompson was killed where he lay, but Mr. Clark came to his senses just before daylight and knew that he had been hurt. He was hot and feverish and wanted water, but on making an attempt to rise fell back and became unconscious again. The moon had risen and was shining brightly, the rain clouds having drifted away, when he first came to himself, but the second time the sun was up. He crawled to Dr. Thompson and shook him, but discovered that he was dead. All had scrambled away from the fire more or less when hit, and it seemed that the doctor had struggled with them some before receiving the finishing blow. His head was beaten into a pulp.

Mr. Clark had three wounds on his head, and Kendall was also badly hurt about the head. Clark crawled to him and tried to get him up to help hitch the oxen to the wagons, but he was not able. Clark was dizzy and hardly able to crawl about on the ground, but realized that something must be done. With slow and painful efforts he managed to unhobble two yoke of the oxen and hitch one yoke to each wagon. He now helped Kendall to get in one wagon in a position that he could drive, and himself drove the other and succeeded in getting to Milstead's house, near San Antonio. The alarm was raised and a party repaired to the scene of the tragedy. An old, rusty scopet barrel was lying in camp, covered with blood—the weapon which did the work. Mr. Clark left a trail of blood wherever he went while getting the oxen and hitching them to the wagons. His pockets were both turned wrong side out. Very little money was taken, as the men had purchased supplies in town, and most if not all of these were taken from the wagons and carried off. The body of Thompson was taken up and carried to San Antonio and buried.

There were a great many desperadoes and robbers around San Antonio in those days, and many people were killed. The two most noted of these characters of the desperado type was Bob Augustine and Bill Hart. A vigilance committee was organized to handle this kind of men, and they came into collision with Hart and had a desperate battle with him. He was killed, but he also killed Phil Stroupe, the city marshal. Hart had eighteen wounds on his body when he finally fell in the streets of San Antonio and expired. Augustine made his escape. Mr. Clark and Kendall remained under treatment until able to return home, but Kendall never entirely recovered and died two years after. The sunken places in Mr. Clark's head still show where the fearful licks were struck with the gun barrel forty-three years ago.

In 1861 Tax Assessor Murry, of Bandera County, was killed by Indians. He had started over to Sabinal Canyon to take assessments. An account of this is given elsewhere.

Captain Mitchell was also chased by Indians and shot with an arrow while out riding in his buggy near Bandera. The Indians kept the settlers nearly broken up in horse stock.

The place where Mr. Clark now lives, four miles southwest from Bandera, was first settled by a man named Hardin. In 1868 his son, about 15 years of age, went out one cold morning bee hunting, and was killed by the Indians. Failing to come in, parties went in search of him, and finally the body was found by O. B. Miles. The youth had made a good fight, judging from the signs around, and his gun and pistol were both empty. If he killed any the balance had carried them off. The body was naked, cold, and stiff when found, and Mr. Miles sat it astride behind his saddle, supporting it with one hand and guiding his horse with the other, until arriving at the home of the stricken parents. Mr. Clark was present when the remains were brought in.

It will be remembered by readers of the history of the Mexican war that some of the American troops deserted near the Rio Grande in Mexico. Some of these were troops that were stationed along the border before the war. Most of these were either killed or captured and shot afterwards. Some were whipped in the American camp. Mr. Clark said he was present when they were whipped and some hung. General Twiggs superintended the flogging and hanging. He made a Mexican do the whipping, and told him if he did not lay it on hard he would have it put on him. The Mexican put in good licks. Colonel Riley was first whipped. He was a burly, stout fellow. The Mexicans gave him his title after he deserted to them. These fellows, Mr. Clark says, fought desperately at Cherubusco, and shot some Mexicans who ran up a white flag. They lay thick around the cannon where they stood. Those that were only whipped and turned loose were those who deserted before war was actually declared. Sixteen of the others were hanged.

Mr. Clark is now engaged in the fruit and nursery business at his place, and has been very successful, especially with apples and pears. He was determined several years ago to show the people that Bandera County was a fruit country. His only regret is that he did not commence sooner. In 1898 at the Center Point fair on the Guadalupe, in Kerr County, he took seven premiums on fruit. He draws a pension of $8 per month for services in the Mexican war, and is justly proud of his record made there. Many more old settlers of Bandera County deserve mention for the part they took in undergoing the hardships of frontier life—watching for, trailing, and scouting after Indians. One of these especially is Mr. George Hay, who lives at Bandera. He did as much scouting and trailing and bringing back stolen property retaken from the Indians almost as any man in Bandera County, but was in no regular Indian battle. Then there was Valentine, Laxons, Mansfield, and many others. All had to take their chances of being scalped by Indians, and they did not know at what hour that event might take place.

KILLED AN INDIAN.

1873.

Taking into consideration the many years that Texas had a frontier infested by hostile Indians and the many combats the rangers and settlers had with them, comparatively few men engaged in these fights killed an Indian that he was certain of. Of course there were personal incidents during these years, and Indians were killed under circumstances where there was no doubt as to who was the slayer of the redskin. For instance, Nick Haby killed one at night while guarding his horses; Xavier Wanz killed one and brought his body home on a horse; Henry Hartman killed one while they had him rounded up alone in a thicket; John Bowles killed three one night at one fire with a shotgun; Big Foot Wallace killed several. But these are exceptional cases, and there were many more like them, it is true. On the other hand, however, where two or more are engaged in an Indian fight they are all shooting generally, and likely four or five at one Indian, who may be exposing himself plainly or performing some daring act. If this particular Indian is killed likely every man who fired at him will claim the honor.

Among those, however, who did kill an Indian that he got, and no one to dispute his claim, is Mr. Edward Tschirhart, who lives in Castroville, Medina County. The circumstance was this: In 1873 he and Joe Tschirhart, Nic. Tschirhart, Louis Tschirhart, and Louis Ahr were freighting from San Antonio to Fort McKavett. On the 5th day of July, 1873, they went into camp near the fort for the night. About midnight they were attacked by a band of Indians, who charged on horseback and commenced firing among the mules, stampeding them badly and killing one horse. At this time Joe Tschirhart, brother to Edward, was on guard and commenced firing with his Winchester at the Indians, and the camp was soon aroused. Edward Tschirhart, who had spread his blanket down near his wagon and was asleep, waked as soon as the firing began and sprang up, seized his Winchester, and ran around the end of his wagon to get a view in the moonlight, as the shooting and yelling of Indians was all on the opposite side of his wagon. As soon as he did this he saw an Indian very near him on a horse, and leaning low towards him to avoid the bullets which Joe was sending in his direction. The Indian had his face turned the other way and did not see Edward as he raised his gun to fire, and who took a fair aim by moonlight at his left side. The Comanche was greatly surprised when this gun fired so near him, and went over to the other side of his horse quickly, and in this position guided him rapidly away and was soon lost to sight. By this time all the men were shooting and the Indians were beaten off. Edward ran around the mules and succeeded in getting them all back to the wagons, and none were lost. At daylight the trail of the wounded Indian was found where he bled as he hung to his horse and galloped away. Two hundred yards from the wagons his body was found, where, when life was extinct, he had slipped to the ground. The ball struck him in the left arm, and going through the body came out where the neck joins the body. No one was firing at this time but Joe, and none of his balls could have taken the course the one did which killed the Indian from the position he occupied. There was no doubt that Edward killed him. He was evidently a chief, and this was one reason the fight terminated so quickly. They supposed he was killed, no doubt, by not hearing anything from him, but could not find the body, or they would have carried it away. The dead Indian had a shield, bow and arrows, six-shooter, and a knife, all of which were taken by his slayer. The bow and shield were sold for $35. The Indian also had three white scalps—a woman's and two children's. The latter were very small. There was also around the dead chief's neck a necklace made of the finger nails of white people strung on a buckskin string.

The teamsters got back all right to San Antonio without having any more trouble with the Indians.

F. L. HICKS.

Came to Texas in 1855.

Fabian L. Hicks was born on the 16th day of April, 1828, in Forrestville, North Carolina, and came to Texas early in 1855. After crossing the Texas line he pushed on towards the west and stopped at San Antonio. Soon after arriving here he learned of an expedition that was on foot to cross the Rio Grande into Mexico for the purpose of chastising the Indians who were depredating upon the Texas settlers and then retreating into Mexico when pursued. Mr. Hicks at once became enthused, and joining the expedition spent a considerable amount in helping to fit out and equip himself and others. The main instigator and leader in this move was Capt. James H. Calahan, an old Indian fighter and one of the survivors of the massacre of Fannin's men at Goliad. Among other leaders were Captains Henry and Benton.

When everything was ready the command set out and crossed the Rio Grande with something more than a hundred men, and went out in the direction where the Indians were supposed to be located. In the meantime, however, the Indians had been informed of this move on the part of the Texans and sent out a force to meet them, assisted by several hundred Mexicans, making a total force of over 600. This force drew up in front of the Texans between Piedras Negras and San Fernando. Captain Calahan ordered his men to charge them, which they at once did, but were met by a severe fire from the opposing force, who then broke their ranks to let them through. Mr. Hicks carried a double-barreled shotgun, well loaded with buckshot, which he held in readiness, determined not to shoot until he went to pass through them, so that he could be certain of execution. As they went through he threw his gun on a Mexican and fired one barrel at a few yards distance, but he squatted and the whole charge went over his head. He then turned and aimed the other barrel at an Indian on the left, and this fellow got the full benefit of the other load and fell in a heap on the ground. After getting through the line of Mexicans and Indians the Texans took up a position in a ravine and continued the battle. They had some men killed and some wounded as they charged, and among the latter was young Eustis Benton, who was shot in the head and fell from his horse. He was the son of Capt. Nat. Benton, who was also wounded, but had made his way to the ravine. Captain Benton was very solicitous about his son, and Mr. Hicks, Hughes Tom and Wesley Harris volunteered to go back and get him. It was a perilous undertaking, for the bullets were flying thick and the wounded boy lay in open ground. The three men made the run from the ravine on foot, and seizing young Benton bore him quickly back while the bullets kicked up the dust all round them.

The Texans remained in the ravine until night and then made their way to Piedras Negras, opposite Eagle Pass, leaving their dead in the hands of the enemy. This place (Piedras Negras) they burned, and then crossed the river back to the Texas side and soon made their way back to San Antonio.

Mr. Hicks now came up into Bandera County, looking at the country, and finally located there and went into the stock business and was very successful. Here he also married. While looking about over the country he one day went through the Bandera pass, at the north end of which he found the skeleton of an Indian which had been dug up by some one. Beads and other things were scattered promiscuously about. Mr. Hicks dismounted, and tying his horse proceeded to gather up the remains of the fallen brave and put them back in the hole they came out of, covering them up and putting two rocks across the place. These remains were those of an Indian chief who was killed in a battle here by the Texas rangers under Jack Hays in the early 40's.

Mr. Hicks was on many scouts after Indians. On one occasion he and others pursued a band to the head of the Medina, and came so close upon them, the trail being very fresh, Mr. Hicks proposed a halt while he reconnoitered. Going down into the bed of a creek where there was water, the Indian sign there was so fresh that Hicks knew they must be in the immediate vicinity. They had watered their horses there and the water was still muddy. In fact it seemed they had run away from the water as if they had detected the presence of the white men. Mr. Hicks now went down the creek a little further and then turned back, as the Indian trail had left the creek, and went among rocks where he could not see it. After getting nearly back to where the Indians had watered their horses he discovered an Indian sitting on his horse on the bluff, not more than thirty yards away, looking and listening. Hicks took a quick but steady aim at his side and fired. At the crack of the rifle the Indian uttered a loud squall and went tearing down into a ravine on his horse, and Mr. Hicks could hear him making a noise down there like a buzzard or something of that sort, as you might say, a kind of squawking noise. Hicks quickly reloaded his gun and went back to where he left his horse and the other men. They now went to look for the wounded Indian and the others, but nothing could be seen of them. Blood was found on the trail where the Indian ran his horse after Hicks shot him, but down in the ravine he had got with companions and they carried him away, the trail continuing towards the divide in a very rough country. Hicks wanted to follow on after, but the other men refused to go, saying the Indians knew of their presence now, and would be certain to ambush them somewhere. They now turned back to Bandera. One of the party had been shot by an Indian with an arrow only a short time before, right in the town of Bandera, just at dark. On the way back they met a squad of soldiers from Camp Verde, on trail of the Indians. They went on and found the Indian dead on the trail after they passed the place where he was shot by Hicks. Mr. Hicks also rendered good service aiding the sheriffs of Bandera in ridding the country of horse-thieves, robbers, etc. He died at his ranch above Bandera on the 2d day of January, 1899. He left a large family, all well provided for. Several of them had families and ranches of their own. Among these were Fabian, who married Miss Lucy Barrow. Gleamer married Miss Garrison; Cleophas married Miss Moody. One daughter married George Fee, owner and publisher of the Bandera Enterprise. Mrs. Hicks and the young children still reside on the ranch.

CALAHAN'S EXPEDITION.

1855.

In 1855 the Indians made a daring raid upon the settlers east of San Antonio and penetrated as far as the Cibolo along and in the western edge of Guadalupe County. Among those killed by them was Doc. McGee, son of a Methodist preacher.

Not long after this raid, and in consequence of which, Capt. James Calahan determined to cross the Rio Grande, and if possible chastise the Indians. Mexico had long been a place of refuge for raiding bands of Indians who were hostile to the Texans. This movement of Calahan was sanctioned by Gov. E. M. Pease, who instructed him to cross the Rio Grande if necessary in pursuit of hostile Indians. Volunteers were now called for, and as soon as Calahan's company was full he advanced as far west as the Leona River, 100 miles from San Antonio. Here he learned that the Indians were continually depredating upon the settlers in this country and then retreating into Mexico when pursued. He now determined to cross into Mexico, and sent back to Seguin and San Antonio for more men. About thirty men at once left Seguin under the command of Capt. Nat Benton and a like number from San Antonio under Captain Henry, all being under the command of Calahan, whom they joined on the Leona, about seventy-five miles from the Rio Grande.

Captain Calahan left part of his men to protect the settlers on the extreme border, which reduced his individual company to sixty men. The three companies now set out and reached the Rio Grande on the evening of the 27th of September, 1855. Here, at the mouth of the Las Moras Creek, they remained for several days waiting for the river to fall, which was considerably swollen on account of recent heavy rains above. Besides the three captains in the expedition there were Eustis Benton (son of Captain Benton), Henry King, Hughes Tom, Ben Patton, John W. Sansom, Fabian L. Hicks, James McCormick, Hal. Holland, Willis Jones, Wesley Harris, Wall, Clopton, Bassham, Smith, Gregor, and of course many others.

On the 30th, the river still being very high and no chance to cross at that point, the command left camp about one hour by sun, and traveling all night at dawn found themselves near the town of Eagle Pass. Here the men were secreted in a cove between two mountains, and the captains went to the river to see if there was any chance to cross in boats.

The captains returned at 3 o'clock and reported the Mexicans unwilling to furnish boats for the men to cross. Captain Henry then proposed to take twenty-five men and secure the boats, while the others would march down the river to an old crossing three miles below. The men then separated to meet at the old crossing. Captain Henry and his party made their way to the boat landing, and the men were concealed behind a bank. The captain was to signal a boat as if wanting to cross, and when it landed was to place his handkerchief over his hat, which was to be the signal for the men to come from their ambush and take possession of it. Accordingly the captain made the signal and two boats put off from the opposite side and landed near Captain Henry, the signal was given to the men, who instantly made a rush for the boats and sprang into them. The Mexicans were then ordered to row rapidly down the river. This they at first refused to do, but being mildly persuaded by a cocked revolver they went to work with a will, and soon the perspiration was rolling from their brows and mingling with the muddy waters of the Rio Grande.

In a short time the boats arrived at the old crossing, just as the command rode up. It was now about dusk. That night men enough to protect the landing were crossed to the opposite side. The next day all crossed over except fifteen men, who were left to guard the pack mules.

This reduced the command to 110 men. At daylight on the following morning, the 3d of October, they set out for the town of San Fernando, distant about thirty miles. At noon, while the men were resting, a Mexican came to them with the information that the Mexicans were in force ahead of them, and would oppose their further progress. Calahan did not anticipate having to fight the Mexicans, but as he had come thus far he determined to proceed and fight anything which came in his way until he got a chance at the Indians, if he could find them.

After leaving this place and proceeding about five miles the command was fired on at long range from a dense thicket, and

the Texans advanced rapidly towards it. They halted in front
of it and were again fired on by Mexicans and Indians, who
showed themselves. One of Calahan's men returned the fire and
broke the leg of an officer's horse, and another shot wounded the
rider, and they all retreated back into the thicket. In a short
time, however, more than one hundred mounted Mexicans and
Indians emerged from the brush and formed opposite the Texans
for a fight. Calahan, believing there were more of them in the
thicket, ordered his men to fall back hastily, as if terror-stricken,
so as to bring the whole force upon him if there were any more
concealed. This had the desired effect, and instantly 750 Mexicans and Indians swarmed out of the thickets with loud and continuous yelling, thinking the white men would be an easy prey.
In this, however, they were badly mistaken. Calahan instantly
halted his men and formed them into line of battle. The Mexicans and Indians then formed in front of the Texans until they
reached the end of their line, and then lapped around them, almost surrounding their position. Calahan now rode down his
line and gave the men a short talk, telling them their only chance
was to make a desperate fight, and at the word of command to
charge the enemy's line. Captain Calahan now placed himself
in front at the head of his column and cried out with a loud
voice, "Now, boys, remember the bloody son of McGee, and
charge!" With an answering yell to this command the men
charged, and in a few moments collided with the enemy and a
desperate fight ensued. Pistols, rifles, and shotguns rang out
on every side, mingled with the yell of the Texans, the warwhoop
of the Indians, and loud imprecations of the Mexicans. The
enemy were completely broken in front, and the Texans went
through them and advanced about 300 yards to a deep ravine, and
there took a strong position and awaited the enemy to act. In
the charge through the Mexicans and Indians, Willis Jones, Hal.
Holland, Clopton, and Smith were killed, and Eustis Benton,
Henry King, Ben Patton, Captain Benton and a man named
Gregor were wounded. Willis Jones was the son of Hon. W. E.
Jones; Hal. Holland was from San Marcos; Clopton lived up on
the Guadalupe, and Smith was from San Antonio. Captain
Benton was wounded in the arm, Henry King in the shoulder,
Eustis Benton in the head, Ben Patten in the neck, and Gregor
in the breast.

While the Texans were dismounting and forming in the ravine and leading their horses into it they were fired on by about 200 infantry who were concealed in a thicket within gunshot of the ravine, and who had not as yet shown themselves. Here the Texans sustained a heavy fire until night, but without serious damage, as they were well protected by the banks of the ravine. The bodies of the dead fell into the hands of the enemy. Wesley Harris, of Seguin, assisted by some others, saved the body of young Benton, who had fallen from his horse and was lying in an exposed position. The ball had struck him over the left eye and remained somewhere in the head. A man named Wall, called by the men "True" Wall, killed the Mexican who wounded Captain Benton. After dark the firing ceased and the enemy drew off in the direction of San Fernando. The Texans then emerged from the ravine, and mounting their horses took the road to Piedras Negras.

Having arrived at this place, the inhabitants made some hostile demonstrations, and the Texans took a position under the banks of the river some 200 yards below the town.

An officer of the American garrison at Eagle Pass (on the Texas side opposite Piedras Negras) came down and called across the river, and asked if they needed any help in crossing. Being answered in the affirmative, he said they should have it, and returning to the fort ran up the Stars and Stripes and pointed six cannon towards Piedras Negras, so as to cover the rear of the Texans while crossing the river. The wounded were soon sent across with part of the force, and went into camp on the Texas side. In the meantime the Mexicans in the town became alarmed and commenced leaving, and soon the road to San Fernando was lined with men, women and children. Some of the Texans pursued them and took the guns from those who were armed.

Calahan now took possession of town and fortified himself in a large stone building, as he had heard rumors of a large force coming to attack him. He had two cannons brought into the building which he found in the town, and pointed them through some of the ground-floor windows. The men found plenty of chickens, eggs, pigeons, and pigs in the town to subsist on.

On Saturday morning, the 7th, Calahan thought it best to cross the river, and at once commenced crossing the horses, and by 3 o'clock had two-thirds of them across. At this time opera-

tions were suddenly suspended by a large force of Mexicans, said
to be about 1200. The Texans had all left the stone house and
were under the river banks, near the boats, when the Mexicans
arrived.

The three captains had no idea of surrendering to this formidable force, but at once made ready to fight, although they
only had eighty-five men on that side of the river. The Mexicans divided their force, sending a large party below the Texans,
and the balance formed in front of them, about 360 yards off.
The Texans at once opened fire on them with two small cannon
which they had brought with them from town, which threw
them into confusion, and they failed to charge, as they were expected every minute to do. Night soon came on and the Texans
determined to burn the town and then cross the river. A heavy
fire was now opened on the Mexicans by most of the men, while
the balance of the men ran through the town and fired everything that would burn. Hughes Tom, from Seguin, applied the
first torch. Many of the houses, being covered with grass and
low, could be fired almost as fast as a man could gallop a horse.
It was like setting a prairie of dry grass on fire. It caught
quick and made a terrific blaze. About 7 o'clock, or a little
after dark, Calahan ordered the men into the boats. The country for miles around the mountains and Rio Grande was lit up
almost as bright as day by the burning town when the Texans
embarked and pulled for the other shore. When about half way
across, the small ropes which held the boat to the large one
broke, and the men and boat went down the river about half a
mile before they could land on the Texas side, which they finally
did by aid of some oars which were found in the large boat.
They now joined the other men at the camp above, where most
of the horses and the wounded men were.

Eustis Benton lay three days from the time he was hit before
he showed any signs of life. The only way they could tell that
he was breathing was by holding a soft, downy feather close to
his lips. On the third day he suddenly opened his eyes as one
waking from sleep, and seeing men standing around him asked
for his gun. He thought the battle was still going on. He remembered the ball striking him in the face, and then all was
a blank until he came to himself on the Texas side of the river
three days after. The ball was never extracted from his head,

but he recovered with the loss of the left eye, behind which the ball was supposed to be. He was a captain in the Confederate army during the war, and married and settled in Arkansas when it was over. His father, Capt. Nat Benton, commanded a regiment during the Civil war, and lost an arm at the battle of Blair's Landing, in Louisiana.

MRS. C. A. WITT.

Came to Texas in 1852.

Among the first settlers on the Guadalupe River above the present town of Comfort was Mrs. C. A. Witt, wife of Rev. J. M. Witt, Baptist minister. Mrs. Witt was the daughter of Thomas Denton, and was born in Kentucky in 1849. She was also a granddaughter of Daniel Boone, of Kentucky pioneer fame. Her father was a soldier in the war of 1812, and died at Merry Oaks, Barren County, Kentucky. Her grandfather, David Denton, was a soldier under Washington, and passed through many of the stirring incidents of the Revolutionary war. When he died the following sketch of his career as a soldier was published:

"Departed this life at the Merry Oaks, at his residence in Barren County, Kentucky, on the 18th day of May, 1838, David Denton, Sr., aged 84 years. He served his country as a private soldier five years and eight months during the Revolutionary war. He was one of the heroic little band that crossed the Delaware in December, 1776, with Washington, and was in the battle of Trenton. He was again with his beloved commander in the battles of Princeton, Brandywine, and Germantown. He was with Wayne at the storming of Stony Point, and was one of the advance guard and with the first that entered the fort. He was at the siege of Yorktown and capture of Cornwallis and his army, and shortly after peace was made immigrated to the West and took part in most of the Indian wars that attended the first settlement of Kentucky, and in a close fight with an Indian was wounded with a tomahawk, that rendered him an invalid for life. He lived and died an honest man, beloved by all who knew him. professing an unshaken confidence in his Redeemer, and died in hope of a blessed immortality. He was buried with the honors of war."

The above glowing tribute to the memory of an honest man, a faithful soldier, and model Christian gentleman, is nicely framed and hangs in a conspicuous place in the home of Mrs. Witt. There is nothing to show who is or was the publisher. It is in large, plain print, and has been well kept during all of these years by members of the Denton family. At the top of the frame just above the head lines of the memorial are the letters I. H. S., but Mrs. Witt does not know their significance.

She says her grandfather went with Daniel Boone to Kentucky and was in the terrible battle with Indians at Boone's fort, and it was there he received the wound from the tomahawk. Her grandmother, Mrs. Denton, was present at this fight, and molded bullets for Boone's men. For two years she could not go to the spring or to milk cows with safety unless Grandpa Denton was along with his gun for her protection. Mrs. Witt does not mean that her grandfather came with Boone to Kentucky his first trip when he discovered and explored the country, but with immigrants he brought to settle the country after the War of the Revolution was over.

Mrs. Witt came to Texas with her mother in 1852, in the spring, and in the fall of the same year settled at the mouth of Cherry Creek, where it empties into the Guadalupe River, four miles below the present town of Center Point. They were the outside settlers, and their nearest neighbors below were Schleador and Weadenfield, two Germans who lived about where Comfort now is. The first two years of their frontier life were spent in quiet, no Indians coming to molest them, as they had no stock and nothing to induce them to make a raid in this isolated place. Her mother had five children—two boys (Joseph and David) and three girls. The oldest boy was 12 years of age. One of her uncles, E. A. McFadin, came to Texas and settled and lived with them. Mrs. Denton also had two negro men, so if the Indians came they calculated to make a good fight with them. Mr. McFadin in after years commanded a ranging company, and Mrs. Denton's boys served as rangers when they grew up and in the Confederate army when the Civil war broke out. Joseph was the older and David the younger. The latter was killed by Mexicans on the Rio Grande. After the country began to settle up and stock to be brought in the Indians began to depredate upon them.

On one occasion they ran the children from the cowpen. David had gone across the creek after the cows, and seeing a steer running, kept a close lookout and soon saw the Indians, and at once ran back and told the girls at the cowpen to run, and they all escaped to the house. The men then armed themselves and went to fight the Indians. They got out of the way, but returned in the night and stole a quarter of beef out of the yard. The beef had been cut up and spread out on a scaffold. Some of the Indians decoyed the dogs off while others went into the yard and got the beef. In doing this they passed within fifteen steps of where De Witt Burney and Captain McFadin were lying asleep in a wagon. They dropped some of the beef in the yard as they were carrying it out. The Indians often came at night and roamed through the field, eating watermelons and roasting ears. They would also pull up potato vines, hunting sweet potatoes, until hardly any vines were left in the patch.

In 1859 the Indians came close to the house in order to get a gentle horse to drive off a bunch on. Captain McFadin and a negro man went to save the horse, and the negro saw something he thought was an Indian and fired at it with a load of buckshot and crippled him. The horses were now carried close to the house and guarded until daylight. As soon as it was light enough to see objects distinctly they repaired to the spot where the negro had fired at the Indian, and there found his shield and other things and plenty of blood. That day two boys coming from Bandera saw nine Indians. One of them was considerably in the rear with a blanket around him, and traveling very slowly, and was evidently the one wounded by Mrs. Denton's negro man.

The old log cabin is still standing where the mother first settled. The two negro men cut and hewed the logs and built the house. There was a fine spring close by at that time, but it is dry now. Just below the spring there is a very large cypress tree, which is a sight to people who have not been used to seeing large timber. Rev. J. M. Witt at one time measured it and found that five feet from the ground it measured thirty-three feet in circumference and would hold this girth thirty feet. It would measure forty feet at the base. Thirty feet from the ground there is a hackberry tree about eight inches in diameter growing out of a fork of this big cypress, probably the largest in western Texas. Rev. Witt settled here in 1867, and the same year married Miss Denton. He has a fine farm and ranch, and lives one mile west of the old Denton home. He accompanied the writer to look at the large tree in 1898, and says many people come to look at it.

JOE WILTON.

Killed by Indians, 1877.

Among the frontiersmen who have figured in Indian history on the Hondo, Black Creek, and other points near Devine, in Medina County, is Mr. Bee Tilley. While not participating in many Indian battles, Mr. Tilley was an actor in connection with one of those distressing frontier tragedies in which the bloody hand of the savage has brought mourning and wailing to the many hearthstones along the border and caused a settled gloom to come over the lives of fathers, mothers, brothers, sisters, and husbands, as all of these different relationships have met the rude shock of the savage and been made to mourn during the advance of the pioneers in settling up this vast State of Texas.

On the 22d day of April, 1877, a young man named Joe Wilton, 18 years of age, started from the ranch of Mr. Dan Patterson, who lived about one mile east from the present town of Devine, to go to a store on the Hondo kept by a man named Segenus, at the Eagle Pass crossing of the river. This place was west of the Patterson ranch, and the young man started there in the morning. His mother was a widow, and her boy not coming back at the proper time, she became uneasy and search was instituted.

On this day religious services were being held at the house of Rev. C. B. Hukill, who was assisted by Rev. Burkitt. Mr. Bee Tilley, who was one of the searchers for the absent Joe Wilton, went to the meeting, thinking likely the boy had gone there, but nothing had been seen of him. It was now nearly night. Rev. Hukill, who had not been on the frontier long, now told Bee that their horses had been carried off that day by men who had tin pans on their arms. "Indians," said Tilley. What they took to be tin pans on their arms where shields. Tilley was now almost certain that the Indians had killed young Wilton, and set out in the night to the ranch of Lon Moore, who lived on the Hondo below the crossing, to see if Joe had been there. On the way Bee saw the horse of the unfortunate Wilton (who had been killed), but did not recognize him in the uncertain light.

The horse was wounded and standing still. Coming to the ranch of Moore and waking him, he could get no news of the missing youth, but as yet no one had gone to the store. From Lon Moore's place Tilley, in company with Rufus Ketchum, went back to Patterson's, arriving there about daybreak, but still no tidings. A crowd of ten or twelve men now gathered to make a thorough search and to fight the Indians if they came in contact with them. There was no doubt now about Indians being in the country. Of those who gathered were Bee Tilley, Cull. Moore, Napoleon Harr, Charles Harr, Frank Jackson, Hay Moore, John Tilley, and Rube Ketchum. This party struck the trail of the Indians near Hondo and followed it to the head of Black Creek, ten miles distant. Here they halted and held a consultation. The Indian trail seemed to be leaving the country, and they now had some hopes that the boy was still alive. Rufe Ketchum and John Tilley were now sent across the country to the store, to see if he had been there, but he had not. Some of the men went back down the country, and the others followed later. When near Black Creek they heard a man hallooing and went to him. This man was Napoleon Harr, and he had found Wilton's horse, which was badly wounded and died soon after. The men now commenced with renewed energy to find the body. They soon found the trail of the Indians, who had made a turn beyond Black Creek and came down the country, and near here had met Wilton and began to chase him. The men soon found where this chase commenced and followed fast. Wilton had run a trail, and the tracks of the Indians' horses were on both sides of it. About 500 yards from here Hay Moore, who was in the lead, said, "Here he is." The body was lying under a liveoak tree with some white chaparral bushes around it. The boy had run in here after leaving his wounded horse, and was there killed, stripped, and mutilated. He had one bullet hole in the lower part of the neck between the shoulders, high up. One arrow in the left nipple went through the body, and the spike pushed the skin out on the opposite side. This arrow was in so deep that it was hard to extract it, so Charley Harr held the body down while Bee Tilley pulled it out. Besides these wounds there was a lance wound through the right breast, and another gunshot wound in the head and one in the hip. This last wound was evidently inflicted when the Indians first met the boy and before he turned to run, as it was in front. The men now left Charles Harr and Cull. Moore with the body and the balance went back to the settlement to carry the news. Bee Tilley went back with a wagon and brought the body in, and it was buried one mile east of Devine, not far from where the International road now runs. A tombstone now marks the spot, with name, date of death, and cause inscribed upon it.

XAVIER WANZ.

Came to Texas in 1845.

Mr. Xavier Wanz (pronounced Sevier Vance) was born in Strassburg, Alsace, in 1844, and came to Texas with his parents as part of Castro's colony in 1845. They landed at Port Lavaca and then came on out to Castroville. Mr. Vance of course does not remember anything of these times, being only one year old. His parents left Castroville and came fifteen miles further west and settled at a place called Vanderburg, four miles northwest from the present village and settlement of New Fountain. Vanderburg was near the old "Wall road," as it was called, an' which marked the route of retreat of Wall's army after his defeat by General Caldwell at the battle of Salado in 1842. At the time of this settlement Mr. Vance says the route could be easily traced, and that the fight on the Hondo between the rear guard of the Mexican army and the rangers under Jack Hays took place two and a half miles west from the Vanderburg settlement and on the east bank of the Hondo. Mr. Vance there found some sabers, broken guns, dishes, and other things when a boy. When the writer passed the site of Old Vanderburg, on the way to see Mr. Vance, he discovered an old rock building nearly hidden by mesquite brush, and the old "Wall road" was 300 yards north of this. The rock house was built by Louis White, an American. When the settlement was made here the creek then called Lucky, but now Verde, was a bold, running stream, and derived its name from the many evergreens that grew along its bank and always gave it a verdant appearance.

This settlement began prosperously, but all at once a strange thing happened, which caused Vanderburg to be abandoned and the houses which they had so carefully and substantially built to go to decay. This was the sudden drying up of Verde Creek. It broke out again, however, four miles below, and most of the people moved there and started another village and called it New Fountain, suggested by the new flow of water. A few remained at the old town and hauled water. They were the Vance family, the two Decker brothers—Joe and Charley—and Louis

White. The latter stayed here until the breaking out of the Civil war, and being a Union man, went to Mexico and remained there until it was over, and then came back and finally died at Castroville. The Vance family remained a long time here, and hauled water from where Mr. Joe Decker now lives, and the elder Vance died here. The country around was open then, and the stockmen were in the habit of climbing to the top of White's stone house to look for their stock on the open prairies around. When Sevier was 14 years of age he had his first Indian scare, and a good one, as he expressed it. On that occasion he went out to hunt mustangs, armed with a six-shooter, and there being plenty of deer, fired five of his loads at them. He saw no Indians that day, however, but came back with an almost empty pistol and failed to reload it. At about 4 o'clock a. m. the Indians came. The dogs first discovered them and commenced barking, and the bells on the horses began to rattle lively. Vance did not think it was Indians, and went out in his night clothing and followed the bell, thinking it was mustangs among his horses. Going four of five hundred yards he discovered mounted men driving them, and some of them with guns on their shoulders. The Indians detected him by his white night garments, and wheeling their horses came towards him. Realizing now that it was Indians he turned and fled, his white figure vanishing before them like a specter of the night, carrying the pistol with the one load in his hand. On the way he came upon one horse the Indians failed to get, and tried to catch and mount him, but being unable to do so, ran on past his own house to that of Joe Decker to arouse him. He was pursued, and Mrs. Vance, who was on the lookout, said three Indians passed the house. These turned back and got the horse which the boy had failed to catch, and went on after their companions. Joe Decker got his gun and he and Vance went in pursuit, the latter still carrying the pistol in his hand, and in the excitement had forgotten as yet to load it. In about one mile and a half they came so close to the Indians they could be heard talking by the boys. Decker proposed to go back, as the Indians were too many and would kill them as soon as it was light enough. So they went back. Next morning Vance, Decker, and a Frenchman named Bushman again followed the Indians. Vance, being the youngest, carried the provisions. The trail was soon lost in the rough country, and they scattered to hunt it. Vance got lost from his companions and had to come back home. His horse was very tired, and he tried to get another to go back that night to McCoy's ranch on the Hondo, as he knew the other two men would have to go there to get something to eat if they did not come home, but failed to get the horse and had to remain. Decker and the Frenchman had found the trail of the Indians and followed it until nearly night without anything to eat, and then abandoned it and went to McCoy's to get provisions. This ranch was in Hondo Canyon, twenty miles from where Vance got lost from his party. The Indians camped a mile from where they quit the trail, but left in the night, and before day appeared at McCoy's ranch and killed some cattle and then left, carrying off some of his and Bandy's horses. Next day a scout was made up and attempted to follow the trail but lost it, and came back to the ranch to await until morning again. The trail was found next day and the Indians caught on the West prong of the Hondo in a dense cedarbrake, so thick they had to walk and lead their horses. When the white men came upon them firing commenced at once on both sides, but the Indians ran and left all of the horses. None of the settlers were hurt, and only one Indian wounded, and he got away, but the horses were all rounded up and brought back.

In 1867 Sevier Vance, Joe Decker, and his brother Charley started in the early part of the week with their wagons and ox teams and a saddle horse apiece to cut grass to cover houses, as they could get no shingles. They located their camp on the Hondo prairie and went to work, the distance from home being six miles. On Saturday morning, having their loads completed, they prepared to return home. The Deckers were to load the wagons, while Vance rounded up the oxen. It was about 10 o'clock when he got to camp with them, and as the water was out he and Charley Decker took the three horses and one keg and went after some, which was some distance off. When about half a mile from camp Vance noticed horses moving in the timber beyond the prairie and just coming out of the hills. Looking close it was discovered that mounted men were with them, and all about a mile distant. Vance said it was Indians, and they had better go back and inform Joe, as he was the oldest. When informed of the presence of the Indians he said it was not prudent to follow them, as they might be in large force and against three of them. Vance thought there were but few Indians, and proposed to follow them. This was agreed to, and the pursuit commenced. When the Indians were again sighted they were crossing a flat and just beginning to ascend a ridge, still driving the horses. They were now nearly within gunshot, and six of them in number. They discovered the white men and attempted to mount fresh horses, two of which turned back, followed by two Indians with lariats trying to rope them. Failing in this they went back, and all went into the brush on a small ridge. Vance had a Mississippi rifle and six-shooter, Joe Decker had a Mississippi rifle, and Charley a Spencer carbine. Vance was in the lead as they advanced, and the Indians fired at him with bullets and commenced yelling and charging, but he sat upon his horse, not being hit, and aimed his rifle. The Indians were all coming on foot, but fell to the ground to avoid the shot, and he held his fire, not being able to see them good, and the Indians arose and yelled and charged again. The fearless white man would not run, and again aimed at them, but they dodged and scattered back to their horses and mounted. All this transpired very quickly, and at this time Charley Decker came up by the side of Vance with his Spencer, having seven shots in it, and was told by Vance to cut down on them, as he had plenty of loads. The Indians lay over on the sides of their horses with only one leg exposed. Charley now fired and shot one of them through the leg, and two left their horses and took to the brush. The balance went on after the loose horses and Vance followed them. Joe Decker, who was in the rear and in a position to see clearly, discovered an Indian on horseback behind a thicket opposite Vance. He shouted to the latter, "Look out! There is an Indian behind the thicket." Vance now turned his horse and rode around to the lower side of the thicket; the Indian did the same on the, opposite side, but neither saw the other until they met at the end of the thicket. The white man raised his gun quickly, but the Indian was also quick, and wheeled his horse into the brush behind some large bushes about fifty yards away. He leaned forward on his horse as he went, and thought he was hid, and partially straightened up. Vance had his gun on him trying to get a bead as he went, not wanting to waste a shot with

35

a muzzle-loader, but now saw part of the Indian plainly, and taking aim fired. At the crack of the gun the Indian's horse jumped out of sight, and Vance could not tell if he hit the Indian or not, but thought he did. Determined to find out where he went, Vance rode out there to hunt him, keeping his revolver ready for instant use, and soon found him dead under his horse's neck. The Indian was on his hands and knees with his face to the ground, and his long hair spread out over the grass. He was a fearful-looking sight, and Mr. Vance said it almost frightened him when he rode up on him, but seeing he was dead, got down beside him. He was lying on a rope which was around the horse's neck, and had on a pair of leggings and a white man's coat. He also had a dressed buffalo yearling skin with the hair on tied around his waist, which with his own mop of hair gave him a very bulky appearance. He had shot the Indian square through the body, breaking his back. He now took the buffalo skin, bow and quiver of arrows and bow case and tied them to his own saddle; also the Indian's knife, which had no handle, but a buckskin string closely wrapped around the hand-hold. Mounting, he again pursued the Indians to try and recover the horses, which he soon succeeded in doing, as they had abandoned them and gone. The Indian that Vance killed had evidently stopped behind the thicket to kill him as he came through in pursuit. He returned to the dead body of the Indian with seventeen head of horses, and found the other two men there. They could not tell where Vance had gone, but finding the Indian he had killed, remained by the body.

After getting back to camp they coupled two wagons together so one man could drive two, and Vance drove the captured horses, and they got home before night. When they told about the fight and killing the Indian, some said they did not believe an Indian had been killed, and that he lost the things Vance had while running. This irritated the men, and on the following morning Vance and Charley Decker took one of the Indian horses, and going back to the spot loaded the Indian on him and brought him to the settlement, so that all the people who wanted to could look at him, and to prove their assertion. The Indian had brass rings in his ears as big as silver dollars. Vance scalped him, and then dragged his body about a mile and covered it up with rocks. The horse off which the Indian was killed belonged to Billy Harper, son of Judge George Harper and brother to Robert A. Harper. The latter still lives on the Hondo, has passed through many stirring scenes on the frontier, and is known to his many friends as "Uncle Bob."

Shortly after this raid the Indians made another one and stole some of Judge Harper's horses, some from Rev. William Fly, and some from negroes who lived in the Harper settlement. They had formerly belonged to the Harpers, and still lived in the country as freedmen. Next morning after the raid Mr. Fly came over to see Mr. Vance to notify him, and get up a scout to follow the Indians. Vance said "All right, we will get men enough." The party who gathered to go in pursuit were Sevier Vance, Rolly Harper, Charles Decker, and six negroes. The trail led towards Sabinal Canyon, and after entering it turned up Little Creek, and then went back towards the Sabinal River, passed through a pecan grove back of John Ware's field, stopped awhile on the river, and then went on towards the Frio Canyon. They crossed below the settlement and went in the direction of Camp Wood, on the Nueces. One place was found where they stopped and killed a mare and took some of the meat along with them, and here some of the negroes began to think they had gone far enough, and wanted to turn back, but Vance saw something on a hill standing still and could not tell what it was, whether an Indian or Spanish dagger, so the balance of the party were told to remain where they were, and he would go on foot up the mountain and see what it was. Decker followed, and then Rolly Harper, leaving the negroes in the valley, and they came on up the mountain, too. When arrived at the summit they were in the midst of an Indian camp, but the Indians were gone. There was their fire and cooked meat upon it. It was evident that they were just preparing to eat when one of them raised up to take a look and discovered Vance and his party. Forty yards away was a bluff, and in the valley beyond were the horses, except those ridden away by the Indians and a few taken along. Rolly Harper went back to bring up the negroes, and Vance and Decker took the trail of the Indians. In about a mile five head of horses were discovered near a thicket, and when all the crowd got together Vance said, "We will have a fight, now," and led the advance, the negroes riding close together in a bunch. Vance noticed this, and said, "Scatter out, there; the Indians will fire into you directly and kill three or four in a pile." They rode up to the horses, but no Indians were there. The horses were tired, worn out, and standing still. The Indians had left them when they saw their pursuers still following. By night all of the horses, eighteen in number, were collected and carried back to the settlement. This was in sight of Camp Wood.

In 1872 the Indians made another raid on the Hondo. They first struck the ranch of Widow Dean below and came on up, and early in the morning appeared in the Vance settlement. The families of Vance and Decker lived on the west side of Verde Creek, and Frank Vogel, Gotlieb Britsch, Louis Mumme, Charles Martin, Tampkes, Hallers, and others on the east side. The Indians first struck the Vogel place. The horses on this ranch had been kept stabled during the night, but had been turned out about daylight to graze, and Vogel had started to the field to work. He saw the Indians riding around the field, and at once turned back in a hurry, but before he could get his gun and return, the Indians had his horses and gone with them. Charles Martin ran over to Vance and Charles Decker, and told them about the Indians. They at once got their guns and pistols and went to the rescue of their horses back of the field, several hundred yards from the house. They soon found Decker's horse, and heard the bell of Vance's in the bed of the creek. The latter told his companion to wait for him until he could secure his horse, and then they would go back to the house and carry them to a place of safety. Both of them, however, ran down to where they heard the bell, but the horse was gone and the bell had quit rattling. The Indians had got the horse and taken the bell off. In this raid there were thirty-four Indians, as was seen afterwards, but were now divided. One party came up on the east side of the creek, and the others on the west. Those on the east got Vance's horse. The two men now followed the Indians to get the horses back if possible. They ran half a mile north, but not seeing them turned east some distance and still not seeing anything, turned back towards home again. While going up a brushy hill they saw the Indians, fourteen in number, not more than 125 yards away. Decker wanted to fire at once, but Vance said, "No; wait till they come closer." By this time the Indians had discovered them, and the two men arose from the squatting position they were in and commenced firing. They had Winchesters and plenty of cartridges. The first shot Vance fired hit an Indian, a large fellow off to one side on a horse. He did not fall, but leaned over to avoid another shot, and made off. The other Indians yelled and returned the fire, and the white men continued to shoot and yell and curse the Indians at the top of their voices. This fight and loud cursing and yelling was heard all over the settlement. The Indians finally retreated and the two fearless settlers pursued them on foot, when they separated, some going east and some west. Vance and Decker followed those who took the west course. Decker soon gave out and dropped behind, but his companion went on and caught up with one Indian who had stopped and roped a fresh horse. He was down putting a bridle on him, and had the bit in his mouth and the headstall over one ear, when Vance opened fire on him. The Indian retreated on foot and was pursued and fired at rapidly, jumping high and yelling at every crack of the Winchester. Vance had run so far and fast and was breathing so hard he could not hold on him, but ran and fired at the Indian for 200 yards, until he joined the balance. Decker was now hallooing to Vance to wait for him, as he had given out and could not catch up with him. The Indian who had been pursued so closely mounted behind another, and several of them now fired at the bold, aggressive white man, who stood his ground and waited for his tired companion to come to him. Some of the Indians who were in this crowd had Decker's horse. He had left him and come with Vance on foot to help him retake his horse. The Indians soon retreated, and waved two red shawls as they went off. Three or four of them hung back and still continued to shoot at Vance and also at Decker, who had just caught up. It was some time before Vance could get his breath back to normal. The Indians seemed to be badly rattled by the pluck of the white men and rapid fire of the Winchesters. They finally all ran away, carrying the loose horses along with them. They raised a dust as they went down into the Hondo valley that looked like smoke on a burning prairie.

The two white men now went back to where the fight commenced, and found fourteen head of mules and horses which the Indians had left in their flight and fright. Three mules stood saddled and packed with horsemeat. They had killed this horse the night before near the Dean ranch. On the horses were also blankets and canteens. On the way back home with the horses the two men met Joe Decker, who had heard the fight and was coming to help them.

This was the best fight that two men ever made with Indians in this country. By their rapid fire and loud cursing they had practically put to flight thirty-four Indians and captured fourteen head of animals from them. It was only equaled by Henry Hartmann in his desperate battle alone. The Indians evidently thought that all the men in the settlement were after them. In the lot of recaptured stock there were three mules that did not belong in this settlement, but had been ridden in by the Indians. The scouts from the Hondo were in hearing of the fight, but they were on the way to the Widow Dean's ranch to strike the trail there, and were not aware that the Indians were in that direction, and that it was a fight they heard. It was a long ways off, and they could only hear the shots, and not those very distinctly. They got on the trail and came on up towards the Vance settlement, and then went on into the mountains. Vance raised a scout and came on behind the Hondo men. The Verde scout went nine miles in a northwest direction and found nine dead horses which the Indians had killed. They were not all together, but scattered along the trail. Seven miles further on they found a gray horse that was not hurt himself, but was sprinkled with blood on the shoulders. An Indian was either shot on this horse or else a wounded one had been carried on him until the animal gave out. Six miles further on, while going over a mountain, a bunch of men and horses were discovered. They were thought to be the Indians, but proved to be the Hondo scouts under the command of Isaac King. They yelled at the Verde men to see who they were. They all got together, numbering thirty-one men, and kept on in the pursuit. Some wanted to turn back, but Vance was not willing, and said he would trail as long as he could see. Two miles from here was Perry Wilson's ranch, where were young Wilson and a negro (some say a Mexican.) The Indians attacked them, but both made their escape, Wilson on horseback and the negro on foot in the brush. The Indians looked for him but could not find him, and this delay caused the white men to overtake them before night. Near this ranch the Indians killed eighteen head of cattle and horses (two of the latter), and cut out their tongues, hearts, and loins. While at this the scouts came upon them. The Indians were badly scattered, but at the approach of the white men collected to give them battle. They, however, dodged the issue and continued their retreat. As they went over an open country thirty-four were counted. Vance, Chris. Schumaker, Billy Johnson, and a Mexican named Casuse followed at a run, and the other men came on, being scattered for a mile back. Some stopped at the dead cattle and got knives and ropes. The Indians ran two miles, crossed the Hondo, went on to a mountain, and commenced firing on the advance of the settlers. By this time the horse ridden by Vance had failed, and he dismounted and went on foot. He had on a pair of leggings, and getting tired of these, stopped to unfasten them, and the Indians fired a volley at the time, hit the ground all around him, and knocked dirt in his face. The Mexican now came up and the Indians fired at him. He dodged and dropped when the puffs of smoke were seen, and was not hit, although the dirt and rocks were knocked up all around him. The Indians cursed him and said, in Spanish, "There, I liked to got you that time." He then took shelter behind rocks, and Johnson, Schumaker and others opened fire on the Indians from cover also. Vance also commenced firing, and twenty-five shots in all were fired. Vance now went back to where he had left his horse and waited for the other men to come, who were approaching as fast as they could, attracted and guided by the firing. It was nearly night when they came, and would not then go up the mountain, as darkness would come on before they could accomplish anything.

Vance saw a horse half way up the mountain, saddled, and a hackamore on his head and nose, and said, "Boys, let's go up and get him." He had seen the Indian jump off the horse and leave him, and was not afraid it was a trap. Vance set out up the mountain to secure the deserted animal, and Schumaker followed him. When they reached the horse Vance wanted to go on up and see where the Indians were. They went on up, and others of the crowd below came on up also to be in the battle, if it was a fight. The Indians were gone and had left four horses and two saddles. The latter were lying on the ground.

Vance thinks most of the Indians went on at first and only left a few to fire at them. They secured the horses, and all went back to Wilson's ranch that night. Wilson's son, who had escaped and raised the alarm, caused the Sabinal and Seco men to come out and strike the trail after the first party had abandoned it. They found where the Indians had camped that night after the fight, and saw beds of cedar and bloody rags lying about where they had been trying to do something with the wounded. The rags were twisted like ropes where they had tried to stop up the bullet holes with them. Mr. August Rothe was with this party, and told the writer about the bloody rags, etc. This was in what is the present pasture of Mr. F. A. Hicks. This was the last big raid by Indians in this part of the country.

Mr. Vance was very energetic after Indians, and vindictive against them. In 1870 they killed his aged mother. At this time the mind of the old lady was somewhat impaired and she would take trips alone in the woods, which caused the members of the family to be uneasy about her. On this fatal day she failed to return at night from a ramble, and Mr. Vance commenced a search in the night and fired guns, but no response came. Next morning a diligent search was made by many settlers and continued all day, but night came again and no tidings came of the missing lady. Large fires were built in the woods in various places, so if still alive they might attract her, but none of this proved availing. This was kept up three days, until finally the body was found by George Byers, three miles from home. She had been killed by Indians and the body was in the channel of Verde Creek between two rocks, where it had been thrown, evidently by the Indians after they had murdered her.

In this same year Capt. H. J. Richarz raised a company of rangers, of which Mr. Vance was lieutenant. His commission was dated September 10, 1870. He was very active as a ranger, and recaptured many head of stolen stock and returned them to their owners. He was on a scout with twenty-three men when part of Captain Richarz's company had their desperate battle with Indians near Carrizo, and says if he had been there with his men they would have given the Indians a good whipping. When the Indians killed Riff and Captain Richarz's son (two rangers), Lieutenant Vance followed them, but could not overtake them. He had just arrived at camp from a seven days' hard scout when news of the death of the boys came, and although the men and horses were tired, they went that night to where the men were killed, and at daybreak took the trail and followed it to the

Nueces. Captain Kelso had a company at this time at Camp Wood in Nueces Canyon. The captain was gone, and the Indians passed out near his camp. The horses ridden by Vance and his men gave out and lay down with them on their backs. Failing to get fresh horses at the post, the rangers went on with their tired horses until night, and next morning the lieutenant took six men and continued the pursuit on foot, but was compelled to return unsuccessful. Part of the dead rangers' clothing was found on the trail. Riff had a violin which he was carrying to camp from D'Hanis. The Indians split this in small pieces and scattered it along the trail. Vance says the murdered boys were good shots and had Winchesters and six-shooters, but thinks both were badly wounded at the first fire of the Indians, who were in ambush. They had been home on furlough and were returning to camp on the Leona, below Uvalde, and were killed on the Blanco between the Sabinal and Frio.

Mr. Vance has a nice ranch, plenty of water and grass, and also a fine farm. His place is five miles northwest from New Fountain. Four miles west is the place where he fought the Indians and killed one. Two miles from the house is where he and Charles Decker fought them. Half a mile away in his pasture is where the Indians killed his mother.

Mrs. Vance, who was a Martin, was raised here, and remembers hearing the guns and the cursing when her future husband and Decker were fighting the Indians. Her brother was a ranger, and was in the Carrizo fight. Mr. Vance has up to this time been fifty-four years in Medina County, and has never moved out of it.

J. B. WERNETTE.

Came to Texas in 1845.

Among those who braved the dangers of the western wilds at an early day, when the Comanche, Lipan, and Kickapoo Indians roamed at will over the vast domain then unsettled which lay between the San Antonio River and the Rio Grande was Mr. J. B. Wernette, now of Castroville. He was born in Upper Alsace, in 1835, and came to Texas under Henry Castro in 1845. The ship in which he sailed was the Robinson, the largest ship then afloat. The start was made from Antwerp, and they landed at New Orleans in fifty-one days from the time of setting sail. From this place he took shipping on a steamer for Galveston, Texas. The number of immigrants who came over in the Robinson was 360. On the way from New Orleans to Galveston Joseph Wernette, 6 years old, brother to J. B., was lost. The little fellow was playing on the deck and fell overboard. The captain stopped the ship and search was made, but the body of the unfortunate young immigrant could not be found. At Galveston, the immigrants who intended to go west took passage on a sail ship bound for Port Lavaca. Before arriving at that place the ship ran on a sandbar and remained fast. The captain ordered all the passengers to leave the front end of the vessel and concentrate at the rear, so that the front would lift and get clear of the bar. This was done and they got off as the captain had anticipated, and proceeded on their way. From Port Lavaca many of the people who were bound for the colony of Castro went on carts, but the Wernette family went in wagons with their household goods, except the elder Wernette and three brothers. They came on foot and carried guns.

One night while traveling in a trail after they had arrived upon the frontier, not far from the San Antonio River, they discovered the faint glimmer of a fire far out in the mesquite brush. The elder Wernette told his companions to remain where they were and he would go to the fire and see who were there. On approaching the spot he saw twelve men all asleep around the fire, and Mr. Wernette stood close to them and observed them with great interest and curiosity, as he had never seen such people before. They were dark-skinned and had long, black hair. Mr. Wernette now retraced his steps to his companions and told them of the strange people he had seen asleep around the fire, and said that he came away without disturbing them. Just think of it! This newly arrived colonist, just from the crowded cities and country of Europe, standing in the midst of twelve sleeping Comanches on the frontier of Texas, far from the habitation of any civilized man, and curiously gazing upon their swarthy faces by the light of their flickering campfire. He did a fine thing not to disturb them. Next evening about sunset the four pedestrians discovered a smoke ahead of them on a hill, and Mr. Wernette again went forward to reconnoiter. They likely by this time had talked matters over and had to some extent realized that there was danger in such a wild country as this, and their scout advanced with more caution. Going through the brush, he arrived near enough to make discoveries without being seen himself. He saw a man beside a small fire broiling a piece of meat on a stick, and as his face was white, boldly advanced in view. The quick eye of the man discovered him, and jerking up his rifle he presented it at him, and said sharply, "Que viva." Mr. Wernette did not know what this word meant, but supposed from the man's action it was a challenge. and answered quickly, "Friend." The gun was lowered and the man said in English, "Come on." They soon came together and found they could understand each other, and had a talk. This man was one of Jack Hays' rangers, who was carrying a dispatch, and the place was on Calaveras Creek, eighteen miles from San Antonio. He saw the man many times afterwards, and they were always good friends. His name was John Lamon, and he afterwards died at Castroville.

The party arrived finally and safely at Castroville and settled there. Mr. J. B. Wernette says he never saw as many deer and wild horses as were in the country at that time. He says it is no use to say thousands—there were millions of them; more game than in any country God created. The settlers soon commenced to build rude picket houses. Some of the Indians pretended to be friendly and often came to the settlement, bringing wild turkeys and deer horns for sale. They would not bring small turkeys, but all large gobblers that would weigh fifteen pounds when dressed, and sold them for ten cents each, and deer

horns the same. They got along all right with the Indians until
the American settlers came from the east. One party of these,
five in number, with their families camped near town. They
had five wagons and some good horses and mares. The grass
was waist-high near town, and the men made a corral of their
wagons and put all of their best horses inside and hobbled the
balance out. The first or second night the Indians came and
got all of the horses which were on the outside and carried them
off. ·Next morning Mr. Wernette, then a boy 11 years of
age, went down to the camp of the Americans to play with some
of their little boys whom he had got acquainted with, and saw
the men trailing the Indians to find which way they had gone
off with the horses. Many cut hobbles were seen lying about
on the grass, and at that time Mr. Wernette did not know what
all this meant. After getting the direction of the trail located,
the Americans went back to their wagons and commenced making
preparations to follow the red thieves and try to recover their
stock. The young German boy saw them putting pones of corn
bread in wallets, which was the first of this kind of bread he had
ever seen. They had long rifles, and pouches and powder horns
across their shoulders, and belts around their waists containing
pistols, and long heavy knives in scabbards, and blankets rolled
up and tied behind their saddles. This was all new and strange
to Mr. Wernette. When all was ready the men mounted, and
telling their wives good-by and to take care of themselves, they
would be back some time, started off towards the west. Their
names were George Hammer, George Allen, two Arnold brothers,
and Dick Thompson. Their trip was not of long duration. They
returned on the following day, bringing their stolen horses, four
Indian scalps, with bows, shields, blankets, etc. The Indians
were found in camp at the Quihi Lake, ten miles west from Castroville, and were not aware of the presence of the white men
until they heard their rifles in their very midst. They were
panic-stricken at the sudden and unexpected assault, and made
but little show to fight, scattering wildly into the brush. These
settlers who made such quick work with them had fought Indians on the Colorado and Brazos, and understood the business.

The Germans had never up to this time fought the Indians.
In fact, they did not know how to trail them, and had no horses
for them to steal. From this time on, however, they had to

learn to trail and to fight them, and many became good Indian fighters, as the history of Castro's colonies will show. The Indians walked the streets of Castroville no more. Mr. Wernette says it would have been a good thing for them if all the Indians had been killed in the fight, for those who escaped told the news of the battle at Quihi Lake, and Castro's colony had to suffer for it. The Americans left and settled near where Lytle is now, and then some of them moved on further west. Every light moon now the Indians would come, and when horses were brought to the settlement the Indians would get them, and the Germans would have nothing to follow them on. One night the men of Castroville, during a light moon, said they would lay for the Indians. So twenty of them took their guns and went out of town near the foot of the hills and stood guard, walking back and forth like regular sentinels. Mr. Wernette's father went out with the old men, and he stayed with his mother. They had one little pony, and he was chained to a hackberry·tree in the yard. The house was not finished, and had slats nailed across the windows several inches apart. Along in the night Mrs. Wernette through this window saw an Indian trying to get the pony, and said to her son, "Come here; the Indian will get the pony." The boy said, "No; let the Indian get him," and covering up his head lay still. The mother now reached between the slats across the window and tried to catch the Indian by the hair, and he ran away and let the horse alone. The old men came in about daylight, and thought sure they had saved the horses this time; but every one in town was gone except Mr. Wernette's, that was chained to the tree. The Indians saw the men on guard in the moonlight and went around them.

The first of Castro's colonists killed by Indians were F. H. Gullett, Vincient Chan, Joe Chan, and a young man named Bassalle. They went up the Medina about seven miles to start a farm and ranch, and the Indians killed all of them the first night. Mr. Nic. Haby found the bodies while turkey-hunting. He saw a camp, and thinking it was Indians, he crawled up to it and found the bodies all stripped and their guns taken away. One of the men, Vincient Chan, had fought them and broken one lance. He was found twenty steps from the fire. His entrails were out, and he had walked on them while fighting the Indians. Gullett had been pinned to the ground by a lance, but whirled over when it entered his body and broke it. He was the oldest man in the party. He has a son of the same given name now living at Lockhart. The piece of the broken lance was still in Gullett's body. The men were careless. They had made their camp in a thick place in a flat at the foot of a hill, but had made their fire against a dead tree, which during the night had burned up to the top and could be seen some distance off, and revealed the location of their camp to a band of Indians that was passing. The men were evidently all asleep and an easy prey. Their guns were stacked around another tree several yards from where they lay, but the Indians did not see them and did the work with lances without firing a shot. This was just before Christmas, 1847.

Before this time Castro took part of his colonists and went on a prospecting tour to Quihi Lake to arrange about putting a colony there and laying off a town. One day at the lake a man named Peter Frigger strayed off and the Indians captured him, and that night made him lie down by a fire, as he did not look like he wished to get away, but that night Peter commenced sliding on his stomach, and when about twenty feet away jumped up and ran and made his escape. Next day a searching party found him coming back.

Mr. Wernette knew Capt. Jack Hays well, and says he was the best Indian fighter in the West, and had the best set of men and as brave a lot as he ever saw. He also knew Big Foot Wallace, and says the Indians were afraid of him and would run when they saw him in command of a fight.

One night after the Civil war, while Mr. Wernette was living in the upper part of town, he carried his horse Bill across the river and belled and hobbled him. Late in the night he heard the bell rattling loud and fast, and said to his wife, "The Indians are after old Bill." Next morning he told his stepson if he would go and get old Bill he would give him a nice present. The boy skipped out and went quickly, but soon came back with the bell and hobbles, saying that was all he could find of him. That night the Indians got all of the horses on the east side of the river, but delayed so long in rounding up and getting them together that by daylight they had only proceeded with them as far as the head of Colevro Creek. John Green, a brave man and good Indian fighter, raised six men, and taking a near cut came upon them at the Verde pass and at once charged them. Green was ahead of his men and first encountered the Indians, but soon scattered them with his revolvers, but was himself severely wounded. The other men soon came up and all the horses were retaken and brought back, and Mr. Wernette got old Bill again. Green afterwards belonged to a company of minute men, and was first lieutenant. On one occasion he wanted to take a night scout and ordered the men to saddle up, but while saddling his horse, was shot and killed by a Mexican who belonged to the company, who then ran and made his escape into Mexico. What the trouble was about the writer has not been able to learn.

About 1847 a company of rangers was stationed on the Medina above town, about where the Haby settlement now is, and on one occasion the captain gave permission for seven of the men to go up the river above where the old Morman camp now is, to hunt bear. The rangers camped near the river, and unsaddling their horses left one man in charge, and the balance scattered in the mountains to hunt. A band of Indians saw the ranger camp, and came down out of the hills and attacked it. The guard ran off and took shelter behind a tree and aimed his gun, but would not fire on account of the Indians being so numerous. They got all the horses, but did not attack the position of the lone ranger, who stayed behind his tree a distance off and watched them. The hunters in the mountains heard the noise in camp and came back, but all of their horses and the Indians were gone. They had to walk back to camp, carrying their saddles part of the way, and then hiding them. The captain was very mad when they returned and told their tale of woe, and said it was a disgrace to the ranger service, and at once took nearly all of the company and followed the Indians.

He had a friendly Indian for a guide named Bill Chism, and the captain said to him, "Now, follow the trail; we want to catch them." Bill said, "Follow me; me catch." The trail was long and tedious to follow, over hills, rocks, and gullies, clear to the head of the San Saba River. But here they came upon the Indians in a village. The attack was made on horseback with great fury, the rangers bursting in upon the astonished Indians like a clap of thunder from a clear sky. As they went in the captain told them not to shoot the squaws, and many of these passed out close to the rangers, running between the charging horses. The bucks were headed off in every direction and many of them killed. They were completely rattled, and hurt but few of the rangers and killed none. One hundred head of horses were captured, but of those lost by the rangers on the Medina none could be found. The others were brought back to camp and there sold to the highest bidder, as no owners could be found for them. The people from Castroville went up to the ranger camp and bought many cheap horses, some for $3 or $4, and so the country was stocked with horses again.

The people in Castroville were not aware that the rangers had gone on this expedition, and two young fellows from town went up there one day. Two rangers had been left in camp, and becoming lonesome built a large bonfire of old boxes and barrels, which made a great blaze. When the two young men from town came in sight of this large fire they ran back and told that the Indians had killed all of the rangers and burned up their camp. There was great excitement in Castroville, and Castro told all the people to come to his place and fort up. Wagons were driven across the streets on both sides of the house and a close barricade made, as they fully expected to have the Indians to fight. One man would not fort up with the balance, but taking his wife got into a canoe and stayed on the river all night. Another who lived above town sent his wife and children in, but would not come himself, saying he would stay up there and let the Indians get him first. He had been a drummer in the army in Europe, and taking an old brass kettle beat on it all night. The people in town from where they were forted up could plainly hear the old kettle, and with but short intervals it continued its lonesome rattle through the night. Next morning a scout was sent up the river, who went to the ranger camp and there found the two young rangers in perfect ignorance of the great tumult they had caused. A swift runner went back to town with the information of the false alarm, and the people scattered back to their various abodes.

Mr. Wernette says that in 1856 he was at the Bandera pass and saw a great many bones there, mostly those of horses. At the north end of the pass, where the grass had recently burned off and exposed them, they were very thick. These bones were those of horses killed there by the rangers in Jack Hays' great battle with the Comanches about 1843.

JUDGE JAMES M. HUNTER.

Came to Texas in 1861.

Judge James M. Hunter, who at this writing lives at Rock Springs and is the county judge of Edwards County, is an old-time Texan, and has many interesting reminiscences of early days along the border.

Judge Hunter was born in Buncombe County, North Carolina, in 1829. The wife of Gov. Bob Taylor, of Tennessee, was his niece, being a daughter of his sister, Mrs. Baird, of North Carolina. He came to Texas in 1851 and first stopped at Fredericksburg, where he had a brother living, John Hunter, who kept supplies and traded with the Indians, who at that time were friendly. In the fall of 1852 he went to Seguin, in Guadalupe County, and put up the first billiard table that was ever there. In connection with the billiard table he also had a saloon, but not liking that business, sold out in the following spring.

At this time Maj. Robert Neighbors was a member of the Legislature, and was employed by the agent of the Peters Colony Company to take charge of a surveying party to locate lands for the company. These lands embraced the country along the Clear fork and tributaries of the Main Brazos and Wichita country. Major Neighbors employed Judge Hunter to raise a company as guards to the surveying party, for at this time the Indians were hostile again. The number of men to be raised was eighteen, and several of the Seguin men volunteered to go. Among these were William M. Rust, William Tom, Frank Biler, and Bud Grinage. They now went to Austin to complete the expedition. Before leaving Seguin Major Calvert presented Mr. Hunter with a pair of pistols that once belonged to his son-in-law Jack Hays, and which he had used in the Mexican war. The surveyors employed were W. M. Rust,,from Seguin; Joe Bledsoe, John Hubbard, and a man named Smith, from Austin. Dr. Baker was physician and surgeon for the outfit, and he and others repaired direct to Fort Belknap on the Main Brazos. The surveyors drove their first stake on Pecan Bayou, and took up a connecting line

36

from there to Belknap. This line was run by Rust and others. The party experienced no trouble with the Indians except a stampede of horses one night, but Hunter and Bledsoe got them back and none were lost. It was a very enjoyable trip. Game of all kinds was in abundance and plenty of fish in the streams. When the work was completed the expedition returned to Austin and disbanded, arriving there the last of November, 1853. The Legislature was in session, and H. E. McCulloch, of Seguin, was a member, and he and Hunter put up at the same hotel.

From Austin Judge Hunter went to San Antonio and was employed by George Giddings, brother to D. C. Giddings, to carry the mail from San Antonio to Santa Fe as conductor. Giddings was a contractor for mail lines, and one trip a month was all that could be made. Big Foot Wallace and Tom Rife had carried it the year before. This was in 1854. Judge Hunter stayed two years in this service, and during that time had three fights with Indians. The first fight took place at Howard's wells, known then as the springs. This vast country then was without an inhabitant from Joe Ney's ranch on the Seco, in the present limits of Medina County, clear on through a distance of 700 miles or more. When the stage arrived at Howard's wells, thirty-six miles from the Pecos, a halt was made to water the stock, and it was then the Indians made the attack, firing on them from the hills close by. There were eight white men in all, including the passengers and regular stage guards. The Indians numbered about twenty, and had three guns and the balance bows. The white men had Yaugers and rifles, and killed several of the Indians when they charged, but they were carried back into the hills and the Indians would come and charge again, but finally got enough of it and drew off. They were Mountain Apaches. The white men suffered no loss except having one mule killed, as they were protected by the stage and some ambulances that were along.

The next fight was between "Dead Man's hole" and Van Horn's well. This was an outbound trip, and the men along, besides the guards and driver, were Captain Skillman and three or four men with ambulances. They nooned together at "Dead Man's hole," and then Skillman and his party went on, but said they would stop at Eagle Springs and wait for the stage, as that was a dangerous place. After the party had separated and Skillman was out of sight, Hunter and his men saw fifty Apaches on the prairie bearing down upon them, and there were but thirteen of the white men. One of these was Dr. Giddings, brother of the contractor. The teams were now whipped up to a lively gait, but the Indians came faster on their ponies, and ran quartering across·the prairie to intercept them, and when about 200 yards off Hunter said, "Stop, boys; we have got to fight these fellows. Side line the mules." The Indians also halted, and the chief said "Amigos." Judge Hunter said to Louis Dickens, who could speak Spanish, to tell that fellow if they were friends to stay where they were; that he was as close as they wanted him to get. The Indians now consulted awhile and all galloped off, but made a circle and came around in the road ahead of them and displayed a soldier's jacket on a spear, and also held up a letter to view, and then dropped it in the road. A week before this they had killed a military express messenger between Fort Davis and Fort Clark, and the jacket was his.

After the Indians dropped the letter they galloped off on the road taken by Skillman and his party, and Hunter was satisfied they knew he was ahead and were going to overtake him, so he pushed on with all speed with his men to the Limpia mountains to help him. The letter which the Indians dropped in the road was an official one directed to Washington by the quartermaster, which they had obtained from the dead body of the messenger. The Indians caught Skillman in camp shoeing mules, and were trying to get the drop on him by playing "amigos," but Skillman told them to get away and not come close, especially when he saw Hunter and his party coming. The Apaches were determined to have a scrape, and before Hunter could get there the fight commenced. The Indians made a complete circle around Skillman's ambulances, but he had brave men with him, and the rapid puffs of smoke that came from the vehicles proved to Hunter that they were making a game fight of it, and he and his men renewed their exertions to reach them, whipping their teams into a gallop and shouting words of encouragement. It was a most dangerous looking circle to attempt to pass through, but they went in firing right and left at the yelling Apaches, who also fired on them, but without effect, overshooting them with the scopets which most of them carried. The combined forces now beat the Indians off, and about sundown they left, having five killed besides quite a number wounded. The stage and ambu-

lances caught most of the bullets and arrows, and some of the
horses and mules were hit. The two parties camped on the battleground that night and continued their journey next morning
without any further trouble from the Indians. The next fight
took place at the head of Devil's River. The Indians attacked the
camp at night and tried to stampede the mules, but were beaten
off, and no damage was done to either side. On these trips
Judge Hunter avoided as many fights as possible, seldom camping
at the regular watering places. Many people were killed along
this route, travelers and immigrants, as the numerous graves
indicated. There were five at Eagle Springs. The only stage
man killed on these trips, said Judge Hunter, was one of the
stage guards of Big Foot Wallace. In 1856 the judge quit this
mail service and went with Pellum and Garrison to New Mexico
to run parallel and meridian lines to base townships and sub-
divisions, and was one year in this business.

In 1858 he went with Col. Earl Van Dorn on his Wichita expedition as contractor and sutler, but was not in the famous Indian
battle that was fought on that occasion, but was coming back
on Van Dorn's trail. The Indians were badly defeated and suffered great loss, but Colonel Van Dorn himself was badly
wounded and had to be brought back on a litter. Ex-Gov. Sul
Ross, then a young man, was in the battle, and was also wounded.
Many more of the whites were wounded and some killed. Judge
Hunter was at a place called Radzminski when Colonel Van Dorn
was brought in, and says it was a wonder he did not die, as the
case of medicine and surgical instruments was lost during the
fight. The mule which carried them and the steward in charge
both disappeared when the battle commenced, and were not heard
of again. They had to send to Fort Arbuckle, in the Indian Territory, for medicine and instruments, the distance being forty
miles. On this expedition they saw a lot of abandoned wagons
and carts which had been left by Col. John S. Ford in one of
his Indian campaigns.

During the Civil war Judge Hunter served as first lieutenant
in the company of Capt. Henry Davis on the frontier and afterwards commanded the company, receiving the commission of captain from Gov. Francis Lubbock. While in command of the
company he was in two fights with the Indians, the first at the
head of the Pedernales and James rivers. The forces were ex-

actly even—eleven rangers and eleven Indians. The trail was started on the Llano River and followed to where the fight took place. Six of the Indians were killed and the balance scattered. A ranger named John Benson was wounded with an arrow in the hip. The spike curled up in the bone like a fishhook, and the doctor had to cut it out. Besides the ranger, one horse was wounded. This was in February, 1863. The Indians were trying to get into a horse country. They only had two poor ponies, and were resting when the rangers came upon them. They stood their ground until the chief was killed, then became confused and ran, but would rally and fight when overtaken, and would run again when the rangers stopped to load their guns. The Indians were all young-looking fellows, and would have all been killed if the powder of the rangers had been good, but it was wretchedly bad. It was what they called in those days home-made powder, or Confederate powder, made in the south. The majority of the rangers were from the Guadalupe Valley, and were a fine set of men. The next fight was on House Mountain, but with no results, the Indians running and getting away. Before the Civil war was over this frontier regiment was sent to the Confederate army and left the frontier exposed. Judge Hunter then received a commission as major from Governor Murrah to serve in the frontier district from Burnet County to the mouth of the Rio Grande. He organized his district effectually for frontier protection, and remained in this until the close of the war.

In 1870 he again served as a ranger captain; had no fights with the Indians but many chases. This wound up his service in the military line. In 1876 he was a member of the Legislature, the district he was sent from being composed of ten counties, to wit, Mason, Gillespie, Kendall, Kerr, Medina, Uvalde, Menard, Edwards, Bandera, and Kimble. Edwards and Kimble at this time were unorganized. He was at one time county judge of Mason County, and also served that county as surveyor. When his present term is out (1898) he will have served Edwards County ten years as county judge.

During Judge Hunter's eventful career on the Texas frontier he has been associated with the following distinguished men: Gens. John B. Hood, Robert E. Lee, Fitzhugh Lee, E. Kirby Smith, Oakes, and Thomas. Robert E. Lee was a captain, Fitzhugh Lee was a second lieutenant, Oakes was a lieutenant, and all held some rank at the frontier posts. Fitzhugh Lee, he says, had a most exciting adventure in a fight with Indians on the Clear fork of the Brazos, in which he killed an Indian chief in a desperate and long-contested hand-to-hand fight.

When the writer saw Judge Hunter in 1898 he seemed to be in perfect health, and was a fine specimen of physical manhood. May he now rest in peace from his labors.

ED. ENGLISH.

Native Texan. Born in 1852.

Mr. Edward English, son of Capt. Levi English, was born in De Witt County, Texas, on the 28th day of April, 1852. His mother was Matilda Burleson, cousin to Gen. Edward Burleson, and for whom the subject of our sketch was named. She was also a cousin to Joe Hornsby, of the early settlers of that name, who lived on the Colorado and figured conspicuously in the frontier history of Texas. Joe Hornsby, it will be remembered, was with Josiah Wilbarger when he was scalped by the Indians, and was the last man to leave him. Mrs. English was a sister to "Buffalo" John Burleson.

Ed. English moved to the Leona River, in Frio County, with his parents when a small boy.

In 1860 the Indians came into that settlement on a raid and killed Leonard Eastwood and a man named Sanders, and wounded a third, John Spears. On that morning the three men ate breakfast at Eastwood's ranch and then separated. Sanders went up the river, and met the Indians, and was killed by them. The other two men went down the river on some business, and on their return met the same party of Indians, who attacked them and killed Eastwood. They gave Spears a hard chase and succeeded in wounding him in the back with an arrow, but he made his escape and ran to the ranch of Capt. Levi English. Young Ed. was there, and saw the arrow sticking in his back as he came up. The people all forted up at the house of Captain English for two weeks and then abandoned the country, most of them going to Atascosa County. The English family only remained away about six months, and then went back to the Leona. Many others came, and in 1865 quite a number of settlers were there. In the above named year the Indians made a raid and were pursued by Captain English at the head of a band of settlers and a desperate battle was fought with them, in which Bud English, oldest brother of Ed, was killed and his father wounded. A full account is given of this fight elsewhere. In this same year, in the fall, Captain English moved to Carrizo Springs.

In July of 1866 Ed., who was attending to the horse stock, took his little brother Joel out with him to hunt for horses on the range. They rounded up all of the horses but two, which were not found, and they continued the search for them until near sunset, and then turned up a creek to go home, and Ed. shot a deer. From here they crossed the creek and went out through a flat on the opposite side, traveling towards the west. Joel Stopped at the creek to water his horse, and Ed. went on about 100 yards with his hat pulled down in front, as the setting sun was shining in his face. At this time he heard the sound of horses' feet in front of him, and looking up saw seven Indians about 150 yards distant, likely attracted in that direction by the report of his gun. They commenced to yell and charged him, coming in the shape of the letter V. Ed. wheeled his horse to go back, and as he did so an Indian fired at him with a six-shooter and wounded the horse in the hip. The Indian continued to fire, and the next shot went through the hindtree of the saddle and wounded Ed. in the hip. The whole band now closed around him, and he fired at the one nearest him on the right with a Ballard rifle and killed his horse, the ball breaking his neck, but the shell hung in the rifle, and it was thus rendered useless. The Indian after his horse fell, who was the same one who had fired the other two shots from the revolver, fired again. This shot cut the wristband from one of Ed.'s shirt sleeves, wounded him in the wrist, and knocked the gun out of his hand, which fell to the ground. All of the Indians now closed around, thinking the young settler had no more arms. He had a six-shooter, however, and began to draw that, when an Indian made a thrust at him with a lance. The pistol scabbard was one of the old-fashioned kind, with a flap that came down over the pistol stock. The lance of the Indian struck this pistol flap and went through it, but Ed. succeeded in getting the pistol out and shot the Indian dead from his horse. The ball went through his head, and he fell in a heap on the ground. The other Indians all ran to this one, and Ed. got clear and started for the ranch. Joel had made an attempt to get to his brother, but was cut off by an Indian, and was still circling around trying to get to Ed. The Indians now left the dead one and came in pursuit again, cutting off Joel, who had made another run to get to his brother. He had no arms of any kind. Ed., however, went to his rescue, and the Indians gave

ED. ENGLISH.

back when they saw the revolver in his hand. While it takes a long time to write these things, it all occurred in a few minutes. When Ed. opened the way for his brother to come to him he let his horse out towards the ranch again, but the Indians again cut Joel off. They made no attempt to kill him, but seemed to want to capture him. Edward again went to his rescue and drove the Indians back with his revolver. He now shouted to Joel to run his horse close in beside him and make him do his best. He did so, and the two brothers ran side by side with the Indians in pursuit. In crossing a muddy flat four of the Indians caught up with them. Ed. had to watch his horse to keep him from falling, and while doing this running through the boggy flat an Indian shot him in the back with an arrow, which struck under the shoulder blade. He turned on the Indians now and fired at them with his pistol, but failed to hit one as he knew of. Wheeling, he again ran towards home, the Indians in pursuit for a mile or more, and when in 300 yards of the house, the Indians turned back, Ed. firing twice more during this last run. Captain English pulled the arrow out of his son and did all that he could for him, but he came near bleeding to death, and had to stay in bed thirty days. This was one of the remarkable escapes so often recorded in frontier history. If young English had not remained cool and kept his head, as the saying is, during all this fearful ordeal through which he was passing, it would have ended like hundreds of others along the border, and he would have lost his scalp and his little brother been carried into captivity, if not slain. No pursuit of the Indians was made, as no other settlers lived there.

The next raid the Indians made was in 1870, about 200 of them. They first struck the ranch of Charley Vivian, fifteen miles above, and killed a Mexican there and captured a Mexican boy. They came down the main road, then to the ranch of Dave Adams. Before they arrived there, however, they came in contact with five cowboys, namely, William Bell, Joe Tumlinson, Si Hay, John Smith, and a Mexican. The boys were not able to make headway against such a band of Indians and retreated before them, and in the pursuit the Mexican was killed. Adams had his horses in the pen and was out there with them when the Indians made their appearance. They came around the pen and Adams left it and tried to gain the brush, but was cut off by the Indians, and took a position behind a mesquite tree to make a fight. His only weapon was a Ballard rifle, and the first shot he fired the shell hung, which left him at the mercy of the savages, and they soon killed him. This was evident from the fact that his gun was found a few days after on the battleground where the rangers fought them, with a shell fast in the barrel.

The Indians still kept their course to within one-half mile of Carrizo Springs. Nine men went to meet them when informed of their approach and fought them, some of whom were as follows: William Pickens, Rube Bell, Caldwell Roberts, Si Hay, and Joe Tumlinson. The names of the others can not be recalled. The Indians drove these back. The men from the upper ranch followed them, and going around beat them to the ranch. At the time the Indians were killing Adams a wagonload of people drove upon the scene, going to Carrizo. They were Jack McCurly (cousin to Ed. English), Jake Burleson, Pat McCurly, Pleas. English (brother to Ed.), Mrs. Matilda English (mother of Ed.). They turned the wagon and ran away from the Indians, and only two followed them, the balance being at this time engaged with the cowboys and Dave Adams. Jack McCurly was on horseback, and rode in the rear of the wagon and fought the Indians, telling those in the wagon to throw everything out that was heavy, so that the team could make better time. The two Indians were kept back by Jack, and they had no chance to shoot at the occupants. The people at the main ranch at the springs stayed together that night and stood guard. Next morning twenty-five men got together, led by "Buffalo" John Burleson, and pursued the Indians below Fort Ewell, eighty miles below the springs.

Ed. English and his father and two or three Mexicans went out and recovered the bodies of Adams and the Mexican that was killed and brought them in. They turned the body of the dead Mexican over to the Mexicans at the main ranch, and Ed. and his father took the remains of Adams to his own house and buried him in the yard. Captain English made the coffin, and while he was doing so Ed. dug the grave, and these two buried him. He was shot in many places with arrows and bullets. One of his fingers was shot off.

On the third day a squad of rangers came from Uvalde, under the command of Dr. Woodbridge, on the trail of the Indians who had committed depredations on Turkey Creek, in Uvalde County, on their way down. Among these rangers were Tom Blakeney, Doc Quebum, Billy Cox, John Whitney, and others, about thirteen in all. They were armed with Winchesters, and Dr. Woodbridge said, "Now, we want to find an Indian." Captain English said, "If you will stay with me three days I will show them to you." They then went out to the main pass and waited for the Indians, to catch them on their return from below. Each day a man was sent east and one west to see if the trail had passed up. About the third day Captain English, Doc. Quebum, and a boy went west and two east. These two saw the Indians coming, and returned and reported the same to the doctor, and he took what men there were in camp and went to meet them. When Captain English and his men came back to camp it was abandoned, and they followed on the trail of the rangers and came to where there had been a battle, several dead horses being there, and one dead ranger. They now took the trail of the Indians, thinking the rangers were still after them. In two miles they were overtaken, and twenty-five Indians came back to fight them, the chief and his warriors circling the white men and shooting at them, but Captain English told his boys not to shoot until they thought they could hit something. The Indians had shields and rode low on their horses, moving rapidly, and were hard to hit. Quebum finally shot at the chief and cut the string which fastened the shield to his arm, and it fell to the ground, and after they passed he ran and got it and waved it at the other Indians, and yelled as much like the chief as he could. The shield had a woman's scalp attached to it, the hair of which was very black.

The Indians now quit the fight and moved on again, followed by Captain English and his men, still thinking the rangers were ahead. The Indians camped at dark, and English rode so close to their camp that he was discovered and chased by fifteen of them, but made his escape and then came on back. It was when he first came onto the ground where the rangers fought them that he found the gun of Dave Adams with the shell hung in it.

Two rangers came to the springs and reported the main battle, and said all of the rangers were killed. They left, it seems, before it was over. Another account of the fight will be seen elsewhere.

Ed. English saw Dr. Woodbridge when he came to the springs after the fight. His hat was gone and he was riding behind Tom Blakeney, and his neck was badly swollen. During the fight an Indian knocked him off his horse with a bow and came near breaking his neck. Captain English furnished two horses to assist the rangers in getting back to their camp.

About 1872 the Indians came again, thirty-five in number, to the springs. Ed. English at this time had 1000 head of sheep and a herd of cattle. He was delivering the cattle to a shipper, and had sent the shepherd out with the sheep. Ed. went out while engaged in delivering the cattle without his gun, and heard shouting and yelling, and also fifteen shots fired. He ran back after his gun, and three men ran in and reported that his shepherd was killed. They were John Bell, Van Neill, and a Mexican. Ed. went to see about his shepherd and sheep, and found the Mexican herder killed and scalped. He brought him in and then went after the Indians, but could not overtake them. This time the pursuit was by United States troops under the command of Major Perry.

In 1874 the Indians came again and killed and captured all of Captain English's horses, about thirty head, and then came on down to within a mile of the springs. Ed. had a stock camp a mile from the route they were coming, and had forty head of horses there. A Mexican ran to the main ranch house and reported that he saw the Indians going in the direction of Ed's camp, and he at once mounted his horse and started over there, and heard shooting before arriving. On coming upon the scene he found his Mexican horse herder shot through with a bullet. Ed. asked what was the matter. "Oh, bad luck," said he; "lost all the horses. Look out, the Indians will kill you." On being asked where the Indians were, he said, "Right behind the brush there, cutting hobbles off the horses." English went around where he could see them, and counted twenty, but not being able to do anything, he withdrew, and next day with a party followed them to the Rio Grande, but they crossed over, and the men had to return without having an opportunity to fight them. The wounded Mexican died and was buried the following day.

In 1876, while Ed. was out on a cow-hunt with two white boys and two Mexicans, driving a bunch of cattle, he saw about forty Indians. One of the white boys and one of the Mexicans ran, but

Ed. told one of the others to hold his horse and he would shoot at them one time, anyhow. Before the boy could get around to hold the horse the Indians charged them, coming in a V shape. English fired one shot, and he and the boys retreated to a large thicket and entered. The Indians followed and fired 100 shots or more, but stopped at the thicket, and Ed. and his party went on through the brush and made their escape back home. This was his last scrape with Indians. He now lives in Kinney County.

HENRY HARTMAN.

Came to Texas in 1860.

In the summer of 1897, while the writer was traveling in the interest of the Galveston News in Medina County, he attended a picnic given by the .thrifty German settlers around Quihi and New Fountain. Arriving on the ground in company with Judge M. Charobiny, quite a crowd had already collected in a beautiful pecan grove near the Verde Creek. The affair being under the auspices of the German Methodist church, nothing but temperance drinks were sold, such as soda water, etc. An abundance of everything good to eat that the country afforded was on hand and free to all. Speeches were made after dinner, and many old timers were present, and these more especially were the kind the writer was looking for. A small, quiet-looking man, who limped as he moved along, was pointed out as one who could give an interesting sketch of his life on the border. This man was Henry Hartman, and the writer was assured, if he could be prevailed on to tell the cause of his crippled condition, that every word would be facts and of more than passing interest.

Upon this the writer sought an interview, but at first was refused, saying it would not be of interest to other people, and to hunt up older settlers, who had a large experience to tell. At the request of his friends he finally consented to tell what he knew.

In giving this true account of one of the most desperate encounters with Indians, one such as but few of our most noted and famous Indian fighters have passed through, it will be clearly demonstrated what a brave and cool man can do under the most trying circumstances, and live to tell the tale.

Mr. Hartman came from the principality of Schaumburg Lipe to New Fountain in 1860. Coming at this rather late date was one reason he thought his experience would not be of as much interest as the older settlers who came with Castro's colony and helped to subdue the wilderness.

The trip across the ocean was made in the sailing vessel Wesser. Many storms were encountered, and at times it seemed that all was lost. The ship landed at Galveston, and Mr. Hartman came on out to the Castro settlements and first stopped at New Fountain. He stayed here several years and then drove stock to Kansas, but still New Fountain was his home for six years, when he moved to the upper Guadalupe, twenty miles above Kerrville, and there for some time engaged in hunting with two companions. This was in a dangerous locality, and they saw Indians several times. One man named Chris. Wachter lived above Kerrville, and on one occasion went to town, leaving his wife, brother-in-law, mother-in-law, and a negro man at the ranch. The white man and the negro next morning after Wachter left went half a mile from the house to make shingles, leaving the women alone. At this time a band of Indians were on a mountain, evidently watching the house, and when they saw the negro and white man leave made a descent on the ranch. One of them was standing in the door before their presence was discovered. Mrs. Wachter was young and stout, and as soon as she saw the savage she ran at him and knocked him backward out of the door and ran away, but did not escape the flight of arrows which followed, two wounding her in the back. She still continued her flight, however, and instead of going to the men who who were making shingles near by, ran to a mill one and a half miles away, where Hartman and others were at work, and was well nigh exhausted on arriving there. Mrs. Huepner was the only woman about the mill, and she pulled the arrows out of the stricken woman. Mr. Hartman and others repaired hastily to the scene of the raid, and on arriving at the house found it burned down and the body of the old lady in it. They now searched for the trail of the Indians, and went to the shingle camp and informed the men there what had happened. They had not even discovered the smoke of the burning house. The mountains were high all round, and the Indians could see from their summit all that was going on in the valley below without being seen themselves, and could easily escape when followed, so this band was not found by the trailers. The bones of the unfortunate woman were taken from the ashes and buried. She was evidently killed by the Indians before they fired the house. Mrs. Wachter recovered from the arrow wounds, and was still living in 1897.

Mr. Hartman came back to New Fountain and engaged in handling stock, and it was while in pursuit of this calling that he experienced one of the most thrilling chapters in his life's history. On the 11th day of June, 1873, he, in company with Louis Harting, Fred Folk, Charles Martin, and a negro named Johnson, went up on Verde Creek, fifteen miles from New Fountain, to gather a bunch of beeves. All were well armed except the negro, having three Winchesters in the crowd. The men, as they hunted the cattle, became careless. They had seen no signs of Indians, but had discovered men a long distance off, but paid no attention to them. They had rounded up some cattle, and Hartman saw some more at a distance, and leaving Charles Martin, a young fellow, with the loose horses which were brought along for a change, the balance went on with the cattle, so if those in the distance were theirs they could round them into the herd. While going to these cattle five or six men were seen in the distance, and Hartman said they were Quihi men looking for their oxen, and as before paid no more attention to them, and in fact was not expecting any Indians. After getting to the cattle another bunch was seen half a mile away on a hill, and Hartman, taking the negro with him, went off at a gallop to round up this bunch, leaving the other men holding the cattle already gathered. After going about 600 yards, and while passing a thicket, still in a gallop, they were fired on from ambush with firearms, ten shots or more being aimed at them. Hartman's horse was hit by a bullet just behind the saddle, breaking his back. The stricken animal gave three jumps and fell, turning on his side, and catching Hartman's left leg under him. The negro's horse was also hit, but he ran about 300 yards and then fell. The negro left him and went to the brush, but the horse regained his feet and ran again, but again fell, and died half a mile away. The Indians, seeing the white man's horse dead and lying on him, thought sure they had him, and came yelling around him, thirteen in number, and all shooting at close range with guns and six-shooters, but in their wild excitement failed to give him a wound, but knocked the dirt all over him. Some were firing pistols at not more than ten paces. Some men under these circumstances would have been powerless through fear to have done anything, and would have fallen an easy prey, but not so Henry Hartman. His Winchester was in the scabbard on the horn of the saddle, and this by a powerful effort he reached and drew out. The Indians, seeing

37

their paleface foe was not dead, despite the fusilade and great
dust they had raised, but on the contrary seemed very much alive
and self-possessed, and with a dreaded Winchester now in his
hands, beat a hasty retreat back to the thicket to reload. There
were twelve on foot and one mounted.

   All of this happened very quickly. Although Hartman had
his gun in his hand and the Indians had retreated, he was still
pinioned to the ground by his dead horse. He knew that as soon
as the Indians reloaded their guns and pistols they would fire
at him from cover and he would have no chance at them, so he
began to make desperate efforts to release his leg, and succeeded
after many trials in quick succession. After getting free from
his horse he ran to a sumach thicket, and the Indians commenced
shooting at him again. Crouching low on the ground, watching
with gun ready to shoot, he waited for further developments on
the part of the Indians, and while so doing saw the negro Johnson crawling in a thicket, and about the same time heard a battle
open back at the cattle. Another band had attacked them besides those who were after Hartman.

   The place in which the hard-pressed man had taken refuge did
not afford any security except to partly hide his body from view.
None of the bushes would turn a bullet, and they were cutting
the twigs all around him, and finally one knocked his hat from
his head. He saw the Indian that did this. He had crawled up
behind some bushes and could see Hartman, and fired at him with
a revolver. As he exposed himself to take another shot Hartman
fired at his face, but went a little too high, wounding him in the
top of the head, and knocking a white man's hat off he had on.
The Indian quickly left this position and crawled away. During all of this time Hartman was watching in front the direction
from which the shots were coming, but the Indians resorted to
a trick to get the white man. They sent one of their number to
crawl around through the bushes and take him in the rear, and
shoot him unawares while he was looking for danger in front.
This would likely have been successful, but the wily savage was
like some hunters who, having slipped upon a deer, begin to
breathe hard just as they are about to shoot. Hartman heard
him breathing close behind him as he was raising up over the
bushes and about to fire. Quickly turning he fired, and the Indian did the same, but his ball hit the ground almost under the

white man, while the Comanche got a Winchester ball through the heart and fell forward on his face, his pistol falling almost on Hartman. The Indians still continued to fire, the balls cutting through the sumach bushes here and there.

Hartman was now determined to leave his place and go to a dense thicket which he could see, but which was beyond the Indians, and he would have to run the gauntlet to get there. He dared not fire much, as he only had six cartridges in the magazine of his Winchester at first, and two of these had been fired. He had a full box in his saddle pockets, but they were under his dead horse. With him, to think was to act, and soon as he made up his mind to leave the place he ran out and boldly charged the Indians with gun presented, and they scattered back towards their thicket and let him pass, but repeatedly fired at him. It was in this run that he got the wound that made him a cripple for life. The Indians behind fired after he passed them, and a ball struck him in the bottom of the foot, coming out in front and tearing the instep all to pieces. The force of the ball knocked him down, and the Indians, thinking they had him this time, came yelling and shooting around him once more. In this, however, they were again mistaken. Their invincible foe regained his feet and faced them with leveled Winchester, and they again scattered back to the thicket. The one on horseback came very close and Hartman intended to kill him, but as the Indian quickly threw himself over on the horse he would not risk a shot, but turned and managed to get into the thicket. Here he lay, with his gun ever ready to shoot, until the sun went down, but the Indians did not assault his position. This was a liveoak thicket with many big saplings in it, and afforded good protection. His foot bled a great deal, and soon after getting to cover he had to cut off his boot on account of its rapid swelling. He now also discovered that he had another wound in the leg, but not so severe. By the time night came he was very thirsty, but could not walk a step. As the hours passed on his thirst became so intense he determined to make an effort to reach water. Taking off his leggings, he cut one of the legs into strips and wrapped them tightly around the wounded foot, drawing the broken bones together as best he could, hoping by thus bracing them he would be able to walk. This, however, failed; as soon as he attempted to bear any weight to step the foot would give way and he would fall. The only chance was to crawl. The Hondo River he knew could not be far, and he determined to make an attempt to get there. His battleground was between the Verde Creek and Hondo. All night long he crept and crawled, carrying his gun along with him. Of course he had to make many halts to rest, as he became exhausted from thirst and painful locomotion. When daylight came and he could get his bearings, he found that he had only succeeded in getting about 400 yards from the starting point, and that in the opposite direction from the water. A shower of rain came during the night, which to some extent relieved his thirst and the high fever which had set in. He would lick the water from the bushes as he crawled. Nothing more was seen or heard of the Indians.

After daylight he crawled out of the brush onto a hill where he could have a view of the country, but kept in some bushes on the top of it, so that he could see without being seen.

The Indians failed to find the negro, but stripped both dead horses. They also defeated the men who were with the cattle, and got all the loose horses. The companions of Hartman had no chance to aid him, although they saw his horse fall with him. A band of nine Indians attacked them about the same time, and they had to give way. This made twenty-two Indians in all of this raiding party.

The negro made his way to the settlement that night and reported that Hartman was killed, and that the Indians had carried him off on a horse. From his place of concealment he saw the Indians place the one Hartman killed on the horse that was in the party and go off, and he thought it was Hartman, not having seen him when he ran from that place.

The other men also reported him killed, and his friends sent out an ambulance to bring in the body and picked out a place to bury him. Guided by the negro, they found the dead horses and the bloody ground where he killed the Indian, but thought it was Hartman's blood, and that, as Johnson said, the Indians had carried him off. They now drove around looking for the body. About two hours after Hartman got on the hill he heard the rattle of the vehicle, and crawling out of the bushes he stood on one foot, leaning on his gun so that they could see him. They were very much surprised to find him alive, and soon had him as comfortably situated in the hack as circumstances would permit, and started back to the settlement. They had found the hat which Hartman had shot from the Indian's head, and it had a bullet hole through it. A party had come up in the night to hunt for the supposed dead body of Hartman, and passed so near him that he saw and heard them, but supposed it was the Indians, and remained quiet. This party was still out, but soon came upon the scene, and all went back together. There was great rejoicing among the people when the hack arrived. The wound in the leg was not severe and soon healed, but the foot was in a bad condition for many months, and will always make him a cripple.

Mr. Hartman was a ranger under Captain Richarz, and missed being in the terrible battle near Carrizo by being on a scout up the Nueces when it was fought.

J. M. ADAMS.

Came to Texas in 1849.

Among those who came to Texas at an early day when the country was wild and full of hostile Indians, none made a better record as brave men and Indian fighters than the Adams brothers, Cood, William, Henry, Dave, and James M., the subject of this sketch. Henry was killed by Indians at the Chalk bluff in Nueces Canyon in February, 1861. Henry Robinson, another noted Indian fighter, was with him at the time and was also killed. Dave was killed in 1870 near Carrizo Creek, also by Indians.

James M. Adams came to San Antonio in 1849. On the way out when he and his party came to the Guadalupe River, opposite New Braunfels, in Comal County, it was found to be badly swollen by recent rains, and a halt was made for it to run down sufficient to be forded without danger. During the time of waiting quite a crowd of travelers collected on the east bank of the river, among whom was Asa J. L. Sowell (father of the writer) and Calvin S. Turner (uncle of the writer), two of Capt. Henry E. McCulloch's rangers who came up from Seguin. The rangers sat on their horses a short time after riding up and surveyed the situation, and then expressed their intention of trying to cross. Some one expressed an opinion that it was not safe, and advised a longer tarry. Turner says, "I do not suppose it would drown a fellow," and they went into it. When the main current was reached the horse ridden by Sowell went down, and he was compelled to abandon him and swim back to the place of starting. The people on shore became greatly excited when they beheld the desperate efforts the ranger was making to gain the shore. He finally succeeded, and to the great surprise of the onlookers brought his gun out with him, which was one cause of his laborious efforts. Turner came back when he discovered his companion could not make it, and tried to swim his horse to his assistance, but seeing it was not needed he turned his attention to the horse, which had landed some distance below, and was trying to get up a bank. The horse was rescued, and nothing was lost ex-

cept a pair of saddlebags. After waiting a short time the two
rangers made another attempt to cross, and were this time successful. The others went over later.

In 1852 Mr. Adams went on a prospecting tour in company
with two men named Daley and J. Snyder. A negro named Tom,
who belonged to Snyder, was also of the party. The object of
this expedition was to look at the country and prospect for gold
and silver in the valley of the Rio Grande near Donna Anna, on
West River, in New Mexico. It is surprising any of them lived
to get back and tell the tale. They went into the very heart of
the stronghold of the Mountain Apaches, who at that time were
very hostile and vindictive towards white men. One day at noon
they camped in the prairie near the head of a long draw that
wended its way to the Rio Grande. The head of this draw was
depressed several feet, and made what we might call a sinkhole.
Having had no trouble as yet with Indians, they were not much
concerned about them. All of a sudden, however, soon after
stopping they discovered a band of 150 Apaches riding over a
swell in the prairie towards them. They soon commenced yelling
and charging. The four men saw no hope, but being well armed,
determined to give them the best battle they could. They retreated towards the draw, firing as they went, and had the satisfaction of seeing several of the redskins fall from their horses.
During this retreat the Indians were firing at them and Snyder
was badly wounded, having his thigh broken by a ball. When he
fell, the negro Tom lifted him up and carried him on his shoulders into the sinkhole. Here the men made preparations to stand
a siege, provided the Apaches did not storm their position at once
and overpower them. Snyder could still use his gun, and so accurate was the aim of the white men that an Indian would fall
at almost every fire. They now began to widen the distance between them and the draw. They shot both arrows and bullets,
but could do no execution, as the white men were entirely hid except when they would go to shoot, and then only the top of the
head and eyes could be seen. The Indians yelled a great deal
and made some weak charges, always wheeling their horses before
getting very near the fatal sinkhole, and make a circle back.

The Indians finally settled down to a regular siege and concluded to starve them out, keeping in plain view during the day
and howling and yelling around them at night. Four days

passed, and the situation was unchanged.   The men were starving
for food and perishing with thirst.   Snyder was nearly dead for
the want of medical aid, and one and all now gave up all hope of
ever getting out alive.   The bloodthirsty Apaches still yelled
and whooped and watched for the palefaces to come out.

Night had come again, and with it some hope.   It had become
cloudy, a slow, drizzling rain set in, and it was intensely dark.
They must not miss this chance to escape.   The Indians were
still on the alert, but a man could not be seen twelve inches from
his eyes.   It was thought escape could be made down the draw
by moving away in perfect silence and keeping in touch with
each other.   But what about the wounded man?   He could not
walk one step.   Nigger Tom solved the problem.   He was a
powerful man physically, 6 feet 6 inches in height, 35 years of
age, weighed 240 pounds, and proposed to carry his master.   The
horses and pack animals had all fallen into the hands of the Indians at the commencement of the fight.   Everything now being
agreed upon and arranged, Tom tenderly shouldered his master,
who dared not groan, no matter how excruciating the pain.
Adams and Daly took the four rifles and went in front, ready to
shoot at a moment's warning, and all moved silently off into the
black night.

Our readers must bear in mind that this draw was not a narrow gully, and that the Indians could place themselves in it and
bar their progress.   On the contrary it was wide and covered
with grass, and was simply the depression between the swells of
the prairie, and in daylight would afford no protection except
the place the men had just vacated, where the sinkholes were.   It
was a desperate undertaking, but this was the last chance for
their lives, and they moved on, hardly daring to breathe.   No
doubt the Indians had warriors posted at various places, but they
were quiet.   Not a sound was heard, nothing could be seen, and
the Indians knew that a sound from them might bring the deadly
rifle ball from out the darkness.   An hour passed away, and they
began to breathe more freely.   No sound had been heard, and
it was several miles back to the dreadful battleground.   The
white men now moved faster, keeping as best they could in the
darkness towards the Rio Grande.   The misty rain had to some
extent alleviated their burning thirst and made them stronger.
When daylight came, which they dreaded to see, it was thirty

miles back to where they had left the Indians. The devoted Tom bore up bravely through this terrible ordeal, but was now well night exhausted, although frequent short halts had been made through the night. One thing which buoyed them up when morning came was the fact that the Rio Grande was near. They managed to cross this, and in eight days more they arrived at the copper mines in Old Mexico. This last traveling was not forced; they took their time and shot game by the way. From here they finally made their way back to their various homes, when Snyder recovered. Tom remained true to his master even in Mexico, and saw him safely back home. He was given his freedom, and never wanted for anything as long as a member of the Snyder family was around.

In 1854 Capt. Henry Skillman, who had a contract to run a stage from San Antonio to Santa Fe, employed Mr. Adams, among others, as stage guard. This was dangerous employment, as the line ran through the Comanche country in Texas and the Apache in New Mexico. The first serious trouble they had with Indians was at Howard's Wells on a return trip. There was a rich Philadelphian's outfit along, making seven vehicles, including the stage, and thirteen men, including the driver, guards, and passengers. The man from Philadelphia was named Henderson, and he had $300,000 in the hacks. Louis Oge was the conductor and driver this trip on the stage. While halted at the wells, seventy-five hostile Indians put in an appearance, and Oge made quick preparations for defense by running the hacks and stage in a circle and making breastworks of them and the mules and horses. The Indians charged at long range, but before they came close enough to do any damage Oge was ready for them, and the battle commenced. The Indians were so badly hit by the first fire from the inclosure that they fought shy and circled the wagons many times, yelling and shooting under their horses as they ran. This was kept up four hours, and then they withdrew with considerable loss. On account of their protection among the vehicles the white men suffered no loss, but there was sad havoc among the mules and horses, five of which were killed and many wounded. During the four years this line was run men were killed nearly every trip. When Skillman gave up his contract Mr. Adams went with a contractor named Butterfield and often met the Apaches again, but had no more serious conflicts with them.

At this time Mr. Adams said Big Foot Wallace ran a line from San Antonio to El Paso, and had a fight on Devil's River in which he had three men wounded. The Indians trapped them in the pass and shot from the bluffs.

In 1855 Mr. Adams was in an Indian fight at the head of the Nueces river. It was fought by citizens and soldiers, twenty-five men in all. It was a hotly contested field for a time, and seven of the white men were wounded. The Indians finally retreated, leaving forty of their number dead on the ground. The lieutenant who was in command was a West Pointer, but his name can not now be recalled.

In 1859 his brother, William C. Adams, led a company of men on an expedition into the mountains of the Nueces, and had a battle on the West prong. The Indians made a poor fight and lost nine of their number without inflicting any loss on the settlers, who numbered twelve, and the Indians many more.

Mr. Adams came from Llano to Medina City, in Bandera County, where the writer interviewed him in 1897. He said he was with Big Foot Wallace many times, and that he was a very intelligent and educated man. His brother, Sam Wallace, he says, was killed with Fannin at Goliad.

The last Indian fight Mr. Adams was in he went out with Lieutenant Johnson and some soldiers. They had stolen some horses from Adams and others. They found the Indians at the head of Paint Creek, not far from South Llano. There were but two Indians—a buck and a squaw—but the former made it very interesting for the soldiers. As soon as he saw the white men, and knew there was no chance to escape, he killed his squaw and then charged the crowd, and succeeded in wounding five of them before they could kill him. He knocked two soldiers off their horses with his bow.

Mr. Adams died near Medina City in the fall of 1899.

FRANK BUCKALEW CAPTURED BY INDIANS.

In about the year 1867 Frank Buckalew, son of Robert Buckalew and nephew of Berry Buckalew, Sr., who brought him to this
country, was at work for Judge Davenport in Sabinal Canyon,
above the forks of the river. His parents had died, and he and
two sisters were all living at the same place on the Davenport
ranch. At the time of which we write an ox had lost a bell, and
Frank and a negro boy were sent to hunt it and instructed to
search around the foot of a certain mountain, near a cedarbrake
where the ox was wont to graze which had been so unfortunate
as to lose his bell, and thereby get a boy into a world of trouble,
as the saying is. The white and the black boy were unable to
find the bell, but located something in a thicket which they
could not make out the nature of, and kept getting nearer for
a closer inspection. It had something red about it, and seemed
to be in a heap on the ground among the bushes. Finally the
white boy said he was going to throw his hat at it, and did so,
but at the same time the inanimate looking lump on the ground
began to materialize and expand, and that very suddenly, and developed into a powerful Indian, who sprang towards them with
a whoop. The boys turned and fled, and terror lent speed to
their legs and they gave the Indian a lively chase, but finally he
struck Frank on the head with a bow and captured him, and
the negro boy made his escape. The lad was now taken up the
mountain by the Indian, who drove him along ahead of him, and
when they arrived at the crest an old chief was discovered sitting
on a rock, and the captive was conducted to him. The chief
took a good look at him, and then addressed him in broken English with the inquiry if he was a German or an American, and
at the same time vouchsafing the information that if he was a
German his life would be spared, but if an American they would
kill him. This was a severe test for a boy of his age, but he told
the Indian he could not help it, that he was an American, and to
do with him as he liked. This rather stumped the old chief, and
he looked at him some moments in silence, and then gave orders
for his clothes to be stripped off. This was at once obeyed, and

the boy was ordered to go out on the brow of the mountain where
he could see the house and call his sisters to come to him, as if
in great distress. By this time several Indians had assembled,
but they were afraid to make an attack upon the house, but no
doubt would have done so had they known Judge Davenport was
gone, who had ridden away after sending the boys to hunt the
bell. Frank did as the Indian bid him and called his sisters,
and they wanted to go to him, but they knew something was
wrong, and were afraid to, and soon found out from the negro
boy about the Indians. The Indians went west from here and
stopped in the head of Nueces Canyon. They wanted more
horses and were going down this valley on a raid, but did not
want to carry their captive along for fear he would give them
the dodge, or they would have a battle with the white men and
lose him. They finally decided to leave him there alone, and to
prevent his escape they placed him face down in a gully and tied
his hands and feet together over his back and thus left him.
They were gone a long time, and the hours were very tedious to
the captive on account of his awkward and strained position and
the thought of his captivity and no chance to help himself, as it
was useless to pull at his cords, as he soon found out. The Indians were very successful, and came back before night with a
bunch of horses, and untied the boy and made him help catch
them. By this time he was very sore and stiff, and his body
full of pear thorns and briers where they had driven him through
them naked. After the horses were caught an Indian motioned
to Frank with his hand. He thought the fellow wanted him to
come up closer to him, and he did so, but was at once knocked
down with a chunk of wood. The Indian wanted him to sit
down by the motion he made, and adopted this forcible plan to
make him understand it. From here the Indians went to the
Pecos River. where was a large camp of them. They were Comanches, and soon a large body of Lipans came over from Mexico to fight them. A hard battle ensued, but the Comanches
were the victors, and drove the Lipans back across the Rio Grande
with a heavy loss. The Indians on this and other occasions discovered that their captive white boy was not a coward, and said
when he grew up they were going to make a chief out of him,
and commenced training him by dividing the Indian boys into

two squads, placing him in command of one, and making them
fight a sham battle with blunt arrows. During a charge and excitement of the fight young Buckalew shot a young Indian in
the head too hard and came near killing him, and was badly
scared in consequence, thinking now for certain the Indians
would kill him, but on the contrary they applauded the act, and
crowding around patted him on the back and cried "Bravo!
Bravo!"

One one occasion a squaw picked him up, and laying him across
her lap drew- a sharp knife along his throat; but as he did not
flinch she put him down again without injury. He thinks that
if he had shown any fear she would have killed him.

During this long stay here in camp on the Pecos part of the
employment of Frank was to make arrows after they had learned
him how to construct them properly, and he soon became an expert at the business, as well as how to shoot them. He made
trips with the Indians into Mexico to sell arrows and other
trinkets, and on one of these occasions was seen by a Texas ranchman who lived on the Texas side of the river, and being satisfied
he was a captive, hired a Mexican to ascertain the fact, and said
if he could get him to the east side of the river and bring him to
his ranch he would give him $150. The next time the boy was
seen by the Mexican he asked him if he was not a prisoner from
Texas and if he did not want to come home, and answering
these questions in the affirmative, he was told to go back with
the Indians, but to get two of the best horses there were in camp
and come back into Mexico with them, and he would conduct
him to a ranch across the river. Frank did this, and in a short
time was back with the horses, and he and the Mexican set out
and swam the Rio Grande, but had some difficulty in getting out
on the other side on account of the steepness of the bank. The
horses could find bottom to stand on, but could not climb out.
They succeeded finally in getting over the difficulty by digging
the bank down with butcher knives. They soon made their way
to the ranch of the generous Texan, and he paid the Mexican for
his services, but he was to conduct the boy home, which he did,
and turned him over to Mr. William Davenport at Bandera,
where he was joined by his sisters. On the way back one night
was spent at the ranch of Judge Newman Patterson on the Sa-

binal, and the judge and other citizens of Uvalde County helped to pay the ransom. He looked very much like an Indian in their garb. His hair was also long and he was much sunburned. He was 12 years of age when captured, and they kept him eleven months. He still lives in Bandera County, and is a Methodist preacher. He is a cousin to Berry Buckalew, Jr.

BERRY C. BUCKALEW.

Berry Champion Buckalew was born on the 15th day of February, 1824, in Laurens County, Alabama, and came to Texas in the early 50's from Arkansas. He had four milk cows, and these he broke to the yoke and worked them in his wagon to Texas, and then traded for some young steers and milked his cows. In 1856 he went to the town of Bandera and then settled on Laxon's Creek, but soon after moved to Sabinal Canyon and lived at the Blue waterhole on a ranch of Judge James Booker Davenport, and kept some stock for him on shares. During this time he went back to Laxon's Creek, where his nephew was making shingles, and carried a load of them to San Antonio and sold them. With the proceeds of the sale of the shingles Mr. Buckalew bought supplies, and loading them into his wagon started back home, and on 26th of January, 1866, arrived at Cosgrove's ranch, on the Seco, at the foot of the mountains, and ate supper there about sundown. His team was very tired, and he borrowed a yoke of oxen from Cosgrove to pull his wagon on home. But a very curious thing happened. He was unable to hitch the oxen to the wagon, although they were perfectly gentle. They continually plunged and tried to get away, and were finally turned loose and Buckalew started on home, the distance being five or six miles. Before he started, however, Cosgrove told him he had better not go, as Indians were in the country and he had seen two of them. "No," said Buckalew, "I have been gone so long I am anxious to get home," and drove on. This was on Friday evening, and he left the ranch about dusk. On Saturday morning Mr. Cosgrove saw a horse across the creek in the flat, and sent a negro after him, thinking it was one of his, but when the boy came back he said the horse did not belong to the ranch. Cosgrove now went over to look at the horse himself, and found that he belonged to Buckalew—one he lead behind the wagon to drive up his oxen on every morning while camping on a trip. Mrs. Cosgrove now said, "I will bet you anything the Indians have killed Buckalew." Her husband thought not, and said she was too easily scared. On Sunday some cowmen ate dinner there, and Mrs. Cosgrove told them she believed Buckalew was killed. A man named Redmond Givens lived at Cosgrove's, and hearing all of this he went over on the Sabinal to the Davenport ranch and asked Mrs. Buckalew where her old man was. She answered that he had not yet returned home from his trip. Givens now told of the circumstance of his passing their ranch, and an alarm was at once raised. Givens went up the canyon to Waresville after men to help hunt, and got Ben Biggs, Joel Fenley, Wilson O'Bryant, and probably some others, and on returning they closely searched the road on both sides of it back towards Cosgrove's. The body was found one and a half miles from home, some distance from the road, down in a gully, as was also the wagon and team. One ox was dead, having been shot by the Indians, but the other three were still hitched to the wagon alive, but unable to get out of the ravine. Mr. Buckalew was lying on his back and a pile of rocks under his head, and three arrows in his body. It was evident he was walking beside his wagon when the attack was made upon him, and the Indians came up in his rear and shot one arrow in his back, and as he whirled around to confront them two more were sent into his breast. Probably then the team left the road and ran away, and he followed, trying to get some protection from the wagon, until it went into the ravine and the oxen stopped from inability to proceed any further, and here the Indians killed him, beating his head badly in doing so. The body was taken home by the men who found it, and washed and dressed in the Sabinal River.

Mr. Berry Buckalew, Jr., who now lives on Pipe Creek, in Bandera County, was 6 years old when his father was killed, and remembers well how he looked when laid out, and went up and kissed him. He thinks his father lived until just before the body was found, and that he placed the rocks under his head himself. His reason for this is, and a very good one, too, that the body was yet warm, although having been there two days and nights. It is likely the led horse broke loose when the team ran, and came back towards Cosgrove's.

After the killing of her husband, Mrs. Buckalew went back to Bandera, bought a lot in town, and sent her children to school. Here after a time (in 1868) she married James W. Siers, a veteran of the Mexican war, and then moved back to Laxon Creek. Their nearest neighbors were William Walker and Harvey Stanard, about one-fourth of a mile away. A widow lady named Moore lived with the family of Mr. Walker. On one occasion she started to visit Mrs. Curtis, who lived in Mono flat, just below where Medina City is now, and not far from Mr. Walker's place. Not more than half a mile of the distance had been made when the unfortunate woman met a band of nine Indians. The place was on top of a hill, and she turned and ran back from them and succeeded in getting within 200 yards of the house before she was killed. Mr. Siers heard the woman scream, and said to his stepson, Berry, "The Indians are killing some one," and all ran out of the house to look, and discovered the Indians going rapidly around a hill, all on foot. Young Buckalew seized his gun and ran in the direction of the noise of the woman when she was killed, but when he arrived on the ground Mr. Walker was already by the body. Mrs. Moore was lanced through the body, going in at the back, and she had fallen on her face and great quantities of blood had issued from the mouth.

Mr. Walker said if he had known what the situation was he might have been able to have saved her, but thought it was the children hallooing and playing when he heard her screams. He now told Berry Buckalew to go and tell Harvey Stanard, and he set out rapidly to do so, but soon met three Indians and aimed his gun at them, and they dodged back and ran away, and he was in doubt as to whether to empty his gun or not unless they charged him. Even if he killed one the others might get him with their arrows before he could reload or get away from them. He then went on to Stanard's, and he said the Indians passed his house in a fast run. A runner was now sent after Mr. F. A. Hicks, who, as soon as he heard the news, raised a squad of men and set out after the Indians and pursued them closely, but finally the trail was lost among the rocks in the mountains.

Mrs. Moore was buried in the Arnold graveyard, on Laxon Creek. Some time before the Indians came upon Mrs. Moore, Berry Buckalew saw the Indians running horses, but thought they were girls, on account of their long hair and being on foot. He was in the field piling cornstalks, and said to Mr. Siers, "What are the girls running the horses for?" He looked towards the hill where they were, and at once exclaimed, "Hell! those are Indians." The horses were rescued and the Indians went on,

38

and the excitement was not over when they ran and killed Mrs. Moore. Some woman on the creek washing also saw the Indians on a hill looking at young Buckalew piling the stalks, and thought they were cowmen. They evidently had a notion of coming down into the field and trying to kill him.

Mrs. Buckalew, left a widow the second time, still survives and lives with her son Berry, on Pipe Creek.

LON MOORE.

Born in Texas in 1844.

Mr. Alonzo Moore, better known as Lon, was born in Prairie Lea, Caldwell County, Texas, in 1844. His father, Daniel Boone Moore, came there in 1843, and built the second house that was built there. The first one was built by Captain James H. Calahan, one of the survivors of Fannin's massacre, and who led an expedition into Mexico in 1855. The elder Moore helped to build Captain Calahan's house, and then built his own soon after. Daniel Boone Moore, father of Lon, was born in Kentucky, and was a cousin of the famous Daniel Boone, the first pioneer of the "dark and bloody ground," and for whom he was named. Lon Moore's mother was a Linscomb, and was a cousin of Col. James Bowie, who died with Travis and his heroes in the Alamo, so Lon has distinguished ancestors on both sides of the house. He has one brother named Haywood Travis and another Rezin Bowie, the latter named for a brother of Col. James Bowie. Cull is another brother and all are old time Texans and Indian fighters. Lon Moore is a plain, unassuming, western stockman, and no one in the West in better known than he and his erstwhile boon companion, "Seco" Smith. Many nights have these two spent around the campfire on the frontier, scouting for Indians and stockhunting. Daniel Boone Moore came to the Hondo with his family in 1852, and settled in Medina County ten miles south of Hondo City, the present county seat of Medina County, at what is now called the Lon Moore crossing on the Hondo River. The elder Moore was an old time Indian fighter, and died at Devine in 1892.

When Lon was 12 years of age the Indians made a raid down the Hondo Valley, and men were gathering to follow them. Lon, although so young, had the spirit of a frontiersman and Indian fighter, and mounting his horse with a long old rifle went with the crowd, ten in number, who soon got on the trail and followed it rapidly. Among the men were Big Foot Wallace, captain; Tom Hale, Manuel Wydick, Howard Bailey, Henry Adams, and Lon. The others can not not now be remembered. They overtook the Indians at the Presidio crossing of the Hondo. They had fifty head of horses, but abandoned them at sight of the white men and made a poor fight. They lost two killed and soon ran and scattered, and the settlers rounded up the horses and drove them back. Lon fired his rifle, but does not know if he hit an Indian or not.

In the early 60's the Indians made another extensive raid and killed many people and carried off a great deal of stock. Among those they killed on that raid was Pete Ketchum. Mark Harper and others were on the trail and found the body of Ketchum, but it was so badly disfigured about the face that no one recognized it but Mark Harper, and he at once said, "That is Pete Ketchum, and no mistake." The body was carried to the house of old man Daniel Moore, who was his father-in-law. The Indians were followed on down towards the Chicon, and the settlers were there joined by Big Foot Wallace, who was placed in command. These same Indians killed a young man named Long and scalped one of his sisters, thinking they had killed her, but she recovered and afterwards married "Seco" Smith. They also killed a negro, besides other white people, and gathered up many horses. Quite a lot of settlers, among whom was Lon, continued the pursuit under Wallace, overtook the Indians at the head of Seco, defeated them, and brought all of the horses back.

The Indians made a raid in the Hondo valley again during the Civil war and killed a boy named Hood, who lived at the Redus ranch. The settlers followed them into the mountains and were joined in Sabinal Canyon by a squad of rangers under command of Lieutenant Patton of Captain Montel's company. Lon Moore was with the rangers and belonged to the company. The Indians were found in camp in the mountains. There were fifteen of them and twenty of the rangers and settlers. The charge was made on them with loud shouts. The Indians strung their bows and tried to outyell the whites, but did not succeed, and soon ran, leaving four of their number dead on the ground, —the chief, one squaw, and two warriors. Lon ran close to one Indian and shot him with a pistol, breaking his leg, and he fell off a bluff. Moore leaped off after him, but made a narrow escape, as the wounded savage made a dangerous thrust at him with a lance, but the active young ranger sprang to one side and shot the Indian three times more, and killed him. He and

others ran one Indian some distance and shot him repeatedly with pistols, but could not kill him. After the fight he told the men he had killed the chief, and showed them where he lay. Lon then tried to scalp him, but his knife was dull and he made slow progress. Some of the men told him it was not his knife but his heart that had failed him, but he finally got it off. The Indians had killed his brother-in-law, Pete Ketchum, and mutilated his face by cutting off his nose and skinning off the beard, and then, not being dead, dragged him through the prickly pears until life was extinct.

The men gathered up the spoils of the Indian camp, among which were twelve American saddles taken from men whom they had killed. Lon got a knife from the chief which had belonged to the boy Hood, whom they killed at the Redus ranch. It was brought back and given to the boy's mother. A party went back to this battleground some time after, who were not in the fight, to look at the dead Indians, and said the bodies of the Indians had been covered with brush. One lone Indian had returned and done this. It had rained since the fight, and all other tracks were obliterated but his, which had been made since the rain. Nearly all of the Indians who got away were wounded. There was so much shooting that Lon said he was as afraid of his own party as the Indians.

Lon Moore, Big Foot Wallace, and six other men had a running fight with Indians on the Seco, ten miles below D'Hanis, but they got into the bottom without much damage being done to them, but had to give up the horses they were driving off.

On one occasion the Indians captured a boy named Monier, on the Francisco, near the Moore ranch. The boy was with his stepfather Monier, and they tried to get to Moore's, but the Indians cut the boy off and captured him, and he was never heard of again by his people. He went by the name of his stepfather, but his right name is not remembered. The Indians were followed to the Llano, but were not overtaken.

On another occasion a band of Indians was followed by settlers from the Hondo to John Kennedy's ranch, and he was placed in command. The Indians were overtaken at the foot of the mountains at sundown and attacked, but escaped into a cedarbrake. These were the Indians that killed Wolf and Huffmann. Lon Moore was of this party, and says no Indian was killed, but they got the horses back, and two saddles, one bow, and arrows. The horses belonged to William Redus.

During the Civil war the Indians made a raid on the Hondo and killed Rube Smith, one mile west of his house, on Liveoak slough. Smith and Manuel Wydick were out on foot hunting horses and had separated, when a large body of Indians attacked Smith. Wydick from the top of a hill saw them running him, and heard his pistol shots, six in number, but could give him no aid against such odds, and ran in with the news. At this time Lon Moore and Nathan Davis were also out and had separated. Moore heard Smith shooting, but thought it was Davis firing at havilinas. A party went back after Wydick came, and soon found the body of Smith, which they carried home, and raised men to follow the Indians. The Indians numbered about thirty-five, and camped the first night on the Hondo and killed three beeves and partly cooked them. While on the trail the settlers found where a wounded Indian bled on a rock, and strips of Smith's clothing, which had been used for bandages and which had been thrown down, very bloody. Lon Moore afterwards went back to the spot where Smith was killed, under a persimmon tree, and cut his name and date of death on the tree. He also found eight spikes in the trees around the spot where he made his stand to fight them.

The Indians were overtaken at 12 o'clock on the day following the killing of the beeves. The men along were William Mullins, Nathan Davis, Lon Moore, Jerry Bailey, Manuel Wydick, Roe Watkins, Zed Watkins, Louis McCombs, Sam McCombs, Wesley McCombs, John Brown, and a schoolteacher named Bradford. The place was in a valley not far from the old Fort Ewell road, between San Miguel and Cescadara creeks. The Indians wheeled around when the white men charged, and the fight commenced. In this first onset the Indians were repulsed and some of their party wounded. The Indians being in large force, the settlers went back in the timber and dismounted to continue the fight there, and sent off two men, John Brown and Louis McCombs, to get the rangers to come and assist them, who were about twenty miles below. In this first charge Lon Moore's horse ran in among the Indians and was shot, and Moore slightly wounded in the arm with an arrow. He shot one Indian at close quarters with a pistol, and he slapped his hand to his breast where the ball struck him. The horse turned when hit and went back to the other men. The Indians retreated in among some rocks. The two men who went after the rangers slipped away without being seen, so the Indians would not pursue them.

When the white men came into view again the Indians discovered that two of them were missing, and yelled and charged, thinking these two had been killed. The fight lasted off and on all evening. The white men would charge and rout the Indians from the rocks, and then would have to retreat and load, and the Indians would charge and rout them. Many arrows stuck in the trees, and the settlers would pull these out and break them to keep the Indians from getting them in case they had to leave their position. During these charges and countercharges and retreats Nathan Davis was badly wounded with an arrow, which went through the right shoulder, the spike coming out on the opposite side. It was taken out by William Mullins. The horse ridden by Mullins was killed in his tracks with an arrow, which went in at the edge of the saddleskirts, and the spike came through on the opposite side. The horses ridden by Davis, Monroe Watkins, and Bradford were all wounded. At length, during a charge on the part of the Indians, their chief was killed by Mullins, which put an end to the fight. He fell close to the white men, and the Indians made one desperate attempt to recover his body, some of them even grabbing at his hair, but were beaten off. This was a strange fight. The Indians and white men swapped positions time and again, and the loose stolen horses were captured and recaptured as often as they changed. In this way Mullins mounted one of Rube Smith's horses, which the Indians had, when his was killed. During the fight, when both parties were keeping close under cover, Lon Moore and Roe Watkins went out to give the Indians a dare to draw them out, but were fired on without the Indians showing themselves. "Uncle Jerry" Bailey, the oldest man in the crowd, and very brave, would go in front twenty or thirty steps and watch for a chance to shoot, but one time would have been caught if it had not been for Lon Moore. The Indians charged, and the guns being empty, the men mounted to leave the timber and take shelter somewhere else until they could reload, but Uncle Jerry was slow to mount, having to run from his advanced position back to his horse, which, being frightened at the near approach and the

loud yelling of the Indians, would not stand.   Moore, seeing his
critical condition, spurred his horse back and held the other
until the the old man could mount, and when they wheeled to
run some of the Indians were close upon them.   The men when
they left the timber would make a circle and dismount among the
rocks which the Indians had just vacated, and there load their
guns.   The Indians finally left the battleground and went to a
waterhole.   One Indian died before they reached the water, and
they hung his bow and shield on a limb and threw his body into
the waterhole when they reached it.   The Indians were followed
to a point above Bandera by the rangers, and there they found
where five Indians had been buried.   Near the graves were two
mules and a horse.

During the war, when Lon Moore was a member of Captain
Montel's company of rangers, an expedition against the Indians
on a large scale was gotten up.   The intention was to invade
the stronghold of the Comanches in the northwest.   Thirty men
were selected from each company on this part of the frontier,
making 130 in all, and all under the command of Captain Montel.
When the command arrived at a point high up on Devil's River
some of the men wanted to come back.   Montel stepped out and
said, "All those who want to go on come and stand on my right."
All of his own company came over and stood by him, and the
other men turned back.   Montel and his men now went on
until they came to a place called the Black Hills, between the
head of Devil's River and the Texas line.   Here they saw many
wigwams in a valley, and the captain said, "Now, all those who
are willing to go down in there and fight them step to the right."
All responded.   "Now, boys," said Montel, "I see that I will have
to say go back, you will not do it.   I was in hopes you would
say go back.   There are too many for us."

The Indians had discovered the presence of the rangers and
followed them back to the Colorado, and one night while they
were camped ran a thousand or more buffalo through the edge
of their camp.   The intention was to run them square over the
rangers, but they turned.   Six pack mules and two saddle horses
were cut off, and went with the buffaloes.   The design of the
Indians was to stampede all the horses and leave the rangers
afoot.   They followed the trail of the buffalos thirty miles to

rescue their stock, but came upon an Indian trail that turned in on the buffalo trail, and knew they would get them, so turned back.

On this trip they subsisted on the return fifteen days on buffalo meat without bread. They were also without tobacco, and the first place they struck where they could get any was Fort Mason, and they had to pay $2.50 a plug for it in Confederate money.

Lon has been on fifty Indian scouts and in seven fights, most all of them under Big Foot Wallace.

THE COX FAMILY AS INDIAN FIGHTERS.

While traveling in the Dry Frio Canyon in 1897, seeking information of the frontier days, the writer was told by several parties of an interesting frontier incident which took place in the Nueces Canyon and that Mrs. Sirrilda Whistler was likely the only person that was accessible that could give an accurate and detailed account of the affair; she was in the battle, and although a small girl at the time had a good memory, etc. The writer sought an interview, and obtained in substance the following facts:

Mrs. Whistler was the daughter of Mr. Wiliam Cox, and was born in Fannin County in 1851, four miles from Bonham. In 1861 her father's family moved to Brackett, and in 1865 to the West prong of the Nueces River. No one lived there at the time, and the country was wild and lonely indeed. Of this new settlement, besides William Cox and family, was his son Henry and his family, and John Bingham and his family. They all lived in tents near each other, and two months passed away before any signs of Indians were seen. Henry Cox's tent was about fifty yards from his father's and John Bingham's a short distance on the other side, the old man being between the two. As is usual on the frontier during a long period of quiet and peace, the settlers became careless, and when the Indians did come were poorly prepared to receive them.

On the eventful morning in question Henry Cox was at his father's tent, and his family were at their own, fifty yards away. No close watch was being kept, and the Indians came over the hills and into the valley near the camps before any one discovered them. They were twenty-five in number, and all on foot. Mrs. Bingham was the first to see them, and exclaimed, "Lord, God! Look at the Indians!" At this time they were about 100 yards from the tent of the elder Cox. He heard the announcement of Indians by Mrs. Bingham, and at once seized his old flintlock rifle and went out to make a fight and defend his family as best he could. Another mistake, however, had been made by the old man. He had fired his gun at a turkey that morning, and had neglected to reload it. Standing, however, in full view of the approaching and now yelling savages, he began hastily to load, but was hit by an arrow in the knee before he could do so, and was badly wounded. Reaching down he pulled it out, but the spike remained in the bone. Henry now came to his father's assistance, but without his gun, it being in his tent. The old man coolly finished loading his gun, and together they charged. A shot from the old rifle wounded one Indian badly, and he ran into a mott of timber close by. At the first discovery of the Indians the elder Cox had shouted for all of them to concentrate at his tent. A little 4-year-old girl of Henry Cox made a run to get to her grandfather's tent, but was caught by the Indians, who were retreating from the old man and Henry, and going into the mott of timber. John Bingham and his wife attempted to reach the tent, and were both shot and wounded by bullets, or a bullet properly, as the same ball wounded both in the legs, but they succeeded in reaching their destination. The Indians now began to plunder the tent of Henry Cox, and got his gun. His wife before this time had made her escape with one of her children to the old man's tent, and it was while making this run the Indians got the little girl. One younger child was left sitting under a wagon. Our readers must remember that all of this transpired very quickly and under great excitement, Indians swarming all around, yelling, shooting, and bullets whizzing. Old man Cox had retreated back to his tent, but seeing Henry's little 2-year-old child under the wagon, made a run and rescued it. Bingham had no gun, the Indians had Henry's, and the old man had to fight the battle alone. The brave old man was equal to the occasion. He would ram another ball home as fast as he would fire, hitting an Indian every shot. He killed one just as he was coming out of Henry's tent with his arms full of things. The Indians certainly did not know the almost unarmed condition of the white men, as they could have made a charge en masse and overpowered them at once. They dreaded the ominous crack of the old rifle, and were soon all out of sight in the bottom, but still within rifle shot. The chief had a whistle, which he would sound when wanting his men to come closer. Old man Cox wanted to kill him, and watched his chance to do so, believing that his fall would put an end to the battle and the balance would take their departure. He had him located by the sound of his whistle. He was behind a tree in the brush, but very close to camp. His warriors seemed to be further back, and he wanted them to come up and charge. Finally he turned to give a blast and exposed part of his body. At that instant the rifle cracked from the tent, and he fell dead in his tracks. This shot also sealed the fate of the little captive girl. She was at once put to death in retaliation for the slain chief. She was killed with a lance, and her screams could be heard as the cruel blade entered her body.

It was about 10 o'clock when the chief was killed, and soon after the Indians took their departure in silence, keeping up the river in the timber, hid from view. Before this they were yelling and keeping a continual noise. When they went to leave the valley they came into view going up a mountain, and the white men watched them until they disappeared. The old man and his son now went into the mott where the Indians were, having fears for the safety of the child, but not seeing anything of her concluded the Indians had carried her off captive. They saw the trail where the chief had been dragged, and followed it until his body was found in a waterhole, which they pulled out and scalped, and then came back, but on the way found the dead body of the little girl. In the evening the sad burial took place, and the survivors made preparations for flight. During all of this time old man Cox was limping around with the spike still in his knee. The Indians had taken all their horses, and nothing was left but one yoke of oxen to convey these three families away. Next morning, however, the start was made for Brackett, the wounded and small children in the wagon and the balance on foot. After a great many hardships they succeeded in arriving at the fort. Three of the Indians shot in this battle died on the retreat, and were afterwards found.

At the time of this fight Mrs. Whistler was 14 years of age, and remembers of all the incidents distinctly. Her family has had a great deal of trouble on the frontier. She had one sister, brother-in-law, and their three children all killed by Indians near Brackett, and a brother 13 years old killed by them on the Eagle Pass road. He was alone at the time, and no particulars can be given. The others were moving in a wagon when assailed and massacred.

Mrs. Whistler has been married twice. Her first husband was Ben Maples. He was killed in a difficulty, and she married Mr.

Ross Whistler, her present husband. They live in Dry Frio Canyon, near her cousin, Capt. Joshua Cox.

Capt. Joshua Cox is a nephew of the old man William Cox, who made such a game and successful fight with the Indians. He is an old settler and Indian fighter himself. When the fight above described took place he was on Elm Creek, seven miles east of Fort Clark. They all come together from Fannin County, and he had his first experience with Indians on Elm Creek in 1864. While out on a horse-hunt nine Indians charged him and Nilus Cantrell. Seven of the Indians ran around a thicket and two charged straight towards them. At nine yards distant Cox and Cantrell both fired, and each hit his Indian. They wheeled, and the white men pursued them until they ran over a bank and disappeared. The other seven ran back the way they came as soon as the guns fired. One of the wounded Indians was shot through the body, which shot also broke his left arm. He took a shirt off which he had on, and tying it tightly around his body rode his horse six miles to a waterhole, and dismounting there tied his horse to a tree, and lay down by it and died. On the seventh day his body and the nearly starved horse were found. The horse belonged to William Pafford. The Indian had seven pairs of moccasins and a flintlock rifle. The head and shoulders of another Indian were found by the cowboys in the Anacatchi mountains, and this was supposed to be the other one shot on that occasion. His horse was also found, and had a short piece of rope around his neck. Cantrell shot the Indian who died at the waterhole.

In 1867 Mr. Cox had another fight with the Indians twenty-six miles from Uvalde, on the Nueces River. His father, Nathan Cox, Tom Bingham, Zood Pulliam, and himself had the fight. Pulliam and a Mexican were herding cattle when attacked by the Indians, and retreated to the ranch of Captain Cox, about one and a half miles away. During the retreat, however, the Mexican was overtaken and killed. When the reinforcements went back the Mexican was still alive, but lanced in seven places, and did not long survive. The Indians were overtaken while crossing the Nueces River. They had a number of horses, and were trying to cross them by pushing them backwards off a bluff into the water. Capt. Josh. Cox shot at two Indians close together, and one of them fell into the river, but swam across to the other side badly wounded, and it was supposed he died. The other men who were in the rear did not fire for fear of hitting Captain Cox, who was between them and the Indians. All were in a trail one behind the other when they came upon the Indians, who scattered when Cox fired and crossed the river rapidly. Only three head of the horses were recovered.

Another fight took place on the Chaparosa Creek, three miles from Pete Bowles' ranch. The men in this fight were Josh Cox, Archie Cox, Hugh Cox, Henry Cox, Irvin Cox, Dave Cook, and William Carter. The Indians, twenty-five in number, were in an open prairie and could be easily counted. There were twelve on horseback and thirteen on foot. The mounted ones were first seen and charged by the whites and fired on. Those on foot were concealed in the grass near by, and then they rose up and commenced yelling and shooting. The fight lasted nearly an hour, and in that time the Indians were beaten back a mile to the brush, and it ended there. The horse rode by Captain Cox was wounded. His first shot broke an Indian's thigh, who was riding a paint horse. He left the fight, and his broken leg could be seen flopping as he galloped off. Two Indians were killed on the ground. The last shot fired by Hugh Cox hit an Indian in the back, but he hung to his horse and was supposed to be lashed on. The white men were armed with Spencers, six-shooters, and Winchesters, some having one kind and some another, but mostly six-shooters. Irvin Cox had no arms of any kind, and there were only three guns in the crowd, and the men who had these did most of the shooting. The Indians avoided a close fight, and the revolvers were mostly saved for that. They ran repeatedly and shot wild. The white men fired many shots with the repeating guns and many Indians were hit. Out of the twelve on horseback only five were left in the last charge. Mexicans from Mexico said these were Kickapoos, and that more than half of them were killed and wounded. They crossed the Rio Grande and went into Mexico after the fight.

DESPERATE RUN FOR LIFE.

Some time during the Civil war occurred one of those desperate chances for life which frontiersmen sometimes have to take and pass through when coming in contact with Indians on the border. On the occasion of the circumstance mentioned above, Billy Allen and one of his cousins, whose given name was Ranse, the other not being remembered, went out horse-hunting from the Allen ranch on the Tehuacana Creek, in Frio County. They were young fellows, being not more than fifteen years of age. The horses which they were in search of had been gone for some time, but had been heard from as being on the Seco prairie, some distance from old man Allen's ranch. When the boys arrived at the place designated as where the horses were supposed to be, they rode out into the prairie and began their search. Off some distance in the prairie a lone grove of timber was seen, and near it grazed several horses. Thinking these to be the horses they were in search of, the boys rode towards them, not apprehending any danger. Neither had defensive arms of any kind, except, as you might say, those which nature had provided them with. When near the horses one of them threw up his head to look at them, and it was discovered that he had on a halter. Ranse at once exclaimed, "Billy, one of those horses has on a halter." "Indians!" exclaimed Allen; "we must run for it." The distance to the grove was about 100 yards, and rank grass grew all around it. The Indians, about a dozen in number, were lying down in the grass near the edge of the timber or small grove, holding their horses by ropes while they grazed. They all sprang to their feet when the horses first gave sign of the approach of something, and by this time the boys had wheeled their horses and were making off. The Indians all mounted and followed them. About 400 yards away was a hill which was bare on top, but had thick brush around the edges. Drowning men will catch at straws, someone has said, and towards this place the boys ran, hoping likely that here they could abandon their horses and conceal themselves. Even this slim chance, however, was not to be. An Indian on a fast sorrel horse ran around them and turned them back on the prairie again, and the whole gang closed in after them. For some time the Indians were distanced, but finally the one on the sorrel came close upon them. Up to this time no attempt to kill the boys had been made. The Indians perceived they had no arms, and wanted to capture them. Fearing, however, they would get to the brush, the foremost one drew a large pistol having a brass handle. This he waved three times around his head, yelling, then presented it and fired. The ball struck Ranse in the back and came out through the stomach. The stricken boy remained on his horse for some time, but when he began to show signs of weakness by swaying in the saddle, Allen took hold of him and held him on. A short distance further, and Ranse begged his cousin to turn him loose and save himself, saying he was killed and could not stay on his horse any longer. But still the gallant Billy held him. At every jump of the horse the dying boy swayed forward or back, to right or left, and then finally with a sudden plunge went to the ground, nearly pulling Allen from his horse, who made a desperate attempt to hold him. During this time the Indians had scattered to right and left, and the one with the pistol was riding in the rear. He had slowed up some, adjusted his rope, and now came close again, swinging it in the air to rope Allen. The boy watched him, and when the lasso was launched gave his horse a dexterous turn and avoided the loop. He was now near two other Indians, who were also twirling their ropes to give him a turn. He ran between the two, ducked his head low when they threw, and they missed. In this way for miles around and around in the prairie they ran. He was headed off in every direction, and had to run the gauntlet of ropes to get through them. This was kept up until the horses of both parties were run down. At this time, after making a most desperate run, with the last remaining strength of his horse Allen gained the chaparral which skirted the big prairie, for the first time since the chase commenced. The Indians entered after him, but they could no longer use their ropes, and Allen soon dodged them. His faithful horse was nearly dead, and soon lay down with him. The Indians could be heard passing around on both sides of him, but the chaparral and prickly pears were so thick they failed to see him. Allen remained here for some time, fearing to leave the spot, as he might be discovered, but finally with some urging induced his horse to get up, and slowly threaded the intricate openings in the brush and made his way back home, without seeing anything more of the Indians. When the saddle was taken from his horse the poor animal walked off a few yards, lay down, and soon died.

A party went back to the scene of the tragedy, but nothing was seen of Indians, and they secured the body of the slain boy and brought it in. He had been scalped and badly mutilated.

About this time Mr. Sam Pue had a terrible run from Indians, was wounded, but made his escape and recovered from his injuries.

ED. TAYLOR.

Came to Texas in 1857.

Thomas Edward Taylor was born in Wilcox County, Alabama, on the 12th day of March, 1831. Came to Texas from Mississippi in April, 1857, and the same year, in June, came to Uvalde County and settled on the Sabinal River, ten miles below the Eagle Pass road. Indians raided the country frequently, and Mr. Taylor scouted and trailed after them at intervals for seven years.

In 1862 he joined Captain Montel's company of rangers for frontier protection. They served a double purpose as Texas rangers and Confederate soldiers, being subject to the then existing Confederate government. Their camp was in Seco Canyon, at a place now known as Ranger Springs. In the summer news came to camp of an Indian raid below the mountains, which extended as far south as Atascosa County. The information was brought to the rangers by Demp. Fenley, then a boy, who had been sent on this errand by his father, John Fenley, who then lived in Sabinal Canyon. The Indians had turned back and were then heading in that direction, driving about sixty head of stolen horses. About a dozen men from camp, under the command of Lieut. Ben Patton, went in pursuit of them, among whom was Ed. Taylor, Pete Bowles, John Cook, Lon Moore, Dan Malone, Jack Davenport, and Harrison Daugherty, a citizen not in the service. In the meantime the Indians had passed up Sabinal Canyon to the head of Salt Marsh, and then took to the mountains, pursued by the settlers from below. The rangers and settlers got together in the mountains between Sabinal and Frio Rivers, and all followed the trail, which led a northwest course, and finally came in sight of the Indians encamped in the valley of a small creek. The men dismounted, and keeping under cover went up the creek to the camp, which was surrounded by a bluff except on the side next to the mountains, and the men had to climb this bluff before they could see the Indians. The latter were taken completely by surprise, and when the white men came upon them ran without attempting much resistance.

A great deal of firing was done by the settlers and rangers, and most of the Indians killed had more than one ball in them. Mr. Taylor ran after one and shot at him with a Mississippi rifle just as the Indian went over the bluff, and he fell to the bottom and was found there after the fight. After the Indians had been scattered and some killed, John Cook, Lon Moore, and Dan Malone all got after one Indian, who had a broken arm, and commenced shooting at him with revolvers. The chase led up a ravine towards the mountains, and soon all parties were out of sight and nearly out of hearing, but at frequent intervals shots could be heard in that direction. After some little time a great racket among the rocks and brush was heard, with shots interspersed. The boys had headed the Indian some distance up the ravine, and were bringing him back on the other side, and here a strange thing happened,—all at once the Indian disappeared and could not be found. He was shot in many places, and no doubt died. The stolen horses were collected and carried back. Three Indians were left dead on the ground and more were wounded, but hid in the brush and rocks and could not be found. Mr. Taylor and others came back to the battleground some days after, and the dead Indians were all covered up with brush. Some who escaped had come back and done this.

Mr. Taylor was made a Mason in 1863 in Hondo lodge, which was on the east bank of the Hondo River, about four miles east of the present Hondo City, county seat of Medina County. He now lives on the Leona River, in Uvalde County, not far below old Fort Inge.

Mr. Taylor is a man of sterling integrity and has many friends, and is known as "Uncle" Ed. Taylor.

JOHN LEAKEY.

Came to Texas in 1847.

Mr. John Leakey, who built the first house in Frio Canyon, and for whom the town of Leakey was named, which was the county seat of Edwards County until removed to Rock Springs, is one among the most noted characters of the pioneers of the Southwest, and was born in Warren County, Tennessee, in 1824. His grandfather was a soldier under Washington, and did good service in the cause of freedom in the long, bloody war of the Revolution. The subject of our sketch came to Texas in 1847 and first settled in Rusk County, but moved from there in the fall of 1853 and came to Uvalde County, stopping at the Dan Brewster place until the following year, and then settled on the Sabinal River below the mountains, where Henry Shane now lives. In 1855, which was a very dry year, he and Mr. Newman Patterson opened up an irrigating ditch, and while living here Mr. Leakey became involved in a difficulty in which he killed one man, wounded another, and was himself badly wounded.

One one occasion in 1856 Mr. Leakey and his wife went on a visit to Sabinal Canyon, and stopped one night at the house of Mr. Aaron Anglin. An old negro woman slept in a small house in the yard, and during the night waked Mrs. Anglin and told her Indians were around. Mr. Anglin was gone at the time, so Mr. Leakey was aroused and informed of the fact in regard to the presence of Indians, and he secured his pistol and walked out into the yard. Three Indians were concealed in the shadow of some trees near the house, and the dogs were barking at them. The barking of the dogs, and the peculiar actions of one that always tried to get into the house when Indians were about, was what excited the fears of the old negress in regard to them. Mr. Leakey could not tell where the Indians were until they began to shoot arrows at him, which struck the ground at his feet, however, and did no damage, the distance being too far. He now began to fire in the direction the arrows came from, and the Indians ran, pursued by Mr. Leakey, who continued to fire at them until his loads were exhausted and then returned to the house and stood guard the balance of the night. When daylight came he examined the ground, and found the trail of three Indians, two of whom were wounded, as the bloody trails indicated. We will say here that at this time Dr. Ben Thomas was in Mexico practicing medicine among the Mexicans and Indians, and one day two wounded Indians were brought to him for treatment, both shot in the hips. He told this when he came back to Texas, and it was supposed these were the ones who were wounded by Mr. Leakey that night. If this was so they were either Kickapoos or Lipans, for these two tribes lived in Mexico and the Comanches in Texas, on the great plains.

After a short search on the morning in question Mr. Leakey notified the settlers in the canyon, who were few at that time, and four of them volunteered to take the trail of the Indians. They wer Gid. Thompson, Sebe Barrymore, Silas Webster, and Henry Robinson, Mr. Leakey making five. They did not expect to find the Indians very soon, unless it was those Mr. Leakey had wounded. They took time to get ready, Mrs. Anglin fixing up some cooked provisions to last several days, which were put in a pillow slip. Their plan was to follow on the trail of the Indians on foot until they found them some night in camp, and then make an attack upon them. There were more of them than those three mentioned, but not so near the house. When the settlers took up the main trail it was found to lead in a southwest direction towards a high range of mountains two miles distant. Mr. Leakey had the provisions strapped across the back part of his neck and shoulders, but not a morsel of it was ever eaten by either of the party. At this time the Indians, about twenty-five in number, were in ambush on top of the mountains, awaiting the approach of the white men, whom they could plainly see following their trail in the valley below. For fear they would not come straight into the trap on account of losing the trail in the bushes and rocks on the sides of the mountain, the Indians cut down bushes at intervals so that it could be easily followed, but still the unsuspecting white men did not "smell a rat," as the old saying is. It was very tedious and exhausting climbing the mountain. There were steep ledges, slanting rocks, huge boulders, scrubby cedar, and tangled vines to surmount and tear through, so that when the five settlers arrived at the crest of the mountain they were hot, tired, wind-broken, and in no first-class condition to commence a battle. Henry Robinson was an old trailer, and in front when the ambush was reached, which was just on top of the mountain in a cedarbrake and short undergrowth of brush, with large rocks here and there. When the Indians began to raise up with bows in hand and arrows adjusted they were quite close and looked to be very numerous. Robinson, who had fought Indians before, saw at a glance that they were in a trap, and confronted by a largely superior force. Quickly aiming his rifle he fired and wheeled back, telling Mr. Leakey to do the same, who was the next man to him. Leakey had, however, sprang forward and was making a vain effort to fire his gun at the jumping, yelling, painted savages, who in a few moments were all around him shooting arrows. Thompson, Barrymore and Webster were in the rear a few yards, and all leveled their rifles and fired, called to Leakey to run, and then went back themselves. The gun which Leakey had was a new, borrowed rifle, and one he had never fired. It was double-triggered, and Mr. Leakey had been used to shooting a single-trigger gun. He had failed to spring the trigger, and therefore could not pull the hammer down. He had the muzzle almost at an Indian's breast and jerked at the trigger hard enough it seemed to break it out, but seeing it was useless, threw it down and pulled his pistol. He shot one Indian fairly in the ribs at only a few yards distance, and he fell. He now began to get in his work on the Indians and backed away from them, keeping them at bay, although repeatedly wounded. He could not go back the way he came and the way his companions went, for by this time the Indians had cut him off from that direction and were forcing him towards a steep and rugged cliff. His pistol finally refused to fire, and thinking he had exhausted his loads, he now for the first time turned his back to the Indians and plunged over the cliff, rolling and tumbling, catching here and there at bushes and rocks for 100 feet or more, and finally coming astride a tall, slender, cedar sapling, which bent with his weight, and he rode this down over a ledge and found a stopping place. He was now nearly dead with wounds and exhaustion, and lay down under a wild cherry tree. Presently he heard the Indians above him, evidently looking to see if they could discover him lodged anywhere. Thinking he would have to fight again, he examined his pistol, which he still held in his hand, and to his surprise found one chamber loaded. The reason of this was the fact that an arrow spike had struck between the cylinder and barrel, and the small point of the spike had broken off and was tightly fixed there so that the cylinder could not revolve to the next load. Mr. Leakey had snapped several times after the pistol failed to fire, not noticing in the terrific combat that the cylinder did not revolve when he drew the hammer back, and that it fell on an empty chamber each time he attempted to shoot. The Indians thought Leakey was dead, and two of them came down by an easier descent than that which the white man had taken, to scalp him. There was life enough in him yet, however, to make another fight, and getting to his feet he charged them, presenting the pistol. The two Indians no doubt thought the white man, as he was not dead, had had ample time to reload, and having had some experience only a few minutes before with what dexterity he could handle a six-shooter, beat a hasty retreat back the way they came, Leakey cursing them as they went. This cursing was the first intimation the other men had that Leakey was not killed. When Leakey got clear of the Indians one of them picked up the rifle which he had thrown away, and coming out on the cliff where he could see down the mountain, discovered the other white men in their retreat. Webster was ahead, Barrymore next, and Thompson in the rear. Robinson could not be seen, having stopped under cover to load his rifle. The Indian understood the gun, and springing the trigger, aimed at Thompson and fired. The ball passed just above his right ear wounding Barrymore in the hip, and they all soon halted, as the wounded man kept falling. Robinson now came to them and wanted to shoot the Indian, who was still in view, but the others objected, saying if he did the others would scalp Leakey. "He is not dead yet," said Robinson; "listen at him cursing the Indians." Those of the party who were not hurt went to Leakey, and Thompson gave him some water. They also pulled the arrows out of him and stopped the flow of blood as best they could, which came from the nine wounds which he now had on his body. Seven of these he received while facing the Indians at close quarters, and two after he began his retreat, one of which was in the head with an arrow, which carried his hat with it. One arrow went lengthwise of his arm while extending it to shoot. When Leakey threw down his gun and pulled the pistol Robinson was still near him, and an Indian was just in the act of shooting the latter with an arrow when Leakey shot him down. Mr. Leakey was carried back to the settlement, and was six weeks recovering from his wounds. The pursuit of these Indians and massacre of them by the settlers in the Leona River is given in the sketch of Mr. Thompson and others. The provisions carried by Leakey were completely saturated with his blood and could not be used.

In 1857 Mr. Leakey moved to Frio Canyon, and was the first settler there. He had been all over the country, explored it thoroughly, and picked upon a lovely spot in a pecan grove on the banks of the Frio River for his future home. He vowed he would live there in spite of the Indians, and his house is there to this day. He had many adventures with the Indians, however, and at times it seemed that he would be unable to sustain himself. But in a few years other settlers came in, and they helped to protect one another. Among those who came next were Kit Stanford, Thacker, Basham, Aldridge, Van Pelt, Dale, Frank Hilburn, Rain, Wall, and others.

On one occasion Basham and Aldridge were camped on the river making shingles, and the latter borrowed Mr. Leakey's gun to kill a deer. He killed one on the spot where the town of Leakey now is, and was about to proceed to skin it, but detected an Indian behind a tree watching him, and not knowing how many more might be around, beat a hasty retreat. A man named Carter, who lived with Leakey, went back with him, but no Indians were seen, and they brought the deer in. Signal smokes were seen on the mountains, and all the men went to look for the Indians but Mr. Leakey. He remained to protect the women and children. Mr. Wall saw some of the Indians and ran them three miles up the river, but did not get any of them. Lieutenant Wood had a fight with them in Nueces Canyon and succeeded in killing some of them, and they stopped raiding for some time.

In 1859 the Indians stole a large drove of horses in the lower part of the canyon, and the settlers began to rally to fight them. The soldiers at Fort Inge were also notified, and a squad of them came to help the settlers. Mr. Leakey and others, including Richard Ware, Clabe Davenport, and Courtney, struck the trail of the Indians on Blanco Creek, east of the Frio, and it led north. While starting the trail in the rough, mountainous country, Mr. Leakey fell down a rocky bluff, and was so badly hurt that he could hardly mount or ride his horse, and announced the fact that he was too badly bruised to proceed in the pursuit, and would return home. Others of the party said if he went back they would, too. Not wishing for the chase to be abandoned or the force weakened too much, Mr. Leakey went on. The trailing was one of the roughest imaginable, all the way through the mountains. Many crippled colts and horses were found along the way. The Indians were overtaken on the divide at the head of Sabinal and Frio rivers, in an open but rocky country. There were about twenty white men, and they outnumbered the Indians, but the latter were game and gave them a desperate fight. They had about eighty head of horses, and ran at first sight of the white men through a very rocky place, and the settlers flanked on both sides and some circled around them, and the Indians went into a burnt cedarbrake, and the fight commenced. Many shots were fired by the white men, and the Indians charged, fighting at close range. They were close observers, and would charge a white man and sometimes run him if his gun or pistol were empty. On one of these occasions Mr. Leakey saw an Indian closely pursuing Courtney, who had exhausted his shots. Although hardly able to ride he ran between them and cut the Indian off, and shot him six times with a revolver at close range, and he quit the fight, and went off about 200 yards and laid down under some young cedar trees. Leakey, while loading his pistol, watched him, and seeing young Clabe Davenport near, told him to go down there and shoot the Indian in the head. The young settler did so, but first advanced on the hidden warrior cautiously, knowing the danger if he was able to fight. Coming into view he fired, but said it was no use, as the Indian was about dead. This was quite a mixed up fight, and many personal combats took place, especially when the Indians were routed from the cedarbrake, where five of them were killed. One powerful Indian, who was called at that time Blackhawk by the settlers, was very brave, coming close to the white men and wounding some of them. During the fight Mr. Leakey came in contact with Blackhawk and shot him eight times, but failed to bring him to the ground. He was one of the few who escaped from the battleground, but no doubt perished. During the latter part of the fight, when the Indians were running, one fell in a gully, having both hips and left arm broken. Leakey was close behind on a splendid mare, and she jumped clear over him. When he passed the Indian held his bow with the right hand and pulled an arrow back with his teeth and shot at him, but missed, the arrow glancing along the rocks ahead of him. A sergeant who belonged to the soldier squad came along and finished the wounded Indian by a shot in the head with his carbine, and was promoted to a lieutenancy for this when it was reported to headquarters. Two white men and several horses were wounded in the fight. The stolen horses became badly scattered during the fight, but were nearly all collected and carried back to the settlement.

Mr. Leakey has been on many scouts after Indians. On one occasion he followed them to the head of the Nueces River, but citizens and soldiers came in ahead of Leakey and his party and fought a battle with them just before they arrived on the scene. They met some of the settlers, who had killed one Indian and recaptured a lot of stolen horses taken from a man named Ragsdale. They also rescued a negro boy who was a prisoner among them. Here a squad was raised to help Ragsdale to Fort Clark with his horses, and Leakey was put in command of it.

On one occasion a man named Hilburn was living with Mr. Leakey, and becoming tired of deer meat, went out to hunt some hogs belonging to Leakey, for the purpose of killing one. The hogs were wild, and Hilburn advanced cautiously while looking for them. The morning was foggy, and when the hogs were found an Indian was also discovered in a stooping position watching them, evidently waiting for a good opportunity to shoot one. Hilburn was a quick shot, always firing when the gun came to his shoulder, and on this occasion at once fired and broke the Indian's back. He went back from here and told the news, and two men went back to where the Indian lay, and he was still alive. They talked to him in Spanish, and he said he was a Kickapoo. When he died these two men buried him, not far from the present town of Leakey.

In 1861 Mr. Leakey went with a wagon to haul cedar poles which he had previously cut in a brake. When he arrived, before commencing work he placed his gun against a fallen tree, and his three dogs lay down near it, but on the opposite side of the log. In driving about gathering up his load Mr. Leakey lost sight of the spot where his gun was, but had two revolvers buckled around him. At this time a band·of Indians was coming down a deep gorge near by, and one of the gang acting as spy and scout was on the high ground, but traveling parallel with the others. He discovered Mr. Leakey's gun, but did not see the dogs, and while in the act, as was supposed by his tracks, of taking the rifle, the three dogs sprang over the log and seized him. The Indian ran and plunged off the bluff into the gorge, carrying the dogs along also, who still held on to him, and followed the other Indians, and the dogs still kept after him. Mr. Leakey heard the scuffle, and thinking the dogs had a bear, ran to his gun, snatched it up, and followed. By this time dogs and Indian had gone over the bluff, and still thinking it was a bear, Leakey followed, a bend in the gorge hiding them from view. The other Indians wounded the dogs, and they came back. The truth now dawned upon Leakey, and looking about him he discovered the gorge full of Indian tracks, and retreating back climbed out of the gorge and got his team and went home. The dogs were able to follow, and all got in safely.

The writer, while collecting these reminiscences, spent a night with Mr. Leakey in Frio Canyon. When asked how many wounds he had on his person, he laughed and said, "You will have to strip me and count." The old man had thirteen prominent wounds on his body, besides bruises and scratches, but the writer took his word without counting. These wounds are all in front from his knees to the top of his head, made with bullets, arrows, knives, etc. The worst one is on the front of the head, several inches in length, and is plainly visible through his scattered gray locks, and this was one inflicted by the breech of a shotgun.

Mr. Leakey has been a member of the church, and firmly believes in the religion of Jesus Christ, and is a Mason of long standing. No man ever left his door in distress when it was in his power to aid him.

C. G. JARVIS.

Came to Texas in 1865.

Among the settlers of Frio Canyon who deserve notice is Mr.
Charles G. Jarvis, not so much on his record as an Indian fighter,
although he has seen some of that, but as one of Lee's veterans
who gallantly and unflinchingly followed the Stars and Bars on
many hotly contested fields, and shed his blood in defense of the
"lost cause." The war has been over for a long time, but still
we read with interest the deeds of valor performed by our devoted Southern boys, and the old soldiers who followed the Stars
and Stripes will many of them join us in giving them praise for
their dashing courage and devotion to the cause which to them
was right and just.

Mr. Jarvis was born in Algiers, La., in December, 1843, and
in 1852 moved to Missouri and settled in St. Francis County.
When the Civil war broke out he joined the State guards, com-
manded by Colonel Schanebel. These were disbanded in six
months, and he then entered the Confederate army under Gen.
Sterling Price. Mr. Jarvis participated in his first battle at
Oak Hills, or Wilson Creek, as some call it. Then in regular
order came the battles of Springfield, Elkhorn, Farmington, Iuka,
Corinth, Grand Gulf, Port Gibson, Baker's Creek (called by the
Federals Champion Hills), Big Black, and siege of Vicksburg.
In all of these battles Mr. Jarvis did his duty as a brave soldier,
as will be attested by his old comrades who may chance to see
this sketch. Charles Jarvis is a man who does not like to make
a display in regard to the part he took in these various engagements, and is too modest to recount any of his own deeds of personal valor, but pays glowing tribute to comrades who fought by
his side. On the 18th of May he was twice wounded at Vicksburg, receiving one ball in the left arm and one in the right
shoulder. In twenty days he reported for duty. After the surrender of Vicksburg he was paroled, and then exchanged in September, 1863. He was in the Georgia campaign, and took part
in the battles of New Hope Church, Latimore, and Kenesaw
Mountain. The latter was one of the bloodiest of the war, con-

sidering the time and numbers engaged. The Federal troops attempted to storm the position of the Confederates on Kenesaw Mountain, but met with a most crushing defeat and a perfect slaughter of men, and without doing much damage to the Confederates. Mr. Jarvis said he saw the blood running down the hill in small rivulets from one ledge to another. The Federals deserve great credit for their bravery on this occasion, coming as they did to the works and attempting to get over them while suffering such great loss of men. Colonel Blood of the Union forces fell near the works, and his dead body fell into the hands of the Southern troops when his men retreated. Mr. Jarvis says he was a fine-looking man, and they buried him with the honors of war, showing their appreciation for the chivalry and almost matchless courage he displayed on that occasion.

The next battles Mr. Jarvis engaged in were Vining's Station, Peach Tree Creek, and siege of Atlanta. He and five others crossed the Chattahoochie River and captured a sergeant, six men and thirteen mules, all within long range rifle shot of the Federal cavalry headquarters. The cavalry came out and pursued them, and they placed their prisoners on the mules. They put two on one mule, and one of them was an Irishman. He began to complain at their rapid gait, and said he could not ride the bloody mule, he bounced so, and began to hump up as if about to fall. Jarvis reached him with his gun, gave him a punch, and told him to straighten up there. "All right, be Jasus," said the Irishman, and at once rode erect.

The Confederates fell back to Lovejoy and an armistice of ten days was agreed upon. From there Mr. Jarvis followed Hood up into Tennessee, and fought in the battles of Big Shanty, Ackworth, and Altoona. In the last named he was wounded in the right thigh, and when his command retreated he followed the army, badly hurt as he was, rather than be captured. A comrade named Johnny Cockery stayed with him to help him along. In the retreat Jarvis pulled off his pants, as they irritated the wound, and all at once discovered some women and children by the roadside watching the soldiers pass. He told his companion to stay between him and the women and to go slow and keep step with him, so that he would not be exposed. His comrade was full of fun, and at the critical moment walked fast and left the wounded man limping along with nothing on but his shirt. When he recovered from this wound he went into the secret service until the final surrender. Among those who were with him in this service were J. M. Bond, a Methodist minister, now living in Granger, Williamson County, and John L. Carlisle, living in Italy, Ellis County.

At the close of the war Mr. Jarvis came to Texas and helped Peck Johnson put up a herd of cattle in Brown County, and started with them to California. He stopped, however, at Las Cruces, N. M., and went to Denver, Col. From there he went to Durango, Mex., and drove a herd of horses; then to El Paso, Texas.

In 1870 Mr. Jarvis had charge of a train belonging to Ward B. Blanchard. At Fort Quitman the Indians made a raid and captured sixteen head of mules belonging to the train. He applied to Maj. A. P. Morrow, who was in command of the fort, for troops to follow the Indians, but the major said, "No use; impossible to catch them." He then asked for horses to follow them on, but this was also refused. Jarvis went back to camp and studied over the situation some time, and finally concluded he must have the mules back, as he could not move his train without them. There was nothing but a few wagon mules in camp, but he mounted himself and four teamsters on these and commenced the pursuit. The route was long and rough, through gorges and over mountains, but so tenacious and energetic was the chase that sixty miles were covered that day, and when night came on they were in sight of the campfire of the redskin marauders. Jarvis got the camp well located, which was in a gorge with bluffs around, and then rested, waiting until daylight to make the attack. The Indians had killed a mule and sat up late that night eating and singing, which could be plainly heard by Jarvis and his men. The light of their campfire above the bluff could be seen. They thought they were safe for the night. Just as day began to break, Jarvis took his men to the bluff and looked over. Only one Indian was up, and he was sitting down on the opposite side of the fire. The others were lying down and away from the fire, and could not be seen. At this time one of the men, some of whom were Mexicans, cocked a Spencer carbine, which made a loud click on the cold, frosty air. The quick ear of the Indian caught the ominous sound, and he looked up towards the top of the bluff and started to rise. No time was now to be lost, and the order to fire was given. One gun went off in the air, sending the bullet towards the stars. One struck the fire in front of the Indian, and the other three went through his body, killing him instantly. The other Indians made their escape, as it was still dark, especially in the gorge. Jarvis collected his mules, and without further incident got back and moved his train.

In 1873 he married Miss Mattie Watkins, of Guadalupe County, Rev. C. Shapard performing the ceremony. He came to Frio Canyon in 1886, and is now engaged in farming and stockraising. He belongs to the Methodist church, and was made a Mason at Frio Town in 1884, made a royal arch in Uvalde, July 3, 1890, and is now worthy master of Leakey lodge No. 622.

CAPT. JOHN H. ROGERS.

Native Texan. Born in 1863.

Capt. John Harris Rogers was born in Guadalupe County, Texas, on the 19th day of October, 1863. His father was Pleasant William Miles Rogers, son of Isaac and Mahala Rogers. His mother was Mary Harris, daughter of John and Laura Harris, all old settlers of Guadalupe County. The father of Captain Rogers was a Confederate soldier during the Civil war, and participated in some hard-fought battles in the Louisiana campaign. In one of these the Confederates got the worst of it, and the boys who carried the "bonny blue flag" were forced to retreat. Mr. Rogers came very near being captured on account of his horse falling into a ditch which he attempted to leap, and was unable to extricate himself. The Federal cavalry was close upon him, but at this critical moment he was rescued and carried safely off the field by his brother-in-law, Lieut. John Wesley Harris, who gave the unfortunate young soldier a mount behind him.

While Captain Rogers is not an old man, he has made a reputation as a brave and gallant Texas ranger surpassed by but few, and deserves a place in the history of southwest Texas. On the 5th day of September, 1882, he joined Company B of the rangers, commanded by Capt. S. A. McMurry. There was no lieutenant of this company, and John McNally was sergeant. Afterwards McNally was made a lieutenant, as was also Sam Platt, of Austin.

Just before young Rogers joined the rangers they had a fight with train robbers at Ranger Station on the Southern Pacific road, wounded one and captured all but one of the balance, as it was supposed.

Captain Rogers remained with this company fifteen months, and then came home in December, 1883, and spent the holidays.

He enlisted again in the following spring in the company of Capt. Joe Sheely, at Cotulla, La Salle County. William Scott was lieutenant and W. T. Morris sergeant. The latter is now sheriff of Karnes County. In 1885 Captain Sheely severed his connection with the company and Lieutenant Scott was made captain. Sergeant Morris married a Miss Harper, of Yorktown, and also resigned, and J. A. Brooks was made sergeant. The company left Cotulla and established a camp in the Nueces Canyon. In the fall of 1885 the command went to Mitchell County, and in the following year went after fence-cutters in Brown County. Captain Scott was in command, and the outlaws were surprised in camp. The captain was in front, and commenced firing as soon as he perceived them. The rangers all followed suit, and when the smoke cleared up two fence-cutters were seen lying dead on the ground. This was the first battle of young Rogers.

From Mitchell County a detachment of the rangers were ordered to Sabine County to arrest a gang of murderers and outlaws who had defied the civil authorities, and in fact the whole country. These desperate men were old man Conner and his three sons—Fred, William, and John. They were splendid shots, and lived almost like Indians in the dense pine forest which nearly covered that part of the country. When the rangers arrived in the vicinity of the Conners they were to meet a man at a certain designated place after dark, who was to pilot them to the camp of the outlaws. He had been with the Conners often, and in fact had been placed in this work by the rangers on a previous trip, when they had failed to locate their men. He was a citizen of this locality, and had bought out the Conners, and they were now living in a camp in the dense pine woods, covered with underbrush. Two other citizens were with the rangers— Judge Polly, from Hemphill, and W. W. Wethered, from the town of Milam. The rangers rode around in the vicinity of the camp in the early part of the night, and their trail was discovered by the Conners while they were out fire-hunting with a torch. Apprehending the significance of this trail, they at once repaired to their camp and prepared for defense. They took off the bell from a pack horse so that its rattling would not betray their position, and awaited developments. On this night the citizen spy had hunted with the Conners, but finally excused himself and said he would go home, but instead came to the rangers, who were a mile or more away. The Conners discovered the trail of the rangers by their torchlight after he left. The spy intended to be guided to some extent by the bell on the pack horse

40

in piloting the rangers through the dark woods to the stronghold of the outlaws. He carried them, as he thought, to within
two or three hundred yards of their camp, and then went back
a short distance, not wanting to be seen by the Conners. Captain Scott had told the man before this to slip down the gully
on which the camp was situated and take observations, but not
hearing the bell, he was afraid he had missed the place. This
was a new camp, and he had only been there in the night time.
While he was gone on this reconnoitering expedition he thought
he heard one of the Conners cough, and so reported. Captain
Scott now told him not to leave the place, as he might be needed
for a guide after the fight, and dismounted his men, who tied
their horses to the trees. The party was now divided. Two
rangers and two citizens were sent to the left, and the captain
and five rangers went to the right. As the latter were the men
who fought the battle, we will follow them and give their names,
which were, besides the captain, Sergeant Brooks, Frank Carmichael, J. H. Moore, John H. Rogers, and William Treadwell.
The intention of the captain was to find the camp between the
two parties, but to remain near enough to each other so that when
firing commenced they would not shoot by accident any of their
own men. The right and left separated too far, and both parties
passed the camp without discovering it. Captain Scott and his
party finally came to a gully, and Sergeant Brooks said if this
was the one they were camped in it was no use to cross, but to
turn back and keep up on this side. This was done, and all
moved cautiously along. It was now nearly day. The time was
the last day of March, 1886. Just at daybreak John Rogers saw
the outlines of a man in a squatting position, and called the attention of Sergeant Brooks to the fact, but at this time the man
raised up and the rangers covered him with their Winchesters.
He backed ten steps to a tree and stopped. Rogers called to him
and asked if he was one of their own men. Without replying
he raised his gun to fire, and was instantly killed by three shots
from Scott, Rogers, and Brooks. One ball went through his
head and two through the body. All struck about the same
time, and he dropped instantly in his tracks. This was Bill Conner, second youngest. Simultaneously with these shots came a
volley from ambush fired at the rangers, which wounded John
Rogers in the side, spinning him around, and killed James H.

Moore, of Center Point, Kerr County, Texas, who was shot through the heart, dying instantly. Captain Scott now received a wound and fell, shot through the lungs. Another volley came quick, and young Rogers was wounded the second time, and he fell to the ground. He had his gun in position to fire, and the ball struck his left arm and went through the muscle between the main artery and the bone, cutting the nerve. Sergeant Brooks now advanced on the hidden marksmen and continued to shoot in their direction, but was soon shot through both hands. He had his gun up to fire, and a ball glanced on the under side of his gun barrel, shot three fingers from his left hand, and lodged in the right. Unable now to work the lever of his Winchester, he sank to the ground to avoid other shots, and crawled back to Rogers on his knees and elbows. Then, with bloody and shattered hand, he drew his pistol, gave words of encouragement to the boys, and renewed the battle with his unseen foes. The bullets were now flying thick and striking the ground around the wounded men. Rogers was paralyzed in the left side and arm, but had use of the right, and with this worked the lever of his gun, holding the barrel between his knees, and fired repeatedly from where he lay on the ground. The Conners finally retreated, and the firing ceased. Captain Scott was lying to the right of Rogers, and the latter made an attempt to reach him, but was unable. The other two rangers who had not been hit and had sprang to cover during the fearful fusilade, now came forward, and Carmichael placed a coat under the head of Captain Scott and elevated him so that he could breathe better, as in the position he was lying he was strangling with blood. He lay there now, and gave orders as to what should be done coolly and calmly. One man was to be sent to Hemphill, the nearest point, for doctors to give immediate attention, and Private Crowder was to go to San Augustine, forty miles away, after the best surgeon there. Crowder had been left at the house of one of the relatives of the Conners, with orders to arrest anyone who came there, and a citizen carried him the message from his captain. A doctor soon arrived on the scene and dressed the wounds of the stricken men, the shot fingers of Sergeant Brooks having to be amputated. The ball was cut out of Captain Scott; it had lodged below the shoulder blade on the left side. A daybook saved the life of John Rogers. The ball would have gone directly through his body had it not first come in contact with the book. , It went through the book, however, but deflected and passed out through the left hip. It will be noticed that all of the men who received wounds were struck on the left side, and it would appear that the Conners were aiming for the heart. This, however, might not have been the case. Men shooting from behind a tree generally aim from the right side of it, and the first part of the man's body he sees at whom he is about to fire is the left side, and in quick, hot work he fires his piece as soon as he covers that part of the body. The trees behind which the Conners stood were thickly peppered with balls, showing with what true aim the rangers sent their shots in the direction from which came those of their foes, who were completely hidden from view during the battle.

The next day after the fight, April 1st, the wounded men were removed to Hemphill, nine miles away. Captain Scott was carried on a litter, and Rogers and Brooks in a wagon. They suffered a great deal on the way. The brave and gallant young Moore, who lost his life in this battle with the outlaws, was carried to Hemphill and buried before the wounded rangers reached there. His was the most largely attended funeral ever known there. Many ladies came and dropped bouquets in the grave of the dead hero. The citizens were all kind and sympathetic, and came to see the rangers in great numbers. The wounded were all kept in one house, and many ladies came every day with flowers and nourishment. The relatives of Moore at Center Point were notified of his death, and Capt. Frank Moore, sheriff of Kerr County, his uncle, came at once. He carried the horse, saddle, and pistol of the gallant boy back home. The horse, a fine sorrel pacer, was kept in the Moore family until he died. When Captain Scott recovered he married Miss Georgia Lynch, of Waelder, Gonzales County, Texas.

When young Rogers so far recovered as to be able to travel he obtained leave of absence, and came to see his mother at Kingsbury, Guadalupe County, his father having died when he was very young. When this leave expired he went back to his company, which had been continuously hunting the Conners ever since the fight, but being unable to find them, the rangers came back west to San Angelo, Tom Green County. Sergeant Brooks was now captain of the company, and John Rogers was made sergeant.

While at San Angelo, Sergeant Rogers and a deputy from Mitchell County followed a couple of horse-thieves and accidentally met them in the road, rather to the surprise of both parties. One of them raised his gun to fire, but Rogers was too quick for him, getting in the first shot, wounding him in the arm, and he dropped his gun. The sergeant then jumped down and caught his horse by the bridle. The deputy had his man covered, also, but turned his head when Rogers fired, and he succeeded in getting his pistol out, but in his haste let it fall, and both were captured and put in jail in San Angelo.

From Tom Green County the rangers moved to Rio Grande City and stayed there two years, and then in 1890 came back to Cotulla. In the fall of 1892 Catarina Garcia raised his revolt, and Sergeant Rogers went out with five men to locate him and his band, who numbered 165. In one of his deserted camps papers were found which disclosed forty names of men and officers. Sergeant Rogers went twice to Laredo and begged for help, and finally a squad of soldiers came under the command of Captain Hardie. This officer was a fine man, and was very popular among the rangers. It will be remembered that Garcia was not making war against the Texans, but was organizing his force in Texas for the invasion of Mexico in the hopeless and useless endeavor of overturning the Diaz government. The rangers and soldiers in conjunction broke up his band in Texas, and many of them were captured. Garcia himself was not taken, but made his escape to Cuba and joined the army of Maceo, the Cuban patriot, and lost his life in battle with the Spaniards.

On the 10th of October, 1892, Sergeant Rogers, having obtained leave of absence, married Miss Hattie Burwell, at Cotulla. Soon after this important event in the life of the gallant ranger the company was sent to Realitos, Duval County. Sergeant Rogers was commissioned captain of the company by Gov. James Hogg on the 1st day of January, 1893. Tupper Harris, of Kingsbury, Guadalupe County, was elected first sergeant. The company was stationed at Alice. Curran Rogers, brother of the captain, belonged to the company, having joined soon after the Conner fight.

The company remained at Alice five years, and then came back in June, 1898, to Cotulla, relieving Captain Brooks, the gallant sergeant in the Conner battle, who had been placed in command of a company, and his command went to Alice.

In September Sergeant Harris resigned, and H. G. Dubose was elected to fill the vacancy.

On the 18th of March, 1899, Captain Rogers received an order from General Scurry to repair to Laredo with a detachment of his men to assist State Health Officer Blunt in enforcing quarantine regulations, there being a great epidemic of smallpox at that place. Mexican citizens of Laredo who had the disease objected to being moved from their homes to the pesthouse or hospital which had been provided for those afflicted. When Captain Rogers arrived at Laredo he quartered himself and men at the Hamilton Hotel. On the 19th he took A. Y. Old ("Augy") and repaired to the scene of moving the patients. The Mexicans had a clash with the city officials, in which several shots were fired on both sides, and hundreds of them now swarmed together on the streets, yelling and hissing. Captain Rogers, having but few men, wired Governor Sayers to use his influence with the war department to call out troops from Fort McIntosh if found necessary. Operations were now suspended until the morning of the 20th. In the meantime General Scurry wired Sergeant Dubose at Cotulla, to proceed with all of the men there to the assistance of Captain Rogers at Laredo. He arrived on the 20th with rangers W. A. Old, W. L. Wright, Creed Taylor, and James Moore (cousin of the James Moore killed in the Conner fight). The ranger companies at this time had been cut down to not more than a dozen men each. Sergeant Dubose reported to Captain Rogers at the Hamilton House, and he and his men were quartered there. Just before starting the pest wagons, information came that at a certain house in East Laredo arms and ammunition were being concealed for the purpose of resisting the officials of the quarantine when the removal of patients commenced. Captain Rogers at once repaired to the place designated, in company with the sheriff and three Mexican officers. One house was searched, nothing found, and no resistance offered. Here A. Y. Old and special ranger Thomas Raglin joined Captain Rogers. The party now proceeded to the house of Agapeta Herrera, and presenting a search warrant, told their business. He then called the sheriff to one side and had a talk with him. Two brothers of Agapita were present, and they commenced pacing back and forth across the yard in a very nervous manner, and at the same time closely watching the rangers. The sheriff finally grabbed Agapita and beckoned to the Mexican deputies. The Mexican in this talk with the sheriff had refused submission to have his house searched. The two brothers now ran into the house, seized their Winchesters, and ran through a gate which was between the street and their yard. Captain Rogers fired on them, and the Mexicans jumped behind a wall, and Agapita got loose from the sheriff and obtained possession of his Winchester. The captain was watching the two Mexicans behind the wall, and did not see Agapita when he secured his gun. The first he noticed of him he was aiming his gun at the captain, and had crossed the street in the rear, and Captain Rogers wheeled and fired at him, wounding him in the breast. Shooting at this time was general, the other two rangers having opened fire. Their hats were covered with lime from the whitewashed walls of the house against which they stood, the balls striking over their heads. About the time that Captain Rogers fired his second shot he was badly wounded in the right shoulder by a shot from Agapita, and another ball also cut his thumb. Augy Old now fired two shots in quick succession at Agapita, hitting him both times in the head, and he fell dead in his tracks. During this time the sheriff and Mexican deputies had left the yard and gone into another street. The ball that struck Captain Rogers broke the bone just below the shoulder joint, rendering his right hand powerless. The left arm had been disabled in the Conner fight and was not strong, and thus left powerless he withdrew and went down the street towards the Hamilton House, where he could get medical assistance, as he was bleeding profusely. The other two rangers held their own with the Mexicans, but finally withdrew. Captain Rogers, becoming very weak, hailed a hack before reaching his destination, and was taken in and conveyed to the hotel. Before reaching there he met City Marshal Joe Bartlow, who asked what was the trouble, and was informed of the fight. Sergeant Dubose and the other rangers were also met coming in a run with Winchesters. They had been 'phoned by Dr. Blunt that a fight was in progress. Although bleeding and suffering, Captain Rogers ordered the hack to stop, and gave orders to his men what to do. He told Dubose that now was the time to call out the soldiers, as they had permission to use them, and to wait and get them; to be prudent, take matters in hand, and do the best he could. At the hotel the wounded captain was met by Frank Earnest and other friends, and assisted to his room, where Dr. McKnight attended him. In about twenty minutes news came that fighting was going on again in town. The rangers under Sergeant Dubose, becoming impatient, repaired to the scene of the late fight, and there found about fifty armed Mexicans assembled around the dead body of Agapita. They opened fire on the rangers when they appeared, and a general fusilade commenced. At the first fire from the rangers the Mexicans scattered quickly and promiscuously to cover behind fences, etc. The rangers, although only a corporal's guard, as you might say, also went to cover and held their own, and quite a battle ensued. One Mexican repeatedly fired a Winchester from cover, and for some time the rangers could not locate him. Creed Taylor, the youngest ranger in the party, had a slide magazine shotgun, and changing his position he obtained a view of the Mexican, as he to some extent uncovered himself to fire, and gave him a load of buckshot, which turned him over. There was more sign on this Mexican after the fight than any that could be heard of that was hit. There was no chance to find out how many were killed or hit. Five had the assistance of doctors afterwards. Sergeant Dubose received one ball through the pants leg, and Special Ranger O. N. Wright was badly bruised by a spent ball in the groin. After the fight the rangers repaired to the hotel and informed their captain what they had done, and was told to go on with the work of removing patients. This was done without any more resistance.

On the 21st Captain Rogers was removed to the Santa Rosa hospital, San Antonio, and placed under the treatment of Dr. Graves. Dr. Wilcox, of Laredo, came as far as Devine with him, and then returned. Dr. Graves told the captain he could save his arm, but would likely have to make it shorter, and that evening at 5 o'clock he operated upon it, cutting out one inch and a half of bone. The captain had to lie in one position six weeks, but when able to sit up, was carried to his mother's house, who lived in San Antonio. In three weeks more he went back to his command at Cotulla, and is there now in command of Company E, doing business at the same old stand, and has up to date (January 3, 1900) served the State as a ranger nearly eighteen years.

Captain Rogers is related to Col. Nat Benton, who lost an arm at the battle of Blair's Landing, in Louisiana, during the Civil war. Colonel Benton and his young son Eustis were in the Calahan expedition in 1855, and were both wounded in the battle of San Fernando, in Mexico,—the son severely in the head. Eustis was a captain in the Confederate army, and faithfully followed the Stars and Bars.

JUDGE M. F. LOWE.

Judge Marcellus French Lowe, the subject of this sketch, was born in Atascosa County, Texas, west from Pleasanton, the county seat, on Padillo Creek. The date of his birth was March 28, 1855, and he was the first white child born in Atascosa County.

From this place he moved with his parents to McMullin County and settled on the bank of the Frio River, nine miles below the old Laredo road. His father, James Lowe, Sr., was a stockman, and had many experiences with Indians—trailing, fighting them, etc. He had extensive cattle interests in the Southwest, and established several branch ranches, one of which was on the Nueces River, about thirty-five miles from his place of residence, and known as the San Jose ranch. It was in charge of an old Mexican, called a "remudada"—one in charge of horses, or a "remuda."

In 1871 the elder Lowe sent his son Marcellus, then 14 years of age, and one of his negro hands, a boy of the same age, named Sam Heritage, to the San Jose ranch after a herd of about eighty head of horses. They were to carry these horses to Alligator Lake,—where they were to meet Moses McLean, a negro in the employ of Mr. Lowe on one of his ranches. Moses had written or sent word to Mr. Lowe that he was in need of the horses, and would be at the lake on a certain day, and would there receive them if he would have them sent down there. Young Lowe and the negro boy arrived at the ranch late in the evening. The ranch house was nothing but a small picket affair, and stood on rising ground overlooking a mesquite flat, across a small draw or ravine, with rising ground beyond towards the east. About sundown a man named Stringfield drove up in an ox wagon, having with him his wife and three children—two boys and a girl, the latter being the eldest. They camped for the night near the yard fence. They were coming from Preata, or Black Creek, and going to Alligator Lake. Early next morning the old Mexican went out and brought up the horses which were sent for, and young Lowe, who was acquainted with the Stringfield family, went out and asked them to come into the house for breakfast. They said no, they had some, and would go on. At this time the old man had the oxen hitched to the wagon and was about starting. Marcellus went back into the house, and in a minute or so the Mexican remudada ran into the yard on a pony, exclaiming, "Indios! Indios!" At this time rapid shots were heard east, in the direction taken by Stringfield. He had crossed the little creek and was on the rising ground beyond about 200 yards, when young Lowe ran to the door to look. The sun was just rising and the wagon was in plain view, surrounded by a large band of mounted Indians, who were shooting towards the wagon with guns and arrows. Mr. Stringfield could be seen fighting them and trying to defend his family, who were all getting out of the wagon and screaming. One of the little boys was riding a horse and attempted to escape on him, but two mounted Indians ran around him, one on each side, and one of them lifted the boy from his horse and placed him behind on the animal he was riding. The little fellow tried hard to pull loose from the painted savage, but was unable to do so. Young Lowe could plainly hear the screams of Mrs. Stringfield, and also calling on him for help, saying, "Oh, for God's sake, Marcellus, come and help us." This was repeated several times, but the boy was totally unarmed, and it would only have amounted to the useless sacrifice of his own life to have responded to the appeal. Judge Lowe says he will never forget this heartrending appeal to him for help in this fearful ordeal, and the tone of the poor woman's voice as it floated out on the early morning breeze has never been erased from his mind. After all was over at the wagon the Indians faced towards the house, as if to make an attack upon it. The old Mexican at once commenced strategy. He had in the house, besides himself and wife, young Lowe, and the negro boy and another Mexican. One Mexican had run away from the place and hid himself in the Nueces River near by, only keeping his head out of the water. He carried a six-shooter with him, and this only left one revolver at the ranch, and was all the firearms at hand. The old remudada, however, determined to make a display of strength. He put a crowbar in the hands of Lowe, gave an old saber to the negro boy, a stick to the Mexican, and himself took the revolver, and marching his crowd out in plain view of the Indians, waved it and dared them to the combat. The rays of the rising sun glinted on the crowbar and saber, and gave the impression that all were armed with firearms. The Indians, however, divided into two parties and approached the house. The old Mexican retired with his force inside again before they arrived near enough to discover his deception, and barred the door. He then, when they came in hearing of his voice, began to give orders in a loud voice in the Spanish language, so the Indians could understand him: "You stand here and shoot, and you there; one stand there and fire; you stand at the door and shoot," etc. The Indians understood, halted, consulted a short time, and then retired, dreading the fire from a foe under cover. They rounded up the eighty head of horses and went away with them.

About this time Lowe heard a little girl crying at the gate, and went to her. It was one of Stringfield's, and she had managed to make her escape to the house, although lanced in several places. Her first thought was about her father and mother, and she asked young Lowe to go back with her to them, as they were killed by the Indians. She was taken into the house and her wounds dressed by the Mexican woman. When there were no longer any Indians in sight, Lowe and others went to the wagon. Stringfield was dead, lying full length, shot both with arrows and bullets. His wife was also dead, killed with arrows. They had left the wagon in a vain endeavor to get to the ravine which ran near the house, but were killed in the mesquites, eighty yards from the wagon. The man was lying with his head west and feet east; the wife with head north and feet south. Her head was close to the middle of the husband's body, the two making a **T**. The two boys were carried off. The bodies of the unfortunate slain were buried where found. The little girl said the Indians broke her father's arm at the first fire, and that he could not shoot good. No doubt his shots were ineffectual.

These same Indians had first made a raid on Moses at Alligator Lake and got all of his horses except two. At noon he arrived at the scene of the tragedy and found all of his horses in a bend of the river, where they had escaped while the Indians were engaged in the battle with Stringfield. The elder Lowe and others followed the Indians, but could not overtake them, but found a small skeleton on the trail, which was supposed to be that of the youngest Stringfield boy. The little girl recovered.

Judge Lowe now lives at Pearsall, county seat of Frio County, and is district judge of the Thirty-sixth Judicial District. He was educated at Bingham's College, in North Carolina, and after returning to Texas was a member of the Nineteenth Legislature. He is very popular, and has many friends in the Southwest.

CAPTAIN ALONZO REESE.

Came to Texas in 1852.

Captain Reese was born in McNairy County, Tennessee, on the 6th day of September, 1837, and came to Texas in January, 1852. His father died in 1842, and he came to Texas with his mother and two older brothers, Sidney and Adolphus. They first settled in De Witt County, on the Guadalupe River, near Clinton. Not having good health in the lower country, the Reese family concluded to move further west in the mountain country. Accordingly Sidney and Adolphus came out and explored the Medina Valley, and liking the country bought land on Bandera Creek, not far from the present town of the same name, and now county seat of Bandera County. They returned home, and the family came out to the new home in 1854. There were but few settlers then where Bandera is now. Among these were P. D. Saner, R. H. and De Witt Burney, — Milstead, — Odum, and Malcolm Gillis. Charles De Montel had a sawmill where Bandera is now, and had quite a lot of hands with him making shingles from the cypress timber which was at that time abundant and of fine quality.

There was one settler on the Helotes, eighteen miles from San Antonio, named Forrester. The Lipan Indians pretended to be friendly, and one day a band of them came to the house of Forrester and came inside of the dwelling. The settler apprehended no danger from them, and when they took notice of his rifle in the rack and wanted to look at it, he handed it to them. No sooner had the treacherous rascals became possessed of the gun than they turned it upon Forrester and shot him dead on the floor. A general massacre of the family then commenced, and only Mrs. Forrester escaped and made her way to San Antonio with the news. The Indians after leaving the place came up the Medina valley and passed out near where the Reese family lived. At this time the Fourth United States cavalry was stationed at San Antonio, and at once came out to the scene of the tragedy and took the trail of the Indians. The Reeses saw the soldiers as they passed by on the trail. This was their first alarm of Indians. Being new comers, they knew nothing about Indian depredations, and were resting in fancied security. The Indians passed out two and a half miles north of Montel's mill.

At this time there lived in the Guadalupe valley, eighteen miles north, near where Center Point now is, Mr. Rufus Brown, an old Texan and brother to John Henry Brown, the historian. A short time after this Lipan raid Mr. Brown came over to the Reese place and warned them of the danger they were in at their present location, and advised them to move over into the Guadalupe valley, near him. This advice was at once acted upon, and the change made. At this time the Reese boys were all young and unmarried. The Burneys also came over, and all grouped together at Brown's ranch for protection.

Soon after this a lot of Mormons came into the country, under the leadership of O. L. Wight. They were originally from Missouri, but before coming here had stayed awhile on the Pedernales River, southeast from Fredericksburg, in Gillespie County. When they came into the Guadalupe valley they stopped on Verde Creek and put up a sawmill for Dr. J. C. Ridley for the purpose of sawing up the cypress timber there. This mill was in about seventy-five yards of the present residence of W. E. Pafford. A settler named George Nichols put up the Pafford house. After the mill was finished the Mormons left and settled at Bandera, but soon moved from there and stopped at a place that still goes by the name of "Mormon Camp," below Bandera.

The Indians made raids on the settlers every light moon, and they were always expected at that time.

About 1855 Governor Pease authorized the raising of minute companies for frontier protection. These companies were to be raised among the settlers themselves and officered by some of their own number. They were to draw pay for the time they were in actual service, scouting or pursuing Indians. In 1855, at the instigation of some of the settlers, for better protection in the Guadalupe valley, a company of infantry was sent out and went into camp on the spot where Camp Verde now is. Seeing the inefficiency of such a force on the frontier, they were recalled in 1856, and Captain Palmer was sent out with a company of cavalry. He built Camp Verde, and it became a permanent station.

The Indians continued to raid on the settlers, and such was

their atrocious deeds of murder, robbery, and carrying off white people—men, women, and children—into captivity, that only the most daring pioneers remained in the country.

In 1861 the State government of Texas authorized the raising of a regiment of men for frontier protection, to be stationed at intervals on the outskirts of the settlements from the Rio Grande to Red River. Scouts were to be kept out all the time and range back and forth between stations, so as to detect any trail of Indians coming out or going into the settlements. This was a good plan, and resulted well. This was kept up until 1862, and then this force was turned over to the Confederate government, but by a reorganization, in which most of the old rangers re-enlisted, was retained on the frontier until 1864.

Mr. Alonzo Reese belonged to one of these companies, commanded by Capt. James M. Hunter, and was lieutenant of the company. On one occasion Captain Hunter sent Lieutenant Reese with ten men on an extensive scout. On James River, a tributary of the Llano, an Indian trail was found and closely followed to the head of the Pedernales River. Here they came upon the Indians, eleven in number, all on foot except two, and they were badly mounted on poor, shabby ponies. Among the men present besides the lieutenant was his brother, Adolphus Reese, J. W. Benson, Jake Banta, and McCann. The Indians, seeing they could not very well make their escape from a mounted force, halted and prepared for a fight. When the charge was made by the rangers, some of the Indians fired at them with revolvers and others with arrows. When the rangers commenced firing, some of the guns failed on account of a damp day and a very poor quality of Confederate powder. After firing a few rounds, however, the Indians turned and ran as the rangers came up close to them. In this fusilade they killed the horse ridden by Adolphus Reese. The rangers kept after the Indians, occasionally some one firing, and others making ineffectual attempts. Lieutenant Reese, coming near an Indian who was running and throwing his shield back and forth around his back and shoulders to ward off bullets, called to Jake Banta close by, who had a good gun and good powder, if he could not kill the Indian. Banta dismounted, so that his aim would be better, and brought him to the ground. Other Indians turned back to the fallen one and stood him on his feet, but as he was not able to go they let him loose again. He fell to the ground again, but as he did so he drew a knife and stabbed himself to the heart. The Indians scattered widely and the rangers scattered after them. Lieutenant Reese had a shotgun, and coming in range of one fired and brought him down. The Indian lay stunned for a few moments, but then began to get up and Reese's gun was empty. At this time Adolphus Reese came up with a loaded gun, and his brother said, "Look out, Dolf, that Indian will shoot you," as his brother started to go up to the Indian, who at this time was resting on his knees. Adolphus, thus warned, stopped, and aiming his rifle shot the Indian through the head and finished him. The Indians, by scattering and taking advantage of the ravines and thickets and the bad condition of the rangers' guns and ammunition, had only one more killed, but several wounded. The dead Indians were scalped and their shields, bows, and other things taken. Of the rangers, J. W. Benson was wounded in the thigh with an arrow, and McCann in the thumb. This terminated the scout and the rangers went back to camp. Lieutenant Reese was afterwards captain of the company, Captain Hunter being promoted to major.

All three of the Reese brother still live in the Guadalupe valley, have large families, and have prospered in stockraising and farming.

BATTLE BETWEEN RANGERS AND INDIANS.

1875.

In the latter part of the summer of the above named year Capt. Rufus Perry was in command of a company of rangers and stationed on the San Saba River. At times, however, when the grass became short in the vicinity of camp, a move was made to better range. On the occasion of which we write the San Saba camp had been abandoned and a new one established in Menard County. One morning while here Scott Cooly and another ranger went out to kill a beef for the use of the company, and while searching for one discovered a band of Indians going west. The camp of the rangers was in the opposite direction, and several miles distant. The two men, seeing the Indians were not disposed to run them, conceived the idea of trying to entice them in the direction of camp by charging towards them, firing their Winchesters, and then turning and running away as if afraid of them. The Indians failed to fall into this trap, and continued on their course. Cooly now told his companion to return to camp and inform Captain Perry of the situation, and he would follow the Indians and keep them in sight until a force could arrive sufficient to fight them. The country was broken, rolling prairie, and the Indians were easily kept in view. At this time Major Jones, who was in command of all the rangers on the frontier, was in the camp of Captain Perry with an escort of thirty-five men, making his tour of inspection and paying off the rangers. When the news of the Indians was brought to camp Major Jones and his men had their horses saddled and were about to take their departure, but mounted instead and set off to find the trail of the Indians. Perry's men followed as soon as they could get ready, under the command of Lieutenant Roberts. Captain Perry remained in camp. The combined force when all got together on the trail was sixty men, which greatly outnumbered the Indians. The latter, knowing they would be pursued, by the absence of one ranger and the other following, traveled fast. Twenty miles were thus passed over before they were sighted by the pursuers. By this time all of the horses except eight had given out or dropped so far behind they could not be seen by those in front. Those in front were all Perry's men, except one citizen of Menard County. None of the escort or any of the balance of Perry's men were in sight. Here at the end of this twenty-mile run the rangers first came up with their comrade, Cooly. He had never lost sight of the Indians during all of this time. Now, with him added, their force was nine and the Indians eleven. Among the rangers present were Lieutenant Roberts, Scott Cooly, Thurlow Weed, Charles Bartholomae, and the citizen. The balance of the names can not now be remembered. A charge was now made, and a run of two miles more brought them close to the retreating Comanches, who, seeing the diminished force and their own horses failing fast, halted, faced about, and prepared for battle. The rangers made no halt, but came up close and commenced firing with Winchesters, the lieutenant shouting, "Give it to them, boys." The Comanche chief charged the lieutenant and commenced, firing at him with a Spencer carbine, and wounded his horse in the shoulder. Roberts also commenced shooting and killed the chief. The Indians had six-shooters, besides bows and a few guns. Their fire, however, was quick and ineffectual. Another Indian fell dead near the chief under the fire of the rangers, and the balance wheeled their horses and once more sought refuge in flight, firing back at the rangers with revolvers. One of the rangers was wounded in the breast during this fusilade with a pistol, and several saddles were hit. One by one the Indians fell on the prairie, and four horses were killed in the long chase. One Indian, when his horse fell dead under him, came back among the rangers making signs of surrender, and was captured. Only three Indians were now left, and they abandoned their played-out horses and continued their efforts to escape on foot. By this time the rangers were again scattered, and only four were around the captured Indian. One of these was left with the Comanche to keep other rangers who were following from killing him when they came up. During the short halt with the captive Indian, the three now on foot were making good time across the prairie, running faster than tired horses. The three rangers, however, spurred up their jaded steeds and again pursued them. Among these three rangers were Charley Bartholomae and Scott Cooly. Bartholomae was on a splendid horse and had fired many times, being always well up in front. Three miles were covered, and again the rangers were nearing the fleeing Indians, who, seeing their case was hopeless, stopped in some rocks and bushes and prepared again to give battle. When the rangers arrived they circled around the place and commenced to look for them. One was discovered and killed by a ranger the first fire. Another ranger rode so close to one he sprang from behind a rock at him, yelling loudly, and attempted to adjust an arrow to his bowstring, but his hand shook so from nervous excitement that he was unable to do it. The ranger fired quickly, but missed the Indian. Charley Bartholomae fired three shots at him in quick succession with his pistol, having exhausted his Winchester ammunition, but also failed to bring him down. The other ranger now fired with a Winchester and killed him. The third Indian could not be found. It was evident he had left the place before the rangers arrived and lay down somewhere in the tall grass on the prairie, and could not be seen. The long return trip was now made on very tired horses. The trailing and long running fight was twenty-nine miles. Ten of the eleven Indians were killed or captured —nine dead on the ground. Most of them were scalped. Scott Cooly took a strip out of one's back for the purpose of trying to make a quirt or something out of it, but when he hung it on a bush in the sun at camp it nearly all went to grease and dripped away. During the fight, as fast as the Indians would empty their revolvers, they would throw them away, and several of these were picked up. The captured Indian was taken to Austin by a squad of rangers, and when they saw the crowds of people come to look at him they conceived the idea of turning it to profit. They carried the Comanche to the operahouse, and there charged 25 cents admission fee for people to look at him. For one day they did a thriving business, but the adjutant-general heard of it, put a stop to the show, and took the Indian away from the rangers and had him sent down to the penitentiary, where he finally died.

Charley Bartholomae was born in Guadalupe County, but now resides in San Antonio.

FROM A PHOTO TAKEN AT REAL'S RANCH, KERR COUNTY.

DISASTROUS BATTLE WITH INDIANS IN KERR COUNTY.

1857.

In 1857 the Comanche Indians made a raid into Kerr County in the vicinity of Kerrville, and then went back up the Guadalupe River valley. A party of seven young men mounted their horses and set out in pursuit of them. Their names were as follows: William Kelso, Spence Goss, Jack Herridge, Tom Wherry, Dan Murff, Tom McAdams, and Newt. Price. All but Kelso were inexperienced in Indian warfare. He had been a ranger and should have been more cautious, and the terrible disaster which followed might have been averted. They trailed the Indians to a point twenty-five miles above Kerrville, and then stopped to cut a bee tree. At this time the Indians were on a bluff near the river, and watched the white men until they left the place where the honey was found and went into camp. This was as-certained afterwards by finding the place where the Indians had congregated on the bluff, and then following the trail to the spot where the unfortunate young men had made their camp for the night. Their camp was in a thicket, and their horses were staked in the open glades around. The night was cold and a bright fire was kept burning for some time, plainly indicating to the Indians the exact location of the camp. The guns of the party were stacked around a tree several yards from the fire. About daybreak Tom Wherry and Dan Murff arose and rekindled the fire, and then taking their guns went out to hunt a deer The balance of the men also got up and stood or sat around the fire. At this time the Indians had crept close upon them, and before the white men were aware of their presence had secured their guns and made the attack upon them. Some of the men had revolvers, and these defended themselves as best they could. Kelso shot an Indian down, and he fell near the fire. The In-dians made such a furious onslaught, and the settlers were so badly shot up at once, that they soon scattered into the brush, each man trying to save himself. When Murff and Wherry heard the firing at camp, and knowing its significance ran back to help their comrades, Murff ran almost among the Indians, and stopping in an open place discharged his gun at them. Almost at the same instant he received a ball in the breast and fell dead on the spot. This shot was from some of the settlers' own guns. Wherry was shot in the breast with an arrow, and after firing his gun escaped into the brush. Spence Goss was sitting down by the fire with his feet drawn up close to his body, facing towards them, and an Indian fired at him with a short Mexican gun called a scopet, carrying a large ball and three buckshot. The charge struck him in the right leg below the knee, broke the bone, and went on out through the thigh. With a powerful effort he dragged himself away into a thicket and lay down. Kelso was shot crosswise through the small of the back with an arrow, but jerked it out, and shooting an Indian down he made his escape into the brush. Tom McAdams was shot in the neck through the windpipe with an arrow, but managed to get away. Newt. Price was standing with his back to the Indians, and was hit in the shoulders with a load of buckshot from one of their own guns. He also made his escape into a thicket. Jack Herridge was sitting by the fire with his shoes off, warming his feet, and only having a small, single-barreled pistol called a derringer, sprang away in flight without being hit. He was the first man to reach the settlement, but his feet were so bruised and lacerated by rocks that before they healed the bottom of his feet came off. The Indians got all of the horses except those of Murff and Wherry. When they started on the deer hunt they turned their horses loose to graze until they got back. They took fright during the battle, ran away, and made their way back to Kerrville. Some time after the fight, when the Indians were gone, Kelso, Wherry, and McAdams got together and started for home on foot, but they made but slow progress. Kelso could scarcely walk, and McAdams was constantly sick and vomiting, caused from swallowing blood from the wound in his neck. Wherry was also badly wounded; the arrow made such a deep wound in his breast, that as he breathed the air would escape through the aperture with a whistling noise. They were several days getting to Kerrville. Goss and Price both escaped into the same thicket, but were not aware of each other's presence. Both were weak from loss of blood and fainted, or, as they expressed it, went to sleep and lay there for several hours. When Goss came to himself again he called for his companions, and was answered by Price near by. These two now got together and went about a mile, Goss dragging one leg after him. Here they found a small cave and spent the night in it. Next morning Price proposed, as he was able to walk, to try and make his way to the settlement and send relief to Goss. He started, but never reached there. He died ten miles from where he had left his companion. In the meantime searching parties were out hunting for Goss and Price, not expecting to find either alive. Goss remained at his cave eighteen days, vainly hoping as each sun ran its course and went down in the west, that before another setting sun help would come. Of course he knew not that his unfortunate companion lay dead ten miles away, where he had sank exhausted to rise no more. No one else knew where he was, and the searching parties had gone round and round his position. During the day he would crawl around in the dense thickets and eat grapes and haws and lie in the cave at night. A small spring branch near by furnished him with water. He had his pistol, but would not shoot anything for fear of attracting a band of Indians. After remaining in this condition for the length of time mentioned above, Goss gave up all hopes of any one coming to him and started towards the settlement, using a forked stick to aid him in getting alone. After traveling several days in this way he was found one day sitting down leaning against a tree by Judge Patton, who was out on a bear hunt. Patton helped him to get to the camp of a man named Miller, eight miles above Kerrville. In the meantime a party of searchers had found the trail of Goss, and could easily follow it by the holes he made in the ground with his stick. They found him at Miller's camp, and from thence conveyed him to the house of his brother-in-law, Joshua D. Brown. Mr. Brown was the founder of Kerrville, which was named after James Kerr, relative of the Browns. Murff was buried where he fell, in a shallow grave, but well covered up with rocks. Shortly after, however, a runaway negro came along, disinterred the remains, stripped the body, and appropriated the clothing to his own use. The negro then placed the body back, but wolves dragged it out again. Hunters found it and brought the skeleton to Kerrville and buried it in the cemetery there. Hunters also found the skeleton or bones of Price two years after, and his boots, with bones in them, were brought

to town.   Also a daybook and 25 cents in money in a purse, and
from these the remains were identified.

When Kelso drew the arrow from his wound during the fight
and threw it down he failed to notice in the excitement of the
time that the spike failed to come with the shaft.   For twenty
years the wound would not heal, until by a surgical operation
the iron arrow head was discovered and removed, and the wound
then healed.

Mr. Daniel Adolphus Reese, who gave the writer the particulars of this most sad frontier episode, was living near Kerrville
at the time, and helped to search for Goss and Price.   He came
to Texas in 1852 from the western district of Tennessee.   He
first settled in Dimmit County, and came to Bandera in 1854,
and he built the first house there out of poles to put corn in.
People had no houses at first, but lived in camps.   He moved
from there into the Guadalupe valley.   In 1856 Kerr County or-
ganished, and Mr. Reese was elected county clerk and helped to
lay off the town of Kerrville, which was the county seat.   In 1863
he belonged to a ranging company commanded by Captain Hunter, and was in an Indian fight on the head of the Pedernales
River, in which three Indians were killed, some of the rangers
were wounded, and Mr. Reese had his horse killed.   His brother,
Alonzo Reese, was in command of the scout.   Adolphus was
commissary and quartermaster sergeant, and only came on this
scout for recreation.   His proper place was in camp.

Mr. Reese also gives the following Kerr County history:

In 1859 there lived, five miles above Kerrville, a settler named
Roland Nichols.   One evening he went out about a mile from
home to kill a turkey.   When he failed to come back at night
the family became alarmed and neighbors were notified.   Mr.
Reese responded, but nothing could be done until morning.   In
company with others the trail of Mr. Nichols was then followed
up a draw to a point about a mile from the house.   Here it
turned abruptly in another direction, and the plain trail of numerous Indian tracks on both sides of it told the tale of the
missing man.   Nearly a mile from here his body was found beside a tree.   He had halted here and got the tree between him
and the Indians, and the tracks showed he had circled around it
repeatedly while they were trying to kill him.   The bark was
raked from the tree all around where he had held to it with both

hands in a vain endeavor to keep the trunk between him and his foes. He had one arrow in the breast, and one arrow and one bullet wound in the body. The bullet and arrow had first struck the left arm about half way between the elbow and shoulder, and then penetrated the body not more than a half inch apart. Going back to the spot where the Indian sign was first discovered, it was evident that here was where the unfortunate settler received the arrow in the breast from ambush. The prints of his knees were in the sandy soil where he had come down either to fire his rifle or from the shock of the wound. If from the latter, he dropped his gun without firing, but recovered and ran to the spot where his body was found. His gun was discovered after a search, covered up in the sand, where the Indians had left it, and it was still loaded.

In 1860 Mr. Samuel Lane lived two miles above Comfort, on the Guadalupe River. In the fall of that year he started on horseback up the river to visit a man named John Conner, who lived near where Center Point is now, above the mill on the north side of the river. The property is now owned by some of the Moore family. Mr. Lane was not armed, and was riding along eating pecans when the Indians rushed upon him from a thicket near the road and shot one arrow into his breast. He now left the road and ran his horse towards a pecan mott several hundred yards away. Before reaching this place the Indians shot several arrows into his back, and forced him from his horse and dispatched him. When he failed to come home on the next day the family became uneasy and sent a runner up to Conner's to see if he was there. Finding no trace of him, the messenger went on to Kerrville and made known the facts there. District court was in session, with Judge Stribbling on the bench, but court was adjourned, and judge, jury, and lawyers went to search for the missing man. Mr. Adolph Reese was one of the searching party, and says they did not find him until the following day, making the third since he was killed. In one hand he had a turkey wing gripped, which he was carrying to Mrs. Conner. In the other hand were pieces of the pecans and hulls, and pecan kernels between his teeth. Mr. Reese and his brother-in-law, Judge Starkey, Foster Cocke, De Witt Burney, and several others took the trail of the Indians, which led a west course through the mountains over a very rough country. They came to one place where the Indians had camped, killed a cow, and eaten her. While riding around in the camp Judge Starkey let his gun go off accidentally, and killed Foster Cocke's horse. Further on the Indians went down such a steep, rocky mountain, they had lanced their horses to make them go down, as was evident from the amount of blood along the way. The white men could not get their horses to go down, so had to leave them with a guard and continue the pursuit on foot. In Hondo Canyon they found the dead body of a Frenchman whom the Indians had killed. The pursuit was kept up to Sabinal Canyon and then abandoned. They would have caught the Indians at the place where they went down the steep bluff if night had not been at hand. The blood from the horses was fresh, not having as yet congealed on the rocks. No doubt they saw the trailers coming, and this was why they forced their horses down such an unreasonable place. Here, however, they entered a cedarbrake, and dark coming on, all trailing had to cease until the morning, and this gave the Indians a long start again.

ROSS KENNEDY.

Mr. Ross Kennedy was born in Monaghan County, Ireland, December 12, 1827, and set sail from Belfast for America when a young man, and arrived at New York about 1850. He came over on the ship Rainbow, commanded by a Yankee captain named Hope. The time consumed in the voyage was twenty-one days and was uneventful, except one fire aboard ship, which originated between decks, but did no material damage. Young Kennedy displayed a decided inclination for the sea and life of a sailor, which attracted the notice of Captain Hope, and he volunteered the advice to the young man that he had better put such notions out of his head; that sailors had a hard life, and that dogs on his place at home were treated better than they.

From New York Mr. Kennedy drifted to Texas and brought up on the Rio Grande, coming up the gulf on the ship John Stroud. Near Powder Horn she was thrown on her beam ends in a squall, but was soon righted without damage. In 1851 he went to Eagle Pass and obtained work from the government, going to Fort Clark and helping to build the garrison there. From Fort Clark he went to Powder Horn and acted as receiving clerk there for the government, and then in the capacity of wagon master of a government train, and finally was put in charge of the United States sutler store on the Pecos. From there he came back to Fort Clark and again served as wagon master, seeing many Indians on these trips, but was not attacked by them. At this time there was a treaty made between Mexico and Texas, by which the latter was to keep Texas Indians out of Mexico, and one one occasion Mr. Kennedy was placed in charge of a band who had passes but had overstepped their bounds, and were being carried back to where they had obtained their passes. On the route a terrible storm was encountered one night, and all of the Indians made their escape. During these years Mr. Kennedy also rode a pony express from Fort Inge to Eagle Pass. On one trip he fell in with Capt. Henry E. McCulloch and a small squad of his rangers and rode some distance with them. During the time a large buck sprang up near the road and went off at a rapid run. One of the rangers wheeled his horse around, and raising his rifle quickly fired and brought the deer down dead in his tracks. It was such a good, shot it was remarked about, and McCulloch asked the ranger if he was in the habit of doing that. He had belonged to another company and only recently joined that of McCulloch, and in reply told him to ask his former captain.

While on this line Mr. Kennedy also had charge of a line up to Fort Clark, and put a man to ride that named Henderson, who on one occasion dismounted at noon, pulled off his saddle so that his horse could cool off and rest, and was about to proceed to make a cup of coffee for himself, when he discovered a band of Indians swooping down on him from the prairie. Hastily throwing his saddle back onto his horse, he vaulted into it from the ground without fastening the girth, and in that manner ran a desperate race with the Indians, the girth popping the horse underneath, which rather aided in accelerating his movements, and arrived safely at the fort.

In after years when Mr. Kennedy was leading parties after Indians, and men slow in saddling and mounting, he would say "Boys, you can't saddle and mount a horse as quick as Henderson."

In 1856 Mr. Kennedy moved to Uvalde County and settled where he is now living, six miles east of Sabinal station, on a tributary of the Sabinal River called Ranchero Creek, but sometimes called Comanche Creek by the old settlers. At this time the Indians were not troublesome to a great extent, and the settlers considered themselves as in no danger of their lives. The first man killed after Mr. Kennedy moved into the country was Louis Thompson, in Frio Canyon. He was a young man lately from Alabama, and had been married but a short time. He had started to Uvalde with a wagon, but stopped on the way to gather pecans, when a band of Indians came upon him, cut him off from the wagon where his gun was, and killed and scalped him. This band of Indians before this killed a man named White in Hondo Canyon, near where the main wagon road is now, thirty-five miles west of San Antonio. He was riding a wild horse when the Indians came upon him, and fell an easy prey and was soon killed and scalped. We stated above that Thompson was killed first, but if the same band of Indians did both murders White was the first victim, as the Indians were going west when they killed Thompson, and the Hondo is east of the Frio.

In 1859, the day before John Davenport was killed by Indians, Mr. Kennedy was out with his wagon after a load of wood, and his brother-in-law, Mr. Ebenezer Rankin, was out on horseback hunting for a bunch of horses which he wished to drive to the ranch of Mr. Kennedy, where he was staying at the time. Before the latter finished loading the wagon Mr. Rankin dashed up excitedly and said, "Did you see those fellows running me?" Mr. Kennedy said "No. Who were they?" "Indians, I think," said Mr. Rankin. The two men now awaited developments a few minutes, but as no one put in an appearance Kennedy finished loading his wood and went home, while Rankin went on, finding the horses, and drove them in.

This band of Indians was evidently the same or part of those who made themselves felt so sadly in the settlement on the following day, which was October 28th, the date of the killing of John Bowles and John Davenport. On this day Mr. Kennedy went to a store on the east bank of Sabinal River, where was also a stage stand on the main road from San Antonio to the Rio Grande country. The Southern Pacific Railroad crosses there now, and the store stood about where the section house now is, one mile west of the present Sabinal station. When Mr. Kennedy left the store to return home Mr. John Davenport was coming down the hill into the channel of the river on the west side. He stopped a short time at the store and then kept on the road towards his home, which was also on Ranchero Creek above Mr. Kennedy's place. The latter was riding a young horse that he was breaking, and the animal showed signs of uneasiness at one place near some thickets. Mr. Kennedy also saw buzzards at this place, and was inclined once to ride by the place to see if anything was dead there, but changed his notion and went on home. If he had done so, riding as he was a young, awkward horse, he would no doubt have been the victim instead of Mr. Davenport, for it was from here that the band of Indians made their onset upon Mr. Davenport when he came along on a slow, stubborn mule. The Indians had meat or something that attracted the buzzards. One reason, it is supposed, why they failed to come out and give Mr. Kennedy a chase was the fact that he was mounted on a horse, and they feared he would escape

and give the alarm of their presence in the settlement. They
had already killed John Bowles, and his mutilated remains were
at this time lying in the prickly pears and chaparral six miles
to the south, near Pilot Knob. When Mr. Kennedy arrived at
home he went on without dismounting and caught another horse
near by, which he saddled and mounted and came on back to
the house, turning the young horse loose where he made the remount. By the time he arrived back at the house again Mr.
Louis Lee was there with the news that Mr. John Davenport had
been killed and scalped by the Indians.

Mr. Lee lived with the Davenports and did blacksmith work for
them. Mr. Kennedy now went in a gallop to Mr. Davenport's
ranch, but when he arrived there his brother John and others
had repaired to the scene of the killing, which was not more than
one mile and a half from where Mr. Kennedy last saw Mr.
Davenport riding down the hill at the river. A man named
Rooney came along with a train and saw the dead body, and came
on to the Davenport ranch, which was near the road, and he or
one of his Mexican drivers reported the fact to Mrs. Davenport,
who was not aware of who it was, but at once had grave fears
that it was her husband, and Mr. Lee at once set out to investigate and soon discovered the sad fact. Mr. Kennedy remained
at the ranch until his brother John and others brought in the
body, and he helped to wash and dress it. It was nude and very
bloody. John Kennedy went with the party that followed the
Indians and fought a battle with them on the edge of the plains,
in which Lieutenant Hazen and others were badly wounded, and
he and Judge McCormick went to Fort Clark, a distance of
eighty miles, to procure surgical aid for the lieutenant.

In the meantime the alarm had been raised in regard to John
Bowles. It was certain he had been killed by Indians, but his
body could not be found. Mr. Ross Kennedy helped the searchers seven days, but the body was not found for three weeks.
Pete Bowles, son of the slain man, continued to hunt, and one
day while standing on Pilot Knob saw a buzzard light down about
half a mile to the south, and repairing to the spot, there found
the remains of his father, reduced to a skeleton. He had been
out hunting his horse about one mile east from the Patterson
settlement, from which place he started, and was ambushed and

killed near some prickly pears and chaparral bushes. A stone now marks the spot.

In 1860 the Indians made another raid and killed old man Schreiver near D'Hanis, and then come on up to the ranch of Mr. Kennedy early in the morning. At this time a young Mexican about 18 years of age, who was in the employ of Mr. Kennedy, was out about 500 yards from the house in a southwest course hunting horses, and was attacked by the Indians and shot with an arrow. He ran and fell within 300 yards of the house. Mr. Kennedy was in the cowpen, and heard the Indians yelling. It was a still morning, and he said he never heard Indians make as much noise as that bunch did. Stock was stampeding all over the flat, bells rattling, and the Indians all yelling. Mr. Rankin was also out hunting horses. The Indians first tried to cut him off from the ranch, and it was then they ran upon the young Mexican. Mr. Kennedy ran from the cowpen and secured his gun, and by that time Mr. Rankin had arrived. The former expressed his belief that the Indians were killing his Mexican and he would go to his assistance, but Mr. Rankin told him it was no use, as he watched him run until he fell, and was satisfied he was already dead. Mr. Kennedy, however, went on, and Mr. Rankin went with him. The Mexican was found on his face, dead, and with the arrow in his hand which he had pulled out as he ran. The body was carried to the house, and Mr. Kennedy and Mr. Rankin at once began to alarm the settlers and organized a pursuit of the Indians.

Now comes in an incident showing the courage and endurance of some of the woman of the southwest frontier. Mrs. Kennedy was left alone at the ranch with the dead Mexican at her own request, urging her husband to leave her and follow the Indians until he caught and chastised them. Among those who gathered and took up the trail of the hostiles were Doc (Louis) Lee, Jack Davenport, L. C. (Clabe) Davenport, Emory Givins, Ross Kennedy, John Kennedy, and Ambrose Crane. On the west side of the Sabinal River this party were joined by William Knox, a man named Glass, and another man whose name is not now remembered, and all kept on in the pursuit of the Indians, but in about six miles the trail became badly scattered and was hard to locate satisfactorily. This was caused from the fact that here the Indians had come upon Huffman and Wolf, two cow-hunters, and a running, scattered fight had taken place for a mile or more across the prairie east towards the river, and finally the bodies of the slain men were found, as was also one dead Indian and his horse standing near, and the shirt which had been taken from the back of the slain Mexican at Kennedy's ranch. The trail was plain from here and was followed rapidly, Ross Kennedy being elected captain and directing the pursuit, and Ambrose Crane was trailer. Twenty miles further on, at the mouth of Blanco Canyon, Crane stopped and pointed to the Indians' horses in a glade between a cedar brake and ravine, and Kennedy motioned for his men to dismount and tie their horses, intending to slip around the Indians and cut them off from the cedar brake. Knox objected to this, and the men who came with him decided with him that it was best to charge at once on horseback, although it was not right for him to hold out against the majority, who had already dismounted and tied their horses at a signal from their rightful captain, Ross Kennedy. Rather than not have a concert of action, however, Kennedy and his men mounted and the charge was made, but a failure to do any good except to capture the horses of the Indians was the consequence. The Indians saw them coming and at once disappeared into the brakes, and none were killed. Quite a lot of horses, bows, shields, and arrows were taken. The Indians were cooking a yearling which they had killed. Huffman's mule, with his pistol on the pommel of the saddle, was taken, but Wolf's horse was not seen. The recaptured horses were driven back that night, and Mrs. Kennedy relieved of her lonely vigil with the slain Mexican. Next day a party went back and buried the bodies of Huffman and Wolf.

In 1861, while the brother-in-law of Captain Richarz was herding sheep three miles from D'Hanis, on the Seco, he was attacked and killed by Indians. The trail was taken up by men from below, and they came by the ranch of Mr. Kennedy and got him, Henry Adams, and others to help in the chase. The Indians had killed Dave, the brother of Henry Adams, and he was ready to go on every scout after them. Capt. Joe Ney commanded this scout. The trail led northwest and passed the Tom Wall settlement on the Frio, and then led up East prong towards the divide. At camping time the trailers were above the main springs in the dry draws, and the only chance for water was at some dripping bluffs, where it would take some time to catch enough for a man to drink, and the horses had no chance for any at all, thirsty as they were. There was just about enough water here for bees, and they were numerous, sucking at the banks. Mr. Kennedy was not satisfied to stay here, so he took a scout farther up and found a little pool with sufficient water for the men, but still not enough for horses. He reported this fact to Captain Ney, and it was agreed to move up to it. The horses were hobbled so they could graze some, but guards were placed to keep them out of the little pool of water through the night, but were to let them have what was left in the morning. There were twenty-five men in the party, and it required a good deal of water for them. During the night horses were heard plunging into water further up the draw, and an investigation disclosed the fact that it was the Frio waterhole, about one mile from where they first stopped at the dripping bluffs that evening. Mr. Kennedy had often been at the Frio waterhole, but had never approached it from that direction and was not familiar with the draw below the pool, which was almost out on the divide, and the last water in that direction for many miles. Daylight disclosed the fact that the Indians had stopped here, cooked meat, and roasted soto heads. The trail now went out onto the divide and led towards the West prong of the Llano. Near the head of this stream they came in sight of the Indians and a general charge was made, but this was abruptly stopped by running onto the bank of a creek which was full of drift and tree tops from overflows, and the horses could not cross it, although there was but little or no water in the channel. With some difficulty a crossing was found, but by this time the Indians had discovered them and made their escape. All of the horses were captured except what they rode off in their flight, and they took time to pick the best ones and got away fast. They could be seen running in the distance, and finally disappeared in a cedar brake. The men now came on back and made a dry camp for two hours. Mr. Kennedy's horse was crippled in the charge in trying to cross the jammed-up little creek, and he had to mount one of the horses captured from the Indians. The head of the crippled horse was tied up so that he could not eat, and when night came he was placed in front on the back track and true to his animal instinct

42

he was not at fault, and before day led the men back to the
Frio waterhole, where man and beast enjoyed its cool waters
after spending one day and nearly a night crossing the dry rocky
divide. The Indians were driving one heifer along which they
intended to eat, and the white men killed it for food, but the
meat was not good on account of the poor animal having been
lanced several times, and the flesh had become feverish from the
wounds. Nothing occurred of interest back to the settlement.
During the pursuit Mr. Kennedy often went on elevated places
to take a view, and finally Henry Adams commenced following
suit, and while on one hill motioned for Ross Kennedy to come
up there. He had found an old-time cart wheel of the Mexican
make, having mesquite hub, and all of a very heavy and clumsy
makeup of not more than three or four parts to the wheel. The
hub was buried in the ground, with the rim resting on the sur-
face. When and under what circumstances the old wheel was
left on this mountain of course no one present could tell, but it
was surmised it was abandoned here by some of the early Spanish explorers and prospectors who at various and sundry times
went all over the country long before the advent of the Anglo-
Saxon. The nature of mesquite is like that of cedar and will
hardly rot.

In 1858 the Indians carried off a large drove of horses belonging to Dr. Isbel, whose ranch was on Frio, at the foot of the
mountains. Men were collected to follow them, and Ross Kennedy, James Davenport, and Emory Givins went from their settlement and joined the other men further up the country. The
trail led through the mountains up the Blanco towards the divide. On a rock in the mountains the men found where the
Indians had made a picture of Dr. Isbel with paint. There were
a few soldiers along from Fort Inge, and after the divide was
reached one of these saw the Indians half a mile away. Mr.
Kennedy now changed rifles with John Leakey at his request,
as the latter had a sore or bruise, likely from falling in the rocks,
under his left arm, and his rifle being very heavy, he could not
hold it well; the other was lighter. When the Indians saw the
white men they changed horses quickly and tried to make their
escape, and also to draw the fire of our men at long range, which
they did. Their intention was to get to a large cedarbrake in
the distance, as the country around them was open, but they

finally stopped, as they saw the white men were well mounted and would run among them. They dismounted in some scattered burnt cedar and the fight commenced. After the first shot from the rifle which Mr. Kennedy carried he found himself in a difficulty. The ammunition for his gun would not fit Mr. Leakey's, and he was unable to reload. By this time the Indians were among the white men, and many close personal combats took place, in which two men were wounded and several horses, including the one ridden by Mr. Kennedy. John Leakey's horse was also wounded, and died from it some time after the fight. One arrow came near wounding Mr. Kennedy in the throat, just grazing the skin under the chin. He finally made his way to Leakey, who had a revolver and was fighting an Indian at close range, but took time to exchange guns again. Most of the men dismounted and took trees on the Indians. Mr. Kennedy got down beside a burnt forked cedar stump, and laying his gun in the fork watched an Indian who had a short gun and was behind a log, trying to get a bead on Mr. Kennedy. Finally he fired, and his ball knocked up so much gravel and with such force into Mr. Kennedy's face that it cut the blood out, and he had the appearance of being badly wounded. He then fired and killed the Indian. They finally retreated, leaving two dead on the ground and another in the chase, and others badly shot. Some of the loose horses were killed and others badly scattered, but most of them were gathered and driven back to the settlement. There were about thirty men in all, but Mr. Kennedy at this late day can only remember the following: Henry Robinson, captain; James Davenport, Emory Givins, John Leakey, John Daugherty (afterwards sheriff of Uvalde County), — Courtney, Lease, Barrow, Isbel, and Tom Wall. When the party arrived at the Isbel ranch, badly worn out and hungry, a bountiful meal was prepared for them, and while eating, the most of them were telling what part they took in the battle and of the Indians that they were certain had fallen by their hand. Mrs. Isbel was greatly interested in all this, and noticing that Mr. Kennedy was eating and saying nothing, turned to him and said, "Mr. Kennedy, didn't you kill any Indians?" "No, madam," he said; "from the number these other men have killed there were not enough to go round, and none left for me to kill."

On one occasion a raiding party of Indians was followed far

to the northwest, Mr. Kennedy in command. They passed around the heads of all the rivers, and finally the leader told the men they were losing ground; that the trail was actually getting old ahead of them. The men had to ride the same horses all of the time and camp at night, while the Indians were changing horses and traveling at night; so the expedition was declared off, and they turned back. They were also out of provisions, and all of the watered country had been passed. One man killed an antelope, and although it was old and tough it was eaten. Among the men were James Davenport, Clabe Davenport, Emory Givens, and others.

In 1861 the Indians made a big raid and went all over the country and far below the mountains. They killed a number of people and secured many horses. The settlers from below followed them under Big Foot Wallace, and Mr. Kennedy got the news, gathered a few men, and met the others between his ranch and D'Hanis, making twenty-five or thirty in all. The trail led up Big Seco, and was followed fast on account of the large drove of horses. The Indians left a spy behind, and he was discovered by Lewis McCombs and others on a mountain in the valley. The Indians had laid an ambush for the white men at the head of the canyon, and they stopped in the valley, rested their horses, and ate dinner in plain view of this ambuscade; but the Indians kept well concealed and watched them from the mountain side in the rocks and bushes. When the men again took up the trail and commenced the ascent of the mountains the advance was fired on and pushed back to the men below. The Indians used shotguns and pistols which had been taken from slain settlers, and all that saved the advance from annihilation was the fact that the Indians overshot them. Wm. Davenport was wounded, also several horses, and all went back to the foot of the mountain and made a stand. Captain Wallace told the men to lie down under a rock ledge and shoot as opportunity offered. The Indians could not see them without coming very close, and finally commenced detaching large rocks from the mountain side and rolling them down among the men. They came crashing through at a fearful rate, and some narrow escapes were made. One struck the breech of Big Foot Wallace's gun and came near breaking it. Mr. Kennedy soon tired of this kind of warfare, and called for volunteers of those who had long-range guns to

ascend the hill in their rear so they could see the Indians and
open fire on them. John Kennedy, Louis Oge, and John Vinton
responded. They all had Enfield or minie rifles, and as soon as
they arrived at a point where they could get a good view, opened
on the Comanches, who at once commenced retreating further
up the mountain, carrying their dead with them. They were
not aware the white men could reach them so far, and several fell
before they could get out of range. One was made to move at a
distance of five or six hundred yards; he was sitting on a mule
on top of a mountain watching the battle. As soon as the fight
was over the settlers went over into Sabinal Canyon and spent
the night, and next day went after the Indians again and got
ahead of them on the divide, but by the impatience of one man
who fired too soon, or let his gun go off accidentally, the ambush
which had been laid by Captain Wallace was discovered and the
Indians scattered, but a large number of horses were retaken
and carried back. Of the men along Mr. Kennedy can remember, besides the captain, Lewis McCombs, Louis Oge, John Kennedy, John Vinton, Judge Davenport, William Davenport, Fount
Tinsley, Chris. Kelley, Malcolm Van Pelt, Frank Hilburn, and
a man named Hill.

In 1866 the Indians made a raid into Uvalde County and
killed a man named John Sanders, who lived on the east bank
of the Frio near the main road. His sons were out near the
Nueces River hunting mustangs, and the old man started to
their camp with a wagon to carry provisions to them. While
en route the Indians came upon him and killed him. He was
bald-headed but had a beard eighteen inches in length, and the
Indians scalped his face and part of his neck to get it. They
then came upon another man named Eastwood, and roped him
and dragged him to death.

In 1873 Mr. Kennedy drove a herd of cattle out to Comanche
Creek, a few miles above Fort Stockton, and left a Mexican to
attend to them, but the cattle drifted towards the Pecos River.
Another cattleman named Frank Rooney had stock on the same
range, and he also had a Mexican in his employ to look after
stock, and when the cattle drifted both Mexicans went in company to the Pecos to look after them, and both were killed by
the Indians and thrown into the Pecos River. After some time
had expired and the Mexicans failed to return, another party

was dispatched to see what had become of them, and their bodies were found lodged against the Pecos pontoon bridge, where they had floated from above. Both of the bodies were in such a state of decomposition one could not be told from the other, except that one had a quirt on his left wrist. Mr. Kennedy said this one was his Mexican, as he was left-handed and always carried his quirt in that way. George Frasier, William Morris, and others went to hunt for the Indians, but could not find them. Morris was in charge of Mr. Kennedy's cattle, and the Mexican was working under him. The Indians took the horses and equipments of the dead Mexicans, even their clothing, and nothing was left on either one of the bodies except the quirt above mentioned.

The wife of Mr. Kennedy was Miss Jane Rankin, who also came from Ireland with some of her people when very small, and landed at New York. She still survives, and has passed through all the dangers and trying scenes of frontier life bravely, and did her part well. One one occasion she cooked breakfast for twenty-two men who came to her house hungry while trailing Indians. Mr. Kennedy says that such things as have been narrated in this sketch were common occurrences for twenty years, being repeated at almost every full moon. He had two sons, George A. and Ross R., and seven girls—Margery K., Jane, Mary E., Rosalie, Clara, Vine V., and Minnie Maud. His sons-in-law are Louis Peters, James Durham, Len Heard, Tom Adams, and C. W. Giffin. Young Ross married Miss Allie Kelso, of Uvalde; Rosalie, now Mrs. Heard, first married Mr. Chas. Barnard, who died in Sabinal; Vine V. married Dave Malone, now deceased, and she and her two children are living with her parents at the old home on Ranchero Creek. Miss Maud, the youngest, is single.

THE FORTY IMMIGRANTS FROM DARMSTADT.

In regard to this immigration scheme we find the following in the San Antonio Express under date of February 27, 1900:

[The following account, taken from the Texas Historical Quarterly, represents the substance of an interview with Mr. Reinhardt, of Arneckeville, De Witt County, who is one of the first settlers in this community. The visionary undertaking here described has become famous among German-Americans in this State on account of the connection with it of Hon. Gustave Schleicher, Dr. Herff, and many other prominent men.—Rudolph Kleberg, Jr.]

This colony owed its origin to the efforts of Prince Solms-Braunfels, Baron von Meusebach, and H. Spies, each successively holding the office of general agent of the Adelsverein.

The Adelsverein, or Union of Princes, was a corporation composed of a number of counts and dukes belonging to the lesser German nobility, and having for its object "the colonization and promoting of German immigration to Texas on a large scale."

The colony was organized in 1846 in Darmstadt. It was named in honor of Bettina v. Armin, a German writer, but was better known as the Darmstaedter Kolonie, while its members were generally called the Vierziger (men of the forties.)

Prince Solms had been in Texas as early as 1814, and his accounts, as well as those of Spies in writing and speeches, caused a sensation among the students of the universities of Giessen and Heidelberg. Solms also made a speech to the students of the industrial school (Gewerbeschule) in Darmstadt, where I was studying, and his extravagant descriptions made the students mad. He remarked that there was no demand in the old country for all the professional men whom the universities were turning out, and that they must find a new and developing country where their services would be in demand. He glowingly described Texas as a land of milk and honey, of perennial flowers, of chrystal streams, rich and fruitful beyond measure, where roamed myriads of deer and buffalo, where the primeval forest abounded in wild fowl of every kind. And what he said was true. It is a glorious land, and I am glad I came here.

PRINCE SOLMS-BRAUNFELS.

It was in this way that Gustave Schleicher, a graduate of the University of Giessen, and already an engineer on the Meinecker road, and Wundt, a student of law, were won for the enterprise. A communistic society was organized, of which friendship, freedom, and equality were the watchwords. It had no regular scheme of government so far as I know. In fact, being communistic, the association would not brook the tyranny of a ruler. But the guiding spirits were by common consent Messrs. Wagner, Herff, Schleicher, and Schenk. Being the youngest of the whole company—I was only 18—I was of course rarely consulted. The general director of the industrial school had purchased my freedom from my father with the understanding that I should botanize in Texas. I was well satisfied as first, and Herff and Schleicher treated me like a son.

In February, 1847, we left for Hamburg and remained there for several weeks until our ship had discharged her cargo. In April we sailed. Our party consisted of about forty men, of whom I remember the following:

Herff, physician.
Schulz, physician.
Schleicher, engineer.
Lerch, architect.
Zoeller, architect.
Freidrich, lawyer.
Wundt, lawyer.
Fuchs, lawyer.
Schleunig, lawyer.
Amelung, lawyer.
Hesse, lawyer.
Wagner, lawyer.
Herrman, forester.
Schenck, forester.
Kuegler, forester.
Voght, forester.
Louis, forester.
Strauss, mechanic.
Flach, mechanic.
Schunk, carpenter.
Neff, carpenter.

Neff, butcher.
Deichert, blacksmith.
Hahn, lieutenant of artillery.
Kappelhoff, ship carpenter.
Michel, brewer.
Ottmer, miller.
Bub, hotel keeper.
Mertins, student of theology.
Backofen, maker of musical instruments.
Lundheimer, naturalist.
Mueller, agriculturist.
Rockan, American who joined in Victoria.

There was no one in our party who could speak English except the cook, who had been in America several times. Dr. Herff had learned the language from books, and could manage to make himself understood.

We had a good voyage, with no incidents of general interest. We landed at Galveston, July 17, 1847. Dr. Herff and Spies, who had sailed ahead of our party, here met us and we were quartered in the William Tell Hotel, kept by a Swiss, and the only inn there at that time. A grand reception awaited us, and being a jolly company, we found no difficulty in showing our appreciation.

As the schooner which was to carry us to Indianola was undergoing repairs, we waited several weeks. When the ship was at last in condition to sail she was pressed into service as a transport by the United States government, the war with Mexico being then in progress. We finally succeeded in getting another ship, but when we were ready to sail the captain was on a "spree." In spite of this, however, we started off, yet before we were far out the ship struck a sandbar and some planks flew out from behind. The captain began to lower the boat on the pretext of going ashore and securing aid, but before he could carry out his purpose Dr. Herff, with drawn pistol, informed him that if it came to drowning the captain would be compelled to stay and perish with us. Here Kappelhoff, who was a ship carpenter, took charge of the vessel, and by keeping close to shore we reached Indianola after five days.

Here twenty-four ox wagons had been waiting for us three weeks, since Meusebach, the general agent of the Adelsverein, had seen to everything. In addition he there bought two wagons with six yokes of oxen each, and two mule teams of eight mules each, for we had an immense amount of baggage. In addition to what we had brought from home and had purchased at Darmstadt we had laid in a big supply at Hamburg and Galveston. We had supplies of every kind imaginable—for instance, complete machinery for a mill, a number of barrels of whisky, and a great many dogs, of which Moro was the largest, being three feet high. We came prepared to conquer the world.

In Indianola $10,000 in American gold was paid to us, as a premium for settling Fisher's grant, by Consul Lee. After a journey of four weeks our train reached New Braunfels in August. Our trip was comparatively uneventful. We camped on the prairie, and sang and drank, and enjoyed ourselves the whole way, as only the German student knows how to do. We lived like the gods on Olympus, and our favorite song on this tour was

"Ein freies Leben fuehren wir,
Ein Leben voller Wonne," etc.

In New Braunfels Schenk and I fell sick with typhoid, while Deichert had the misfortune of being thrown from a horse and breaking his leg. Thus we were unable to move for nearly five weeks, but the whole company waited for us, having no thought of leaving the sick. In New Braunfels on the Verein Shegel (Union Hill) a treaty was made between Meusebach, Spies, and von Koll, representing the colony, and the Comanches, by which the Indians agreed to vacate to our party the tract lying between the Llano and San Saba, and known as Fisher's grant. The Indians were here represented by their chief Santana (also written Santa Anna) and two others, accompanied by Baron v. Kriewitz, Santana's squaws, and his doctor.

Kriewitz had been among the Comanches several months as commercial agent of the colonists at New Braunfels and Fredericksburg, according to the wish of the savages themselves. But the Indians did not trust him, looking upon him as a spy, and it is said that his life was thrice saved by Santana's daughter. Kriewitz at the making of the treaty was dressed like an Indian, but at last one of our party recognized him and gazed intently

at him. Hereupon Kriewitz touched him under the table with
his foot. Kriewitz was then handed a piece of paper and pencil,
and wrote back that he was Kriewitz, but that he could not hold
open communication with them now; that on the journey back
to the Indian camp he would try to get away. He went back
with the savages as far as Comanche Springs, and escaped and
lay hid in New Braunfels three days while the Indians came to
look for him. They came to our own room, and there I saw Santana for the first time. But as far as the treaty went they kept
that to the letter, and later they visited our settlement, as they
had stated at the time of the treaty. We were also faithful to
the compact.

After the sick had recovered we set out for Fredericksburg,
stopping a few days at Comanche Spring, later Meusebach's farm.
Kriewitz was our guide, and as he rode ahead of us one could not
have told him from an Indian. Having again spent several days
in Fredericksburg, we set out for our tract, Kriewitz again being
our guide. Of course we had to move slowly, and when we arrived at the Llano we hunted a ford for three days. The best
one finally proved to be but a few yards from our camp, where
we had to lift the wagons four feet on a rock in the bottom of the
river by the aid of windlasses, and this work took us from
morning until night.

The Llano then was a beautiful stream, clear as crystal, and
known in our party as the "silver Llano." One could see the
bottom at the deepest places. The whole country was covered
with mesquite grass as high as the knee, and abounded in buffalo
and deer.

On the other side we came to a big liveoak, and here camped.
Putting our wagons in a circle, we constructed a big tent in the
center, planted our cannon, and put out a guard. Feeling perfectly secure in our fortified camp, we celebrated that night until
3 o'clock. A bowl of punch was prepared and we sang our
favorite songs, while those who could performed on musical instruments, of which we had a whole chest. We gave "Lebe Hoch,
United States! Lebe Hoch, Texas!" for we were all good patriots.
This was in the early part of September, 1847.

We built a large structure of forks and cross beams, which we
covered with reed grass. It was forty feet long and twenty-two

feet high. Afterwards we constructed an adobe house, covered with shingles. A large pecan tree supplied us with 10,000 of these. In this house was a fireplace twelve feet broad and built of rock. On the roof Strauss put an artistic weather vane. Here we celebrated the Christmas of 1847, and again had a glorious time.

As I have said, the Indians kept their agreement to the letter. In November, 1847, they visited us, as they had promised. At the time I was herding cows, several miles from our camp, when two Indians rode up. From their signs I supposed they wanted something to eat, and I handed them some bread out of the pouch I carried. Evidently not trusting me, they made signs that I should eat first. The fact was that a great number of Waco Indians had been treacherously poisoned by a band of cowboys. It was a dastardly deed, and the Waco's thereafter became the most hostile of the tribes, as before they had been the most amicable. Well, the end of my interview was, they took everything I had and galloped off. They were hardly out of sight when I saw a big crowd of savages riding up, and as they drew nearer I recognized the chief Santana. Upon my asking him if he were not the chief, he seemed greatly surprised that I should know him.

The Indians camped only a short distance from us. During the night a number of our utensils were stolen by the squaws, but the next day the men returned them. For everything we gave them we were paid back threefold. As they stayed some time, we became well acquainted. Whenever we came into their camp they would spread out their deer skins, bring out morrals full of the biggest pecans I ever saw, and tell us to help ourselves. They even tried to learn German from us, in spite of the difficulty they found in pronouncing some of the words.

Several Mormons arrived in the early spring to settle, but did not carry out their intention. Shortly afterward Bickel, who had made himself notorious in Fredericksburg, came with some of his followers and began a settlement, known as the Bickeliner. The leader, however, soon disappeared. He had two wives, who constantly quarreled. Next came the Castellaners, who founded the settlement of Castell, which still exists. Their families came in March, 1848.

In the summer of 1848 our colony of "Bettina" went to

pieces like a bubble. As I have said, it was a communistic society, and accordingly had no real government. Since everybody was to work if he pleased, the result was that less and less
work was done as time progressed. Most of the professional
men wanted to do the directing and ordering, while the mechanics
and laborers were to carry out their plans. Of course the latter
failed to see the justice of this ruling, and so no one did anything. We had made a field and raised 200 bushels of corn—
our whole year's crop. According to our contract with the
Adelsverein, this company was to furnish us with supplies for
the first year, but the next we were to shift for ourselves. As
it was, we still had a plentiful supply of everything, yet that
was bound to end some time, and there was absolutely no prospect of our ever providing for ourselves. I began to see this
plainly. Having made arrangements with some teamsters who
had brought us some goods, I started for Fredericksburg. Before I got there eight others were on their way thither, and
thus our colony went to the four winds. Bub was killed on the
road by Indians.

I went to Mayersville, De Witt County, Texas, and in that
neighborhood I have lived ever since. When after forty-eight
years I met Dr. Herff in San Antonio, we found, as far as both
of us could determine, ten of our company were still living.

THE OLD CHURCH AT FREDERICKSBURG.

This old church, a true cut of which is shown, was built in
1847, and was nonsectarian. Any and all people of whatsoever faith in religious belief were welcome to worship there,
and the laying of the cornerstone was observed as a great gala
day by all the people who had commenced this settlement at
Fredericksburg, far out on the Texas frontier, and one of the
curious and unique features of the occasion was the presence of
a large band of Comanche Indians, who helped to celebrate the
occasion. A treaty had been made with them by Baron von
Meusebach a short time before, and he was called the savior of
Fredericksburg, for no doubt but for this timely treaty the place
would have been destroyed and the people slain and driven
away. When the town built up and the streets were laid out
in order it was found that the old church was in the middle of

OLD CHURCH AT FREDERICKSBURG.

the main street, and four years ago, in 1896, it was decided to remove it. A photo was taken of it, and with another jubilee it was removed, but this time without the presence of the Comanches. Where were they? The bones of the most of them lie scattered along the Texas border, where they met death at the hands of soldiers, citizens, and Texas rangers, for they soon broke their treaty.

J. D. FENLEY.

Came to Texas in 1853.

Mr. Joel D. Fenley was one of the early settlers of Sabinal
Canyon, and deserves a place in history among the pioneers of
southwest Texas.   While not having the opportunity of participating in the bloody battles with savages as others had done, it
was no fault of his.   He was ever ready to mount his horse and
go in pursuit of raiding bands of Indians, or go and help to
bring in and bury his unfortunate neighbors who met death at
their hands.   It was his misfortune or good fortune to always
fail to get into a close fight with the numerous bands whom he
trailed many long and tedious miles over the mountains and
through tangled brakes and gorges.

Mr. Fenley was born in Fairfield district, South Carolina, in
1828, and came to Texas and to this region in 1853.   His ancestors served as scouts in the Revolutionary war.   When Mr.
Fenley came to this valley but few settlers had preceded him.
Of these was Capt. William Ware, whose daughter he married
in 1854, and Gideon Thompson.   Indians were numerous and
very hostile, and he soon learned to watch and trail and guard
against their frequent inroads.   One Sunday morning in 1858,
as Mr. Fenley was mounting his horse to go to church, a rapid
rider came from up the West, or Anglin, prong of the river,
bringing the news of an Indian raid in their settlement ten
miles above.   Mr. Fenley called to his wife, telling her to fix
up the cold victuals on hand, while he got his gun and ammunition, mounted again, and set out rapidly with the messenger to
the scene of the raid.   Other settlers rallied to the call, and
when they arrived at the upper settlement and all came together
there were present Robert H. Kinchaloe, Jack Kelley, Chris Kelley, James Davenport, Gid Thompson, Green Snow, and likely
a few others.   The Indians had passed the ranch of Aaron
Anglin and gone across the mountains towards the Frio.   This
was an old route of the Indians going and coming from one canyon to the other.   This old trail is still to be seen, and is called
by the mountaineers "the old Indian trail."

After the settlers had gotten through the pass and come to the valley of the Frio, near the river, they discovered a crowd of dismounted men in an open prairie near the river. From this distanse, nearly half a mile, they were unable to determine if they were Indians or white men, but as they were directly on the trail which the party was following, it was decided they were Indians and they charged them. Great confusion was noticed among the other crowd, and they commenced to mount their horses. As fast as a man would vault into the saddle he would run towards the river, until all were strung out in that direction west except two, and they ran back through the prairie at a most terrific speed up the river north. The Sabinal men were coming in a charge from the east. One red-headed fellow attempted to mount, but his girth broke and his saddle fell off. Leaving his horse, he followed the crowd on foot, and arrived there almost as soon as they did. His red hair looked like a flying meteor as he sailed through the open flat close on the heels of the horses. These Frio men, however, were not so badly frightened as to run clear away. They were going to cover to fight a battle, and dismounted in the timber along the river. When the Sabinal men came over the slope of the river bank into view, from every cypress tree along the margin of the stream protruded a human head and long rifle. Of course this close inspection revealed the identity of each party, and the Frio men with much laughter came from cover and all got together. The two men who had run off up the river had stopped on a hill to take observations, and seeing the mixing of the two bands came back also. In the wild charge of the men from the Sabinal they failed to notice the cause of the dismounted men in the prairie. Out where the Frio men ran from stood a wagon, and beside it lay a dead man. They had seen the wagon, it is true, but passed below it, not knowing the situation. The slain man was named Thompson, and he had been killed a few hours before by the Indians whom Mr. Fenley and his party were trailing. Mr. Thompson was on his way to the lower settlement and had a yoke of oxen to his wagon, and was crossing the open ground as the Indians came into it from towards Sabinal Canyon. From the sign of the circling horse tracks they had surrounded him, and he had no chance for his life. As is usual with the victims

43

of the fierce Comanches, he was horribly mutilated and his yoke of oxen gone. A man named Kit Stanford was to have gone with him, but was delayed in starting and came on afterwards on horseback and discovered the dead body soon after the killing. Mr. Stanford then galloped back and gave the alarm. The upper Frio men assembled, and had just arrived upon the scene and dismounted when charged by the Sabinal trailers. This occurred just about where the Patterson irrigating ditch now leaves the river, and about one mile and a half from the present Rio Frio postoffice, and five miles below Leakey, the former county seat of Edwards County before it was moved to Rock Springs, at the head of the Nueces River. Some of the men now carried the body of Mr. Thompson back to his bereaved family, and the others went on in pursuit of the Indians. From here the trail led northwest across brushy and rock mountains until near the head of the West prong of the Nueces, when the hostile camp was located in a cedarbrake. They had stopped, killed Thompson's oxen, and were cooking the meat. The white men would have surprised the Indians had it not been that at the time they were advancing cautiously upon the camp they met the Indian's horses being driven out to graze, and those in charge gave the alarm by loud yelling when they saw the white men, and the others scattered into the brush. Only one squaw and a captive white boy were seen when the camp was charged, and they both ran and were soon hid in the thick brakes. The boy could have been easily killed, as he was very close to them, and some said they believed he was an Indian, but when he looked towards them his face was too white for a redskin. This boy had been seen several times by white men in Indian battles, but he always ran and they could never get hold of him. He was finally killed—mistaken for an Indian—an account of which is in the sketch of Richard Ware. Who he was no one knew. On his present occasion thirty-two head of horses were captured, all of which belonged to settlers, and they were returned to their owners.

When Berry Buckaloo was killed on Seco, Mr. Fenley went with others and helped bring in the body. They washed it in the Sabinal River where the wagon road now crosses going to the station. Many arrow spikes were in the body, which were all carefully extracted before burying it.

When Mrs. Kinchaloe, his sister-in-law, was so badly wounded, he helped to bring her away, and she stayed at his house part of the time while recovering from the fearful wounds inflicted by the Indian lances.

On another occasion Mr. Fenley and others followed the Indians from Sabinal Canyon to the Nueces and located their camp, but they discovered the white men and left. They had killed a mare and were eating her. Demp. Fenley, in scouting around, discovered thirty wigwams which they had left, and had the scouts known it they were in a trap and in great danger of being all killed between bluffs in a gorge, but it seemed the Indians did not take advantage of it. They were winding about in these hills for some time and the Indians were watching them. Another scout came back afterwards and found painted on a rock at this place the pictures of the nine men who were looking for them. On another rock was painted two hands turned back to back, indicating to other Indians who were expected to come there that nine white men had been there, and that they had gone one way and the Indians another. On another occasion Mr. Fenley followed the Indians west to Nueces Canyon and was joined there by the noted Indian fighter Edward Westfall, who was then the only settler in Nueces Canyon. They abandoned the trail too soon, as was afterwards learned. Had they gone over one more mountain they would have found them. Westfall said that on this occasion the Indians had 600 head of horses.

Mr. Fenley kept his horses in a strong pen built of split logs, with the gate close to the gallery of the house, but almost worn out with constant watching, and getting careless, one night the Indians got them. His brother-in-law, Mr. R. H. Kinchaloe, came to his house that day riding a very good horse which he had just paid $80 for. He liked the animal very much, and was bragging on him. He spent the night with Mr. Fenley, and this horse was taken also.

Mrs. E. A. Fenley, wife of Mr. Joel Fenley, was born in Montgomery County, Texas, in 1841, and came to Sabinal Canyon in 1852 with her father, Capt. William Ware, one of the famous twenty-two captains who led their men to victory on the plains of San Jacinto. Mrs. Fenley was one of the first white children that ever saw this beautiful valley, and of course has been familiar with all of the attending horrors of a border life.

On one occasion, after she was married and living down on Onion Creek, her brother Richard Ware, who lived there also, was digging a ditch, and one day was surrounded by a band of Indians. Drawing his pistol, he commenced firing and backing towards the house. He succeeded in hitting two of them and keeping them off. Mrs. Fenley heard the firing and yelling of the Indians, and running into the house told Mr. Fenley the Indians was after her brother, and to go and help him. Mr. Fenley seized his shotgun and pistol and started to him, but Mr. John Ware told him to come back and get on his horse. He did so, but thinks this delay kept him from killing an Indian, for if he had kept on at the time he would have met four of them face to face in a trail. As it was, while he was getting his horse the Indians were getting other horses near by, and Mrs. Fenley was standing looking at them. The wife of Richard Ware, when she heard the firing of his pistol, got his gun and started to him with it. John Ware also went. Mr. Fenley tried to stop Mrs. Ware from going, but she went and got to her husband with the gun, but he had already whipped the Indians.

It was here Mrs. Fenley lived when her sister, Mrs. Kinchaloe, had her noted battle with the Indians and Mrs. Bowlin was killed. That morning one of the children was sick with sore throat or diphtheria, and Mr. Fenley was going after Mrs. Binnion, who was the only doctor in the country. When passing the house of John Ware, where Rev. John L. Harper was preaching, Mr. Ben Biggs galloped up and told the news of the killing of Mrs. Bowlin and the wounding of Mrs. Kinchaloe. He galloped back, hitched up his wagon, and came with all haste, the distance being ten miles. When Mrs. Kinchaloe saw her sister, Mrs. Fenley, she said: "I wanted to die before you all came, but now since I have seen you again I want to live."

Mrs. Fenley still lives in the canyon, honored and respected by all who know her as a model Christian lady. Mr. Fenley died in 1899.

DEATH OF CAPT. PHILIP DIMMITT.

1841.

When the American pioneers began to settle in southwest Texas they not only had the Indian tribes to contend with, but also freebooting bands of Mexicans who often crossed the Rio Grande and killed and carried off the property of the Texans and sometimes the settlers themselves, and confined them in loathsome dungeons in Mexico, where sometimes they spent years before being liberated.

In the year 1841 Capt. Philip Dimmitt, long distinguished as a pioneer and gallant defender of Texas, became their victim. He was engaged with some workmen on the 4th of July in erecting a mercantile establishment on Corpus Christi bay, about fifteen miles below the present town of Corpus Christi (then known as the rancho of Aubry and Kinney), when the place was visited by Captain Sanchez, aid-de-camp to General Ampudia, with a party of fifteen cavalry, who took Captain Dimmitt and his men prisoners, and after plundering the establishment conducted them to Matamoros. From this point they were taken, with others, to Monterey and delivered over to General Arista. By his order they were ironed and started to the interior under a guard commanded by Captain Chaffind. That officer was a humane man, and had the irons taken off after the first day's march. On the third day they arrived at Saltillo. Here their anticipations of a long imprisonment and horrid treatment were such that they resolved to attempt their escape. They proposed to procure a quantity of mescal (a Mexican liquor), well drugged with morphine, and give it to the guards, and while they were affected by it to make their escape. Two physicians who were among the prisoners were charged with this part of the programme. After being supplied with this mixture, they arrived at the place where they were quartered for the night. In the night, after the guard had been well supplied with the liquor from water gourds, the signal was given to make the attempt to escape. By some means, however, the morphine proved inefficient, and the mescal alone had only served to keep the guards more wideawake and to stimulate their courage. There were nineteen of the Texans, and a few of them had guns that they had succeeded in picking up as occasion offered, and they succeeded in getting out of their quarters, although the guards were more than a hundred. They succeeded in getting off some distance before daylight came, and a messenger came to them from Captain Chaffind, stating that if they returned they would be forgiven; if not, he would have Captain Dimmitt shot, who had been confined separate from his men, and therefore not able to escape with them. The captain heard of this threat, and knowing Mexican treachery generally, and that it would be carried into execution and likely all of the others shot if they returned, determined to end it all and relieve his men by taking his own life. He had morphine about his person, and at once took a large dose of it. He then wrote a letter to his wife in San Antonio, made disposition of his property, and lay down on his blanket to die. A few prisoners were in confinement with him, and these he requested to convey his letter and manner of death, if they ever returned, and tell the Texans to throw the mantle of charity over his act. "I do not fear death," he said, "but dread the idea of ending my life in a loathsome dungeon. Tell them I prefer a Roman's death to the ignominy of perpetual imprisonment, and that my last wish is for my country's welfare." Soon after he sank into a sleep from which he never awoke.

Thus died Capt. Philip Dimmitt, a noble spirit, who virtually died for his men, and by whose hands the first Lone Star banner of Texas was unfurled to the breeze on the height of La Bahia (Goliad). The other prisoners, when they learned of their captain's death, continued their flight and reached Texas.

One of these murdering bands of robbers was met by Capt. Jack Hays and about twenty-five of his rangers. A battle ensued, in which the Mexicans were defeated with loss and driven to the Rio Grande. None of the rangers were hit, as the robbers fired as they ran. This took place ten miles below Laredo, and the Mexicans were commanded by Capt. Ignacio Garcia. Six of the party were killed and twenty-five captured.

Captain Dimmitt owned property in San Antonio and also

in Seguin. He had four sons—Texas, Alamo, Napoleon, and James. One daughter was named Josephine, who married Mr. William Medlin of Seguin. He died there some years ago and left his widow and two sons, William and Philip. William died, but Philip and his mother still reside there.

TRAILING INDIANS.

Mr. G. P. Hodges, an old settler of Uvalde County, and who was raised in the west, furnishes the facts for this detailed account of Indian trailing by the settlers. He says that in those days, especially during light moons, if a gun was fired at night the near neighbors were up and listening. The presence of Indians was made known by firing guns, blowing horns, or yelling. Runners on swift horses would go day and night to alarm the isolated settlers of a raid, and men would gather to fight them. In 1871 the Indians made a raid, coming east from the Nueces and Frio country towards the Hondo. When they got to the Frio Canyon they stole horses from Mr. J. F. Patterson, and the recollection of Mr. Hodges is that they killed a boy there who was working for Mr. Patterson, taking care of his cow ponies. Coming on east, the Indians struck the Hondo at the ranch of widow Dean, and about dusk shot at Joe Dean, who was standing by the yard gate talking to his brother-in-law, Jesse Campbell. The latter, seeing the Indian near by, drew a pistol and fired at him as he began to retreat, and wounded him. He jumped high and dropped his bow. Other Indians were now seen, and several shots were fired at them by Dean and Campbell. That night they sent runners up and down the Hondo to alarm the settlers. At that time Mr. Hodges was very young and lived on the Hondo with his uncle, Judge Harper. He joined the men, nine in all, that went from their settlement.

The party had agreed to meet at Joel Fenley's place, who lived where Hondo City now is. They were to collect and get there as soon as possible next morning, so as to strike the trail early. They arrived without breakfast, which Mr. Fenley furnished them, and also provisions to take on the trip. The men in this party were Isaac H. King, Jesse Campbell, Joe Dean, William Johnson, Hardy Cocke, Phil. Hodges, one Mexican, and two negroes. When they made the start from Mr. Fenley's, Isaac King was elected captain. The objective point now was Mrs. Dean's ranch, so as to be certain to get on the trail. It was taken up here and was very tedious to follow, as the Indians had scattered in gathering up stock. About seven miles from the Dean place a halt had been made by the Indians to dress the wound of the one shot by Campbell. This had been done in the night, soon after the Indian was wounded, and blood was seen here on the ground, where they had worked with him.

The men kept on, and arriving at the Verde Creek found there had been a terrible scattering among the Indians, and evidently they had trouble there. It was afterwards ascertained that Sevier Vance and Joe Decker had fought them there early in the morning. King's party got the trail together again and kept on, and about noon turned in towards the Hondo river and came to it at Barnes bluff. This place takes its name from an old miser who used to live there in a cave and kept his money in a hollow tree in the river channel. During an overflow the tree washed away, but after the water subsided Barnes found his tree lodged in a drift, and got his money again.

During this halt at the bluff Vance come up with a party on the trail and all went together. Late in the evening, while on rising ground, Elam's and Wilson's ranch on Ward's Creek could be seen, and that many men and horses were there and badly scattered. At first it was supposed to be Wilson's outfit, until the distant men began to collect at sight of the settlers and make off.

At this time the trailers were scattered for half a mile. Joe Dean, Bill Johnson, and Phil. Hodges were ahead, and the first to see them. They intended to wait until their captain and other men came up, but seeing the Indians commence to run, put spurs to their horses and followed them, at the same time waving their hats for those in the rear to come on. They ran about five miles, and by this time most of the horses ridden by the white men had given out. Finally, when the Indians went to the top of a mountain, but few were in front, but they at once commenced the ascent and crowded the Indians so close they turned back on them and a lively fusilade commenced. There were but six men in this fight on the side of the mountain, and about thirty-five Indians. There was a continual pattering of bullets around them, but they held the ground until reinforcements came up and fourteen men then charged to the top of the mountain. It was expected when they arrived at the summit that a hard fight would take place, as the Indians had the advantage of position and numbers, but when they saw the whites reinforced and coming to them, they retreated to the other side of the mountain and continued their flight. The settlers now returned to Wilson's ranch to see what discoveries they could make there. They knew that young Tom Wilson and a Mexican were on the ranch, and expected to find them killed. They could not be found about the place, and were supposed to be dead somewhere. It was afterwards learned that they saw the Indians coming in time to make their escape. Tom Wilson's horse was hitched near by, saddled, and he sprang on him, gun in hand, and waved it at them to let them know he was armed, and galloped away towards a thicket, where he dismounted and tied his horse, then pushed back in the brush and lay down and watched, but they did not follow him. The Mexican also ran away on foot and hid himself in a thicket. They heard the men fighting the Indians on the mountain, but supposed it was the latter killing cattle. Wilson lay in the thicket until night, and then came out and silently went away, leaving his horse, as he would make too much noise on the rocks. It was twenty-five miles to Judge Harper's ranch, and to that place the young settler walked in the darkness and reported the Mexican killed, as he thought it was impossible for him to escape, the Indians were so near when discovered.

The Mexican walked to old D'Hanis and reported there that Wilson was killed. They both kept so close in the brush they were not aware that the settlers were at the ranch, although only a few hundred yards away. The Mexican went out at the back door as the Indians were coming up in front and making a play at Wilson, and escaped unobserved. A party returned to the ranch a few days after and found Wilson's horse still tied where he left him. These were an unusually cruel set of Indians to stock. They killed eighteen head of cattle and only cut out the loin steak of each, and every horse they had to leave they killed. If a horse gave out they would throw a lance into him and leave him thus to die. Quite a lot of things were captured, such as lariats and leggings, and also the saddle and clothing of the boy they killed on the Frio.

JUDGE HENRY MANEY.

Came to Texas in 1851.

Judge Henry Maney, who at this writing lives at Pearsall, Frio County, is an old-time Texan, and has passed through many stirring scenes. He was born in 1829, in Rutherford County, Tennessee, seven miles from Murfreesboro. He was a son of Maj. Henry Maney, and came to Texas and to Seguin, Guadalupe County, in 1851, arriving there on the 16th day of April, and was living there when the Indians made their last raid east of San Antonio, which terminated on the Cibolo, without penetrating far into Guadalupe County. In 1852 Judge Maney married Miss Mary Malinda Erskine, daughter of Maj. Michael Erskine, one of the most prominent families of Guadalupe County. He went back to Tennessee in 1853, and returned in the following spring. At this time Major Erskine was on the eve of starting overland to California with a drove of beeves, and requested his son-in-law to make the trip with him. This was agreed to, and the start was made.

The country west of San Antonio at that time was all frontier and infested by hostile Indians, and it required a strong escort to pass safely through. The escort obtained consisted of thirty-five men, and was commanded by Capt. James H. Calahan, who was employed by Major Erskine for a consideration of $1500 for the trip.

Only twelve men of this guard were under pay, the balance working their way to California.

The expedition started from San Antonio on the 25th day of April, 1854. The cattle consisted of something more than 1000 head of beeves, half of which were purchased from Tom O'Conner on the coast, and had never been inside of a pen except to be branded.

Nothing of interest occurred until reaching the Hondo River, forty miles west of San Antonio. Here, while in camp, a terrible storm came up at 1 o'clock in the morning, with a great deal of rain. The keen claps of thunder startled the cattle, and they broke away in a violent stampede, and when daylight came not a hoof could be seen except one, and he had a broken shoulder, and that was all that kept him there.   He was killed for beef. A week was spent here collecting the scattered cattle, and all but 40 head were recovered.   These made their way back to Guadalupe county.

During the trip a halt was made every Sunday to rest.   The cattle stampeded many times and gave a great deal of trouble until the open prairie country was reached, and nothing of interest transpired until they arrived at the head of Limpia Creek and made camp in the canyon, on the spot where Fort Davis was afterwards built.

A halt was made here two nights and one day.   On the second night the Indians found the herder asleep and cut off three head of work oxen and made an attempt on the main herd, but failed. They carried away the three oxen.   The next morning their trail was taken up and pursuit commenced.   The trailer was a young Mexican, twenty years old, who led Captain Calahan and eleven men.   The trail led to a deep chasm in the mountains, ten miles from camp, and here the Indians had slaughtered the oxen, and were having a feast when Calahan and his men came upon them.   A charge was at once made and the battle commenced.   The Indians were in large force and met the onset with a countercharge, and fired many shots with firearms and with arrows.   Calahan was an old Indian fighter, and one of the survivors of Fannin's massacre.   Seeing, however, that he was not able to stand against the Indians with a small force, he ordered a retreat, but carried the horses of the Indians with him for some distance in a desperate attempt to get clear of the canyon with them.   Seeing the Indians were about to cut them off by making a detour through the hills, he dropped all but two mules and ten horses, which he succeeded in getting into camp.   One of the party, named Mann, had his clothing pierced with an arrow, which was the only casualty among the white men, and as they could not hold the ground, they were unable to tell what damage they inflicted on the other side.   These Indians were Muscalara Apaches.

From this place to the Rio Grande, a distance of ninety miles, there was no water for the cattle, but they had water enough along with them for the horses and men to make out on, so that they would not suffer to any great extent.

After leaving the tableland at the head of Limpia Creek it took four days and nights, lacking four hours, to reach a canyon six miles from the Rio Grande. This was a good place to hold the cattle, as they had begun to smell the water and were hard to control. Four head became violently insane and escaped to the mountains. The beeves were now cut off into detachments of sixty head and driven to the water, and one was lost on arriving there. He swam the river and went into Mexico.

By 8 o'clock in the morning all the cattle, mules, and horses were watered. There were 100 head of the latter. All came quietly out and lay down after quenching their thirst, and were very tame on account of being so full of water. Skittish beeves heretofore would allow themselves to be touched; in fact, were not able to run away.

From there the cattle were carried up the river to Fort Thorn. Major Richardson, in command there, cautioned Mr. Erskine about the Apache Indians, who could not be relied on, although a treaty had been made with them, and advised him to keep them out of camp. They went on from here and crossed the Mimbres River and came to a point about fifteen miles east of the village of Santa Cruz, and there went into camp. Here they found a letter torn up and scattered in the grass. The fragments were collected and put together so it could be read, and it proved to be a letter from Dunlap warning them to be on their guard against Indians, stating that the day before, while their party were at dinner at this place, the Indians came down upon them and cut off 120 head of cattle from their herd, besides forty head of mules and horses, and killed his brother-in-law and partner, Houston, while he was attempting to recover them. Erskine's party now looked around and discovered the grave of Houston. Dunlap and Houston had started through with a herd some time before, and knew that Erskine was behind them.

Major Erskine and his party now went on to Santa Cruz village and found Dunlap in camp on the river of the same name, below town, in company with John James of San Antonio, who was also with beeves for the California market. They remained several days here to recruit stock. The other outfits also remained. There was another dry stretch ahead of forty-five miles from the town of Tucson to the Gila River. While waiting here Captain Calahan went among all the herds and called for volunteers to follow the trail of the Indians who got off with the stock of Dunlap and Houston. Eighteen men responded, of whom were J. Box Roberts, Ig. Johnson, John Lewis, J. H. French, and Henry Maney, all from Guadalupe County. From other places was a sergeant of the regular army whose time of enlistment had expired, and who had joined the cowmen to make a trip to California. Also from Guadalupe County was J. Mann and a Mexican called "Teck." In addition to these men who were willing to go was a lieutenant from the Mexican garrison with twenty-five men, who acted as guides.

As the sun was going down the party set out up the Santa Cruz River, traveling that way three hours, and then turned to the right at an angle of 45 degrees and moved steadily on. After the turn of the night, about 1 o'clock, an alarm of Indians was raised in front and a charge was ordered. The enemy fled across the plain, and after half an hour's chase it was discovered that the supposed Apaches were a bunch of mustangs.

Calahan now ordered the men to dismount and rest, but just as they were about to stretch their weary limbs on the grass the sharp crack of a rifle was heard in the rear, and the cry of "Indians! Indians!" was again raised. Every man was again soon mounted and on the alert for a fight, and a cautious reconnoissance was made around the spot from which the sound of the rifle seemed to have come. Instead of Indians in the grass, however, greatly to their surprise they found old Teck down on the ground beside his horse, drunk, where he had fallen during the charge on the mustangs. He became intoxicated during the long night ride on mescal, which he got from one of the Mexican soldiers. Old Teck, not being able to mount after he fell off, and fearing to be left, fired his gun to bring his crowd back. Calahan was a man of high temper, and roundly cursed the old Mexican, and told him if he did not return to camp he would kill him. Teck went back as soon as he was able to ride. A three hours rest, and then again in the saddle, following the lead of the Mexican soldiers. They knew the country so well and the general route of the Indians when going out, that they saved time by this night ride, even if they could see no trail. They knew it would be found in some of the valleys when daylight came, or likely discover the Indians from the summit of some lofty mountain. When daylight came they found themselves in a postoak-timbered valley, with a ridge on the right and high mountains on the left. At 11 o'clock that day one of the men killed a cub bear, but large enough for all to have meat for dinner.

After leaving the noon camp a short distance, the spies returned and reported Indians beyond the ridge to the right in the San Pedro River valley, which the men were now rapidly approaching. As it drew nearer the river the ridge began to decline into a valley. The Indians were coming into the San Pedro valley, and toward the end of the ridge which terminated in the valley. The spies discovered the Indians when several miles away, and Callahan's men slowed up so as to give them time to approach the end of the ridge, for there was where the captain wished to fight them. The Indians had not as yet discovered the Texans and Mexicans. Spies were still kept ahead, and in about half an hour returned again and reported the Indians going into camp on the San Pedro, and near the end of the long ridge which was between the Indians and the pursuers, and distant from the command not more than 150 yards. The order was now given by Callahan to dismount, tighten girths, fix guns, etc. Command to mount was then given. Calahan moved to one side, but in front, pulled off his hat, put spurs to his horse, and said "Charge!" During this time the Indians were not aware of the near proximity of an enemy. The men of Calahan were hid behind the end of the aforesaid ridge in the timber. They went into the Indians at full speed around the point, and took them completely by surprise, but a hand-to-hand fight at once commenced. About ten of the Indians had not dismounted, and these at once fled from the fight and crossed the San Pedro. They were not again seen except in the distance, after the battle was over. The Indians who had dismounted and partly unpacked their horses had no chance to remount, and the only thing for them to do was to fight or die. Those who were left to fight the battle alone were about twenty, and they yelled defiantly and sent flights of arrows. Only one Indian had a gun and with this he shot a Mexican soldier dead from his horse, firing over his shoulder as he turned to run. The ball struck the soldier between the eyes. The lieutenant who was in command of the Mexicans was a slender, delicate man of the Castilian type, and fought only with a saber, with which he killed one Indian, and cut and hacked others badly. The man French, who was mounted on a mule in the charge, came in contact with an Indian, and his animal stopping suddenly, the girth broke, and French was precipitated violently over his head to the ground, breaking his shotgun off at the breech above the guard, leaving the lock and triggers intact. Near him an Indian was attempting to mount a horse on the opposite side from French, who raised his broken gun and fired over the horse, killing the Indian. There was just enough of the rear of his gun left to draw back the hammer and pull the trigger. About the time that French fell the men all dismounted and turned their horses loose, as the Indians commenced retreating towards the bank of the river. They rolled on the ground like hoops, discharging an arrow each time as they went over. They went over the bank onto the second ledge, and went on rolling through the high grass and still shooting arrows. The men advanced on foot to the bank of the river, which was not more than a creek in size, and fired at the Indians when they could see them. During this time the sergeant who had joined the expedition at Fort Thorn received an arrow in the left shoulder, and several others were hit about their clothing. One horse belonging to Major Erskine was wounded by an arrow. The sergeant was standing close to Henry Maney when the arrow struck him, and he said "Oh!" quick and loud. Maney looked and saw the arrow sticking above the collarbone. It had gone through a heavy overcoat and cape and remained transfixed in the body, where it remained until the fight was over, he not being able to withdraw it. Near the bank of the creek on the opposite side and in front of the men, grew thick bushes, in which some of the Indians hid themselves and in the crevices of the bank. One Indian climbed to the top of the bank and was shot in the head by a man named Walters, and fell with his brains running out. Henry Maney was the first man to cross the creek where the Indians did, and saw two on one horse making off. He gave chase after them, as he had again mounted his horse for the purpose of crossing. He ran about 200 yards and came close enough to shoot and was about to do so when called by a Mexican who belonged to the command named Pedro, who said "Stop! Stop! My Indian, my Indian!" He was accompanied by two Mexican soldiers with lances. Maney stopped and gave place to them. In the chase which now ensued one Indian was shot by Pedro and fell from the horse, and the other was wounded and soon overtaken. One of the Mexicans on a roan horse threw a lariat over him which settled around his arms, and wheeling his horse quick, jerked him to the ground and set off at almost full speed, the wretched Apache bounding along on the ground. The other Mexican soldier followed with a lance and threw it into him every time he hit the ground, until he was dead, and then dismounted and scalped him. Mr. Maney could plainly hear the rasping sound of the lance each time it entered his body.

Judge Maney could now hear no more firing, and went back to the other men. Captain Calahan said he believed some of the Indians were hid in the bushes, and called for volunteers to beat up the brush and kill them. Several went, among whom was Ig. Johnson of Seguin, who was killed at the battle of Manassas during the Civil war. French and Lewis also went, Calahan leading. The latter finally crossed the creek himself and left the boys to hunt in the brush. Going down the river, he looked into a crevice where water had been during an overflow, and found two Indians in there. One charged him with a lance and was shot and killed. Then the other came out. Calahan attempted to shoot him with a pistol, but it failed to fire, and the Indian came at him with a lance, when the captain had to call for help. Maney was in forty steps of him and raised his gun to fire. He was in the act of touching the trigger, and could barely hold his fire, when the wounded sergeant raised up in front of the muzzle of the gun, and he had to desist. The sergeant was lying down in the grass, and not knowing that Maney was about to shoot, raised up to look at Calahan when he called for help. The captain snapped twice with his pistol, knocked the lance aside with it as it was about to enter his bowels, and then jumped into the river. Maney, who had dismounted, again sprang on his horse and dashed to the opposite side of the stream. While this was taking place, the other men were killing Indians whom they had found in the brush. Maney thought the Indian was going out at the gap or horseway up the bluff and watched for him there, but instead he walked slowly toward the ford and seemed perfectly devoid of fear from the bullets that clipped around him, fired from across the river, and one from Maney's gun, who was in thirty steps of him. The brave finally sank down and died. This ended the fight, Henry Maney firing the last shot. The dead

44

Indians were all scalped, mostly by the Mexicans, who did it for the reward offered for them by the Mexican government. Twenty-one dead Indians were counted on the ground. In the beginning of the fight a Mexican boy 15 years old, who had been captured four years before, fell down and cried out with a loud voice in Spanish, "I am a Mexican! I am a Mexican!" and continued to do so as long as the guns were popping around him. Sixty-five head of cattle, ten horses, and two mules were gathered up by order of the captain, who also ordered an immediate return to camp, as they were in the heart of the Apache country. It was now 3 o'clock in the evening. They arrived at Santa Cruz next morning at 9 o'clock, forty-five miles, bearing the dead body of the Mexican soldier tied across the horse. His family was there, and they, with many others, gathered around and set up a wailing cry by the women and groans by the men. The parents of the captive boy lived at Tucson, and he was carried there by the Mexicans. The balance of the trip from there on was uneventful, and the return to Seguin was made by Maney and Calahan by way of New Orleans from San Francisco.

Judge Maney was by profession a lawyer, and practiced in Tennessee before coming to Texas. When the Civil war broke out he served the Confederacy in the company of Wm. P. Hardeman, Riley's regiment, Sibley's brigade, in the Arizona expedition, and took part in the battle of Val Verde, where he received a severe wound in the left leg. There were six in his mess, and three of them were wounded. He stood and witnessed the charge of the lancers commanded by Captain Scarbrough. Lieutenant Long led the charge with forty men, and Judge Maney could plainly see the Federal troops when they raised their guns and fired at them. Twenty saddles were emptied by the discharge and ten of the lancers died on the field. The charge was a failure and the survivors came back in disorder.

Col. Tom Ochiltree was in this battle, and before this came off the boys thought he was a coward. They thought the "Red-headed Ranger," as they called him, had no pluck, but after they saw his red head flaming like a meteor on the battlefield, as he dashed from point to point carrying dispatches, or urging his foam-covered horse where the battle raged hottest and bullets flew thickest in the deadly onset of charging lines, they changed their opinion. When the Confederate troops retreated, although they had gained the victory here but were not able to hold the country, their wounded fell into the hands of the Federals, but were paroled.

Judge Maney was paroled by the famous Kit Carson, who was in command of the men who had charge of the prisoners. One company was cut off and captured at the battle of Glorieta, after the Val Verde fight. After the wounded recovered sufficiently, fifty men were started back home together, Judge Maney being elected captain. All came near being drowned while crossing the Rio Grande on a raft. They had to stay here four days and eat mustang meat, but finally arrived at Seguin on the 15th day of August.

Mrs. Maney came to Texas in 1840, and has also witnessed many exciting scenes. She was in sight of the burning of Linville by the Indians, and saw the vast host of painted savages as they started back to the mountains, and saw them pursue and kill Dr. Bell on the prairie.

CAPTURED AN INDIAN.

1876.

Mr. James A. Hudspeth of Kerrville tells the following interesting incident of border life.

In December, 1876, his cousin, Joseph B. Hudspeth, lived in Hondo Canyon, eighteen miles west of Bandera, having moved to that place several years before. One night in the above named year and month, in the early part of the night before the family had retired, Mr. Hudspeth was sitting by the fire, and was attracted by the furious barking of a young dog that he had. On going out in the bright moonlight to learn the cause, he discovered what he thought to be a blanket lying on the ground a short distance from the house. Thinking the children had left it there, he advanced to the spot and stooped to pick it up, but to his surprise the blanket got up and attempted to get away, and seizing it in his arms a struggle commenced, and he knew he had an Indian. He now called to his wife to come and bring the gun. She did so and made an attempt to shoot the Indian, placing the muzzle of the gun against his head and pulling hard on the trigger, but it would not fire, although the hammer had been drawn back, or cocked, to use a more common expression. The reason of this was the fact that it was a double-triggered gun, and Mrs. Hudspeth had failed to spring the trigger. Mr. Hudspeth now told her to desist, as he could hold him, and at once carried him in the house to the light, and saw that it was an Indian boy about 13 years of age, but wiry and strong. He was nearly naked, only having a leather clout about his waist and the old blanket. He was guarded all night, and next day carried to Bandera and placed in the house of Mr. James Hudspeth. The young Indian could neither speak Spanish nor English, and was kept here several days without being able to get any information out of him. About this time a squad of Texas rangers came along. Their guide could speak Spanish, besides several Indian dialects, and came in to see what he could make out of him. After trying him on several, he finally addressed him in the language or dialect of the Tuscalaro Indians. This he understood, and at once commenced conversing, saying he was of that tribe, and had been a captive among the Comanches since he was six years of age. He had been on a raid with them and had become lost, and was trying to steal a horse from Mr. Hudspeth to get out of the country on. Only a few days before this time the Indians had killed Jack Phillips six miles west of Mr Hudspeth's house, and it was supposed this was the band he was with, although the young Indian said nothing about this killing. Now the rangers were after this band of Indians, and crowded them so close that several of their horses gave out and were left on the trail, and it was supposed it was at this time the boy was left, but before the killing of Phillips. The horses of the rangers gave out also, and they turned back at Wallace Creek.

After a few days the young Tuscalaro was turned over to a Mexican named Polly Rodrigues, who was also guide and trailer for soldiers, rangers, or citizens in their pursuit of Indians. He stayed with Rodrigues about two years, and then left the country on one of his horses—borrowed, stolen, or bought, I can not say which. In about the same length of time, however, he returned again and lived with him. He seemed to have no inclination to leave again, and is in the country somewhere yet. Mr. James Hudspeth has been in Kerrville about four years, and saw him there once since. He was glad to see Mr. Hudspeth, and shook hands with him, as he always did when meeting him. Mr. Hudspeth gave him clothes while at his house in Bandera, and the Indian had never forgotten it.

Mr. James Hudspeth came to Texas in 1864 from Arkansas and settled in San Saba County in November of 1865. This was then the frontier, and he was on many scouts and trails after Indians, but never got into a battle with them. He settled on Wallace Creek, and in 1869 was still living there and teaching a country school. One evening he had just arrived at home from the schoolhouse, and had unsaddled and hobbled out his horse, when he saw Wiley Williams, one of the neighbors who lived about 300 yards above, running toward him with a gun in his hand, and when within speaking distance, he exclaimed: "I've salivated one of them." "Salivated one of what?" said Mr. Hudspeth. "An Indian," said Williams; "I have killed an Indian, and I want you to go with me to get him." "All right," said Hudspeth, "but you go first and get William Harkey, and

I will saddle my horse and be ready when you return to accompany you." Harkey lived down the creek three or four hundred yards. While the horse was being saddled, Mrs. Hudspeth, who was out looking around, suddenly exclaimed: "Come here, Mr. Hudspeth, and look. I see a lot of Indians, and they are putting another one on a horse." He did not come in time to see them, as he was hurriedly saddling his horse. When Harkey and Williams came the three proceeded to the spot where the latter said he had shot the Indian. The circumstances, he said, were this: He noticed some cattle on a hill with heads up looking at something, and thinking it was a wolf, got his gun and slipped up there to get a shot at it. While so doing he discovered the Indian in a crouching position watching the horse that Mr. Hudspeth had just hobbled out. Williams laid his gun against a mesquite tree and took aim. He could see the Indian's shield pressed against his left side, but fastened to his left arm, as they always carry them. He aimed above the shield and fired. The Indian at once sprang to his feet, but fell again and lay there. When they came to the spot the Indian was gone, but plenty of blood was found. The balance of the band was near by and carried him off, and this was what Mrs. Hudspeth had witnessed. Some dogs had come with the men, and they at once took the trail of the Indians, followed by the three settlers. Two miles up the creek they came to a cedarbrake which the trail entered and the dogs and men followed. The dogs, however, soon came back with their hair up, and scared. Mr. Hudspeth, who was in the lead, stopped and said: "Boys, if we go in there we will be killed; they can see us and we can not see them." It was now dusk. Williams said if anyone would follow he would go on in. Harkey said he would go, but Mr. Hudspeth turned his horse around and said, "All those that want to go in there and get killed, can do so; I am going back," and with that rode off and the other two followed. Next morning they returned and made a thorough search, but could not find the dead Indian, but found his shield covered with blood, and his bow and quiver of arrows. The bullet had struck the shield high up and went through it. It was braced against his body, was the reason of this. When used in battle with the arm bent in front, the shield hangs loose on the elbow and gives to a ball, and it will glance off.

Three weeks after this, six miles from here, a man while riding in the hills found the body of an Indian where it had been placed under some rocks, directed to the spot by buzzards.

After this Mr. Hudspeth lived on the San Saba River, four miles above the town of San Saba, and one night discovered an Indian by moonlight in a stooping position coming down the fence for the purpose of getting a horse which was inside the inclosure near the fence, and also near the house. Now, before this time Mr. Hudspeth had traded for a Spencer carbine, which was a repeating gun, the cartridges being in the breech, and which had to be thrown into the barrel by a lever. His first thought was, "Now I will kill an Indian," and cocked his piece, without throwing in the cartridge, having been used to a muzzle-loader, and at the moment had forgotten. He intended to let him come to a certain panel in the fence and then cut him nearly in two if he could. He had time to take careful aim, as the Indian was coming slow, slipping along half bent, and of course the gun snapped, and the Indian vanished like a vision of the night, but pursued into a thicket by the dog. The dog soon came back, however, with hair the wrong way, and taking a position in the yard, barked the balance of the night. The Indians (for more were around) finally got to mocking him. Mr. Hudspeth watched the most of the night, but would occasionally drop off to sleep, and Mrs. Hudspeth would keep him roused up. He told her there was no danger of them approaching the house any more that night, knowing they were discovered. Next morning Indian tracks were thick all around.

On one occasion Mr. Hudspeth came very near getting into an Indian fight. He and Harkey and Williams and a man named Henderson and his son got on an Indian trail and finally divided, Hudspeth and Harkey going one way, and the balance of the party the other. Williams and his party found the Indians, ten in number, and fought the battle. They were compelled to retire, and the elder Henderson was badly wounded with a bullet.

DR. J. C. NOWLIN.

Came to Texas in 1855.

Dr. James Crispin Nowlin was born in Caldwell County, Kentucky, April 16, 1817. In 1821 he went with his parents to the western district of Tennessee, but came to Texas from Mississippi, by way of Missouri and Kansas, in 1855. Dr. Nowlin was a slaveholder, but not liking the situation in Kansas, came on to Texas and first settled in Gonzales County, and in 1856 moved to Kerr County and settled near the present town of Center Point. Those who were living in the settlement at this time were the Reese family, Dr. Ridley and family, Joshua Brown and family, and De Witt Burney. Tom Saner was the outside settler up the river above Kerrville. At the settlement of Kerrville there was nothing but a few cabins and camps. George Phillips and Dr. Scott and family lived at the mouth of Silver Creek and Mrs. Denton lived at the mouth of Cherry, below the present town of Center Point, and was the first settler in this part of the country. A Mr. Long and George Nichols lived on Verde Creek, and Nichols had a sawmill there. A company of United States cavalry was stationed at Camp Verde, commanded by Captain Parmer. Henry Moore, a single man, nephew of Dr. Nowlin, came with him to this country.

About February 12, 1857, the Comanche Indians made a raid through the settlement and stole quite a lot of horses, getting seven from the doctor and two from Henry Moore. Captain Parmer of the regulars was notified of the raid, and at once sent fourteen men to get after the hostiles. The captain also sent two horses to mount Dr. Nowlin and Henry Moore, who were anxious to go on the chase. He also sent Polly Rodrigues, a Mexican guide and trailer, who knew all the country and was an experienced Indian fighter. One of the horses stolen by the Indians was taken from near the chimney where he was tied for safety. When the soldiers and guide came from Camp Verde the start was made and the trail taken up at the crossing of the Guadalupe, one mile from Dr. Nowlin's house. Here the Indians had tied ropes to the trees around in a circle so as to catch horses and mount them.

This place is now in the pasture of Alonzo Reese. The Indians went a northwest course and confined themselves to the roughest country they could find, and killed and ate two horses on the way. For seven days the pursuers followed the trail until they came to the head of South Concho.

About 4 o'clock in the evening of the seventh day the doctor and the guide were ahead, both trailing and separated about eighty yards, when the doctor discovered the Indians. They were in camp, but saddling their horses to leave. At a call from Dr. Nowlin the guide came to him, and they charged. By this time the Indians had discovered them and met the charge in fine style and the border battle commenced. Dr. Nowlin fired the first shot from a shotgun at an Indian who was coming towards him, yelling and throwing up his shield in front of him. The Comanche jumped high at the fire of the gun but did not fall, although badly hit. The guide now made a rush for the horses, telling the doctor to keep firing while he secured them. He tried the other barrel of the gun, but it failed to fire. By this time all of the men had dashed up and were firing rapidly. Dr. Nowlin now dismounted, but the guide yelled to him not to leave his horse, as the Indians would charge and get him. This he had no intention of doing, but stood by his side and tried to pick powder into the tube of the barrel of his gun that failed to fire. While doing this an Indian fired at him with a flintlock musket loaded with slugs, one of which struck his horse in the neck near the throatlatch of the bridle, and he fell dead in his tracks.

Dr. Nowlin noticed when his horse fell that he had also been struck by an arrow. The Indian who killed the horse began to reload again in a hurry, but put his ball down first, and when he tried another fire at the doctor it flashed in the pan. Dr. Nowlin at the same time was playing on the Indian with a six-shooter, and soon moved him further off. Three of the Indians were very brave, and charged within twenty-five yards of the main body of the white men. A good deal of firing was done on both sides, the Indians yelling and jumping from side to side as they fought, and trying all the time to scare the white men's horses. A Mexican named Jim Tafoyia charged an Indian and ran him about 100 yards, snapping his six-shooter at him repeatedly, putting the muzzle of the pistol against the Indian's side, but it failed to fire. The Comanche, seeing he had a chance for life, pulled an

arrow as he ran and quickly shot it over his left shoulder, and
would have killed the Mexican if it had not been for an overcoat
which was rolled up tightly and lay across the saddle in front of
him. The arrow went through this, cutting thirty-two holes in
the folds, and slightly wounding Jim. This stopped him, and the
Indian got away. When the Indians quit the fight they went
quickly and soon disappeared, leaving none dead on the ground.
No doubt some received mortal wounds and ran away to die, or
were assisted away by the others, which they always do if they
can make a stand-off and have time. Badly wounded Indians
leave a battle at once as soon as hit, and sometimes will travel
for miles before lying down.

After the battle was over a badly wounded man named Martin
was brought to Dr. Nowlin to receive medical aid. He was a
soldier from Camp Verde, and was wounded with a bullet. The
ball had passed through the left lung, and blood was running
from his mouth, and he was vomiting blood. This fact puzzled
the doctor, blood coming from a man's stomach, and the wound
in the lung. The doctor could do but very little to relieve him.
Fort McKavett was the nearest point where shelter and better attention could be given the wounded man, and it was decided to
take him there. He lived to make the trip of thirty miles or
more, but died the same night of arrival. Dr. Nowlin was still
curious to know the cause of Martin vomiting blood, and after
the man died he and the post surgeon made an examination of
the body and found that the upper part of the stomach had also
been cut by the ball, which let blood into it from the perforated
lung. Now the next thing was, how did the same ball do both
with the man in an upright position? The cause was finally figured out. During the pursuit of the Indians at one time the
men suffered very much for water, and when they found some
this man, as Dr. Nowlin expressed it, "drank like a cow," and
his stomach was so powerfully distended that it came up under
the lung, and the ball passed through the upper part of it. They
were then close upon the Indians, and the fight commenced a
few minutes after.

Dr. Nowlin says he never saw but five Indians in this fight.
There might have been more, as it was brushy in places. He heard
men tell at Fort McKavett that there were twenty Indians, and
that five were killed. The spoils were five horses, two mules, and

five buffalo skins. The horses and mules were all they had, and the doctor did not believe these were the Indians they were on the trail of, from the fact that none of the stock belonged in the Guadalupe valley. He thinks this band was coming from another direction and happened to stop for a rest near the trail of the others. No search was made at the time to ascertain.

Henry Moore displayed great bravery during the fight, although suffering from consumption, which finally killed him.

In 1859 Dr. Nowlin moved his stock to Kendall County and settled on Curry's Creek.

In October, 1868, the Indians made a raid on Curry's Creek, first showing themselves at Mr. Ammond's, on the Guadalupe River, ten miles from Nowlin's ranch, killing some stock and carrying off others. This was about the 28th of October. On the same night a runner was sent to the doctor's neighborhood, informing the people there that Indians were in the country. On the following day a company of rangers, commanded by Captain John W. Sansom, hunted all day for the Indians, and in the evening found where they had crossed Curry's Creek. The people were then notified that the Indians were in their settlement, and guards were put out at the different ranches. At this time Dr. Nowlin had two young men hired, named Francis Keiser and Charley Williams, and put them on guard at his horselot at night. He had gathered up his best horse stock and put some of them in a small pasture near by and locked others in stables. In the early part of the night it was evident Indians were around on account of the commotion among the horses in the pasture. The Indians were in there after them, and had made gaps in the fence and were trying to drive them out, but the horses would run by these places. The two boys on guard at the lot got in a corncrib with their guns and thought best to remain quiet and await developments, but as the night wore on they fell asleep.

About 2 o'clock in the morning, the Indians failing to get the horses out of the pasture, two of them came to the lot to see what chance there was of getting some there. They took down the fence to the field lot and orchard, so they could get out easy if discovered. About this time a dog on the place discovered the presence of Indians, and set up a furious barking which awakened little Kate Nowlin, and she began to cry. At this time the two young men were fast asleep at their post in the crib. The doctor waked up and told his little daughter not to cry, as the dogs would not hurt her, and to go to sleep again. But all at once the stillness of the night was broken by "Bang! bang!" in the direction of the corncrib. Dr. Nowlin sprang clear into the middle of the floor, and seizing his gun ran out without dressing and shouted, "What's up, boys?" "We have killed an Indian," came a voice from the crib. On coming to the spot an Indian was discovered down on his hands and knees, but not dead. Not wishing to shoot him again, the doctor picked up a hoe-handle and struck him a powerful blow on the side of the head, and he fell over. He repeated the blows until he was dead, exclaiming with each lick, "We will show him up! We will show him up!" The barking of the dog had awakened the boys, and looking out through a crack they saw the two Indians by the moonlight. One was in plain view near a fodder stack, and the other was behind the fence with only the top of his head visible. At this Indian behind the fence Keiser said he would shoot, and Williams was to shoot the other. The ball from Keiser's gun struck the Indian at whom he aimed in the top of the head and he fell; but Williams was a little slower to fire and his Indian started to run and he missed him. He made his escape, followed by the dog, who ran him several hundred yards. The dead Indian had on a polecat-skin cap, and his companion one just like it, which he lost in his run from the dog. The Indians had no weapons, they having been left in their camp on a hill, which was afterwards found.

The doctor now sent his son to notify the people that the Indians had been to his ranch, and to "look out." They had divided and scattered all over the country, being at the ranches of Sansom, Calahan, Reese, and Judge Jones on the same night, and two at each place, and succeeded in getting off with some stock. Calahan had a fine horse tied to the gallery post which he was watching, but went to sleep and the Indians got him. He also had two fine mules close by, but they failed to get these on account of the approach of Dr. Nowlin's son, who came at full gallop to give the alarm.

The camp of the Indians was found less than a mile from the doctor's and the same distance from Wesley Calahan's. On a rock near by were twenty marks, and one of them crossed out. Also one bow and quiver of arrows were found by the doctor.

These no doubt belonged to the dead Indian and had been left, thinking he might have escaped and would need them.

In 1870 Dr. Nowlin was appointed surgeon to a company of rangers commanded by Capt. John W. Sansom and stationed at Camp Verde. In the spring of 1871 the company was ordered to Fort Griffin, on the Clear fork of the Brazos, and soon after arriving there went on a long scout to the head of the Big Wichita River. The Tonkaway chief, Castile, was along, as was also one of his warriors named Bill. This fellow was a good scout and trailer, and kept ahead of the company all of the time. One evening the rangers stopped to pick mulberries, and while engaged in this Tonkaway Bill came back and reported that two Comanches were coming just over the hill. The rangers at once mounted, and on coming to the crest of the rising ground or small hill saw the Indians and gave chase. After running one and a half miles and turning down another hill one of the Indians was dismounted by his girth breaking, and was soon killed. The other one ran across the prairie nearly two miles before he was overtaken. Many shots were fired at him without effect, and he was nearing the timber when his horse was killed by William Causten. The Indian was brave, and charged the rangers, making the arrows fly, but was soon killed and scalped, and left on the prairie where he fought his last battle with his paleface foes. Dr. Nowlin turned him over and saw three bullet holes in him. He also had an old wound in the leg, which caused it to draw, and was shorter than the other. The only damage among the rangers was one with a sprained wrist, caused by his horse falling with him. This the doctor soon set right.

In 1872 and part of 1873 Dr. Nowlin was in command of a minute company. In 1876 he was appointed physician and surgeon for Capt. Neal Caldwell's company of rangers. On one scout during this time at the head of South Llano the rangers got word that the Indians had captured some horses from a party of buffalo hunters, and at once went in pursuit of them. On Saturday they struck the Indian trail at the "buffalo pond," and filling all of the canteens, pushed on after them. A camp was made that night on the plains, and all the water used up. No more could be found, and they were compelled to quit the trail and travel down one of the draws of Devil's River in search of some. On Sunday night they made another dry camp and tied up all the horses. The trailer, Alexander Merritt, walked a good deal, and having drank up all of his water the first day, was now suffering intense thirst. Captain Caldwell had a little water, and Dr. Nowlin told him to give it to Merritt. The trailer was called and the water offered to him, but he would not accept of it, because the other boys had none. All the next day the men suffered so much that they crossed a large Indian trail and paid no attention to it. All eyes were scanning the country in search of water. On the next day they found plenty of water, a large spring coming out from under a mountain. The doctor said, "Boys, drink light, and do not let your horses have much." Some did not hear this order, and going to a pool below the spring, drank so much it made them sick. The command stayed here one day and a half, and then the men did not want to go back the way they came, but seeing a black cloud up that way thought it might rain and furnish water, and were finally prevailed on to start. William Layton was on the left flank as spy, but had to head so many ravines that he became lost and was unable to find the command. The rangers were uneasy about Layton, for fear he would perish for water. The lost ranger, however, found water and filled his canteen, and camped alone when night came. Next morning, not knowing which way to take among such a network of ravines and hills, he gave his horse the bridle, and the instinct of the animal carried him directly to the trail of the rangers. He had to spend another night alone, however, as the command was some distance ahead, but on the next day overhauled them.

In 1876 Dr. Nowlin belonged to Capt. Henry Moore's company of rangers, and was stationed at the head of Bear Creek, fifteen miles from the present Junction City, in Kimble County. On the day before Christmas of the above named year, in the morning, the Indians made a raid into the settlement where Junction is now and killed a boy half a mile west of town, and two miles further killed a man on North Llano. The people were afraid to leave the settlement to notify the rangers until late in the day, but finally one man ventured out and arrived at the ranger camp about an hour by sun. The rangers at once got out and crowded the Indians so close they were compelled to abandon some of the stolen stock, which stood on the trail covered with sweat when the men came upon them.

It was hard trailing through the cedarbrakes and over rocks, and finally the horses played ont and the pursuit had to be abandoned. The rangers turned back at Wallace Creek (named for Big Foot Wallace, who owned a tract of land there), one of the tributaries of the Medina River. This was the band of Indians that killed Jack Phillips between the Hondo and Sabinal, ten miles or more south from where their trail was abandoned.

In 1869 the Indians made a raid, and one of them was killed at Judge Jones' ranch. The Blanco men followed the Indians and kept in sight of them all day, and when night came crossed the divide and notified the settlers on Curry's Creek of the raid. Pink Jones and a Mexican named Serelda went out at night and took a stand at the corner of the field fence to watch for the Indians, and finally saw two coming towards them. They let them came close, and both fired. Just at the moment, however, the Indians discovered them and turned. Jones missed his, but the one which the Mexican fired at was badly wounded, leaving a trail of blood for some distance. He lost his scalping-knife, which was picked up on the trail. Some time afterward the skeleton of an Indian was found in the hills with a belt and empty knife scabbard around the waist. The knife picked up on the trail of the wounded Indian just fit the scabbard, and no doubt this was him.

Dr. Nowlin has lost stock altogether while living on the frontier valued at $13,000, and never recovered but one animal back from them. The doctor was an active, stirring man, however, and always had plenty. He died at his home at Center Point, Texas, on the 8th day of December, 1898, in the eighty-second year of his age.

JACK HARDY CAPTURED BY INDIANS.

Negro boy. Born in Kerr County.

When the great State of Texas was being settled by white men who were continually pushing to the front along the border from nearly every State in the Union, there were those who brought their negro slaves with them, and some of these had thrilling experiences with Indians. They were killed, scalped and carried into captivity the same as white men, and had to meet all the dangers of frontier life as well as their masters, and often fought bravely around the frontier cabin in defense of white women and children.

Among others of these slaves and ex-slaves who have been carried into captivity, and who have a tale to tell, is Jack Hardy, who now lives in the Guadalupe valley near Center Point.

While the writer was on the hunt for frontier history in the Guadalupe valley country, several of the prominent citizens there told me of Jack Hardy, and would like for me to get a history of his captivity among the Indians, and also said that they would vouch for the truth of his statements, and that no colored man stood higher in their estimation than he.

Jack Hardy was born on the Guadalupe River, in Kerr County, half a mile above the town of Center Point, forty-two years ago, and belonged to Dr. John Ridley.

After the Civil war, when all the slaves were free, Jack lived near Comfort, below Center Point. On one occasion, when he was about 12 or 13 years of age, he was sent to mill with a turn of corn, and it was then the Indians got him. He was in sight of home on his return, and saw the Indians when some distance, and could then have made his escape, but thought they were white men, as some of them had on hats. He paid no more attention to them, but jogged along the road, not apprehending any danger, until four of them came up behind him. While some laid hold upon him others jumped down and caught his horse by the bridle and threw his sack of meal to the ground, and said something he could not understand. Up to this time he had never seen Indians, and still did not know who they were.   He noticed they were curious-looking men, but to keep on the good side of them he removed his hat and spoke to them as politely as he could, but as they did not return his salutation he supposed they did not like niggers much. He soon discovered they had long hair, carried bows and shields, and the truth dawned upon him that they were Indians, from descriptions he had heard of them from old settlers and Indian fighters. He cast one glance towards home and could see some of his people in the yard, but it was too far off for them to detect what was transpiring. The young negro, when he realized that he was a prisoner and would have to go with the Indians, adopted a wise course, and that was to be obedient and not get scared at anything they might do to him. He noticed that there were fifteen of them, and that they were tall, fine-looking men except two, and they were very low in stature and very ugly. His first initiation to captivity among Comanches was a severe whipping with a liveoak stick, the scars of which are still to be seen on Jack's head. They now gave him bow and arrows, and made signs that if the white men came upon them he must help fight. They also had guns and pistols, and one of them could talk English. Jack thinks he was a white man, as he would not talk to him much.

This was on Saturday, at 1 o'clock, and the captive had nothing to eat until Sunday at 3. The Indians took a westerly course through the hills below the mouth of Verde Creek, leaving Center Point, or the settlement there, about three miles to the right north. On a tributary of the Verde now inclosed by the pasture of Messrs. McElroy and Vaughan, and in charge and run by Mr. James Crotty, they came upon the cabin of Ed. Terry, due south from the present town of Center Point, about two and a half miles. Mr. Terry was a short distance from the house, sitting down riving boards from cypress blocks which he had brought from the Verde Creek, one mile north of his place. As he had his head down he did not see the Indians when they approached, and one of them stopped his horse and aimed a gun at him. Jack sat on a horse near by and with bated breath watched the whole proceeding, but dared give no warning note to the doomed man. When the gun fired Terry sprang to his feet, ran about forty yards, and fell. Another Indian now went to him and lanced him, and he soon expired. By this time the

45

other members of the family were screaming and running away
from the house, pursued by others of the Indians, who killed two
of the children and captured a little girl about 8 years old. Mrs.
Terry made her escape, and as she sprang over the yard fence
she threw her baby boy Joe into high weeds, and the Indians
failed to discover it. They shot many times at her, but she
sprang into a deep gully near by and eluded them. When she
reached the settlement and the alarm was given, a small party
of settlers repaired to the scene of the killing and buried the slain
man and his children, and also rescued the little boy, who was
crawling about in the grass and weeds not far from the spot
where he was thrown.

The Indians from the cabin went towards the Bandera pass
and ascended a high mountain to the left of it and there halted
awhile. While here they placed Jack on a rock, and pulling off
his hat jerked his head back and put a sharp knife to his throat,
as if about to cut it. The negro was badly scared but showed
no outward sign, and even leaned his head back further so as
to give them a better chance to cut it good. The Indians now
laughed, and turning him loose, said "Bravo! Bravo!" They
now pulled a lot of wool out of his head, and holding it up, let
the wind blow it away as they sifted it through their fingers.
At this they also laughed very much. From here they went
down the mountain and took the Bandera road, and after dark
went through the town two and two abreast, and crosed the Medina River a little above. They now came back on their trail
and captured a sorrel horse in the edge of town. They had
killed a cow somewhere, and when they finally stopped to rest
they ate her paunch. They had one horse along that would
pitch every time an Indian got on him, and one morning they
put a rope on this horse with a loop over his nose as they were
about to start, and sat the little Terry girl astride him. Jack
thought sure the vicious horse would kill the poor child, but
strange to say he went along perfectly docile. An Indian now
tried him, and he pitched all over an acre of ground.

When the Indians would camp at night Jack thought sure the
white men would catch them by morning, but no pursuers came,
and in this way they traveled through the mountains and crossed
Hondo, Seco, and Sabinal canyons, the latter just below where
Utopia is now. When they came to the Blanco, still further west,

they made another halt on top of a mountain, and three of them took Jack and went down into the valley after water. While doing this they saw a white man coming up the valley towards them. The three Indians howled like wolves when they saw him, and all of the other Indians came to them. One Indian was left with the captives, and fourteen of them ambushed the white man, who came along all unconscious of the trap laid for him. The Indians all had guns and pistols, and raised up and commenced firing at him at not more than thirty steps distant. The white man turned quickly and made a terrible plunge through the brush, pulling his Winchester as he did so and firing one shot, but was then seen to fall from the left side, and then both horse and rider were lost to sight. The Indians yelled fiercely and went in pursuit, and soon came back leading his horse with blood on the saddle, and one of them had his hat, which was a brown plush. Well, thought Jack, one more white man dead. He soon found out, however, that they did not get him. They failed to show up his scalp or gun. The scabbard was hanging to the horn of the saddle. The Indians would point to the blood on the saddle and gloat over that. They fired fourteen shots with guns and pistols, and Jack says if they had used their bows they would have got him, for he had seen them shoot deer and never miss. They handled firearms awkwardly.

The writer expects to get a full account of this remarkable escape from Indians, but will say here that the man was Chris. Kelley, who lived on Sabinal, and that he was not wounded, and got home all right. The blood on the saddle was from deer hams he was carrying.

The weather had now turned very cold, for it was in December, and commenced to sleet and snow. The little girl's bare legs were about to freeze as she rode across the bleak mountains behind one of the Indians. They made her a pair of moccasins which came above her knees, and she fared some better. That night when the Indians camped it was very cold and sleet was falling rapidly, but despite all this they tied Jack down as usual flat of his back, legs stretched one way and arms the other, to stakes in the ground, with his upturned face exposed to the bitter blast. He had his hat on, and by working his head back and forth managed to bring it over his face and held it there with his teeth to keep the wind from blowing it back, and by that means kept the·sleet out of his face and to some extent alleviated his sufferings.

During this cold spell the Indians killed a steer, and ate all of it up from 2 o'clock one day until 2 the next. They ate all the time while in camp. The rascals did not seem to fear pursuit. They carried water in cow paunches, and it was as cold as ice. When Jack went to take a drink he took but little on account of it being so cold, and the Indians, noticing this, made him drink a quart without stopping. He said it nearly killed him, and he felt like his head was going to come off.

One of the Indians made a hair rope, one end of which he gave to Jack and he took the other, and made signs for him to pull hard. He wanted to let loose his end and give Jack a fall, but the boy turned loose his end and let the Indian fall after giving one strong pull. He was very mad, and Jack had to keep out of his way to keep from getting hit. One of the Indians made a girth, and Jack was lying on his stomach watching him, and when the Indian got through he pulled out a six-shooter, put the muzzle of it in the negro's mouth at a full cock, and then placed his finger on the trigger. Still retaining his presence of mind, Jack opened his mouth wider so the Indian could push it further if he wanted to, and they all laughed as he drew it out, and said, "Mucho bravo!" The Indians were very mean, and tried to annoy their captives as much as possible. They made them throw rocks at each other, but Jack would miss the little girl every time on purpose.

After the weather moderated the Indians came on over into Frio Canyon and robbed a cow camp, and then crossed the Frio and went on to a high mountain overlooking the settlement on the Patterson ditch farm. Some of the Indians had stopped in the valley to catch some horses, and four of them who had the captives stopped on the mountain to wait for them, and here Jack made his escape. He was about fifty yards behind, and all at once concluded to make his escape. He jumped down and pulled off his bow and quiver and laid them on the ground so he could run well, but at this time an Indian looked around and ordered him back on his horse. The negro made signs to him that he was fixing his blanket, and the Indian looked down the valley to see where the others were. About this time they were just getting on top of the mountain, and the Indians saw some houses up the valley and had their eyes on them. Jack now ran down the mountain through the brush, and when the Indians looked around again he was gone; they were not aware which way he went, and could not find him. The little girl saw him when he started, but said nothing. Down near the foot of the mountain he hid under a bluff, and he thought sure he heard the Indians coming after him and gave up all hope, but when he looked around it was an old muley cow coming under where he was to lick. He was nearly starved, and broke icicles from the rocks and ate them, and then coming on down into the valley he went to an old house which he could see in the distance. When near the place he saw a man riding near him and carrying a Winchester, and being afraid of him, he began to whistle so as to attract his attention without coming up to him too suddenly. At the sound of his voice the man turned his head quickly and Jack cried out "Good evening, sir."

The white man said, "Who are you?"

"I am a little nigger boy, sir, and just got away from a bunch of Indians that had me," said Jack.

"The h—l you say," said the man with the gun. "I thought there were Indians over there, the way them d—d horses were cavorting around."

This man was John Dickson. He was a kind-hearted man, and took the half-frozen, half-starved negro to his house and gave him warm clothes and plenty to eat, and getting all the information he could in regard to the Indians, mounted his horse and alarmed the settlers.

How the Frio men gathered and pursued the Indians, fought a battle with them in Dry Frio Canyon, and rescued the little girl, will be found in the sketch of John Patterson.

Jack finally drifted back to the Guadalupe Valley, hiring himself for a time to James McLemore on the Hondo.

CAMP VERDE.

Established in 1855.

This old, historic frontier post, around which cluster so many reminiscences of ante-bellum days, is situated in Kerr County, on the Verde Creek, twelve miles south of Kerrville, two miles north of the famous Bandera pass, and six miles west of Center Point, on the Guadalupe River.

This post was established by an act of Congress in 1855, for frontier protection and for a camel post. In 1856 forty camels arrived, with twelve Armenian drivers and their families. A sketch had been made of an eastern caravansary in Asia Minor, and it was reproduced at Camp Verde in every minute particular. It was built in a rectangular shape except the north wall, which made an angle, the distance from each corner to this angle being 150 feet. This wall was sixteen feet high and made of concrete and timber, called "pise" work. The timber came from Pensacola, Fla., and it cost the government $125 per thousand to get it here. The south walls were not so high, and in front was an open court, in which was a well with the old-style Egyptian sweep. This project of using camels on the Texas frontier was an idea which originated with Jefferson Davis. He thought that camels could cross the desert country with more ease and quicker than horses and go longer without water, which would greatly facilitate carrying dispatches and following Indians. This was all true enough. The camel could cross these desert stretches better than a horse if it had all been desert sand, but Camp Verde was situated too far east, and was in a mountainous, rocky country, over which the camel with his soft, spongy feet, only suited to sand, could make but little headway. The tough Spanish pony could beat him. Later it might have succeeded, when the line of posts was extended out to the great plains, but the project at Camp Verde was a failure.

Capt. I. N. Palmer was the first commander at this post, and he rose to the rank of general in the United States army during the Civil war. Major Bowman next occupied the position, and died here. Lieutenant Wheaton, afterwards a general, also commanded here. Gen. Robert E. Lee and Gen. Albert Sidney Johnston were also at this post, and it was from here that General Johnston started on his expedition across the plains to operate against the Mormons in 1857. The Johnston fork of the Guadalupe was named after him.

The post was surrendered to the Confederates in 1861, and occupied by them until 1865, when the United States government again took possession of it. The camels being a failure as far as following Indians was concerned, they were sold in 1868 to Bethel Coopwood. Up to that time they had increased to 125. The price Coopwood paid for them was $12 and $14 around. Part of the breeding stock was then sold to a man here in Texas, who raised them for a circus, and the remainder was bought by a Californian (that is, of the breeding stock), who raised them for their hair value. The strong camels were sent to Mexico to be used by a transportation company, a scheme of Mr. Coopwood's, but it failed. They were left some time in Mexico, and their feed bill ran up to $800, when they were sold to cover it. They were redeemed by the Vance brothers, and brought back to the United States and placed with a bunch in California.

Some of the camels escaped, and their offspring are now wild on the plains of Texas, New Mexico, and Arizona. They are occasionally seen by cowboys, and some few have been run down and wrongfully shot by them. Some few escaped from Camp Verde and went into the mountains here, and a good price was paid to have them brought back in case anyone found them. At that time they had not become wild, and could be easily managed when found. A German boy living near Castroville caught one and carried it to San Antonio, and the authorities paid him a good price for it.

During the cholera score of 1892 General Wheaton, who was in command of the department of Texas, sent some officers to Camp Verde, who took an option lease on the property for a year, with a privilege of longer time, so they could absolutely have a quarantine camp by closing roads and stopping all travel to this place. This arrangement was made with the Commissioners Court through Mr. J. A. Bonnell, who then owned the Camp Verde property. He purchased it in 1875. It is now owned by his son, W. H. Bonnell. After the purchase of the property by the elder Bonnell, one day while the hands were at work the skeleton of a camel was turned up by a plow. An old negro man in the settlement said he knew how it came there, but at first would not tell his tale until he was assured that nothing would be done with him for any wrongdoing on his part. He said soon after the war he, in company with several other negroes, one night went out on a chicken-stealing expedition, and along towards day sat down in an open glade to rest. A dense fog had arisen, and objects could not be distinctly seen at more than a few feet distant. Directly a hideous object came out of the brush towards them, and they were all greatly frightened, thinking it was the devil. At first they all prayed, thinking it was no use to run. When the poor old camel, however, for such it was, came and poked his cold nose in some of their faces, and they realized what this nocturnal visitor was, their courage came back, and being armed with pistols, all commenced shooting and soon killed the old camel. The washings from the hills soon covered the remains and there he found a grave—the last of his race. He had come back from the hills near the old caravansary, where he had spent so many days.

Part of the old caravansary was still standing when the writer was there in 1898. The timber was all taken out and carried to San Antonio and sold, leaving the wall unsupported, and most of it had fallen down.

The present owner of the property, Mr. W. H. Bonnell, has a large establishment and keeps a public house. He has many summer and winter boarders. The latter come from the far North to escape the long winters there, and others come from the South and interior of Texas to escape the heat of summer. The place is beautiful, warm in winter and cool in summer, with plenty of game near in the hills.

REV. A. L. JAMES.

Rev. Andrew Larkin James was born in Comanche County, on Restly's Creek, near the Erath County line, March 4, 1860. This place was a cow-ranch fort, where the people assembled in times of Indian raids, and as all lived in one settlement near together, they could take refuge on short notice when the alarm of Indians in the country was heard. Of the families in and near the fort were those at Croos' mill, Braggett's ranch, Galbreth's ranch, Barbee's ranch, Monroe Whitesides, Ratliff's ranch, Enoch James, father of our subject, and William M. Stone, his grandfather. These two were partners in business under the firm name of Stone & James. In this same year, 1860, several members of the Braggett family were killed by Indians, including men and women. Most of the people after this assembled at the "cow ranch fort," which was eighteen miles east of the present town of Comanche, which at that time was not in existence. Old Cora was the county seat, twenty-two miles southeast, and Restly's Creek was twelve miles north of this place. At the commencement of the Civil war the Indians were more hostile than usual, and Enoch James, with many others, moved to the town of Comanche, which was just starting. Some of the families moved east and left the frontier. The Indians raided around Comanche constantly, killing people and carrying off stock, and even coming into the town on moonlight nights and carrying off stock. During these raids the James family had an old, gentle hack horse which was carried off three times, but on each occasion he would give out in a half day's travel and they would turn him loose, and the faithful old animal would come back home.

It was among such scenes and incidents as these that young James was raised until he was about 12 years of age, when he became a participant in one of those bloody chapters of frontier history. At this time, about 1872, two young men employed as teamsters by James & Stone, who had a store in Comanche, started to San Saba with two wagons and mule teams loaded with wheat and corn. The young men were George Wallace and Frank Brown, and a young man named Bush. Grissum, who was out for his health, was with them. One of the teams consisted

REV. A. L. JAMES.

of six mules and the other four, the former having the wheat. It was fifty miles to San Saba. The boys traveled half the distance the first day, and just before sundown drove out of the road to make their camp for the night. Before they commenced to unharness the mules a man named John Roach rode up on a pony just from San Saba, and said he would camp with them. Of course this was agreeable, and he unsaddled his pony and turned him loose to graze. The Indians had made no raids for some time, and the fear of them was about over in that country. At this time, however, there were about thirty Indians in a ravine near by, watching the movements of the three young men. They had evidently discovered the wagons coming and ambushed them, thinking they would pass near, and even let Roach pass so as not to give the alarm to the drivers too soon, for fear they would make their escape. When, however, Roach met them and turned his horse loose they perceived the white men were going to camp, and came out of the ravine and advanced towards them, thinking no doubt to make easy work with the four white men. About this time Brown, who was a new comer in the country, asked Roach if he was not afraid of Indians, to travel alone in that way, and his reply was that he had not lost any Indians and was not hunting for any. At this moment Grissum discovered the Indians, and said to Roach, "Whether you are hunting for them or not, you will be apt to find them, for here they come now." Brown knew nothing about Indians, but was brave, and said, "Boys, we will have to sell out the best we can," and took the shotgun out of the wagon, the only weapon they had. Roach had a five-shooter, and was also a fearless man. The Indians came yelling and were soon close upon them, shooting both bullets and arrows. Brown was wounded twice with bullets, once in the face and once in the arm, but he stood his ground and told the other men to cut the mules out of the wagon and each of them would mount one and try to make their escape, and let the loose mules follow them. In doing this several mules escaped and ran to the Indians, as did also the pony of Roach, but Brown held on to one and aimed his gun at the Indians. The chief was in front, finely dressed, and had his shield up in front and advancing, having dismounted from his horse. Brown now aimed under the shield and fired the last load from the shotgun, and, as he expressed it, hit the Indian in the flank and inflicted a mortal wound. The chief caught hold of a sapling to keep from falling, and jumping up and down uttered a peculiar noise, and many of the other Indians crowded about him. Brown says, "Now, boys, is your chance to get away." During the firing George Wallace was shot in the arm, and Grissum had a ball to pass through his coat under the arm. The mule which Brown had held on to during all of this confusion of yelling Indians, firing, and plunging mules, was a wheeler, and had on a saddle, which he succeeded in getting into and started off, as did all the others except Roach. The mule which he mounted was wounded and threw him, and he himself had an arrow shot through his body. Brown turned back to stay with him, but the wounded man begged him to leave and save himself while he could, as he himself was killed and no assistance could be rendered. The brave friend now reluctantly turned and galloped away after his companions. The Indians did not follow, but at once came all around Roach and commenced a desperate battle with him. He had not as yet fired a load from his pistol, reserving it for just such a hand-to-hand struggle as was now inaugurated, and succeeded in keeping them at bay, and again mounted his wounded mule and dashed away, and succeeded in getting clear of them. In a four-mile run the mule fell dead in his tracks from the wound which he had received, and Roach succeeded in dragging himself half a mile further and then sank down exhausted. He was unable to extract the arrow, as it was through the body, the spike protruding on the opposite side from the shaft, and here he had to remain in the most excruciating agony for many long hours. Out of the five shots in his pistol during his desperate battle he killed four Indians. The men who escaped up the road back towards Comanche arrived there just before day with the news, and a party was at once raised and went back to the wagons. Frank Brown, not being familiar with the dress of Indians, supposed the one he shot was a woman, on account of the long hair parted in the middle and the loose, gaudy dress with many fixtures and beads, and told the men who went back if they found a dead Indian woman there full of buckshot, it was him who killed her. He also said he hated to do it, but she was in front and coming at them with a shield before her, and that he aimed under it and fired. The party expected to find the dead and mangled body of Roach. They were unable to do so, but discovered many bloody signs of the desperate battle. A short distance off a grave was found, with a dead horse near it, with a rope around his neck and the other end in the covered grave. This was a rather peculiar circumstance, and when the grave was opened the dead body of the chief was found in a sitting position and holding the other end of the rope in his hand. He was taken out and examined, and twelve buckshot holes were found in his body around the waist. He had on a breastplate made of several pieces of ivory or bone, crossed and lapped in such a way that a bullet would not penetrate it. His arm shield, which he held in front of him, was found with him, and it had five scalps of women attached to it, one of which was that of a red-haired woman. John Roach was found the same day, nearly perished for water, by one of the negro cowhands of Captain Cunningham. He was brought in, and the arrow taken out of him and the wound dressed by Dr. Montgomery. Strange to say he recovered, as did also all the balance of the wounded men. The graves of the four Indians Roach killed were also found.

Twenty-three men now gathered from Comanche and South Leon to follow the Indians, all under the command of Capt. James Cunningham. Among the number were four or five of the captain's sons, all good Indian fighters. After the men had left Comanche, several boys of that place from 12 to 14 years of age were determined to go on this chase, and made up a crowd of their own. They were Andrew James, the subject of our sketch, then not quite 12 years of age, Freeman Clark, Joel and George Cunningham, and a young fellow named Neighbors. They were delayed in getting off on account of one of them having no saddle, and it was some trouble to find one they could get. They also had to rustle for firearms. Young James got a shotgun and the others got old cap and ball six-shooters, or as some called them, "snap and ball." They now set off rapidly on the trail of the others, but had their ardor somewhat dampened when they did catch up by the old fellows trying to drive them back. They begged and even cried to be allowed to go. Captain Cunningham, who was an old Indian fighter, said, "We had better drive you back now than to have to bring you back dead. Boys are like young hound pups, hard to manage, and will run off after every rabbit that jumps up." This is certainly the first instance on record where young Texas lads cried for an opportunity to fight Indians. The two Cunningham boys went back, but James, Clark, and Neighbors followed on in spite of all. The latter was the eldest of the three. The trail of the Indians led into the Salt Creek mountains, in Brown County, and Captain Cunningham and his men camped near them when night came and used the utmost caution, so that their presence was not discovered. A complete surprise was the result early on the following morning, so much so that some of the Indians had not yet arisen when the onset was made, led by Aaron Cunningham, one of the sons of the captain. The Indians had no time to mount horses, and scattered on foot in various directions, fighting as they went. Three Indians ran off to one side in company, and were charged by the kids who had cried to come. Freeman Clark was on the best horse and took the lead, closely followed by Andrew James, while Neighbors came in the rear. Clark soon caught up with his Indian and aimed his old pistol at his breast, and it snapped. The Indian also had a pistol, and passing under the neck of Clark's horse, shot the unfortunate boy dead from his saddle. In the meantime the other two Indians had sprang behind trees and opened on the other boys, one with a pistol and the other with arrows, and killed both of their horses and wounded young James twice, one bullet and one arrow wound. But the lad who cried to fight Indians did not lose his head in this terrible dilemma, but fired both barrels of his shotgun at an Indian who had left his tree and was running and shooting back, and no doubt got in his work, for the Indian was killed. About this time, however, a reinforcement came to the boys. Larkin Stone, uncle of young James, seeing the terrible havoc that was being made of the young Indian fighters by the three experienced warriors, dashed in at full speed with a shotgun and two revolvers and commenced a rapid fusilade. He first killed the Indian who had just killed young Clark, and then the one behind the tree, picking him out nicely with a pistol shot as he partly exposed his body to shoot. This Indian had fired at Stone with a pistol just as he killed the Indian that shot young Clark, and struck the hilt of one of his pistols with such force that it bruised his side considerably. All three of these Indians were killed. In the meantime the fight, though badly scattered, was going on with the balance of the band, and it was an hour before the pursuit was ended. Nine more Indians were killed, making eleven in all. About twenty bows and shields were picked up, besides pistols and some Spencer carbines. When young James was examined it was found that he had one ball through the leg below the knee and one arrow above the knee, which had penetrated to the bone and was still fast in the wound, and was with difficulty withdrawn. He was placed on a blanket between two mules and slowly conveyed back home to his parents, where by good nursing he soon recovered. The funeral of young Freeman Clark was the largest that was ever seen in Comanche up to that time. He was a teamster for James & Stone, and was liked by all who knew him. Only one Indian raid was made after this in that part of the country.

Andrew James was converted in 1885, and has been in the ministry as a Baptist preacher since 1892. He now lives near Center Point, Kerr County, Texas, and is in the Southwest Missionary work in the Medina River Association.

He has an old rifle which belonged to his grandfather Stone, which has killed many Indians, the last one being in Comanche County. On that occasion Mr. Stone was out hunting in the Leon bottom, and discovered an Indian sitting on a log with a gun across his lap. The old man took aim at him and tumbled him off and then beat a retreat back, as he knew not how many more might be around. He returned with a party and found the dead Indian by the log.

CAPT. NEAL COLWELL.

Came to Texas in 1860.

Captain Colwell was born in Dade County, Missouri, in May, 1844. His father, Thomas Colwell, was a soldier under General Jackson in the war of 1812, and participated in the famous battle of New Orleans, fought on the 8th of January, 1815.

In 1850 Thomas Colwell immigrated to California, going the overland route across the plains. His was quite a large outfit, consisting of five wagons with five yoke of oxen in each, and one spring wagon and ambulance for the members of the family to ride in. Besides this, he carried extra horses for the vehicles and 100 head of Missouri cattle. In his pay also, as guards, were fifteen men under the command of Captain Stockton.

This was a long, tedious trip, and fraught with many dangers and hardships. Many Indians were met on the route, but most of them were friendly. Near Carson River, however, one night a hostile band made a raid and stole all of their horses and part of the cattle. Next morning the guards followed them on foot and succeeded in getting the cattle back, but not the horses, and they now had to work oxen to everything. Finally Mr. Colwell bought several head of horses from some friendly Indians and continued his journey, but was followed and overtaken by another band, who claimed the horses, saying they had been stolen from them by the ones who sold them. There was no other alternative but to give them up, and the Indians drove them back.

The subject of our sketch was then but 6 years of age, but distinctly remembers all of these things, and says one circumstance which made a most vivid impression on his mind was crossing the desert, which consumed two days and nights of travel. It was a sandy country with no water on the route, and was strewn with abandoned wagons and other possessions of those who had gone the trail previous. Feather beds had been ripped to save the cloth, and the feathers had been scattered promiscuously by the winds across the sandy wastes. He saw men chopping spokes out of wagon wheels for fuel, and yokes and chains were lying in front of abandoned wagons where they had been dropped and the given-out teams carried on to water and grass. These wagons were public property for anyone who was disposed to pick them up, as the owners never returned for them, not being worth a trip back in the deep sand to recover them. The elder Colwell exchanged wagons several times, finding some he liked better than his own among the hundreds that strewed the desert plain. Twelve miles from Grass valley an enterprising individual was found by the roadside selling grass and water, the latter at $1 per gallon. The Colwell family finally reached their destination, and Mr. Colwell went into the stock business. His cattle were the first Missouri stock to cross the plains, and some of them sold for $150 per head. None but Spanish stock had been here previously. Gold dust was the circulating medium in trade, and each dealer, in whatsoever business he was engaged, had his scales to weigh gold dust.

In 1852 the elder Colwell died, and in 1856 Mrs. Colwell went back with her family to Tennessee, her native State. Here young Neal Colwell attended the Black Grove and Newmarket schools until 1859, when his mother with her family came to Texas, and reached Kerr County in 1860.

In 1862, during the progress of the Civil war, young Colwell enlisted in the company of Captain Eugene B. Millet, Thirty-second Texas cavalry, the regiment commanded by Col. P. C. Wood. Their field of operation was in Louisiana, opposing the invading army under General Banks. He participated in all of the battles and skirmishes, thirty-two in number, with the exception of Mansfield, his last fight being at Yellow Bayou. During one of these battles, while the regiment was under fire and not replying to it, awaiting orders, one man became very nervous, and said there was no use talking, he could not stand it, and would have to move back. Sergt. John C. Douglas of Seguin told him to come and stand with him, and he would try and keep him up to the fighting point. He stood for a few minutes until a bucketful of canister shot tore up the ground in front of him, when he wilted again, and Douglas told him to go, and he went. Their horses were tied in the rear, and this man rode a swayback he called Rainbow. He was a humorous fellow, and telling afterwards of his flight from the battlefield, said that when he

46

mounted he picked old Rainbow up with his spurs and shook him three times, and when he let him down he fairly flew, only hitting the road in high places. After the war Captain Colwell came back to Kerr County and engaged in farming and stock-raising.

In 1875 a frontier battalion was organized to operate against the Indians, and he was appointed captain of Company F. Pat Dolan was first lieutenant, F. C. Nelson second, and there were seventy-five enlisted men. There were six companies in all, the whole being under the command of Maj. John B. Jones. Their station (Captain Colwell's men) was the headwaters of the Guadalupe River. Their scouting territory embraced the country from the mouth of the Pullium prong of the Nueces to the mouth of the South fork of the Llano, where Junction City now is. Much scouting was done, and with such energy that the Indians were kept in check without any fights, but came very near getting one band. On this occasion George Danner, William Baker, and Joe Moss were camped with a wagon four miles east of the Frio waterhole hunting game and wild honey. They had found a bee cave in a gorge and were robbing it, when they were attracted by the barking of a dog at their wagon on the hill. Climbing out to see what was the matter, they discovered a band of nine Indians, who had taken their wagon horses and were carrying them off, the dog following and barking at them. The distance to the Indians was about 600 yards, but Joe Moss had a buffalo gun, and taking a pop at them, he killed one of their horses. The Indians now killed the dog and rode on. At this time Baker was out on a hunt and riding their only remaining horse. When he returned and learned the situation he at once rode to the camp of Captain Colwell, nine miles distant, and informed him of the presence of the Indians. He set out at once to the scene with thirty men. The trail of the Indians was taken up at 5 o'clock and followed until night. It led south towards the head of the Sabinal River, and the trailing was tedious and slow, being in a timbered country abounding in high grass. The rangers camped on the divide at the head of the river, having no water, and were moving again as soon as the trail could be seen on the following morning. As they turned down into the head of the canyon a belled mare and colt were seen, and had they known the situation here they could have waited and caught the Indians, for the latter had only gone down in the valley to camp by water, and came back to the divide next morning, but not on their own trail of the previous evening. They crossed over into another valley and came out near enough to see the mare, which they captured, and killed the colt. While they were doing this Captain Colwell and his men were trailing them to where they camped and back on the divide, where the dead colt was found, and the mare gone. Part of this time only a ridge intervened between the Indians and the rangers. The trail now led down the divide between Cypress Creek and the Frio, which came in above the town of Leakey. Here on a high point the Indians stopped for noon, having a good view of the country for several miles, and evidently saw the rangers on their trail and hastily decamped, which fact was indicated by signs of cooked meat, etc. They intended raiding Frio Canyon that night, for as yet they only had one horse besides those they were riding. This one they had stolen from Sam Larrymore on the head of the Pedernales, and had been pushed out from there by citizens who were now on their trail behind the rangers, but went back when they learned that Captain Colwell was after them. At the noon camp of the Indians the captain left the pack mules with Sergt. W. G. Coston and five men to follow on, and he and the others pushed on as rapidly as the rough nature of the country would admit.

To give an idea of the difficulties which had to be surmounted in crossing these rocky mountains, the following incidents will be a fair sample: In many places the rangers had to lead their horses, and in one of these Captain Colwell was leading his by the rope with the bridle reins over the horn of the saddle, and coming to a four-foot ledge, the horses had to make a powerful spring to clear, and all succeeded but the captain's horse. When he made his spring the bridle reins tightened and pulled him backwards, and he fell in such a position with his feet up hill that he had to be turned over before he could get up. At a similar place, one of the pack mules with Sergeant Coston's party fell backwards and rolled to the foot of the hill with his pack.

The Indians were crowded so close that the water in the little branches which they crossed was still muddy when the rangers would cross. If there had been any open country they would have been caught, but all was brakes, mountains, and canyons.

Much blood was on the trail where the Indians had spurred their horses. On the West prong of the Frio two men were discovered some distance off in a little valley, and not knowing whether they were Indians or white men, and wanting to be sure to get them if the latter, Captain Colwell deployed his men and completely surrounded them. When the cordon was drawn close and they were caught in the circle, it was discovered that they were white men. The latter were greatly surprised to see armed men riding towards them from every direction, and at first were alarmed. They were busy cutting a bee tree, and did not notice the approach of the rangers until they were close upon them. They were also on the trail of the Indians, but had not noticed this fact, having come into the valley after the Indians crossed it. One of the men was named Ragsdale. The rangers made another dry camp. They had no provisions, but about 10 o'clock in the night Sergeant Coston caught up with the pack mules, and they got something to eat.

The Indians had the advantage of the night, when the trail could no longer be followed, and got another good start ahead. They were followed, however, until 3 o'clock on the following evening, when a heavy rain came up and obliterated all signs of the trail. Captain Colwell now went down the Nueces, hoping to find the trail again, but could not do so, and the pursuit was abandoned. The Indians were not heard of any more.

In December it became necessary to reduce the ranger force, and the company of Captain Colwell was cut down to forty men and the lieutenants thrown out. Afterwards Major Jones allowed one, and W. K. Jones, who is now county judge of Val Verde County, was appointed. He was brother to the ranger captain, Frank Jones, who was killed in Mexico. Soon after the company was reduced Captain Colwell was sent down into the Rio Grande counties with his men to stop the depredations of bandits. The territory to scout over was from Ringgold barracks to Brownsville. By vigilant work the outlaws were kept in check during the winter. The command was now ordered in to be disbanded, and Captain Colwell instructed to turn over State government property, mules, etc., but with the view of organizing a new company for further operations against Indians and lawless characters. The home of Captain Colwell was near Center Point, in Kerr County, and here he had the government mules and a man employed to look after them. They were turned out during the day and rounded up and penned again at night. On one occasion a mule failed to show up, having strayed, and that night the Indians made a raid through the valley and carried him off, and also a horse belonging to Monroe Surber. Captain Colwell followed the Indians far towards the west, over the rugged mountains, but failed to overhaul them, as they scattered and went various ways.

At this time Lon Spencer and a companion, whose name can not now be recalled, were out on the head draws of South Llano hunting game or mustangs, and saw two Indians coming towards them a long way off, and ambushed them. When they came within gunshot each selected his man to shoot at, and both fired. Spencer killed his Indian, but the other man missed, and one got away. Now, it happened that these two Indians had the mule and horse which were stolen at Center Point, and they were recovered. Spencer brought back the recaptured property, as also the scalp of the Indian and his rigging.

In 1876 another company was organized with Captain Colwell as commander. Their scouting territory was the same as before, and they did a great deal of it. On one scout of ten days, while returning, they came upon some cattlemen at Paint Rock, on South Llano, who were carrying a herd to Kansas. They informed the rangers that the Indians had made a raid on another cow outfit at Green Lake, six miles above, and captured eleven head of their horses. Captain Colwell at once repaired to the scene with his scouts and took the trail. Their only chance for carrying water was in canteens, and as the Indians had gone out through a dry country, the captain cautioned the men to be saving with the water. It was warm weather in April, and the water soon gave out. On the second day, at night, a dry camp was made in a draw, and the men were suffering very much with thirst. They looked bad—skin dry and lips swollen. During the night they were very restless, and moaning in their sleep. Some arose and scratched in the dry gravel of the draw, trying to find moisture. Aleck Merritt, the trailer, had walked a great deal in following the trail, and had long since used up all of his water, and was suffering more than the others, who had ridden their horses. Captain Colwell and Dr. Nowlin were lying on their blankets together, a little apart from the rest, and were commenting on the long distance Merritt had walked and trailed, and expressed an opinion that he was certainly more thirsty than the balance. The captain had preserved some water in his canteen for an extreme emergency if it came, but now called Merritt and made known to him the fact, and offered him some of the water and explained to him the reason. This unselfish and true Texas ranger refused it, because he thought it would look wrong in him to accept it when the other boys had none, and went back to his pallet and suffered on through the long night and until 9 o'clock the following day. When the water was found the men could not very well be restrained, and many of them drank until they were sick. Eighteen Indians had camped here the night before, as was indicated by the imprint of their bodies in the rank grass where they slept. Just below, in the same little valley, a like number had spent the night and held a bunch of horses there. It is likely well enough that the rangers did not come into contact with this band, numbering thirty-six to their twelve, in the famished and weakened condition they were in. The scout was held here two days.

George Beakley's horse had given out and was not able to keep on the trail of the Indians, and the captain did not want to leave him alone, so a return towards camp was made, Beakley riding a pack mule and slowly leading his jaded horse. The captain had flankers on both sides while on the move, and one of these, William Layton, became lost from the command. He was seen during the greater part of the day, but finally he was missed and the command halted. The captain got on an elevated place and searched for him with a spy glass, but could not discover him. He hated to leave the man, but it was useless to go back to hunt for him, as they could not even guess where to look. The grass was fired with the hope that the smoke might be seen by him and to some extent guide him, and the scouts moved on. The men would soon be out of water again, and it was twenty-five miles back to it. Provisions were left in a tree, so that if the lost ranger should strike their trail he could find it. Two nights passed before anything was seen or heard of him, and he was about given up as lost in fact, when on the third day he overtook them. He had crossed the trail of the rangers once and did not see it, and turned back when he discovered that he was going too low down the country. His horse took the trail when he came to where the grass was burned, and followed it as true as the needle to the pole. It was at the next water that the provisions were left in the tree, and by the time he reached that place they were very acceptable to the hungry ranger. Layton had not been in the service long. An old-time Texas ranger would not have gotten into such a scrape as that.

In the following December Captain Colwell was put in command of Company A, which acted as escort to Major Jones, and was almost constantly employed in going from one post to another, inspecting, paying off, etc.

In 1877 Major Jones, with Captain Colwell's command, Pat Dolan's, and Frank Moore's companies, were ordered to concentrate. Captain Dolan was in Nueces Canyon and Capt. Frank Moore was on the Llano, where Junction City is now. The purpose for assembling the rangers was to round up the whole country around the heads of the Nueces and Llanos, and arrest every man in it. This part of the country had become headquarters for all the desperadoes, outlaws, horse and cattle-thieves, and fugitives from justice in the whole Southwest and from the East, and the intention of apprehending every man was to be certain to get the right ones, as the rangers could not distinguish the guilty parties. Each man was examined, and he had to give a satisfactory account of himself before he was turned loose. Forty men out of this round-up proved to be the persons wanted, and they were carried to Junction City and there confined in shackles in a place called the "bull-pen." Junction City was just being laid off. There were only a few houses there—no jail or court house— although it was designated as the county seat of Kimble County. Judge Blackburn had arrived there to hold court, and the rangers remained to give protection in case any of the outlawry kind gave trouble. But these at the time were all in durance vile in the "bull-pen," and everything passed off smoothly during this first term of court in Kimble County. Court was held under a large liveoak tree, and to give color to this primitive court of justice in the wilderness, a swarm of wild bees were working in the tree under which were assembled judge and jury, lawyers and witnesses. The arrested men were all turned over to the civil authorities.

After this Captain Colwell went to Frio Town and operated in surrounding counties, capturing outlaws and desperate characters in that part of the country. During this service he and his scouts apprehended more than forty men and brought them to justice.

These last rangers were different from the first—the Indian-fighting rangers. Many of them were detectives from other States and different parts of this State. The first ones were of the cowboy style—good riders, trailers, and shots, wearing leggings, many of them, and buckskin. The last ones, however, did splendid work in their line, which was fraught with as much danger as fighting Indians. This service was continued by Captain Colwell until 1879.

Governor Roberts was in the executive chair during the last mentioned date, and Major Jones was made adjutant-general and Captain Colwell quartermaster of the frontier battalion. His business was to make tours of inspection, furnish rations, and recommend changes of men or companies from one place to another.

During this service information was received that lawless characters were operating south of Fort Davis, in the Chenati mountains, where there were no rangers. General Jones ordered Sergt. Ed. Seiker to take four men and one Mexican guide and repair to the scene. As these men figure in a fight with the outlaws in which one of them lost his life, their names will be given, as follows: Sam Henry, Tom Carson, L. B. Caruthers, — Bingham, and the Mexican, name not known. At Fort Davis Sergeant Seiker learned that the most daring of the desperadoes were four in number, one of whom was named Jesse Evans, from New Mexico. They would rob stores in daylight in Fort Davis and terrorize the citizens generally, and the latter had offered a reward of $500 for their capture.

The rangers learned through a negro named Louis, who occupied a neutral position between the two parties, that the outlaws' stronghold was in the Chenati mountains. He also told the latter that the rangers were after them. They believed the negro was wholly on their side, and that their position was not known. They also told him if only four rangers came to hunt for them he need not put himself to the trouble to inform them, but to keep them posted in regard to a larger force.

From the fort the rangers went south about eighty miles to

near the Rio Grande, on a little creek in the Chenati range, and there, while hunting for trails, discovered four men on horseback above them. As this corresponded to the number of men they were hunting, and in their range, they turned and started towards them. The outlaws, for such they were, turned and ran, and soon commenced firing at the rangers who were in pursuit. This settled their identity, and Sergeant Seiker and his men put their horses to the utmost speed to overhaul them, firing as they went. The chase lasted two miles, until the outlaws came to a mountain which was flat on top, but on the opposite side was a ledge of rock four feet in height which ran around the circle of the mountain. The fugitives went up the mountain, across its flat crest, down the ledge to near the base, and there dismounted, tied their horses, and came back up to the ledge and took a position behind it to fight the rangers. When Sergeant Seiker and his men arrived at the mountain and found out the position of the desperadoes, they went up to near the crest, dismounted, tied their horses, and advanced to assault their position on foot. The Mexican had stopped back with the pack mule. The rangers deployed as they went, but were soon fired on, and a desperate charge was made across the open ground, in which Bingham was killed. His comrades were charging straight ahead, firing rapidly with their Winchesters, and did not notice his fall. The bullets flew so thick along the rim of the ledge that it was death to an outlaw to get his face above it.

The leader, Jesse Evans, kept his head above, and was fired at by Sergeant Seiker, who was charging straight towards his position, but his first ball hit the rock in front of him too low. For an instant the outlaw ducked his head and then raised it again, but only to receive a ball between the eyes from the Winchester of the sergeant. The other three became rattled when he fell and ran around under the ledge, keeping their heads below, and almost ran against the muzzle of Tom Carson's gun, who had charged to the brink of the ledge and was looking over, with his gun cocked and finger on the trigger, trying to see them. Before he could fire, they begged for life, and began to throw down their arms. The other rangers congregated at this point, and Sergeant Seiker ordered them to hand up their guns and pistols and come out from under the ledge. This all happened in a very short time, and now for the first time it was discovered that Bingham was killed. The others then wanted to kill the prisoners, but were prevented by the sergeant. The sad duty of burying a dead comrade now consumed several hours, as they had nothing to dig with except bowie-knives. The horses of the outlaws were brought up, on which they were mounted, securely tied, and the rangers took their departure, leaving the dead desperado under the ledge where he fell. The trip back to Fort Davis was made without further incident, and the captives put in jail there.

To take into consideration the disadvantage under which the rangers had to charge across open ground upon a sheltered position of desperate men armed with the best repeating guns and the members nearly equal, and the rapidity with which they made themselves masters of the situation, this fight has but few equals in any warfare.

The jail at Fort Davis was of Mexican model, and was a regular dungeon. The main building was square and made of dobies, with rooms in the center and doors opening on the outside into the courtyard. The jail was in one corner of the building, and blasted out of the solid rock to a proper depth and then covered over the top by strong timbers securely fastened. The egress was by a trap door. No light was in there. Into this place in utter darkness the captured outlaws were placed.

At this time Captain Colwell had just arrived, having been sent down there by General Jones to ascertain if any more men were needed at that place. Finding the necessity, General Jones was informed of the fact, and Capt. Charles L. Neville and his men were sent. The rangers were quartered at the court and jail inclosure, and some of them stood guard there all the time. The citizens of this place and Fort Stockton greatly rejoiced at th changes which had been wrought, and had a great respect and admiration for the Texas rangers. Before this they were afraid to open their mouths in condemnation of the lawless acts which were constantly being committed in their midst. They were murdered by these desperadoes on the least provocation. The $500 reward which they had offered for the apprehension of the four leaders of this gang they cheerfully paid to the five rangers, or to the four survivors of the desperate battle. Of course such service as this was expected of rangers without any compensation except their monthly pay, and it was not for any reward that they ran the bandits down and killed and captured them, and they did not expect anything. They accepted the gift in the spirit in which it was given. The donation was from wealthy men—merchants and stockmen.

INCIDENT OF VICTORIA'S RAID.

After the incident above narrated Captain Colwell was ordered by General Jones to Ysleta to inspect the company of Capt. George W. Baylor. At that time Victoria, the famous Muscalera Apache chief, was in Old Mexico, south of the Rio Grande, with a strong band of desparate warrors. He had been fighting the United States troops in New Mexico, and getting the worst of it, had run down in there for safety. His presence there being a menace to citizens of Mexico, troops were sent up from Chihuahua by order of the Mexican government to attack him. Officers of the United States troops in Texas, believing that if he was driven out of Mexico he would cross the Rio Grande into Texas, had troops scattered through the mountains at all of the watering places to intercept him. Colonel Grierson was in command of these forces, with headquarters at Eagle Springs, forty-five miles east of Fort Quitman, on the Rio Grande. On the El Paso stage route a buckboard was run one day, and a jerky, or two-seated hack, the next. Captain Colwell went down from Fort Davis on the jerky. The captain only had on his revolver, but one of his men put a Winchester in the vehicle, saying he might see Indians on the route. A man named Baker was driver. Nothing of interest occurred on the trip down, and they arrived all right at Ysleta. Several days were spent here attending to business, and then the start was made on the return trip to Fort Davis. At Fort Quitman news was received that the Mexican forces had fought Victoria and his band, making a stand-off affair, and had gone back to Chihuahua, and also that after the fight Victoria had crossed the river and was now in Texas. Captain Colwell now knew that the trip back to Davis would be fraught with much danger. Besides him in the jerky was one negro soldier, a boy named Graham on his way to Fort Davis to act as hostler there, and the driver. The latter thought the Indians would attack them at Quitman Canyon, but if they passed that place all right they might get safely through. They expected to meet the buckboard at dusk at Eighteen-mile waterhole, where a short halt was to be made to get water. In the evening five men were seen on large horses, who at a distance had the appearance of United States soldiers on account of the horses. One came towards them a short distance and then went back. The captain now felt somewhat relieved, thinking the country was being well patrolled by the regular troops. About dusk the waterhole was reached, but Baker and his buckboard were not there. This caused some uneasiness, but Captain Colwell got out and said he would fill a vessel with water and they would continue their journey. I will here describe the peculiar team which worked to the vehicle. They were small mules, and had been trained to run all the time on the road, and when they were harnessed and turned loose from the hitching post they started off at once in a gallop, and could not be stopped quietly until they reached the next station, so when Captain Colwell alighted and was filling his canteen the driver had to let the mules run around in a circle until he was ready to mount again. One startling fact which the captain and his party were not aware of at the time, was that on this very day a battle had been fought with Victoria's band in a few hundred yards of this waterhole, in a little canyon just back of it, in which a squad of the Tenth cavalry had been routed with the loss of five or six men and horses, and they had retreated back to Eagle Springs. The dead horses were lying almost in view of the road, and the men in the valley back, who had been taken for soldiers, were the scouts of Victoria mounted on United States cavalry horses which they had captured. It had been agreed by the party in the hack, if the Indians came upon them, that the driver should give his gun to the boy Graham and let the team run in the road, and the balance to fight the Indians as they went, unless a mule was killed, and then to stand and fight to the best advantage, but with little hope of ever coming clear. If they had known what was ahead the situation at this time would have seemed more desperate. The non-appearance of Baker with the buckboard was ominous. After leaving the waterhole the mules in the jerky went at a lively rate for three miles, and then shied at something by the road. It was the buckboard with one mule dead, the other gone, and beside it lay two dead men—the driver

Baker and a passenger. They were evidently killed about sundown, as they should have been at the waterhole at the time the other vehicle was there. No doubt they ran and fought the Indians until one mule was killed, and then died beside the vehicle. Very little time was taken to look around here. The situation was appalling for the captain and his party. Indians were all over the country, battles being fought and men killed in various places. The driver was told to slow down his team. The captain sat with his Winchester in hand, admonished the men to keep cool, have their guns in readiness, and to keep close watch on both sides of the road; they were in for it, and must face the situation and get out of it the best they could. They arrived all right at Eagle Springs, and reported the killing of the two men in the buckboard. Baker was warned by the soldiers who had fought the battle near the waterhole not to start on his trip, and they told him he was certain to be killed there. For four days Victoria's band swarmed along this road, and finally crossed it at Van Horn's pass and went in the direction of Rattlesnake Springs. The troops, being informed of the route, went around them and laid an ambush at the springs. Here impatient, restless men spoiled all, as is the case on many occasions of ambuscades. Firing commenced too soon, and the Indians turned back and recrossed the Rio Grande at the same place where they did in coming over. Victoria was quite a general; he knew the Mexican troops were gone by this time, and the coast would be clear on that side.

In the following winter Captain Baylor came down from Ysleta with his men to investigate the killing of one man and the wounding of another in the Quitman pass. At the same time Captain Neville came down from Fort Davis with his men, and the two commands met at Eagle Springs. The combined forces now, after finding the trail of the Indians, which were Victoria and his band, again followed in rapid pursuit to the Guadalupe mountains, and here located the camp of the Indians by their smoke and surrounded them. A fight ensued, but the hostiles soon discovered that it was a considerable force of Texas rangers that was upon them, and began to scatter and break through the cordon and get away. Six were killed on the ground and many wounded. One wounded squaw was cap-

tured and brought back. , Some of the United States officers
paid the rangers a compliment when they returned by saying
they had done more good in ten days than the United States
troops had all summer. Victoria was finally killed and his
band scattered.

Captain Colwell's service ended on the frontier in 1883, and he
has since lived at the old home, near Center Point, Kerr County.
He has had many offers of honorable positions, but has refused
them all, one of which was the nomination to represent his district in the Legislature. He accepted some public work in the
organization of the Center Point Fair Association, and served as
its president four years. He married Miss C. E. Martin of
San Marcos, sister of Judge W. W. Martin.

Mrs. Colwell witnessed a rare sight during the frontier days,
which few women every had the opportunity of doing. On one
occasion she accompanied the captain and his escort far out on
the border, where he went to inspect some posts, and saw the
rangers running and killing buffalo.

FRONTIER INCIDENTS.

The following incidents of frontier life were obtained from Mrs. Elizabeth Fessenden, who is familiar with all of the facts. She is the widow of Mr. Samuel Fessenden, an ex-ranger, old frontiersman, and Indian fighter, who came from Guadalupe County in 1862 and settled on the frontier. Prior to this, however, when a young single man, he had been all over the Texas frontier in the early 50's with a surveying party around the forts of Graham, Griffin, Belknap, and others, and had much experience with Indians. In 1859 he went south and married Miss Lizzie Tate, in Victoria County, and then came to Guadalupe, and from there to San Saba County and settled near Richland Springs, and soon after joined a company of rangers commanded by Capt. Riley Woods. This company scouted a great deal, and Mr. Fessenden was in many chases and fights with Indians.

In 1863 they followed a band of Indians and overtook them near the "Peg-leg" crossing of the San Saba. They were surprised in camp, but ran and dodged and hid so quickly that none of them were hit by the fire of the rangers except one. This fellow took refuge behind a tree and prepared to fight, and some of the rangers stopped to fight him. The Indians had no time to mount their horses, and all went off on foot. The white men scattered in pursuit, but soon came back to where the lone Indian had made his stand, and all commenced shooting at him, but took trees on him also, as no one wanted to be killed by a wounded Indian if it could be avoided. Many balls struck the tree behind which he stood, and he was hit many times, but continued to yell defiance and shoot an arrow at every man that exposed himself the least bit, and kept them dodging continually and keeping close behind their trees. Finally Jesse Poe said he was going to get out from behind his tree so that he could see the Indian good, and put in one good shot and finish him. But as soon as he left his place and exposed himself fair the Indian shot an arrow into his forehead, and he sprang back behind the tree again. Two other rangers, seeing he was wounded, went to him, and both had to pull at the arrow before it would come out. It had struck just above the eyes, firmly and fast in the skull, but the spike did not reach the brain. This was the last shot of the Comanche, for he was in a dying condition, and the rangers went to where he was and finished him.

Mr. Fessenden and another man were sent back to the settlement with Poe, and the others again went in pursuit of the Indians. The wounded man was brought to Mr. Fessenden's house, and the wound washed and dressed again. Mrs. Fessenden can remember how pale he looked, and said his head was badly swollen, and his eyes closed up when the bandage was removed. The party also had the scalp of the Indian with them.

In the same year another band of Indians was followed and overtaken where Brady City is now, in McCulloch County. It was in an open country, and the Indians saw the rangers coming at some distance, and a long chase commenced. Only two of them could be overtaken—a warrior and his squaw, both on the same horse. Many shots were fired, and finally the horse was killed and the warrior wounded; but he was able to get to a thicket and put up a game fight. The squaw went in with him and helped to fight the rangers, and they had to do some fine dodging to keep from being hit, but they fired continuously into the thicket, not being able to see the Indians, but located them by the arrows that came out. Finally the warrior was killed and the squaw ran out with hands up; no one fired at her, but took her prisoner. The man was supposed to be a chief from the fine rigging he had on, all of which was taken off and brought back. Mrs. Fessenden saw this rig, earrings, scalp, etc., of the slain brave. The captive squaw was sent to a reservation.

KILLING OF BEARDY HALL BY THE INDIANS.

In the spring of 1864 Mr. Hall lived in San Saba County, on Richland Creek, three miles from Mr. Fessenden's place. He had a good horse, which he never allowed to run on the range for fear the Indians would get him. Still he did not believe so many reports about Indians being in the country, when men were continually coming in and reporting "Indian sign." One morning, however, he met his fate. He had started to San Saba town, fifteen miles distant, and was riding his good horse. He also carried a six-shooter, but said he did not expect to find or see any Indians. He did not go the direct way, but took devious windings, and had proceeded about five miles when he was suddenly confronted by a band of Indians at a place called Round Mountain. He made a desperate attempt to get away, and was supposed to have fought the Indians as he ran. By some means, however, they went round him and cut him off in a circle of yelling Comanches, and they killed him in half a mile of Uncle Jimmy Wood's place. Some members of the family heard the Indians yelling and supposed it was coyotes, and even thought it strange that they would yelp at this time of day, as it was about 10 o'clock in the morning. These same Indians had stolen all of the best horses on Harvey Creek, and only a few men were on their trail, but they came upon the body before it was cold. One of these men was Pick Duncan and another one was named Hall, but no relation to the slain man. The Indians got his horse, pistol, and shoes, and also scalped him. A scout of rangers were out at that time, but did not strike the trail of the Indians as they were going in, but got after them as they came back. Mr. Fessenden was along, as this was the same company mentioned before. These rangers were home men, and took turn about scouting, half a dozen or more at a time, and when one scout returned another one took their places and went out, while those just returned went home until their turn came again. Mr. Fessenden had been at home, but took his turn with this second scout, which now found the trail. The Indians were overtaken near the head of the San Saba River and surprised in camp. A sharp running fight took place for some distance, in which three Indians were killed and all of the horses recaptured, including Mr. Hall's horse, as was also his hat, clothing, moral, and pipe.

THE HOUSE OF YOUNGBLOOD ATTACKED.

In 1864 Mr. Fessenden moved to Blanco County and settled on Hickory Creek. Three miles from him, on Grape Creek, lived the family of Youngblood. He had died, and a man named Sam De Buss was a hired hand on the place, but at the time of

47

which we write he was away.　Three of the children—a boy and
two girls—were about a quarter of a mile from the house when
the Indians came upon them.　They soon killed the boy, but the
girls ran swiftly towards the house, followed by the Indians, who
kept shooting at them with arrows until both were wounded, but
they succeeded in getting into the house, the mother holding the
door open for them and screaming for them to "Run! run! run!"
during the desperate race.　There were two rifles in the house,
and Mrs. Youngblood took up one of these and at once commenced a battle with the Indians.　They succeeded in getting to
the door, and were trying to force it open, when the brave woman
killed one of them.　After firing both guns the woman would
pick up first one and then the other, and present it when they
advanced, and the Indians would skip back around the corner.
There were six of them when they came to the house, and when
they left and were last seen only five were together, but what they
did with the one who fell in the yard and they carried away could
not be ascertained.　Up to the time the Indians left the mother
had no time to attend to her wounded children, but now pulled
the arrows out of them.　One was shot in the head and the other
in the body.　Both got well, but the one wounded in the head
was ever after partially deranged.　De Buss came back before
night, and went out and brought the body of the little boy in.
He was 10 years of age, and the girls were 8 and 6.　After night
De Buss came to the house of Mr. Fessenden and waked him up
and told him the news, and they went to the camp of the rangers
on Cypress Creek and aroused them.　Mr. Fessenden's eyes were
very sore, and as soon as daylight came he went back home, but
on the way came very near falling into the hands of the Indians.
He crossed their trail, but did not see it on account of his eyes,
and was not aware of his danger at the time.　The rangers saw
the trail as they came on behind him, and it was so fresh that De
Buss, who was with the rangers, declared his belief that the Indians had killed Fessenden, and a search was made for his body.
Not being able to find it, the trail was taken up and the Indians
overtaken.　A fight commenced, but the Indians ran at the first
fire and made their escape, with some wounded but none killed
on the ground.

MRS. ALEXANDER KILLED BY INDIANS.

In the winter of 1867 there lived in Kerr County, eighteen miles above Kerrville, William Alexander and his wife. Also in the same house lived his son-in-law, Mr. Wachter, who had married his daughter, Nancy. At the time the Indians made the raid Wachter and Alexander were both away, having gone to Fredericksburg with shingles, leaving the two women alone. The first intimation they had of the presence of Indians was one standing in the door. Mrs. Wachter was a stout young woman, and at once ran at the Indian and knocked him out of the door with a smoothing iron which she had in her hand, and then ran on through the balance of the band who were in the yard, at the same time calling to her mother, who was in the back yard, to run. The Indians were shooting arrows at her, and as she turned to look back for her mother she fell over a log and remained there for a few moments, and then crawled to a thicket near by without being perceived by the Indians, who, thinking they had killed her, were after the old lady in the yard, who had come around the house at the call of her daughter, instead of running the other way into the brush, which she could have done and made her escape, as evidently the Indians did not know where she was until she came among them around the corner of the house. The daughter did not remain long in her hiding place, but made her way three miles down the river to where her brother, Wren, and a negro were in camp making shingles. Wren came on back, but ascended a mountain where he could overlook the valley to see if anything could be seen of the Indians. No signs of them were visible, but he made the discovery that the house was burned.

Now in the meantime, between this event and the last one narrated, Mr. Fessenden had moved from Blanco County and settled in ten miles of the Alexander place. Thither a messenger was sent to notify him and other scattered settlers, and he and others came to the scene. The house was reduced to ashes, and in the yard near it were the remains of Mrs. Alexander, partly consumed by the intense heat of the burning house. Her clothing had burned off, and Mr. Fessenden and others had to handle the remains carefully to keep the arms and legs from coming off, but which they did finally as they went to place her in a box that had

been prepared for reception of the remains.   Mr. Fessenden and
others followed the Indians, but a snowstorm soon came on and
they were forced to return.   Others were sent to notify the absent men, and they were met coming back.

FOUR OF THE DOWDY FAMILY KILLED.

In 1878 a man named James Dowdy moved to Kerr County
and settled on the Johnston fork of the Guadalupe River, two
miles from the home of Mr. Fessenden, who lived on Stockman's Creek, near the Johnston fork.

Mr. Dowdy had a large flock of sheep, and had only been in
his new home a short time when the fearful tragedy occurred
which we now relate.   On that day four of his children, three
girls and one boy, went out with the sheep to keep them together
while they grazed about a half a mile from home on a hillside.
The oldest girl, named Fanny, was 20 years of age.   The next
was Alice, aged 18, Rilla 15, and the boy James 12.   There was
a grown son named Richard at the house.   Before noon a band
of Indians came upon the unfortunate children and killed every
one of them.   At the house that day it was the intention to eat
an early dinner, and Richard and another young man present,
who was engaged to Fanny, were to go and relieve the girls and
the boy while they came to the house for their dinner.   The meal
was partaken of at 11 o'clock by the young men, and then they
set out to hunt the flock of sheep.   They soon returned, however,
somewhat alarmed, and said they could not find the children, and
that the sheep were badly scattered.   The mother then hurried
to the hills, and soon found her murdered children.   Two of the
girls, Alice and Rilla, were lying together, Fanny 200 yards from
them, and James some distance from her.   All were in a horrible condition from bullet, lance, and arrow wounds, but none
were scalped.   A runner was sent for Mr. Fessenden, and he and
Louis Nelson came with a wagon and team and hauled the bodies
home.   Mrs. Fessenden also went up there and helped to wash
and dress the girls and comb out their hair, and then sat up all
night with them.   All were buried the next day.   Many arrows
were lying around on the hillside where the victims ran and were
pursued and shot at.   The Indians had a drove of horses, and

came from towards the Pedernales and went towards the head of the Guadalupe. Mr. Fessenden and others followed the Indians, but so much time had been consumed in getting in and burying the bodies that they were not overtaken. Some are of the opinion that it was not Indians who did the murder, but Mr. Fessenden was an old Indian trailer, and pronounced them such from the sign they left. The Dowdy family were from Goliad County.

Mr. Fessenden died in Bee County in 1897, and was buried at Beeville. He was in bad health and had gone on a trip down there to see if he could not be benefited.

Mrs. Fessenden still lives on the old place near Johnston fork, with some of her children.

FIGHT BETWEEN SETTLERS AND INDIANS.

1855.

In the above named year the Indians made a raid in the vicinity of Selma, on the Cibolo Creek, near the line of Guadalupe and Bexar counties, and carried off a large drove of horses, mostly belonging to Johnny B. Brown and Capt. William Davenport. The latter was in command of a small company of minute men for frontier protection. Among the men who belonged to this company was William Hale, second in command, George Murchason, Hood Murchason, William Turner, J. W. Smith, and others. Captain Davenport soon got nine of his men together and set out on the trail of the Indians. Those who are known to have been along were William Hale, George Murchason and his brother Hood, and J. W. Smith. The trail led northwest towards the mountains, and was followed as rapidly as possible, Captain Davenport himself being the trailer. Soon after starting it commenced to rain and continued to do so for several days, greatly to the hindrance of the pursuers, who had no way of keeping their guns and pistols dry, which was very essential in the days of muzzle-loaders. The tubes, however, were protected by keeping something tightly bound around them. The hard showers of rain would almost put out the trail, which caused slow progress until a point was reached where the Indians had traveled after the rain. They passed out near the new settlement at Boerne, and then took to the mountains over the roughest country they could find. So many of the horses were cut and locerated by the sharp rocks in the mountains that a trail of blood was left behind them. They were driving a hundred head, and would force them down places where they could not keep their feet without bracing themselves and sliding down stiff-legged. It was down these long, rugged mountain slants that the trails of blood were left. The white men had a like difficulty; their horses suffered very much, and the one ridden by Hood Murchason gave out and he had to walk and lead him. The trail finally came out into the Medina valley and passed north of where Bandera is now. There was a small

Mormon settlement there then, and likely a few other American settlers. The Indians went out onto the divide after leaving the valleys, and went into camp on a creek somewhere near the head of Paint Creek. The camp was in a thicket, but the white men located it by the smoke from an elevated position on a mountain, and also the large drove of horses which were grazing near. The pursuit had now lasted nine days and the Indians were resting in fancied security, thinking the white men were not coming on account of such long delay. They were making moccasins to put on the feet of the crippled horses that were the worst hurt in their desperate drive across the mountains. The settlers hid themselves from view as soon as possible and advanced upon them, but the Indians did not discover them until a charge was made into camp and rifles were cracking. There were only six Indians in camp, two of whom fell at the first volley and the others ran, not having time to string their bows. The white men followed them. The Indians went over the bank into the creek and took shelter under the bluff, which was of solid rock and sloped under. Here they strung their bows and made ready to fight, while the white men dismounted, tied their horses, and advanced to assault their position. It was a most admirable place to make a stand, as the assailants could not see them without advancing close and looking over. There was no chance to cross the creek and take them in the rear, on account of the bluff banks on both sides. After the first charge the white men saw that it was going to be difficult and dangerous to dislodge them. The Indians were on the watch, and as soon as they appeared on the bank over them they shot arrows at them, and one of the men was wounded in the arm. The men would shoot quick, and then dodge back and load. This was repeated until another man was wounded in the stomach, and still some of the Indians survived. They now resorted to strategy. The men that were not hurt advanced, crawling, with loaded rifles and their hats on sticks above their heads. As soon as the Indians saw the hats they let fly their arrows, and before they could adjust more the white men sprang to their feet over them and fired. This volley settled all of the Indians save one, and he left the position and crossed the creek, and commenced the difficult ascent of the bluff on the opposite side. Guns were quickly loaded and fired at him, but he hung on and slowly pulled himself up, although several times hit, and succeeded in getting up and disappearing in the brake beyond. On a return to camp it was found that one of the Indians who had fallen at the first fire was gone, but he was soon found about fifty yards away and still alive, only having been shot through the hips. Another shot finished him, and he was found to be the chief. Hood Murchason cut his long hair off, which was profusely decorated with thin silver plates. There was a feathered ornament on his shield which, when loosened and the wind allowed to blow it out, was eighteen feet in length. The other Indian was scalped, but the three dead ones in the water were not molested. The water where they stood and fought was as red as blood itself. The horses were all collected and the slow return commenced, the wounded men being taken care of as best they could under the circumstances. At the Mormon camp on the Medina all of the crippled horses were left, to be brought in later. Two days were consumed in getting to this place, but the balance of the trip was easier. Both wounded men recovered. The scalp of the Indian warrior and the shield and ornaments of the chief were given to the Rev. John S. McGee, who had lost a son a short time before, killed by Indians on the Cibolo. Rev. McGee carried these trophies a short time afterwards to Kentucky.

We often read about Indians being surprised and not having time to string their bows, and being put to great disadvantage in consequence, and some might ask why they did not keep them strung at all times and be ready for a fight at any moment. For the information of those who have had no experience in such things or taken no thought in regard to the matter, we will say that if a bow was kept strung at a high tension all the time the stick would become weakened, and the arrow could not be sent with much force. It is only when a party of men so completely surprise Indians and are among them before their presence is known, that they are unable to string their bows to meet the charge, for they can do so very quickly.

CHARLES PETERS.

Mr. Charles Peters was born in Hanover, Germany, in 1842, and came to America in 1855. When the Civil war broke out he joined the Confederate army at Savannah, Ga. The command he belonged to was called the Georgia Hussars, an old organization of a hundred years standing. At this time it was commanded by Capt. Fred Waring, and they were sent to Virginia. After the first battle of Manassas Mr. Peters joined the Jeff Davis Legion, which was composed of three companies of Mississippians, two of Alabamians, and the Hussars. This organization was commanded by Lieut.-Col. W. E. Martin, in the brigade of Gen. Wade Hampton, and all under the command of the famous cavalry leader, Gen. J. E. B. Stuart. Mr. Peters was in the Peninsula campaign and in many small battles and skirmishes; also at Williamsburg and the seven days' fight around Richmond, second battle of Manassas, Chancellorsville, Sharpsburg, South Mountain, and the Maryland campaign. In 1862, at the Blue Ridge, Virginia, near Salem, in a cavalry fight, he was wounded in the left thigh, the ball stopping against the bone, and was cut out by a surgeon. At the time the wound was received, Mr. Peters and a lieutenant were about to be cut off in a lane and were running to get out, being fired on from both sides. The lieutenant was killed and fell from his horse, shot through the head. After being wounded Mr. Peters stuck to his horse and ran through this terrible gauntlet of fire, with the balls whistling on every side, and succeeded in getting clear. At Gettysburg he was captured by General Custer's cavalry. He arrived during the last day's battle, their command having been delayed capturing wagon trains. When captured he was riding in company with a colonel, who escaped, but Mr. Peters was on a slow horse and was overtaken. He was bugler at the time, and was carried to Fort Delaware and kept until the war was over, being liberated on the 13th of June, 1865. He took transportation for New York, where he had two brothers, Louis and Nicholas, and came on from there to Texas in 1867. During the years 1868 and 1869 he drifted towards the frontier, and in the latter date was at Ben Fickland, when that place was just starting. During this time the stage driver from Fickland, or Fort Concho, a man named Melon, was killed by the Indians, and Mr. Peters took his place. This route was across the plains to a point further west, and was one of extreme peril and hazard both from Indians and stage robbers, but Mr. Peters was lucky in his trips, and for six months never failed to deliver his mail. By that time, however, he was tired of the business and gave up the contract, which was at once filled by a man called "Dutch Jake," and in ten days he not only lost his mail but the stage also. On one trip out the coach was overhauled by a band of Mexicans, Indians, and one white man. The latter was riding a fine black horse, and he rode along by the side of the vehicle and told Jake and his one guard to jump out and run and they would not be killed. This was acted upon as soon as a favorable place was reached, where there was protection of brush, not wishing to leap out into the open ground for fear of the Indians, who were coming close in the rear, while the white outlaw was advising them to abandon the stage and run. No attempt was made to follow them, and they arrived safely back at the fort and reported the disaster to the military. A squad of soldiers was sent out, and on arriving at the scene of the hold-up the stage and mules were gone. The Indians had carried the stage away, and at this time were riding about in it over the plains and having a fine time. The soldiers found them, but their force was not sufficient to make an attack with any chances of success, and they had to return without accomplishing anything, except as to finding out where the coach was carried to. The stage was full of Indians, yelling and making the mules gallop over the prairie, followed by a numerous band on horseback, also yelling, when the soldiers saw them. A stronger party was sent back, and after considerable search and trailing the stage was found in a gully with the tongue and part of the spokes cut out. The team of four mules had been carried away by these gay aud festive Comanches when they tired of the sport and novelty of riding in a United States mail coach across the grassy plains.

The dilapidated vehicle was carried back to Ben Fickland and repaired by Mr. Peters, who was at that time working in a shop.

Mr. Peters was very lucky during his experience on the frontier in never coming into serious contact with the Indians During one winter he and some companions, among whom was Chas. Hank, stayed for months along the western streams killing buffalo, deer, and antelope, and also gathering pecans, without meeting any Indians, who at that time were numerous along the edge of the plains, and from there made their incursions upon the settlers further east. Hank was an old stage-driver, and had arrows shot into the stage on some of his trips. On one occasion during the winter hunt above mentioned he and Mr. Peters became lost while out and spent twenty-four hours on the plains without water, but finally struck the Concho River. Mr. Peters was so hot and thirsty that he waded into the water and lay down, and as he expressed it, "let the water run into him." When he got up he was as big as a barrel, and could hardly walk. He sat down for some time, thinking he had overdone the business, and that it would kill him, but finally came around all right and they made their way back to camp.

One night in Ben Fickland he saw a man killed named William Thompson. Peters and others, among whom was Sam Ragland, were in a shanty playing cards for amusement, when Thompson came, under the influence of liquor, and asked if Ragland was in there, the door being shut. No satisfactory reply was given him, and he went away, but soon returned and said he was going to smash the door and come in there and kill Ragland. The latter now said to his companions to open the door and let him in, and as they did so Thompson stepped in, pistol in hand, and Ragland shot him dead in his tracks. During another row one night old man Ben Fickland, for whom the place was named, had his boot heel shot off.

After Mr. Peters left Ben Fickland he worked four years for the same company, on a line from San Antonio to Eagle Pass. Two years of this time were spent on the Nueces, keeping the stage stand, attending to the teams, etc. From there he came down to the Sabinal River and kept the stage stand there for the same company, and remained there two years, and then, quit-

ting this business in 1874, he went into camp alone in the Blanco
Canyon, near his present home, about twenty miles northwest
from the present Sabinal station. This was an exposed place
for a lone man to remain, but Mr. Peters had made up his mind
to settle down, and was willing and fearless enough to brave all
the dangers and inconveniences of a frontier life to carve out
the valuable home and ranch which he now occupies and enjoys.
One night the Indians passed so near his little cabin he could
plainly hear them talking, and at once blew out his light and
awaited developments. His dog barked and showed signs of
uneasiness, but the Indians passed on, either not locating the
cabin or else afraid to make an attack. Mr. Peters had his
horse staked out not far away, and arming himself with shotgun and pistol, brought him up and tied him near the cabin
door, and there sat with gun and pistol ready for instant use
until daylight. The shotgun once belonged to John Bowles, and
was the same with which he killed two Indians and crippled another at his ranch on the Sabinal in 1859. After daylight came
Mr. Peters went out to investigate, and found the trail of the
Indians in 150 yards of his cabin.

After Mr. Peters commenced his settlement here others come
in, among whom was Frank Jones, who settled and lived alone
one mile above Mr. Peters. Sometimes Jones would have the
companionship of a hired hand, as would also Mr. Peters. On
January 12, 1875, Jones, Ben Brown, and Josh. Hastings went
up the left prong of the creek about two miles, bear hunting.
Hastings lived with Peters, and Brown with Jones. After
rambling and hunting for some time unsuccessfully Brown and
Hastings returned, but Jones said he would go on to a certain
bluff and hunt for bees which he had been coursing. When night
came and he did not return, no especial uneasiness was felt, as
it was supposed he had joined a party of Frio hunters. Next
day, however, a man came over from the Little Blanco east and
reported that Indians were in the country. The impression now
was that the Indians had killed Jones, and a search was instituted
for him. This was kept up unsuccessfully for three days, but at
the expiration of that time the body of the unfortunate man was
found by Mr. Peters, William Garrett, and others. The body

was found on the bluff, whither he had gone in search of bees in a low depression of the hills. It was entirely nude and lying face down. The marks of violence on the body were one bullet hole clear through it, breaking both arms in its passage, and one arrow in the back, which penetrated four inches. Mr. Peters drew this out, and so firmly was it fixed that the body was raised clear of the ground in doing so, and the spike then was detached from the shaft and remained in the body. The man met his death at the hands of Indians, as was verified by their tracks. Evidently they were on the bluff and saw Jones coming up the creek and laid an ambush for him, concealing themselves in different places so as to be certain of him, not knowing at what point he would make the ascent. Jones came up between two of them, and the one who lay behind a bunch of soto with a gun was the one who did the work. His imprint was seen in the rank grass where he lay, and the top of the soto stalk was cut off by the bullet when he fired at Jones, not more than a few yards distant, and in line with the body where it fell. Jones had his side towards the Indian, as the ball hit one arm, broke it, went through the body, and broke the other arm in its exit. Beyond, in various places, was the imprint of other Indians where they lay in the grass. Mr. Peters and Ben Brown were the first to discover the body, and Mr. Peters said they had evidently seen the body several times in their search before they ascended the bluff, as it lay in plain view, but being naked, resembled the white rocks which lay around it. One of Mr. Jones' dogs was the cause of them finally ascending the bluff, for he repeatedly went up to the body, but would return again when they failed to follow him. The men had lost the trail of Jones, and were trying to locate it again in the rocks and ravines below. Mr. Peters finally noticed the action of the dog and suggested a search on the bluff. The Indians had not entirely stripped the body, but, as was their strange custom, had left one sock, which had not been removed from the foot. The arrow was shot into the back after he was dead and stripped. The searchers were all called in now, and some of them went back to the cabin of Jones and there found some planks, which they converted into a rude box, and returned and placed the body in it. Near the spot was a sink or wide crack between solid walls of rock, and on cleaning out the trash and small stones from this fissure it presented a natural grave in width, depth, and length, and into this the body was placed and covered up carefully, and a mound of rocks heaped over it.

These same Indians had killed a paint mare belonging to Ed. Meyers and cooked and eaten her in 150 yards from the spot where they killed Jones, and had evidently been here several days before the unfortunate settler came upon them, and it was from their elevated camp that they discovered him and laid the scattered ambush to intercept him as before described. While in this camp the Indians had made ropes from the mane and tail of the animal which they had killed. They also stole sixteen head of horses belonging to Ed. Meyers, and carried them away. His ranch was at the foot of the mountains, near the Frio. Jones had a fine Springfield rifle and plenty of cartridges when killed, but being shot from ambush, had no chance to use it, and the Indians got possession of it. Jones had no connection in this country, and but little was known about him. There was nothing among his few effects that gave a clew as to where he came from. He had five or six dogs with him when murdered, but none of these were molested by the Indians, and they all came back home. Mr. Peters remained alone with the body while the others were gone to make a coffin, and they tried to get him to leave also, expressing a fear that the Indians would kill him, but he said, "No; lightning does not strike twice in the same place."

During his lonely life in the hills, surrounded by dense cedarbrakes and dark canyons, Mr. Peters killed many bear, panther, deer, turkey, and other game, and really enjoyed himself. He was a man of education and intelligence, and had the company of books and papers with which to pass away the time when tired of hunting and rambling, and was also raising cattle and hogs, having an unlimited range for both and plenty of water from the bold mountain streams. He finally changed his state of single blessedness and married the widow Allison, a lady from Mississippi, with whom he has lived a quiet and contented life. He was engaged in the mercantile business for twenty years at

Sabinal, in partnership with his brother Louis, under the firm name of Peters Brothers, but lived here on his ranch all the while and attended to the stock interests, and has been very successful in all of these things.

Mr. Peters relates a very sad incident which occurred while he was at Ben Fickland. A young man named Murray Mason came there from Virginia, and on one occasion, being on a trip up the country, intended to board the stage at Lipan Springs, which was about twenty miles from Fort Concho, and come on to Ben Fickland. There was a ranch near the springs but no stage stand, and the stage passed that place in the night. Mason intercepted it, but the driver, not hearing his hail on account of the rattling of the coach, he attempted to climb into it, not wishing to be left. The guard who sat on the seat with the driver, seeing his action, supposed he was a robber, and at once drew his pistol and fired at him. The ball entered the right breast, inflicting a mortal wound, and Mason turned loose and fell to the ground. The driver whipped up rapidly, thinking a band of robbers might be on hand, and when he arrived at Fickland reported killing or shooting a man at Lipan Springs who was attempting to climb onto the stage. Mr. Peters and others knew that Mason intended coming back in the stage on that trip, and at once said they would bet the guard had killed him. A party was at once made up and went back and found it to be so. The people at the ranch had found him, and said he lived an hour and a half after being shot. The body was then brought to Ben Fickland and buried. Mason was a fine young man, and well liked by all who knew him.

Mr. Peters showed the writer the famous gun which killed two Indians at one shot in the hands of John Bowles. It seems to have been a very dangerous kind of a gun, and generally killed things by the wholesale when turned loose. Mrs. Peters let it go off accidentally on one occasion while trying to shoot a rattlesnake, and killed two dogs.

PAUL VOGHT.

Mr. Paul Voght was born in Germany in 1844, came to Texas in 1854, and first settled on the Cibolo, eighteen miles east of Boerne. At that time the following settlers were there, all in a radius of four miles: A. Piper, Henry Voges, John Kabelmacher, William Gerfers, Peter Poss, R. Kurtzer, Sr., G. Obst, all in Bexar County. As a matter of course the Indians made raids, killed people, and stole stock as they did in all parts of the Texas frontier as soon as a settlement was commenced by the pioneers of those days. During one of these raids the Indians shot a horse belonging to Mr. Kabelmacher, and the animal ran home with the arrow in him. The intelligence of this raid was carried to San Antonio and reported to the military there, and a squad of United States soldiers was sent out, who scouted all over the country but failed to locate the hostiles. The old man Voght, father of Paul, had one favorite mare called Minnie, and the Indians passed her by several times without molesting her; the old man said the Indians did not want her, and that she was safe. Paul said, however, that the Indians would get her some time. Next time the Indians came the nag was missed, and the elder Voght, after a diligent search, was compelled to own that the Comanches had undoubtedly got off with Minnie this time. Paul said, "I told you so," but also went and took a look for the missing favorite, and to his surprise, after getting out in the range, heard the familiar sound of Minnie's bell. Arriving near the spot from which the sound emanated, he was sorely puzzled. The country was open, the bell still rattling, but no animal in sight. The mystery was soon solved. The Indians had taken off the bell when they caught the mare and hung it on a bush, and the wind was rattling it. Paul took it home and the old man said, "Yes, Minnie is gone," when he saw it and learned of the circumstance of finding it. Minnie, however, was not gone for good; the Indians rode her and rounded up horses all over the country, and when ready to commence their retreat back to the west, turned her loose and she came back home, to the great joy of the family, especially the old man, who said to Paul, "I knew the Indians did not want Minnie."

On one occasion, when the old man and Paul were out in the woods and without firearms, they suddenly came upon an Indian who had a gun in his hand. He looked at the white man and boy a few moments without saying anything or making any demonstrations of a hostile nature towards them, and then turned and walked slowly off through the forest. Paul now ran home and procured a shotgun, and came back with the intention of hunting the Indian and having a battle with him. He met the old man, however, who took the gun away from him and told him to go home; that if he followed that Indian he would stop behind a tree somewhere and kill him.

On a Sunday morning, when the Indians captured the two Smith brothers, Jeff and Clint, Paul saw them go out across the hills towards Spring Creek. The Indians were followed by the Gorley boys, Sam Patton and one of his brothers, John Lawhon, and August Knippe. In a dense cedarbrake near Curry's Creek the Indians ambushed the party and fired on them, and they were unable to do any damage to them on account of not being able to see them, and finally gave up the pursuit. When the Indians fired on the white men one ball struck the stirrup of August Knippe, split it open, and drove a splinter into his ankle, wounding him severely.

In 1867 the Indians attacked the ranch of George W. Kendall, for whom the county was named, and killed two men there, Schlosser and Baptiste.

In 1868 suspicion rested on Mexicans who lived in the country that they were committing some of the murders and depredations laid to the charge of Indians, and this was almost verified when a man named William Smith unexpectedly walked into a Mexican's house and found him making arrows. He quickly pushed them under the bed, but Smith pulled them out and examined them, and the maker gave no explanation of why he was making them. Not long after this the Bickle family were killed, supposed to be by Indians, and also a man named Spanneberg, at the same time and place, making four people in all. One

48

boy made his escape, but ran so far and exerted himself to such
an extent, being closely pursued by a Mexican or Indian, that his
lungs were affected, from which he never entirely recovered, although he is living yet, but speaks with a wheezing noise. This
wholesale murder occurred five miles east of Boerne. The boy
who made his escape came first to old man Zoeller's place and told
the news. Many people gathered around the place where the
slain people were, and after they were buried a party was made
up on the spot to take the trail of the murderers and punish
them, whoever they might be, as soon as found. There were men
from Kendall and Comal counties, and two or three from Bexar,
sixteen in all who went in pursuit. The trail from the scene of
the murder was so conflicting, and scattered in so many different
directions, that the avengers were more than ever satisfied now
that it was Mexicans, and at once commenced rounding up and
capturing all of that race then living in the country. Arrows
and many other things found in their possession fastened the
guilt on them, and their captors had no scruples in executing
them, and accordingly seven of them were put to death. Texas
at that time was under military rule, and many of the men concerned in the raid on the Mexicans were arrested on affidavits,
furnished it is supposed by Mexican women, none of whom were
killed. A squad of United States soldiers came out from San
Antonio and arrested the men, and they were taken back and
confined about two weeks; but when the trial came up there was
so much conflicting testimony among the witnesses against the
men that they were all turned loose and allowed to go back home.

There is also a noted place in this county, called "Robbers'
Camp." Here three horse-thieves were captured in their camp
by the settlers and hung. "Dead Man's Hollow," another noted
place, is where a horse-thief was killed and his body left there
during the Civil war. It is fifteen miles below Boerne, on the
Cibolo River, and is now included in the property and pasture
of Mr. Chris. Pfeuffer.

Before this, in 1855, the Indians made a raid eight miles east
of where Mr. Voght lived, and attacked the Hill ranch, in which
they killed four persons—two men, one woman, and one child.
One negro woman on the place made her escape.

The Indians made their last raid in Kendall County in 1872, and sixty men gathered under Lieut. Charles Rompel to follow them. The trail led through a dense cedarbrake, and when they were in the midst of it one of the men commenced blowing a bugle which he had with him. The men commenced laughing, and said the man was blowing up the Indians like a man with a horn calling hogs, as they used to do in the olden time. Captain Rompel was a soldier, and wore a sword, which he drew and rushed back furiously on the man and made him desist, and asked him if he was letting the Indians know they were coming. This scout was fruitless of results as far as catching Indians was concerned, for they made their escape.

About the same time a party of Indians made a raid above Boerne, and went out towards the Medina and stole one horse from Mr. Chris. Anderson, on Red Bluff Creek. The horse, however, was recovered. He gave out on the trip, and was left near Castroville.

In 1864 Mr. Voght was in the hills near where Sisterdale is now, late in the evening. He had eaten nothing since morning, and was very hungry. Seeing a deer, he dismounted, put the foot of his horse through the bridle reins, so that he could not run off, and taking cover, slipped upon the deer, thinking if he could kill it he would cook some and eat. When he arrived at a point from which he supposed he would be in gunshot of the game, he cautiously raised his head to look, but the deer was gone, and instead were five or six horses. He kept concealed and peeped, and soon discovered an Indian on one of the horses, lying low on the opposite side, but his hair visible under the horse's neck. Turning now, he ran back towards his own horse, followed by the Indians, who all straightened up in pursuit, yelling as they came. Mr. Voght had no time to throw the reins back over his horse's neck after disengaging the foot, but mounted and fled. The Indians followed in two parties, cut him off on Black Creek, and ran him in on a bluff of the creek. The distance down was ten feet, and the Indians thought sure they had him, but now was the time to take all chances, and he forced his horse over the bluff. His forefeet went into deep gravel as

he struck, which kept him from falling or getting hurt. He
now rode fifty yards and dismounted, tied his horse, and went
back to the protection of the bluff to fight the Indians. They
rode close along the bluff over his head and looked at the horse,
but were afraid to go to him, for they knew the white man was
was near with his gun, but they could not see him and finally
went away, and he came out, mounted his horse, and went to a
ranch.

Two old bachelors lived for many years in Kendall and Bexar
counties, and were among the first settlers. Their names were
Hermann and Bartenstein. Their cabins were five miles apart,
and the latter lived just across the line in Bexar County. They
often visited one another, but neither ever married. Hermann
was engaged to a young lady once, but before the wedding day the
Indians killed her, and the young man lived to be old and gray
alone. Both are now dead.

During the Civil war Mr. Voght belonged to the Third infantry, company of Capt. Hermann Kampmann of San Antonio.

In 1871 Mr. Voght went to Fort Concho with Mr. Hartberger,
who had a contract with the government to haul hay, and here
he had some more Indian experience. An ox was lost, and the
two men went down the river, one on each side, to hunt for him.
Hartberger came in contact with an Indian. Voght saw him
lay his hand on his six-shooter, and knowing that it was an Indian from his actions that he was about to shoot, commenced
trying to disengage a Spencer carbine which was fastened to the
pommel of his saddle, but it hung, and was with difficulty released. The Indian in question was on Mr. Voght's side of the
river, but under the bank from him, and he could not see him.
He ran from the man on the other side and came up the bluff
onto the open prairie near Mr. Voght, not knowing he was there,
and then dashed passed him at a rapid rate before he got his gun
ready. He followed, however, and commenced shooting as soon
as he could. His companion dashed across the narrow river and
followed, and being on a fast horse soon came in range and also
joined in shooting at the Indian with a revolver. In this way
a mile or more of country was covered, and finally the Indian

disappeared in a thicket. The motion of the running horses spoiled the aim of the white men, and this was one reason they failed to bring the Comanche down. They now rode around the thicket he was in and discovered a large band of Indians and a drove of horses in a valley, and at once went to the fort and reported to the commandant. A force of twenty-five United States cavalry was at once sent out and got on their trail. The Indians had a good start, and before the troops could overhaul them they captured a Mexican train on the El Paso road, killed the drivers, and burned the carts. The cavalry finally rounded them up in a canyon as it was getting dark and stationed guards around, but during the night they escaped, a few at a time, by crawling out and leaving the horses, which the soldiers rounded up when daylight came and carried them back to the fort.

In 1869 Mr. Voght went up the trail to Kansas, and had another experience with Indians. On the way back, and when near Belton, the Indians made a raid in five miles of that place and carried off about sixty head of horses. One very fine one was taken from a man named Blevins. Mr. Voght and about twenty other men took the trail, but soon divided. Part of them kept up the divide between the Colorado and Brazos and the others came up the river, each following different trails, as the Indians had also divided. The first party going up the divide overtook their Indians and got all the horses back except what they rode off, and got back without a fight. The other party also came up with their Indians on Pecan Bayou, but had a battle. The Indians had halted at noon and were shoeing horses with raw hide. A man named Williams was along who had a dog that would trail Indians, and there was no difficulty in following them, whether the trail was plain in places or not. There was one negro along named Ben, who was very brave and a good Indian fighter. The battle soon commenced and was hot for a few minutes, but the Indians were defeated and ran, leaving two dead on the ground and having some wounded. All of the Indians' horses were taken except one, and he was killed in the fight. The negro Ben was wounded in the shoulder with a bullet. He ran in among the Indians and charged one who was on his (Ben's) horse, which had been taken in the raid below, and while firing at the Indian killed his own horse, shooting him through the head with a pistol ball. There were twenty-nine Indians in the fight, and all went off on foot. On the San Saba River, as the men came back, an Indian was discovered sitting on a large rock on the bluff and watching them, but out of range. Voght dismounted and took cover, approaching a tree that was in range, but when he peered around it to shoot, the Indian was gone and could not be found, although a search was made for him. The return trip was very slow on account of the condition of the recaptured horses, which had been badly treated by the Indians. Bread gave out, and the men had to subsist on meat alone. On the Colorado many wild turkeys were seen and several of them killed and carried to a ranch, where the men tried to swap them for meal, but the people there did not have any. The men were four days on the trail of the Indians and much longer in returning, but finally arrived all right, and their wounded negro got medical attention.

Mr. Voght was on this cattle driving trip with Capt. James Ellison. In the Indian Territory, beyond the Washita River, a wagon broke down, and Mr. Voght volunteered to go back to a trading post twenty-three miles distant after an auger to use in fixing it. He went in the night, so as to better avoid Indians, and arrived there about daylight. Several Indians were there, and also two tramps who were traveling across the country on foot. Five dollars was paid for an auger, and Mr. Voght started back on the return trip. He had remained long enough to get breakfast, but the two footmen had started on, going in the same direction, and he calculated to soon overtake them, but before doing so heard two shots ahead and at once left the road and went into a ravine, where he remained concealed all day, and then went on again in the road at night. He soon met a herd coming, and the men with it reported finding the dead bodies of two men on the road. There were the two footmen who had been killed by the Indians, just as Mr. Voght had expected would be their end.

He arrived all right at their camp. He came near being

drowned crossing the Canadian River. A small boat he was in turned over, drifted down the river, and hung up on a poplar tree. Here his foot caught in the fork of a limb, and not being able to release it he was about to drown, when a negro came to him and, diving down, succeeded in getting the foot out, and he made it to shore.

Mr. Voght has a nice place about five miles south of Boerne, and seems to very much enjoy life.

JAMES C. CARR.

COL. J. C. CARR.

Col. James C. Carr was born in Fayette County, Tennessee, and came to Texas January 1, 1845.

Colonel Carr has lived fifty years on the frontiers of Texas, and is an old-time Indian fighter, not only in Texas, but in Oregon and California. In every position and condition of life, whether as a friend, a soldier, or a civilian, Colonel Carr has been equal to the emergencies, and conducted himself in such a manner as to win the respect and approbation of his fellow-citizens. During his long experience on the frontiers of Texas he has exhibited all those qualities of prudence and manhood that are so characteristic of the pioneers of civilization. Colonel Carr, being a newspaper correspondent, is well and favorably known throughout the Rio Grande counties as "Locomotive," "Buckskin," or "Leather Breeches."

Colonel Carr was in the prime of manhood when the tocsin of war sounded in the South in 1861, and with that readiness which has always distinguished his patriotism and love of his adopted State, he immediately enlisted in defense of the homes and altars of the South. He was soon appreciated as a soldier, and elected lieutenant of Company I, Thirty-second Texas cavalry, commanded by Col. P. C. Woods, De Bray's brigade. He participated in all the battles throughout that brilliant campaign, opening at Pleasant Hill and closing at Yellow Bayou.

The following is an extract from Colonel Carr's graphic description of the dedication of the new State capitol, published on the twelfth anniversary of that most interesting occasion to all Texans:

"Twelfth anniversary of the dedication of the new State capitol of Texas. Twelve years ago to-day, May 16, 1888, the broad avenue, well named Congress avenue, in Austin, was filled from sidewalk to sidewalk with gaily caparisoned bands of music, filling the air with sweet sounds and martial notes, preceding in line of march the State officials, invited guests, and military companies with banners waving, marching up and performing military evolutions en route to the capitol building. The side-walks, the doors and windows of the business houses and offices, were filled with the beauty of Texas, waving handkerchiefs and clapping their hands in applause of some intricate movement of some favorite company, and standing at the head of this avenue, upon which the procession and massing crowds were congregating, the new, graceful, and magnificient capitol building, like a young bride waiting for her lover, and truly were lovers and admirers gathering about her to do her honor in dedicating her a temple—a monument to the magnitude and grandeur of Texas. The building itself and the capitol grounds were filled with the hardy citizens of Texas, mingling with the utmost freedom of our manners with faculties of colleges, members of the learned professions, representative men and women from every part of the State.

"They came from the region of the whispering pines of the East; from the classic banks of the Rio Grande; from the flowery, grass-covered plains, the Panhandle, the Gulf, the interior, the snowy waters of Canada, the tropical Florida and the golden sands of California, to witness the dedication of the new Texas capitol. With its imposing grandeur, elegant design, and beautiful finish—the wonder, astonishment, and admiration of all—this building is mammoth, massive, magnificent, and sublime. That is, it is mammoth in size, massive in structure, magnificent in appearance, and sublime in conception. All combined, with other attractions on that occasion, has made the 16th of May a day long to be held in proud remembrance by every true patriot within our borders,—a day that will ever be commemorated as one of the grandest and most eventful in the history of our State; a day in which the chain of unity that binds the east and the west and the north and the south of our empire State was forged anew, and its binding links of love, pride, patriotism, and mutual interest united and blended all in one might whole. Texas undivided, now and forever.

"Texans who are proud of the immensity of their State can with true justice to themselves be prouder of their beautiful solid granite and marble capitol, which rivals the grandest capitols of the ancient or modern worlds. Yes, it was on the 16th

day of May, 1888, in the city of Austin, that the grand pageant
of honor commenced to move in beautiful order up Congress
Avenue towards the new capitol, preceded by the Masonic fraternity of Sir Knights and members of the grand lodge in brilliant regalia. Then next came the military, fifty-two companies,
in gay uniform, martialed in all the pride, pomp, and circumstance of glorious war, the whole being led by the following
bands: The famous Mexican National, the celebrated Gilmore,
and fourteen others, with over seven hundred instruments, all
discoursing the most enlivening martial music. The procession
moved up the avenue to the grand stand at 9:30 a. m., where
stood in waiting the speakers, Gov. L. S. Ross, Judge A. W.
Terrell, Col. Abner Taylor, Hon. Temple Houston, and other
orators of the day. This, together with the dedication cere-
monies by the assembled members of the Masonic Grand Lodge
of Texas, the military, with bands playing and colors flying,
made complete a most magnificent scene—the grand dedication
of the Lone Star State capitol."

We extract the following from the San Antonio Express in
regard to the fair held in San Antonio in November, 1899:

"Col. J. C. Carr ('Locomotive') was boiling over with enthu-
siasm yesterday over the success of the Fair, and when a reporter
for the Express ran across him he was perfectly willing to talk.

" 'Yes, sir, she's a success from start to finish; a great, big,
rip-roaring, all torn-up success.' That is the way he put it, by
way of introduction. Continuing, he said:

" 'It was grand in all its departments, representing the various resources of southwest Texas and Mexico. There were the
long-horn and improved short-horn; the mustang pony and
thoroughbred race horse; primitive and improved machinery;
everything from a wooden-axle wheelbarrow to a steam engine.

" 'The fair grounds composed a real live city, attractive and
instructive. The pictures in the art department were many and
varied, not only the one bought by Col. George W. West, entitled
"Cattle Drifting," but others, showing beautiful valleys, lakes,
foothills, mountains, distant and towering trees appearing to
be tossing and bending with the wind, their evergreen branches
outlined in a golden mist formed by rain following through the

shining sun. There were other pictures of stock of all kinds, not drifting in a snowstorm, but grazing in pastures green. In fact, so real were the paintings that you could almost hear the singing of the birds and see the conquetting butterflies moving among the flowers from bloom to bloom. From the first entrance on the first day, October 28th, to the closing of the gates to-day, the thousands of visitors were all satisfied.

" 'Due to what? The management, the committee, and others of this city; to the press; railways, especially the Aransas Pass, International & Great Northern, and Southern Pacific, including the splendid service of our street car lines and the patronage of San Antonio and the people of southwestern Texas generally. I met at the fair and talked with farmers and stockraisers from every county in the southwestern portion of our State, and many told me that at our next fair they would be on hand with exhibits competing for blue ribbons and prize money.

" 'On ranger day it afforded me great pleasure to meet so many old veteran rangers whose service dates back into the 40's and 50's,—men who in years gone by protected our frontier settlers from the wild Comanche and other depredating Indians; men whose markmanship settled the warwhoop of the depredators and stayed the tomahawk and scalping knife that had caused cries of murder from women and children. I was also pleased to meet and hear Lanham, Chilton, and Bailey; and to say that the old Confeds enjoyed the talk of that distinguished comrade, Hon. S. W. T. Lanham, does not sorter express it.

" 'I must mention and recommend that the Sons of Veterans of this city adopt as a member the Hon. Theo. Harris.

" 'On with the San Antonio and Brownsville Railroad, and our International Fair in October, 1900.' "

Colonel Carr resides in the Alamo city, ripe in years and reminiscences of the past.

In the next chapter read Colonel Carr's courtship in Arkansaw.

COL. J. C. ("LOCOMOTIVE") CARR'S FIRST COURT-
SHIP IN "ARKANSAW."

It was in the early 40's, when just in my teens, I left my native State, Tennessee, with my father and family, for Texas, by way of Arkansaw, where we were water-bound a few years, and lived up to the time of our departure for this State. All our household goods, on leaving Tennessee, were shipped from Memphis by steamboat down the Mississippi River to be delivered at Alexandria, on Red River. The steamboat was sunk, and in her we lost all we had, save and except a few wagons and ox teams by means of which the Carr family were trying to pull overland through to Texas.

Being delayed in Arkansaw by high water and other things, the Carr family stopped, built houses, bridges, rolled logs, and tried to cultivate the soil and live as others of that section and time did, shut off from the outside world. There were but few people in that country, but neighbors would gather from ten to fifteen miles around to help at a log rolling, house raising, or bridge building. Lived! you bet we did, on hog and hominy, bear meet, deer, turkey, etc. We made our own "licker," tanned our own leather to make shoes, dressed skins for clothing, used herbs for medicine, made our tar, wagons, trucks, hats (of oat straw), coonskin caps; in fact, produced and made about everything we used. We ground corn for meal on old fashioned steel hand mills, and hand-picked our cotton to make cloth on old-fashioned hand-made looms. We made our own furniture, bedsteads, chairs, buckets, baskets, and dishes. We raised our own lard cans,—fat gourds,—from which were made cups, dippers, and a great many things, including gourd-covered buttons for all purposes, which were put on old time hand-made clothing. Socks, stockings, and underwear, such as drawers and other things, were never seen,—that is, we never had such things. What few were had were used only by the very old people. Yet notwithstanding all these primitive conditions, there lived in

the State of Arkansaw at that time some of the best people that
ever blowed a horn or paddled a canoe.

It was here at a log-rolling and quilting that I met my first
love, Miss Peggy Roarer, a handsome young lady about five years
my senior. I was only a little up in my teens, while Miss Peggy
was just passing out of hers. She was tall and her complexion
resembled turkey eggs, a hue of which I was a great admirer.
It was at night, and when the log-rolling and quilting were over,
when the house was cleared, the fiddle started and the dancing
in full blast, I was standing outside the door, like a poor boy
at a corn shucking, looking wistfully on, too bashful to go in or
say anything after going in. Miss Peggy, who sat on the end
of a bench near the door, observed me for some time, and making room for me, said, "Sit down on the bench." After a little
while she asked me if I could dance. Greatly embarrassed and
stammering somewhat, I finally replied, "Yes'm." So the next
cotillion was a "Piny Wood Reel," and she said, "Let's dance,"
and we did, after which we took our same seat on the end of the
bench.

We—I mean myself and Miss Peggy—talked a little and
danced again and again; talked and talked, danced and talked,
neither Miss Peggy nor myself dancing with anyone else but
each other from start to finish, from dark to daylight. Of course
we told each other our names and where we lived. She lived
ten miles west and I lived ten miles east from where we had on
that occasion met.

This was about the middle of December, 1844, and I told her
before parting that if I did not come to see her the following
Sunday I would Christmas, sure. She kinder put her head over
on my shoulder and said, "Oh, that's so long." Bidding each
other good-by we parted, one going east, one west.

Think of it! A poor, bashful boy, who only learned to dance
with nigger boys in the kitchen after such music as the Arkansas
Traveler, Nigger in the Woodpile, Dinah Had a Wooden Leg,
Great Big Taters in the Sandy Land, for the first time ten miles
from home, for the first time going home after dancing all night
with a ringing in his ears, "Oh, that's so long," the last words
spoken by his first sweetheart.

Well, long before reaching my home I, too, wanted to put my head up against Miss Peggy's shoulder and whisper, "Yes, yes, any time is too long." My thoughts ran thus, soliloquizing with myself: "Our tan leather is just out and my dressed buckskins are about ready to be made into breeches, and I can have ma plat me a new oat straw hat, and wash my white cotton coat, and well, that's all,—shoes, hat, coat, breeches." I forgot my shirt, apron-checked and nearly new, and a white cotton coat that had only been washed once. That was all, and more than I ever had at one time before in all my life, and when I got them on, and washed and combed back my long hair, placing my new straw hat up and a little to one side on my head, I walked to and fro in front of the glass and fancied myself the best dressed and best looking boy in all that neck o' the woods. True, my naked ankles showed just a little, and I have since that time thought if I only had socks, my pants would have made connection—but I had none. Being accustomed to the old long plow shirt, which was only doffed on Sundays, in this instance a little naked show of ankles didn't amount to much.

I then got my traveling rig together, getting the plow gear and old Charlie (the horse) hitched to an old buggy that had been standing under a tree for six months or more. I assure you it took not only work, but rope and rawhide. However, I made it, and all was ready to start west at 10 a. m. The weather was dark and threatening, and after proceeding a few miles a cold north wind and rain was on me. It grew stronger and finally took away my buggy top, leaving me without any protection. I was not only wet and cold, but hungry, but the thought of Miss Peggy and a good warm supper at least was consoling, and for the time supplied the vacuum in my stomach. Continuing my journey, at about 2 p. m., and a little off my route, I found a house where I stopped and for several hours warmed. Of course I was too late for dinner, but, as before stated, the thought of my loved one and those last words, "Oh, that's so long," and the short end of my day's travel still being westward, I struck out in the rain for Mr. Roarer's, where I arrived about sundown.

On nearing the house I got a glimpse of Miss Peggy. I struck old Charlie with the whip, ran over a hog pen, turned over the buggy, broke off two wheels, and spilt myself out in the mud. The old gentleman, old lady, a little boy, and Miss Peggy, and all the dogs, something less than a dozen in all, got around me. Old man Roarer poured water over me and washed and scraped off the mud, and it was found that I was not otherwise hurt.

The old horse was caught, and of course Miss Peggy introduced me to her father and mother, and we all went into the house. It was still raining and a cold north wind was blowing. Mr. Roarer was from Missouri, and he too, a few years previous, like the other settlers, had got waterbound on his way to Texas.

Mr. Roarer's house was a one-story, one-room log cabin. The chimney and fireplace were of the old style, built with jams or hobs on either side, the fireplace to be used by the women to put cooking utensils on when not in use, such as skillets, ovens, coffee pots, etc. I was seated on one side of said fireplace and Mr. Roarer on the other, with the little boy on his knee, while Miss Peggy and her mother were cooking supper. I was not only wet and cold but hungry, and the old gentleman, appreciating the situation and to make me feel at home, was quite talkative. I was a very bashful boy, and boy-like sat silent. To break somewhat my timidity I got to fumbling with my fingers at the end of an old long-handle frying pan that projected near me from the jam of the fireplace, sticking my finger in and out of the hole in the pan handle. Finally I got my finger in over the joint and couldn't get it out, so there I was.

Of course the old gentleman nor anyone else knew I was fastened to the pan handle, but sure I was, and to make my predicament still worse, about that time the old lady announced supper. Great goodness, what a fix I was in. However, as luck had it, the chair in which I was seated, not being needed at the table, I was made happy by being told. "Well, if you won't have supper, keep your seat." My finger getting worse and worse, what should I do? There was only one remedy—pull it out—and while the family was at supper, with a determined twist, bringing off all the hide, out it came. I carelessly wrapped my hand in my handkerchief so as not to attract attention. The table was then cleared, and the old gentleman resumed his corner with the ladies and little boy in front. Time passed on, and finally the little boy and the two old people went to bed, leaving Miss Peggy and myself up at the fire, all in the same room, as it was a one-room house. There we sat, Miss Peggy and me, she on one side of the fireplace and I in my same seat on the other. I kept thinking what to say and how to say it without the old folks hearing it. On and on the time passed in perfect silence, until finally Miss Peggy ask me what I was thinking about. I told her nothing, and then she said she was thinking of going to bed, and that I could sleep in the back room, she at the same time opening a side door and pointing to a little house out in the field some fifty yeards distant. Said she. "You will find a bed in that room. Good night."

Away I went through the cold north wind. I found the door shut with a wooden pin about a foot long, with a string tied to one end and the other end sticking in a hole. I found that the "back room" was built for a shuck pen or cotton house, and that it was built of round logs, leaving large open cracks. The bed was of a one-legged pattern, a sort of corner scaffold with grass mattress, cotton pillow, and with one thin cover. Nevertheless Miss Peggy called it a back room where I slept. My, but it was cold, cold out there, and my teeth fairly rattled as I got off my cotton coat, hat, and shoes, and lastly, my partly wet and partly dry buckskin breeches. Thinking to break off some of the cold wind, I stuck my breeches in a large crack near my head and bounded into the rude bed, with nothing on but a short, thin, apron-check shirt. Winding up in the aforesaid thin cover, it was with me a stand-off whether I would starve or freeze. However, I lived through the night, and on the following morning, seeing everybody but me up, out of bed I jumped. I looked at the crack first for my breeches, and much to my dismay I found them gone. Upon second thought, I fancied they had fallen through the crack on the outside.

Watching my chance, as the door of my room fronted toward the house, out I went around the corner, with the cold north wind making the tail of my shirt flutter breezily around my waist. I looked hurriedly around for my breeches, but nowhere were they to be found. There I was. What a fix I was in. Presently

49

I discovered all that remained of my missing breeches, to wit, a few pieces of buckskin, with here and there a button sewed to it, evidence conclusive that my breeches had been chewed up by the cows. Great drops of water larger than blue whistlers came out of my eyes and rolled down my cheecks as I watched back around the corner for another opportunity to get back into my aforesaid back room, which I did, and again got to bed. To my seeming it was "Oh, so long," that dreary time rolled heedlessly on, until finally that same little boy was sent down to wake me up. I told him I was sick. Of course the little boy went back to the house and reported, when the old gentleman Mr. Roarer, a 260-pounder, with a stomach on him like a bass drum, came waddling down and remarked as he got to the door. "Say, young man, get up. I am satisfied you are sick, but get up and come up to the house and drink some coffee."

I sorter turned over, and in a sniffling, stuttering, cold kind of voice, told him I was not only sick, but the cows last night had eaten my breeches.

Of course the old gentleman promptly took in the situation. He got a pair of his own breeches to put on me. It was my only show to get out of bed. The breeches Mr. Roarer gave me were brought from Missouri. They were old-timers, hand-made cotton jeans, dyed with walnut bark and snakeberries, and were built with open barn-door front, or buttoned-up flap. This flap buttoned up on either side, where the pockets went in, and they had galluses. Imagine such a garment on me, a body weighing ninety pounds. When I put them on they reminded me of the first breeches my mother ever made me, even in the bosom, only the opening here was too great. So I about-faced. In other words, I took them off, changed fronts, and put them on again, buttoned up the aforesaid flap around my waist, rolled up the legs, put on my shoes, hat, and coat, and went to the house. Hungry? You bet I was, but too sick and mortified to eat.

Mr. Roarer was out in the horse lot, and Miss Peggy and her mother had just come from the cow pen and set on the table two large buckets of milk. These buckets, like nearly everything else about the place, were doubtless made by Mr. Roarer. They were made of cedar, with large, tall, broad handles put on with wooden peg fastenings, and when these buckets were carried by the handles and set down, the handles would stand erect. In this instance the buckets of milk sat on the table with the tall handles erect. Just about this time some one—a traveler on horseback—was passing in front of the house. All the dogs went barking after the traveler, and the old lady, Miss Peggy, the old gentleman, who was in the yard, and the little boy, all went out hollering at the dogs and looking to see if they could recognize the traveler. Being left alone in the house, and being nearly famished, I stealthily stuck my head under one of said bucket handles and begun drinking milk. Just at that moment the big bucket handle fell, from some cause, striking me on the back of the neck. The blow startled me, and my first thought was that Mrs. Roarer had hit me with a stick. Quickly straightening up, in my excitement I brought the bucket and milk all over my head and face. Blinded by the milk and bucket I fell over a chair, turned over the table, and with it spilt more milk, all amidst a crash of breakfast dishes. The general uproar brought Miss Peggy, the old lady, and the little boy, all slapping their hands and crying. When I did finally extricate myself and get loose from the bucket, there was Mr. Roarer, that old 260-pounder, chasing me around in the house. I verily believe he thought I was an escaped lunatic. But the old gentleman never succeeded in capturing me. I made for the fence, jumped clean over it, mounted old Charley, and cut out.

Taking Greeley's advice, I started west, and never stopped until I was safely on the west side of the Sabine River in Texas, where I have lived on the frontier to this day, June 1, 1900.

J. C. CARR.

Toast of Col. James C. Carr at the reunion of the San Jacinto Veterans, in the Alamo city, April 21, 1900.

"Here is to Texas. Looked upon by all christendom as the largest and grandest State and garden spot of the universe, and to-day throughout our broad land, and even beyond the blue and briny waters, she attracts more attention than any other portion of the habitable globe. Made so by what? The heroes of the Alamo, San Jacinto, and the fairest of God's creation—the ladies—a chivalrous, patriotic, liberty-loving people, and the Press."

THE SIEGE AND FALL OF THE ALAMO.

BY IDA RAND WILSON, ABBOTT, TEXAS.

Kindness of COL. J. C. CARR, *of the Alamo City.*

Eloquent indeed was the letter that Colonel Travis sent;
He had waited, watched and hoped, 'till his strength was nearly spent.
"Compatriots," he had written, "Come, our force is very small,
The enemy are all around us—nothing now divides us but a wall.
They have asked us to surrender, surrender at Santa Anna's will;
We have answered with a cannon shot and our flag waves proudly still.
Though our call may be neglected, as long as we have life and breath,
We'll fight for our country and honor, and it shall be victory or death."
Day after day within the fort in vain for hope they watch and wait,
The Mexican forces increase, and they soon shall know their fate;
The god of day, descending, sank slowly in the west,
Santa Anna's troops cease firing, the Texans pause to rest.
Brave Travis stood among his men, with low-bowed head and folded arm,
For to him had come the knowledge that 'twas the lull before the storm.
Then followed there the grandest scene that our history doth record:
It was one to inspire a poet, it was one to thrill a bard!
"Death is inevitable!" Travis cried. "In vain I've waited day by day,
The reinforcements will never, never come, and help is very far away;
Forgive me if I've raised false hopes; I knew not this should be our fate,
In deceiving you I deceived myself, and see my mistake now all too late!
But we can die but once, my boys," and his voice rang clearly then,
"Who will cross the sword line, boys; who will die with me like men?"
One by one they cross the sword line—even the wounded, all save one.
"Lift me over, too!" cried Bowie, and Travis answered "Boys, well done!"
Against four thousand human fiends what could they hope to do?
It was the hour of midnight, and the great struggle was at hand
That was to bring the Mexicans victory and death to the Texas band.
Hark! Listen! What is the terrible sound they hear?
'Tis the dreadful duello, ringing so loud and clear.
Closer they come and closer, now trying in vain to scale the wall,
But before the Texans' steady fire the advancing soldiers fall.
"Kill them!" ordered Santa Anna, "all who shirk the fight,"
As from the Texans' volleys they try to turn and run in flight.
Again they come, again they slowly try to scale the wall,
But the Texans fight like demons, and the enemy swiftly fall.
The fury of despair had nerved them, and they fight with might and main;
The Mexicans almost falter, and they hesitate to renew the fight again.

But Santa Anna's voice rebuked them. "Advance! Advance!" he cried,
Until the dead numbered hundreds, and the ground with blood was dyed,
But there's a limit to human endurance, and the noble Travis falls.
The Texans' strength is exhausted, and the enemy scale the walls.
One by one they fall, those heroes, and the spark of life has fled—
The last of that brave, gallant band is numbered with the dead.
Oh, God! What pen could picture the sight the sun shone on?
The brave hearts, stilled and silent, would never greet the dawn!
It shone on sights to wring the heart, and cast its golden flood
Across the silent battlefield bathed in life's crimson blood.
One feels a start of horror, it was so like some fearful dream,
The Mexicans won the victory—death and Santa Anna reigned supreme.
And thirsting still for vengeance, did they build a funeral pyre
And consign the brave Texans' bodies to the cruel tongues of fire.
The smoke ascended heavenward as the Sabbath sun sank slowly,
And from that sacred fire arose a smoke both bright and holy,
'Twas a flame that burned in every heart, and for it hundreds died.
It cost the Mexicans many a battle, and humbled Santa Anna's pride,
And this is written to their memory, whoever they may be,
Who gave their lives, their precious lives, that Texas might be free.

COL. T. F. SEVIER.

Came to Texas in 1848.

Theodore Francis Sevier was born February 22, 1832, in the town of Russellville, Logan County, Kentucky, and was related to the famous Col. John Sevier, one of the heroes of King's Mountain, commanding a regiment there on that occasion when the men of Sevier, Shelby, and others routed the British troops with great slaughter and killed their commander, Colonel Ferguson. Colonel Sevier was afterwards elected Governor of Tennessee, and served with distinction and honor in tnat capacity.

William Peter Sevier, father of Col. T. F. Sevier, served as second officer on the famous privateer Fox, which rendered such valuable and meritorious service during the war of 1812.

The subject of our sketch came to Texas in 1848, when but 16 years of age, and joined the United States army, which was then doing service on the Texas frontier. Young Sevier was an active soldier and did a great deal of hard scouting service, and was in most of the principal Indian battles of that time, in the late 40's and early 50's. In one Indian battle near Laredo fifteen soldiers engaged forty Indians and a most desperate fight took place, in which the Indians were finally driven off, but the troops were terribly cut to pieces, Sevier and two others alone escaping without injury. After this young Sevier became attached to the commissary department of the army, and in 1856 returned to the States and located in Nashville, Tenn., and in 1859 married Miss Mary Benton Douglas, daughter of Gen. Kelsey Harris Douglas, who served with such distinction in the Indian wars of the later 30's, holding his commission as brigadier general from the Republic of Texas. It was he, in conjunction with Gen. Thomas J. Rusk, who fought the decisive battle with the Cherokees in eastern Texas in 1839, in which both of the principal chiefs, Bowles and Big Mush, were killed, and which put an end to the war and forever crushed the power of the great Cherokee nation.

At the outbreak of the Civil war for State's rights Colonel

AFTER THE LAST GUN WAS FIRED AT THE ALAMO.

Sevier was captain of the Rock City Guards, of the Confederate forces, who so often distinguished themselves on hotly contested fields of slaughter, especially at Perryville, Ky. This company was the nucleus for the First Tennessee regiment, being divided into three companies, and Sevier was elected lieutenant-colonel, but was virtually its commander, and served with it until the spring of 1862, when he was made inspector general of Gen. Leonidas Polk's corps. After the death of General Polk he held the same position under Gen. A. P. Stewart, who succeeded Polk. Colonel Sevier participated in most of the battles of the war except Shiloh, and was wounded at Caswell, Ga., while on a tour of inspection.

After the war he was a member of the faculty of the University of the South, at Sewanee, Tenn., remaining with that institution for ten years.

He returned to Texas in 1889, and now resides at Sabinal station, in Uvalde County, and in consort with his son Hal publishes the Sabinal Sentinel.

CAPT. FRED METZGER.

Came to Texas in 1844.

The subject of this sketch was born in Germany, on the Rhine, in 1833, at a place called Nassau, then a dukedom but now belonging to the German empire. William Metzger, great uncle of Frederick, was a rear admiral in the navy of Holland under Prince Orleans.

Mr. Metzger came to Texas with his parents in 1844, as part of Castro's colony. His father had a brewing outfit which he intended to bring on to Castroville or San Antonio, but as transportation was not readily obtained, the family had to remain some time in tents, and all became sick at Port Lavaca, and they left there and went to Galveston, and there the elder Metzger died, and in 1846 Frederick enlisted in the army of the United States to fight Mexico, in the company of Captain Hornsby, Colonel Bonham commanding the regiment and General Lally the brigade. He went through the war and was in many battles and skirmishes, the hardest being at the village of Huamantla, where Lieut.-Col. Sam Walker of the Texas troops was killed. Metzger was near him when he fell, and says that he had a canteen hanging over his shoulder, and the ball went through this first and then through his body, and that he fell in his tracks and died at once. The body of the gallant officer was brought back to Texas and buried at San Antonio. Another hard fight was at the National Bridge, where Captain Hornsby had twenty-five men out of his company killed. One sergeant was shot in the knee by a brass ball while resting on one knee to fire, and blood poison set in and killed him. Another man was shot in the right eye, the ball passing through the side of the head and coming out of the ear. Lally's brigade captured the National Bridge fort.

While in Mexico Mr. Metzger visited the prison of Perote, where Big Foot Wallace and other Texans were confined a few years before, and says it was a very strong place, and at the corners of the prison were large mortars for throwing shells that a man could crawl into. He also examined the place where some of the captive Texans dug under the walls and made their escape.

Mr. Metzger came back to Galveston after the war was over, and in 1849 set out for California, but was taken sick at Fort Leavenworth and all of his outfit was stolen, as he had no one to take care of it for him. After many reverses, in 1851 Mr. Metzger was back at Galveston and sailed for the West Indies, and at Martinique saw some of Walker's men who went on the ill-fated expedition to South America, where the "gray-eyed man of destiny" met his fate and his men scattered. This party claimed French protection to save themselves and remained there some time, but finally went aboard of the United States sloop-of-war Portsmouth and sailed away, Metzger going on the same ship. He made the acquaintance of one of Walker's men named John Ecker, and they afterwards served in the same cavalry troop on the Texas frontier.

They enlisted in the United States service in Company D, Captain Enos. The regiment was commanded by Colonel Parmer, and was ordered to Texas. Hardee was lieutenant-colonel, Pap Thomas major, Robert E. Lee captain, Earl Van Dorn captain, Kirby Smith brevet major. Oaks was captain of Company C. Eagle lieutenant, John B. Hood adjutant, and Menter quartermaster. These were some of the distinguished men who served on both sides in the Civil war with whom Mr. Metzger served on the Texas frontier. Part of these troops went to Fort Mason and others to Camp Verde, in Kerr County, Metzger coming to the latter place. Captain Whiting also cammanded a company in this consignment of troops to Texas.

Soon after arriving at their Camp Verde quarters a runner came and informed them that the Indians were in the country, and thirty men were at once sent out under the command of Lieutenant Van Camp, with Polly Rodrigues as guide and trailer. The Indian raid was in the Medina valley, fifteen miles south of the post, and when the troops arrived on the scene a band of settlers led by F. L. Hicks was already on the trail and had fought the Indians at the head of the Medina and defeated them, Mr. Hicks killing the chief in the skirmish. Rodrigues found the body of this chief and scalped him and took his head dress, and afterwards let the scalp hang attached to his bridle. The soldiers followed on after the Indians three days, but could not overtake them. This was in 1857.

Lieutenant Van Camp afterwards went on the expedition with Major Van Dorn to the northwest, and was killed in the great Indian battle at the Wichita village.

In 1857 the Indians again came down on a raid, this time southeast from the post in the Guadalupe valley, and again a runner was sent to notify the soldiers. A detachment of twenty-five men was sent out under Sergt. William McDonald, Polly Rodrigues again being guide and trailer. The settlers, as before, were on the trail, among whom was Dr. J. C. Nowlin and a man named Moore. Among the soldiers a strange thing occurred just before they got the news of the raid. A man named John Martin said to Metzger, "I had a vision last night, in which I saw my sister, who lives in Baltimore, come to my tent door and beckon to me with her hand, and begged me to come home." Metzger said, "You get a furlough and go home."

When the news of the Indian raid came Metzger said to Martin, "You had better not go. Something will happen to you. Go home." Martin, however, said he would go this time, and then go home. The soldiers and citizens got together and followed the Indians in a northwest direction towards Kickapoo Springs, which was in the Fort McKavett country, and came upon them near the springs. The guide was ahead, and when he gave the alarm the men all rushed in and captured the mules and horses of the Indians, but the latter met the whites bravely, and although being surprised in camp and largely outnumbered, gave them a sharp fight, and the horse ridden by Dr. Nowlin was soon killed. Part of the men dismounted, among whom was Metzger, and opened fire from their horses. Jim Lafoyo, bugler, ran his horse to the left and engaged an Indian at close quarters and attempted to fire at him with a pistol, but it failed several times, and the Indian shot him in the stomach with an arrow, which would have killed him but for the intervention of an overcoat which was rolled up and in front of him, and the wound was only slight. The bugler after receiving the wound threw his pistol at the Indian's head and left him. Metzger now ran around on that side, and seeing an Indian, fired at him and he fell, but could not tell whether he killed him or not, and he then ran back past the dead horse of Dr. Nowlin and saw Sergeant McDonald fighting an Indian with his gun empty and trying to keep him off by pointing the empty weapon at him. Metzger went to his assistance and killed the Indian, who was the chief. John Martin fell mortally wounded to the right of where Dr. Nowlin's dead horse lay. The fight was soon over, and the Indians ran and scattered. Metzger picked up the pistol of the bugler, and also secured the scalp and fine head dress of the chief, which was covered with silver plates, one of which he afterwards had adjusted to the handle of a walking stick with his name engraved on it.

After the fight the wounded man Martin was carried to Fort McKavett, where Dr. Nowlin and the post surgeon there did all they could for him, but he died and was buried there. On the way to the fort Jim Lafoyo rode behind the wounded man and held him on his horse, as he was shot in the stomach and could not lie on a stretcher.

About two months after this Mr. Metzger was in another fight with Indians in the Guadalupe mountains. Three Indians were killed, one of whom was a squaw. One man named McKeen was shot in the back with an arrow, and Metzger's horse was wounded in the neck with an arrow.

When the Civil war broke out Mr. Metzger was captain of a frontier company commissioned by General Huffman. When these were disbanded Captain Metzger joined Colonel Duff's regiment, and was elected orderly sergeant in Capt. Frank Robinson's company, John C. Ware being lieutenant.

Captain Robinson is now county judge of Uvalde county. John C. Ware lives in Sabinal Canyon, and Captain Metzger lives in Hondo City, Medina County.

THE GILLELAND CHILDREN CAPTURED BY INDIANS.

1837.

In 1837 Johnston Gilleland and his wife, Mary Gilleland, came from Pennsylvania and settled in Refugio County, near the Don Carlos ranch. They had two children, Rebecca and William. Mr. Gilleland soon joined a ranging company commanded by Captain Tumlinson, and materially aided in protecting the frontier from hostile Indians.

One evening in 1840 Mr. Gilleland and his wife and children were a short distance from the house, about sunset, when suddenly a band of Indians with a loud warwhoop dashed upon them. The father and husband made a run for the house to get his gun with which to protect his family, the others following, but he and his wife were killed before they could get there, and the children captured and placed on horses and carried off, screaming. The Indians did not like this crying, and said they would cut off their hands and feet if they did not stop it, but an old Indian woman took their part and made the other Indians let them alone. The Comanches did not stop, but pushed on through the settlement all night, and the first halt they made was after daylight. During their flight, however, a band of soldiers and a squad of rangers, among whom was "Mustang" Grey, had struck their trail and were in hot pursuit of them, and came upon them during this halt and a furious battle commenced. The Indians soon ran and went into a dense forest, and here lanced the boy and knocked the girl in the head and left them both for dead; but they soon returned to consciousness. They had been taught to ask God to help them when in trouble, and now prayed for that deliverance. They knew that white men were not far off, for they saw them fighting some of the Indians while others were running into the bottom with them. The girl was the oldest, being eight years, while her brother was only six, and badly wounded and unable to walk, but the brave child took him in her arms and made an attempt to get out of the timber so that the white men could see them. Her strength soon failed and she sank down, but after resting she renewed the effort and kept on in this way until she came to the edge of the prairie, and saw many horsemen on it, riding about. Thinking they were Indians, she took up her little brother again and ran back into the brush and hid. The soldiers and rangers knew the Indians had the two children, for they had been informed by special courier of the killing and capture. The company of soldiers was commanded by Capt. Albert Sidney Johnston, afterwards the famous Confederate general, and he had sent out this squad under Lieut. Hannum to follow the Indians, and they had met Mustang Grey and some of Captain Price's rangers, who had seen the Indians, but were not strong enough to warrant an attack upon them, and were coming to Johnston's camp, but all now went together, and the battle above narrated was the consequence. The scattered men on the prairie were hunting for the children and calling them, not knowing what the Indians had done with them. When they came to the edge of the woods and called them loudly by name the little girl, knowing now it was friends, arose from the ground where she was lying hid, and lifting her little weak and badly wounded brother in her arms, carried him out to the men, many of whom shed tears at the sight as they raised them to their saddles and hurried them back to camp. Here they were kept until the following day and then carried to the Don Carlos ranch, and the little boy placed under the treatment of Drs. Axsom and Hammond. The girl was conveyed by General Johnston to Victoria, and was there joined by her brother when he recovered, and both placed in the care of a Presbyterian minister, Dr. Blair, and his good wife. They were like a father and mother to them.

Many years after this the boy accidentally shot himself in the hip, badly shattering it, but recovered from it and survived both wounds many years, but was always a sufferer.

The girl married a man named Fisher, and has relatives in Sabinal Canyon—the family of Orceneth Fisher, who was a Methodist preacher, and died there about 1880.

THE ETTER FAMILY.

Came to Texas in 1851.

Samuel Etter, Sr., was born in Switzerland in 1801, and started from Bremen, Germany, to Texas in 1851, in the fall of that year. His wife was Elizabeth Rocbet, and they had five sons and five daughters, namely: Samuel, Jr., John, Peter, Jacob, Gottlieb, Mary, Elizabeth, Anna, Rosina, and Magdalena. Mr. Etter was first under a contract to settle in the highlands of Illinois, a man named Grossniklaus being the head agent for that colony, but another agent advised him to settle at San Felipe, and Peter Heinerman, who was on the same ship, advised a different locality, which was Castro's colony in southwest Texas, whither he was himself bound. Mr. Etter decided on the latter suggestion, and came on to Galveston in a two-masted ship, the Herschel, having been on the ocean seven weeks, and landing on Christmas day. The trip to San Antonio was uneventful, and here Mr. Etter remained for some time and rented nine acres of land from Mr. Groesbeck, on Garden Street, and cleared it and planted a crop on it. There was a new house on this tract of land at the time, and all of it could have been bought for $400.

After the crop was planted Mr. Etter left the boys to cultivate it, and came on out to Castroville and bought, for $1.50 per acre, 350 acres of land from Charles Montel, which was situated five miles east of Castroville, north of the San Antonio road. Here he built a house out of elm planks, cutting the logs and hauling them to the sawmill of Mr. Montel on the Medina River, and having them converted into lumber. The family came out from San Antonio when it was finished, and occupied the new home, which was pleasantly situated and in a very desirable locality, and a farm was soon opened up in the black, rich prairie soil.

Mr. Etter was not bothered much by Indians, but had to keep on the lookout, and lost one horse during a raid. In this settlement on the east side of the river, but badly scattered, were James Brown, Mr. Woodward, who lived back towards Castroville, but below the road, old man Adams, who lived on Medio, towards San Antonio, and Sam Lytle, who lived low down on the Medina at the mouth of Protrancko Creek, and these were the nearest neighbors. Big Foot Wallace and Jeff Bond at this time had left their place down on the west bank of the Medina and settled on the Chicon, still further west. Jacob Droitcourt lived on the east bank of the Medina, opposite Castroville, and this was the only house between Mr. Etter and town. A battle with Indians took place seven miles north of Mr. Etter's place, in which a young lad named Jac Huffman killed two, but Mr. Etter was in no fights with them. He stayed close about home and attended to his farm, and he and his wife both died there at a good old age. Mr. Samuel Etter, Jr., the oldest son, now lives on the old place, and his wife, who was Augusta Tschoepe, was born in Prussia in 1833, and had four brothers—Louis, William, Rudolf, and Henry. Her sisters were Agatha, Louise, Lena, and Bertha, the latter dying in Germany six months before the balance of the family left the old home for Texas. She was a grown young lady, and cried all the time when the decision was made to hunt a new home across the water, and continually said that she would never go to Texas, and pined away and died. There were ten of the family on board the ship Von Fink when the start was made, which was in 1852, and they were nine weeks crossing the ocean. Among the passengers two children died and one was born on board the ship, and one great storm was encountered. Mrs. Etter liked sailing on the ocean, and was sorry when land was made, and would like to have gone on nine weeks more. The ship anchored in front of Indianola, on the coast of Texas, on the 14th of December, 1852, but could not come nearer than five miles on account of its size and lack of deep water, and had to unload passengers and freight on two schooners and convey them into port.

The trip from the coast was made in ox wagons to New Braunfels, in Comal County, and they arrived there on the 1st of January, 1853, and stayed three months, and then moved down into Guadalupe County, where Mr. Tschoepe was employed by Colonel Young to make furniture. Some time after this he bought land on Long Creek, two miles from Schumanville, in Guadalupe County, at $2 per acre, and moved the family out there, about 1884, but the old man and his son Louis, who was also a good wood workman, stayed in Seguin about three years off and on, from 1884 to 1887, and during this time did a good deal of carpenter work for General Jefferson, and Louis built the Faust mill in New Braunfels, but died just before it was completed, and the father and mother of Mrs. Etter died on the farm near Schumanville.

Before Louis died, however, the Civil war came on, and he and his brother Rudolf joined Sibley's brigade and were in nearly all of the battles in which it was engaged during the campaign in New Mexico and Louisiana, Rudolf being in twenty-two engagements and Louis in nineteen. Louis had his horse wounded badly once and himself twice slightly, and Rudolf, who belonged to the Val Verde battery, which he helped to capture, had two horses killed under him.

Lieutenant Sayers was adjutant to General Green and Rudolf was assistant, and he and Louis were held in high estimation by the adjutant, the former staying in the tent with him and General Green. When provisions became very scarce, and only one piece of bread was in the general's part of the commissary, he divided it into four parts, for himself, Sayers, Rudolf, and the negro cook.

Rudolf still lives in Guadalupe County, as also does Louise, who married Mr. Wolfort. Lena, who married Mr. Lindeman, died in Guadalupe County, and her children are there now. Agatha lives in Victoria; she married Mr. Schadwitz. Mrs. Etter first married Mr. Blum, and he died in Lockhart. She married Mr. Etter in Medina County.

Jacob Etter married Katy Keller, and she was the first child baptized in Castroville and the second one born. The first one born died in a few days. When Castroville had its fiftieth anniversary Mrs. Jacob Etter was placed in a wagon in the procession with the godmothers around her, and another wagon was for the oldest men. Judge Herman Haas made a speech in nice form showing the difference in the early settlement and the present,—the hostile Indians, rude shelters and wagons, farm implements, etc.

THEODORE THE SHEPHERD KILLED BY INDIANS.

During the first settlements on the Sabinal, near where the station is now, but in what year we are not able to find out, a young man named Theodore was killed by Indians. His other name also is not now remembered, but his taking off was very sad, and some of the old settlers remember the circumstance. At this time James Davenport lived at what was afterwards known as the Thompson place, about four miles north of the present station of Sabinal, on the road to Sabinal Canyon. This young man Theodore was hired to Mr. Davenport to herd sheep, and on the day that he met his death was up the Sabinal River several miles, and there came in contact with a band of Indians. The circumstance of his killing is not known, only by signs afterwards discovered. When he failed to come in at the proper time with the sheep a search was made for him, and he was finally found sitting against a hackberry tree, dead. His trail from the tree led back up the river nearly a mile, marked in many places by blood spots, to the place where the Indians had chased and shot him with arrows. Why they did not pursue and finish him on the spot is not known, for the country was tolerably open. He evidently traveled as long as his strength would permit down the river towards the Davenport ranch, and then, sitting down, leaned his back against the tree and died. His people lived on the Medina, and were notified of his death and the body buried under the tree where he was found. His people, however, soon came and removed the remains to his home and re-interred them.

At the time Theodore was killed Mr. George Dillard and his father-in-law, Mr. Chris. Kelley, had hauled a load of cypress lumber from Sabinal Canyon, where at that time was a sawmill, and unloaded it in a liveoak grove on the opposite side of the river lower down, but not a great ways from the spot where Theodore died, and narrowly escaped coming in contact with the Indians themselves. After finding out the circumstance of this

50

THE TREE UNDER WHICH THEODORE THE SHEPHERD DIED.
From Photo by Miss Edith Dillard.

raid and killing of the young man they abandoned the idea of
settling where they had unloaded the lumber, which was at first
their intention, and moved it back to the canyon, where it was
more thickly settled. Mr. Dillard afterwards settled on the
spot where Theodore died, his house being about one hundred
yards north of the hackberry tree. In the picture the view is
east towards the barn and hay stack, and the dwelling not visible.
Mr. Dillard sold this place and now lives further out in the
prairie, where he runs a farm and ranch.

WATKINS AND RICHARDSON KILLED BY INDIANS.

1860.

In August, 1860, B. F. Watkins and J. H. Richardson started from the mountains in the Frio and Sabinal country to Uvalde for the purpose of taking the oath of allegiance to the Confederate government. After crossing the Frio River they went into camp for the night about eight miles from Uvalde, and during the night or early next morning they were attacked and killed by Indians. Some time during the day after the killing a man named George Robinson, also on his way to Uvalde, came upon the bodies. They were most horribly mutilated and stripped and fifteen arrows were scattered around, besides what were in the slain men, showing a stand-off was made with the Indians for some time. Robinson galloped on to town with the news, and a party came out and brought the remains of the unfortunate settlers in and buried them in the cemetery at Uvalde. The stone which marks the spot was put there by friends and relatives of the deceased.

George Robinson, mentioned above, was the son of Henry Robinson, Sr., the famous scout and Indian fighter of the Southwest, and who was finally killed by the Indians in Nueces Canyon. The same Indians who killed him and Henry Adams at the same time attacked the Robinson ranch and were fought and kept off by George Robinson, then a boy, who succeeded in shooting two of them and was himself wounded in the arm by an arrow. A family named Kelsey was in a camp near by and one of the girls was wounded and scalped by the Indians, but was carried to Fort Inge and by careful attention recovered. Judge James McCormick, who still lives in Uvalde County, helped to remove the unfortunate girl to the fort and then helped to wait upon her until she recovered. Henry Robinson, Jr., another son of Henry, Sr., was killed by Indians near where the ranch of Joe Richarz now is, at the foot of the mountains on the Frio. This party of Indians was pursued by a squad of men from Sabinal

THIS ST NE MARKS THE SPOT WHERE WATKINS AND
RICHARDSON WERE KILLED BY THE INDIANS.

Canyon under command of Capt. John C. Ware, who overtook
them and had a fight, in which the horse of Demp Fenley was
killed. Among others along was Joe Kelley, Jack Kelley, and
Wilson O'Brien.

ANCESTORS OF THE AUTHOR.

The name of Sowell, or Sewell proper, is of Celtic origin, and originated in the highlands of Scotland many centuries ago. In the Scottish war against King Edward of England they followed the fortunes of Sir William Wallace, and when he was taken and executed they espoused the cause (in an humble way as private soldiers) of Robert the Bruce, and helped to retain the crown to him on the bloody field of Bannockburn. When Oliver Cromwell broke up the British Parliament and raised an army to oppose King Charles, the Scottish Sewells joined his standard, and seven of them distinguished themselves in the charge of the highlanders at the great English battle of Lynn.

They came to the colonies of America at an early day, and two brothers settled on the Yadkin River in North Carolina, and their descendants moved to Virginia and Tennessee. The Virginians retained the original name of Sewell, while the Tennesseeans, by some cause, in after years spelled it Sowell. When the war of the Revolution broke out in 1776 our branch of the family were in North Carolina, and many of them joined the army of Washington. John Sowell, great-grandfather of the writer, was severely beaten by the Tories on account of a speech he made on one occasion at a country schoolhouse, in which he denounced them in most bitter terms.

We were also related to the Champes of Virginia, one of whom, John Champe, was a noted patriot soldier and warm friend of "Light Horse" Harry Lee, under whom he served. On one occasion Champe penetrated the British lines and undertook to capture Benedict Arnold after his treason and bring him back to the American lines, but failed on account of a violent storm which set in just as he had all of his plans laid.

John Sowell, grandfather of the writer, was born in Rutherford County, Tennessee, and when the war of 1812 broke out joined the army of Gen. Andrew Jackson and fought the Indians at the "Horseshoe Bend." There were many other Sowells in the army, one of whom, Shadrach, a powerful man physically, with long arms, killed three Indians with his clubbed rifle at the

ASA J. L. SOWELL.

breastwork of logs. William and Louis were both killed in battle with the Indians, the latter at Mackinaw Island and William under General Harrison, probably at Tippecanoe, for many of the Sowells fought in that battle. Joe Sowell, a captain of rangers, was killed in a fight with Indians in Fannin County, Texas, and his son John captured by the Indians and kept three years.

When the army of General Jackson went to New Orleans, grandfather John and others of the connection went with it and fought in the battle there. Grandfather was a gunsmith and made thirty rifles to arm a Tennessee company, and they were used at New Orleans.

My father, Asa J. L. Sowell, was born in Davidson County, Tennessee, in 1821, near the home of General Jackson, called "The Hermitage." Also four of my uncles was born there,— Andrew Jackson, William, Lewis, and John. Andrew was the oldest and was named by the wife of General Jackson after her distinguished husband, who was a warm friend of our family. This is where we get the family name of Andrew Jackson. I was named for my uncle, and have nephews named for me. My father's middle name was Lee, named for "Light Horse" Harry Lee, who was the father of Robert E. Lee, the great leader of the armies of the Confederacy in the Civil War.

From Tennessee grandfather moved to Missouri, and from there to Texas as part of the colonists of Green De Witt, arriving at Gonzales, Texas, in 1829. Here he put up a shop and made and mended guns, and also made a knife for James Bowie, which took his name.

When the Texas revolution broke out in 1835 and the battle of Gonzales was fought, grandfather made slugs of bits of iron to load the cannon with. His sons, Andrew, William, Lewis, and John, were in the fight, my father being too young to go. In the war with Mexico and the Indians Andrew became a noted scout and trailer, and was a companion of "Kit" Carson, with whom he swapped hats on one occasion. He served under Hays, Burleson, Caldwell, McCulloch, Mason, and Calahan, and was in the battles of Gonzales, Plum Creek, Blanco, Sabinal, Nueces, Mission Conception, Powder House, Grass fight, Council House, and Salado. In the Civil War he served in the Confederate army.

A. J. SOWELL AS A RANGER, 1870.

THE WRITER IN 1900. LAID DOWN THE WINCHESTER
AND TOOK UP THE PEN.

The Sowell league was located in the bend of the Guadalupe
River below the present town of Seguin, and they helped to build
that place in 1838. My father served as a ranger under Hays,
McCulloch, and Calahan, and was the orderly sergeant of Capt.
Henry McCulloch's company. He was the first district clerk
of Guadalupe County, and afterwards at various times held
every office in the county,—assessor, sheriff, mayor, county judge,
etc.

My great-grandfather on the side of father's mother was John
Carpenter, who was one of Francis Marion's men, and was killed
in a fight with the Indians and Tories in the war of the Revolution. His daughter, my grandmother, was the fifth white
woman to cross the San Marcos River in Texas.

My mother was Mary Mildred Turner, born in Nashville,
Tennessee, and daughter of Major William S. Turner, who served
on General Jackson's staff in the militia, and served under him
in the war with the Creek Indians, participating in the battles
of Talladega, Tallahassee, Horseshoe, and New Orleans. In the
battle of Talladega he was twice wounded with arrows in the
neck and head. His wife was Elizabeth Smith, and among her
people were noted lawyers and doctors ; of the former was Calvin
Smith and the latter Dr. Goodlow Smith. Among the Turners
were also noted lawyers, one of these being Jack Turner, of Nashville, Tennessee. My mother's brothers were William, Calvin,
Hardin, and John, and one sister, Lucinda. They came to Texas
in 1840. My father's sisters were Sarah and Rachel. My
mother's great-grandfather, James Turner, was Governor of
North Carolina in the early days, and one of her ancestors, John
Turner, came over to America in the Mayflower.

There were nine children of our family, four boys and five
girls, as follows: Andrew Jackson (myself, eldest), Leroy
Polk, Pleaman Smith, and John; sisters, Adaline (older than
myself), Lucy, Isabel, Laura, and Molly.

I was born on the 2d day of August, 1848, near Seguin, and
when quite young father moved to the Blanco, in Hays County,
and here in 1853 I came near being captured by an Indian.
Five of us children,—my sister Adaline and three of Uncle Andrew's children, Asa, Elizabeth, and Mary,—were on a small hill
near uncle's house getting cedar wax and pulling the bark from
a slippery elm tree, when suddenly my sister says, "Look there;

what an ugly man," and ran. We all took one look and started, too. The Indian was coming out of a cedar brake very near, and almost got his hands on me, as I was the youngest and short-legged, and fell several times while running across an open glade on top of the hill. Our screams soon brought father and uncle Andrew with their guns, and the Indian ran back into the brake before they could get a shot at him, but they trailed him about a mile.

I served the State of Texas as a ranger in the Wichita campaign of 1870-71, and experienced some hard service in the northwest, almost freezing on several occasions in sudden blizzards while scouting in the Panhandle. On one occasion we spent three days and nights in a draw or depression of the prairie while a fierce storm of snow and sleet swept across the plain. Our only chance for fire was a few stunted mesquites, which we burned to the last twig and root. On another occasion we were caught and spent a fearful night in a sleet that cut and stung almost like shot, and our blankets and slickers were a sheet of ice. When daylight came my horse had succumbed to the blast, and I was a dismounted ranger. At another time I lay on the frozen ground with pneumonia, and sleet falling constantly all over me, and my hair frozen fast to my blanket; but I had true and brave companions with me who carried me 100 miles across the ice-covered prairies to Big Sandy Creek, where we went into camp in the heavy timber.

In 1871 I was detailed with fifteen others as scouts and was sent to the outside limit to watch along the spurs of the Wichitas for the Kiowas and Comanches, who were trying to beat back the settlers in Montague, Wise, and Jack counties, and it was while on this service that we had that terrible fight at the "Keep Ranch" in Wise County, ten rangers and one citizen from Montague County fighting forty-one Kiowas and Comanches on the open prairie for more than an hour, and witnessed by terror-stricken women and screaming children. In the end we were the victors, killing and wounding more than one-third of their number, including two chiefs in the slain,—Sittanke and Oska Horseback,—who both died on the field fighting us at only a few yards distance. Nearly half of our men were stricken but none fatally, although the life of Billy Sowell hung long in the bal-

THE WOUNDED RANGER.
Helping a Comrade at the " Keep Ranch " Battle.

ance, he having been shot badly in the side with a bullet. Our gallant little sergeant in command of the scouts, Edward H. Cobb, had his horse shot from under him, but mounted the horse of the chief Sittanke, who had just been killed in our front, and his horse broke through our squad to the rear.

I was on the forty-four days' scout, and after the fight between the cowboys and Indians in Battle Creek Canyon, which we tried to get into but were overrun and forced back by 300 head of stampeded horses, myself and Dan Woodruff were sent out by Sergt. Joel R. Payne, who was in command of this scout, as spies, and were ambushed near the head of Foyle's Creek, I think likely not far from where Albany is now, either in Taylor or Shackleford County. I can not tell, as I have never been back there since. Anyway, we had to run and keep them off for six miles, and our horses almost died under us, but we finally got away. On this same scout one night we got torn up in a cyclone and four saddle horses and a pack mule got away, my horse being one of the four, and we had to walk 151 miles and live on game without salt until we got to camp, consuming fifteen days during the time. I was also one of the dozen scouts who rode all night facing a sleet to succor the Keenon ranch, but

TEXAS RANGERS TRAILING INDIANS.

when we arrived the Comanches had done their bloody work, and seven women and children lay scattered around, scalped and mutilated.

This family history I suppose will be of more interest to my numerous relatives than other people, but here it is.

My father died at Seguin, as did also my mother and sister Lucy. Brother John died in Parker County at sister Isabel's. Pleaman Smith is a lawyer and lives at Seguin, and served his district in the Twenty-fourth Legislature as a Democratic nominee. Leroy Polk lives in San Antonio and is engaged in the mercantile business. Laura and Molly live in the Panhandle. Laura married Lem Smithers; Molly, Cliff Abbott, sheriff of Dallam County; Isabel married Milford Nichols, now deceased; John married Ida Rogers; Leroy married Almedia Tinsley; the writer married her sister, Mary Lillian; Pleaman Smith married Henriette McLean; Adaline married James A. Sowell, now dead. He helped to capture the Harriet Lane at Galveston and was wounded in Louisiana, and was in many battles there.

Father was a Royal Arch Mason, and was buried by that order. It was the largest funeral procession that ever went out of Seguin.

THE LOST VALLEY FIGHT.

1874.

The following facts of one among the most desperate Indian battles ever engaged in on the Texas frontier were furnished the writer by Mr. Walter M. Robinson, one of the participants, and who still survives and distinctly remembers all of the terrible scenes through which he passed and witnessed on that day.

This battle was fought on July 12, 1874, in "Lost Valley," Jack County, between the Texas rangers, thirty-five in number, commanded by Maj. John B. Jones and Captain Stephens, and 200 Comanche and Kiowa Indians, as near as their number could be estimated during a five hours battle, the Indians being led by Chief "Lone Wolf." On the day before the battle Major Jones, who was in command of all the rangers on the frontier, and who went from post to post with an escort inspecting the different companies and paying them off or adjusting any other matters needing his attention along the border, arrived at the camp of Captain Stephens, in command of a ranger force stationed in Jack County, northwest from Jacksboro about fifty or sixty miles. On July the 12th a report came to Captain Stephens that Indians were in the country, and Lieutenant Wilson was detailed with six men by the captain to take a scout into the vicinity from which Indians were reported and make an investigation, Walter Robinson, a member of Capt. Rufe Perry's company, being one of the members of this scout. The detail proceeded about six miles and came upon a large Indian trail which denoted a raiding band of Indians of unusual large force, and a runner was sent back to camp by the lieutenant to inform Major Jones and Captain Stephens of the fact, and advising a force to be sent out of all the men that could be spared from camp to take up the trail of the Indians and give them battle in case they could be overtaken. In the meantime, while the messenger was speeding on his mission, Lieutenant Wilson and the other five men followed slowly on the trail, and in about twelve miles Major Jones and Captain Stephens with thirty men overtook them, making the ranger force now about thirty-five all told.

The combined force now kept on the trail rapidly until twenty minutes before 12 o'clock a. m., when they came upon the Indians in a timbered but rough and rocky country in the Lost Creek valley, where the Comanches and Kiowas had placed their force in ambush to try issues with the rangers whom they had discovered on their trail. Before doing this, however, the wily chief had divided his force into three bands and crossed and recrossed Lost Creek several times on purpose to disconcert and bother the rangers and cause them to scatter their force in pursuit, following the meanderings of the different trails, but finally he consolidated his whole force in a mott of timber on the west side of the creek. Before locating the Indians Major Jones divided his force into three squads to follow as many different trails, but admonished each party to remain in touch with each other and be ready at any moment to reunite in case of an emergency. The major with thirteen men went to the right and skirted around the foot of some hills and came in close range of the timber in which the whole Indian force was concealed, and was fired on by them, which was the first intimation he had of their presence. This volley wounded some horses, and on the heels of it came the charge, the Indians leaving cover and attacking Major Jones with great fury in the open prairie, but he stood his ground and the gallant squad around him opened up a hot fire from their Winchesters into the very faces of the yelling and advancing savages. The other two parties of the ranger force were not long in rushing to the scene of the fierce fight which was now being inaugurated, and the main battle opened with terrific fury on both sides, the yelling of the Indians almost drowning the noise of the carbines, which popped and cracked like a canebrake afire, and in a few moments Lee Corn was badly wounded with a bullet and his horse killed, besides other horses being wounded. A sweeping charge was now made by the rangers on horseback almost in among the Indians, who were thickly massed, and such was their rapid and fatal fire both with revolvers and Winchesters that the Comanches and Kiowas gave way and started in rapid and disordered flight through open ground towards the hills, followed by the now yelling rangers, who killed them here and there as they were overtaken on slow horses, or having them killed or disabled un-

der them. In about a mile another skirt of timber was passed
through, in which was a ravine made by washings from the
hills, but the Indians crossed this and kept on through an open
glade for a hundred yards or more, and then made a stand on
the side of the hill amid rocks and bushes and opened a severe
fire on the rangers from cover, which checked them, and they
wheeled back to the ravine and there dismounted. During this
fire from the Indians the horse ridden by Walter Robinson was
killed, being hit by five bullets, and he went back to the ditch
on foot, and a gallant young ranger of Stephens' company named
Glass was killed, falling in front before the turn back was made.
Also another ranger named Moore was wounded. The ravine
or ditch was shallow, and while the rangers to some extent could
protect themselves by lying down, it was not sufficient to cover
the horses, and they were hit repeatedly. The Indians fairly
swarmed around on the sides of the hills yelling and shooting,
and some of them gradually worked around the rangers and
shot at them from various points. This gallant little band,
however, worthy the name of Texas rangers, were not dismayed,
but would raise their heads above the ravine, take aim at some
particular target, fire, and down again to adjust another charge,
at the same time shouting defiance to their dusky foes. In
about twenty minutes after the ravine was reached Zack Waddell
noticed that ranger Glass, whom they thought dead, was kicking
about on the ground, and expressed his intention of making a
run and bringing him into the ravine. This looked so much
like a man throwing his life away and doing no good that even
the officers tried to persuade him from the rash act, but Waddell
had his eye on his friend, and all at once leaped out of the ditch
and ran rapidly to him, gathered him up in his arms, and started
back amid a perfect shower of bullets and demoniac yells of the
Indians, and the rangers in the ditch sprang to their feet, regardless of exposure, returned yell for yell and shot for shot
with the Indians, and loudly cheered their gallant comrade, who
came staggering with wounds and his burden in among them.
He was hit with five bullets, but none inflicted serious wounds,
and one of his boots was nearly shot off of his foot, so much so
that he could hardly keep it on. Poor Glass never spoke, but
lay there and breathed awhile, and then died there in the ravine

with his comrades around him, with the noise of cracking carbines, whistling bullets, and savage yells in his dying ears.

Here for five hours the battle was kept up with only short
intermissions. The Indians had plenty of good guns and ammunition, and the balls were almost·constantly kicking up the
dust around the margin of the ravine or hitting rocks and sending
showers of scattered lead among the rangers. As before stated,
some of the Indians went around the head of the ravine, surrounding the rangers and cutting off Lee Corn and Wheeler and
two others who had stayed with Corn when his horse was killed
and himself wounded, and they were forced to retreat back to
the creek and hide themselves in the rank grass and bushes and
mud and water in the bed of the creek. The rangers fighting
the battle in the dry ravine suffered greatly for water, remaining
five hours with the hot July sun beaming down on them. Their
tongues swelled, and such was their thirst that they dug in the
bed of the ravine with their Bowie knives to moist earth and
sucked it between their parched lips, which gave some relief.
During all of this time Major Jones exposed himself greatly and
made several narrow escapes. Once he left the ravine and went
to a tree and was watching the chief Lone Wolf to see if he could
tell from his actions what his intentions were or what his next
move would be, and talking to the boys and telling them to be
careful now of their cartridges and not shoot all of them away.
Captain Stephens also encouraged the boys by word and example,
and in fact neither officers nor men showed the white feather
during this trying time. While Major Jones was watching Lone
Wolf he sat down and leaned against the tree, with the balls
occasionally skipping around him, and Walter Robinson and
Flint Damon said, "Look out, major, they will hit you directly,"
and about this time a hissing ball came and struck the tree near
the major's head, filling his eyes and face full of bark and splint-
ers, and with such force that he fell backwards on the ground as
if killed, but quickly recovered himself.

About one hour by sun some of the rangers expressed a determination to leave the ravine in spite of the Indians and go to Lost
Creek after water, but all were persuaded out of this notion except two, Bailey and Porter, and they mounted their horses and
rode off. Two hundred yards from the ravine the Indians ran

51

upon them and killed Bailey in plain views of his companions, his mare, though fleet, failing to run when the Indians came close, on account of fright, and reared and plunged until they shot and lanced her unfortunate rider from her back. Porter had better luck, but had a narrow escape for his life. The Indians ran him so close that he was compelled to abandon his horse when near the creek and leap from the high bank into it, one Indian who was very close saying, "Me git you! Me git you!" in broken English as he went over. Now it happened that the place Porter went over was close to the spot where Lee Corn was in hiding, and thinking it was an Indian hunting for him, shot at him as he hit the mud and water a few yards away, but fortunately missed, as he had to aim his gun with one hand, having the other arm badly shattered. In throwing the cartridge from the magazine into the barrel he had to hold the gun between his knees to do so. When night came the rangers back at the ravine were in a terrible strait, and a council was held to determine what was best to do. They were nearly exhausted with thirst and strain and shock of the battle, ammunition nearly all gone, dead and wounded comrades scattered here and there, and fourteen dead horses besides the wounded lying around and in the ditch. The Indians had drawn off at dark and nothing now could be heard of them, and Major Jones asked the boys which they had rather do—remain there until daylight and renew the battle again if the Indians did not leave, or until soldiers could come from Jacksboro to their relief, for a ranger named John P. Holmes had ridden out of the ravine on a wounded horse in sight of the Indians before night, and gone to the fort where United States soldiers were quartered to ask for assistance. After canvassing the situation thoroughly, the rangers concluded to leave the ravine and make an attempt to get to Jacksboro or meet the soldiers. The dead ranger, Glass, was strapped to an Indian horse whose rider had been killed, and he dashed down among the rangers and stayed there. When all was ready they silently departed down the ravine, more than half of them on foot, and succeeded in quenching their thirst at a small spring they found, and then kept on fifteen miles to a ranch, and there remained until the following morning and buried their dead comrade, this sad rite being performed by Walter Robinson and others, who were then to return to the battleground with a ranch wagon to bring in the wounded, being preceded by some of the rangers and a squad of soldiers who had arrived at the ranch before daylight, having been informed of the situation by the gallant Holmes, who had got through safely. Uneasiness was felt for the boys who had been left scattered in the Lost Creek bottoms, and a hurried return was made to the place by the rangers and soldiers, but on arriving there they were all gone and could nowhere be found. The fact was developed later that they had left some time during the night and made their escape to Loving's ranch. The body of Bailey was found near where the fight commenced, badly mutilated, scalped, and full of arrows, besides numerous lance wounds. He was buried near the spot where he met his fate, and since the country has settled up in that locality, a schoolhouse and church stand near his grave, or near the spot where he was killed. It was afterwards learned that forty-two Indians were bullet-stricken during the battle, nineteen of them dying on the field.

The rangers went back to Jacksboro, bought horses to replace those killed, and then went on into the Llano country.

It is related of Lee Corn that when his horse was killed and himself down beside him, with his left arm shattered, he still continued to work the lever of his gun, holding the barrel between his knees to load, and firing with one hand at the Indians who were swarming around them and yelling most fearfully. and during this time Major Jones passed him and the young ranger looked up and says, "We're givin' 'em hell, major."

Mr. Walter Robinson, who was one of the escort of Major Jones, and who took a prominent part in this fearful battle, belonged to Capt. Rufe Perry's company, and was in the Salt Creek fight in Menard County, and several others. He was cousin to Major Jones and nephew of Mrs. Julia Lee Sinks, who has contributed so many interesting sketches of the early times on the Texas frontier, especially around Austin. Mr. Robinson was born in Austin, and comes from an old historic family of pioneers of the place. His wife was a Hornsby, another noted frontier family, among whom a braver or more gallant set of men never settled on a frontier.

CREED TAYLOR,

CREED TAYLOR.

Came to Texas in 1824.

Creed Taylor was born in Tennessee in 1820, on the 10th of April. His father, Josiah Taylor, was born and raised in Virginia, in James County, on the James River, and was related to Gen. Zachary Taylor, so the general himself said. The occasion of his saying this was during the Mexican war when Creed Taylor, as a dispatch-bearer, brought a message to the general, and he asked the young courier what his name was, and on being told it was Taylor he asked several questions as to where his people came from, and if his father had a brother named William, and on being told that he had to the latter question, said, "Well, I and you are kinfolks, then."

Capt. Josiah Taylor, father of Creed, came to Texas in 1811 on an exploring expedition with many others from the States at that time to look at the country, and many Americans had already settled in the eastern part of the State. In the following year a revolution was inaugurated by the Mexicans to throw off the Spanish yoke, and many Americans and Indians in Texas joined them. The army collected at Spanish Bluff, and after an organization set out for Goliad to attack the Spanish army there. The opposing force to Spain in this body of men were mostly Americans and commanded by American officers, of whom were McGee, Kemper, Ross, Gaines, McFarland, and Captain Josiah, who had joined the expedition and commanded a company. One of the Mexican commanders was Bernardo and another was Manchaca. The American force, as we will call it, for they largely predominated, numbered 800 when they left the bluff, and many battles were fought with the Spaniards with various successes until 1813, when the Spanish army retreated to San Antonio and the Americans followed. Reinforcements had been sent to the Spanish Governor of Texas, Salcedo, and he now sent his army to meet the advancing Americans. The Spanish army, which was at the mouth of Salado Creek where it empties into the San Antonio River, consisted of 1500 regulars and 1000 militia, all under the command of

the officer who brought the reinforcements from Mexico. He
had solicited this position, and pledged his head to the Governor
that he would kill and capture the entire American army.

The American army consisted of 800 Americans led by
Kemper, 180 Mexicans commanded by Gaines and Manchaca,
and 325 Indians under McFarland. The Americans, expecting
an ambush, marched slowly in order of battle. The left wing
moved in front under Ross, in which was Capt. Josiah Taylor
and his men, all good rifle shots. The right, under Kemper,
was in the rear, and a company of riflemen under Captain
Luckett acted as flankers on the right. Their left was protected
by the San Antonio River. About nine miles from San Antonio
there was a ridge which divided the river and creek and the side
next to town was prairie, while the other side, bordering the
Salado Creek, was covered with chaparral brush. Here in this
place the Spanish army lay in ambush while the Americans were
coming up the river on the east side of the creek, and were not
aware of their presence until they crossed and began to enter
the ambuscade. They were first discovered by Luckett's riflemen, who at once fired on them. The Spaniards then arose and
formed in front of the Americans about 400 yards below, their
line extending nearly a mile, and in their center was twelve
cannons. The Indians were now placed in front of the Americans to receive the charge of the Spanish cavalry, but they all
ran at the first onset except the Cooshattas and a few others,
who stood firm and received two more charges. By this time
the Americans had formed at the foot of the ridge, and orders
were given to advance to within thirty yards of the Spaniards,
fire three rounds, load the fourth, and then charge all along
the line.

This order was obeyed in silence and with such coolness that
it struck terror to the Spanish army, and the volleys they fired
at the Americans went over their heads on account of the advance being up hill. They did not wait for the charge, but
broke up into disordered squads all along their line and fled in
terror towards San Antonio. They were hotly pursued and
hundreds of them killed in the disordered rout, and the wounded
were butchered by the Indians. When the Spanish commander
saw his army flying from the field and realized that the day

was lost, he drew his sword and, turning his horse, rushed upon the ranks of the pursuing Americans. He first attacked Major Ross and then Colonel Kemper, and as his sword was raised to strike the latter he was shot dead by William Owens, a private in the company of Capt. Josiah Taylor. In this great Southwest Texas battle one thousand of the Spaniards were killed and but few taken prisoners, on account of the Indians, who followed in the rear of the Americans during the disordered flight.

The American army then went on to San Antonio and demanded the surrender of the place, and the Governor and his staff came out to comply, and the first Americans they came in contact with was the company of Capt. Josiah Taylor, drawn up in their front, and to their leader Salcedo offered his sword, but Captain Taylor would not receive it and referred him to Colonel Kemper. He refused it and referred him to General Bernardo, the Mexican commander, whereupon the Governor stuck it in the ground and went off and left it, and Bernardo took it up.

It is not the intention to give a full history of these stirring events of that time, but only to mention them on account of the part taken by the father of the subject of this sketch. Suffice it to say, another Spanish army came from Mexico and was defeated by the Americans on the Alazan Creek with great loss, and then a second army came but stopped on the Medina, and the Americans went out there to fight them, but were drawn into an ambush and almost annihilated. The Americans fought like tigers, and continued the battle after the day was lost and everything in confusion. The Mexicans, commanded by Manchaca, fought well and were nearly all killed in the center of the deadly ambuscade. The Spanish cavalry pursued and fought the remnants until nearly all were killed. Capt. Josiah Taylor rode his horse and stayed on him during all of this fearful slaughter, and was wounded seven times, but made his escape with about ninety other Americans to eastern Texas, where he had two large musket balls cut out of his body, and as soon as he recovered he went back home to Virginia.

In 1824 Captain Taylor returned to Texas with his family, and died in the winter of 1830 on his ranch, below Cuero.

Creed Taylor, after the death of his father, was sent to Gonzales by his mother to attend school, and he boarded at the house of Almon Dickinson, who was afterwards killed in the Alamo. His schoolteacher was named Miller, and his schoolmates were the Sowell boys,—Andrew, John, and Asa,—Highsmiths, Pontons, John Gaston, Galba Fuqua, and Dave Darst. In 1835 when the Mexicans came to take the cannon, Creed was in the fight five miles above the town near Zeke Williams' place, since called the Dikes place. He says they loaded the cannon at John Sowell's shop and carried it with them, and fired it three times during the fight.

When Stephen F. Austin went on out to San Antonio with an army to continue the war, Creed Taylor was along in the company of Capt. John J. Tumlinson, and was in the battle of Mission Concepcion, the Grass fight, and storming of San Antonio, and was about one hundred yards from Ben Milam when he was killed. The company he belonged to was really that of John A. Coleman, but he was not present in any of the fighting on account of sickness, and his lieutenant, Tumlinson, commanded and was called captain by the men. Creed went back home to his mother on the Guadalupe after the surrender of the Mexican army, and was there when the Alamo was taken and Santa Anna came on down with an army after General Houston. He moved his mother to Kennard's prairie, and then in company with Joe Tumlinson took the trail of Houston's army and caught up with them in camp on Buffalo Bayou the night before the battle of San Jacinto, and went through the battle on the following day without being attached to any particular company. He fired many shots, and part of the time was mixed up close in among the Mexicans. After the battle he went back home and attended to the stock and farmed some until 1840, when the Indians burned Linnville. He was in the pursuit and battle with the Indians on Plum Creek in the company of Capt. D. B. Fryer. Among the men whom he remembers seeing in the battle was Robert Hall, French Smith, Zeke Smith, Andrew Sowell, James Nichols, Ben McCulloch and his brother Henry, and Matthew Caldwell. Mr. Taylor killed several Indians in personal combats during the long running fight.

In the fall of this same year he went on an Indian expedition commanded by Col. Tom Howard, and belonged to the company of Capt. Matthew Caldwell. There were 170 white men on this Indian hunt, and they located a large camp of them where Brackett is now. A considerable battle took place and a great deal of noise was made, but none of the white men were killed and but few wounded. Twenty Indians were killed and 700 head of mules and horses were captured. Among the men along from the Guadalupe were William Tumlinson, Dan Grady, Calvin Turner, and John Gattes. A great many of these mules and horses had been carried off by the Indians from below in the settlements along the rivers, and were returned to their owners.

After this expedition Mr. Taylor joined the rangers under Jack Hays and was in the fight at Bandera Pass. The men that he can remember who were in the fight were, besides Captain Hays and himself, two of his brothers, Josiah and Pipkin, Andrew Erskine, Peter Fore, Ad Gillespie, Kit Ackland, Sam Luckey, George Neill, James Dunn, Sam Walker, and George Jackson. His recollection is that the time was June of 1841, that twenty-five rangers were in the fight, and that it lasted more than an hour. The Indians fired on them first and soon showed themselves in large force and came close, and the rangers had all they could do to manage them. About 11 o'clock the Indians began to give back towards the north end of the pass, pursued by the rangers, who constantly mixed with them and hand to hand conflicts took place, in one of which, near the north end of the pass, Kit Ackland killed the chief, and many horses were killed and wounded. Among the rangers killed was Peter Fore and George Jackson. The latter was a son of Tom Jackson, who was killed in the Alamo. Peter Fore was shot through the body with an arrow, the spike being on one side and the feather on the other. Sam Walker was thrust through with a lance and Andrew Erskine was wounded in the thigh with an arrow. He charged the Indian with a five-shooter, but the barrel dropped off without his knowledge, and he almost touched the Indian trying to shoot, but failed. The Comanche had his bow-stick shot in two and was also unable to shoot, but noticing the condition of the ranger's pistol, grasped an arrow in his hand and tried to stab him with it, but was at this time

shot and killed by Creed Taylor.   Mr. Taylor says other rangers
were wounded and had to be carried to San Antonio to be
treated, but he does not remember their names.   He can only
remember two that died on the ground.

When Wall captured San Antonio in 1842 the rangers were
quartered in San Antonio, but most of them were out on a scout
with Jack Hays and made their escape.   When the Texans were
gathered on the Salado to fight them and Captain Hays drew
them out, Lieut. Henry McCulloch covered the retreat with ten
picked men, four of them Taylors,—Creed, Pipkin, Josiah and
James.   Towards the last of the race Creed Taylor and McCulloch were alone in the rear, and 200 shots or more were fired at
them by the Mexican cavalry, but neither were hit.

In the main battle that came off on the creek Creed Taylor
had his arm broke, shot in the middle of the elbow, and the ball
split on the bone, half going out and the other remaining.   As
it would never permanently heal, years afterwards he had the
other part of the ball taken out by Dr. Herff of San Antonio.
After the battle Mr. Taylor went to Seguin and stayed until
his arm apparently got well, staying with Tom Nichols during
the time.   On the way to Seguin he passed over Dawson's battle
ground, and said he never saw such a sight of mangled men and
horses.   He says in the Salado battle Calvin Turner was glanced
on the side of the head with a grape shot and knocked down, and
that one of the Sowell boys was wounded in the hand.   When
the Mexican war of 1846 broke out Mr. Taylor joined the regiment of rangers commanded by Capt. Jack Hays, and passed
through nearly all of the battles in Mexico, the last he was in
being at Buena Vista.   The first one he says was at Palo Alto,
and there he saw more men together than he ever saw before,
and it was a grand sight.   Both armies met each other with
all the regimental bands playing at once on both sides, and five
hundred flags were in sight.

Mr. Taylor still survives at this writing (April 27, 1900),
and lives at the head of James River, in Kimble County, and
has been there about thirty years.   His life is being written by
a gentleman of Fort Mason, and no doubt will be very interesting when all of the facts are brought out of his eventful life, of
which this article is only a shadow.

M. SAATOFF.

Came to Texas in 1846.

Among the first settlers in the town of Quihi, and who still resides there, is Mr. M. Saatoff. He was born in the province of Hanover, Germany, in 1839, and on April 15, 1846, came to Texas with his father, M. M. Saatoff, and other members of the family. The elder Saatoff had contracted with an immigration agent named G. D'Hanis, as part of the colony of Henry Castro. From this agent the town of D'Hanis derives its name.

They sailed from Bremen on the ship Leo with eighty passengers, and the time consumed in the voyage was nine weeks. One child was born and named Leo, after the ship.

Like most of the others, they first landed at Galveston and then took shipping for Port Lavaca, staying there three weeks, eating and resting being furnished by Castro. Here young Saatoff heard bullfrogs and thought they were buffalo bellowing, as they had heard of those animals before arriving. The family made it through in Mexican carts to Castroville in August, 1846, and soon after went on out to the Quihi Creek, where a new settlement was to be made, reaching there the same day they started, and went into camp on the spot where their future homes were to be built. That first night a hard rain fell and almost spoiled all of their bedding and clothing, and on the following morning the wagons which had conveyed them there went back and left them in this water-soaked condition in this wild, Indian-infested country, with their belongings piled up on the ground in the mud and water; but there were brave hearts there, and they made the best shift 'they could under the circumstances and looked with hope to the future. The first thing to be done was to build small, rude shelters covered with grass and try to open up farming land, but the following year no crop was made. Some corn was planted with hoes, but the deer ate it up. Game, honey, and fish were plentiful and there was no danger of starving, and the next year a good crop of corn was made on new land. One ox team served five or six families to break land with. The elder Saatoff had one yoke of oxen, and he would lend these to his neighbors to help get their land ready for planting. The Delaware, Tonkaway, and Lipan Indians often came and traded with them before the latter became hostile. The Tonks lived on the Blanco, Delawares on Pedernales, and the Lipans further south.

Mr. Saatoff has an old document in his possession which stipulates that the settlers were, inside of three years, to put fifteen acres of land in cultivation, and to sell no intoxicating drinks or firearms to the Indians, and in case they did this their lands would be forfeited. The people suffered some before crops could be made, and would have suffered more if it had not been for the Texas rangers who were stationed there for their protection, and who divided their rations with them and killed game for them, as the settlers were poorly provided with guns and ammunition. It was fifty miles to mill and corn scarce at $2 per bushel. When the rangers were disbanded the Indians came and stole nearly all of the horses in the country, and being now thrown on their own resources they had to defend themselves and rely on their own exertions. All of Mr. Saatoff's horse stock was stolen in 1866 except one mule, and this was all he had to cultivate a crop with in 1867. Mr. Gerdes was killed by the Indians while out hunting horses which they had already carried off. It was a very cold day, and the Indians stripped the old man and carried him one mile in that condition and then killed him, inflicting twenty-eight wounds. Mr. Saatoff found the trail of the Indians while out and came back to report, and learned that Mr. Gerdes was lost, and said then he was sure the Indians had killed him. A party who were out soon came in with the body, and Mr. Saatoff helped to bury him. The farmers at first only raised corn, having a good market for it at Forts Inge, Clark, Duncan, and Lincoln. In 1858 wheat, oats, and rye were cultivated and did well, but during the progress of the Civil war farming was neglected, there being more money in freighting by those who remained at home, and in consequence of this the farms grew up in weeds, and in 1865 no crops of any kind were made, and the want of them was soon felt. In 1866 six families went down in to Guadalupe County and made a good crop of corn on the Wilcox farm, and took notice how the people worked down there, having clean crops.

They went back to Quihi in September and carried a good deal of corn with them and sold to the people who had failed, and told them, "When you work your farms like they do in Guadalupe County, you will make good crops here." Next year wheat, oats, corn, and sorgum were planted, and all made a good crop, cutting the small grain with scythes, and in this year (1867) the first threshing machine was brought into the country, and in the following year several more, as crops were still good, and it became an agricultural county. Cotton was tried and it did well, but they had to haul it to the Cibolo, forty-five miles, to a gin, and the farmers now agreed with their merchant, Mr. Fred Muennink, at New Fountain, only two miles from Quihi, that if he would put up a gin they would plant 200 acres in cotton. This was agreed to, and in 1870 more than a bale to the acre was made, one man saying he made two bales to the acre; and so cotton raising was an established fact and the acreage increased each year.

The last Indian raid was in 1874, and they carried off and killed together fifty head of horses in the Quihi settlement, and killed one boy on Black Creek. On one occasion Mr. Saatoff and others made a famous ride of eighty miles in one day after Indians, but the latter went one hundred and got away.

JOHN E. WILSON.

Come to Texas in 1832.

John Ewing Wilson was born in Wilson County, Tennessee, one mile east of Lebanon, on the 6th of July, 1828, and his father, Joseph Wilson, was born in the same county in 1799. The county was named for his grandfather James Wilson, a soldier of the revolution, and who was killed in battle during that long struggle. The father, Joseph, was in the battle of New Orleans and was wounded in the leg, being the only man in his company hit. The mother of our subject was Margaret Barton, and her father was killed in the battle of Horseshoe Bend, when General Jackson defeated the Indians there. When young Sam Houston called for volunteers to storm a log fort where a number of Indians had collected near the river, Mr. Barton was one of the men that responded and went with the charge, and was killed with many others, and Houston was desperately wounded. Mr. Wilson's grandmother was Anna Bradley.

Joseph Wilson came to Texas with his family in 1832 and first settled four miles from San Augustine, but later, in 1837, moved to Bastrop. While en route on the main road from San Augustine to the settlements on the Colorado Mr. Wilson, then a boy, saw his first Indian, and he was a dead one. There was a log fort on the route where Anderson is now, called Fort Lacy, after the man who built it, and here the elder Wilson put up for the night on arriving there with his wagons and family. The fort was inclosed and Lacy told Mr. Wilson to come inside with his family, as there was danger from Indians. He also placed two young men in a fodder house to watch the horses, which were tied outside. Late in the night the Indians came and made an attempt to carry off the stock, but were discovered and fired on by the guards, and one was killed and another wounded. Joseph Wilson and Mr. Lacy ran out with their guns when the shots were heard and also fired on the Indians, but without effect, as they were making off in the moonlight across the prairie. When morning came the body of a large dead In-

dian was found near by, and Mr. Lacy told one of his negroes
to bring a yoke of oxen and a log chain and drag him off. When
the team came they were afraid of the Indian, and could not be
driven near enough to fasten the chain to the body until they
were blindfolded. The chain had a ring in one end, and a loop
was made and slipped over the Indian's head and then drawn
up. The blinds were now taken from the oxen's eyes, but as
soon as they caught sight of the Indian close behind them they
gave a loud snort, and, jerking loose from the negro, dashed
off across the prairie with the Indian bouncing in the air behind
them, and did not stop until exhausted. Suffice to say they carried the body as far from the fort as was necessary. Mr. John
Wilson can distinctly remember how the Indian looked as he
bobbed up and down behind the oxen as they ran with him across
the prairie.

When the Wilson family arrived at Bastrop the Perry family,
Manloves, Wilbargers, and others, and a German named Dietze,
were there. General Burleson lived fifteen miles below and
John H. Moore above La Grange. He and the mother of Mr.
Wilson graduated at the same school at Lebanon, Tenn. One
night shortly after getting here, while John Wilson and one of
his brothers and two negroes belonging to their father were
sleeping in their wagons a short distance from the balance of
the family, who were in a small house, they had an Indian alarm.
The horses had been tied to the wheels of the wagon, and in
the night they began to snort and pull on the ropes, which
caused the wagon to rock violently, and young John Wilson
raised the wagon sheet and looked out and saw a big Indian
standing very close who "shooed" at him and ran off, and John
then jumped out of the wagon and ran to the house. This was
in 1840, and was part of the large force of Comanches who were
going on a big raid down the country which culminated in the
burning and sacking of Linnville on the coast, and the battle of
Plum Creek on their return. The Wilson family had before
this gone out to San Antonio and tried to settle, but Indians
and Mexican robbers and raiding bands from Mexico had caused
all of the Americans and some of the Mexican settlers to vacate
the place and move back east.

On one occasion, about the time of getting back from San

Antonio, in May of 1840, John Wilson and his brother James and one of their negroes were planting corn for a man named Johnson, three miles from home. After night the two brothers saddled their horses and started home across the prairie, although warned by Johnson not to do so, as he had been out that day and saw Indians. While riding across the bright moonlit prairie their horses suddenly stopped and threw up their heads, and about thirty men were seen running on horses, but soon disappeared from view. Next day it was learned the horsemen were Indians and that they were running Gen. Ed. Burleson, and made him lose his hat and saddlebags, but he recovered them by searching the ground next day. Had General Burleson not been ahead of the boys and the Indians came in contact with him first they would have had a race for life, and likely been caught.

When the Indians were coming back from Linnville nearly all of the men were collecting from the Colorado, Guadalupe, and other places to fight them. A large company left the Colorado under Burleson, and another composed of old men and boys were concentrated on Buckner's Creek, eighteen miles above Bastrop, as a reserve in case the first men that went out got whipped. Of this party were three boys—John Wilson, Jasper Berry, and Leander Herrill—who wanted to go with the first party and be in the battle, but were restrained by the older men. They, however, made up their minds to go, and hid their saddles and horses out that evening, and when night came mounted and started. From what they heard the men say they knew about where the Indians would be intercepted, and made rapidly for that point on Plum Creek, about twenty miles distant. It being night, however, and having no road to guide them, they became lost and wandered all night in the sand hills between Plum Creek and the Colorado, and when they finally arrived on the scene the battle was over. Mr. Wilson says that large crowds of men were scattered all over the country coming back from the battle, which was quite extended, covering many miles of country. The boys got to see some of the dead Indians.

Shortly after this many Americans settled at San Antonio, and Jack Hays was commissioned by General Houston to raise a company of rangers for their protection, and John Wilson and

Leander Herrill, hearing of this, mounted their horses and set out for San Antonio, and from there to the camp of Hays, on the Medina, and offered themselves as rangers. Herrill was accepted, but Wilson was too young and could not be enlisted, but he would not leave, and stayed three months with the rangers and went on many scouts with them, killed deer and buffalo, and had a good time generally.

In 1842, when Wall captured San Antonio and men were hurrying to the front to repel the invader, young Wilson again mounted his horse and offered his services to Gen. Matthew Caldwell, who used him as a messenger or express rider, and placed him on the San Antonio and Gonzales road at the crossing of Nash's Creek, to give information to all who came along and tell them what to do as to the concentration of the forces at the Salado Creek, near San Antonio. He was the first to carry the news of Dawson's defeat and the victory of Caldwell to La Grange, and as soon as that was accomplished started back for his post, but met Gonzalvo Woods, who made his escape from Dawson's massacre, and was badly wounded. He was shot in the shoulder and wounded in three places on the head with a saber. His horse was killed in the fight and himself hit with a bullet and badly sabered, and he tried to surrender, but a Mexican lancer dashed upon him with leveled lance, and Woods caught it and gave such a quick, strong pull that it jerked the Mexican from his horse to the ground, and he wrenched the lance from his grasp and ran it through his body and pinned him to the earth, and then, pulling it out, mounted the Mexican trooper's horse and made his escape, carrying the lance with him, which he still had, and which was very bloody. His wounds had not been dressed, and young Wilson at once washed all the blood from his head and poulticed the wounds with prickly pear, and then went back with Woods to La Grange. Norman Woods, a brother, was also in the fight and had his back broken and was carried a prisoner to Mexico, and died in the Perote prison. Zadock Woods, father of the boys mentioned, was also in the battle and was killed. The lance which Gonzalvo brought back is now in the possession of some of the Woods family near Yorktown, and is highly prized by them, as it should be.

In 1848 John Wilson was living with his father and family

52

on Peach Creek, in Gonzales County, where Waelder is now, and
in that year Henry E. McCulloch raised a company of rangers
and he joined. Their station was in Hamilton's valley, on
Hamilton Creek, sixty miles from Austin, near where Burnet
is now. Their officers, besides the captain, were First Lieutenant John King, Second Lieutenant Calvin S. Turner, Orderly
Sergeant Asa J. L. Sowell. They did a good deal of scouting,
but had no battles with Indians. Mr. Wilson says that while
here Sergeant Sowell and Joe Williams caught the largest cat-
fish he ever saw, and that it took both of them to hold it and
get it out. He speaks in high praise of their orderly, and says
he was the best man he ever saw, and covered all of the ground
he stood on at all times and under all circumstances. The company was mustered out December 23, 1848.

In 1849, on the 23d day of August, Mr. Wilson joined a
company of rangers commanded by Capt. John S. Ford, at Austin, and they went south and were stationed between Brownsville and San Patricio, near King's ranch, on the Santa Ger-
trudes Creek.

In November of the same year Mr. Wilson, Dave Steel, Charles
Wiedenmiller, and John Dickens were on their way back
to camp with a wagonload of supplies, and one evening camped
and Wiedenmiller went to water the wagon horses in a little
creek not far away, and they soon heard him scream for help.
Wilson and Steel ran to him and found him surrounded by Indians, but drove them away by a well-directed fire, and all made
their way quickly back to the wagon with the horses. The Indians rallied, and seeing that only two men had put them to
flight, made a charge and the rangers went into a thicket. Here
the Indians kept them all night, charging around, yelling, and
shooting arrows and bullets into the brush. Occasionally the
rangers would slip to the edge and shoot, and the Indians would
run. Dickens left and went to camp at the commencement of
the trouble and told Captain Ford that he thought the other
three men were killed, and next morning the captain came to
them with fifty men. The trail of the Indians was taken up
and Captain Ford had a fight with them and killed several, but
none of his men were hurt. Of this company Andrew Walker
and Ed. Burleson were lieutenants.

During this term of service Mr. Wilson and James, his brother, and Ed. Stevens got on the trail of a band of Indians and followed them to the Rio Grande, stripped and swam over to see what discoveries they could make on the other side, and were arrested by the Mexican soldiers and confined in an old Mexican hut made out of poles. Here they remained until night, naked, and then Wilson and Stevens began to plan an escape. The soldiers all went to sleep except one guard, and he walked to and fro in front of the harcal with his musket, and it was agreed to kill him if they could. Each armed himself with a heavy hard stick, pulled out of the old house, and as the guard passed the door Wilson hit him a terrible blow on the back of the neck and killed him in his tracks. All three then made a run for the river, Wilson carrying the soldier's gun to make a fight with if pursued. It was all done so silently that none of the soldiers were aroused, and they gained the river without any signs of pursuit, and all plunged in and swam over to the Texas side, Wilson throwing the gun away as they entered the water. Their camp was six miles below on the river, and they soon made their way back. Captain Ford had sent them out to trail these Indians and see where they went to. This was in 1850.

In the same year the rangers followed another band of Indians and overtook them where Campbellton is now. They had been two days on the trail without anything to eat, and by this time were getting very hungry. There were fourteen rangers and thirty Indians. The Indians were in camp about daylight, roasting a colt which they had killed, and had 200 head of horses. They made no fight when the rangers charged them, but scattered, and all of the stock was retaken. It was about forty miles to Fort Merrill on the Nueces, and to that place the rangers went to get something to eat, and carried the horses with them. After getting all they wanted to eat they went into camp and concluded to rest until morning, and John Wilson, Jack Taylor, Mat Nowlin, and Lieutenant Burleson stayed among the horses to guard them. To pass away the time a blanket was spread and a deck of cards produced, and the party played by moonshine while the balance of the men lay near by asleep. Before any one was aware of it two Indians slipped up and got a horse apiece and started off, but at this time were dis-

covered by Wilson, and he and others fired at them, killing one
and wounding the other. The wounded one got into the brush
and lay down, badly wounded in the body and in the hand, and
his bowstick shot in two. The rangers had a Mexican guide
and interpreter with them called "Old Roka," who had been a
prisoner among the Indians nearly all of his life and could
speak several Indian dialects, and when the wounded Indian
was found "Old Roka" was told to converse with him in Comanche and see what he had to say, but being badly wounded
he made but little reply, and soon died. This occurred outside
of the fort limits, and at the time a whole regiment of dragoons
were stationed there. They heard the firing at the ranger camp,
but thought they had got up a row among themselves and paid
no attention to it, but on the following morning, when some of
them came down there and found a dead Indian in camp, they
cut his head off and placed it on a pole. This made the rangers
mad, and some of them went to the colonel and got him to order
some of his men to take the head down and put it and the body
together and bury them, which he did.

After the return to camp Captain Ford sent Mr. Wilson and
Jack Taylor to see if any Indians could be found in force, and
they soon located forty of them in ambush on the Nueces River,
being the same the rangers had taken the horses from, and the
Indians had followed them back. As soon as this was reported
Captain Ford took fifteen men and went to fight them, and arrived there at 4 o'clock p. m., but the Indians were gone, the
trail bearing south, which was followed rapidly until dark and
then camp was made. On the following morning it was resumed, and in three miles came upon the camp of the Indians
where they had stayed the night before in the edge of some timber. The trail still tended south and the rangers followed and
shortly came in sight of them, but held back until the Indians
got out on the prairie, as there was too much brush and timber
to make a good fight. They finally, however, entered a more
open country, and the rangers spurred up and came close upon
them near the Agua Dulce Creek. The Indians were all on foot
except a few, their horses having been taken by the rangers as
before stated. Two mounted ones were in the rear to watch
for the rangers, and these were charged but made their escape

to the main body, and all of them came out into open ground and formed for battle. The rangers went in among them at a charge and several were killed at the first volley, but the Indians fought well and rapidly both with guns and bows. In the second round Dave Steel shot a chief in the head and killed him, and the balance began to get into confusion, and many personal combats took place. Captain Ford pursued one who was on horseback and aimed his pistol at him, but the Comanche leaned low down behind his horse to avoid the shot and his girth broke and he fell to the ground, but he was on his feet in an instant and aimed an arrow, but the captain shot him in the head and he fell, sending his arrow straight up as he went down. When the fight was over William Gillespie was found to be killed and Jack Spencer and one other ranger wounded. Gillespie was a nephew of Ad. Gillespie, a famous ranger under Hays, who was killed in Mexico. This was "Old Yellow Wolf's" band, and was in charge of a sub-chief. His son was also in the fight and was wounded and captured. Eight dead Indians were found on the ground and many were wounded. Gillespie killed one Indian, and a wounded Indian killed him. This fellow was on the ground and nearly dead, but bent his bow with his feet and shot the ranger through the heart, who was close and coming towards him. The rangers buried their gallant comrade on the banks of the Agua Dulce Creek. Mr. Wilson passed all through this hotly contested fight but was not hurt. In about two weeks after the rangers got back to camp Mr. Wilson was on guard one morning about daylight, and saw a white rag held up on a stick by two Indian squaws. He put his handkerchief on the end of his gun and held it up and they came in. They were the mother and aunt of the young Yellow Wolf, who was a captive, and the old chief, his father, had sent them to exchange all the captives he had, thirteen in all, for his son. Captain Ford agreed to this, and they were brought in and the exchange made. Most of their prisoners were Mexicans, one negro, and two or three whites. One of the latter was James Hart, captured near Refugio.

In 1851 Mr. Wilson, Andrew Wheeler, Andrew Walker, and two Mexicans were sent out by Captain Ford to capture wild cattle for beef for the company, and on a creek south of the Nueces called La Garta, in a very brushy place, a bunch of

hobbled horses were discovered which belonged to a band of Indians. Lieutenant Walker told Wheeler to take the two Mexicans and round up the horses and unhobble them, and he and
Wilson would watch for the Indians and protect them if any
were near and should make a charge upon them. The horses
were hobbled with strips of buffalo hide, and were all taken,
thirty-five head in all, and no Indians put in an appearance.
A trail, however, was discovered leading into a thicket, and Walker and Wilson followed it and found the saddles, ropes, and
lances of the Indians who had gone off on foot to get some more
horses. A runner was now sent back to camp for more men.
and Captain Ford sent a squad and they lay there in ambush
to await the return of the Indians, all the rangers being under
the command of Lieut. A. J. Walker. On the fifth day John
Wilson and Andrew Wheeler were on guard watching for the
approach of the Indians, and discovered one coming down a
draw at full speed on a horse. Lieutenant Walker was now
notified of the approach of this Indian, and he said to let him
pass and then cut him off so that he could not get back and
notify the others, as no doubt they were near. The balance of
the Indians, forty in number, soon came along, driving 200 head
of horses, and the rangers got out of their ambush and charged
them, greatly to their surprise. They split in two and rallied
in two bunches to fight. Lieutenant Walker and part of the
men attacked one party, and John Wilson, D. M. Level, Robert
Rankin, Andrew Wheeler, and another ranger named Good
wheeled to the left and attacked the balance, fifteen in number.
These, seeing the small force assailing them, charged fiercely,
and one of the rangers ran, and a doubtful battle now took place
on this part of the ground. Wilson's horse was soon shot down
and he had to abandon him, and Level's horse was killed and
fell on him. He called to the ranger who ran to help him and
not let an Indian lance him, who, seeing his condition, was
coming to him for that purpose, but the ranger went on. John
Wilson, who had just got clear of his fallen horse, heard the
call and at once charged the Indian and killed him, having a
repeating gun and several loads left. He then pulled the horse
off of Level and he got on his feet and once more took part in
the fight, although himself wounded in the thigh. Mr. Wilson

COL. JOHN S. FORD.

killed one more Indian during the fight and Wheeler killed one, and Walker's party killed five. Wheeler and an Indian faced each other a few yards apart and the ranger shot the Comanche in the mouth, knocking his teeth all out, the ball going out at the jaw. The Indian had quit his horse and this shot knocked him down, but he turned his head in time to partly escape a second shot from Wheeler, but the ball took his nose off in a side shot, but he raised to a sitting position and sat there until the fight was over. Lieutenant Walker then told John Wilson to finish him, but he refused, and the lieutenant threatened to put him under arrest, but still he would not comply and told him to arrest and be d—d. Wheeler was then told to shoot him, but he said he had shot him as many times as he wanted to or was going to. The lieutenant then handed a large holster pistol to a Mexican who was along and told him to go and finish that Indian, as he did not want to leave him in that condition. The Mexican took the pistol and rode up close to the Indian, who looked up, and, seeing the pistol in the Mexican's hand, knew what his fate was, and dropped his head down on his breast and the Mexican sent a ball into the crown of his head. These Indians when the fight commenced had a Mexican boy tied naked on a mule, and the mule loose without anything on him but the boy, and was running here and there, and the captive yelled manfully for the rangers not to shot him, that he was not an Indian. The rangers had to rope the mule and then cut the strings loose before he could be taken from the back of the animal. Years afterwards an Indian skull was found near this battleground and carried to San Antonio by Mr. E. R. Lane, and on being shown to Mr. Wilson he recognized it as that of the Indian whom Wheeler shot and the Mexican finished by order of Lieutenant Walker, by the bullet hole being in the crown of the skull.

The horses which were retaken from the Indians in this battle, 197 in number, belonged to a wealthy Mexican in Mexico, and this was the reason they were gone so long from their camp, and how they came by the Mexican captive. Captain Ford notified the Mexican that the rangers had recaptured his horses and for him to send after them. Three of the rangers had lost horses in the fight—Wilson, Level, and Roundtree. (The latter fought

with Walker's party.) Captain Ford told these three men to
select three of the best horses in the captured lot and appropriate
them to their own use, and they did so, selecting the best they
could find. The rich old Mexican came in person to receive
his horses, and although there were no charges for getting them
back and keeping them under herd, he made a great fuss about
the rangers taking three of them. This made Captain Ford
mad, and he told the old Mexican to take the balance of his
horses and get back into Mexico as soon as he could or he would
let his men hang him, which they were anxious to do, anyway.
No use to say he did so, and did not stand on the order of his
going.

At this time or the time of the fight Lieutenant Burleson
had been sent to San Antonio by Captain Ford with ten men
to bring $13,000 up to El Vacas, commissary money for the use
of the rangers for supplies, pay, etc. The trip there was made
all right and they got back to a point twenty-five miles west of
where Walker had his fight west of the Nueces, in a salt marsh.
Here they met trouble and fought one of the most desperate
battles that is recorded on the Texas border, with the same Indians that Walker and his men had fought and whipped the day
before. The men with Burleson were James Carr, Jack Spencer, Baker Barton, Warren Lyons, William Lackey, Alf. Tom,
a German named Miller, and Givens, known in camp among the
rangers as "washtub." Lyons had been a captive among the
Indians and almost raised by them, and knew all about them,
and had been in many fights with other Indians. When these
Indians were first discovered they were in full retreat from
Walker's fight, but stopped and began to make demonstrations
toward Burleson's men, and Lyons, who was closely observing
them, said to Burleson, "These Indians have been in a fight, mad,
and are going to give us hell." Lyons then got down from his
horse and pulled off his boots and Burleson thought he was
fixing to run, but he was only making preparations for the fight,
as the Indians were coming at a charge and yelling fiercely.
They made no halt, and engaged the rangers hand to hand, and
a most sanguinary battle took place. Wounds were received
and given at close quarters on all parts of the ground, but
finally the shattered remnants of the Indian braves drew off and

quit the field, half of their number being killed and nearly all of the balance wounded. The first man killed of the rangers was Baker Barton. James Carr was wounded in two places, one with an arrow which cut out his bowels. William Lackey was badly wounded in the lungs with an arrow, and died at Laredo. Alf Tom was shot in the leg with an arrow, and Lieutenant Burleson was wounded three times in the head and arms. Spencer and Lyons were also wounded, the latter slightly. He knew how to duck and dodge among the Indians from his experience in fighting with Indians against Indians, and escaped many arrows that were aimed at him, and the wounds he received were glancing, and his hat was shot from his head. The most of the wounded rangers were so badly hurt they had to remain on the ground until a runner could be sent to Captain Ford, and he sent ambulances and conveyed them away.

Some time after this another scout was sent out under Lieutenant Burleson along the Rio Grande. Mexicans reported that the Indians had made a raid and killed two families below and carried off two women and a boy. The Indians were overtaken and a running fight commenced. One of them, who had been acting as a spy in the rear, was behind on a fine horse, and was crowded close by Burleson and John Wilson. Finally the lieutenant told Wilson if he could to kill the horse, and then they would be sure of the Indian. This he succeeded in doing and Burleson wounded the Indian, but he got into the brush and they could not find him. The balance of the Indians were caught up with and rapid firing commenced, and they tried to kill the prisoners but only succeeded in wounding the boy, and all were retaken. The Indians got into a big thicket and most of them escaped across the Rio Grande.

In 1852, when the rangers were discharged, Mr. Wilson went on an expedition into Mexico under Carabahal, mostly Mexicans, and they had a battle in which he was badly wounded in the arm by a bullet. Mr. Wilson's mother died in Gonzales County in 1848, and his father in the same county in 1855. He ranched in Bee County and then in the Panhandle and has ranches up there yet in Brewster County, but lives on Beacon Hill, San Antonio, Bexar County.

Colonel Ford had many more battles with the Indians, one of

which, in 1858, occurred in the northwest part of the State, on the South Canadian River, in which a large number of Indians were killed. During the Civil war he commanded a regiment on the Rio Grande and fought the last battle of that great struggle. He was a native of North Carolina, and died at his home in San Antonio in 1898. On account of his vim and quick actions he was called "Old Rip" by the rangers.

JACK HUFFMAN.

Came to Texas in 1845.

Jacob Huffman, or Jack as he is called by those who know him, was born in Prussia, in the town of Hilbringin, near the Saar River, in 1838, and came to Texas in 1845. Many storms occurred during the passage and the vessel leaked badly, and finally a great storm drove them back 300 miles onto the coast of England, and they stayed there ten days for repairs near a great chalk bluff. Jack became very expert during the voyage. climbing ropes and masts, and the captain wanted to keep him, but his parents would not consent, so he became a pioneer and Indian fighter on the Texas frontier instead of a sailor.

The landing on Texas soil was made at Port Lavaca, and they found Prince Solms there waiting for them, and he took charge of them in the name of Henry Castro, whose colonists they were. and brought them out to Castroville in carts. The prince wore a uniform and sword, and amused himself and the people by the way killing tarantulas with his sword, they being very numerous along the route, and their bite was very poisonous. He would pin them to the ground with the keen point of the blade, or toss them up and cut them in two in the air.

The carts were covered with raw hides in lieu of wagon sheets, and being repeatedly drenched with rain, a most disagreable smell emanated from them. When it thundered loud the Mexican cart drivers would yell, and Mrs. Huffman would cry and wish she was back in Germany. When they arrived in Castroville the elder Huffman had $5 in money, with which he bought provisions and went three miles above town and planted corn, living in a picket hut covered with grass. His small farm of a few acres produced abundantly of corn, melons, and pumpkins, and he had plenty to live on, trading for meat from the Indians. 500 of whom were camped on the Medina River near by.

Jack remained at home until he was 14 years of age, and then worked around at anything he could find to do. He made one trip to Camp Verde with corn for the soldiers there, and re-

turned by way of Bandera to load with lumber at Montel's sawmill, and when five miles below town on the way home his team
stalled at a steep hill. and two Polanders came along and told
him

HIS BROTHER JOHN WAS KILLED BY THE INDIANS,

And then helped him to get his wagon up, and he came on
home with a heavy heart. for he was greatly attached to his
brother. John was older than Jack and was married, and at
the time he was killed was building a house on the Medina at
the foot of the mountains in a very exposed place. as the Indians were now hostile. The walls of the house were up and
John was on the roof nailing on boards, when six Comanche
Indians suddenly appeared and attacked him and shot one arrow through his body before he could descend and get his gun.
which was in the house. He made the attempt and got to the
door, but here he received another arrow in the temple and fell.
His gun was an eight-shooting rifle which he had purchased
from Big Foot Wallace, and had he carried this on the house
with him no doubt he could have kept off the Indians. A man
named Dan Turner was helping him to build the house and at
this time was bringing an armful of boards from the river
bottom, and when he came into view some of the Indians made
a charge on. him, but he threw the boards down and ran back
to the board tree and secured his gun, which he had left there,
and then made his escape. intending to go to the Haby settlement below, but they lived on the opposite side of the river,
and it was up from recent rains. Turner could not swim but
made the attempt to cross anyhow, and came near being drowned,
and lost his gun. He only saved himself by catching the limb
of a cypress tree as he went down. and climbed up into it above
the water. Here he stayed two days and nights waiting for the
river to fall, and then tore up his clothing, and twisting them
into a rope broke off a limb, fastened it to one end. and threw
it repeatedly to the bank until it fastened in some bushes. and
then drew himself over and again set out for the settlement.
In about a mile he met a party of men going to see about John,
who was in the habit of coming home on Sunday. and it

was now Monday, and his wife and others were very uneasy about him. When they met Turner and heard his story
they knew almost beyond a doubt that John was killed, for he
said he saw John down when he turned to run from the Indians.
On arriving at the cabin the body was found near where it fell,
stripped and scalped, and the fine gun and Hoffman's mule
gone. The body was now taken up and carried to Castroville
and buried. The mule got away from the Indians and came
back home in a few days.

JACK KILLS TWO INDIANS.

There were a great many mustangs in the country and Jack
tried many times to catch one, and while out on this business
one day rode up on two Comanche Indians lying down in the
grass asleep, with their bows and arrows beside them. He was
at a loss at first as to what action he would take, thinking at
first to shoot one, but finally backed off quietly, as he only had
one shot in a muzzle-loading gun, and the other Indian might
get him with his arrows before he could run out of range of
him. He now started to Castroville after help, but on the way
found the horses of Dr. Bimm, whom he had been working for,
and drove them in for fear the Indians would get them. When
the alarm was raised four men mounted their horses and started
back with young Huffman, but without carrying any ammunition except the loads in their rifles. The men were Chipman, Reinhart Swartz, Turpie, and Tom Outer. Jack was still
a boy in his fifteenth year. When they arrived near the place
the Indians had waked up but were still lying in the grass, and
discovered the white men just as Jack waved his hand indicating
to his companions the spot in the prairie where he had seen the
Indians, and they, supposing this meant their discovery, sprang
up and made a run for a thicket 200 yards away and a lively
chase commenced, the men all firing their guns except Jack and
Chipman. The latter was a Mormon, and seemed to have some
scruples about taking human life, but said, "Jack, you shoot
them and I will keep them cut off from the thicket." Young
Huffman knew the value of a shot now, and running close to an
Indian, dismounted so as to take better aim, and fired, and the

Indian fell, but sprang to his feet again and went on, making a fearfully curious noise. Chipman tried to cut the Indians off from cover, but one of them shot him twice with arrows, inflicting only slight wounds, but which caused him to lose his scruples about shooting Indians, and he fired at one but missed. In the meantime Huffman was reloading his gun as fast as he could, and as soon as he got it ready fired again at the Indian whom he first shot and badly wounded, and this time he killed him, the Indian falling with his face in a thorny bush. The other men with empty guns were idle spectators of the battle which young Huffman was now making, and he shouted to them to catch his horse, which, becoming frightened, was running off across the prairie, and he again commenced loading his gun for a third shot, and yelled to Swartz to charge the other Indian, who was about to get into the thicket, and shoot him with a little self-cocking pistol which he had. The man said the pistol was no good; he had tried it and it would not shoot. "Keep in sight of him then," said Jack, "until I get my gun loaded." Swartz now took off after the Indian, but soon ran over a big rattlesnake and turned back, telling Huffman, who was coming in a run with loaded gun, there was the biggest snake he ever saw. "Let the snake go to the devil," said Jack; "follow the Indian." Again he did so, but as he rode under a tree the Indian shot two arrows at him almost as quick as lightning, both of which would have struck his body had they not hit a small limb first and glanced upward. Jack now came up and fired and hit the Indian, but he succeeded in getting into the thicket out of sight. The white men now all got together again, one of them having Huffman's horse in charge, and they went back to the dead Indian and got his bow and arrows and other things, and went back to town, where the people gathered around them, and young Jacob was quite a hero in their eyes. Next morning a party went back to the scene of the fight and a diligent search was made for the other Indian, but he could not be found, but his buckskin leggings were, and covered with blood, proving he was badly wounded. Several days after this Captain Beck came out from San Antonio to buy cattle, and while riding over the range and through the thickets in the vicinity of the fight found the dead body of the other Indian not far from where Huffman last saw him, and brought his bow and arrows and rope to Castroville.

After this Jack went on many scouts after Indians and acted as guide and trailer for the soldiers from San Antonio, but got into no fights while with them, as they were too slow, and had sergeants with them who did not wish to catch Indians, preferring to stop at ranches and drink buttermilk. During one full moon, however, Jack had his

SECOND BATTLE WITH INDIANS.

On this occasion he found a dead cow at a place called "Government Canyon," deriving its name from Gen. Albert Sidney Johnston, who made a government road through it out towards Fredericksburg. The cow had not been long killed, and by Indians, he knew 'from their trail, and at once hurried to his ranch on the Helotes and told his neighbors the Indians were in and to tie up their horses and come to his house at daylight and they would take an Indian hunt. They were on hand at the time designated and the start was made, the trail being found out in the prairie, and which led back past where the cow was killed and then on towards Verde Creek. The Indians had a large drove of horses, and the settlers in pursuit were Jack Huffman, John Green, Frank Heibner, Christian Aves, John Huffman, Jr., Ed. Galagher, Chris. Schuhart, and Garland Odum. The trail was followed rapidly and they came upon the Indians at 4 o'clock in the evening, who, when they saw the white men, stopped on the side of a hill 400 yards away and prepared to give them battle. The charge of the settlers was led by Huffman and Green, and they advanced to within eighty yards of the Indians, and, dismounting, commenced the battle, expecting the balance of the men to come up to where they were, but the others stopped too soon and commenced firing at long range. The Indians saw this advantage and came yelling and firing at close quarters, and Green was soon badly wounded, having his arm shattered by a ball while loading his gun and could do nothing more, and Huffman had to meet them alone. To add further to his discomfiture his gun snapped twice when he had a good aim on the foremost Indian, but at this time the

other men began to come near and one of them ran to Huffman
with a gun, which he took and snapped in an Indian's face,
and as he turned to run snapped it again at his back. This
gun was not loaded. Green was down by a tree and the Indians
charged again, thinking they had the whites whipped, but this
time Huffman's gun began to fire and he opened up on them
right, his gun being a repeating Henry rifle, and soon had one
of them down badly wounded, but he got up presently and ran.
The cause of his gun failing at first to fire was an empty shell
in the barrel, which, as soon as he discovered it, he threw out
and it worked all right. Schuhart and Odum now came to his
side and opened fire, and the Indians ran, with four more of
their number wounded, which could be ascertained by them
throwing their things away and running to the brush when the
balls would strike them. There were two squaws in the band,
and when the fight commenced they screamed and squealed like
pigs and ran away over the mountain, both being mounted on
horses, one of which belonged to old man Gillis, a white man,
and the other to Toras, a Mexican. Jack shot twice at them
as they ran away up the mountain, but failed to bring either
down, and they all collected in a ravine beyond the mountain.
One ball glanced Huffman's head, but he was not injured. The
Indians made the fight with guns instead of bows, and made
some close shots considering the excitement that prevailed and
the bullets which were whistling around their own ears. Only
ten Indians were seen, including the two squaws, and they left
all of their horses, sixty-three, and some of their own, saddled.
Green was very weak and sick, but came to Huffman during
the fight and asked him to load his gun for him, but on
turning around to do so discovered the man had left his gun
at the tree that he had been leaning against. One Indian had
left his horse with saddle and a canteen of water on him, and
Huffman caught him and led him as they started to leave the
ground, Green riding close beside him and very sick. Suddenly
he said, "Catch me!" and commenced falling from his horse,
but Huffman got hold of him and eased him to the ground,
where he lay and called for water. Jack told him there was
no water except that on the Indian's horse, and it might be
poisoned. "I don't care if it is," said the wounded man; "I will

53

die anyhow if I do not get some water." It was given to him
and he soon revived, the water being all right. At this time
the other men were rounding up the horses and getting them
down the mountain, and some of the Indians still in sight.

Green recovered from his wound, but was afterwards killed
by a Mexican.

For want of space we can not go through all of the frontier
incidents of Mr. Huffman's life, but can say he was ever on the
alert and was a typical border man, and now lives twenty miles
west of San Antonio, where he owns a fine ranch, and says here
he has killed many mustangs for their tallow to grease wagons,
lariats, etc.

He knew Big Foot Wallace well, and often hunted with him
and his famous dog Rock, and says when the dog died Wallace
buried him and covered his grave with the skins of wild animals.
Mr. Huffman married Miss Caroline Ernst, who was also a
Castro colonist, and passed through many stirring scenes. On
one occasion she watched a band of Indians rounding up horses
near their ranch while her husband was away.

MRS. AMANDA L. SCULL.

Came to Texas in 1825.

Mrs. Amanda Scull was born in Jackson County, Mississippi, November 4, 1822, and was the daughter of Capt. Theodore Dorsett. She came to Texas with her father in 1825, and first settled in the Red lands on Irish Bayou, near Nacogdoches. Mrs. Scull is one of the few who still survive and can tell of the times of W. B. Travis, Patrick Jack, and Monroe Edwards, and of San Jacinto—a connecting link between the past and present. The writer had the pleasure of meeting and conversing with Mrs. Scull in April, 1900, at the house of her son, Mr. Gambia Scull, near Lavernia, Wilson County, but the residence of Mr. Scull was in Guadalupe County.

Mrs. Scull passed through those troublesome times in eastern Texas called the Fredonian war, and the Regulators and Moderators. Her father, Captain Dorsett, commanded a company in the Fredonian war.

The American settlers in east Texas and the Mexican population in the years from 1830 to 1835 were not on the best terms with each other and often open ruptures occurred, and during these times three prominent Americans, namely, W. B. Travis, Patrick Jack, and Monroe Edwards, were placed in prison at Anahuac. Now, at the time of their arrest they were boarding with Captain Dorsett, and he obtained the contract of feeding them while in confinement. Also in prison at the time was a man called "Jawbone Morris," and it seems that one particular Mexican guard had charge of him, and Morris finally commenced negotiations with him in the way of a bribe for escape. The price of $10 was agreed upon for the guard to let Morris escape, but he was not possessed of that amount of money in the prison, but had an empty pocketbook of well-dressed leather. In the town at this time Morris had a friend named W. D. Scull, whom the subject of this sketch afterwards married, and he was allowed to converse with the prisoners, but no notes were allowed to pass between them, nor were the guards allowed to carry anything but verbal messages to anyone. Mr.

Scull and Morris, however, had an agreement that in case the
Mexican guard brought the pocketbook to Mr. Scull he was to
pay him $10 and keep the book. This was all accomplished
a few days after, and Morris escaped and was never seen or
heard of by Mr. Scull afterwards, but he kept the pocketbook
and wrote on it the date of the transaction, which was the 5th
day of April, 1832. It is now in possession of his son, Mr.
Gambia Scull, and was shown to the writer, and the writing,
which was with ink, is still very plainly visible.

Mr. Scull during these times acted in the capacity of messenger from place to place, going most of the time in a boat
from point to point around Galveston Bay, and was a member
of a company commanded by Captain Erskine. Colonel Travis
and Mr. Scull were schoolmates at Mobile, Ala., and he said
that Travis was the brightest boy in school, was tall and manly
in appearance, and had no difficulty in getting his lessons; even
Latin was easy for him. Mrs. Scull says she can remember him
as a very handsome man,—tall, well proportioned, light hair,
blue, smiling eyes, broad white forehead, nice rounded chin and
mouth, and it seemed to her like he ought to have been a
woman. Their families were acquainted before they came to
Texas, and Travis used to wait on her sister Ellen. He married
in Alabama but his wife did not accompany him to Texas, and
he often spoke tenderly and with great solicitude about a little
son he had back there, saying he hoped some day to be able
to do something for him in the way of lands and property.
When he and the others were released from prison they came
direct to Captain Dorsett's house, where they had formerly
boarded, and greatly surprised the family, and at the same time
rejoiced them, as they were very popular among all of the
American settlers.

Mrs. Scull, then a girl, saw them approaching the house and
exclaimed, "Oh, mamma! Yonder comes Mr. Travis, and Mr.
Jack, and Mr. Edwards." The mother, not having any idea
the Mexicans had released them, or were going to do so, soon
replied, "Amanda, hush; what makes you want to talk that
way?" In a few moments the three distinguished gentlemen
entered the door and were warmly welcomed, and ate their first
meal with the family after getting out of the prison. They re-

mained here several days, and William Jack, brother to Patrick, came and carried him to his home on the Brazos. Travis and Edwards also went away, and that was the last time Mrs. Scull saw Travis, and all grieved sincerely when they heard of his tragic death in the Alamo. Monroe Edwards went to New Orleans and she saw him no more.

During the retreat of the families from Santa Anna Captain Dorsett went to Galveston, and Mrs. Scull says there was no town there then, only one house on the island, but many people in tents, and a brig anchored near by was a boardinghouse. The Dorsett family, with their tent, occupied some mounds that were thrown up by the pirate Lafitte and his men, and one of them named Campbell was still there. When rumors came of the near approach of the Mexicans, Captain Dorsett took his family in a boat and went out into the bay and plainly heard the cannon when the battle of San Jacinto was being fought, and Mrs. Scull can remember how the artillery sounded, and with what great anxiety they listened to it, for they knew that the fate of Texas was at issue, and that before the sun went down Texas would be free or lost. Next morning the news of the great victory was announced to all the people, and loud shouts and great rejoicing was heard.

Captain Dorsett went to the battleground and viewed the scene of the terrible slaughter, and then went to Gen. Houston's camp in the timber on Buffalo Bayou. Mrs. Scull says that a widow named McCormick lived near the battleground, and a little boggy branch over which the Mexicans had to pass, and in which so many of them mired and were killed in the retreat, was called McCormick's Creek.

While Captain Dorsett was in the camp of the Texans he learned a strange and unique feature of the war. The Mexican prisoners, 700 in number, were being given away to anyone that wanted them to work for them, and the captain took three. Their names were Hosea, Martines, and Bibee. This one was called "Baby" by the Dorsett family. Martines was wounded in the leg, the leaders being cut by a ball so that he could not walk, and Captain Dorsett did not want to take him, but he cried and begged until he did so for pity. He said he could do a great many things on the place if he was hurt in the leg;

that he could shell corn and feed chickens, etc. When the Mexicans were brought home Mrs. Dorsett told the captain that he ought not to have brought the wounded one, but he said, "If you had been there and heard him cry and beg to be taken, you would have done as I did."

Captain Dorsett moved from Galveston Island when things began to be settled again and went to Liberty County, and the Mexicans worked for him there on a farm. Martines died there on the 19th of August, 1843, of fever.

Miss Amanda Dorsett married Mr. W. D. Scull on the 8th of January, 1840, at her father's farm on the Trinity. Colonel Bradburn acted as goodfather to Mrs. Scull when she was baptized.

Mrs. Scull says that in 1835, when hostilities commenced with Mexico and men were concentrating and marching upon San Antonio, three Taylor brothers, all boys or youths, were picking cotton for her father, and as soon as they finished the job made preparations to go to the war, and many neighbors came in to see them off. Their names and ages are as follows: Edward, 21; James, 17; George, 15. These gallant boys died with Travis in the Alamo.

The mother of Mrs. Scull died in Liberty County in 1843, and in 1851 Mr. Scull came to Guadalupe County and settled on the Cibolo. In the following year Captain Dorsett came and lived with them until he died.

In 1855 the Indians made a raid down the Cibolo valley and killed Lewis McGee, young son of Rev. John S. McGee, and a negro girl 14 years old, named Lucy, who belonged to Mr. W. R. Elam. All this occurred in about two and a half miles of Mr. Scull's house, and the news was brought to them by Ed. Tarver. Most of the people in the settlement were gone to a barbecue at Seguin and but few men could be raised to follow the Indians, and great excitement prevailed. Mr. Scull, Jim Umphreys, and Silas Harmon loaded their guns and went to hunt the Indians, and Mr. Scull's family and others started to Seguin on foot. In this party were Mrs. Scull and her family, William, Mary, Sarah, Gambia, and Charley, Mr. Patton's negroes and his wife, Julia Shaw, her sister, Monroe Dorsett and his wife and four children, and three or four negroes.

The word had come that a large body of Indians were coming
down the valley and for the people to leave their homes. Mrs.
Scull and her party only went about one half mile from the
house, and then all entered a deep gully at the head of a ravine
and hid. Captain Dorsett had remained behind to get the
horses, and joined them here with a negro boy named Homer
and another negro, bringing the horses along. Guns were heard
while here, and the people thought sure the Indians were close
upon them. A messenger now arrived and told the people to
fort up at the house of Mr. James Newton, and many of them
went there and spent a wakeful, uneasy night. Major Montgomery loaded his wagon that night with the intention of starting back to Mississippi when daylight came, but changed his
notion, and is here yet. On the following morning Mrs. Scull
brought her family back home, and in a few days Mr. Scull came
back and said the Indians were all gone out of the country and
there was no more danger. They had followed the Indians to
the Sabinal River, in Uvalde County.

The negro girl who was killed was a house girl and had been
raised by Mrs. Elam, who thought a great deal of her. At the
time that she met her death at the hands of the savages she
was carrying water to work hands in the field of Robert Floyd.
There was a small stream near by called Lipan Creek, near the
Cibolo, and it was from this place she was coming with a bucket
of water on her head when the Indians came upon her. She
thought they were cowboys and stopped to look at them, and
they at once surrounded her. The first thing the painted
rescals did was to rope the bucket and jerk it off of her head.
They then began to rope at her, but she threw the rope off several
times, but they finally succeeded in fastening her, and her
screams was answered by the men in the field. The Indians
then lanced her and cut her across the bowels, and left. It was
evident they intended to capture and carry her along, but her
resistance and screams caused them to fatally wound her. She
lived several hours, was perfectly conscious, and told all about
the circumstance, but Mrs. Elam, her mistress, never saw her
alive any more, but gave her a nice burial. Mr. Elam was at
Floyd's, and was soon upon the scene and assisted the poor unfortunate as best he could, and sent young Tarver to warn the
people below.

In 1859 Mr. Scull moved to the San Antonio River and settled five miles below Floresville.   On the 13th day of July, 1861,
the Indians made a raid and killed one of Captain Wayman's
negroes and carried off another.   Mr. Gambia Scull saw the
dead negro and helped to bury him.   He had four or five arrows
in him.   One had struck a joint of the back bone, and was the
one that killed him.   The others were in the shoulders.   All
of the horse stock in the country had been rounded up by the
Indians, but they had stampeded and many of them were shot
with arrows and some recaptured and carried off.   Among these
were the entire lot of John Peters.   This was the last bad raid
made in that part of the country.   West of there, on the Lucas,
the cow hands, among whom was Gambia Scull, were nearly
rounded up by a large body of Indians, but the boys scattered
and got away.

When the Civil war broke out William Scull, brother of Gambia, joined the regiment of Terry rangers in the company of
Capt. William Houston, and was killed in the battle of Murfreesboro.

The elder Scull, father of Gambia, died on the 4th day of
January, 1886.   Mrs. Amanda Scull now lives with her
daughter, Mrs. Emma Mattox, two miles from Lavernia, and
near her son Gambia.   There are four boys and two girls still
living, all married, and all near by.   Mrs. Mary Ellen Richardson, a daughter, lives in Lavernia.   Mr. Gambia Scull has a
fine farm near the old road along which marched the army of
Santa Anna after the fall of the Alamo, when he was marching
to the conquest of the balance of Texas.   They encamped on the
Cibolo River, near the present home of Mr. Scull, and many
things have been found there from time to time, among which
was a large chunk of lead weighing several pounds.

R. H. BURNEY.

The name of Burney has been closely connected with the history of Kerr County since a very early date. They passed through the frontier days and were used to Indian alarms, scouts, trails, and battles with the red men, and materially aided in settling and developing the country.

Robert H. Burney, one of the representative men of the large connection of the family of Burney, was born October 22, 1854, in McNary County, Tenn. His father, Judge H. M. Burney, came to Texas and settled in Kerr County in 1856, when Robert was but two years of age, and has passed the most of his life on the Texas frontier. His first schooling was of course only such as could be afforded in a sparsely settled country on the border, but he finally entered the Southwestern University at Georgetown, Texas, in 1875 and received medals for proficiency in mathematics and oratory. He graduated in 1879, with the degree of bachelor of arts, at the Southwestern University, and also in 1879 was made bachelor of laws after a course of lectures in the law department of Vanderbilt University, at Nashville, Tenn.

In 1874 Judge Burney joined a company of Texas rangers commanded by Capt. Neal Caldwell, and made many scouts after hostile Indians over the rough mountain country, and in all kinds of weather, suffering alike with heat and cold—sometimes almost scorching on the desert plains, suffering with thirst and hunger, and at other seasons of the year almost perishing in some sudden, driving blizzard far out in the open country of the plains and divides. With the money earned as a ranger he paid his tuition fees and part of his other college expenses. His experience as a ranger enabled him to gain an intimate knowledge of frontier life and the needs of the west, which has been of great service to him as a State senator. He was nominated by the Democracy and elected to represent the Twenty-eighth senatorial district in the Twentieth and Twenty-first Legislatures, and in 1890 was re-elected for a term of four years. His district was composed of sixteen counties, embracing

an area of over 63,000 square miles. In the Twentieth Legislature he was chairman of the select joint committee of the senate
and house charged with an examination into the conduct of the
Comptroller's office. This thorough examination and exhaustive
report was due largely to his labors and direction. It was the
openly expressed opinion of the highest State officials that this
report was most important and beneficial to the State.

He was the author in the Twentieth Legislature of the measure under which the geological department is operated. In the
consideration of the vexed school land question he was considered by his colleagues an eminent authority, his opinion were
listened to with marked respect and carried with them great
weight, and he was finally placed upon the free conference committee of the two houses to adjust conflicting opinions and
formulate a State policy.

In the Twenty-first Legislature he was chairman of the senate
committee on education, and in the Twenty-second Legislature
chairman of the senate committee on State asylums. He took
an active part in the leading debates and important legislative
work of these bodies, and added further strength to his well
earned reputation as an able legislator.

On one occasion Judge Burney met with an accident which
came near rendering him a cripple for life, and which few men
under like circumstances survive. On this occasion he and
others were out turkey-hunting in the mountains, and Judge
Burney arose before daylight and repaired to a turkey roost
alone, and unfortunately stepped off into a deep, rocky gorge
and fell many feet, landing on the solid rock bottom below.
His hip was crushed and other parts of his body badly bruised,
so much so that he was unable to arise and was compelled to
remain there for many hours until his calls for help finally
attracted his companions, and it was then with great difficulty
that he was rescued, on account of the steepness and ruggedness
of the cliff over which he fell, and it was years before he recovered. Senator Burney married Miss Mattie Prather, of Pales-
tine. He is a member of the Masonic fraternity, a good lawyer,
and still resides in Kerr County, in the town of Kerrville,
county seat.

CONCLUSION.

Owing to the size this present work has assumed, many worthy sketches have to be cut short, but the writer hopes at some future time to write them up at length. Among these are the following:

Hon. B. F. Cocke, who came from Tennessee to Texas with his family and settled in Kerr County in 1857, near Comfort, in the Guadalupe valley. His sons were Jack, Foster, James, Fred, and William. They were good frontiersmen, and had many scrapes with the Indians. On one occasion Foster and Fred ran fourteen Indians by waving their hats and calling to an imaginary force in the valley below, and at the same time boldly charging the Indians, who at once beat a hasty retreat. William was also closely pursued by three Indians about dusk between Center Point and Comfort, but he outran them, keeping his pistol in hand ready to shoot if they overhauled him. In 1872 he was ordained to the ministry by the Methodist church, and has been serving in that capacity since, and resides at Center Point, Kerr County, Texas.

Dr. J. Clark Ridley, who still survives at a very advanced age, at Center Point, was one of the first settlers in this country, and did as much to develop and settle up the country as anyone who came here at that early day.

John Tedford, one of the early settlers on the Verde Creek, near Center Point, was wounded and his horse and saddle captured by an Indians as he was going from his home to that of his sister, Mrs. Reese, wife of Sidney Reese, who lived on the Guadalupe above Center Point.

Capt. Charles Schrenier, one of the most successful business men of Kerrville, came at an early day and passed through some stirring scenes during the frontier days, serving as a Texas ranger part of the time along the border.

Capt. L. P. Sieker, now of Austin, spent nearly all of his young manhood days on the Texas border, trailing, scouting, and fighting Indians. He was captain of a company of rangers and was ever on the alert after the hostiles, following them with a tenacity and endurance that was most remarkable. On one

occasion he pursued a band so fiercely across the plains for seven
days that when finally the chase was abandoned it took the
captain and his men three weeks to retrace their steps with their
played-out horses and pack mules, but he had driven the Indians
beyond the Pecos River.   Many interesting incidents in the life
of Captain Sieker will be written later.   He is now captain and
quartermaster of the frontier battalion.

Capt. Robert Hall, who spent more than half a century on
the Texas frontier, is well known to the people of southwest
Texas, and whose history has already been written in book form.

Capt. William Pitts, who now resides at Austin, is one of the
old-time Indian fighters who served under Gen. Ed. Burleson
and Capt. James H. Calahan, and is widely and favorably known
in the west.

Thurlow Weed, who resides in Austin, was a gallant Texas
ranger, serving as sergeant in Capt. Rufe Perry's company.
He participated in the second Lost Valley fight and also in the
long battle and chase of Comanches in Menard County, in which
he killed an Indian at close quarters during a stand made by
the Indians in a desperate attempt to drive back the rangers.
Mr. Weed also has the honor and distinction of being one of the
pallbearers in the reinterment of Big Foot Wallace at Austin,
when his remains were moved from Devine by an act of the
Legislature.

Ben and Henry McCulloch, the two brothers whose names
are interwoven in nearly every chapter of the book, as others
told of their heroic deeds along the border for more than fifty
years.   They were natives of Tennessee, and in their young days
hunted and frolicked with David Crockett.

Among others who can not now be written, who deserve a
chapter, are Wm. Davis Drown, Milford Day, Jr., Braxton
Nicholson, Louis Oge, Judge P. D. Saner, R. H. Hunter (one
of the old three hundred), Mr. Cole, veteran of the Mexican
war, and Mrs. Braen, one of the old-time pioneers.   Also some
other incidents in the life of Col. James C. Carr while in California and Oregon, where he got the name of "Buckskin."

Hoping that my efforts to perpetuate the name and fame of
these heroes of the border will be appreciated by my readers,
I remain, yours truly,

                                        A. J. SOWELL.

Roberts, J., 416
Roberts, J. Box, 686
Roberts, James, 322
Robins, _____, 50
Robins, George, 224
Robinson, Dr., 15
Robinson, Frank, 212, 213, 779
Robinson, G. W., 42
Robinson, George, 787
Robinson, Henry, 106, 206, 212-219,
    286, 354, 366, 466, 582, 613-615,
    649, 787
Robinson, Jesse, 6
Robinson, Walter M., 798, 800, 802, 803
Robinson (vessel), 554
Rochjen, Capt., 139
Rockan, _____, 666
Rocksprings, Texas, 561
Rodrigues, Gil, 250
Rodrigues, Justo, 249
Rodrigues, Polly, 693, 696, 777, 778
Roebet, Elizabeth, 782
Roemel, Henry, 433
Rogers, Ida, 797
Rogers, James, 15, 16
Rogers, Capt. John H., 624-633
Rogers, Martin, 432
Rogers, Mike, 432
Rogers, Pleasant William Miles, 624
Rogue's Grave, 423
Rogue's Hollow, 423
Rompel, Lt. Charles, 755
Rooney, Frank, 661
Rosec, N., 138
Ross, _____, 805-807
Ross, L. S., 564, 763
Rothe, _____, 381, 441
Rothe, August, 119, 186, 229, (port.)
    232, 233-241, 552
Rothe, Fritz, 233, 234, 239, 240
Rothe, H., 116
Rothe, Henry, Sr., 233
Rothe, Henry, Jr., 233, 234
Rothe, Louis, 186, 233, 234
Round Mountain, 737
Roundtree, _____, 824
Roundtree, Vol., 399
Rowan, William, 75
Rowe, Mrs., 414
Rudlinger, John, 281, 283
Rudlinger, Joseph, 452
Ruggles, Col., 483
Rump, _____, 128
Runaway Scrape, 296
Runnels, David, 417
Rusk, Gen. Thomas J., 14, 292, 774
Russell, John, 416
Russell, William, 285
Rust, _____, 248, 427
Rust, William M., 561, 562
Rutinger, _____, 182
Rutinger, Josie, 445
Rutledge, _____, 251
Rutledge, William, 271
Ryman, Jacob, 250

Saatoff, _____, 441
Saatoff, M., 811-813
Saatoff, M. M., 811
Sabinal Canyon, 30, 90, 106, 109, 111,
    112, 199, 206, 208, 21, 218, 229, 257,
    263, 286, 288, 290, 292, 307, 322,
    337, 381, 386, 401, 402, 463, 466,

476, 503, 511, 547, 587, 596, 612,
    661, 672, 779, 781, 785
Sabinal Mountains, 402
Sabinal River, 90, 93, 109, 117, 188,
    192, 198, 207, 208, 239, 241, 251,
    323, 331, 384, 388, 410, 423, 483,
    489, 495, 547, 610, 785
Sabinal Sentinel, 775
Sabinal Station, 106, 291, 292, 775
Sabinal, Texas, 401, 503, 785, 839
Sabine County, 625
Sabine River, 292
Sacramento Mountains, 144
Saddler, Doc, 381
Saddler, Joe, 326
Saddler, John, 322, 381, 382
Saffold, Gen. William, 414
St. Clair, R., 416
St. Joseph's Island, 159
Salado, battle of, 24, 25, 252, 423
Salado Creek, 9, 59, 171, 420, 442, 805,
    806, 810, 817
Salado River, 315, 384
Salado, Mexico, 49, 66, 67, 72
Salcedo, Gov., 805, 807
Salizar, _____, 494
Salt Branch, 251
Salt Creek Mountains, 718
Saltillo, Mexico, 66, 677
Salucia, (vessel), 233
San Angelo, Texas, 628
San Antonio Express, 663
San Antonio Herald, 498
San Antonio River, 5, 7, 13, 141, 806,
    840
San Antonio, Texas, 2, 5-10, 20-24, 28,
    39, 54, 57-59, 86, 95, 97, 115, 116,
    121, 126-129, 136, 141-143, 146,
    151-153, 156, 159-164, 170-172, 182,
    185, 187, 206-208, 214, 249, 250,
    280, 281, 284, 291, 308, 315, 319,
    331, 335, 345, 380, 419, 422, 477,
    480, 481, 522, 523, 530, 678, 683,
    763, 782, 806, 807, 810, 815, 817
San Augustine, Texas, 627, 814
Sanchez, Capt., 677
Sanders, _____, 567
Sanders, Frank, 516
Sanders, George, 432
Sanders, John, 661
Sanders, Lee, 206
Sanders, Steward, 432
Sandies Chapel Church, 242
Saner, Capt., 166
Saner, Judge P. D., 521, 638, 844
San Felipe, 39, 782
San Fernando, Mexico, 531, 533
Sanford, Ben, 173
San Gabriel River, 422
San Geronimo Creek, 414
San Jacinto, battle of, 11-12, 14, 32, 35-
    37, 41-43, 48, 292, 837
San Jose Ranch, 634
San Juan d'Ulloa, Mexico, 249
San Lucas Springs, 328, 376
San Luis Potosi, Mexico, 76
San Marcos, Texas, 113, 284, 314, 438
San Marcos River, 44, 409
San Miguel Creek, 37, 498, 501, 598
San Miguel Creek, battle of, 252
San Miguel Ranch, 485
San Pedro River, 586
San Saba County, 693, 736

San Saba River, 178, 642, 695, 735,
    737, 758
San Saba, Texas, 713, 715, 736
Sansom, John W., 530, 699, 701
Santa Gertrudis Creek, 818
Santana (Indian), 667, 669
Santa Anna, Gen., 77-79, 250, 297
Santa Fe Expedition, 66
Santa Cruz River, 686
Santa Rosa Mountains (Mexico), 267,
    506
Santiago Creek, 13
Santitas' Ranch, 131
Sauce Creek, 486
Sauer, Capt., 166
Sauer, Tom, 696
Saump, John S., 414
Saunders, Adam, 432
Saunders, Frank, 432
Sauter, _____, 275, 576, 450
Sauter, Tobe, 234
Sawyer, _____, 192, 194
Sawyer, Lon, 194
Sayers, Lt., 784
Scallorn, Eliam, 316, 421
Scallorn, Wesley, 316, 421
Schadwitz, _____, 784
Schalkhausen, _____, 275, 450
Schanungga, (vessel), 140
Schenck, _____, 665, 557
Schleador, _____, 537
Schleicher, Gustave, 663, 665
Schleunig, _____, 665
Schlosser, _____, 753
Schmidt, Baptiste. 350
Schneider, H., 350
Schram, _____, 459
Schreiber, John, 275-277, 450, 451
Schreiber, Mike, 234
Schreiner, Capt. Charles, 843
Schreiver, _____, 655
Schuhart, Cris., 832, 833
Schulz, _____, 665
Schumaker, Chris., 551
Schumaker, John, 452
Schumanville, Texas, 783, 784
Schunk, _____, 665
Scott, Dr., 696
Scott, John, 471
Scott, William, 624, 627
Scott, Gen. Winfield, 183, 184
Scull, Mrs. Amanda L., 835-840
Scull, Charley, 838
Scull, Gambia, 835, 840
Scull, Mary 838
Scull, Sarah, 838
Scull, W. D., 835
Scull, William, 433, 838, 840
Scurry, Gen., 630
Seco Creek, 87, 102, 109, 111, 156,
    165, 166, 182, 186, 195, 198, 199,
    203, 205, 220, 280, 283, 289, 322,
    327, 349, 381, 422, 444, 478, 511,
    591, 597
Segenus, _____, 539
Segler, James, 345
Segler, Texas, 308, 343, 345
Seguin, Juan N., 13, 14, 25, 416
Seguin, Texas, 15, 59, 155, 156, 171,
    248, 249, 255-257, 335, 409, 410,
    414, 416-420, 422, 426, 258, 530,
    561, 679, 783, 794, 797, 810, 838
Seguin Mercury, 246